W9-CAJ-448

THE LEGAL ENVIRONMENT OF
BUSINESS

NINTH EDITION
JOHN BLACKBURN & ELLIOT KLAYMAN

092

PEARSON
Custom
Publishing

Cover photographs courtesy of Corbis.

Copyright © 2008, 2006, 2005, 2003 by John Blackburn and Elliot Klayman
Copyright © 1998 by Simon Schuster Custom Publishing
Previously published by McGraw-Hill Companies, Inc.
All rights reserved.

Permission in writing must be obtained from the publisher before any part of this work may be reproduced or transmitted in any form or by any means, electronic or mechanical, including photocopying and recording, or by any information storage or retrieval system.

All trademarks, service marks, registered trademarks, and registered service marks are the property of their respective owners and are used herein for identification purposes only.

Printed in the United States of America

10 9 8 7 6 5 4 3 2 1

ISBN 0-536-06304-4

2007160591

CS

Please visit our web site at *www.pearsoncustom.com*

PEARSON CUSTOM PUBLISHING
501 Boylston Street, Suite 900, Boston, MA 02116
A Pearson Education Company

This edition fills the need for quality teaching material for the legal environment of business course. It combines highly readable text with interesting cases suitable for business students.

The Book Responds to Accreditation Standards

This is a mainline legal environment of business book. It responds to the accreditation standards of the American Assembly of Collegiate Schools of Business (AACSB), as well as those of the Association of Collegiate Business Schools and Programs (ACBSP).

The Book Is Organized Logically

This book consists of 21 chapters, organized into six parts.

- *Part I, Law and Ethics in a Global Environment,* covers ethics and international business law.
- *Part II, The American Legal System,* presents the nature of law and legal reasoning, and the legal system. It also surveys American constitutional and administrative law.
- *Part III, Introduction to Private Law and the Regulatory Environment,* presents the subjects of contracts, torts, and property. They are the legal base for many areas of government regulation. Part III also includes a chapter on product liability and advertising and a chapter on environmental law. These chapters show the integration of private and public law, typical of other substantive areas of law.

- *Part IV, Business Organizations and Financial Markets,* consists of chapters on business associations, securities regulation, special topics in corporate law, and debtor-creditor relations.
- *Part V, Business and Its Employees,* contains chapters on the employment relationship, equal employment opportunity, and labor-management relations.
- *Part VI, Business and the Marketplace,* discusses economic regulation of a business's relations with its customers, competitors, and suppliers. It contains chapters on trade restraints, monopolies and mergers, and other antitrust topics.

However, the book's organization is not sacred. Instructors can rearrange the chapters without harm.

The Book Continues Its Proven Pedagogical Features

In revising the book we have retained the following features that proved so successful in the earlier editions:

- *Part introductions* orient the student to a part's subject matter and organization.
- *Excerpts of statutes set off in the text* allow easy reference to legislative material.
- *Charts and illustrations* help students visualize concepts.
- *Questions after cases* point out important aspects of a case.
- *Problems at the end of each chapter follow the chapter sequence,* allowing for an orderly review of the chapter.
- *Each chapter includes a list of the chapter's objectives.* Experts in education point to the need for clear goals to focus student learning. One way to do this is with behaviorally described learning objectives.
- *Chapter outlines appear on the opening page of each chapter.* Students can see at a glance a chapter's headings.
- *Important terms appear in bold within chapters.* They later appear in the chapter problems as terms the student must define. This helps students grasp major concepts.

The Book Provides a "Building Block" Approach to Learning

The pedagogical elements contained in the text provide the building blocks for learning. The text combines part introductions, learning objectives, chapter outlines, concept illustrations, cases, case questions, and chapter problems. These organize a student's learning. The student sees what to learn, how to organize study, and where to review. The book gives the student the "building blocks" that educational experts say help students learn, by aiding students to recall, apply, analyze, synthesize, and evaluate the concepts in legal environment courses.

The Book's Cases Are Carefully Edited

Professors and students will enjoy reading the cases in this book. We edited the cases carefully. We summarized the facts and court proceedings at the beginning of each case. Ellipsis points show where we omitted language from an opinion. (Where major omissions occur, the ellipsis points are in the form of blocks.) In general, we omitted citations and footnotes from the cases.

Acknowledgments

We have had considerable help in writing this book. Amanda Runyon, a student of the Moritz College of Law, The Ohio State University, deserves special mention for her valuable research assistance. A special thanks also goes to our editor, Jackie Grisvard, without whose services this edition could not have been so efficiently produced. None of these people is responsible for the views expressed or material used.

John D. Blackburn
Elliot I. Klayman

B R I E F   C O N T E N T S

*Dedicated to our faithful adopters
and our past, present, and future students.*

C O N T E N T S

PART III

INTRODUCTION TO PRIVATE LAW AND THE REGULATORY ENVIRONMENT

7   Contracts   175

8   Torts   204

9   Product Liability and Advertising   234

INTRODUCTION

Learning Objectives

After learning this chapter the student should be able to:

- Explain why law is studied in a business school.
- State the objectives of a course on the legal environment of business.
- Read a case.
- Brief a case.

Legal study differs from other business study. Thus, business students need an orientation to the nature of legal study before they turn to the subjects of the business legal environment. This introduction provides a frame of reference that business students can use to analyze, apply, synthesize, and evaluate the various areas of law affecting business. The following discussion explores the objectives of legal study by business students, before explaining the nature of legal study.

Objectives of Legal Study by Business Students

It is particularly appropriate at the beginning to inquire into the educational objectives of a book or course on the legal environment of business. Thus, the following discussion focuses on the rationale and the objectives of legal study by business students.

Why Study Law in a Business School?

It is generally assumed that law is a subject taught only to aspiring attorneys in a professional law school program. Historically, however, law was considered important to the lay public as well. In earlier days, legal study was an integral part of a liberal education. Today, legal study outside law schools is gaining renewed interest. This trend is a manifestation of a simple fact of modern life: law is too important to be left to lawyers.

Business colleges have long recognized the importance of legal study in the curriculum. Business managers must realize that their business relations are also legal relations.

Business students should particularly study material on law and regulation. Managers deal not only with suppliers and customers, but also with an array of state and federal agencies. A list of the acronyms and initials of these agencies (e.g., SEC, NLRB, FTC, OSHA, and EEOC) sounds more like an alphabet soup than a collection of government entities. Woe to the uninitiated manager who does not even know what these abbreviations stand for, let alone shorthand jargon (e.g., insider trading, price discrimination, and bona fide occupational qualification), used by the bureaucrats who work for those agencies. The plethora of regulations emanating from various government agencies requires managers to understand how public regulation affects their work. The language of business includes not only the items of the balance sheet but also the legalese of government regulations.

What Are the Objectives of a Course on the Legal Environment of Business?

A course on the legal environment of business has many objectives. Some are general and resemble the objectives of other business law courses; others are unique to a course on the legal environment of business. The following list includes both types. Two points should be noted: (1) the list is not exhaustive, and (2) the formulation of course objectives should be a cooperative effort involving the text authors, the instructor, and the students—it should not be an exercise that a text author or an instructor does alone. The following list is the authors' contribution toward such an effort. A course on the legal environment of business should help you to:

1. *Apply conceptual knowledge to problems.* A principal goal of legal environment courses is to teach conceptual knowledge for future use in decisionmaking situations. This is accomplished by communicating the concepts in a case-oriented setting and by giving you practice in applying the concepts to case problems. The use of case study makes you sort out relevant and important facts, determine the issues involved, and reach conclusions based on known rules, regulations, standards, and principles.

2. *Acquire a vocabulary of terms and concepts that make it possible to understand further communications.* This facilitates a continuation of learning beyond the limits of the classroom. A working knowledge of the legal terms and concepts used in business helps in understanding the sources that businesspeople read

every day. These sources include business papers and periodicals, technical journals, and financial reports.

3. *Develop the principles of inquiry, restraint, objectivity, and regard for considerations of public policy.* Understanding the legal method of resolving conflicts helps managers to develop restraint by not reaching conclusions too quickly on the basis of narrow thinking, to be more objective, and to consider not only the immediate issue but also the broader considerations of economic and social benefit.

4. *Develop an understanding of the philosophy underlying the legal rules and regulations controlling business activity.* This helps managers understand their roles in the improvement of the legal system. Legislative bodies, administrative agencies, and courts should ensure that the legal system reflects the consensus of public thought. Therefore, everyone should think critically about the present system and the desirability of change.

5. *Facilitate interdisciplinary communication in business.* Accountants, financial executives, marketing experts, and other business specialists must constantly communicate with one another. Frequently, the subject matter involves legal concepts with which all of them must be familiar.

6. *Develop an understanding of the principal area of law and regulation affecting business transactions.* This enables business managers to improve their managerial performance. Legal rules and regulations affect almost every business activity. Ignorance of these rules and regulations leaves a large void in the formal education of a business manager. The fact that there is a professional field of law practice does not free managers from the need to know about the legal environment of business. Many will not have lawyers on retainer; even those who do cannot rely on their lawyers to instruct them on every business matter in which law is involved. Almost every business decision is affected in some way by existing rules of law.

7. *Develop an awareness of legal pitfalls.* This enables managers to seek legal assistance before losses occur.

8. Satisfy the intellectual curiosity that drives every person to learn more about the principles and concepts that give meaning to observations and experiences. Legal environment courses show how law interacts with the business sector of the social order and gives you a better understanding of the relationship between business practice and social development.

9. *Develop an awareness of the legal aspects of international business practice.* Because business is conducted in a global economy, the study of the legal environment of business necessarily includes appropriate reference to international business law.

10. *Develop a deeper attitude of the social responsibilities of business, and a high standard of business ethics.* Successful and sophisticated business leaders consider the impact of their business decisions upon society. The law informs members of the business community of their social responsibilities. Beyond law's limits, business executives must apply ethical standards. The principles and analytical methods used in studying the legal environment of business help students learn to recognize and resolve business ethical issues.

Nature of Legal Study

The peculiar feature of legal study is the inclusion of excerpts of legal cases in the text. These cases are unlike the business cases usually included in business school case courses. In fact, these legal cases are not really "cases" at all—they are legal opinions written by judges (usually on appellate courts). These opinions resolve the legal issues in disputes brought before the courts, and they constitute the cases presented in this book. The cases illustrate the application of the principles of law (provided in the textual material preceding each case) to particular legal disputes. These cases, plus the text and the discussion by instructors, form the fundamental substance from which you learn about the legal environment of business.

The cases selected have been chosen by the text authors for their value in teaching. Most of the cases in this text are recent cases illustrating trends in the law. These permit both business students and their instructors to evaluate the decisions against the background of their own current experience. Some cases have been selected because they proceed on unsound assumptions or somehow fail to solve the problems at hand—they maximize opportunities for class discussion and criticism. Others have been included because they are the great landmark cases—from these you learn sound law and come into contact with prevailing legal principles.

Reading Cases

The first thing you should do is read the textual material immediately preceding a case. This material presents the fundamental legal principles in a general manner. Second, read the case following the textual presentation. Do not read a case as you would read a novel, skimming lightly for the thread of the plot; read the case as carefully as you would read a page of statistics, accounting, or finance. You should read each word, looking up the unknown words in the glossary. The old proverb, "To read many times is not necessarily to understand," is worth cherishing, plain as it is.

In reading cases, bear in mind the points of law you are seeking. It does not suffice to read legal opinions merely as narratives. The cases are presented to illustrate particular areas of the law, and your legal analysis of the cases should be structured to make your reading profitable. You must not only know what you are looking for, but also have a method to help you in your search. As the learned Justice Cardozo once said, "Cases do not unfold their principle for the asking. They yield up their kernel slowly and painfully."[1]

Your reading of these cases, then, must be systematic. Keep in mind that an appellate judge does *not* always write his or her opinion with an eye toward functional, simple, orderly legal analysis. Our American legal system is one of the few in the world in which people are not specifically trained to become judges.

---

[1] Benjamin N. Cardozo, *The Nature of the Judicial Process* 29 (1921).

Our judges have usually been trained to become lawyers (though even this is not always a prerequisite). Then, depending on the particular judicial procedure, some of these lawyers are either elected to judgeships or appointed to these offices of honor and power. When people become judges, lightning does not strike them with the knowledge and expertise necessary to write meaningful (or even lucid) legal opinions. They sometimes experience great difficulty in formulating their decisions.

Even so, important decisions may be made by judges. Problems in case selection arise when an important decision is contained in an opinion written by a judge who may have had great difficulty in committing his or her thoughts to paper. We have included some such cases within this text. In these instances, your analysis may be impeded by obscure language. Also, many of the legal opinions in your text have been edited to conform to space limitations or to illustrate only one of the many points of law addressed. Therefore, realize that sometimes a case may appear confusing because it is confusing.

A Sample Case

At this point, it is helpful to actually read a case. The case that follows is fairly typical of those you encounter in the rest of the book. You should, however, know a few things before reading it.

The case involves an area of law known as the *law of torts*. Tort law is basically the law of accidents. You can read more about this subject in Chapter 8.

Before a court requires someone to compensate the victim of an accident, the court must conclude that the person who caused the victim's injury was under a duty to protect the victim from the very injury that occurred. Thus, the concept of a duty is basic to an understanding of when one person is liable to another.

There are several kinds of duties. There are social duties, such as when two people agree to go out to dinner. There are moral duties, such as the duty to come to the aid of another. There are voluntary duties that we agree to undertake, such as when we enter into business contracts. And there are duties that society imposes on us by law.

Not every moral duty is recognized by the courts as creating a legal duty that can be enforced by the courts. The case that follows addresses the question of whether a duty should be recognized so as to require one party to pay for the other's injury. The case involves a lawsuit known as *a wrongful death action*. This type of lawsuit is brought on behalf of a dead person's beneficiaries (e.g., spouse, parent, or children) against someone who negligently caused the death of another. Thus, a husband can bring a wrongful death action against someone who negligently caused the death of his wife and recover compensation for the loss of his spouse.

One final note is in order here. In a lawsuit, the party who brings the lawsuit is called the *plaintiff;* the party who is being sued is called the *defendant.* Now, on to the case.

OTIS ENGINEERING CORP. V. CLARK[2]
668 S.W.2d 307 (Tex. 1983)[3]

Donald Roy, a foreman for Otis Engineering Corporation (Otis), suggested to Robert Matheson, an Otis night-shift employee, that he go home. Roy made this suggestion after several of Matheson's co-workers complained following their lunch break that Matheson was intoxicated at his machine. While escorting Matheson to the company parking lot, Roy asked if Matheson was all right and could drive home; Matheson answered that he could. Roy knew that Matheson had to drive on the heavily traveled Belt Line Road to reach home. Thirty minutes later, some three miles away from the plant on the Belt Line Road, Matheson was involved in an automobile collision in which he and the passengers of the other car were killed. The county medical examiner's report showed that Matheson had a blood alcohol content of 0.268 percent, which indicated he had ingested a substantial quantity of alcohol, an amount representing 16 to 18 cocktails if consumed over a period of one hour, or 20 to 25 cocktails if consumed over a period of two hours.

Larry and Clifford Clark (plaintiffs) brought suit against Otis (defendant), claiming that Otis was liable to the Clarks for the wrongful death of their wives, who were the passengers in the other car involved in the collision with Matheson. The trial court awarded summary judgment for Otis. (A summary judgment is a judgment made by the judge after a hearing, but without the benefit of a trial. It is granted if the judge decided that no dispute about the facts exists and one party is clearly entitled to judgment as a matter of law.)

The Clarks appealed to the Texas Court of Appeals, which reversed the trial court judgment and ordered that the case be sent back to the trial court for a trial. Otis appealed this decision to the Texas Supreme Court, which affirmed the appellate court's decision. What follows is the opinion of the Texas Supreme Court,

---

[2] The title of the case reflects the parties of the lawsuit. The first name is usually the name of the party that brought the appeal, which in this case was Otis Engineering Corp., the defendant in the case. A party who appeals a case is referred to as the *appellant*. The party who responds to the appeal is called the *appellee*. Clark is the appellee in this case. Some courts keep the caption the same as the trial court. In that case, the first name will be the name of the plaintiff, the party who brought the lawsuit.

[3] The second line in the case title contains the citation to the legal report where the case may be found in a law library. In legal citation, the first number is the volume of the publication containing the opinion, the abbreviation is the publication, and the number that follows is the page where the opinion is located. Thus, the case of *Otis Engineering Corp. v. Clark* may be found in volume 668 of the *South Western Reporter,* 2d series, page 307. The abbreviation and number in the parentheses is an abbreviation of the court that decided the case and the year in which the case was decided. In the case of *Otis Engineering Corp. v. Clark,* the opinion is that of the Supreme Court of Texas, which decided the case in 1983. Students should not need to consult the full opinion of the case by going to the library, because the authors have edited the necessary parts of the opinion and excerpted them for inclusion in this book.

which is in turn followed by a dissenting opinion. (A court's opinion, or majority opinion, is the legal decision in a case. A dissenting opinion reflects the views of a justice or justices disagreeing with the court's majority.)

Justice Kilgarlin

[S]ummary judgment was granted on the basis that as a matter of law Otis owed no duty to the Clarks. In order to establish tort liability, a plaintiff must initially prove the existence and breach of duty owed to him by the defendant. As a general rule, one person is under no duty to control the conduct of another, even if he has the practical ability to exercise such control.

Though the decisional law of the State has yet to address the precise issue presented in this case, factors which should be considered in determining whether the law should impose a duty are the risk, foreseeability, and likelihood of injury weighed against the social utility of the actor's conduct, the magnitude of the burden of guarding against the injury and the consequences of placing the burden on the employer.

While a person is generally under no legal duty to come to the aid of another in distress, he is under a duty to avoid any affirmative act which might worsen the situation. One who voluntarily enters an affirmative course of action affecting the interest of another is regarded as assuming the duty to act and must do so with reasonable care.

■   ■   ■

What we must decide is if changing social standards and increasing complexities of human relationships in today's society justify imposing a duty upon an employer to act reasonably when he exercises control over his servant. . .

■   ■   ■

[T]he standard of duty that we now adopt for this and all other cases currently in the judicial process, is: when, because of an employee's incapacity, an employer exercises control over the employee, the employer has a duty to take such action as a reasonably prudent employer under the same or similar circumstances would take to prevent the employee from causing an unreasonable risk of harm to others. . . . Additionally, we adopt the rule in that the duty of the employer . . . is not an absolute duty to insure safety, but requires only reasonable care.

Therefore the [jury] in this case should be left free to decide whether Otis acted as a reasonable and prudent employer considering the following factors: the availability of the nurses' aid station, a possible phone call to Mrs. Matheson, having another employee drive Matheson home . . . and the foreseeable consequences of Matheson's driving upon a public street in his stuporous condition. . . . [A] factual issue is present and summary judgment is improper.

Justice McGee
(Dissenting)

The sole question is whether an employer is under a duty to control the conduct of an intoxicated, off-duty employee.

■   ■   ■

In my opinion, Otis was under no legal duty to restrain Matheson or to refrain from sending him home before the end of his shift, as the majority holds.

■   ■   ■

The unstated premise of the majority opinion is that holding parties such as Otis liable will somehow reduce the number of accidents caused by drunk drivers and will assure adequate compensation for victims such as the Clarks. As a practical matter, however, reducing the number of such accidents and compensating accident victims can and should be accomplished in a more direct and efficient manner by comprehensive legislation.

■   ■   ■

The result the majority reaches in this case will no doubt reinforce cynical public attitudes that tort liability is not based upon fault, but upon ability to satisfy a judgment. Further, by allowing the Clarks to shift the burden of liability from Matheson's estate to Otis, the majority erodes the concept that an individual is responsible for his or her own actions. I would adhere to the rule that an employee is not acting in the course of his employment while traveling to and from work and that the employer will not be held liable to one injured by the employee's negligent operation of an automobile during these trips to and from work.

Case Questions

1. Which standard of duty did the court adopt? Explain.

2. Assume that an employee has a history of heart trouble and has had open-heart surgery. He comes to work, experiences chest pains, complains to his employer, and is asked to leave or is sent home to rest. If, on the way home, he suffers a heart attack and is involved in a wreck, does the rule pronounced by the court's majority make the employer liable? Explain. Assume the same facts except the employee left his glasses at home, is sent home to get them, and is involved in a wreck. As a result of the court's decision, would the employer be liable for the injuries to a third person? Explain.

3. What is the likely effect of this case on the hiring practices of employers in Texas? If you were an employer in Texas, how would this case affect your hiring practices with regard to those who are alcoholics, drug addicts, or who might otherwise become incapacitated while working? Explain.

4. The dissent maintains that the issue should be dealt with by the legislature, not the courts. Do you agree? Explain.

Briefing Cases

To assist in your case analysis and note taking, you may be expected to prepare a brief of the case. This is a digested version of the case. Almost all instructors have their own ideas of what a well-formed brief should be. Sometimes your instructor tells you how to brief cases in an introductory lecture. More frequently, you learn what your instructor expects through criticisms of your own products in class.

Even so, let us approach the problem of briefing by examining the functions it should perform for you. The brief is intended to remind you in class of the salient facts and points of law raised and decided in the case. One timeworn request of instructors is to ask you to "state" a given case; here, a well-drawn brief can help refresh your memory. If your brief is too long, you lose the salient points in the verbiage.

A further function of the brief is to serve as an aid in reviewing the course for examinations. Instead of attempting to accomplish the impossible task of rereading all the cases, you can recall the problems to mind by referring to your briefs. Hence, each brief should contain enough details to help you recall the nature of the dispute, the legal principles it invokes, and their application to the facts of the case.

Topics Typically Covered in a Brief

The following is an annotated list of the topics typically covered in a brief. The points do not always appear in the same sequence, and some may not be relevant to a particular case.

Parties

Who is suing whom? Who is the plaintiff? Who is the defendant?

Legal Proceedings

Is the litigation civil or criminal? Which remedies are being sought? What was the result in the trial court? If the case was reviewed before reaching the reported appellate court, what was the result of that review? How did the case come before the appellate court?

Issues

Which issue or issues are presented for decision? These can often be presented in a series of questions. Some cases involve only a single issue; other cases entail several issues. In either event, the court attempts to resolve the issue or issues presented before it. Starting with the arguments of the contending parties is a useful way of discovering the issues of the particular controversy presented; many judges include the arguments of the parties in their written decision.

Holding

How were the issues decided? Who won, and what was the nature of the award? What general rule does the case lay down? The holding is the court's decision that answers these fundamental questions about the decision and its ramifications.

Rationale

What is the reasoning behind the court's decision? The court weighs the issues raised in the case and makes its decision within a conscious legal framework. On the appellate level, where these legal opinions are often presented in a formal, written format, the judges usually feel compelled to back up their decisions with what they consider to be the reasons for them. The appellate court looks not only to further appellate review of its opinion (if this is possible) but also to the principle of legal precedent. In an important case, a court realizes that the ramifications of its decision may be far reaching and that the case may set a precedent for decades to come. Realizing the importance of such a powerful act, a court often feels compelled to explain why the decision was reached—thus, the reasons for the decision.

Concurring and Dissenting Opinions
If there are any concurring or dissenting opinions, what do they say? Concurring and dissenting opinions are the opinions of individual judges who do not join in the court's opinion. A concurring opinion is written by a judge who agrees with the court's result but disagrees with its reasoning. A dissenting opinion is written by a judge who disagrees with the court's decision.

A Sample Brief

The following is a brief of *Otis Engineering Corp. v. Clark.* You may use it as a guide for briefing the other cases in the book.

OTIS ENGINEERING CORP. V. CLARK
Texas Supreme Court, 1983

Parties
Plaintiffs (husbands of victims of a car collision) sued defendant (employer of the driver of the other car involved in the collision) seeking compensation for their wives' wrongful death.

Legal Proceedings
Appeal from the trial court's granting of summary judgment for the defendant.

Facts
Plaintiffs' wives were killed when their car collided with another driven by an employee of the defendant. The defendant had sent the employee home in the middle of his shift because he was obviously intoxicated at his machine.

Issue
Does an employer who sends an obviously intoxicated employee home during the middle of his shift owe a duty to others who may be harmed as a result of a collision with the employee's car while the employee is en route home?

Holding
Yes. The summary judgment that was granted on the basis that the defendant owed no duty to the plaintiffs was improper.

Rationale
Changing social standards and the increasing complexities of today's society justify imposing a duty on an employer to act reasonably when it exercises control over an employee.

Dissenting Opinion

An employer has no duty to others for the actions of an off duty employee. By allowing the plaintiffs to shift the burden of liability from the employee to the employer, the majority erodes the concept of individual responsibility. A policy decision to impose liability on employers because it will reduce drunk-driving accidents is one that should be made by the legislature, not the courts.

General Comment

Note that in *Otis Engineering Corp. v. Clark* terms such as *summary judgment* have specific legal meanings. As you read this and other cases throughout the text, consult the glossary at the back of the book for precise definitions of key legal concepts.

Finally, class discussion may not always, or even usually, follow the preceding outline of topics or sample brief. Your professor may not require that you utilize these. The important thing is the result—understanding the cases—and not the technique by which that result is attained.

I LAW AND ETHICS IN A GLOBAL ENVIRONMENT

Business education today differs from what it was a generation ago, in two important ways—there is a greater emphasis on the subjects of international business and business ethics. These developments are somewhat interrelated. As business expands globally, encounters with diverse cultural values raise inevitable ethical issues.

Although interrelated, the emphases on international business and business ethics arose independently. News accounts of unethical conduct by business school graduates in the 1980s and 1990s prompted business educators to focus on ethics. Furthermore, that even the smallest company may be doing business with foreign firms has required business schools to internationalize their course offerings.

Courses on the legal environment of business have emphasized business ethics for many years. There is a natural fit between law and ethics. All law reflects values. Law forms an index of a society's value system. Chapter 1 starts the study of the legal environment of business by presenting the subject of ethics. In later chapters throughout the book, ethical issues are included in the material.

Following the discussion of business ethics in Chapter 1, international business law is covered in Chapter 2. International business relations require a body of international law. Chapter 2 examines this legal environment of international business transactions.

The subjects of business ethics and international business law can be deferred until later. However, we have included them at the outset for the following reasons. First, we believe the subjects of ethics and international law are of primary importance. Second, ethics and international law can be understood without a background in American law. And, third, additional material on ethics and international business law can then be integrated into later chapters. For these reasons, the book starts with a discussion of these two important subjects.

1   BUSINESS ETHICS

Chapter Outline

Learning Objectives

After learning this chapter the student should be able to:

- Define ethics and appreciate the importance of the application of ethics to business decisions.
- Engage in rational discussions of business ethics issues.
- Describe the cost/benefit model of ethics, apply it to ethical dilemmas involving business fact patterns, and evaluate the model as a means of solving ethical problems.
- Describe the rights model of ethics, apply it to ethical dilemmas involving business fact patterns, and evaluate the model as a means of solving ethical problems.
- Describe the various models of justice, apply them to business situations, and evaluate them as models for ensuring fair distributions of the things of value.

There exists a relationship between business ethics and the study of the legal environment of business. What is perceived as unethical business behavior often spurs public outcry for increased government regulation of business. Virtually every law on the books that businesses find onerous—the environmental laws, the securities laws, the employment laws, and the antitrust laws—can in some way be linked to some past business abuse and negative public reaction to the abuse.

Justified Moral Positions

Ethics is the study of standards of conduct and moral judgment. Morals are views of what is right and wrong, good and bad, just and unjust. Ethics is concerned with whether moral positions can be rationally justified. Ethics aims to develop reasonable moral standards.

Business ethics is the application of ethics to business and the study of the moral justification of business decisions. Thus it develops reasonable moral standards for business.

Instruction in ethics involves analyzing the strengths and weaknesses of justifications provided for moral positions. Students are frequently called on to formulate and defend their positions on moral issues. They are required to give reasons and support for the moral positions they take. This enables a rational discussion of moral issues. Ethical instruction often requires assumptions to be stated, accurate factual evidence to be offered, and conclusions to be logically developed from premises. This is what is meant by *justification in ethics*. It requires mature, rational discussions and respect for the opinions of others; it demands that opinions be developed and defended. In this way individuals and groups can develop a better understanding of the moral views of others, as well as a better understanding of their own moral views.

Ethical Models

An ethical model is an attempt to develop a fundamental rule or standard for determining what ought to be done. Several models developed by ethicists exist for answering ethical questions. However, there are two that ethicists consider the standard operational models: the cost/benefit model and the rights model.

The Cost/Benefit Model

The cost/benefit model (sometimes called the *utility model*) analyzes ethical issues by focusing on the costs and benefits of an action. Any action that increases the overall good is right. When encountering ethical dilemmas using this model, a person selects the action that brings about the greatest amount of good for the greatest number of **stakeholders**—those affected by the action.

The cost/benefit model measures the moral correctness of an action by its consequences. The cost/benefit model determines correctness in terms of social benefit: Thus, the model seeks to maximize benefits to the greatest number of people. Because consequences can extend indefinitely, the cost/benefit model

---
FIGURE 1-1   Applying the Cost/Benefit Model

When applying the cost/benefit model, you would:
1. Identify the facts.
2. Identify the ethical issues.
3. Identify the alternative courses of action.
4. Identify the stakeholders (those affected by the action).
5. For each alternative, calculate the costs by identifying who would be harmed and determining how great their harm would be.
6. For each alternative, calculate the benefits by identifying who would benefit from the action and determining how great the benefit is.
7. Decide which alternative would likely yield the greatest overall benefit to stakeholders; or, if there is no benefit, the least harm to stakeholders.

---

extends only to foreseeable consequences (see Figure 1–1). Those favoring this model maintain that the purpose of morality is to promote human welfare by maximizing benefits and minimizing harms.

The cost/benefit model has played a prominent role in current economic and legal thought. For example, the tendency to consider cost/benefit analysis in the development of regulatory policy is an application of the model.

Many people, especially those in the business community, favor the cost/benefit model. Many others, however, reject the idea that moral positions may be justified solely on the basis of consequences. They favor an ethical model grounded on moral standards that apply regardless of consequences. This model is known as the *rights model.*

The Rights Model

The **rights model** analyzes ethical issues by focusing on an action's impact on human rights. Under this model, human rights are the rights all people have. An action that maximizes respect for human rights and minimizes their violation is morally correct. When encountering ethical dilemmas, a person applying the rights model selects the action that minimizes the violation of stakeholders' rights (see Figure 1–2).

FIGURE 1-2   Applying the Rights Model

When applying the rights model, you would:

1. Identify the facts.
2. Identify the ethical issues.
3. Identify the alternative courses of action.
4. Identify the stakeholders (those affected by the action).
5. Determine to which extent each alternative respects the dignity of stakeholders or violates their rights.
6. Choose the alternative that maximizes respect for the dignity of stakeholders and minimizes the violation of their rights.

TABLE 1–1   Rights of Liberty

The following rights are often included within the category of liberty rights:

- *Privacy:* The right to control both one's private life and what is known about one's private life.

- *Free consent:* The right to be treated according to how one freely and knowingly consents to be treated.

- *Free speech:* The right to express one's view to the extent that such expression does not violate someone else's rights.

- *Freedom of conscience:* The right to refuse to act in any manner that violates one's moral beliefs.

Those who argue for the rights model maintain that what sets humans apart from all other creatures is that we are rational. Exercise of this rational nature requires human autonomy, or freedom. Further, if people possess an autonomous, rational will, each person must be treated with dignity. Respect for human dignity implies that each person possesses certain fundamental human rights.

Rights model advocates argue that the two necessities to be fully human are freedom and well-being. Thus, two basic categories of human rights exist within the model: (1) rights of liberty, and (2) rights of welfare. People often disagree as to whether one category of human rights is more important than the other, or which rights should be included within each category. Tables 1–1 and 1–2 list the rights that are often included in the categories of liberty and welfare.

Critics of the rights model claim that it is too idealistic and abstract—impracticable in making everyday moral choices. However, the model's emphasis on respect for the inherent dignity of persons has made it a major ethical model that can be seen reflected in business and legal decisions recognizing fundamental human rights (see Figure 1–3).

TABLE 1–2   Rights of Welfare

The following rights are often included within the category of welfare rights:

- Employment
- Food
- Housing
- Education

FIGURE 1–3   **Ethical Models for Business Decisions**

Model	Description	How Applied
Cost/Benefit Model	The greatest good for the greatest number of stakeholders	Estimate the impact alternative actions would have on all stakeholders and select the one that optimizes the benefits of all those stakeholders
Rights Model	Stakeholders' rights to be respected	Reject any alternative that violates a stakeholder's rights

Models of Justice

Justice is an important concept in ethics. But what is justice? To most people, justice refers to a sense of fair play, of getting or giving what is owed or due. It includes a principle of equality—people in like situations are treated alike. However, problems occur when we try to determine when people are in equal positions. The two types of justice are procedural justice and distributive justice.

Procedural Justice

The form of justice that deals with the process used in deciding outcomes is referred to as **procedural justice**. For example, in a business context, the process used in making promotions is an issue of procedural justice. In law, the procedures followed in passing legislation or in lawsuits are matters of procedural justice.

Several concepts are often included in descriptions of procedural justice, such as

- To give advance notice to stakeholders before an action is taken.
- To provide an opportunity for stakeholders to give input before an action is taken.
- To be consistent in the administration of the rules.

Distributive Justice

Distributive justice concerns how things of value are distributed. When confronting questions of how to pay workers, whether to declare a dividend to shareholders, and whether to vote for a particular tax proposal, we are confronting questions of distributive justice. The three major models of distributive justice are merit, capitalist, and Marxist.

Merit

A popular model of justice asserts that if any distribution of things of value is based on merit, the distribution is just. This is the **merit model of justice.** For example, employers commonly say they use merit selection to choose employees or merit pay to pay them. Critics of the merit model point to the problem of specification of merit. For example, suppose a company decides to pay its chemists in the research and development department on the basis of merit. How is merit to be determined—by the number of patents obtained, the number of products invented, the academic qualifications of each chemist, or how many hours each chemist spends in the laboratory?

Capitalism

Milton Friedman expressed this model of distributive justice as follows: "The ethical principle that would directly justify the distribution of income in a free market society is, 'To each according to what he and the instruments he owns produces.'"[1] This is the **capitalist model of justice.** Stated differently, this model asserts that any distribution of things of value resulting from unfettered economic competition is just. Critics question how this concept of distributive justice would treat those who cannot compete, such as the sick and the elderly.

Marxism

Karl Marx expressed his model of economic justice as follows: "From each according to his ability, to each according to his needs!"[2] This is the **Marxist model of justice**. Critics of the Marxist model of distributive justice maintain that it fails to address the problem presented when resources are inadequate to satisfy everyone's needs. Critics assert that under conditions of scarcity and incompatible needs, the Marxist model suffers the same problem that afflicts a merit model: the problem of specification. With the merit model, the problem is how to specify merit. With the Marxist model, the problem is how to determine whose needs matter (see Figure 1–4).

Ethics in Action: Selected Ethical/Legal Issues

This section of the chapter focuses on two ethical/legal issues that have resulted in litigation. The first concerns the issue of when a duty to act arises. The second concerns the issue of keeping promises. As you read this case material, try to determine which ethical model is reflected by the opinion. Also try to determine how the other, competing model would have approached the issue.

---

[1] Milton Friedman, *Capitalism and Freedom* 161–62 (1962).
[2] Karl Marx, *Critique of the Gotha Programme* 10 (1936).

<u>FIGURE 1–4</u>   **Justice Models for Business Decisions**

Model	Description	How Applied
Procedural justice	Requires fairness in decision-making procedures	Gives advance notice in the form of rules for actions to be taken, provides an opportunity for stakeholder input, consistently administers the rules
Distributive justice	Fair distribution of benefits and burdens	Various models are available, including making distributions according to merit, wealth, or need

Application of this analytical approach should not be limited to only the cases in this chapter. You should also be alert to the ethical issues involved in later cases throughout the book.

The Duty to Act

"Am I my brother's keeper?" Many assert that the moral answer to this question is yes. When raised in the context of someone's duty to render assistance, however, the law's answer may surprise you.

The following case involves the issue of when a person should be held to a duty to render assistance to another. The case is a tort case for wrongful death, the same type of tort case that the plaintiff brought in *Otis v. Clark,* presented in the Introduction.

SOLDANO V. O'DANIELS
190 Cal. Rptr. 310 (Calif. App. 1983)

Darrell Soldano was shot and killed by Rudolph Villanueva at Happy Jack's Saloon. An eating establishment, the Circle Inn, was across the street from Happy Jack's. On the date of the shooting, a patron of Happy Jack's came into the Circle Inn and informed the bartender that a man had been threatened at Happy Jack's. The patron requested the bartender to either call the police or allow him to use the Circle Inn phone to call the police. The telephone was not in a private office but positioned where it could be used by patrons without inconvenience to the Circle Inn's owner or guests. The bartender refused this request. Soldano's son (the plaintiff) sued the owner of the Circle Inn, Howard O'Daniels (the defendant),

Ethical Dilemmas/Issues

The following questions were included in a Gallup Organization poll conducted for *The Wall Street Journal*.[3] The poll surveyed the opinions of the general public as well as business executives. To compare your responses with those of the survey's participants, see Appendix K in the back of the book.

Family versus Ethics.   Jim, a 56-year-old manager with children in college, discovers that the owners of his company are cheating the government out of several thousand dollars a year in taxes. Jim is the only employee who would be in a position to know this. Should Jim report the owners to the Internal Revenue Service at the risk of endangering his own livelihood, or disregard the discovery in order to protect his family's livelihood?

The Roundabout Raise.   When Joe asks for a raise, his boss praises his work but says the company's rigid budget won't allow any further merit raises for the time being. Instead, the boss suggests that the company "won't look too closely at your expense account for a while." Should Joe take this as an authorization to pad his expense account on grounds that he is simply getting the same money he deserves through a different route, or not take the roundabout "raise?"

The Faked Degree.   Bill has done a sound job for over a year. Bill's boss learns that he got the job by claiming to have a college degree, although he actually never graduated. Should his boss dismiss him for submitting a fraudulent resume or overlook the false claim since Bill has otherwise proven to be conscientious and honorable, and making an issue of the degree might ruin Bill's career?

Sneaking Phone Calls.   Helen discovers that a fellow employee makes about $100 a month worth of personal long-distance telephone calls from an office telephone. Should Helen report the employee to the company or disregard the calls on the grounds that many people make personal calls at the office?

---

[3] Ricklefs, "Ethics in America," *The Wall Street Journal,* November 27, 1983. Reprinted by permission of The Wall Street Journal, Dow Jones & Company, Inc. All rights reserved.

for the wrongful death of his father. He alleged that the actions of the Circle Inn bartender were a breach of the legal duty that the Circle Inn owed to the decedent. The trial court dismissed the suit and awarded judgment for O'Daniels. The California Court of Appeals reversed the trial court decision and returned the case to that court for trial. What follows is the appellate court decision.

Associate Justice Andreen

Does a business establishment incur liability for wrongful death if it denies use of its telephone to a good samaritan who explains an emergency situation occurring . . . and wishes to call the police?

■   ■   ■

There is a distinction, well rooted in the common law, between action and nonaction.

> The fact that the actor realizes or should realize that action on his part is necessary for another's aid or protection does not of itself impose upon him a duty to take such action. . . .

The distinction between malfeasance and nonfeasance, between active misconduct working positive injury and failure to act to prevent mischief not brought on by the defendant, is founded on "that attitude of extreme individualism so typical of Anglo-Saxon legal thought."

Defendant argues that the request that its employee call the police is a request that it do something. . . .

The refusal of the law to recognize the moral obligation of one to aid another when he is in peril and when such aid may be given without danger and at little cost in effort has been roundly criticized. . . .

[S]pecial relationships which create a duty to render aid [include] that of a common carrier to its passengers, an innkeeper to his guest, possessors of land who hold it open to the public, or one who has a custodial relationship to another. A duty may be created by an undertaking to give assistance.

Here there was no special relationship between the defendant and the deceased. It would be stretching the concept beyond recognition to assert there was a relationship between the defendant and the patron from Happy Jack's Saloon who wished to summon aid. But this does not end the matter.

It is time to re-examine the common law rule of nonliability for nonfeasance in the special circumstances of the instant case.

■   ■   ■

Crime is a blight on our society and a matter of great citizen concern.

■   ■   ■

"[T]hat attitude of extreme individualism so typical of Anglo-Saxon legal thought" may need limited re-examination in the light of current societal conditions and the facts of this case to determine whether the defendant owed a duty to the deceased to permit the use of the telephone.

■   ■   ■

[T]he reluctance of the law to impose liability for nonfeasance . . . is in part due to the difficulties in setting standards and making rules workable.

Many citizens simply "don't want to get involved." No rule should be adopted which would require a citizen to open up his or her house to a stranger so that the latter may use the telephone to call for emergency assistance. As Mrs. Alexander in Anthony Burgess's *A Clockwork Orange* learned to her horror, such an action may be fraught with danger. It does not follow, however, that the use of a telephone in a public portion of a business should be refused for a legitimate emergency call. . . .

A business establishment such as the Circle Inn is open for profit. The owner encourages the public to enter, for his earnings depend on it. A telephone is a necessary adjunct to such a place. It is not unusual in such circumstances for patrons to use the telephone to call a taxicab or family member.

■ ■ ■

We conclude that the bartender owed a duty to the plaintiff's decedent to permit the patron from Happy Jack's to place a call to the police or to place the call himself.

It bears emphasizing that the duty in this case does not require that one must go to the aid of another. That is not the issue here. The employee was not the good samaritan intent on aiding another. The patron was.

■ ■ ■

The possible imposition of liability on the defendant in this case is not a global change in the law. It is but a slight departure from the "morally questionable" rule of nonliability for inaction absent a special relationship.

Case Questions

1. Which ethical model or models do you see reflected in the court's opinion? Explain. How is the concept of justice involved in this case? Explain.
2. Analyze the issue of whether one should be under a duty to render assistance to another using the cost/benefit model. What conclusion do you reach? Explain.
3. Analyze the issue of whether one should be under a duty to render assistance to another using the rights model. What conclusion do you reach? Explain.
4. Suppose that the bartender at the Circle Inn had allowed the patron to use the phone, and the patron called for an ambulance. Suppose further that the ambulance crew arrived and refused to render assistance to Darrell Soldano, because Soldano was bleeding profusely and the crew was concerned about the possibility of contracting HIV (the virus that leads to AIDS). Should the ambulance crew and the ambulance company be held liable for Soldano's wrongful death if emergency medical service could have saved his life? Explain. Is the crew under a moral obligation to come to Soldano's rescue? Explain.

Keeping Promises

Is one ever morally justified in breaking a promise? The business community considers the contract as essential to a functioning economic system. Expressions such as "A deal is a deal," "Freedom of contract," and "But you promised!" convey the moral sentiment that promises are forever. Yet, one need only look inside the typical divorce court, strewn with the shattered promises of lasting marital fidelity, to see contradictory evidence.

The law of contracts (discussed in Chapter 7) addresses the question of which promises should be enforced by courts. The following case involves the issue of whether a surrogate motherhood agreement should be recognized as a binding contract. To state it differently, the issue involved in the case is whether a woman who promises to have a baby for another couple in return for payment is justified in breaking her promise to give the baby to the couple.

IN THE MATTER OF BABY M
537 A.2d 1227 (N.J. 1988)

William and Elizabeth Stern were two upwardly mobile professionals who wanted to have a baby. Elizabeth Stern, a 41-year-old pediatrician, had a mild form of multiple sclerosis, and she and her husband worried that pregnancy would aggravate the disease and leave her paralyzed. William Stern was a 40-year-old pediatrician. The couple had been married for 12 years when they entered into an agreement with Mary Beth Whitehead in 1985 for her to conceive a child through artificial insemination and carry it on the Sterns' behalf. Mary Beth Whitehead, 29, was a housewife with two school-age children by her husband Richard.

The Sterns and the Whiteheads signed a six-page agreement negotiated by Noel Keane, the attorney who brought the Sterns and Whiteheads together. Under the agreement, the Sterns and the Whiteheads agreed that for $10,000, plus more than $10,000 in fees and expenses, Mary Beth Whitehead would be inseminated with William Stern's sperm. The $10,000 fee was to go into an escrow account until he got custody. The agreement also stipulated that the Sterns would assume all legal responsibilities for the baby, even if it was born with serious defects. Whitehead was required to undergo an amniocentesis; if the results showed problems, she agreed to have an abortion if the Sterns insisted. The Whiteheads would give the baby to the Sterns. Mary Beth Whitehead acknowledged that the child would be conceived "for the sole purpose of giving the said child to William Stern."

After the birth, Mary Beth Whitehead changed her mind. Whitehead gave the baby girl to the Sterns three days after the birth—only to beg for her return a day later. The Sterns complied. However, the Sterns sued to have the agreement enforced in court. The trial court held the contract was valid, ordered Whitehead's parental rights terminated, and awarded sole custody of Baby M to William Stern and authorized adoption of Baby M by Elizabeth Stern. The Supreme Court of New Jersey decided that the best interests of the child justified awarding custody to the Sterns and giving Mary Beth Whitehead visitation rights. The court, however, decided that the surrogate contract conflicted with state public policy. The portion of the court's opinion discussing the legal status of the surrogate motherhood agreement follows.

Chief Judge Wilentz

The policies expressed in our comprehensive laws governing consent to the surrender of a child stand in stark contrast to the surrogacy contract and what it implies. Here there is no counseling, independent or otherwise, of the natural mother, no evaluation, no warning.

The only legal advice Mary Beth Whitehead received regarding the surrogacy contract was provided in connection with the contract she previously entered into with another couple.

■   ■   ■

Under the contract, the natural mother is irrevocably committed before she knows the strength of her bond with her child. She never makes a totally voluntary, informed decision, for quite clearly any decision prior to the baby's birth is, in the most important sense, uninformed. . . .

Worst of all, however, is the contract's total disregard of the best interests of the child. There is not the slightest suggestion that any inquiry will be made at any time to determine the fitness of the Sterns as custodial parents, of Mrs. Stern as an adoptive parent, their superiority to Mrs. Whitehead, or the effect on the child of not living with her natural mother.

This is the sale of a child, or, at the very least, the sale of a mother's right to her child, the only mitigating factor being that one of the purchasers is the father. . . .

Intimated, but disputed, is the assertion that surrogacy will be used for the benefit of the rich at the expense of the poor. . . .

[I]t is unlikely that surrogate mothers will be as proportionately numerous among those women in the top twenty percent income bracket as among those in the bottom twenty percent.

■   ■   ■

The point is made that Mrs. Whitehead *agreed* to the surrogacy arrangement, supposedly fully understanding the consequences. Putting aside the issue of how compelling her need for money may have been, and how significant her understanding of the consequences, we suggest that her consent is irrelevant. There are, in a civilized society, some things that money cannot buy. In America, we decided long ago that merely because conduct purchased by money was "voluntary" did not mean that it was good or beyond regulation and prohibition. Employers can no longer buy labor at the lowest price they can bargain for, even though that labor is "voluntary," or buy women's labor for less money than paid to men for the same job, or purchase the agreement of children to perform oppressive labor, or purchase the agreement of workers to subject themselves to unsafe or unhealthy working conditions. There are, in short, values that society deems more

important than granting to wealth whatever it can buy, be it labor, love, or life. Whether this principle recommends prohibition of surrogacy, which presumably sometimes results in great satisfaction to all of the parties, is not for us to say. We note here only that, under existing law, the fact that Mrs. Whitehead "agreed" to the arrangement is not dispositive.

The long-term effects of surrogacy contracts are not known, but feared—the impact on the child who learns her life was bought, that she is the offspring of someone who gave birth to her only to obtain money; the impact on the natural mother as the full weight of her isolation is felt along with the full reality of the sale of her body and her child; the impact on the natural father and adoptive mother once they realize the consequences of their act. Literature in related areas suggests these are substantial considerations, although given the newness of surrogacy, there is little information. . . .

The surrogacy contract is based on principles that are directly contrary to the objectives of our laws. It guarantees the separation of a child from its mother; it looks to adoption regardless of suitability; it totally ignores the child; it takes the child from the mother regardless of her wishes and her maternal fitness; and it does all this, it accomplishes all of its goals, through the use of money.

Beyond that is the potential degradation of some women that may result from this arrangement. In many cases, of course, surrogacy may bring satisfaction, not only to the infertile couple, but to the surrogate mother herself. The fact, however, that many women may not perceive surrogacy negatively but rather see it as an opportunity does not diminish its potential for devastation to other women.

In sum, the harmful consequences of this surrogacy arrangement appear to us all too palpable. In New Jersey, the surrogate mother's agreement to sell her child is void. Its irrevocability infects the entire contract, as does the money that purports to buy it.

Case Questions

1. Which ethical model or models do you see reflected in the court's opinion? Explain. How is the concept of justice involved in this case? Explain.

2. Analyze the issue of whether surrogate motherhood contracts should be recognized as enforceable promises using the cost/benefit model. Which conclusion do you reach? Explain.

3. Analyze the issue of whether surrogate motherhood contracts should be recognized as enforceable promises using the rights model. Which conclusion do you reach? Explain.

4. Suppose that the Sterns and the Whiteheads had agreed that an embryo created from the sperm of Mr. Stern and the egg of Mrs. Stern would be implanted in Mrs. Whitehead. Under these circumstances should the Sterns-Whitehead agreement be enforced? Explain.

Ethics in Action: Ethics Codes and Compliance Programs

How seriously do business organizations and their executives take business ethics? There was a time when the words *business ethics* were thought to be mutually exclusive terms. However, today a manager will not be considered a sophisticated executive if he or she maintains a cavalier attitude toward business ethics.

A prominent concern of many of America's largest corporations is developing corporate cultures that encourage ethical behavior and discourage unethical behavior. Organizations have developed and enforced codes of ethics, instituted formal ethics training programs, hired ethical consultants, maintained standing ethics committees, and their top managers have actively addressed ethical problems confronting their organizations. Ninety percent of Fortune 500 companies now have a code of ethics in place, and nearly half have added chief ethics officers or chief compliance officers to their management rosters.

One motive for developing corporate ethics codes and compliance programs is the federal sentencing guidelines for corporate crime, which hold companies liable when employees are convicted of felonies or Class A misdemeanors. The guidelines also permit dramatic increases in penalties—400 percent or more—for companies that do not have in place an effective program to prevent and detect violations of the law.

Whatever the motivation, many businesses and their executives take seriously the management of a company's values. Corporate ethics codes and compliance programs show that companies are dealing with ethics in a systematic way.

Business Ethics in a Global Economy

In today's global economy, corporations and executives encounter ethical issues that arise when different cultural traditions are confronted. How should American companies and their employees respond when doing business in countries where bribery of political officials is common, or in countries that permit discrimination against certain ethnic groups?

Some argue that **cultural relativism**, which holds that no culture has better ethics than any other, is the answer. Their position is captured by the old saying, "When in Rome, do as the Romans do." On the other hand, others, like Tom Donaldson, professor of business ethics at the Georgetown University School of Business, reject the notion of relativism.

Donaldson recognizes that many cross-cultural conflicts do not implicate fundamental rights, and therefore tolerance of minor ethical differences should be practiced. However, some conflicts involve fundamental values, and that is where Donaldson advises companies and their employees to draw the line. Donaldson maintains that there are "certain norms so fundamental to the human condition that they have transcultural implications." According to Donaldson:

> Companies encounter this kind of situation frequently. [For example] surveys of people in Central America show that the average Central American went to work at the age of eleven. If we believe in the right to a minimum education, which includes, at the very least, the ability to read and write, then surely hiring very young children for ongoing full-time labor fails the moral threshold test. The corporation doing this has failed to protect the basic human right to a minimal education from deprivation.[4]

When encountering cross-cultural ethical conflict, companies and managers often seek creative solutions to ethical problems. For example, companies can negotiate with their international trading partners regarding concerns about unethical practices. Companies sometimes try to establish international standards through organizations like the International Chamber of Commerce. At times, American companies have asked the U.S. government to negotiate treaties to have American ethical standards (e.g., labor standards) of business adopted abroad.

Chapter Problems

1. Define the following terms:

a. Ethics	*f.* Distributive justice
b. Cost/benefit model	*g.* Merit model of justice
c. Stakeholders	*h.* Capitalist model of justice
d. Rights model	*i.* Marxist model of justice
e. Procedural justice	*j.* Cultural relativism

2. Roussel-Uclaf, a French pharmaceutical company, developed RU-486, commonly known as the *abortion pill*. By inducing menstruation, RU-486 prevents a fertilized egg from being implanted on the uterine wall; it also causes eggs already implanted to be shed. RU-486 is most effective during

---

[4] Thomas Donaldson, "When in Rome, Do . . . What?" a paper delivered at an international conference for business leaders on ethics of business in a global economy, conducted by the Council for Ethics in Economics, March 25–27, 1992, in Columbus, Ohio.

the first seven weeks of pregnancy. The pill was attacked by antiabortion groups but widely hailed by the health-care community. Antiabortion groups argue that the pill's only use is solely for the killing of an unborn baby. Health-care professionals assert that the pill facilitates the life of a woman, who will otherwise have surgery with side effects. Abortion had been legal in France for 15 years when Roussel-Uclaf developed and marketed the pill. However, when antiabortion groups threatened to boycott Roussel-Uclaf, it suspended marketing of RU-486. Do you think Roussel-Uclaf's management was morally justified in suspending the pill's marketing? Explain.

3. Jim Davis is a research and development chemist employed by Acme Chemical Company. Acme has a range of chemical products marketed strictly in the northeastern region of the United States. Davis has developed a chemical that he knows will generate a high demand in the United States and, perhaps, worldwide. However, he feels Acme does not have a reputable enough name to market his discovery. Davis decided to approach a large, western-based chemical corporation. They are willing to hire him, provided they obtain the rights to produce and market the chemical. In return, Davis will be given a large block of the corporation's common stock and his salary will be tripled. Davis is considering the offer. He figures the most Acme will do is give him a bonus for his discovery. Do you feel that Davis is morally justified in considering an offer from the western corporation? Explain. If you were in his position, would you feel obligated to notify Acme of your discovery and not search for alternatives? Explain.

4. Sam Abbott worked 20 years in the sales division of a major soft drink bottling company. He retired three years ago, having risen to the position of vice president of sales. Sam's dream has been to start his own business. So on retirement, Sam used his savings and pension funds to buy the Overland Truck Stop. As a result of the construction of several fast-food restaurants nearby, the Overland Truck Stop has been losing business.

    Robert Grubb approached Abbott offering to sell him the patent rights on a product Grubb named the Stealth Car Bra. This car bra is a rubber covering that stretches over the front of an automobile. What distinguishes the Stealth Car Bra from other car bras is that it contains a chemical that deflects radar beams. When placed on the front of an automobile, the Stealth Car Bra makes the automobile invisible to police radar.

    Abbott asked his attorney, Mary Margolis, for an opinion on the legality of producing and selling the Stealth Car Bra. Margolis responded that no state or federal law forbids the manufacture or sale of such a device. Margolis also reported that five southeastern states prohibit the manufacture and sale of radar detection devices.

    Abbott recently received an offer from Scott Jennings to buy the Overland Truck Stop. With the money from the sale of the truck stop, Abbott can accept Grubb's offer, set up production, and begin marketing the Stealth Car Bra.

Do you think Abbott would be morally justified in using the proceeds of the sale of the Overland Truck Stop to accept Grubb's offer and produce and sell the Stealth Car Bra? Explain.

5. Your company is considering selling its product in a foreign country. To do business in this country, your company needs a license from the government. It is accepted practice, and expected by the officials, that to get the license you must hire a certain local individual and pay him $250,000. If payment is not made to this official, and your company decides to go through proper channels, your company can expect the granting of the license to be delayed by two years. Once the license is obtained, your company can expect to make at least $20 million a year from sales in that country. You are the vice president of marketing for your company. What will be your recommendation regarding making this payment to the foreign individual? Explain.

6. Sid Chiarella, a printer for Pandick Press, was responsible for printing five announcements of corporate takeover bids. (A takeover bid is where a person or company offers to buy a controlling share of the stock from the shareholders of another corporation—called the target company—in a bid to take over control of the target company.) The names of the target companies were omitted or replaced with false names. The real names were not sent to Chiarella until the final night of printing. Despite these precautions, Chiarella was able to figure out the names of the target companies from other information in the documents. He immediately purchased stock in those companies and then (without informing the sellers of the forthcoming takeover bid) sold the shares after the takeover attempts were made public. As a result, he realized a $30,000 profit. Do you feel that Chiarella's conduct is morally justified? Explain.

7. Continental Airlines Corporation has lost over $500 million in recent years. One cause of the loss is that Continental's competitors have lower labor costs and, thus, are able to charge lower fares. Continental is not able to pay its debts as they become due. Consequently, some of its creditors have threatened to cut off services. Continental has made efforts to adjust its collective bargaining agreements with the unions representing Continental employees. Continental has proposed that the collective bargaining agreements currently in force be modified to reduce pay and work benefits for employees; however, the unions have refused to accept Continental's proposals.

Continental is entitled by law to file a bankruptcy petition requesting what is referred to in bankruptcy law as a reorganization. In such a petition, Continental can seek to have the court reject its collective bargaining agreements and other employee contracts. If the request is granted, Continental would no longer be bound by its collective bargaining contracts. Under such a bankruptcy reorganization, Continental would continue to do business while arrangements were being made by the court to adjust Continental's contractual obligations.

   Would Continental be morally justified in filing for protection under the bankruptcy laws in an effort to avoid its costly labor contracts? Explain. If you were the president of Continental, what would you do?

8. Skyhigh Construction Corporation specializes in multifloor office buildings predominately located in major cities throughout the United States. Skyhigh is a very respected firm in the high-rise construction industry. It has the reputation of completing all contracts on time and on budget. Frank Cook, a site supervisor for Skyhigh, comments, "Skyhigh employs an average of 240 construction workers per site. For those who work up on the beams, this is a high health-risk occupation. There is a small but considerable number of serious and sometimes fatal accidents at every site before the job is completed. To meet deadlines, I sometimes must send the crew up when weather conditions are not favorable. My crew members are working in a potentially dangerous environment, but they are compensated with attractive wages. If one of them complains about going up every time it gets a little windy, I fire that person. When Skyhigh signs a contract, my job is to ensure completion of it on time!" Do you feel that Skyhigh's policy as reflected in Frank Cook's comments is morally justified? Explain.

9. Kaiser Steel Corp. has a plant in Gramercy, Louisiana. Kaiser's policy has been to hire as craft workers in the plant only people who have had prior experience. As a result, almost all of these workers are white. The work force in Gramercy is 40 percent African-American. You are the director of human resource management at Kaiser's Gramercy plant. You have been asked to consider establishing training programs to teach unskilled workers the skills necessary to become craft workers. The program would reserve 50 percent of the openings for African-American employees. This aspect of the program would continue until the percentage of African-American in the craft work force approximated the percentage of African-Americans in the local labor force. Would you be morally justified in establishing such a program? Explain.

10. Frank Senour is the president of Intercontinental Oil Company. Intercontinental maintains its corporate headquarters in the United States, but also has offices in several Southeast Asian and South American countries, where Intercontinental does much of its business. Intercontinental is looking for a manager of international marketing for its Southeast Asian and South American operations. The position requires that the manager travel to Intercontinental's several Southeast Asian and South American offices and interact with present and prospective customers of the company. Joyce Reichman is qualified for the position, has been with the company 12 years, and has been the manager of Intercontinental's marketing operations in the United States for the last four years. She is the only applicant for the position.

Frank is aware that according to the practices currently in force in several Southeast Asian and South American countries where Intercontinental does business, many of Intercontinental's customers would prefer to do business with men rather than women. As a result, Frank realizes that Joyce will have great difficulty performing the job of international marketing manager. Nevertheless, Joyce tells Frank that she can do the job, if given the chance. What should Frank do? Would he be morally justified in refusing to promote Joyce? Explain.

2 INTERNATIONAL LEGAL ENVIRONMENT OF BUSINESS

Learning Objectives

After learning this chapter the student should be able to:

- Describe the sources of international law.
- Describe the various ways a business may enter a foreign market.
- Describe the operation of import and export trade regulation.
- Describe the methods of international dispute resolution.

Economic conditions in the United States, as in all other nations in the world, have increasingly been affected by the global economy. This chapter introduces the processes and environment of international business, beginning with a consideration of international law.

Sources of International Law

The sources of international law are international conventions, general principles of law recognized by civilized nations, decisions by domestic courts, and the rules of supranational organizations.

    International conventions or treaties are agreements between two or more nations. They generally result from much negotiation, create a private legal system for the parties (frequently including a method of resolving disputes), and are generally contained in a signed writing. Treaties affect more than purely political issues; they often affect trade relations between countries.

In certain cases, nations recognize international customs that have been generally accepted by a majority of nations for a long time as binding upon them. For example, the meaning of such terms as *seaworthy* or *good faith* are also a product of international custom.

Civilized nations recognize certain general principles of law. To find such principles, one must examine various domestic legal systems. An illustration of a general principle of law recognized by civilized nations is that of not admitting coerced confessions into evidence.

A source of international law that has been developed recently is the supranational organization. A supranational organization is created by a treaty entered into by several nations to form a regional trade bloc. The supranational organization contains an institutional structure for making and administering law that directly covers individuals within a member country.

An example of a supranational organization creating a regional trade area is the **European Economic Community**, or European Community (EC), which was created in 1957 by the Treaty of Rome. Today the EC includes Belgium, Germany, France, Italy, Luxembourg, the Netherlands, Denmark, Ireland, the United Kingdom, Greece, Spain, and Portugal. The EC forms a common market for the free movement of goods, people, capital, and businesses. Institutional structures within the EC carry out its law-making, executive, administrative, and judicial functions. For example, the European Commission makes regulations and issues directives. Regulations apply directly to member countries, while directives maintain that the countries bring their national law into harmony with the standard set in the directive. The European Court of Justice interprets EC law and resolves conflicts between national law and EC law. In 1986, the EC passed a law known as the *Single European Act,* which set a goal of eliminating remaining trade barriers by 1992 to form a single market.

Examples of other regional trade agreements include the Andean Common Market (ANCOM), the Association of Southeast Asian Nations (ASEAN), and the United States-Canada Free Trade Agreement.

The United States, Canada, and Mexico negotiated the North American Free Trade Agreement (NAFTA) in 1992. NAFTA will become effective January 1, 1994, if it is approved by the legislatures of these countries. By reducing trade barriers among the three countries, NAFTA creates the largest free trade area in the world.

Entering a Foreign Market

Suppose Dampers, Inc. has recently designed a disposable diaper guaranteed to produce "a drier, happier baby." Dampers's marketing director, Stocton Gamble, has determined that the growing South American middle class would be receptive to this new Dampers product. Which methods are available to Dampers in marketing its diapers overseas? The following discussion examines various methods of entering a foreign market.

The Direct Sales Contract

If Dampers wishes to export its diapers directly to several large grocery chains in Venezuela, it would have to be concerned with the risks of not being paid and of loss of goods in transit, along with the law governing contracts and the means of resolving disputes that might arise. Each of these concerns is discussed in this section. Other concerns, such as tariff and nontariff barriers to Dampers, are considered later in this chapter.

The Sales Contract

Dampers first negotiates a sales contract with the Venezuelan grocery chains. Frequently, the contract is created by an exchange of forms. Dampers sets forth the terms of its performance in its invoice, including such items as price, shipping terms, and risk of loss. The Venezuelan stores ordering the diapers set forth the terms of their performance in a purchase order form.

Several key provisions of the sales contract should be noted. One is a **choice-of-law provision**, which specifies the body of law that governs the contract. In some cases, this provision names a particular country's domestic law. The parties may also choose to have specific clauses governed by a treaty or by rules developed by an international organization, such as the International Chamber of Commerce (ICC). Parties are generally free to choose the law they wish to govern their transaction. Here, they might choose United States or Venezuelan contract law to govern the contract.

Unless the parties to an international contract opt out or specify otherwise, **the United Nations Convention on Contracts for the International Sale of Goods** automatically applies international legal rules for the sale of goods if the buyer and seller have places of business in different countries that have ratified the convention. Many countries, including the United States and Venezuela, have ratified the convention.

Another key provision in the sales contract is shipping terms. Shipping terms determine the point where the risk of loss passes and forms a basis for quoting prices and defining when a seller's performance is completed. A long commercial history lies behind the meaning of such shipping terms as *F.O.B.* (free on board), *F.A.S.* (free along side), *C. & F.* (cost and freight), and *C.I. & F.* (cost, insurance, and freight).

The governing rules covering most American overseas contracts, the Revised American Foreign Trade Definitions of 1941 (RAFD), are being rapidly replaced both here and overseas by an International Chamber of Commerce publication known as *INCOTERMS* (International Rules for the Interpretation of Trade Terms) *of 1980.* Because precise definitions vary, it is wise to specify governing law, as in the following clause: "This contract shall be governed by I.C.C. INCOTERMS (1980 edition)."

The following case involves a suit brought by the seller against a carrier for damage to merchandise.

MEXICAN PRODUCE CO. V. SEA-LAND SERVICE, INC.
429 F. Supp. 552 (D. Puerto Rico, 1974)

Fourteen hundred cartons of garlic were shipped via the maritime carrier Sea-Land Service, Inc. from San Juan, Puerto Rico, to Trinidad. This was a C.I. & F. transaction, and the goods were damaged en route. The seller, Mexican Produce Co. (plaintiff), sued Sea-Land Service, Inc. (defendant). In the opinion that follows, the trial court grants a summary judgment in favor of Sea-Land. The court dismissed the suit because Mexican Produce did not possess any rights in the damaged merchandise, and therefore had no right to bring this lawsuit.

Chief Judge Toledo

There is no doubt . . . that the terms of the sale in this particular case were cost, insurance and freight Trinidad. Gilmore and Black state in *The Law of Admiralty,* the following:

> Under a C.I. & F. term property passes at the port of shipment and the buyer (for whose benefit the insurance is carried) bears the risk of loss in transit. Where buyer prefers to take out his own insurance . . . the term used is "C. & F." (Cost and Freight). The "C. & F." term has the same meaning so far as seller's performance and the passage of property are concerned, as C.I.F. except that the seller does not see to the insurance coverage.

In the Revised American Foreign Trade Definitions adopted July 30, 1941, by a joint committee representing the Chamber of Commerce of the United States of America, the National Council of American Imports, Inc., and the National Foreign Trade Council, Inc., it will be found that what C.F. and C.I.F. mean, among other things, is that title to the merchandise passes to the [buyer] upon the delivery made by the seller to the carrier of the merchandise at the port of origin. Pursuant to the aforementioned, under a C.I.F. contract naming the point of destination the seller quotes a price

including the cost of the goods, the marine insurance and all the transportation charges to the named port of destination. Under the quotation the seller must:

1. provide and pay for transportation to a named point of destination;
2. pay export taxes, or other fees or charges, if any, levied because of exportation;
3. provide and pay for marine insurance on behalf of the [buyer];
4. provide war risk insurance as obtainable in seller's market at the time of shipment at buyer's expense, unless the seller has agreed that the buyer will provide for war risk coverage;
5. obtain and dispatch promptly to the buyer, or his agent, a clean bill of lading to the named point of destination, and also the insurance policy for negotiable insurance certificates;
6. where received-for-shipment ocean bill of lading may be tendered, be responsible for any loss or damage, or both, until the goods have been delivered in the custody of the ocean carrier;

7. where on-board ocean bill of lading is required, be responsible for any loss or damage, or both, until the goods have been delivered on board the vessel;

8. provide, at the buyer's request and expense, certificates of origin, consular invoices, or any other documents issued in the country of origin or of shipment, or of both, which the buyer may need or may require for importation of goods into the named point of destination and, where necessary, for their passage in transit through another country.

Under the C.I.F. quotation, the buyer must:

1. accept the documents when presented;

2. receive the goods upon arrival, handle and pay for all subsequent movements of the goods, including taking delivery from the vessel in accordance with the bill of lading clauses and terms and pay all costs of the landing including any duties, taxes and other expenses at the named point of destination;

3. pay for war risk insurance provided by seller;

4. be responsible for loss of or damage to goods, or both, from the time and place at which seller's obligations under number 6 and number 7 above have ceased;

5. pay the cost of certificates of origin, consular invoices or any other documents issued in the country of origin or of shipment, or of both, which may be required for importation of the goods into the country of destination and, where necessary, for their passage in transit through another country.

The fact that the . . . buyer is responsible for the loss or damage to goods, or both, from the time and place at which the seller delivered the goods to the ocean carrier at the port of origin, has been decided by this Court.

It appearing . . . that the [one who has the right to sue in] this litigation is not the plaintiff . . . summary judgment shall be entered on behalf of defendant. . . .

Case Questions

1. How does a C. & F. contract differ from a C.I. & F. contract?

2. Which key elements of the C.I. & F. contract led to the court's determination in this case?

3. Why did the seller bring this action?

Letters of Credit

Dampers wants to assure itself that it will be paid if it ships the diapers. On the other hand, the Venezuelan stores want assurance that they will not have to pay unless the seller complies with the terms of the sales contract. How can both parties achieve their goals?

If payment is made in advance, the buyer is trusting the seller to carry out the terms of the contract, and the risk of nonperformance is on the buyer. In contrast, if payment is made after shipment, the seller is trusting the buyer to pay, and the risk of nonperformance is on the seller.

If both parties wish to reduce their mutual risks to a minimum, they may decide to use a **letter of credit** to facilitate payment. In a letter of credit, a bank substitutes its credit for that of the buyer. The seller thus relies on the bank's credit for payment rather than on the buyer's credit.

The buyer (a Venezuelan grocery chain) would enter into a contract with its bank (the issuing bank) to arrange a letter of credit on its behalf to ensure payment to the seller if certain conditions are met. The type of letter of credit is prescribed in the sales contract. Typically, the contract calls for an irrevocable letter of credit, which means that the letter cannot be cancelled without the agreement of both the buyer and the seller. In addition, the sales contract frequently calls for a confirmed letter of credit, which means that the issuing bank forwards the letter of credit to a bank near the seller's place of business, the confirming bank. The confirming bank then notifies the seller that it will pay if the correct documents are presented.

Bills of Lading

The notice the confirming bank sends to Dampers includes the requirement that Dampers deliver certain documents to the confirming bank as a prerequisite for payment, documents listed in the sales contract between the buyer and the seller. These typically include an insurance certificate, an invoice, a packing list, and relevant bills of lading.

A **bill of lading** is a document issued by a person engaged in the business of transporting goods. The bill of lading serves several functions: as a receipt by the shipowner acknowledging that goods have been received, a memorandum of the contract between the seller and the shipowner for shipping, and a document of title that is typically negotiable. If the bill of lading is negotiable, the shipowner promises to deliver the goods to whomever is in possession of the properly endorsed bill of lading. Control of the bill of lading thus controls the right to the goods. The sales contract typically specifies the types of bill of lading to be used. In the United States, the relationship of the shipper and the shipowner is governed by the Carriage of Goods by Sea Act of 1971 (CAGSA). The CAGSA adopts rules known as the *Hague Rules,* which also have been adopted by many other countries.

Obtaining Payment

Letters of credit typically specify that payment will be made to the seller by the seller's presentation of a sight draft or a time draft. A sight draft is the seller's demand for immediate payment drawn on the confirming bank. A time draft is a demand for payment after a certain period of time (e.g., "pay after 180 days"). The confirming bank has promised to pay either a sight or a time draft in its confirmed letter of credit if Dampers meets the conditions of the letter (e.g., if Dampers delivers all relevant documents). In turn, the confirming bank draws a draft on the buyer's issuing bank demanding payment and sends the issuing bank all relevant documents. Finally, the issuing bank either deducts money from the buyer's account or draws a draft and demands payment from the buyer as a condition for turning the negotiable bill of lading over to the buyer. The entire direct export sales contract is summarized by Figure 2–1.

A rule of strict compliance is followed in making payments under a documentary sale involving a letter of credit. The documents the seller provides must

FIGURE 2–1   **Direct Export Sales Contract**

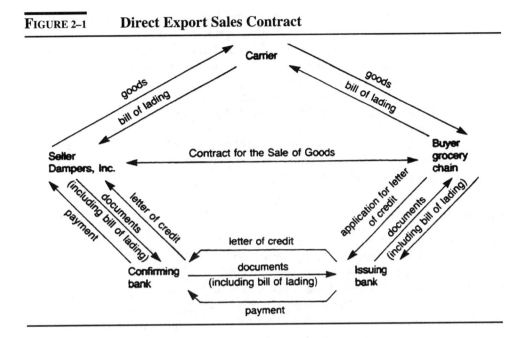

match precisely the terms of the letter of credit before the issuing bank is required to make payment. If there is a difference (called a *discrepancy*) in the documents and the letter of credit, the bank may refuse payment. If the bank pays where there is a discrepancy, the buyer does not have to pay the bank. Where a discrepancy exists, the issuing bank may ask the buyer to waive the discrepancy in order to proceed with payment. In the perilous international marketplace, it is a sacrosanct rule that payment by the bank is made on the documents, not on whether the goods conform to the order. If the documents are in order, payment is made. If the documents are discrepant, payment may be refused. The following case illustrates the importance of accurate documents in international sales.

ALASKA TEXTILE CO., INC. V. CHASE MANHATTAN BANK, N.A.
982 F.2d 813 (2nd Cir. 1992)

Alaska Textile Co. is a New York-based textile company that exports fabric from India. Lloyd Williams Fashions, Inc. ("Lloyd"), a manufacturer of women's clothing, contracted with Alaska in early 1988 to buy Indian silk to be delivered to Lloyd's facility in Hong Kong. To make payment, Lloyd arranged for Chase Manhattan Bank to issue two letters of credit in favor of Alaska.

Alaska shipped the silk from India to Hong Kong on April 2, 1988 and forwarded the necessary documents to its confirming bank, Merchants Bank of New York. Merchants informed Alaska of several discrepancies in the documents.

Alaska directed Merchants to present the documents to Chase and ask Chase to request Lloyd to waive the discrepancies and authorize payment.

Chase promptly advised Lloyd of the discrepancies, and asked whether it would waive them. Over the next two weeks, Alaska and Lloyd continued to negotiate over payment for the silk.

On May 18, 1988, Chase sent a telex to Merchants Bank restating the discrepancies justifying dishonor and stating that the documents were being held at Alaska's disposal.

Alaska sued Chase for wrongful dishonor of the letters of credit. The trial judge decided in favor of Chase. Alaska appealed, and the appellate court affirmed the trial judge's decision.

Circuit Judge McLaughlin

A brief description of what a letter of credit is and how it works may illuminate the discussion. Suppose that B, a Japanese buyer, wants to buy cloth from S, a New York seller. S does not know B and is reluctant to ship the cloth to Japan on credit, with no solid assurance that B will ever pay him.

To allay S's concerns, B may arrange to have a bank issue an irrevocable letter of credit in favor of S. S may then ship the cloth to Japan, secure in his own mind that he will be paid by the bank. The commercial letter of credit, then, is a common payment mechanism in international trade that permits the buyer in a transaction to substitute the financial integrity of a stable credit source (usually a bank) for his own.

In its classic form, the letter of credit is only one of three distinct relationships between three different parties: (1) the underlying contract for the purchase and sale of goods between the buyer ("account party") and the seller ("beneficiary"), with payment to be made through a letter of credit to be issued by the buyer's bank in favor of the seller; (2) the application agreement between the bank and the buyer, describing the terms the issuer must incorporate into the credit and establishing how the bank is to be reimbursed when it pays the seller under the letter of credit; and (3) the actual letter of credit which is the bank's irrevocable promise to pay the seller-beneficiary when the latter presents certain documents (e.g., documents of title, transport and insurance documents, and commercial invoices) that conform with the terms of the credit.

■   ■   ■

Because the credit engagement is concerned only with documents, the terms and conditions of a letter of credit must be strictly adhered to. . . . If the documents do comply with the terms of the credit, the issuer's duty to pay is absolute, regardless of whether the buyer-account party complains that the goods are nonconforming. Issuers, moreover, must swiftly and carefully examine documents submitted for payment; and they are [prevented] from complaining about discrepancies they did not assert promptly.

■   ■   ■

These developments are embodied in the UCP [Uniform Customs and Practices for Documentary Credits], a compilation of internationally accepted commercial practices, first issued in 1930 by the International Chamber of Commerce and revised approximately every ten years since. The UCP enjoys a unique status. Although it is not law, the UCP applies to most letters of credit (including the ones at issue in this case) because issuers generally incorporate it into their credits.

■   ■   ■

The UCP provides that "the issuing bank shall have a reasonable time in which to examine the documents and to determine, as above, whether to take up or to refuse the documents." If the issuer does not act in accordance with this provision, it "shall be precluded from claiming that the documents are not in accordance with the terms and conditions of the credit," i.e., it must honor the credit.

■   ■   ■

We hold that Chase acted reasonably under the circumstances. Until either Lloyd decided whether to waive, or Alaska requested action (one way or the other) on its demand for payment, Chase was proceeding as it had been requested, and the matter was out of its control.

■   ■   ■

The letter of credit is intended to grease the wheels of trade and commerce. As many as half of the demands for payment under letters of credit are discrepant, yet, in the vast majority of cases, the account party waives the discrepancies and authorizes payment. This process is efficient, and the law should encourage it, particularly when the beneficiary has acknowledged that its documents are discrepant and has specifically requested that the issuer consult the account party.

We acknowledge that this result is not altogether satisfactory because it leaves open the issue of when, having heard neither from the account party nor the beneficiary, the issuer must nevertheless act on the beneficiary's demand for payment. . . . [T]his uncertainty is likely to be short-lived because the newest revision of the UCP, which is to take effect no later than January 1, 1994, provides that an issuer shall have a reasonable time, not to exceed seven banking days following the receipt of documents, to examine the documents and determine whether to accept or reject them.

Case Questions

1. Why did Chase refuse to make payment to Alaska?
2. Under what circumstances would Chase have made payment to Alaska?
3. According to the UCP, what is the obligation of the issuing bank for inspecting the documents and making payment?
4. Suppose you were the executive in charge of purchasing for Lloyd. What would be your strategy in this situation? Explain.

Indirect Export Sales

Some firms may be unable or unwilling to assume the risks of exporting. Intermediary companies exist to facilitate the export of products from smaller American firms to overseas buyers. Several methods of indirect exporting are available, including export management companies, export trading companies, and piggyback marketing.

An export management company (EMC) in the United States is typically a small company specializing in the sale of a particular product in a foreign market, having contacts with foreign buyers and a foreign distribution network in place. Some larger EMCs finance foreign sales for other companies.

Like an EMC, an **export trading company** (ETC) acts as an intermediary to market goods overseas. An ETC is typically larger than an EMC and provides more services. The major difference between the two is that an ETC traditionally takes title to the goods in this country, while the seller retains title to goods sold through an EMC. The Export Trading Company Act permits banks to be involved

Ethical Dilemmas/Issues

The H.B. Fuller Company is a Minnesota-based manufacturer of industrial adhesives. It produces an industrial glue called *Resistol,* which it sells to Central American shoe manufacturers.

Glue sniffing is widespread among poor youths in Latin America. For at least a decade, street kids in Central America have become addicted to inhalants, the most popular being Fuller's Resistol. It is estimated that 8 million to 16 million of the 40 million street children in Latin America are addicted to Resistol. Abuse is so widespread that the addicts are called *Resistoleros.*

Central American activists have pushed Fuller to add oil of mustard to its Resistol formula on the theory that the oil would make Resistol intolerable to addicts. The Honduras legislature passed a law requiring that oil of mustard be added to Resistol. However, toxology reports show that inhaling oil of mustard produces potentially fatal side effects.

Fuller has tried different glue formulas with other ingredients. However, the other formulas affected the effectiveness of Resistol.

Fuller has also spent $100,000 annually on an education program aimed at telling kids about the danger of addiction.

The countries in Central America where Resistol is sold are characterized by poor economies and unstable governments. It is estimated that two thirds of households live in poverty. Pulling out of the market would cost the economies of these countries badly needed jobs.

Fuller's board of directors is scheduled to meet soon. On the board's agenda is a motion that will be introduced by one of the board members that Fuller discontinue sales of solvent adhesives wherever those products are known to be used as inhalants.

What are the issues? If you were a Fuller board member, what would you do?

in setting up ETCs, encourages the formation of ETCs, and reduces ETCs' antitrust liability.

A third option available to the exporter is called *piggyback marketing,* in which one company distributes another company's products through its overseas distribution facilities. Usually, the piggyback product complements a product already manufactured by the distributor, thus enhancing the marketability of both products.

Manufacturing in a Foreign Market

Suppose that instead of exporting its diapers to Venezuela, either directly or indirectly, Dampers, Inc. decided to invest in Venezuela through some form of direct presence there. Various forms of operation are available.

Foreign Subsidiaries and Branches

In a wholly owned branch or subsidiary, a U.S. firm exercises complete control over the marketing and production of the foreign facility through 100 percent stock ownership. Technology, such as trade secrets and patented processes, may be transferred with complete protection, depending on local law in the foreign market. The crucial element in the choice of this form of operation is control—it is opted for when control is necessary to accomplish the firm's goals.

The Joint Venture

A **joint venture** may be defined as two or more firms contributing assets toward the conduct of a business. The endeavor becomes an international joint venture when one or more of the firms is not a resident of the foreign country targeted as a market. Frequently, a joint venture involves a U.S. firm and either a foreign government or foreign private-sector firm operating in the foreign country. It could, of course, exist in other forms, such as a U.S. firm and a firm from somewhere other than the targeted foreign country.

The joint venture provides several advantages over wholly owned subsidiaries. First, the foreign partner may contribute its knowledge of the targeted market, its contacts, and its distribution network. Second, the U.S. partner may wish to limit its costs and risks of operation.

The major drawback to the joint venture is the loss of control, not only concerning management of the enterprise but also over technology. Increased liability may also result, because in the worst case the loss of control can diminish the quality of the product produced or result in increased safety or environmental hazards.

Franchising and Trademark Licensing

Dampers, Inc. may decide to license its trademark to a Venezuelan producer for a price. Licensing is simply a contractual arrangement in which a licensee pays royalties (compensation) to a licensor for the right to use the licensor's property. Licensing is a way to make trademarks, patents, copyrights, technology, or trade secrets available to a foreign licensee. The value of licensing is that, in comparison with other forms of foreign investment, it involves much less financial risk. In addition, the know-how of the licensee in its home market is maximized.

Problems with licensing may occur because of the loss of control over the licensed property, resulting in poor quality or the disclosure of secrets to the licensor's competitors. Protection from unfair use can be found in the Vienna Trademark Registration Treaty (TRT). The TRT provides for a firm filing for an international trademark, and the force of the trademarks is governed by national (U.S.) law. Treaties, such as the Paris Convention, also grant holders of international patents the rights they would have in their home countries. Both the TRT and the Paris Convention are administered by the World International Property Organization (WIPO) in Geneva. Thus, the extent to which a company is protected from unfair use of its patents and trademarks depends on whether the country in which the goods are marketed honors the TRT and the Paris Convention.

If Dampers has a product that might be franchised, or if technology is licensed, U.S. and foreign antitrust laws would have to be consulted. The European Economic Community in particular has strict antitrust laws applying to licensing and franchising within it.

International Trade Regulation

After World War II, national leaders understood that it would be advantageous to promote world trade. To do this, it was essential that obstacles to trade, such as high tariff barriers, import and export duties, and nontariff barriers (quotas and licensing procedures), be torn down. The framework for removing these trade barriers is the General Agreement on Tariffs and Trade (GATT).

General Agreement on Tariffs and Trade

In 1947, along with 22 other countries, the United States signed a protocol entitled **General Agreement on Tariffs and Trade (GATT),** which is designed to set limits on tariffs and remove nontariff barriers. GATT deals primarily with the trade of goods, not services. Currently more than 110 nations are members of GATT. GATT's provisions have never been expressly adopted either by Congress or by a U.S. treaty; U.S. adoption rests on a presidential executive order. GATT has been amended from time to time through multilateral negotiations, called *rounds.*

The heart of GATT is the principle of nondiscrimination among all member nations. Each member of GATT agrees to unconditionally grant the same rate of duty and treatment to other GATT members' products, regardless of the country of origin. This nondiscrimination principle is expressed through a most-favored-nation clause (MFN). MFN treatment is the normal, or general, treatment given to a product. As we show later, better or worse treatment (e.g., in the form of lower or higher tariffs) may be granted.

GATT permits numerous exceptions to this nondiscrimination principle. Regional zones, such as a free-trade area, may be designated by a country to grant lower tariffs to an area. The Caribbean Basin Initiative is an executive order by which the United States allows duty- or tariff-free entry of products from the Caribbean. Departures from the nondiscrimination principle are also permitted to protect national security. In addition, nations may favor less-developed countries by granting preference to them in the form of lower tariffs.

Imports

Rates of tariff on goods imported into the United States are set by tariff schedules. The schedules first classify items by product category. Most countries have adopted the Brussels Tariff Nomenclature (BTN) as a means of classifying products. The

United States still uses its own tariff schedules (TSUS) but is moving together with the rest of the world to adopt a new Harmonized Commodity Description and Coding System (HS).

Once a product category is determined, the rate of tariff is set by the product's country of origin. Essentially, three different rates prevail: the lowest rate or duty-free rate for products from least-developed countries or free-trade zones, the normal or MFN rate, and the full rate to non-MFN countries.

The third step in calculating the applicable duty is the valuation of the item. At each step disputes can arise between the importer and the U.S. Customs Service, which assesses and collects the duties and importation fees. Appeals of the Service's determinations may be made to the Court of International Trade (CIT). CIT decisions are appealable to the U.S. Court of Appeals for the Federal Circuit and, ultimately, to the U.S. Supreme Court.

U.S. Trade Remedies

Under GATT and U.S. statutes, remedies may be imposed that are directed at unfairly traded imports. These remedies include antidumping duties (AD), countervailing duties (CVD), Section 337 remedies, and escape clause proceedings.

Antidumping Duties

Dumping is defined as selling exported goods for a price lower than in the home market. The major problem with such pricing policies is the harm caused to competing companies in the importing country. Selective, predatory dumping may drive these competitors out of business, leaving the foreign producer in a monopolistic or oligopolistic position.

Antidumping duties (AD) are imposed on unfairly priced imports if:

- The price in the home market is higher than in the U.S. market.
- The dumped import is causing a material injury to a domestic industry.

The determination of comparative prices is made by the Department of Commerce's International Trade Administration (ITA). The determination of a material injury is made by an independent federal agency, the International Trade Commission (ITC). Typically, an affected industry files a petition with the ITA and ITC, but the Commerce Department may initiate the action as well. A final antidumping order by the Commerce Department (appealable to the Court of International Trade) terminates the procedure.

Countervailing Duties

At times, a government pays subsidies to product manufacturers in the form of bounties or grants to encourage exports. These subsidized goods then can be sold for a lower price in the American market or some other foreign market.

To counteract these subsidies by governments (or by any corporation or individual) **countervailing duties** (CVD) may be imposed on the importation by the importing country. Two issues must be resolved. First, an unfair subsidy's existence and amount must be found by the Commerce Department's ITA. The definition of unfair subsidies and whether they include various forms of tax rebates, credit financing, government training, or research help, for example, is a major definitional problem. Second, the International Trade Commission (ITC) must find that an American industry is materially injured by the subsidized product.

The following case considers the requirement of material injury in the context of the imposition of a countervailing duty.

BRITISH STEEL CORP. V. UNITED STATES
593 F. Supp. 405 (Int'l Ct. Trade 1984)

British Steel Corp. (plaintiff) alleged that the International Trade Commission erred in finding that the U.S. steel industry was materially injured by steel imports from the United Kingdom. The Commerce Department had calculated the amount of subsidy by the British government. British Steel sought review of the Commission's finding in the Court of International Trade. The Court of International Trade affirmed the Commission's determination and dismissed the action.

Senior Judge Newman

The following observations in *American Spring Wire Corporation* concerning "material injury" are also pertinent to the present review:

> In its final antidumping and countervailing duty investigations, the ITC is required to determine whether:
> (A) an industry in the United States
>   (i) is materially injured, or
>   (ii) is threatened with material injury; or
> (B) the establishment of an industry in the United States is materially retarded, by reason of imports of the merchandise with respect to which the administering authority (ITA) has made an affirmative determination. . . .

■   ■   ■

"Material injury" has been defined by Congress as "harm which is not inconsequential, immaterial, or unimportant." Congress has directed the ITC to consider "all relevant economic factors which have a bearing on the state of the industry. . . ." In making an injury determination, the Commission is required to consider, among other factors, the following:

> (i)   the volume of imports of the merchandise which is the subject of the investigation;
> (ii) the effect of imports of that merchandise on prices in the United States for like products, and
> (iii) the impact of imports of such merchandise on domestic producers of like products.

■   ■   ■

Volume of Imports

We first consider plaintiffs' challenge to the Commission's findings relative to import volume.

The Commission collected and evaluated data on the absolute volume of imports of stainless steel plate from the United Kingdom and the proportion of the United States market captured by these imports (viz., market penetration). Upon the basis of such data, the Commission found that the absolute volume of imports of British stainless steel plate, on an annual basis, increased substantially in the last two full years covered by the investigation. Indeed, 1982 imports of British plate rose to the highest point since 1970. The Commission further found that the absolute volume of imports and levels of market penetration by the imports are significant in terms of section 1677(7)(c)(i). There can be no doubt that the Commission complied with the volume criterion in section 1677(7)(C)(i) (1982).

Plaintiffs advance the position that the Commission erred as a matter of commercial reality in making its analysis of import volumes on a calendar year basis and by not considering the most recent quarterly data on import volumes.

The "commercial reality" allegedly not considered by the Commission was that in 1980 Great Britain was affected by a nationwide steel strike, the effects of which lasted throughout 1980 and into the first quarter of 1981. According to plaintiffs, during the strike British exports to the United States "were virtually nonexistent" and in the first quarter of 1981, imports of British steel began returning to "normal levels." Further, plaintiffs emphasize that prior to 1980, import volumes were suppressed by import quotas and a severe exchange rate imbalance in 1979.

[We] point out that (1) the decline in plate imports that plaintiffs attribute to the 1980 strike, in fact, began in 1979, one year prior to the strike; and (2) the quarterly levels of imports after the strike (viz., in 1981 and 1982) were generally significantly higher than pre-strike quarterly levels. Consequently . . . it appears that the strike fails to fully explain the sharp 1982 increase in volume of imports. . . . [W]hatever the reason for the increase in imports, the record shows that annual imports of British plate in 1981 and 1982 reflected substantial increases over all the preceding years as far back as 1970.

Price Undercutting

Turning to the price criterion for determining material injury that is in dispute, the statute directs the Commission, in evaluating the effect of imports on prices, to consider whether "there has been significant price undercutting by the imported merchandise as compared with the price of like products of the United States."

In its decision the Commission found:

> Imports of plate from the United Kingdom undersold the domestic products in all four specifications for which BSC [British Steel] provided data. Underselling occurred throughout 1980–1982 with the exception of one quarter in one specification.

The Commission contacted eight firms which had purchased British plate and one firm which stated that it had used a price quote from BSC to negotiate a more favorable price from a U.S. producer. Four firms gave price as the primary reason for purchasing British plate. Two other firms stated that favorable credit terms or the availability of a refund of duties on its own exports were the reason for its purchase. One firm stated that the primary reason that it purchased British plate was the availability of smaller tonnage orders without paying a premium.

■   ■   ■

The Court agrees with the contention of the Commission that an absence of a direct correlation between price depression and the volume of imports does not necessarily exonerate the imports as a casual factor of the price depression. The statute's causation prerequisite to an affirmative injury determination is satisfied if the subsidized imports contribute, even minimally to the conditions of the domestic industry, and the Commission is precluded from weighing the causes of injury.

■   ■   ■

The Court finds there is substantial evidence that the significant volume of imports of stainless steel plate from the United Kingdom was a contributing factor to the price depression experienced by the domestic industry.

■   ■   ■

For the foregoing reasons, the Commission's determination that imports of stainless steel plate from the United Kingdom have caused material injury to an industry in the United States is affirmed. Accordingly, this action is dismissed.

Case Questions

1. Is a subsidy of a foreign country to its industries helpful or harmful to the American economy? Explain.

2. Which criteria are necessary to find a material injury to an American industry?

3. How did the plaintiff seek to explain the recent increase in its share of the American market?

4. Did the British Steel Corp. cause the decline in the American industry's prices? Explain.

Section 337

Section 337 of the U.S. Tariff Act is designed to stop unfair methods of competition in connection with imported products. Unfair methods of competition include such things as patent, copyright, and trademark infringement, as well as such anticompetitive activities as false advertising and stealing trade secrets.

U.S. companies or the ITC may initiate an action against the Section 337 violator. The ITC is authorized to order that either the goods be barred from import or the violator of Section 337 cease and desist from its anticompetitive activity.

Escape Clause Proceedings

A variety of products are prohibited or restricted from entry into the United States to protect the public's health, safety, or welfare, or to promote American foreign policy interests. Thus, for example, illegal drugs, obscene literature, insects, viruses, and various plants and animals may be banned from entry. Weapons and radioactive materials may also be banned or restricted from entry.

Subject to ITC recommendations, the president also may restrict the entry of any product whose import is determined to cause serious injury to domestic industry. No dumping or subsidy need be found. Under what is known as *escape clause proceedings,* the president has restricted the import of motorcycles, stainless steel flatware, and oil. The proceedings are called an *escape clause* because as a consequence of them tariff concessions granted under GATT may be escaped, that is, revoked.

Resolving International Disputes

Frequently, despite parties' attempts to resolve their own conflicts through preventive means (e.g., contract drafting and risk allocation) as well as informal post hoc (after the fact) means, their differences are irreconcilable. Two basic dispute-resolution mechanisms exist: arbitration and litigation.

Arbitration

Arbitration is where disputing parties agree to submit their disagreement to a private person or persons for decision. Arbitration has enormous advantages as an international dispute-resolution mechanism. Parties may be unfamiliar with any selected country's laws. Publicity from litigation may be unwanted. A particular court system may decline jurisdiction. Judgments may be difficult to enforce.

Through a contractual arbitration clause, parties to an agreement may provide that arbitration is the exclusive remedy for any disputes arising between them. A well-drafted arbitration clause includes a mechanism for selecting an arbitrator; the rules governing procedure, place, language, substantive law, division of expenses, and the time in which arbitration is to be held; and a waiver of any judicial review of the arbitration award.

Various treaties, including the United Nations Convention on the Recognition of Foreign Arbitral Awards (which the United States has signed), encourage American recognition of international arbitration agreements and awards. Model rules for arbitration have been issued by the United Nations, the World Bank, the International Chamber of Commerce, and many nations. The ICC has a permanent and busy court of arbitration established to handle international disputes.

Litigation

Sometimes arbitration is not available, perhaps because there is no agreement to arbitrate or the arbitration agreement has been invalidated by a court. In such cases, litigation (the bringing of a lawsuit in a nation's court of law) is the only alternative to resolving disputes.

Before a nation's court can decide a lawsuit, the court must have jurisdiction to hear the case. Jurisdiction is the lawful power or authority of a court to hear a case. Parties to international agreements usually try to control this by inserting a **choice-of-forum provision** in their international contract. A choice-of-forum provision simply notes the particular nation's courts in which disputes are to be resolved. National rules must be consulted to determine the circumstances in which the parties' choice can or cannot be recognized. The following case illustrates the approach federal courts in the United States have taken to determine whether to recognize the validity of a choice-of-forum clause.

M/S BREMAN V. ZAPATA OFF-SHORE COMPANY
407 U.S. 1 (1972)

Zapata Off-Shore Company, a Houston-based American corporation, contracted with Unterweser, a German corporation, to tow Zapata's ocean-going, self-elevating drilling rig *Chaparral* from Louisiana to a point in the Adriatic Sea off Ravena, Italy.

The contract contained the following provision: "Any dispute arising must be treated before the London Court of Justice." In addition, the contract contained two clauses protecting Unterweser from liability for damages to the towed barge.

While Unterweser's deep-sea tug *Bremen* towed the *Chaparral* in international waters in the middle of the Gulf of Mexico, a severe storm arose. The sharp roll of the *Chaparral* in Gulf waters caused its elevator legs, which had been raised for the voyage, to break off and fall into the sea, seriously damaging the rig.

Zapata sued Unterweser in admiralty (the law of maritime commerce) in the U.S. district court at Tampa, Florida, seeking $3.5 million, alleging negligence and breach of contract. The district court ordered Unterweser not to bring any lawsuit in the London Court of Justice. The circuit court of appeals affirmed the district court decision, and Unterweser appealed to the U.S. Supreme Court. The Supreme Court ruled in favor of Unterweser and reversed the lower court decisions.

Chief Justice Burger

For at least two decades we have witnessed an expansion of overseas commercial activities by business enterprises based in the United States. The barrier of distance that once tended to confine a business concern to a modest territory no longer does so. Here we see an American company with special expertise contracting with a foreign company to tow a complex machine thousands of miles across seas and oceans. The expansion of American business and industry will hardly be encouraged if notwithstanding solemn contracts, we insist on a parochial concept that all disputes must be resolved under our laws and in our courts. . . . We cannot have trade and commerce in world markets and international waters exclusively on our terms, governed by our laws and resolved in our courts.

Forum selection clauses have historically not been favored by American courts. Many courts, federal and state, have declined to enforce such clauses on the ground that they were "contrary to public policy. . . ." Although this view apparently still has considerable acceptance, other courts are tending to adopt a more hospitable attitude toward forum-selection clauses. This view . . . is that such clauses are prima facie valid and should be enforced unless enforcement is shown by the resisting party to be "unreasonable" under the circumstances. We believe this is the correct doctrine to be followed by federal district courts sitting in admiralty. . . .

This approach is substantially that followed in other . . . countries including England. It is the view advanced by noted scholars. . . . It accords with ancient concepts of freedom of contract and reflects an appreciation of the expanding horizons of American contractors who seek business in all parts of the world. Not surprisingly foreign businessmen prefer, as do we, to have disputes resolved in their own courts, but if that choice is not available, then a neutral forum with expertise in the subject matter. Plainly the courts of England meet the standards of neutrality and long experience in admiralty litigation. The choice of that forum was made in arm's length negotiation by experienced and sophisticated businessmen and absent some compelling and countervailing reason it should be honored by the parties and enforced by the courts.

■   ■   ■

Thus, in light of present day commercial realities and expanding international trade we conclude that the forum clause should control absent a strong showing that it should be set aside. . . .

We note, however, that there is nothing in the record presently before us that would support a refusal to enforce the forum clause. . . . A contractual choice of forum clause should be held unenforceable if enforcement would contravene a strong public policy of the forum in which suit is brought, whether declared by statute or by judicial decision. It is clear, however, that [is] not this case.

Case Questions

1. As a result of the Supreme Court's decision, where will any lawsuit between Zapata and Unterweser be tried? Explain. Which law will apply to such a lawsuit? Explain.

2. Why did the Supreme Court uphold the choice-of-forum clause in the contract between Zapata and Unterweser?

3. Suppose that the two clauses protecting Unterweser from liability would not be enforced in the United States but would be enforced in England. Should the choice-of-forum clause be upheld under such circumstances? Explain.

4. Suppose that no specific negotiations concerning the choice-of-forum clause took place. Should the clause be upheld under these circumstances? Explain

Chapter Problems

1. Define the following terms:
    a. European Economic Community (EC)
    b. Choice-of-law provision
    c. United Nations Convention on Contracts for the International Sale of Goods
    d. Letter of credit
    e. Bill of lading
    f. Export trading company
    g. Joint venture
    h. General Agreement on Tariffs and Trade (GATT)
    i. Countervailing duty
    j. Choice-of-forum provision

2. Ace Manufacturing Company wishes to build a factory in Spain, which is a member of the European Community. Ace is concerned about the environmental, labor, and consumer protection laws that may affect its manufacturing plant. What areas of law should Ace be concerned about? Explain.

3. The Native American Company, a small company specializing in selling products made by Native Americans, wishes to export Native American pottery to foreign markets. What forms of export sales should Native American consider? Explain.

4. High-Tech, Inc. is a computer manufacturer considering selling its products to Middle Eastern and African markets. It is concerned about maintaining control over technological trade secret information. How might High-Tech undertake to accomplish its objectives? Explain.

5. An American importer entered a sales contract with the maker of Swiss typewriters. After the contract was entered, the exchange rate of dollars to Swiss francs radically changed so that the American importer's costs for purchasing the typewriters doubled. Which law is applicable to this contract? Why? Is there any escape route for the American importer? Which kinds of clauses ought to have been in the sales contract to deal with this particular problem?

6. T-shirts were imported into the United States C.I. & F. They were then subcontracted to a printer who put a picture of a famous person on them. A number of costs were incurred, not only for the making of the shirts, but also for freight, brokerage, and duty. In addition, royalties, printing, and packaging charges were incurred in the United States. Which charges should be included for valuation purposes by the Customs Service? Explain.

7. KMW entered a contract to sell telephone poles to the Iranian government. Shortly after the contract, the Iranian government fell and a new government replaced it. KMW was obligated under the contract to pay $350,000, via an irrevocable letter of credit, in case of its nonperformance of the contract. Such nonperformance was determined by the Iranian government. KMW alleges that the issuance of any letter of credit should be enjoined since the change of governments in Iran made a fraudulent claim of nonperformance a real possibility. Should the court enjoin the issuance of a letter of credit in this case? Explain.

8. North Carolina National Bank issued an irrevocable letter of credit on behalf of its customer, Adastra Knitting Mills. It agreed to honor 60-day time drafts of Courtalds North America, Inc. that were accompanied by a "commercial invoice in triplicate stating that it covers . . . 100% Acrylic Yarn." The invoice that was presented to the bank stated that the goods were "imported Acrylic Yarn." The packing lists that were stapled to the invoice contained the following description: "Cartons marked—100% Acrylic." Must the bank make payment on the draft? Explain.

9. The ITC determined that an industry of the United States was being threatened with material injury by the dumping of French-produced sodium silicate at less than its fair market value. Bardot and Bridget, two French companies, argue that the ITC erred in examining future trends when determining a threat of material injury. Their position is that only present injury standards are appropriately considered by the ITC. Should threats of injury include trends and predictions about the future? If so, which kinds of data should the ITC examine to make these predictions?

10. Soler Chrysler-Plymouth, Inc. entered into a distributorship agreement with Chrysler International S.A. (CISA), a Swiss subsidiary of Chrysler Corp., to sell Plymouth automobiles in Puerto Rico. The agreement authorized Chrysler to have Soler's orders filled by any Chrysler affiliate. Chrysler and Mitsubishi Motors Corp. had earlier formed a joint venture for the production of certain vehicles. At the same time Soler entered into contract with

Chrysler, Soler, CISA, and Mitsubishi entered into a sales contract. A clause in the sales contract provided that all disputes that might arise between Mitsubishi and Soler would be "settled by arbitration in Japan in accordance with the rules and regulations of the Japan Commercial Arbitration Association."

When a dispute between Soler and Mitsubishi later arose, Mitsubishi requested arbitration. Soler claimed that Mitsubishi conduct amounted to a violation of the Sherman Antitrust Act, which protects competition by prohibiting restraints of trade. Soler felt that its right to a trial in U.S. court under U.S. antitrust laws should prevail over the arbitration clause. Is Soler correct? Explain.

II THE AMERICAN LEGAL SYSTEM

Modern management functions in a legal environment. Sensitivity to legal issues must be a central part of business decision making. This does not mean that managers must be lawyers, and most are not. However, managers must make decisions within an increasingly legalized environment, and they must often consult with attorneys.

Part II introduces the American legal system. It examines the nature of law and legal reasoning, presents the legal system, and looks at constitutional and administrative law.

Chapter 3 introduces the nature of law and legal reasoning. Just as a science student must understand what is meant by the scientific method, and a student of literature must know the method of formal criticism, those who study law must know about the basic nature of law and legal reasoning.

Ours is a litigious society. One wag once remarked, "Litigation is the basic right which guarantees every corporation its decade in court." A manager is quite likely to be involved in litigation during his or her career. This involvement may take a variety of forms, including being a party to a lawsuit, testifying as a witness, or compiling information for trial. A manager who understands the context of his or her participation in a lawsuit is in a better position to cooperate with counsel. Thus, Chapter 4 explains the attorney-client relationship, describes the court system, discusses the litigation process, and—of increasing importance today—describes alternatives to litigation for resolving business disputes.

The fundamental law of the land is the United States Constitution, covered in Chapter 5. Keep in mind that there persists a debate between those who maintain that the Constitution should be interpreted strictly to adhere to its original meaning and those who maintain that the Constitution should be interpreted broadly to conform to contemporary needs. The debate comes to the fore when a Supreme Court appointment is announced or when the Supreme Court announces a decision that touches the values held dear by many Americans.

Chapter 6 concludes the introduction to the American legal system by focusing on the legal framework that applies to all federal agencies: administrative law. At times, the public mood has been to encourage administrative efforts to solve social problems. At other times, the public sentiment has been skeptical of administrative solutions.

From this debate, four views may be identified: one favors giving agencies greater flexibility to carry out their public mandates. Another favors requiring that agencies follow more formal procedures when implementing public policy. A third view focuses on making agencies more politically responsive by requiring greater public participation in the administrative process. Still another emphasizes the result of agency action and would require that agency decisions be efficient. As you read Chapter 6, identify the legal developments that reflect these four views. As administrative law has evolved during this century, each of these views has left its mark.

3 NATURE OF LAW AND LEGAL REASONING

Chapter Outline

Learning Objectives

After learning this chapter the student should be able to:

- Compare and contrast the following conceptions of law: ideal conceptions, positivist conceptions, historical conceptions, sociological conceptions, realist conceptions, economic conceptions, and critical conceptions.
- Describe how the legislature, the executive, the judiciary, and administrative agencies are sources of law.
- Describe the doctrine of stare decisis and why it is important to managers.
- Describe some of the rule-based rationales, precedent-based rationales, and policy rationales commonly used in legal reasoning, and recognize these rationales when they are used in court opinions.
- Compare and contrast formalistic and purposive methods of interpreting legislation.

This chapter considers the nature of law and legal reasoning. Not everyone would agree on how to define *law*. Therefore, we first examine the various definitions and conceptions of law that have developed over the years. Second, we discuss the sources of law. Finally, we conclude with an examination of legal reasoning, an analytical method distinctive to the legal system.

The Nature of Law: What Is Law?

The simple question, "What is law?" leads to a complex answer that reveals the many-faceted nature of the subject. Each person seems to have his or her own answer to this question. Some think law is a body of rules. Others see it as a means of restricting human conduct. Still others see it as an instrument for protecting basic freedoms. Similar to other basic concepts dealing with human behavior, law is susceptible to many definitions. A historian may regard law as a reflection of a society's mores at a particular time. A sociologist may regard it as a social institution.

When defining law, one can refer to several schools of jurisprudence. **Jurisprudence** is the study of legal philosophy. The following discussion outlines several major philosophical conceptions of law, namely:

- Ideal
- Positivist
- Historical
- Sociological
- Realist
- Critical
- Economic
- Feminist Jurisprudence

Ideal Conceptions: Natural Law

Natural law philosophers think law is ordained by nature. For them, law consists of a body of higher principles existing independently of human experience, and it exists as an ideal condition that is either inherent in human nature or derived from a divine source.

According to this conception of law, people cannot create natural law, but they can discover its principles through reasoned thinking. Knowledge of natural law is thus an informed intuition of what is fair and just. The principles of natural law, discoverable by reason, are universally valid. Thus, **natural law** is a body of principles of right and justice existing for all peoples irrespective of time and culture. It transcends human notions of what is right and just.

Positivist Conceptions

In word-association exercises, the word *law* often evokes the response *rules,* because most people think of law as a body of rules.

In jurisprudential terms, this is the positivist conception of law. The *positivist* school of jurisprudence regards law as any body of rules imposed by a sovereign or sovereign body. The term *positivist* stems from the root word *posit,* which means to place, put, or lay down something. A **positive law** is a law laid down by the duly constituted authority. A legal positivist might point to a speed-limit sign as an example of law.

Positivists distinguish between the law as it is and the law as it ought to be. They believe that an immoral command of a duly constituted authority is still law. In this regard, they differ from natural law theorists.

For example, in its early history, the United States enacted the Fugitive Slave Act, requiring the return of escaped slaves to their slaveholders. Positivists regarded the Fugitive Slave Act as law even though it was immoral. Natural law theorists did not regard it as law because it was immoral.

Historical Conceptions

Those who define law only as the current command of a sovereign may be criticized for ignoring the many rules that bound people in the past. Because law is often older than the state, some argue that the state is an incidental product of more mature legal systems rather than the distinguishing characteristic of all law.

The historical school of jurisprudence defines law as the embodiment of a society's customs. Historical jurisprudence asserts that custom is the chief manifestation of law, and that law evolves with social development. Custom may influence and become the basis of positive law. According to this conception, as customs and cultural values change, so does the direction of positive law. Laws patterned after custom are likely to meet with greater social acceptance.

Sociological Conceptions

Closely associated with the historical view is the sociological view of law. Sociologists define law in present human conduct. Thus, law is the sum of what the lawbooks permit and what human behavior provides. Under this view, for example, if you wanted to know what constitutes a business contract, you would look at business conduct to ascertain when people in business treat their agreements as binding, as well as when courts would declare such agreements to be contracts. Under this approach, formal law should reflect present human conduct; therefore, it might be necessary to bring about law reforms to have legal rules that reflect human experience.

The similarity between the historical and the sociological conceptions is obvious—both treat human conduct as the source of law. However, the historical conception embodies a long-range perspective, whereas the sociological view focuses on more immediate experience.

The sociological approach to law is not necessarily in conflict with the positivist approach. Positive law may reflect current human conduct. However, where human conduct is not in accord with a formal proposition of law, those adhering to the sociological conception would change the law to bring it into line with human conduct. Stretched to its limits, this logic would reduce formal law to its least influential level if people chose to ignore it.

Realist Conceptions

A conception of law closely allied to the sociological school is the realist conception. Realism looks beyond logic and reasoning and examines what actually occurs in the legal process. Both sociological and realist jurisprudence view life experiences as affecting the development of law. However, the realist conception focuses primarily on the social influences affecting the judicial decision-making process. It views law as the product of various social influences on official discretion. For example, if a speed-limit sign on a highway stated that the speed limit was 55 mph, but a police officer on patrol would not pull drivers over unless they drove over 65 mph, a legal realist would say that the law was 65 mph.

Critical Conceptions

A school of jurisprudence called *critical legal studies* is a type of legal realism. Its proponents contend that law is the product of political and sociological judgments made by judges. Critical legal theorists contend that judges make law in such a way as to preserve the existing political and economic order. Critical legal scholars claim that what appear to be legal reforms actually perpetuate the status quo by avoiding reconsideration of the basic assumptions behind the economic system.

Economic Conceptions

The law and economics school of jurisprudence affirms a link between law and economic activity. It contends that good law reflects good economics. It sees law as an instrument by which efficient economic outcomes are achieved. A concern for efficiency is an important, if not overriding, value for those who subscribe to this conception of law. Those belonging to the law and economics school turn to the study of economics in the belief that it can provide a stable basis for legal decisions.

Feminist Jurisprudence

There are three branches of feminist jurisprudence. Liberal feminists focus on traditional legal doctrines of individual rights, expose ways in which women have not been treated equally with men, and seek to correct the injustice.

Cultural feminists argue that the law's focus on individual rights reflects a male perspective. They contend that women, primarily due to their roles as bearers and caretakers of children, do not emphasize individualism to the same extent as traditional notions of law; rather, women emphasize a "culture of caring." Cultural feminists call for reevaluating the law in light of this culture of caring. For example, they call for a reevaluation of the traditional legal rule that a person has no duty to rescue a stranger even though he or she has the ability to do so.

Radical feminists view women's roles as caregivers as a source of their oppression. They view the law as a means of male dominance that perpetuates the oppression. For example, they consider the First Amendment's protection of pornography not as a guarantee of free speech, but as a protection of violence against women.

Sources of Law

It is often said that the legislative branch of the government makes the laws, the executive branch enforces them, and the judicial branch interprets them. Although this is a valid outline of the separation of powers among the three branches of government, it is not entirely accurate. In reality, each branch makes law. Additionally, administrative agencies, which collectively have come to be called the fourth branch of government, often have lawmaking authority. The following discussion focuses on the four primary sources of law, namely:

- The legislature
- The executive
- The judiciary
- Administrative agencies

The Legislature

One source of law is the legislature. A legislature is an organized body of persons having the authority to make laws for a political unit (e.g., Congress). It often exercises other functions, such as the control of government administration (e.g., Congress approves funding for federal agencies and oversees their regulatory efforts).

The Legislative Process

Laws created by a legislature are called *statutes, enactments, acts,* or *legislation.* Such law is sometimes called *written law.* The term **legislation** refers either to the process by which a statute is enacted or to the statute itself.

The procedure by which the U.S. Congress enacts a statute is typical of the legislative process. A federal statute begins as a bill introduced in either the House of Representatives or the Senate. Many bills are introduced by sponsors who realize that they have little or no chance of passage. These sponsors use such bills to satisfy constituent demands or to call public attention to particular issues.

After a bill is introduced, it is referred to the appropriate committee. Most bills die in committee from inaction. Those that receive serious consideration result in public hearings and, not infrequently, studies by the committee's staff. The committee then meets in executive session to "mark up" the bill, reviewing it line by line and rewriting it.

Finally, the committee sends the bill to the floor of the house of Congress in which it was introduced. It is accompanied by a committee report detailing the policy reasons for the bill and explaining the bill's intended effect on existing law. A minority report may also be included, if members of the committee disagree with the majority view. Following debate, the bill is voted on. If it receives support, it is sent to the other house of Congress for similar treatment.

When both houses pass similar but different bills, a conference committee consisting of members of both houses is established. This committee develops a compromise bill that satisfies both houses, and then submits it to each house for a vote.

Bills that pass both houses of Congress are forwarded to the president for signature. Pursuant to Article I, Section 7, of the U.S. Constitution, the president may sign the bill into law or return it to the house in which it originated (i.e., veto it). If the president takes no action within 10 days following the bill's transmittal, the Constitution states that the bill becomes law "unless the Congress by their Adjournment prevents its Return, in which case it shall not be a Law." Thus, if Congress adjourns after transmitting a bill to the president, the president may pocket-veto the bill by simply doing nothing.

State laws are enacted through similar procedures, specified in state constitutions.

The Executive

The executive branch of government also makes law. However, its lawmaking authority is limited by applicable constitutional provisions. For example, Article II of the U.S. Constitution provides that "the executive Power shall be vested in a President." The executive branch of the government consists of the president, the cabinet, and the agencies and bureaus operating under the president's authority. The president's exercise of official discretion is a source of law. In addition, the Constitution gives the president limited authority to make law in foreign and domestic affairs.

Presidential Authority over Foreign Affairs

The president's ability to make law regarding foreign affairs derives from the presidential power to make treaties, subject to the advice and consent of two thirds of the Senate. By virtue of the Supremacy Clause in Article VI of the U.S. Constitution, treaties confirmed by the Senate become part of the supreme law of the land, along with the Constitution and congressional enactments. All lawmakers of every state are bound by a treaty, notwithstanding any state law or state constitution to the contrary. The treaty controls, whether its ratification precedes or follows the enactment of state law.

Treaties are an important source of law for international businesses. They often determine the type and quantity of goods that may be sold in foreign markets.

Presidential Authority over Domestic Affairs

The president's authority over domestic affairs is yet another source of law. Article II of the Constitution of the United States provides that the president "shall take Care that the Laws be faithfully executed." Executive lawmaking in domestic affairs is exemplified by the executive orders issued and implemented by presidents throughout U.S. history.

Presidential power to make law has been limited by the Supreme Court's interpretation of the Constitution. For example, during the Korean Conflict, President Harry Truman directed seizure of the nation's steel mills to prevent a threatened strike. The Supreme Court held the seizure unconstitutional for two reasons: first, the Court found no constitutional basis for the seizure; and second, the Congress had refused to confer such authority on the president.[1] The Court stated that the president's power to issue such an executive order must stem from an act of Congress or from the Constitution itself.

The Judiciary

Courts are also a source of law. When a court decides a dispute, it makes law. Through the application of general legal principles to actual controversies, these principles are refined and shaped into a more precise statement of law. A court's application of a statute to a particular case gives meaning to the statute.

Judge-made law is referred to as **common law**. Following the Norman Conquest of England, William the Conqueror sent his court officials throughout the realm to keep the king's peace. William's purpose was to bring the various parts of his newly conquered country under one law. These court officials resolved disputes by applying custom. Thus, there developed in England a body of judicial decisions that constituted the country's common law. As England had no Parliament or written constitution at that time, these decisions became the law of the country. Today, the term *common law* refers to those areas of law that have been developed principally by the courts.

Administrative Agencies

Administrative agencies have the power to affect the rights of private parties. Administrative agencies are housed in the executive branch of government but are created by the legislature. An administrative agency may have functions that are

---

[1] 72 S. Ct. 863 (1952).

traditionally executive, such as investigating, administering, and prosecuting. It may also have functions that are traditionally legislative or judicial, such as rule-making and adjudication.

Later chapters discuss lawmaking by administrative agencies in more detail. However, it is helpful to realize that administrative agencies may make law in much the same way that the legislative, executive, and judicial branches. For example, if Congress confers rulemaking authority on an agency, that agency's duly authorized rules and regulations have the same legal stature as if Congress itself had acted on the matters.

Interaction among the Various Sources of Law

The various sources of law in the United States do not operate in a vacuum. The three branches of government frequently interact. This interaction provides a system of checks and balances in which the branches may aid or block each other. For example, as already noted, a congressional enactment needs presidential approval to become law, and a treaty negotiated by the executive branch needs Senate ratification.

People often think that the judiciary stands isolated from the other two branches and has the final word on any issue. Students often accept appellate court opinions in their casebooks as the final word on the law. In reality, a dynamic interaction occurs between the judiciary and the other branches of government. Congress, for example, can overrule a Supreme Court decision by legislation or constitutional amendment.

The judicial opinions presented in this book should be assessed carefully. You should question not only what the law is but also what it should be.

Legal Reasoning

The rest of this chapter looks at a method of thinking called *legal reasoning.* Legal reasoning cannot be precisely defined. Because it is a method of reasoning, the most that can be hoped for is a functional description of the process. Indeed, it is ironic but true that generations of law students have been taught to "think like a lawyer" without ever having been told explicitly just what is meant by that statement.

Although the method of reasoning that underlies legal reasoning is not unique to the legal system, we find the method most prominently displayed there. This is due in part to the methods and doctrines developed by courts to guide their decision making. Because courts explain their decisions in written opinions, we turn to court opinions for examples of legal reasoning.

Thus, to understand legal reasoning, we must first understand that judicial decision making uses prior cases to decide a present controversy. This method of decision making is referred to as the *rule of precedent,* or more frequently, the *doctrine of stare decisis.*

The Doctrine of Stare Decisis

The doctrine of **stare decisis** (Latin for "let the decision stand") is a policy that courts have developed as a general rule; thus, past judicial decisions are applied to decide present controversies. Consequently, a rule of law decided by the highest court of a jurisdiction subsequently binds all lower courts within that jurisdiction. It also generally binds later cases decided by that same court. Unless a court overrules itself, the decision is followed in all future cases presenting the same material facts and legal issues. Thus, a decision is a full-fledged precedent only for future "like" cases, that is, for future cases involving the same material facts.

The decision is not binding on courts in other jurisdictions. However, they may find its reasoning persuasive and follow it when considering similar cases in their jurisdictions. For example, although the Supreme Court of California is not bound by the decisions of the Supreme Court of Pennsylvania, it may adopt the Pennsylvania court's reasoning in a particular case.

Several bases underlie the doctrine of stare decisis. One is fairness. Inconsistent decisions of the same kinds of factual disputes seem unfair. Another basis for the doctrine is predictability. When a court decides a present case the way it decided a similar one before, parties are better able to anticipate and plan for the future.

Although a policy of applying prior cases to decide present controversies appears to look backward, it is important to recognize the way in which the method looks forward. A court's decision today will be tomorrow's precedent. A court, therefore, often carefully considers the future effects of a decision.

Obiter Dictum

Only the decision of a court is binding on future courts. What a court says and does that is necessary to its decision to settle the parties' dispute has precedential, or binding, effect. However, sometimes a court makes statements by way of explanation that are not really necessary to its decision. These remarks are referred to as **obiter dictum** or **dicta** (in the plural), which is Latin for "a remark by the way." Although these statements lack precedential value, they nevertheless indicate what the court is likely to do in the future. These statements may have some persuasive effect on a future decision of the court.

Some Common Rationales Used to Support Legal Reasoning

Although one of the justifications for the doctrine of stare decisis is that it advances the law's predictability, one quickly discovers decisions of appellate courts in which the judges are divided in their decisions. For example, it is not unusual for the nine justices on the Supreme Court of the United States to be divided five to four over the outcome of a case. If stare decisis works, why are there split votes?

The answer rests in the fact that those cases clearly controlled by precedent are usually either settled before trial or are disposed of routinely by the trial courts. The cases that go to the higher appellate courts involve issues where there are disagreements about the application of precedents or what constitutes sound legal policy.

Just as the parties may disagree about what the rule of law is or should be in a given case, so do judges often disagree. When the court announces its decision, the majority opinion states the court's rationale for reaching its result, and any dissenting judges may register their rationale for their disagreement in dissenting opinions. Although dissenting opinions have no precedential effect, a dissenting judge may register a dissent in the hope of persuading a future court to overrule the present decision. Thus, the majority and dissenting judges may each argue that the other has misread the cases or the rules established by them. This form of argument or rationale relies heavily on rules and precedent.

Judges may also disagree on the probable social effects of their decision. This type of argument or rationale relies heavily on policy. The following discussion describes three of the rationales found in legal opinions: rule based, precedent based, and policy based.[2]

Rule-Based Rationales

Rationales or arguments that are based on rules deal with the meaning to be given to the words in cases and statutes. (More is said about the interpretation of statutes later in this chapter). Typically, one side asserts that the language of a past case or statute established one rule, while the other side disagrees, asserting that the rule is something else altogether. The reasoning typically falls into one of two broad categories: *formalist* reasoning or *purposive* reasoning.

Formalist reasoning takes the words in a case or statute out of context and defines them without taking into account their purpose, much in the way you would define the words in a sentence by using a dictionary. For example, consider the question of whether the Constitution's First Amendment provision that "Congress shall make no law . . . abridging freedom of speech, or of the press" applies to commercial advertising. A formalist approach to this question might be to look up the definition of the terms *speech,* or *press,* and *advertising* in various dictionaries to ascertain what these words mean. Notice that different meanings can be provided depending on whether you use a current dictionary or one from 1791, the year the First Amendment went into effect.

Purposive reasoning, in contrast, attempts to define the meaning of words in a case or a statute by ascertaining the purpose underlying them. Notice that, as with formalist reasoning, different meanings can be derived, depending on how one might characterize the purpose of a given statement. In the example of commercial advertising and the First Amendment, one might assert that the purpose of the First Amendment's free speech clause is to promote an open society with access to all forms of information. Hence, laws forbidding certain forms of advertising would be unconstitutional. On the other hand, one could also assert that the purpose of the constitutional protection of speech is to provide for open com-

---

[2] Much of this discussion was drawn from J. Boyle, *Anatomy of a Torts Class,* 34 Am. U. L. Rev. 1003 (1985).

munication of political ideas, which is necessary for the functioning of a democratic society. Hence, laws restricting political speech would be unconstitutional, but laws regulating commercial advertising would be constitutional.

As noted earlier, rule-based rationales are found in court decisions where a court is called on to interpret language in its prior cases, as well as in court decisions involving the interpretation of statutes or regulations. In disagreements over the interpretation of language in cases, the formalist approach typically quotes the language of a prior case without elaborating on its context. In contrast, in the purposive approach, the court emphasizes the asserted purpose the court had in mind when it decided the earlier dispute. With regard to statutes, the formalist approach tends to focus on the literal language of the statute, while the purposive approach argues that the legislature or Congress had a certain purpose or intent in mind when it wrote the law. This discussion of formalist and purposive rule-based rationales should be reviewed when examining the material on legislative interpretation later in this chapter.

Precedent-Based Rationales

Rationales or arguments based on precedent deal with the basic question of whether an earlier decision applies to the present case, or if it is in some significant way different from the present controversy. If one side wishes to justify a decision on the basis of a past case, it argues that the earlier and current cases have essentially similar facts and issues and concludes that the earlier case controls the current case. The other side may be expected to argue that the cases have essentially different facts and issues, or are distinguishable. Much, therefore, depends on how the two sides characterize the facts and issues of the earlier decision and the current case. Thus, the side that treats the earlier case as similar may give it a broad reading, for example, by drawing analogies. The other side may argue that the earlier case is distinguishable by tying the rule of the earlier case so closely to its facts that it cannot be given a broader application.

A similar form of reasoning involves disagreement over the facts of the current case. The majority and dissent may differ in their descriptions of the facts of the case under consideration. For example, the majority may emphasize facts that the dissent ignores and, in that way, fit the case under consideration into the mold of prior **case law**. The dissent might emphasize factual characteristics of the earlier case that differ from those of the current case. Of course, the majority may be the side that distinguishes the earlier case, while the dissent may regard it as controlling.

Policy-Based Rationales

Some arguments or rationales in legal opinions involve disagreements over policy rather than precedents. These arguments tend to focus on who should be making policy rather than on the policy issues themselves. However, a careful reading of an opinion reveals the policy choices being made.

One common rationale deals with judicial administration. An opinion, for example, may assert that what is needed is a firm rule, that this rule can be easily administered by the legal system, and any other rule would "open the floodgates of litigation" and bring down the judicial system or otherwise bring about social ruin. In contrast, the competing opinion's view may reason that what is needed is a flexible rule, that the courts are capable of deciding the matter on a case-by-case basis, and the public confidence in the judicial system would erode if courts did not assume the responsibility of administering justice.

A similar policy argument deals with institutional competence. One opinion may reason that the rule should be developed by the courts because the judiciary is the only legal institution that combines the capability of determining complex factual issues and the capability of considering changing circumstances. However, the other opinion may assert that the issue involves public policy, which should be left to the legislature because it is the governmental body closest to public opinion and best suited for the task of considering the broader social implications.

Ethical Dilemmas/Issues

Howard Ross is a sales representative for the Page Printing Company. Page's employee handbook provides a progressive discipline procedure for employees. Under this procedure, if an employee violates the rules contained in the manual, he or she receives harsher penalties for each new violation. The company can discharge an employee after three violations of company rules.

The county prosecutor indicted Ross for rape. Ben Johnson, Ross's supervisor, suspended Ross from his duties pending the outcome of his criminal case. Johnson told Ross, "You will have your job back if there is a satisfactory outcome to your case."

The jury in Ross's trial could not reach a verdict, so the judge dismissed the indictment against Ross.

Ben Johnson went to see Donald Mehling, Page's vice president of human resources, and asked what to do about Ross. Mehling contacted Page's attorney, Anne Penn, who wrote an opinion letter.

Penn's letter concluded that under present state law, Page could fire Ross and disregard the employee manual and Johnson's statement. Her letter also mentioned that the law in this area was dynamic. Some states had recently declared employment manuals and supervisor's statements binding on the employers. Even under these views, it is unclear whether Page would have to honor the statements in the manual or those made by Johnson.

What are the ethical issues? What would you do?

An Example of Legal Reasoning

To fully appreciate what is involved in legal reasoning, consider the following three cases, which deal with a single issue: whether the husband or wife of an injured person is entitled to compensation from the wrongdoer for the loss of the victim's spousal services—what the law labels *loss of consortium.*

Deciding a Case of First Impression

Sometimes a court must decide an issue with no statute or prior judicial decision to guide its determination. When this occurs, the court is faced with a **case of first impression**. A court confronted with this novel situation must determine what the law should be. That situation confronted the Supreme Court of California in the following case involving loss of consortium.

DESHOTEL V. ATCHISON, TOPEKA & SANTA FE RAILWAY CO.
328 P.2d 449 (Calif. 1958)

Eloyce Deshotel's husband was severely injured when a taxicab in which he was a passenger collided with a train. He sued the railway company, the taxicab company, the train engineer, and the cab driver, obtaining a judgment of $290,000. While his case was pending, Eloyce Deshotel (plaintiff) brought a lawsuit against the same defendants. She alleged that as a result of their negligence her husband was injured in such a manner that she had "been denied his care, protection, consideration, companionship, and society" and that "by reason of the loss of consortium of her husband" she had been damaged in the sum of $100,000. The trial court dismissed her claim and awarded judgment for the defendants. Eloyce Deshotel appealed to the Supreme Court of California, which affirmed the trial court decision.

Chief Justice Gibson

The sole question presented is whether a wife whose husband has been injured as the result of the negligence of a third person may maintain an action for loss of "consortium," a term which is used in the opinion to refer to the noneconomic aspects of the marriage relation, including conjugal society, comfort, affection, and companionship. The question is one of first impression in this state, but it has been answered by the courts in many other jurisdictions. In England and in the vast majority of American jurisdictions the wife has been denied the right to recover for loss of consortium.

■   ■   ■

In a number of jurisdictions where the wife has not been allowed recovery, the husband is given

such a right if his wife is negligently injured. Plaintiff argues, in effect, that the courts which withhold relief from the wife have relied upon medieval concepts of the marriage relation, that in modern time the marital status of the wife has changed, placing her in a position equal to that of her husband, and that there is no longer any reason to refuse her the kind of redress which he may obtain. Some jurisdictions, however, have denied recovery to the husband as well as to the wife. The law in California with respect to the right of the husband is not settled. In *Meek v. Pacific Electric Ry. Co.,* it was said that damages "could not be obtained by a husband for the loss of his wife's society, or what is termed the *consortium.*" This statement was rejected as "inadvertent dictum" in *Gist v. French* [a decision of a lower-level California court of appeals], which held that a husband whose wife had been negligently injured could recover not only for the loss of services but also for the loss of cohabitation and society. We agree that the quoted statement in the *Meek* case is dictum, but a statement in the *Gist* case which indicates that the wife may recover for loss of consortium resulting from a negligent injury to her husband is also dictum, and for the reasons hereafter given, the language in the Gist case relating to the wife's rights is disapproved.

It is clear that the granting of relief to the wife for loss of consortium caused by negligent injury to her husband would constitute an extension of common law liability, and the courts are justifiably reluctant to depart from established limitations on recovery. Obviously, such an extension would also involve problems of policy or procedure. A judgment obtained by a husband after he is injured by a third person might include compensation for any impairment of his ability to participate in a normal married life, and, if his wife is allowed redress for loss of consortium in a separate action, there would be danger of double recovery. Any harm she sustains occurs only indirectly as a consequence of the defendant's wrong to the husband, and the measurement of damage for the loss of such things as companionship and society would involve conjecture since their value would be hard to fix in terms of money. Moreover, if a cause of action in the wife were recognized on the basis of the intimate relationship existing between her and her husband, other persons having a close relationship to the one injured, such as a child or parent, would likely seek to enforce similar claims, and the courts would be faced with the perplexing task of determining where to draw the line with respect to which claims should be upheld. . . .

In our view the Legislature rather than the courts can best deal with these problems. For example, the Legislature, if it found this type of suit to be desirable, could define the extent of the liability, designate who may maintain the action, and provide safeguards against the danger of double recovery. . . .

■   ■   ■

The Legislature has not seen fit to alter the common law rule that the wife cannot recover for the loss of consortium resulting from a negligent injury to her husband, and we are of the opinion that any departure from the overwhelming weight of authority in support of that rule should be left to legislative action.

Justice Carter (Dissenting)

I dissent.

It was held in *Gist v. French* [a lower California court of appeals decision] that a husband may recover for loss of consortium resulting from a negligent injury to his wife. This court unanimously denied a hearing on December 14, 1955. The statement in the majority opinion that "The law in California with respect to the right of the husband is not settled" would appear to ignore the very definite holding in the *Gist* case that the husband may recover for the loss of his wife's consortium since only the statement therein concerning the *wife's* cause of action for loss of her husband's consortium is disapproved.

There is no sound reason for denying either husband or wife a right of recovery for the loss of consortium of the spouse. "The parties to a marriage are each entitled to the comfort, companionship and affection of the other. Any interference with the right of either spouse to the enjoyment of the other is a violation of a natural right as well as a legal right arising from the marriage relation" [Gist *v. French*]. . . . The statement in the majority opinion that the "granting of relief to the wife for loss of consortium caused by negligent injury to her husband would constitute an extension of common law liability" ignores the present-day status of the wife and her emancipation from old-world concepts that the wife was but a chattel of the husband without either feelings to be injured or rights to be considered.

Case Questions

1. What did the majority opinion mean when it described the issue in the case as "one of first impression in this state?"

2. What did the majority opinion mean when it described as dictum certain statements contained in two earlier cases?

3. Did the majority opinion rely on any precedent-based rationales for its decision? Why or why not?

4. How do the majority and dissenting opinions differ in their discussion of *Gist v. French*?

5. Which policy-based rationales did the majority opinion rely on for its decision? How did the dissenting opinion differ from the majority with respect to the policy questions?

Applying Precedent

Two years after deciding in *Deshotel* that a wife could not sue for loss of consortium, the Supreme Court of California revisited the issue-only this time it was a husband's claim for loss of consortium that was under consideration. An interesting question at that point was should *Deshotel* have applied so that a husband, too, would not be able to recover for loss of consortium, or would the California court join the majority of states in allowing the husband this recovery? Consider the following case:

WEST V. CITY OF SAN DIEGO
353 P.2d 929 (Calif. 1960)

Dorothy West was seriously injured and rendered incompetent as the result of a collision between an automobile she was driving and one operated by a police officer killed in the accident. Her husband brought suit on her behalf against the City of San Diego (defendant) to recover damages she sustained, and, in addition, he sought redress for himself, alleging permanent loss of his wife's services. As a result of the collision, Mrs. West sustained massive brain damage, which reduced her mentality to that of a child four or five years of age. She had been married to Mr. West for 10 years and was 57 years old when she was injured. The jury returned a verdict in favor of the Wests (plaintiffs), awarding $57,828.89 to the wife and $5,000 to the husband. The City appealed to the Supreme Court of California, contending that Mr. West should not have been awarded damages for loss of consortium. The Supreme Court of California reversed that part of the jury's verdict awarding Mr. West compensation for loss of consortium.

Chief Justice Gibson

At common law in England, based on the now out-moded theory that the wife was the husband's inferior and occupied a position in relation to him akin to that of a servant to a master, the husband, but not the wife, was allowed to recover for loss of consortium caused by negligence, and a number of American jurisdictions have followed the common law rule. A few courts grant relief to the wife as well as the husband. Some jurisdictions deny recovery of both spouses.

■　　■　　■

In 1958 this court was called upon to consider the question of recovery for loss of consortium in *Deshotel v. Atchison, T. & S. F. Ry. Co.,* where a husband had been negligently injured. We held that a wife was not entitled to recover, disapproving the dictum to the contrary in the *Gist* case. In so holding, we discussed the various problems of policy and procedure involved. For example, there is a danger of double recovery, and the loss of such things as companionship and society is indirect only and is difficult to measure in terms of money. In the absence of a statute . . . courts would be faced with the perplexing task of determining where to draw the line with respect to similar claims by others having a close relationship to the one injured. We concluded that the Legislature rather than the courts could best deal with these problems and determine whether the wife should be allowed relief. It was pointed out that some of the objections to an action by the wife apply with equal force to one by the husband and that legislation in this field with respect to the husband as well as the wife would be preferable to piecemeal determination of the problems of judicial decision.

There is no sound reason to depart here from the principle that the Legislature is the proper body to decide whether recovery for loss of consortium should be permitted and, if so, under what terms and conditions. Drawing a distinction between spouses on the ground that the husband, unlike the wife, had a right of recovery at common law would be extremely inequitable and, further, would ignore the fact that recognition of his right was based upon the wife's subservient position in the marriage relationship, whereas, under present-day law, spouses are generally regarded as equals.

Justice Peters (Dissenting)

I dissent. . . .

The majority, in concluding that the judgment as to Mert West should be reversed, hold that, in this state, a husband has no cause of action for the negligent interference with those noneconomic aspects of marriage usually included within the term "consortium." Stated another way, the majority hold that a husband, in this state, is not entitled to recover on his own behalf for a negligent injury to his wife that results in depriving him of his privilege of sexual intercourse with his wife; of the possibility of becoming a father; and of the right of society, care, and comfort of his wife. This holding is unrealistic and unsound.

A large portion of our family law is devoted to protecting the spouses against intentional interference with these conjugal rights. If a wife were to deprive her husband of these rights it would, of course, be a ground for divorce. But, according to the majority, negligent interference resulting in the deprivation of these rights is not compensable. This holding is contrary to the common law, is contrary to the overwhelming weight of authority elsewhere, and is contrary to the public policy of this state.

■　　■　　■

There can be no doubt, and the majority concede, that the common law rule was and is that a husband has such a cause of action. Such right was recognized as early as 1619 in the [English] case of Gay against Lively.

■　　■　　■

The majority opinion is predicated on the false premise that such a right should not exist in the husband because the Legislature has not expressly provided for such a right. . . .

Apparently the majority have overlooked section 22.2 of the Civil Code, which provides: "The common law of England, so far as it is not repugnant to or inconsistent with the Constitution of the United States, or the Constitution or laws of this State, is the rule of decision in all the courts of this State. " If the Legislature has not seen fit to change a common-law rule, at least a common-law rule existing at the time this state was admitted into the Union in 1850, the courts should not repudiate such rule but should follow.

Apparently, in the realization that they are repudiating a common-law rule, and that this should not be done without some good reason, the majority state that because the wife had no such right at common law it "would be extremely inequitable" to grant the right to the husband. This solicitude for symmetry in the law may be laudable but it carries little weight against a settled rule of common law. The common law itself created this lack of symmetry. The point does not have to be labored that the law is not necessarily logical nor symmetrical. Lack of symmetry alone is no sound reason for this court, by judicial fiat, to enter into the legislative field by repudiating a common-law rule that the Legislature itself has not seen fit to repudiate. . . . Moreover, it can be argued with what I submit is sounder logic, that, if symmetry is to be secured, it should be secured by holding that the wife as well as the husband is entitled to maintain such an action. Such a result . . . could be justified on the reasoning that the Legislature, by its many laws freeing women from their common-law disabilities, had evidenced an intent to place the wife in the same position as the husband so far as the right of consortium is concerned.

■   ■   ■

That a husband should recover under the facts of this case for loss of consortium is justified by reason, logic, authority, the common law, and by the public policy of this state. For these reasons I would affirm the judgment in favor of Mert West.

Case Questions

1. What effect did the *Deshotel* decision have on the court majority in *West*?
2. Did the majority opinion rely on a precedent-based rationale for its decision? Explain.
3. Did the majority opinion rely on any policy-based rationales for its decision? Explain.
4. How could the *Deshotel* case have been distinguished from the situation confronting the court in *West*? How did the majority respond to this point? If the court had distinguished *Deshotel,* how would that have affected the precedential weight of the *Deshotel* decision on the court? How did the refusal to distinguish *Deshotel* affect the court's decision?
5. How does the dissenting opinion rely on a precedent-based rationale? Does the dissenting opinion rely on any policy-based rationales? Explain.

Overruling Precedent

The doctrine of stare decisis expresses the policy preference of the courts to stand by precedents and to preserve settled points of law. However, where a court concludes it has made a mistake or that the rule needs to be changed, the court may correct or change the rule. Thus, a court may overrule an earlier case where there is good reason to do so. For example, technological change or changes in social conditions may dictate that the law be altered; or events occurring after an earlier decision may prove that the decision was wrong. It would be ironic if appellate courts, which are empowered to correct the errors of lower courts, lacked the power to correct their own errors. If appellate courts could not correct erroneous or outdated precedents, the law would stagnate.

When a court overrules its earlier case law, it usually goes to great length to explain its action. This usually involves explaining why the earlier decision is wrong, outdated, or otherwise exists as a fishbone in the throat of the law. Having wiped the slate clean, the court then considers the issue anew and explains why it is adopting a new rule in place of its earlier decision. The following case involving a reexamination of the consortium issue shows a court undertaking this rare task.

RODRIGUEZ V. BETHLEHEM STEEL CORP.
525 P.2d 669 (Calif. 1974)

While at work, Richard Rodriguez was struck on the head by a falling pipe weighing over 600 pounds. The blow caused severe spinal cord damage, which left him totally paralyzed in both legs, totally paralyzed in his body below the midpoint of the chest, and partially paralyzed in one of his arms. The injuries were permanent. Because he needed assistance in virtually every activity of daily living, his wife, Mary Anne (plaintiff), gave up her job and undertook his care on a 24-hour basis. At the time of the accident Richard was 22 years old and Mary Anne was 20. The accident occurred only 16 months after their marriage. Mary Anne sued Richard's employer, Bethlehem Steel Corp. (defendant), for loss of consortium. The trial court dismissed her claim, and a California appellate court affirmed the dismissal. She appealed to the Supreme Court of California, which reversed the lower court decisions.

Justice Mosk

In this case we are called upon to decide whether California should continue to adhere to the rule that a married person whose spouse has been injured by the negligence of a third party has no cause of action for loss of "consortium."

■   ■   ■

In affirming the judgment the Court of Appeal . . . indicated its dissatisfaction with the *Deshotel* rule, but correctly deferred to this court for any reconsideration of the doctrine: Presiding Justice

Kaus, writing for a unanimous court, stated that "In spite of counsel's eloquent exhortations to the contrary, we must hold that it is up to the Supreme Court to qualify or overrule its decisions. We say this in full recognition of Mary Anne's argument that several Supreme Court cases since *Deshotel* and *West* can be read as undermining the rationale of those holdings." This is a perceptive and accurate reading of our decisions, as we shall explain.

To begin with, we delineate the rationale of *Deshotel* and *West*. . . .

In *Deshotel* . . . the court devised . . . reasons of "policy and procedure" to justify . . . the rule. . . .

We shall show that each of these reasons has been rendered untenable by developments subsequent to *Deshotel.*

Stare Decisis and the Role of the Legislature

■　　■　　■

First and foremost, the *Deshotel* court emphasized that the "overwhelming weight of authority" supports the common law rule, and "the courts are justifiably reluctant to depart from established limitations on recovery." In the 16 years since *Deshotel* was decided, however, there has been a dramatic reversal in the weight of authority on this question. At the time of *Deshotel* the majority of the states denied the wife the right to recover for loss of consortium, while the right was recognized in only five jurisdictions. Today those 5 have grown in number to at least 31. . . .

In these circumstances we may fairly conclude that the precedential foundation of *Deshotel* has been not only undermined but destroyed. In its place a new common law rule has arisen, granting either spouse the right to recover for loss of consortium caused by negligent injury to the other spouse. Accordingly, to adopt that rule in California at this time would not constitute, as the court feared in *Deshotel,* an "extension" of common law liability, but rather a recognition of that liability as it is currently understood by the large preponderance of our sister states and a consensus of distinguished legal scholars.

The second principal rationale of the *Deshotel* opinion was that any departure from the then settled rule denying the wife recovery for loss of consortium "should be left to legislative action." But in the years since *Deshotel* the argument has fared badly in our decisions. As we summarized in *People v. Pierce,* "In effect the contention is a request that courts of law abdicate their responsibility for the upkeep of the common law."

The judicial responsibility to which we referred in *Pierce* arises from the role of the courts in a common law system. In California as in other jurisdictions of Anglo-American heritage, the common law is not a codification of exact or inflexible rules for human conduct, for the redress of injuries, or for protection against wrongs, but is rather the embodiment of broad and comprehensive unwritten principles, inspired by natural reason and an innate sense of justice, and adopted by common consent for the regulation and government of the affairs of men.

"The inherent capacity of the common law for growth and change is its most significant feature. Its development has been determined by the social needs of the community which it serves. It is constantly expanding and developing in keeping with advancing civilization and the new conditions and progress of society, and adapting itself to the gradual change of trade, commerce, arts, inventions, and the needs of the country. . . ."

Whenever an old rule is found unsuited to present conditions or unsound, it should be set aside and a rule declared which is in harmony with those conditions and meets the demands of justice. Although the Legislature may of course speak to the subject, in the common law system the primary instruments of this evolution are the courts, adjudicating on a regular basis the right variety of individual cases brought before them.

■　　■　　■

If upon further analysis it appears the remaining reasons given in *Deshotel* no longer support that rule . . . we shall have no hesitation in abrogating it. Such a step would not be an usurpation of legislative authority, but a reaffirmation of our high responsibility to renew the common law of California when it is necessary and proper to do so.

The Injury Is Indirect, the Damages Speculative, and the Cause of Action Would Extend to Other Classes of Plaintiffs

[T]he *Deshotel* court asserted that "Any harm [the wife] sustains occurs *only indirectly* as a consequence of the defendant's wrong to the husband." The argument was negated 10 years after

Deshotel in *Dillon v. Legg*. There the issue was whether a driver who negligently runs over a small child in the street is also liable to the child's mother for emotional shock and resulting physical disorders suffered by the latter when she personally witnessed the occurrence of the accident. Finding such liability, we in effect rejected the argument that the injury to the mother was too "indirect." The critical question, we explained, was foreseeability. . . ." Such reasonable foreseeability does not turn on whether the particular [defendant] as an individual would have in actuality foreseen the exact accident and loss, it contemplates that courts, on a case-to-case basis, analyzing all the circumstances, will decide what the ordinary man under such circumstances should reasonably have foreseen. The courts thus mark out the areas of liability, excluding the remote and unexpected."

Applying these rules to the facts alleged, we were of the opinion in *Dillon* that "Surely the negligent driver who causes the death of a young child may reasonably expect that the mother will not be far distant and will upon witnessing the accident suffer emotional trauma." By parity of reasoning, we conclude in the case at bar that one who negligently causes a severely disabling injury to an adult may reasonably expect that the injured person is married and that his or her spouse will be adversely affected by that injury.

■　　■　　■

The next rationale of the *Deshotel* court was that "the measurement of damage for the loss of such things as companionship and society would involve conjecture since their value would be hard to fix in terms of money." This argument, too, has fared badly in our subsequent decisions. Although loss of consortium may have physical consequences, it is principally a form of mental suffering. We have fully recognized that "One of the most difficult tasks imposed upon a jury in deciding a case involving personal injuries is to determine the amount of money the plaintiff is to be awarded as compensation for pain and suffering.

. . . In a very real sense, the jury is asked to evaluate in terms of money a detriment for which monetary compensation cannot be ascertained with any demonstrable accuracy." (*Beagle v. Vasold*) "Yet," we emphasized in *Beagle,* "the inescapable fact is that this is precisely what the jury is called upon to do."

■　　■　　■

The third argument of this group set forth in *Deshotel* is that if the wife's cause of action were recognized "on the basis of the intimate relationship existing between her and her husband, other persons having a close relationship to the one injured, such as a child or parent, would likely seek to enforce similar claims, and the courts would be faced with the perplexing task of determining where to draw the line with respect to which claims should be upheld." Here again the answer was subsequently given in *Dillon v. Legg*. In that case it was likewise urged that any cause of action granted to a mother who witnesses her child's injury could also be asserted by other close relatives present at the scene such as siblings or grandparents, thus involving the courts "in the hopeless task of defining the extent of . . . liability."

We rejected this argument in *Dillon* on the ground that . . . "proper guidelines can indicate the extent of liability for such future cases." Those guidelines . . . are the general principles of negligence law limiting liability to persons and injuries within the scope of the reasonably foreseeable risk.

The Fear of Double Recovery

[T]he *Deshotel* court expressed the concern that "A judgment obtained by a husband after he is injured by a third person might include compensation for any impairment of his ability to participate in a normal married life, and, if his wife is allowed redress for loss of consortium in a separate action, there would be danger of double recovery. . . ."

It is true the rule against double recovery fore-closes the wife from recovering for the loss of her husband's financial support if he is compensated for his loss of earnings and earning power, "because the *source* of the wife's right to support is the husband's earning capacity, for impairment of which *he* is entitled to recover." But there is more to the marriage relationship than financial support. "The concept of consortium includes not only loss of support or services, it also embraces such elements as love, companionship, affection, society, sexual relations, solace and more." As to each, "the interest sought to be protected is per-sonal to the wife," so that to compensate her for damage to that interest cannot result in double recovery.

■   ■   ■

All that is necessary to avoid double recovery "is to insure that each element of the damages is separate and distinct from all the others," and in particular that the wife's recovery does not include any damages for loss of her husband's financial support or other items for which he is primarily entitled to be compensated. . . .

We therefore overrule *Deshotel v. Atchison, T. & S.F. Ry. Co.* and *West v. City of San Diego* and declare that in California each spouse has a cause of action for loss of consortium, as defined herein,

caused by a negligent or intentional injury to the other spouse by a third party.

Justice McComb (Dissenting)

I dissent. I adhere to the view that any change in the law denying the wife recovery for loss of con-sortium should be left to legislative action. (*Deshotel v. Atchison, T. & S.F. Ry. Co.*)

Case Questions

1. Why did the lower-level court of appeal not simply decline to follow the *Deshotel* and *West* decisions?
2. How did the *Rodriguez* court use precedent-based rationales in overruling its earlier precedents of *Deshotel* and *West*?
3. How did the *Rodriguez* court confront the policy-based rationales used earlier by the court in *Deshotel*?
4. *Deshotel* was decided in 1958. *Rodriguez* was decided in 1974. Which changes in the social conditions in California occurred during this period? Could these changes have influenced the court's decision making? Explain. Do you see any evidence of this in the various major-ity and dissenting opinions? Explain.

Legislative Interpretation

Legal reasoning is not confined to the interpretation of case law; it is also used to interpret and apply legislation to legal disputes. Thus, the meaning of a statute is not fully known until the statute is interpreted by the courts.

In interpreting statutes, the courts begin by attempting to determine the leg-islature's intent, which may be expressed explicitly in the statute. However, the legislature may not have envisioned the particular controversy before a court, so legislative intent may be nonexistent. In such cases, the court attempts to deter-mine how the legislature would have wanted the statute applied in the given case.

The most obvious indirect indication of the legislative intent is the statute's language. Where the language is clear, a court does not go beyond the plain mean-ing of its words to determine what a statute means. This is known as the **plain**

meaning rule. A court will not apply a statute literally, however, where doing so produces an absurd result or renders the statute unworkable.

In examining the statutory context, a court considers the statute as a whole, not merely the particular clause at issue in the case. In this way, the court avoids considering a particular statutory clause out of context. Thus, courts do not divorce a single phrase or section of a statute from its other portions.

Where the context of the statutory language does not reveal legislative intent, courts frequently consider the statute's legislative history. This includes the social conditions that gave rise to the legislative response and any documents, such as committee reports, proceedings, and records of legislative debates.

The following case involves the interpretation of Title VII of the Civil Rights Act, which forbids discrimination in employment on the basis of race, color, sex, religion, and national origin. Three years earlier, in the case of *McDonald v. Santa Fe Trail Trans. Co.,* the Supreme Court had interpreted Title VII to apply to racial discrimination in employment directed against whites.[3] In *McDonald,* several white employees were discharged for misappropriating their employer's property, but their black accomplice was not dismissed. The Court stated that "Title VII . . . prohibits the discharge of `any individual' because of such 'individual's race. . . .' Its terms are not limited to discrimination against members of any particular race."[4] *McDonald* left open the issue of the legality of voluntary affirmative action programs. That issue was addressed in the following case.

UNITED STEELWORKERS V. WEBER
443 U.S. 193 (1979)

Kaiser and the United Steelworkers of America (petitioners) entered into a collective bargaining agreement that established training programs to teach unskilled production workers the skills necessary to become craft workers. The program reserved 50 percent of the openings for black employees. This aspect of the program was to continue until the percentage of blacks in the craft work force approximated the percentage of blacks in the local labor force. Before the program began, Kaiser hired only experienced craft workers, almost all of whom were white.

Weber (respondent) brought a class action alleging that junior black employees were accepted into the program ahead of more senior whites. The trial court held that this violated Title VII, and the Fifth Circuit Court of Appeals affirmed. The Supreme Court reversed the circuit court decision.

---

[3] 427 U.S. 273 (1976).
[4] Id. at 278–79.

Justice Brennan

The only question before us is the narrow statutory issue of whether Title VII *forbids* private employers and unions from voluntarily agreeing upon bona fide affirmative action plans that accord racial preference in the manner and for the purpose provided in the Kaiser-USWA plan. That question was expressly left open in *McDonald v. Santa Fe Trail Trans. Co.*

Respondent argues that Congress intended in Title VII to prohibit all race-conscious affirmative action plans. Respondent's argument rests upon a literal interpretation of 703(a) and (d) of the Act. Those sections make it unlawful to "discriminate . . . because of . . . race" in hiring and in the selection of apprentices for training programs. Since, the argument runs, *McDonald v. Santa Fe Trail Trans. Co.* settled that Title VII forbids discrimination against whites as well as blacks, and since the Kaiser-USWA affirmative action plan operated to discriminate against white employees solely because they are white, it follows that the Kaiser-USWA plan violates Title VII.

Respondent's argument is not without force. But it overlooks the significance of the fact that the Kaiser-USWA plan is an affirmative action plan voluntarily adopted by private parties to eliminate traditional patterns of racial segregation. In this context respondent's reliance upon a literal construction of 703(a) and (d) and upon *McDonald* is misplaced. It is a "familiar rule, that a thing may be within the letter of the statute and yet not within the statute, because [the thing is] not within its spirit, nor within the intention of its makers." The prohibition against racial discrimination in 703(a) and (d) of Title VII must therefore be read against the background of the legislative history of Title VII and the historical context from which the Act arose. Examination of those sources makes clear that an interpretation of the sections that forbade all race-conscious affirmative action would "bring about an end completely at variance with the purpose of the statute" and must be rejected.

Congress' primary concern in enacting the prohibition against racial discrimination in Title VII of the Civil Rights Act of 1964 was with "the plight of the Negro in our economy." Before 1964, blacks were largely relegated to "unskilled and semi-skilled jobs."

It plainly appears from the House Report accompanying the Civil Rights Act that Congress did not intend wholly to prohibit private and voluntary affirmative action efforts as one method of solving this problem. The report provides:

> No bill can or should lay claim to eliminating all of the causes and consequences of racial and other types of discrimination against minorities. There is reason to believe, however, that national leadership provided by the enactment of Federal legislation dealing with the most troublesome problems will create an atmosphere conductive to voluntary or local resolution of other forms of discrimination.

Given this legislative history, we cannot agree with respondent that Congress intended to prohibit the private sector from taking effective steps to accomplish the goal that Congress designed Title VII to achieve. The very statutory words intended as a spur or catalyst to cause "employers and unions to self-examine and to self-evaluate their employment practices and to endeavor to eliminate, so far as possible, the last vestiges of an unfortunate and ignominious page in this country's history," cannot be interpreted as an absolute prohibition against all private, voluntary, race-conscious affirmative action efforts to hasten the elimination of such vestiges. It would be ironic indeed if a law triggered by a Nation's concern over centuries of racial injustice and intended to improve the lot of those who had "been excluded from the American dream for so long," constituted the first legislative prohibition of all voluntary, private, race-conscious efforts to abolish traditional patterns of racial segregation and hierarchy.

Our conclusion is further reinforced by examination of the language and legislative history of 703(j) of Title VII. . . . The section provides that nothing contained in Title VII "shall be interpreted to require any employer . . . to grant preferential treatment . . . to any group because of the race . . . of such . . . group on account of" a *de facto* racial imbalance in the employer's work force. The section does not state that "nothing in Title VII shall be interpreted to *permit*" voluntary affirmative efforts to correct racial imbalances. The natural inference is that Congress chose not to forbid all voluntary race-conscious affirmative action.

The reasons for this choice are evident from the legislative record. Title VII could not have been enacted into law without substantial support from legislators in both Houses who traditionally resisted federal regulations of private business. Those legislators demanded as a price for their support that "management prerogatives and union freedoms . . . be left undisturbed to the greatest extent possible." Section 703(j) was proposed by Senator Dirksen to allay any fears that the Act might be interpreted in such a way as to upset this compromise. The section was designed to prevent 703 of Title VII from being interpreted in such a way as to lead to undue "Federal Government interference with private businesses because of some Federal employee's ideas about racial balance or imbalance." Clearly, a prohibition against all voluntary, race-conscious, affirmative action efforts would disserve these ends. Such a prohibition would augment the powers of the Federal Government and diminish traditional management prerogatives while at the same time impeding attainment of the ultimate statutory goals. In view of this legislative history and in view of Congress' desire to avoid undue federal regulation of private businesses, use of the word "require" rather than the phrase "require or permit" in 703(j) fortifies the conclusion that Congress did not intend to limit traditional business freedom to such a degree as to prohibit all voluntary, race-conscious affirmative action.

We therefore hold that Title VIIs prohibition in 703(a) and (d) against racial discrimination does not condemn all private, voluntary, race-conscious affirmative action plans.

Justice Rehnquist (With whom the Chief Justice joins, dissenting)

The operative sections of Title VII prohibit racial discrimination in employment *simpliciter*. Taken in its normal meaning, and as understood by all members of Congress who spoke to the issue during the legislative debates, this language prohibits a covered employer from considering race when making an employment decision, whether the race be black or white. Several years ago, however, a United States District Court held that "the dismissal of white employees charged with misappropriating company property while not dismissing a similarly charged Negro employee does not raise a claim upon which Title VII relief may be granted." *McDonald v. Santa Fe Trail Trans. Co.* This Court unanimously reversed, concluding from the "uncontradicted legislative history" that "Title VII prohibits racial discrimination against the white petitioners in this case upon the same standards as would be applicable were they Negroes. . . .

We have never wavered in our understanding that Title VII "prohibits *all* racial discrimination in employment, without exceptions for any particular employees. . . ."

Today, however, the Court behaves much like the Orwellian speaker earlier described, as if it had been handed a note indicating that Title VII would lead to a result unacceptable to the Court if interpreted here as it was in our prior decisions. Accordingly, without even a break in syntax, the Court rejects "a literal construction of Section 703(a)" in favor of newly discovered "legislative history," which leads to a conclusion directly contrary to that compelled by the "uncontradicted legislative history" unearthed in *McDonald* and our other prior decisions. Now we are told that the legislative history of Title VII shows that employers are free to discriminate on the basis of race; an employer may, in the Court's words, "trammel the interests of white employees" in favor of black employees in order to eliminate "racial imbalance."

As if this were not enough to make a reasonable observer question this Court's adherence to the oft-stated principle that our duty is to construe rather than rewrite legislation, the Court also seizes upon Section 703(j) of Title VII as an independent, or at least partially independent basis for its holding. Totally ignoring the wording of that section . . . and totally ignoring the months of legislative debates . . . which demonstrate clearly that it was enacted to prevent precisely what occurred in this case, the Court infers from Section 703(j) that "Congress chose not to forbid all voluntary race-conscious affirmative action."

Thus, by a *tour de force* reminiscent not of jurists such as Hale, Holmes, and Hughes, but of escape artists such as Houdini, the Court eludes clear statutory language, "uncontradicted" legislative history, and uniform precedent in concluding that employers are, after all, permitted to consider race in making employment decisions.

Case Questions

1. What is the basis for the Court's conclusion that the Kaiser affirmative action plan did not violate Title VII?
2. Which kind of legal reasoning (formalist or purposive) did the Court use? Explain. Which kind of legal reasoning (formalist or purposive) did the dissent use? Explain.
3. Suppose you had been plant manager of the Kaiser plant involved in this case. Would you have agreed to the proposal to adopt the affirmative action plan that actually was adopted by Kaiser and the United Steelworkers? Explain.
4. How would you have decided the issue of the legality of the Kaiser affirmative action program? Explain.

Chapter Problems

1. Define the following concepts and terms:
   a. Jurisprudence
   b. Natural law
   c. Positive law
   d. Legislation
   e. Common law
   f. Stare decisis
   g. Obiter dictum
   h. Case law
   i. Case of first impression
   j. Plain meaning rule

2. What conception of law is embodied in the following statement from the Declaration of Independence?

   When in the Course of human events, it becomes necessary for one people to dissolve the political bonds which have connected them with another, and to assume among the powers of the earth, the separate and equal station to which the Laws of

Nature and of Nature's God entitle them, a decent respect to the opinions of mankind requires that they should declare the causes which impel them to the separation. We hold these truths to be self-evident, that all men are created equal, that they are endowed by their Creator with certain unalienable Rights, that among these are Life, Liberty and the pursuit of happiness.

3. In 1973, the U.S. Supreme Court was called on to decide the constitutionality of a state statute making it a crime to obtain an abortion. In deciding that the statute was unconstitutional, the Court stated:

We forthwith acknowledge our awareness of the sensitive and emotional nature of the abortion controversy, of the vigorous opposing views, even among physicians, and of the deep and seemingly absolute convictions that the subject inspires. One's philosophy, one's experiences, one's exposure to the raw edges of human existence, one's religious training, one's attitudes toward life and family and their values, and the moral standards one establishes and seeks to observe, are all likely to influence and to color one's thinking and conclusions about abortion. . . . Our task, of course, is to resolve the issue by constitutional measurement free of emotion and predilection.

Which conception of law best describes the Court's statement? Do you think that the Court can resolve the issue "by constitutional measurement free of emotion and predilection?" Explain.

4. Martin Luther King, Jr., once wrote: "I think we all have moral obligations to obey just laws. On the other hand, I think we have moral obligations to disobey unjust laws because noncooperation with evil is just as much a moral obligation as cooperation with good." Lewis F. Powell (retired associate justice of the Supreme Court of the United States), when he was president of the American Bar Association, deplored the doctrine "that only just' laws need to be obeyed and that every man is free to determine for himself the question of 'justness.'" He added, "An ordered society cannot exist if every man determines which laws he will obey." Which conception of law was Justice Powell expressing? Which position was Dr. King espousing? Explain. With which position do you agree? Explain.

5. The president of the United States concludes a commercial treaty with Russia. The treaty is subsequently ratified by the U.S. Senate. After ratification, a group of citizens files a lawsuit in a federal court attacking the treaty as unconstitutional. Will the citizens win? Explain.

6. The Federal Trade Commission, a federal agency, brings action against Conglomerate Car Company as a result of a complaint filed with the commission by Bigdome Car Company. After reviewing the complaint, the commission concludes that Conglomerate is guilty. The commission's opinion provides its reasons for reaching this conclusion. Is the commission's opinion law? Explain.

7. Arthur and Ava Strunk have two sons, Tommy, age 28, and Jerry, age 27. Tommy is married, employed, and a part-time college student. He suffers from a fatal kidney disease and is being kept alive by frequent dialysis treatment, a procedure that cannot be continued much longer. Jerry is incompetent and has been legally committed to a state institution for the mentally retarded. He has an IQ of approximately 35, which corresponds to a mental age of approximately six years. He is further handicapped by a speech defect that makes it difficult for him to communicate with people who are unacquainted with him. When it was determined that Tommy would need a kidney transplant to survive, doctors looked for a donor. Possible donors include cadavers as well as live persons. Because of compatibility of blood type and tissue, the only acceptable live donor is Jerry. The parents petitioned a court for authority to proceed with the operation. The case is one of first impression; there are no statutes or prior case law to guide the court's determination. How should the court decide?

8. Scott Lieding and Karey Lieding, husband and wife, sued Commercial Diving Center, Inc., claiming that on April 14, 1980, Scott sustained personal injuries in a diving accident while he was a commercial diving student under the instruction and supervision of Commercial Diving Center. Karey claimed that as a result of her husband's injuries, she was deprived of his "services, social and consortium." At trial, Karey testified that Scott asked her to marry him on March 9, 1980; that she accepted his proposal that day; that at that time they selected May 31, 1980, as their wedding date; but because of Scott's accident the wedding was postponed until August 2, 1980. Upon learning this, Commercial Diving Center asked the court to deny Karey's claim for loss of consortium. The case is being tried in California. How should the court rule? Explain.

9. Paul Forte was walking across the street when he was struck by Ralph Butcher's Volkswagen. Forte suffered a fractured neck, forearm, and leg, as well as a severe cerebral contusion. Forte sued Butcher for personal injuries. Cindy Forte, Paul's wife, sued Butcher for loss of consortium. At trial, Cindy testified that, although she and Paul did not have a valid legal marriage, they did have a common-law marriage. Cindy and Paul began living together in 1969. Since that time, Cindy has used the name Forte. At the time of the accident in March 1981, Paul and Cindy had been living together as husband and wife for 11 1/2 years. They had two children together, filed joint tax returns, and maintained joint savings and checking accounts. Paul acknowledged and referred to Cindy as his wife. On learning that there had been no valid legal marriage between Cindy and Paul, Butcher asked the court to deny Cindy's claim for loss of consortium. The case is being tried in California. How should the court rule? Explain.

10. In 1975, Don and Betty Hair took their nine-year-old son, Michael, to Dr. John Mead for the performance of oral surgery in the facilities of Monterey County General Hospital. During postoperative care, Don and Betty were

told that Michael was suffering from an unknown injury described to them as temporary. Two days later Michael developed convulsions, culminating in permanent injuries including blindness, brain damage, quadriplegia, and petit and grand mal seizures. Don and Betty sued Dr. Mead and Monterey County General Hospital, seeking, in addition to compensation for medical expenses and emotional shock, compensation for lost society, companionship, and comfort of their child—in essence, loss of consortium. Dr. Mead and Monterey County General Hospital have asked the court to deny the Hairs' claim for compensation due to loss of consortium. The case is being tried in California. How should the court rule? Explain.

4 BUSINESS AND THE LEGAL SYSTEM

Learning Objectives

After learning this chapter the student should be able to:

- Recognize when a business should consult an attorney and how to select one.
- Determine whether particular communications are protected by the attorney-client privilege.
- Evaluate whether a firm not directly transacting business in a state is likely to be subject to suit in that state.
- Recognize the different stages of the litigation process and their importance to a firm facing possible litigation.
- Determine in particular settings the advantages and disadvantages of using alternatives to litigation for settling disputes.

Businesses come into contact with the legal system under a variety of circumstances. Disputes with suppliers or customers may result in lawsuits that bring the manager face to face with the legal system and its process. Contact with the judicial system creates a need for legal advice.

This chapter begins by explaining the attorney-client relationship. The next sections describe the judicial system. Finally, the chapter surveys alternatives to litigation (the traditional way to resolve disputes).

The Firm and Its Attorney

Businesses call on lawyers to assist them through the red tape of government regulation. In the past, a business usually did not contact lawyers until a problem arose—for example, when it was sued or when a distributor would not pay an outstanding debt. However, now more and more businesses are concerned with preventive law. By contacting lawyers early and following their legal advice, companies may avoid the consequences that accompany uninformed business practices. Business managers today have more of an ongoing relationship with lawyers than in the past; hence, they need to know more about lawyers.

Lawyers have a common base of education: law school. There, law students receive generalized training that enables them to adapt to a wide range of tasks. The average person thinks that lawyers know the law. It is more accurate to say that lawyers are versed in general legal principles and methods. They are trained to find the relevant law and to apply it to particular circumstances.

Corporate Legal Strategy

A long-standing tension has characterized the relationship between lawyers and business managers. Lawyers tend to be conservative in their advice and often dampen a business's desire to do creative things. Many business executives believe that attorneys should be consulted only to find out what cannot be done. Because they use attorneys only on an *ad hoc* basis, they do not know how to incorporate them into their business organization charts.

Some businesses, however, recognize the need to develop a comprehensive corporate legal strategy. This corporate strategy may appear in any of several forms. A *preventive* strategy employs attorneys to review new programs and documents with an eye to avoiding legal problems. An *enforcive* strategy uses legal activity to protect a company against patent infringement and other violations of its rights. A *creative* strategy employs legal counsel to help formulate corporate goals. An *active* strategy brings the manager and the attorney together to explore various ways of achieving those goals, through, for example, a merger with another corporation, legal loopholes, or lobbying for a change in the law. The preventive, enforcive, creative, and active corporate legal strategies may be used together, depending on the circumstances that confront the company.[1]

---

[1] This discussion of corporate legal strategy is derived from F. Sturdivant and C. Green, *Building a Strong Corporate Strategy,* College of Administrative Science, The Ohio State University, Working Paper Series 83–70 (October 1983).

The Lawyer's Roles

Lawyers play many roles in relation to the business firm. They counsel the firm's managers regarding transactions, compliance with regulations, and similar matters. They draft and review legal documents. Their primary goal as counsellors and drafters is to prevent legal problems from developing.

Lawyers also represent their clients as advocates. They negotiate to settle disputes with other parties on terms favorable to their clients. They represent their clients before courts, administrative agencies, and arbitrators. As advocates, their duty is to present the facts and argue the law in the light most favorable to the client. Counsel for opposing parties will do the same for their clients. Lawyers serve as partisan advocates in a legal system that is based on an adversarial model.

To perform their various roles, lawyers often must investigate relevant facts. Because of the need to investigate, communication between a firm and its attorney is very important.

Communicating with Lawyers

A person needing a lawyer's services should contact counsel early, before the problem intensifies. It is better to have a lawyer draft a contract than to call in a lawyer to solve a problem caused by a contract poorly drafted by the client.

The client should fully disclose the facts relevant to the question at hand. If an attorney's opinion is based on less than full information, the opinion is incomplete. A general understanding of the law affecting the business helps a client detail the material facts and avoid irrelevancies when communicating with a lawyer. Understanding the lawyer's role also facilitates communication.

The client should actively assist the lawyer's search for solutions. Also, the client should inform the lawyer of the company's goals so that the lawyer seeks solutions compatible with those goals. Finally, the client should expect high-quality service from counsel and should communicate that expectation. After all, the client is paying the bill.

The Attorney-Client Privilege

The law protects confidential communications between the attorney and client from disclosure to a third person. Without the client's permission, the attorney may not divulge communications made during the attorney-client contact. The client may, however, waive the privilege and authorize the attorney to make disclosure. The privilege applies only to confidential communications; it does not include statements made to an attorney in the presence of third parties other than the client's or attorney's agents or employees.

A corporation communicates with its lawyers through its employees. The courts have grappled with the question of which employees speak for the corporation so that their statements are protected by the privilege. Some states limit the privilege to statements from senior management who guide and integrate the firm's operations.

In federal court, however, the Supreme Court has refused to limit the privilege to the senior managers who control the firm.[2] The Court applies the privilege on a case-by-case basis, inquiring:

- Was the employee directed by his or her superiors to speak with counsel?
- Was the communication to enable the firm to get legal advice?
- Did the communication concern matters within the scope of the employee's job?
- Did the employee know the reason for the communication?
- Was the communication confidential?

The attorney-client privilege is the highest privileged communication in the law. The physician-patient privilege, for example, may be broken by a court subpoena and the physician forced to testify. However, once the attorney-client privilege attaches, the attorney cannot divulge the privileged communication. In fact, to do so would be considered a breach of professional conduct, for which the attorney may be disbarred. There are some limited exceptions to the privilege, but as the next case makes clear, the privilege is strong enough to survive the death of the client.

SWINDLER & BERLIN AND JAMES HAMILTON V. UNITED STATES
524 U.S. 399 (1998)

White House Counsel, Vincent Foster, met with James Hamilton (Petitioner), an attorney with Swindler & Berlin (Petitioner), to seek legal representation in connection with investigations of the dismissal of White House Travel employees. Hamilton took three pages of handwritten notes during the meeting. Nine days later Foster committed suicide. Thereafter, a federal grand jury issued subpoenas for the handwritten notes as part an investigation by the Office of Independent Counsel into whether various individuals made false statements, obstructed justice or committed other crimes during the investigation into White House Travel firings. Swindler & Berlin and James Hamilton, Petitioners, moved to dismiss the subpoenas on the basis that the notes were protected by the attorney-client privilege. The District Court agreed. The Court of Appeals for the DC Circuit reversed, reasoning "that there is a posthumous exception to the privilege for communications whose relative importance to particular criminal litigation is substantial." The United States Supreme Court granted certiorari.

---

[2] Upjohn Co. v. U.S., 449 U.S. 383 (1981).

Chief Justice Rehnquist

The attorney-client privilege is one of the oldest recognized privileges for confidential communications. The privilege is intended to encourage "full and frank communication between attorneys and their clients and thereby promote broader public interests in the observance of law and the administration of justice." The issue presented here is the scope of that privilege; more particularly, the extent to which the privilege survives the death of the client. . . .

The Independent Counsel argues that the attorney-client privilege should not prevent disclosure of confidential communications where the client has died and the information is relevant to a criminal proceeding. There is some authority for this position. One state appellate court, and the Court of Appeals below have held the privilege may be subject to posthumous exceptions in certain circumstances. In *Cohen*, a civil case, the court recognized that the privilege generally survives death, but concluded that it could make an exception where the interest of justice was compelling and the interest of the client in preserving the confidence was insignificant.

But other than these two decisions cases addressing the existence of the privilege after death—most involving the testamentary exception—uniformly presume the privilege survives. . . .

Such testamentary exception cases consistently presume the privilege survives. They view testamentary disclosure of communications as an exception to the privilege: "The general rule with respect to confidential communication . . . is that such communications are privileged during the testator's lifetime and also, after the testator's death unless sought to be disclosed in litigation between the testator's heirs."

■   ■   ■

Indeed, this Court, in recognizing the testamentary exception, expressly assumed that the privilege continues after the individual's death. The Court explained that testamentary disclosure was permissible because the privilege, which normally protects the client's interests, could be impliedly waived in order to fulfill the client's testamentary intent.

The Independent Counsel contends that the testamentary exception supports the posthumous termination of the privilege because in practice most cases have refused to apply the privilege posthumously. He further argues that the exception reflects a policy judgment that the interest in settling estates outweighs any posthumous interest in confidentiality. He then reasons by analogy that in criminal proceedings, the interest in determining whether a crime has been committed should trump client confidentiality, particularly since the financial interests of the estate are not at stake.

But the Independent Counsel's interpretation simply does not square with caselaw's acceptance of the privilege's survival and with the treatment of testamentary disclosure as an "exception" or an implied "waiver." And the premise of his analogy is incorrect, since cases consistently recognize that the rationale for the testamentary exception is that it furthers the client's intent. . . .

■   ■   ■

Despite the scholarly criticism, we think there are weighty reasons that counsel in favor of posthumous application. Knowing that communications will remain confidential even after death encourages the client to communicate fully and frankly with counsel. While the fear of disclosure, and the consequent withholding of information from counsel, may be reduced if disclosure is limited to posthumous disclosure in a criminal context, it seems unreasonable to assume that it vanishes altogether. Clients may be concerned about reputation, civil liability, or possible harm to friends or family. Posthumous disclosure of such communications may be as feared as disclosure during the client's lifetime.

■   ■   ■

The contention that the attorney is being required to disclose only when the client could have been required to disclose is at odds with the basis for the privilege even during the client's lifetime. In related cases, we have said that the loss of evidence admittedly caused by the privilege is justified in part by the fact that without the privilege, the client may not have made such communications in the first place. This is true of disclosure before and after the client's death. Without assurance of the privilege's posthumous application, the client may very well not have made disclosures to his attorney at all, so the loss of evidence is more apparent than real. In the case at hand, it seems quite plausible that Foster, perhaps already contemplating suicide, may not have sought legal advice from Hamilton if he had not been assured the conversation was privileged.

The Independent Counsel additionally suggests that his proposed exception would have minimal impact if confined to criminal cases, or, as the Court of Appeals suggests, if it is limited to information of substantial importance to a particular criminal case. However, there is no case authority for the proposition that the privilege applies differently in criminal and civil cases. . . . In any event, a client may not know at the time he disclosed information to his attorney whether it would later be relevant to a civil or criminal matter let alone whether it will be of substantial importance.

■   ■   ■

It has been generally, if not universally, accepted, for well over a century, that the attorney-client privilege survives the death of the client in a case such as this. While the arguments against the survival of the privilege are by no means frivolous, they are based on large part on speculation . . . as to whether posthumous termination of the privilege would diminish a client's willingness to confide in a attorney. In an area where empirical information would be useful, it is scant and inconclusive.

. . . [D]irection to look to "principles of the common law as they may be interpreted by the courts of the United States in the light of reason and experience" does not mandate that a rule, once established, should endure for all time. But here the Independent Counsel has simply not made a sufficient showing to overturn the common law rule embodied in the prevailing caselaw. Interpreted in the light of reason and experience, the body of law requires that the attorney-client privilege prevent disclosure of the notes at issue in this case. The judgment of the Court of Appeals is Reversed.

Justice O'Connor, with whom Justice Scalia and Justice Thomas join dissenting.

I agree that a deceased client may retain a personal, reputational and economic interest in confidentiality. But after death, the potential that disclosure will harm the client's interests has been greatly diminished, and the risk that the client will be held criminally liable has abated altogether. . . .

As the Court of Appeals observed, the costs of recognizing an absolute posthumous privilege can be inordinately high. Extreme injustice may occur, for example, where a criminal defendant seeks disclosure of a deceased client's confession to the offense. In my view, the paramount value that our criminal system places on protecting an innocent defendant should outweigh a deceased client's interest in preserving confidences. . . .

A number of exceptions to the privilege already qualify its protections, and an attorney "who tells his client that the expected communications are absolutely and forever privileged is oversimplifying a bit." In the situation where the posthumous privilege most frequently arises—a dispute between heirs over the decedent's will—the privilege is widely recognized to give way to the interest in settling the estate. . . .

Accordingly, I would affirm the judgment of the Court of Appeals. . . .

Case Questions:

1. What is the purpose of the attorney-client privilege? Who does it protect?

2. Are there good reasons for the court to extend the posthumous exception to the privilege to certain criminal cases? What would the dissent say and why?

3. What does the Court mean when it says that principles of law as interpreted by the courts in the light of reason and experience "does not mandate that the rule . . . endure for all time?" What could change to change the rule?

4. How would empirical evidence have helped the Court? What might it show to alter the Court's decision?

5. The U.S. Patriot Act authorizes the eavesdropping on conversations between attorneys and their clients, who are in federal custody. In conjunction with the Patriot Act, the Bureau of Prisons allowed federal agents to tape conversations between a convicted terrorist held in a federal penitentiary and his attorney. Some of the conversations were used to convict the attorney of smuggling communications from his client to his client's followers in violation of the prison rules and law. How do you think the U.S. Supreme Court would rule in this matter? Should this portion of the Patriot Act be upheld? Explain.

Work Product Doctrine

A doctrine akin to the attorney-client privilege is the work-product doctrine. Any materials that have been prepared in anticipation of a lawsuit fall under this doctrine, and are privileged. Neither the attorney nor the client can be compelled to disclose these materials. The doctrine covers not only materials that have been prepared by the client or the attorney, but also any materials prepared by, for example, consultants.

In some cases a party to a lawsuit may obtain these materials if there is a substantial need and there is no other way to obtain them without undue hardship. However, even in this case the court will still protect against disclosure of the mental impressions, conclusions, opinions or legal theories of an attorney or other representative of the party concerning the litigation.

Codes of Professional Conduct

Every state has ethical codes of conduct governing lawyers' professional behavior. Lawyers have certain responsibilities to their clients, to the legal system, and to their own consciences. These responsibilities often result in ethical dilemmas. To guide attorneys and bodies that regulate their conduct, the American Bar Association, a national organization of attorneys, has approved The Model Rules of Professional Conduct (usually known just as the Model Rules). Most states have adopted the Model Rules, with variations from state to state.

The Model Rules require the lawyer to provide competent representation to a client. According to the Model Rules, competent representation "requires the legal knowledge, skill, thoroughness and preparation reasonably necessary for the representation." The lawyer must act with commitment to the client's interest and zealously advocate the client's cause. This must be accomplished while abiding by the client's decision regarding the objectives of the representation and while exercising candor to the tribunal hearing the case.

Lawyers may not represent clients whose interests conflict with those of other clients. The Model Rules require lawyers to adopt reasonable procedures to determine whether there are any conflicts of interest.

Under the Model Rules, a lawyer must keep confidential all information relating to the representation, unless the client consents to its disclosure. This rule does not apply if a lawyer knows that a client intends to commit a crime that would result in death or substantial bodily harm. A client has the right to discharge a lawyer with or without cause.

The Court System

The judicial system in the United States, includes the federal system and the judicial systems of the 50 states. Separate federal court systems exist for the District of Columbia and U.S. territories such as Puerto Rico, the Virgin Islands, and Guam. This means there are more than 50 distinct judicial systems. It is not unusual for a firm to do business in a number of states and, hence, to be subject to the judicial processes in many jurisdictions. The business manager therefore needs a general understanding of the workings of federal and state judicial systems.

Jurisdiction

Jurisdiction is the power of a court to hear and decide a case. To exercise this power, a court generally must have jurisdiction over both the subject matter of, and the parties to, the dispute.

Jurisdiction over the subject matter is accomplished by selecting a court that has power to hear the type of case. State courts of general jurisdiction are usually empowered to hear any type of case. The federal courts, as discussed in the next section, have limited subject-matter jurisdiction.

Jurisdiction over the person may be accomplished by serving the defendant with notice of the suit within the state in which the court is located. The notice is called a *summons*.

The requirement that the process be served on the defendant in the state in which the court is located poses a severe limitation. Suppose a defendant who resides in Alaska strikes a pedestrian while driving a car in Florida. If the Alaskan resident returned home, the injured pedestrian might be forced to sue in Alaska. To combat this shortcoming, states enacted long-arm statutes. A **long-arm statute** is a means of gaining service over an out-of-state defendant. Most states have long-arm statutes that subject an out-of-state defendant to the jurisdiction where the defendant is doing business or has committed a civil wrong. Long-arm statutes must comply with the Constitution's requirement of due process. In *International Shoe Co. v. Washington,* the U.S. Supreme Court held that the U.S. Constitution requires a defendant, if not present within the state, to have certain minimum contacts with the state where the suit is filed.[3] The next case involving the use of the long arm statute grapples with what satisfies minimum contacts.

WORLD-WIDE VOLKSWAGEN CORP. V. WOODSON
444 U.S. 286 (1980)

Harry and Kay Robinson (Respondents) purchased a new Audi automobile from Seaway Volkswagen (Seaway), in Massena, New York. The following year the Robinsons left their residence in New York and relocated in Arizona. While passing through the state of Oklahoma, another car struck their Audi in the rear causing a fire which severely burned Kay Robinson and her two children.

The Robinsons sued a number of parties, including the manufacturer of the Audi, its importer, its regional distributor, World-Wide Volkswagen Corp. (World-Wide) (Petitioner), and its retail dealer, Seaway (Petitioner), alleging that the accident was due to the misplacement of the gas tank. World-Wide is incorporated and has its business office in New York, and it distributes vehicles, parts and accessories to retail dealers in New York, New Jersey, and Connecticut. Seaway also is incorporated in New York, and has its place of business in that state. Neither World-Wide nor Seaway does any business in Oklahoma. They do not do any advertising calculated to reach Oklahoma.

Seaway and World-Wide claimed that Oklahoma's exercise of jurisdiction over them would offend the limitations of Due Process Clause of the Fourteenth Amendment. The Oklahoma trial judge rejected that constitutional claim and the Supreme Court of Oklahoma in effect upheld that ruling. It based its holding on Oklahoma's long arm statute which conferred jurisdiction to the limits permitted by the United States Constitution. Petitioners sought a writ of certiorari which the United States Supreme Court granted.

Justice White delivered the opinion of the Court.

The issue before us is whether, consistently with the Due Process Clause of the Fourteenth Amendment, an Oklahoma court may exercise *in personam* jurisdiction over a nonresident automobile retailer and its wholesale distributor in a products-liability action, when the defendants' only connection with Oklahoma is the fact that an automobile sold in New York to New York residents became involved in an accident in Oklahoma.

■   ■   ■

As has long been settled, and as we reaffirm today, a state court may exercise personal jurisdiction over a nonresident defendant only so long

---

[3] 326 U.S. 310 (1945).

as there exist "minimum contacts" between the defendant and the forum State. The concept of minimum contacts, in turn, can be seen to perform two related, but distinguishable, functions. It protects the defendant against the burdens of litigating in a distant or inconvenient forum. And it acts to insure that the States, through their courts, do not reach beyond the limits imposed on them by their status as coequal sovereigns in a federal system.

. . . We have said that the defendant's contacts with the forum State must be such that maintenance of the suit "does not offend 'traditional notions of fair play and substantial justice.' ". . .

The limits imposed on state jurisdiction by the Due Process Clause, in its role as guarantor against inconvenient litigation, have been substantially relaxed over the years. . . . [T]his trend is largely attributable to a fundamental transformation in the American economy:

> Today many commercial transactions touch two or more States and many involve parties separated by the full continent. With this increasing nationalization of commerce has come a great increase in the amount of business conducted by mail across state lines. At the same time modern transportation and communication have made it much less burdensome for a party sued to defend himself in a State where he engages in economic activity."

■　　■　　■

. . . [T]he Due Process Clause "does not contemplate that a state may make binding a judgment *in personam* against an individual or corporate defendant with which the state has no contacts, ties or relations.". . .

. . . Petitioners carry on no activity whatsoever in Oklahoma. They close no sales and perform no services there. They avail themselves of none of the privileges and benefits of Oklahoma law. They solicit no business . . . [n]or does the record show that they regularly sell cars at wholesale or retail to Oklahoma customers or residents or that they indirectly, through others, serve or seek to serve the Oklahoma market. In short, respondents seek to base jurisdiction on one, isolated occurrence and whatever inferences can be drawn therefrom: the fortuitous circumstance that a single Audi automobile, sold in New York to New York residents, happened to suffer an accident while passing through Oklahoma.

It is argued however, that because an automobile is mobile by its very design and purpose it was "foreseeable" that the Robinsons' Audi would cause injury in Oklahoma. . . .

If foreseeability were the criterion, a local California tire retailer could be forced to defend in Pennsylvania when a blowout occurs there . . . ; a Wisconsin seller of a defective automobile jack could be haled before a distant court for damage caused in New Jersey . . . ; or a Florida soft-drink concessionaire could be summoned to Alaska to account for injuries happening there. . . .

This is not to say, of course, that foreseeability is wholly irrelevant. But the foreseeability that is critical to due process analysis is not the mere likelihood that a product will find its way into the forum State. Rather, it is that the defendant's conduct and connection with the forum State are such that he should reasonably anticipate being haled into court there. The Due Process Clause, by insuring the "orderly administration of the laws," gives a degree of predictability to the legal system that allows potential defendants to structure their primary conduct with some minimum assurance as to where that conduct will and will not render them liable to suit.

When a corporation "purposefully avails itself of the privilege of conducting activities within the forum State," it has clear notice that it is subject to suit there, and can act to alleviate the risk of burdensome litigation by procuring insurance, passing the expected costs on to customers, or, if the risks are too great, severing its connection with the State. Hence if the sale of a product to a manufacturer or distributor such as Audi or Volkswagen is not simply an isolated occurrence, but arises from the efforts of the manufacturer or distributor to serve, directly or indirectly, the market for its product in other States, it is not unreasonable to subject it to suit in one of those States if its allegedly defective merchandise has there been the source of injury to its owners or to others. The forum State does not exceed its powers under the Due Process Clause if it asserts personal jurisdiction over a corporation that delivers its products into the stream of commerce with the expectation that they will be purchased by consumers in the forum State.

But there is no such or similar basis for Oklahoma jurisdiction over World-Wide or Seaway in this case. . . . It is foreseeable that the purchasers of automobiles sold by World-Wide and Seaway may take them to Oklahoma. But the mere "unilateral activity of those who claim some relationship with a nonresident defendant cannot satisfy the requirement of contact with the forum State."

. . . [I]t is contended that jurisdiction can be supported by the fact that petitioners earn substantial revenue from goods used in Oklahoma. The Oklahoma Supreme Court so found, drawing the inference that because one automobile sold by petitioners had been used in Oklahoma, others might have been used there also. . . .

This argument seems to make the point that the purchase of automobiles in New York, from which the petitioners earn substantial revenue, would not occur *but for* the fact that the automobiles are capable of use in distant States like Oklahoma. Respondents observe that the very purpose of an automobile is to travel, and that travel of automobiles sold by petitioners is facilitated by an extensive chain of Volkswagen service centers throughout the country, including some in Oklahoma. However, financial benefits accruing to the defendant from a collateral relation to the forum State will not support jurisdiction if they do not stem from a constitutionally cognizable contact with that State. In our view, whatever marginal revenues petitioners may receive by virtue of the fact that their products are capable of use in Oklahoma is far too attenuated a contact to justify that State's exercise of *in personam* jurisdiction over them.

Because we find that the petitioners have no "contacts, ties, or relations" with the State of Oklahoma, the judgment of the Supreme Court of Oklahoma is *Reversed.*

Justices Brennan, Marshall, and Blackmun dissent.

Case Questions

1. What is the issue that this case presents?
2. What is the policy behind the Constitution's Due Process Clause in relation to jurisdiction?
3. Would not the respondents know that the automobiles they placed in the stream of commerce would wind up in another state? Why then, is "mere awareness" insufficient to constitutionally confer jurisdiction upon the Petitioners?
4. Change the facts of the case so that there would be jurisdiction in Oklahoma based upon the "purposefully avail" test.
5. CEA is a French research agency that patented a technology for the design and manufacture of liquid crystal displays (LCDs), a type of flat panel display used in computer monitors and television screens. CMO is a Taiwanese manufacturer of LCD products that CEA contends infringes on its patents. CMO's LCD products are sold to original equipment manufacturers (OEMs) that incorporate the LCDs into computer monitors. Although CMO does not have any direct contact with Delaware, it does derive substantial revenue from sales of its products to Delaware. Does this present a case of "sufficient minimum contacts" to justify jurisdictional power by a Delaware court? Is it distinguishable from World-Wide Volkswagen? Explain.

Venue

Jurisdiction must be distinguished from venue. *Venue* is concerned with the geographic locality within the jurisdiction where an action should be tried. Venue is specified by statute; it may require that the case be heard in the county where the defendant resides or where the property that is the subject of the action is located. When the location of a trial would result in an inconvenience and a hardship, the doctrine of **forum non conveniens** permits a defendant to transfer the case to another geographic location where venue is proper.

The Federal System

The federal judicial system derives from the U.S. Constitution. Article III provides that "the judicial Power of the United States shall be vested in one supreme court, and in such inferior courts as the Congress may from time to time ordain and establish." Pursuant to Article III, Congress has created 14 circuit courts of appeal and 94 district courts (see Figure 4–1).

FIGURE 4-1   Federal Court System

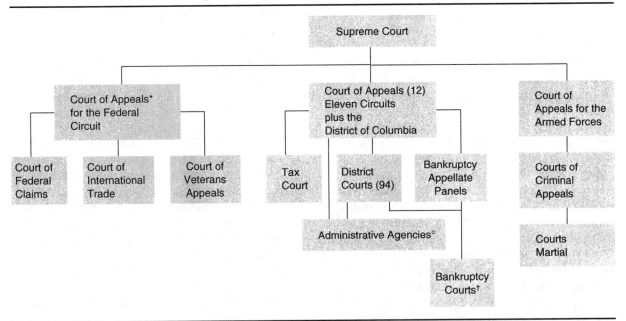

---

*Cases invoving patents, trademarks, copyrights, and contract claims against the United States are reviewed by the Court of Appeals for the Federal Circuit.

†Some appeals proceed to the Bankruptcy Appellate Panel; others go directly to the District Court.

°Most appeals are reviewed by the Court of Appeals; some are reviewed de novo in the District Court.

District Courts

The basic federal trial court is the U.S. district court. There is at least one district in every state and territory. Many states are divided into more than one district, depending on size, population, and number of lawsuits filed. District courts also hear appeals from a few federal agencies, such as the Social Security Administration.

The district court has subject matter jurisdiction only if a statute gives it jurisdiction. The two broadest statutes give district courts jurisdiction over cases involving a federal question and diversity of citizenship.

Federal question jurisdiction cases include any claim arising under a federal statute, a treaty, or the U.S. Constitution. Cases involving robbery of federal banks, federal antitrust violations, and interpretations of U.S. treaties with foreign nations are all properly heard by a federal district court because they present federal questions.

U.S. district courts also have **diversity jurisdiction** over cases between citizens of different states where the amount in contest exceeds $75,000. A corporation is considered a citizen of the states in which it is incorporated and in which it has its principal place of business. A partnership, even a limited partnership, is considered a citizen of every state in which a partner is a citizen. There must be complete diversity of citizenship; no plaintiff (the party who initiates the suit) may be a citizen of the same state in which any defendant (the party who is sued) is a citizen. If there are multiple plaintiffs, each must claim, in good faith, damages exceeding $75,000 (not counting interest or court costs).

For example, assume that four individual plaintiffs sue Chemical, Inc. because wastes it dumped into a waterway ultimately polluted the plaintiffs' property. Each seeks more than $75,000 in damages. Three of the plaintiffs are citizens of Ohio, and the fourth is a citizen of Michigan. Chemical, Inc. is incorporated in Delaware and has its principal place of business in Michigan. Here, diversity of citizenship is not present because a plaintiff and a defendant are citizens of Michigan. If the Michigan plaintiff were eliminated from the suit, then diversity jurisdiction would be present.

The federal district court sitting in a diversity case hears and resolves the case according to the law of the state in which it sits. This is known as the *Erie Doctrine,* named after a case in which this principle was first announced.[4] The court does, however, apply its own procedural rules, such as rules of evidence and rules of conduct regarding the administration of the trial.

Plaintiffs are not required to sue in federal district court, even though that court would have jurisdiction. In most cases, they may elect instead to file suit in a proper state court. The district court has concurrent jurisdiction, with the state courts, as opposed to exclusive jurisdiction. However, if plaintiffs sue in a state court, the defendant may have the case removed to the federal court as long as the case could have originally been brought in that court.

---

[4] Erie Railroad Co. v. Tompkins, 304 U.S. 64 (1938).

Court of Appeals

Appeals from the district courts are heard by the U.S. circuit courts of appeals. There are 11 numbered circuit courts of appeal, the District of Columbia circuit, plus the Courts of Appeals for the Federal Circuit and for the Armed Forces. They also hear appeals from the Tax Court and review most administrative agency actions. The Tax Court hears disputes involving tax deficiencies assessed against a taxpayer. Federal administrative agencies are discussed more fully in Chapter 6.

U.S. Supreme Court

Sitting atop the federal legal system is the U.S. Supreme Court. Review in the Supreme Court is not automatic. Parties seeking review must request that the Court hear the case by filing a petition for **certiorari**. The Court has absolute discretion to grant or deny certiorari, and it rarely gives a reason for a denial. Certiorari is granted if any four of the nine Supreme Court justices are in favor of it. Certiorari is likely to be granted when a constitutional issue of national importance is posed or when an issue has been decided in a conflicting manner by the circuit courts of appeals.

The State System

State trial courts consist of courts of general and limited jurisdiction (see Figure 4–2). A court of general jurisdiction is one that can hear any type of case unless specifically prohibited by statute. Some cases, such as admiralty, bankruptcy, and patent infringement actions, may be brought only in federal court. Most state trial courts of general jurisdiction are organized at the county level. Their names vary

---

FIGURE 4-2   Typical State Court System

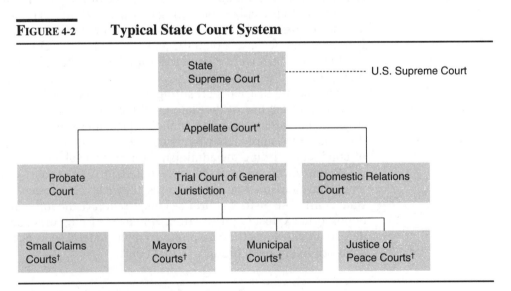

*Not present in the system in smaller, less populous states.

†In some cases, appeals are made directly to the Appellate Court.

from state to state. The most popular names are circuit court, court of common pleas, and superior court.

State trial courts of limited jurisdiction are those that can hear only specific types of cases. A probate court, for example, cannot hear a divorce case; a small claims court cannot try a felony case. Some courts are limited in that they can only hear disputes up to a maximum monetary ceiling.

Many states have an intermediate court of appeals, similar to the federal circuit court of appeals. Following a decision by the court of appeals, review may be sought in the state supreme court; similar to the U.S. Supreme Court, it reviews most cases by certiorari. In the smaller and less populous states, which lack intermediate courts of appeals, appeals from trial courts are taken directly to state supreme courts.

A state supreme court is the highest authority on the law of its state. The U.S. Supreme Court has no power to decide issues of state law. State supreme court decisions interpreting federal statutes, treaties, and the U.S. Constitution are, however, subject to U.S. Supreme Court review.

The Civil Process

A dispute must involve a case or controversy before a court will decide it. Courts do not act when there is no real dispute.

Courts are best equipped to decide cases when the parties have a personal stake in the outcome. Under these circumstances, the parties have the incentive to expend their best efforts in prosecuting or defending a case. This is the adversary system. In this adversarial environment, courts are in the best position to examine the arguments, find the truth, and apply justice.

When an event triggers a dispute, the potential for a lawsuit exists. A lawsuit is a civil case. Table 4–1 contrasts civil and criminal cases. The civil process is the sequence of events from the beginning of the suit to the final appeal. It consists of four stages: the *pleading stage*, the *discovery stage*, *trial stage*, and *appellate stage* (see Figure 4–3).

The Pleading Stage

The *pleadings* are the documents that tell each party's claims or defenses against the other parties. See Table 4–2 for a summary of the pleadings.

Class Action Suits

Under certain circumstances, a person may bring a suit on behalf of a class of people who have been similarly injured. This is known as a **class action suit.** For example, assume that many members of the public have been injured as a result of illegally inflated utility prices. It may not be feasible for every injured person to sue the utility company individually, and not everyone may be aware of the illegal activity. The cost of maintaining the suit also may discourage people from suing, especially if the amount of potential recovery is too small to be worth the effort. The law in these cases may permit one or more persons to undertake a suit

TABLE 4–1   Civil versus Criminal Cases

	Civil	Criminal
Who institutes the action?	Individual or business enterprise	Sovereign
Who has been wronged?	Individual or business enterprise	Society
What is the burden of proof?	Preponderance of the evidence*	Beyond a reasonable doubt†
What is the remedy?	Damages, injunction, or other private relief	Punishment (fine and/or imprisonment)

* By the greater weight of the evidence.

† To satisfy this burden the trier of the facts (judge or jury) must have an abiding conviction amounting to a certainty of the guilt of the accused. This is a greater burden of proof than "preponderance of the evidence."

FIGURE 4-3   The Civil Process

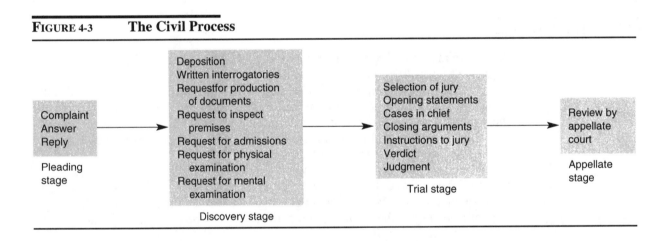

against the utility company on behalf of all the injured customers. By consolidating in one suit the claims of many, the class action suit avoids the potential for repetitious, inefficient litigation.

Class actions have involved thousands and even hundreds of thousands of people. The administration of a class suit is often very difficult because of the number of persons involved. The distribution of the proceeds of a settlement or judgment may be equally difficult. Not all members of the class may be identified or found. Additionally, the amount of distribution to each individual may be disputed. Some courts, aware of this problem, have ordered that damages be distributed to benefit the public. For example, in a case where a utility company charges illegally high rates, a court might order the company to reduce its rates to all consumers for a period of time.

TABLE 4–2	**Pleadings**	
Pleading	*Who Files against Whom*	*Purpose*
Complaint	Plaintiff against defendant	States the factual basis for the claim.
Answer	Defendant against plaintiff	Admits or denies the allegations of the complaint; may also raise affirmative defenses.
Counterclaim	Defendant against plaintiff	States basis for claim by defendant against plaintiff.
Reply	Plaintiff against defendant	Answers counterclaim.
Cross claim	Defendant against another defendant	States basis for claim.
Impleader	Defendant against a nonparty	Defendant adds another party to the lawsuit.
Intervention	Nonparty against a party	Another party seeks to join the lawsuit.
Interpleader	Plaintiff or Defendant against two parties	Forces the court to determine the rightful holder of monies.

Motions

During the pleading stage it is not unusual for a party to file a **motion to dismiss** or a **motion for judgment on the pleadings.**

A motion to dismiss may attack any number of deficiencies in a pleading. It may be used, for example, by a defendant questioning whether the court has jurisdiction over the defendant or over the subject matter. Or, it may allege that the matter should be dismissed because the Complaint fails to state facts that would constitute a reason for the Plaintiff to win the lawsuit. In effect this motion, says, "So what. Even if you prove what you said, the law does not recognize this as actionable." For example, in a jurisdiction where a surrogate mother contract is not recognized, a complaint seeking relief under such a contract should be dismissed for failure to state a cause of action.

A motion to dismiss will also be warranted when it is clear on the face of the Complaint that the statute of limitations has run. In a jurisdiction where the statute of limitations for a wrongful discharge of employment is four years, for example, a motion to dismiss should be granted if it is clear from the Complaint that it was not filed within that time period. Finally, there are consequences when the defendant fails to answer the Complaint in a timely manner, or the Plaintiff fails to Reply to the Counterclaim within the time specified by law. In such a case a motion for default judgment may result in the movant winning.

A motion for judgment on the pleadings may be filed by either party. It is similar to the motion to dismiss, however it alleges that on the basis of an examination of all the pleadings, the movant should prevail. For example, assume that the plaintiff alleges in its complaint that defendant owes it a sum of money. Defendant, in his Answer, pleads poverty, but does not deny the debt. Based on these pleadings a motion for judgment on the pleadings should be granted in Plaintiff's favor.

Remedies

Most people sue for money damages, but in some cases a plaintiff asks the court for an **injunction**—an order compelling the defendant to do something or to refrain from doing something. The plaintiff is not entitled to a permanent injunction until the end of the case. In a proper case, however, the plaintiff may obtain a preliminary injunction by demonstrating that: (1) the plaintiff is very likely to win on the merits of the case, (2) the plaintiff will suffer irreparable harm if the preliminary injunction is not issued, (3) the injunction will not be unjustly harsh on the defendant, and (4) the injunction is in the public interest.

The Discovery Stage

Discovery refers to the process where each party attempts to learn what the other party knows. Each party may direct written questions, known as *interrogatories,* to the other party, who must provide written answers under oath. Each party may also ask the other parties to allow inspection of documents, or the premises, admit or deny specific facts, or submit to a physical or mental examination. Parties may also take each other's deposition, a procedure whereby individuals are questioned under oath before a court reporter.

The discovery process contributes substantially to the costs of litigation. In an effort to control these costs, the U.S. Supreme Court approved changes to the Federal Rules of Civil Procedure. The changes impose on parties a duty to disclose to the other party, without being asked, the following:

- names, addresses and phone numbers of individuals with knowledge relevant to disputed facts alleged with particularity in the pleadings
- copies or descriptions of documents relevant to disputed facts alleged with particularity in the pleadings
- computations of all monetary damage claims
- copies of liability insurance policies covering the dispute
- names and copies of reports by expert witnesses
- names of witnesses the party plans to call

The changes to the Federal Rules rely on automatic disclosure as the primary means of discovery.

Motions

During the discovery stage, it is common for parties to file a **motion for summary judgment**. This motion is not confined to an examination of the pleadings. It calls attention to the discovery materials, and may include additional sworn statements not part of the discovery. It is not unusual for both parties to file a motion for summary judgment and seek a favorable ruling based upon the sworn facts as applied to the law. Movants are required to file a memorandum that argues why the court should rule in its favor, based upon the uncontroverted facts, as applied to the law.

In a motion for summary judgment, the court is required to construe the facts in the light most favorable to the party against whom summary judgment is sought. Hence, if the question is whether the traffic light was red or green, and there is sworn testimony to both versions, then the court will overrule the motion since these facts are contested.

Pretrial Conference

The judge is interested in an efficient trial. Toward that end, the court will seek out ways to decrease the length of the trial. Parties will be asked to mark their exhibits beforehand and to provide the opponent a copy. Stipulations of evidence whereby the parties agree to the admission of certain documents, or to certain findings, is another way to streamline the trial. The number of witnesses should be realistic and duplication of testimony by different witnesses should ordinarily be avoided.

The court is also interested in the status of settlement negotiations, and will strongly encourage settlement. Of course, settlement will avoid the time and the risk of trial. Usually, the court will be proactive in moving the parties to agreement, and may even suggest or require ADR. *[handwritten: alternative dispute resolution]*

The Trial Stage

If the plaintiff is seeking monetary damages (known as *legal relief*), the parties are ordinarily entitled to a trial by jury. They may, however, waive this right and try the case to the court. If the plaintiff is seeking equitable relief, such as an injunction or other court order, the parties are not ordinarily entitled to a jury trial.

In most civil cases, the plaintiff has the burden of proving the case by a preponderance of the evidence. Preponderance of the evidence means by the greater weight of the evidence. To sustain that burden of proof, the plaintiff must convince the judge or jury that the facts are probably as the plaintiff alleges. If at the end of the case the trier of the facts is undecided, then the defendant wins.

After selection of the jury (if a jury trial is proper and not waived), counsel for the plaintiff makes an opening statement, explaining what he or she intends to prove. Defense counsel may make an opening statement immediately thereafter, or reserve opening statement until the close of plaintiff's case. Plaintiff then presents a case-in-chief by calling witnesses who testify and by presenting other evidence, such as business records, photographs, or other tangible objects, called *exhibits*. The defendant is given the opportunity to cross-examine the plaintiff's witnesses. The judge decides on the admissibility of the evidence, based on the law. The plaintiff rests after completing the case-in-chief.

The defendant then proceeds with an opening statement, if previously reserved, and presents his or her case-in-chief. When the defendant rests, the plaintiff may offer evidence to rebut the defendant's case-in-chief. The defense may follow with surrebutal.

When all of the evidence is in, the parties' lawyers deliver their closing arguments. If the case was tried without a jury, the judge makes findings of fact and conclusions of law. In jury trials, the judge instructs the jurors on the relevant law; they then deliberate and reach a verdict.

Motions

At the trial stage two motions are common: motion for directed verdict and motion for judgment notwithstanding the verdict. Both motions basically say the same thing, but come at different times during the trial.

The **motion for directed verdict** may sound like this in the voice of the attorney moving for it:

> Your Honor, based upon the evidence that has been presented, reasonable minds cannot differ. There is nothing to send to the jury because the evidence is clear, and as a matter of law, your Honor must find for my client.

The motion requesting that court direct a verdict in the movant's favor is customarily made by both parties at the end of the opponent's case-in-chief. Of course, if either party's motion is granted, that ends the case.

The **motion for judgment notwithstanding the verdict** is ordinarily made by the losing party after the return of an unfavorable verdict. It states in essence that the case should never have been sent to the jury because reasonable minds could not differ on the facts, and as applied to the law, the movant should win. In effect this gives the judge another opportunity to rule in favor of the movant, whose motion for directed verdict was previously overruled. It is rare that the court would upset the jury verdict and enter a judgment notwithstanding the verdict, but it does happen from time to time.

The Appellate Stage

Once the trial court makes a final judgment in the case, the losing party may not institute a new suit against the same parties involving the same issues. This would be barred by a doctrine called *res judicata* (the matter has been decided), which bars a second suit involving the same parties and the same issues.

However, the legal system provides an opportunity for a party to ask a higher court to review a case for error committed by the trial court judge. The basis for such a request might be that the judge's ruling on a motion was wrong, the judge improperly admitted or excluded evidence, or the judge's instruction to the jury misstated the law. The courts that review trial court decisions are called *appel-*

Ethical Dilemmas/Issues

Burger Town, Inc. is a chain of hamburger stands with 20 establishments located in 15 towns in Kentucky. Big Time Burgers, Inc. is an international hamburger restaurant chain with over a thousand restaurants located throughout the United States, Canada, and Europe. Last week Burger Town started running full-page ads in newspapers stating: "Burger Town hamburgers and fries are healthier than Big Time's Burgers. An order consisting of a Burger Town hamburger and french fries contains less saturated fat than a Big Time hamburger and fries."

John Swickard is the vice president of operations for Big Time Burgers, Inc. Swickard's department includes the legal department. Teresa Valentine, an attorney in the department, has informed Swickard that Big Time could bring a lawsuit against Burger Town for false advertising. However, the success of the lawsuit would depend on the evidence presented in court.

Big Time cooks its hamburgers and fries in beef tallow. It is quite likely that a Big Time hamburger and fries contain more saturated fats than Burger Town's, if Burger Town cooks its hamburgers and fries in vegetable oil.

Swickard knows that Burger Town is a small, regional chain and cannot withstand the expense of a lengthy lawsuit. However, Big Time's financial and legal resources could enable it to sue and tie up Burger Town in costly litigation for years. Swickard is considering filing a lawsuit against Burger Town and immediately seeking to negotiate a quick settlement. Swickard tells Valentine, "Teresa, if I were in Burger Town's shoes, I would settle the case quickly even if it cost me several thousand dollars rather than face us in court with all the expense that would involve. Also, suing Burger Town would teach those small fries who's the boss of burgers."

What are the ethical issues? What would you do?

---

late courts. An appellate court does not hold a new trial, nor does it hear additional evidence; it merely reviews the record of the trial and listens to the arguments of the party (called the *appellant*) claiming some serious error in that trial. The appellate court also listens to the arguments of the opposing party (called the *appellee*), who may be claiming that no serious error occurred.

After reviewing the record of the trial and the arguments of the parties involved, the appellate court has several alternatives. It can: (1) affirm the verdict of the trial court, that is, accept it as is and change nothing; (2) reverse the verdict, that is, decide that the outcome of the trial was wrong and enter judgment for the appellant; (3) modify the legal remedy provided by the trial court; or (4) reverse and remand the case to the trial court for further proceedings.

Abuse of the System

In recent years, courts and legislatures have tried to curb parties from abusing the judicial system. Rule 11 of the Federal Rules of Civil Procedure is typical of these efforts. It requires that a party or lawyer sign every document filed in the lawsuit and attest that to the best of the signer's knowledge, after reasonable inquiry, the document is well grounded in fact and law and is not being filed for an improper purpose. If the other party believes the rule was violated, it must so advise the alleged violator. If the violator fails to withdraw the offending document, the lawyer and client may be liable for the other party's expenses, including reasonable attorney's fees. Additionally, many states by statute or common law permit parties who have been subjected to frivolous lawsuits to sue for attorney fees and costs, and other damages.

Alternative Dispute Resolution

Two problems plague our civil justice system: delay and expense. These problems result from the heavy volume of lawsuits and the formalities and technicalities of the discovery and motion practice. Consequently, parties and courts have developed a number of alternative dispute resolution (ADR) techniques for resolving legal disputes.

ADR Techniques

Most legal disputes never actually go to trial. Instead, they are settled. A variety of procedures have developed to assist the parties in settling disputes. If the parties are unable to settle, they can avoid court by agreeing to one of the many alternatives to litigation.

Mediation

Mediation involves an intermediary to assist the parties in resolving the conflict. The mediator has no power to force a solution; his or her job is to persuade the parties to come to agreement. A skillful mediator helps the parties understand their opponent's perspective; grasp the strengths of their opponent's case and the weaknesses of their own; and assess the benefits of settlement and the costs of continuing to fight. Often, the success of mediation turns on the mediator's ability and the parties' desire to settle.

Early Neutral Evaluation

Parties using early neutral evaluation submit written memos detailing their positions to a neutral evaluator. The evaluator issues a report on the strengths and weaknesses of each side's case. The parties use the report in an effort to settle their dispute.

Minitrials

The minitrial is a procedure structured to convert a legal dispute into a business problem. Lawyers argue their case to business executives of the disputing companies. These executives are usually high-level officers and have the power to settle the dispute. Time limitations are agreed on in advance. A neutral advisor (a judge or an expert in the topic of dispute) presides at the hearing and offers opinions and suggestions to the executives. After the case has been presented, the executives retire to deliberate. At this stage, the business executives settle the dispute, often by negotiation. The minitrial has been used successfully in several multi-million-dollar disputes.

Summary Jury Trial

In this procedure, each side is given a limited time to present its best case to a jury. Then each party meets with the jury to discuss the strengths and weakness of its case. This is followed by a settlement conference.

Arbitration

Arbitration replaces the judge and jury with a private arbitrator, who holds a hearing and decides the dispute. Many associations, such as the American Arbitration Association, and the Better Business Bureau, provide arbitration services.

Disputants may voluntarily agree to use one or more ADR techniques, either on their own or at the suggestion of a court. Arbitration is the most extensively used voluntary ADR technique. Ad hoc arbitration occurs when the parties agree to submit a particular dispute to arbitration. Increasingly, however, parties are agreeing, before any disputes arise, that all disputes will be arbitrated. These blanket arbitration agreements are standard practice in some industries, such as construction, securities, and commodities.

In voluntary arbitration, the parties control the procedures, the timing, and even the identity of the arbitrator. Thus, arbitration provides greater flexibility than litigation and can solve the problems of delay, cost, and lack of expertise. For example, the parties can require that the arbitrator hear and decide the case by a specified date. If the arbitrator is unable to do so, they can select a different arbitrator. The parties can agree to limit or eliminate the formal discovery process. This can save a great deal of time and expense. Parties can also save money in appropriate cases by limiting or eliminating transcripts and briefs.

The parties can require that the arbitrator have expertise in the technical matters involved in the dispute. This can save the parties the time and money they would spend on educating a generalist judge and jury. It would also provide for a more informed decision.

In addition, the parties can also control whether the arbitration is public. They can agree to exclude the media and to keep the record confidential.

On the other hand, arbitrators do not have the same powers that judges have. Judges have the power to swear witnesses and issue subpoenas. Judges can hold witnesses who refuse to obey subpoenas in contempt and jail or fine them until they agree to comply.

More than three fifths of the states and the District of Columbia have adopted the Uniform Arbitration Act (UAA). The UAA gives arbitrators the power to swear witnesses and issue subpoenas. But an arbitrator has no contempt power. If a witness refuses to obey a subpoena, the parties must sue the witness in court. If the court orders the witness to obey and the witness persists in refusing, the court can then hold the witness in contempt.

An arbitrator's decision is called an *award*. The award may order a party to take action, such as paying money to the other party. However, an arbitrator has no power to enforce the award. As with subpoenas, a party must sue in court if the other party refuses to comply with the award.

Arbitrators have the power to award compensatory damages. There is considerable uncertainty, however, over whether an arbitrator has power to award punitive damages, attorney fees, or equitable relief. The trend in court decisions is to recognize broad arbitrator authority, but the law in this area is still developing.

Courts will not overturn arbitration awards for errors of law or fact. Arbitrators need not give reasons for their decisions. A court will only overturn an award if it displays a manifest disregard for the law.

The next case concerning baseball arbitration illustrates the extent to which state courts are required to defer to arbitrator decisions.

MAJOR LEAGUE BASEBALL PLAYERS ASSOCIATION V. STEVE GARVEY
532 U.S. 504 (2001)

In the late 1980s, Major League Baseball Players Association (Association) filed grievances against the Major League Baseball Clubs (Clubs) claiming that the clubs had colluded in the market for free-agent services in violation of the industry's agreement. A free agent is a player who may contract with any Club, rather than one whose right is restricted to a particular Club. In a series of decisions, arbitrators found collusion by the Clubs and damage to the players. Thereafter, the Association and the Clubs entered into an agreement, whereby the Clubs established a $280 million fund to be distributed to injured players. The Association also designed a "Framework" to evaluate the individual player's claims.

The Framework provided that the players could seek an arbitrator's review of the distribution plan. The arbitrator would determine "only whether the approved Framework and the criteria set forth therein have been properly applied. . . ." Under the Framework claims were only legitimate "where evidence exists that a specific offer of an extension was made by a club prior to collusion only to thereafter be withdrawn when the collusion scheme was initiated."

Steve Garvey, a retired highly regarded first baseman, submitted a claim for damages of approximately $3 million. The matter was submitted to arbitration under the Framework. To provide his claim that the San Diego Padres offered him a contract, which was later withdrawn because of collusion, he submitted a copy of a letter from Ballard Smith, the Padres' president and chief executive officer, which stated that Smith offered to extend Garvey's contract, but thereafter the Padres refused to negotiate with Garvey due to collusion of the Clubs.

The arbitrator denied Garvey's claim, stating that there was substantial doubt as to the credibility of the statements in the Smith letter. Garvey appealed to the Federal District Court, who upheld the arbitrator's decision. The Court of Appeals for the Ninth Circuit reversed and remanded the case back to the arbitration panel for further hearings. The case arose to the U.S. Supreme Court when the Major League Player's Association petitioned the court for a writ of certiorari and it was granted.

Per Curiam*

The parties do not dispute that this case arises under . . . an agreement between an employer and a labor organization. Although Garvey's specific allegation is that the arbitrator violated the Framework for resolving players' claims for damages, that Framework was designed to facilitate payments to remedy the Club's breach of the . . . agreement. Garvey's right to be made whole is founded on that agreement.

Judicial review of a labor-arbitration decision pursuant to such an agreement is very limited. Courts are not authorized to review the arbitrator's decision on the merits despite allegations that the decision rests on factual errors or misinterprets the parties' agreement. We recently reiterated that if an " 'arbitrator is even arguably construing or applying the contract and acting within the scope of his authority,' the fact that 'a court is convinced he committed serious error does not suffice to overturn his decision.' " It is only when the arbitrator strays from interpretation and application of

the agreement and effectively "dispense[s] his own brand of industrial justice" that his decision may be unenforceable. When an arbitrator resolves disputes regarding the application of a contract, and no dishonesty is alleged, the arbitrator's "improvident, even silly, factfinding" does not provide a basis for a reviewing court to refuse to enforce the award.

In discussing the courts' limited role in reviewing the merits of arbitration awards, we have stated that " 'courts . . . have no business weighing the merits of the grievance [or] considering whether there is equity in a particular claim.' " When the judiciary does so, "it usurps a function which . . . is entrusted to the arbitration tribunal." Consistent with this limited role, we said . . . that "[e]ven in the very rare instances when an arbitrator's procedural aberrations rise to the level of affirmative misconduct, as a rule the court must not foreclose further proceedings by settling the merits according to its own judgment of the appropriate result."

---

*Literally, "by the Court." In this case it is a decision that is not authored by one justice but by the majority of justices.

That step, we explained, "would improperly substitute a judicial determination for the arbitrator's decision that the parties bargained for" in their agreement. Instead, the court should "simply vacate the award, thus leaving open the possibility of further proceedings if they are permitted under the terms of the agreement."

To be sure, the Court of Appeals here recited these principles, but its application of them is nothing short of baffling. The substance of the Court's discussion reveals that it overturned the arbitrator's decision because it disagreed with the arbitrator's factual findings, particularly those with respect to credibility. The Court of Appeals, it appears, would have credited Smith's . . . letter, and found the arbitrator's refusal to do so at worst "irrational" and at best "bizarre." But even "serious error" on the arbitrator's part does not justify overturning his decision, where, as here, he is construing a contract and acting within the scope of his authority.

. . . [E]stablished law ordinarily precludes a court from resolving the merits of the parties' dispute on the basis of its own factual determinations, no matter how erroneous the arbitrator's decision. Even when the arbitrator's award may properly be vacated, the appropriate remedy is to remand the case for further arbitration proceedings. The dissent [in this case] suggests that the remedy . . . is limited to cases where the arbitrator's errors are procedural . . . If a remand is appropriate *even* when the arbitrator's award has been set aside for "procedural aberrations" that constitute "affirmative misconduct," it follows that a remand ordinarily will be appropriate when the arbitrator simply made factual findings that the reviewing court perceives as "irrational." The Court of Appeals usurped the arbitrator's role by resolving the dispute and barring further proceedings, a result at odds with this governing law.

For the foregoing reasons, the Court of Appeals erred in reversing the order of the District Court denying the motion to vacate the arbitrator's award, and it erred further in directing that judg-

ment be entered in Garvey's favor. The judgment of the Court of Appeals is reversed, and the case is remanded for further proceedings consistent with this opinion.

It is so ordered.

Case Questions:

1. What is the scope of review of a labor arbitration dispute?

2. Under what circumstances in this case would the decision of the arbitrator be overturned by a court? What is the arbitrator's "own brand of industrial justice?"

3. Assume that a contract for an automobile contained sub-microscopic print on the backside that said: "In the event of a dispute the parties shall submit to binding arbitration and not have the right to institute an action in court." The arbitration clause was never brought to the attention of the consumer. How do you think a court should rule in this instance when the consumer seeks to sue in court because of false misrepresentations made by the car dealer concerning the odometer reading? Must it defer to an arbitrator? Why, or why not?

4. Assume that an agreement between a bank and a customer reads:

   > All disputes, or claims, or controversies arising from this contract shall be resolved by binding arbitration by one arbitrator selected by the Bank with the consent of the Customer.

   A customer maintains that she did not receive certain notifications by the Bank required by law. In order to resolve the dispute the company selects an arbitrator, and the customer agrees to the selection. The customer seeks to certify the case as a class action so that other consumers may take advantage of the arbitration. Is it within the realm of the courts or the arbitrator to determine whether the class action is permissible? Explain. How do you interpret the language of the agreement? To permit this or not?

Mandatory ADR

Many courts and administrative agencies are now requiring parties to use various ADR techniques. It is likely that these requirements will increase in the years to come. The Federal Civil Justice Reform Act requires every federal district court to adopt an expense and delay reduction plan. Many of these plans impose mediation or arbitration on certain types of cases.

When a court imposes arbitration on the parties, it usually does not bind them to the result. The losing party may reject the arbitration award and proceed to trial. Typically, however, there is a disincentive for doing so. In some jurisdictions, the party must pay a fee for rejecting the award. In others, if the rejecting party loses at trial, it must pay the winner's costs and attorney fees for the trial. Due to overcrowded dockets it is very likely that the incidence of mandatory ADR imposed by the courts will continue to increase.

Chapter Problems

1. Define the following terms and concepts:
    a. Jurisdiction
    b. Long-arm statute
    c. Federal question jurisdiction
    d. Diversity of citizenship jurisdiction
    e. Certiorari
    f. Class action suit
    g. Discovery
    h. Injunction
    i. Mediation
    j. Arbitration

2. Plastic Corporation manufactures plastic containers sold to bottling companies. The bottling companies fill the containers with liquid and secure them with leakproof caps. John T. purchased from Ace Hardware a bottle of Prevention Plus, a sulfuric acid-based liquid drain unstopper. While carrying the bottle home, it leaked, causing severe burns to John T.'s body. The container was manufactured by Plastic Corporation and the Prevention Plus was bottled by Sure Bottle Company. John T. threatens to sue. Plastic Corporation seeks to hire an attorney. How should Plastic Corporation select an attorney? As a managerial executive in Plastic Corporation, what is your objective in this conflict? Assume that your lawyer informs you that John T.

is willing to settle the case for $10,000. What other information do you need to determine whether to settle or not?

3. Al Ladin, attorney for Spray Lawn, Inc., suspected that two of Spray Lawn's lower-echelon employees were diverting the corporation's funds to their own use. Ladin confronted the employees with his suspicions, and they both confessed. At Ladin's insistence, the employees wrote a detailed account of their activities involving the diversion of company funds. Their employment was then terminated. Subsequently, the IRS conducted an audit of Spray Lawn, Inc. and issued a summons for the written statements in Ladin's possession. Must Ladin produce the statements? Explain. Could the IRS derive the information in any other way?

4. Robert Balla was general counsel of Gambro, Inc., a distributor of kidney dialysis equipment. In July 1985, appellant was advised by an affiliated German company that it was shipping appellant certain defective dialyzers. Appellee told appellant's president to reject the shipment because it did not comply with Food & Drug Administration (FDA) regulations. Initially the president agreed, but later he decided to accept the shipment. What should Balla do? What are the consequences? Explain.

5. UHF, Inc., a citizen of the state of California, manufactured weather insulation. It sold the insulation to contractors who installed it in buildings throughout the United States. The insulation was found to be hazardous to health. Thousands of people suffered injury as a result of being exposed to it. Hundreds of thousands more have been exposed to the insulation, but have no symptoms at this time. What are the potential consequences to UHF, Inc.? Explain.

6. Helicopteros Nacionales de Colombia (Helicol) is a Colombian corporation that has its principal place of business in the city of Bogota. It provides helicopter transportation services for oil and construction companies in South America. Four U.S. citizens were killed when one of Helicol's helicopters crashed in Peru. The crash victims were working for Consorcio/WSH at the time of the crash. Consorcio/WSH was building a pipeline in Peru and needed helicopters to move personnel, materials, and equipment to and from the construction area.

About two years before the accident, the chief executive officer of Helicol traveled to Houston, Texas, and conferred with representatives of Consorcio/WSH. They negotiated a contract later signed in Peru. It stated that controversies arising out of the contract would be decided by the Peruvian courts. It also provided that Consorcio/WSH would make payments to Helicol's bank account with Bank of America in New York. More than $5 million in payments received in these accounts were drawn on a Texas bank. Over an approximately seven-year period, Helicol purchased helicopters and spare parts for more than $4 million from Bell Helicopter Company in Fort Worth. Helicol sent pilots for training to Fort Worth. It also sent management and maintenance personnel to visit Bell Helicopter in Fort Worth. Are there sufficient contacts to confer personal jurisdiction over Helicol in Texas? Explain.

7. Asahi Metal Industry, a Japanese manufacturer of tire valve assemblies, sold them to Cheg Shin Rubber Co. in Taiwan. Cheng Shin used the assemblies in making tires, which it distributed worldwide. Asahi knew that its assemblies would be incorporated into tires sold in California and other states.

   Gary Zurcher sued Cheng Shin in the Superior Court in California for injuries he sustained allegedly caused by a defective motor cycle tire manufactured by Cheng Shin. Cheng Shin, through the use of the California long arm statute, sought to add Asahi to the lawsuit, alleging that the valve assembly was defective. Are the contacts with California sufficient for the California court to exercise jurisdiction over Asahi? Why or why not?

8. Professor Ephriam Cross is employed by New York University to teach French, Spanish, and Romance linguistics. He and his wife sailed from New York for France via Portugal, Morocco, Algeria, and Italy. On arriving in Marseilles, they split up. Mrs. Cross continued to tour, and Mr. Cross, though not pursuing a formal course of study, visited schools, courts of law, churches, book publishers, and restaurants; read magazines; listened to radio broadcasts; conversed with students and teachers; and attended political meetings. Cross and his wife returned to New York in time for Cross to resume his teaching schedule at NYU. Cross filed his income tax return and deducted the full cost of the trip he and his wife took to Europe.

   The IRS objected to the deduction and brought suit against Cross, demanding payment of the amount he allegedly underpaid. Cross contended that the deduction was pursuant to the Internal Revenue Code provision that allows deductions for all expenses incurred in carrying on a trade or business. Cross presented affidavits of other professors that indicated the desirability and necessity of foreign travel for a professor of foreign languages. He then moved for summary judgment. Cross contended that the summary judgment was appropriate under the circumstances. Do you agree? What is the criterion for granting a summary judgment? What if Cross listed separately the expenses incurred by his wife and himself and sought to deduct only his own expenses? Would additional information still be required? Explain.

9. Stanford University had a contract with Volt Information Sciences, Inc. to install electric conduit as part of a construction project. The contract contained a broad arbitration clause. Volt billed Stanford for extra work. When Stanford refused to pay, Volt demanded arbitration. Stanford filed a lawsuit against Volt and two companies that designed and managed the construction project. The suit accused Volt of fraud and alleged that the other two companies were responsible for the extra costs and should indemnify Stan-

ford. Stanford's contracts with the other two companies did not have arbitration clauses. Should Stanford be forced to arbitrate the Volt claim? Why or why not?

10. XYZ Corporation is negotiating a contract with Computer Consultants, Inc. (CCI). Under the contract, CCI will provide customized computer programming, software support, and hardware consulting for five years. XYZ will pay an hourly fee. CCI has proposed that the contract require submitting all disputes to arbitration. Should XYZ agree to this? Explain.

5   CONSTITUTIONAL LAW

Learning Objectives

After learning this chapter the student
should be able to:

- Describe the nature of the U.S.
  Constitution and the role of the
  Supreme Court.
- Identify the source of the federal
  government's power to regulate
  commercial activity, and describe
  the approach used by the Supreme
  Court to analyze the
  constitutionality of legislation
  regulating commercial activity.
- Describe how the Supreme Court
  determines the validity of economic
  regulation under the Fifth and
  Fourteenth Amendments of the
  Constitution.
- Explain the nature of the
  constitutional protection available
  to commercial speech under the
  First Amendment of the
  Constitution.
- Describe the constitutional
  protections available to businesses
  under the Fourth and Fifth
  Amendments of the Constitution
  when encountering governmental
  inspections.

The U.S. government derives its power to regulate business from the Constitution of the United States. Thus, the first question underlying any attempt to regulate business is whether the regulation is constitutional. This chapter focuses on the constitutional provisions that are especially important to business.

Constitutionalism, the Constitution, and the Supreme Court

Constitutionalism is a concept that government power is limited by law. Its central principle is that government officials are not free to do as they please. In the United States, this higher law is the U.S. Constitution. This document establishes and empowers the federal government. It also contains a Bill of Rights in the form of its first 10 amendments.

The Nature of the U.S. Constitution

The Constitution establishes the federal government and distributes its powers among three branches: the legislative branch, the executive branch, and the judicial branch. This division of governmental powers is known as the concept of **separation of powers.** The Constitution's drafters feared the tyranny of unbridled power in one person or group. Therefore, they separated the governmental powers into three branches, with each serving as a check and balance against the other. The interrelationship of the three branches is called the **doctrine of checks and balances.**

The legislative power (the power to enact laws) resides in Congress, which consists of two bodies, or houses: the Senate and the House of Representatives. The executive power, the power to execute or carry out the law, resides in the Office of the President. The judicial power, the power to interpret the law, resides in the Supreme Court and the lower courts.

The Constitution enumerates (lists) the powers of the federal government. Thus, the federal government is said to be one of enumerated, or limited, power. The Constitution expressly reserves the powers not delegated to the federal government to the states or to the people. This division of governmental responsibility between the federal government and the states is called **federalism.**

Although the U.S. Constitution is the governing document for the federal government, each state also has its own constitution. The U.S. Constitution originally applied only to the federal government. However, after the Civil War, the Thirteenth, Fourteenth, and Fifteenth Amendments were directed toward the states. These Reconstruction Era amendments outlawed slavery, established rights of citizenship, and protected the right to vote, respectively.

The Supreme Court has interpreted the Fourteenth Amendment as incorporating or absorbing those liberties provided in the Bill of Rights that are fundamental and necessary to the ordered liberty of a free society. By doing so, the Court has interpreted these provisions as limitations on the states. While not every right contained in the first 10 amendments is applied against the states, most are. This process of applying those provisions of the U.S. Constitution to the states through the Fourteenth Amendment is known as the **incorporation doctrine.**

Fourteenth Amendment, Section 1

No State shall make or enforce any law which shall abridge the privileges or immunities of citizens of the United States; nor shall any State deprive any person of life, liberty, or property, without due process of law; nor deny to any person within its jurisdiction the equal protection of the laws.

Although the Constitution reflects certain fundamental values of American society, it limits only government conduct. Government conduct is frequently called **state action.** The Constitution does not apply to purely private conduct. Thus, while the government cannot interfere with a person's freedom of speech, a private employer can forbid its employees to talk while working.

The Role of the Supreme Court

The Supreme Court assumed the task of interpreting the Constitution in its 1803 decision of *Marbury v. Madison.*[1] There the Supreme Court reserved for itself the power to declare laws enacted by Congress to be unconstitutional. This is known as the *power of judicial review.* This means that the Court can prevent the enforcement of laws or other governmental decisions that it determines to be in violation of the Constitution.

A persistent debate continues over the proper role of the Supreme Court when interpreting the Constitution. Critics of what are viewed as overly broad constitutional decisions claim that such decisions represent judicial legislation, and that the Court is rewriting the Constitution. Critics of decisions that appear to stand in the path of progress portray the Court as applying the dead hand of the past to the need for a living Constitution. Also, the ambiguity of some constitutional provisions further fuels the debate over what the Constitution means and how the Court should apply it.

Federal Power to Regulate Commerce

Every power exercised by the government must be authorized by the Constitution. Whenever the federal government seeks to regulate business activity, the first issue posed is: what is the constitutional basis for the regulation? The Constitution's commerce clause is the most frequent answer.

---

[1] 1 Cranch 137 (U.S. 1803).

The Commerce Clause, Article I, Section 8, Clause 3

The Congress shall have Power . . . [t]o regulate Commerce with foreign Nations, and among the several States.

The Supreme Court has interpreted the Commerce Clause as granting Congress the power to regulate any activity that has any appreciable effect on interstate commerce. This is called the **affectation doctrine.** When applying the affectation doctrine the Court uses a generous analysis that usually results in finding federal economic legislation constitutional.

For example, the affectation doctrine has been applied to uphold the following forms of federal regulation of business: purely intrastate marketing of local products that compete with similar products moving in interstate commerce, price-fixing of commodities, regulation of branding, the regulation of manufacturing, regulation of insurance, regulation of real estate transactions, and regulation of coal mining.

In *Wickard v. Filburn,*[2] the Supreme Court decided that the federal government can regulate activity that, in the aggregate, has a substantial effect on interstate commerce. In *Wickard v. Filburn,* a farmer (Filburn) brought suit seeking an injunction against the enforcement of a penalty imposed against him by the secretary of agriculture. The secretary had fined Filburn for exceeding a limit for the amount of wheat that he could grow on his farm. Filburn's quota had been set at 11. 1 acres, but he sowed and harvested 23 acres. Some of the wheat was sold, but most of it was used by Filburn's family or as feed for his livestock. The Supreme Court noted that the primary purpose of the federal regulation was to increase the market price of wheat. Limiting the volume of wheat could affect the market. Although Filburn was a small farmer, when all the small farmers who grew wheat for home consumption were viewed in the aggregate, their activity had a substantial affect on the demand and therefore the price of wheat that is sold in interstate commerce. Because the activity of growing wheat for home consumption had a substantial effect on interstate commerce, the federal government could regulate the activity. The case shows that the federal government's power to regulate commerce under the Commerce Clause is broad.

Another case that shows the breadth of the federal government's power to regulate business under the Commerce Clause is *Heart of Atlanta Motel, Inc. v. United States,*[3] where in 1964 the Supreme Court upheld the constitutionality of the Civil Rights Act, which forbids racial discrimination in public accommodations (for example, hotels, restaurants). In *Heart of Atlanta Motel,* the motel owner sued, seeking a federal court order declaring the Civil Rights Act unconstitutional. The motel had 216 rooms available to guests. It was located in downtown Atlanta and

---

[2] 317 U.S. 111 (1942).
[3] 379 U.S. 241 (1964).

was readily accessible to interstate highways. Approximately 75% of its guests were from out of state. Before the passage of the Civil Rights Act, the motel had refused to rent rooms to African-Americans, and it intended to continue that practice. The Supreme Court pointed out that while the law was being debated in Congress, people testified before Congressional committees about the effects of racial discrimination on interstate commerce. The testimony included the fact that African-Americans often had been unable to obtain motel rooms and had to call upon friends to put them up overnight. This had the effect of discouraging travel by a substantial portion of the African-American community, which impeded interstate travel. The Court said:

> *The commerce power invoked here by the Congress is a specific and plenary one authorized by the Constitution itself. The only questions are (1) whether Congress had a rational basis for finding that racial discrimination by motels affected commerce, and (2) if it had such a basis whether the means it selected to eliminate that evil are reasonable and appropriate. If they are, appellant has no 'right' to select its guests as it sees fit, free from government regulation.*

Using the above quote as a guide in analysis, substitute the particular activity that the federal government is trying to regulate (for example, auctions on the web, pesticide warnings by lawn care companies, little kid lemonade stand practices) for the terms "racial discrimination by motels" in the quote. If the answers to the questions in the quote are "yes," Congress can regulate the activity.

Even though it seems that Congress has cradle to grave power to regulate activity under the Commerce Clause, there are limits, as the following case shows. The case is significant, because in the fifty years preceding the case, the Supreme Court had declared only one federal statute unconstitutional under the Commerce Clause. As the 5–4 split among the justices shows, the case was not an easy one for the Court to decide. The justices voting in the majority were Rehnquist, O'Connor, Scalia, Kennedy and Thomas. One of the justices voting with the majority, Thomas, wrote a separate concurring opinion indicating that he is willing to go so far as to throw out the affectation doctrine entirely. The four dissenting justices were Souter, Stevens, Ginsburg, and Breyer. They characterize the majority's opinion as giving name-only recognition to the substantial effects test.

UNITED STATES V. MORRISON
529 U.S. 598 (2000)

Christy Brzonkala (Petitioner), a woman who had been a student at Virginia Polytechnic Institute (Virginia Tech) filed suit in the United States District Court against Antonio Morrison and James Crawford, two male students at Virginia Tech who were on the university's football team. She alleged that she had been raped by the two individuals while she and they had been attending the university, and that this attack violated 42 USC Section 13981, which provided a federal civil remedy for the victims of gender-motivated violence.

The United States (Petitioner) intervened to defend Section 13981's validity under the Federal Constitution. Although the District Court decided that the complaint stated a claim against the two alleged attackers under Section 13981, the District Court, in dismissing the complaint, reasoned that Congress lacked authority to enact 13981 under the Constitution's Commerce Clause (Art 1, § 8, cl 3). The Court of Appeals affirmed the District Court's determination that Congress lacked authority under the Constitution to enact Section 13981's civil remedy. The United States Supreme Court affirmed. In a 5–4 opinion, the Court decided that Congress had no authority to enact 13981 under the Commerce Clause.

Chief Justice Rehnquist

Petitioners . . . seek to sustain Section 13981 as a regulation of activity that substantially affects interstate commerce.

■   ■   ■

Congress found that gender-motivated violence affects interstate commerce "by deterring potential victims from traveling interstate, from engaging in employment in interstate business, and from transacting with business, and in places involved in interstate commerce; . . . by diminishing national productivity, increasing medical and other costs, and decreasing the supply of and the demand for interstate products."

Given these findings and petitioners' arguments, the concern that Congress might use the Commerce Clause to completely obliterate the Constitution's distinction between national and local authority seems well founded. The reasoning that petitioners advance seeks to follow the but-for causal chain from the initial occurrence of violent crime (the suppression of which has always been the prime object of the States' police power) to every attenuated effect upon interstate commerce. If accepted, petitioners' reasoning would allow Congress to regulate any crime as long as the nationwide, aggregated impact of that crime has substantial effects on employment, production, transit, or consumption. Indeed, if Congress may regulate gender-motivated violence, it would be able to regulate murder or any other type of violence since gender-motivated violence, as a subset of all violent crime, is certain to have lesser

economic impacts than the larger class of which it is a part.

■   ■   ■

We . . . reject the argument that Congress may regulate noneconomic, violent criminal conduct based solely on that conduct's aggregate effect on interstate commerce. The Constitution requires a distinction between what is truly national and what is truly local. In recognizing this fact we preserve one of the few principles that has been consistent since the Clause was adopted. The regulation and punishment of intrastate violence that is not directed at the instrumentalities, channels, or goods involved in interstate commerce has always been the province of the States. Indeed, we can think of no better example of the police power, which the Founders denied the National Government and reposed in the States, than the suppression of violent crime and vindication of its victims.

Justice Thomas (Concurring)

I write separately only to express my view that the very notion of a "substantial effects" test under the Commerce Clause is inconsistent with the original understanding of Congress' powers and with this Court's early Commerce Clause cases. By continuing to apply this rootless and malleable standard, however circumscribed, the Court has encouraged the Federal Government to persist in its view that the Commerce Clause has virtually no limits. Until this Court replaces its existing

Commerce Clause jurisprudence with a standard more consistent with the original understanding, we will continue to see Congress appropriating state police powers under the guise of regulating commerce.

Justice Souter (Dissenting)

■   ■   ■

The fact that the Act does not pass muster before the Court today is proof, to a degree that the Court's nominal adherence to the substantial effects test is merely that. Although a new jurisprudence has not emerged with any distinctness, it is clear that some congressional conclusions about obviously substantial, cumulative effects on commerce are being assigned lesser values than the once-stable doctrine would assign them. These devaluations are accomplished not by any express repudiation of the substantial effects test or its application through the aggregation of individual conduct, but by supplanting rational basis scrutiny with a new criterion of review.

Justice Breyer (Dissenting)

The majority holds that the federal commerce power does not extend to such "noneconomic" activities as "noneconomic, violent criminal conduct" that significantly affects interstate commerce only if we "aggregate" the interstate "effects" of individual instances. . . . The majority's holding illustrates the difficulty of finding a workable judicial Commerce Clause touchstone— a set of comprehensible interpretive rules that courts might use to impose some meaningful limit, but not too great a limit, upon the scope of the legislative authority that the Commerce Clause delegates to Congress.

Consider the problems. The "economic/non-economic" distinction is not easy to apply. Does the local street corner mugger engage in "economic" activity or "noneconomic" activity when he mugs for money?

■   ■   ■

More important, why should we give critical constitutional importance to the economic, or noneconomic, nature of an interstate-commerce-affecting *cause*? If chemical emanations through indirect environmental change cause identical, severe commercial harm outside a State, why should it matter whether local factories or home fireplaces release them? The Constitution itself refers only to Congress' power to "regulate Commerce . . . among the several States," and to make laws "necessary and proper" to implement that power. Art. I, § 8, cls. 3, 18. The language says nothing about either the local nature, or the economic nature, of an interstate-commerce-affecting cause.

■   ■   ■

This consideration, however, while serious, does not reflect a jurisprudential defect, so much as it reflects a practical reality. We live in a Nation knit together by two centuries of scientific, technological, commercial, and environmental change. Those changes, taken together, mean that virtually every kind of activity, no matter how local, genuinely can affect commerce, or its conditions, outside the State—at least when considered in the aggregate. And that fact makes it close to impossible for courts to develop meaningful subject-matter categories that would exclude some kinds of local activities from ordinary Commerce Clause "aggregation" rules without, at the same time, depriving Congress of the power to regulate activities that have a genuine and important effect upon interstate commerce.

Case Questions

1. What does the majority opinion decide? Can the majority opinion be reconciled with *Wickard v. Filburn* and *Heart of Atlanta Motel v. United States* (discussed in the text just before the *U.S. v. Morrison* opinion)?
2. What is the significance of Justice Thomas's concurring opinion?
3. What is the basis of the dissenting opinions?

4. Would it make any difference to the outcome of the case if Congress had before it studies showing that three-quarters of women never go to the movies alone after dark because of the fear of rape, nearly 50 percent do not use public transit alone after dark for the same reason, and that almost 50 percent of rape victims lose their jobs or are forced to quit because of the crime's severity?

5. Does *United States v. Morrison* represent a major shift in the Supreme Court's approach to interpreting the federal government's power to regulate commercial activity under the Constitution's Commerce Clause; or, does the case represent a narrow exception to the Court's Commerce Clause case law?

The Relationship between State and Federal Regulation

The previous discussion focused on federal power in national and local matters. Now the discussion turns to the power of the states to regulate business. The individual states have a strong interest in protecting the health, safety, and welfare of their people. When they do act, they are said to be exercising their **police power.** That power, though broad, is not unlimited. It may not be exercised in a manner contrary to the Constitution.

Some state activity is specifically prohibited by the Constitution. For example, only the federal government has the power to coin money, declare war, and impose tariffs. Other provisions of the Constitution have been interpreted to implicitly limit state action. The following discussion focuses on two such provisions: the commerce clause and the supremacy clause. These claims have been construed to limit the states' exercise of their police powers.

The Commerce Clause

The commerce clause only contains an express grant of federal power over interstate commerce. By implication, however, it limits the authority of states to regulate in a manner that unduly restricts the free flow of interstate commerce. Without the commerce clause, individual states could establish regulatory barriers against interstate commerce to give local commercial interest an economic advantage.

When Congress remains silent on a subject of interstate commerce, and a state enacts legislation affecting that subject, the Supreme Court sits as umpire of the competing national and state interests. In distinguishing between legitimate exercises of a state's police power and unconstitutional restraints on interstate commerce, the Court balances the need for national uniformity in law against the state's interest in protecting its people from health and safety hazards. On some occasions the court has carved out areas of exclusive federal control, and on other occasions it has struck down state statutes that discriminate against or obstruct interstate commerce. In the following case, the Supreme Court in 1992 reaffirmed that the compact agreed upon in Philadelphia 200 years earlier implied a common understanding that no state would try to solve its problems at the expense of the people of other states.

FORT GRATIOT SANITARY LANDFILL, INC. V. MICHIGAN DEPT. OF NATURAL RESOURCES
504 U.S. 353 (1992)

The Waste Import Restrictions of Michigan's Solid Waste Management Act (SWMA) provide that solid waste generated in another county, state, or country cannot be accepted for disposal unless explicitly authorized in the receiving county's plan. After St. Clair County, whose plan did not include such authorization, denied Fort Gratiot Sanitary Landfill's (petitioner) 1989 application for authority to accept out-of-state waste at its landfill, petitioner sued seeking a judgment declaring the Waste Import Restrictions invalid under the Commerce Clause and enjoining their enforcement. The district court dismissed the complaint, and the court of appeals affirmed. The Supreme Court held that the Waste Import Restrictions unambiguously discriminate against interstate commerce and are appropriately characterized as protectionist measures that cannot withstand Commerce Clause scrutiny.

Justice Stevens

As we have long recognized, the "negative" or "dormant" aspect of the Commerce Clause prohibits States from advancing their own commercial interests by curtailing the movement of articles of commerce, either into or out of the state. A state statute that clearly discriminates against interstate commerce is therefore unconstitutional unless the discrimination is demonstrably justified by a valid factor unrelated to economic protectionism.

Both on its face and in its plain effect, ch. 363 violates this principle of nondiscrimination. . . . The Waste Import Restrictions enacted by Michigan authorize each of its 83 counties to isolate itself from the national economy. Indeed, unless a county acts affirmatively to permit other waste to enter its jurisdiction, the statute affords local waste producers complete protection from competition from out-of-state waste producers who seek to use local waste disposal areas. In view of the fact that Michigan has not identified any reason, apart from

its origin, why solid waste coming from outside the county should be treated differently from solid waste within the county, the foregoing reasoning would appear to control the disposition of this case.

Respondents Michigan and St. Clair County argue, however, that the Waste Import Restrictions . . . do not discriminate against interstate commerce on their face or in effect because they treat waste from other Michigan counties no differently than waste from other States. Instead, respondents maintain, the statute regulates evenhandedly to effectuate local interests and should be upheld because the burden on interstate commerce is not clearly excessive in relation to the local benefits. We disagree, for our prior cases teach that a State (or one of its political subdivisions) may not avoid the strictures of the Commerce Clause by curtailing the movement of articles of commerce through subdivisions of the State, rather than through the State itself.

Michigan and St. Clair County . . . contend that the differential treatment of out-of-state waste is reasonable because they have taken measures to conserve their landfill capacity and the SWMA is necessary to protect the health of their citizens. We may assume that all of the provisions of Michigan's SWMA prior to the 1988 amendments adding the Waste Import Restrictions could fairly be characterized as health and safety regulations with no protectionist purpose, but we cannot make that same assumption with respect to the Waste Import Restrictions themselves. Because those provisions unambiguously discriminate against interstate commerce, the State bears the burden of proving that its further health and safety concerns that cannot be adequately served by nondiscriminatory alternatives. Michigan and St. Clair County have not met this burden. . . . Michigan and St. Clair County assert that the Waste Import Restrictions are necessary because they enable individual counties to make adequate plans for the safe disposal of future waste. Although accurate forecasts about the volume and composition of future waste flows may be an indispensable part of a comprehensive waste disposal plan, Michigan could attain that objective without discriminating between in- and out-of-state waste. Michigan could, for example, limit the amount of waste that landfill operators may accept each year. There is, however, no valid health and safety reason for limiting the amount of waste that a landfill operator may accept from outside the State, but not the amount that the operator may accept from inside the State.

Of course, our conclusion would be different if the imported waste raised health or other concerns not presented by Michigan waste.

Case Questions

1. Why did the Court conclude that the Michigan law discriminated against interstate commerce?
2. How did the Court respond to Michigan's argument that its law did not discriminate against interstate commerce because it treated wastes from other Michigan counties no differently than waste from other states?
3. Why did the Court not accept Michigan's argument that its law was necessary to protect the health of its citizens?
4. Would the result of this case have been different if the imported waste raised health concerns not presented by Michigan waste?
5. Suppose Michigan imposed a tax on the producers of hazardous waste, and taxed out-of-state producers at twice the rate it taxed Michigan producers. Would such a tax be constitutional? Explain.

The Supremacy Clause

The previous section on the Commerce Clause discussed to what extent a state can regulate an area of interstate commerce when Congress is silent. Where both Congress and a state enact laws regulating a field of interstate commerce, which law controls? Must managers obey both laws? If complying with one law means violating the other, which law should be followed? The answers are in the Supremacy Clause of the Constitution, which embodies the **preemption doctrine.**

Supremacy Clause, Article VI

This Constitution, and the Laws of the United States which shall be made in Pursuance thereof . . . shall be the supreme Law of the Land; and the Judges in every State shall be bound thereby, anything in the Constitution or Laws of any State to the Contrary notwithstanding.

When Congress enters a field of regulation, the extent that a state may also regulate that field depends on whether Congress intends to preempt state law in the field. State law can be preempted in either of two ways: (1) if Congress indicates an intent to occupy a given field, any state law falling within that field is preempted; and (2) if Congress has not entirely displaced state regulation of the field, state law is still preempted to the extent that it actually conflicts with federal law—that is, when it is impossible to comply with both state and federal law, or where the state law stands as an obstacle to the accomplishment of the congressional objectives.

Sometimes Congress specifically declares a state regulation to be preempted. At other times Congress specifically declares that it does not intend to preempt a state regulation. Absent explicit preemptive language, determination of congressional intent to preempt state law is left to the courts.

Property Rights and Economic Regulation

Economic regulation frequently restricts the use of property or lessens its value. Property owners sometimes resort to the Constitution's Fifth and Fourteenth Amendments to prevent such impairment of property rights. Under the incorporation doctrine discussed earlier, the Supreme Court applies the Fifth Amendment to the states. Among the Fifth Amendment's list of activities prohibited of government is the Takings Clause, which states "nor shall private property be taken for public use, without just compensation." Both the Fifth and the Fourteenth Amendments contain a Due Process Clause, stating that no person shall be deprived "of life, liberty, or property, without due process of law. . . ." The Fourteenth Amendment also contains the Equal Protection Clause, which makes it unconstitutional for any state to "deny to any person within its jurisdiction the equal protection of the laws."

The Takings Clause

Eminent domain is the power of a government to take, or to authorize the taking of, private property for public use. The Takings Clause of the Fifth Amendment recognizes this basic governmental power but requires that just compensation be given to the owner.

The Takings Clause states, "nor shall private property be taken for public use, without just compensation." Private property must be *taken* for public use. Once that has happened, government must pay *just compensation* to the property owner (usually the fair market value of the property).

The Supreme Court's decisions defining what is a "taking" leave a lot of uncertainty and unpredictability in this area. At one end of the spectrum are *direct appropriations* of private property—where government appropriates or makes use of private property. If government wants to convert a privately owned building into a post office, that is a taking, and government must compensate the owner.

However, government rarely takes property by appropriation. Most government activity affecting business is regulation. For example, zoning regulations that restrict the use of land, rent control laws that limit the amount of rent a landlord can collect, historic preservation laws that require property owners to get approval before modifying historic buildings, or environmental laws that restrict development or require land owners to clean up toxic waste spills—may lower property values.

The 1922 Supreme Court decision of *Pennsylvania Coal Co. v. Mahon,*[4] expanded the range of government action that can create takings to include what are called *regulatory takings*. In the *Mahon* decision, Justice Holmes stated "while property may be regulated to a certain extent, if regulation goes too far it will be recognized as a taking." Holmes did not say how far was "too far." Since that time, the Court has looked at each situation on a case-by-case basis.

In *Penn Central Transportation Co. v. New York City,*[5] the Court noted that no "set formula" exists to determine when regulation becomes a taking of property, that the Court engages in essentially ad hoc, factual inquiries. However, the Court said that the inquiry is not standardless. The economic impact of the regulation, especially the degree of interference with investment-backed expectations, is of particular significance.

In *Penn Central Transportation,* the owner of Grand Central Terminal in New York City sought permission of the New York City Landmark's Preservation Commission to build a 55-story office building above it, but its plans were rejected. New York City's law provided owners of landmark sites additional opportunities to transfer development rights to adjacent parcels on the same city block. Because full development of the terminal site was prohibited, the owner was entitled to exceed zoning limits on the development of other parcels of land. Because of these "transfer development rights," for adjacent property, the Supreme Court decided that New York City's law did not prevent the owner from realizing a reasonable return on its investment.

The Supreme Court has carved out two categories of regulatory takings where a case-by-case approach is *not* followed. The Court calls these *categorical* or *per se* takings.

The first categorical taking is where a regulation causes a property owner to suffer a physical invasion of the property. For example, in *Loretto v. Teleprompter Manhattan CATV Corp.,*[6] the Supreme Court held that a New York statute authorizing a cable company to install cables on the property owner's building was governmental action that amounted to a permanent physical occupation of property, and therefore was a taking.

The second categorical taking is where regulation denies all economically beneficial or productive use of land. An example of this type of regulation is found

---

[4] 260 U.S. 393 (1922).
[5] 438 U.S. 104 (1978).
[6] 458 U.S. 419 (1982).

in *Lucas v. South Carolina Coastal Council.*[7] In *Lucas,* the property owner bought two residential lots on beachfront property, and later the South Carolina legislature passed a law that barred him from erecting any permanent habitable structure on his land. The law made his land worthless, and therefore was a taking.

In the following case, the Supreme Court confronted the question of whether a 32-month moratorium on development in Lake Tahoe, Nevada fell under the case-by-case approach of *Penn Central* or was a categorical taking under *Lucas.*

TAHOE-SIERRA PRESERVATION COUNCIL, INC. V. TAHOE REGIONAL PLANNING AGENCY
535 U.S. 302 (2002)

The Tahoe Regional Planning Agency (TRPA) was created by California and Nevada to regulate development in the Lake Tahoe Basin. While the TRPA was studying the impact of development on Lake Tahoe and designing a strategy for environmentally sound growth—the TRPA imposed two moratoria, the first of about 24 months and another one of about another 8 months, on virtually all residential development in the area. Plaintiffs, area landowners, filed suit against the TRPA. They claimed that the two TRPA moratoria constituted takings without just compensation, in alleged violation of the Takings Clause of the Federal Constitution's Fifth Amendment. The District Court ordered the TRPA to pay damages to many of the affected landowners with respect to the two moratoria. The District Court found that the landowners were temporarily deprived of all economically viable use of their land; therefore, the two moratoria constituted categorical takings, for purposes of the Takings Clause. On appeal, the United States Court of Appeals reversed. It expressed the view that because the two TRPA moratoria had only a temporary impact on the landowners' fee interest in the affected properties, no categorical taking occurred with respect to the mere enactment of the two moratoria. On certiorari, the United States Supreme Court affirmed. It decided that the two TRPA moratoria did not constitute per se (or categorical) takings requiring compensation under the Fifth Amendment's Takings Clause.

Justice Stevens

Petitioners . . . contend that the mere enactment of a temporary regulation that, while in effect, denies a property owner all viable economic use of her property gives rise to an unqualified constitutional obligation to compensate her for the value of its use during that period. . . . Petitioners assert that . . . *Lucas* ha(s) already endorsed their view, and that it is a logical application of the principle that the Takings Clause was "designed to bar Government from forcing some people alone to bear burdens which, in all fairness and justice, should be borne by the public as a whole."

---

[7] 505 U.S. 1003 (1992).

■   ■   ■

The text of the Fifth Amendment itself provides a basis for drawing a distinction between physical takings and regulatory takings. Its plain language requires the payment of compensation whenever the government acquires private property for a public purpose, whether the acquisition is the result of a condemnation proceeding or a physical appropriation. But the Constitution contains no comparable reference to regulations that prohibit a property owner from making certain uses of her private property. Our jurisprudence involving condemnations and physical takings is as old as the Republic and, for the most part, involves the straightforward application of *per se* rules. Our regulatory takings jurisprudence, in contrast, is of more recent vintage and is characterized by "essentially ad hoc, factual inquiries," designed to allow "careful examination and weighing of all the relevant circumstances."

When the government physically takes possession of an interest in property for some public purpose, it has a categorical duty to compensate the former owner, regardless of whether the interest that is taken constitutes an entire parcel or merely a part thereof. [W]hen the government appropriates part of a rooftop in order to provide cable TV access for apartment tenants; or when its planes use private airspace to approach a government airport, it is required to pay for that share no matter how small. But a government regulation that merely prohibits landlords from evicting tenants unwilling to pay a higher rent; that bans certain private uses of a portion of an owner's property; or that forbids the private use of certain airspace, does not constitute a categorical taking. "The first category of cases requires courts to apply a clear rule; the second necessarily entails complex factual assessments of the purposes and economic effects of government actions."

. . . Land-use regulations are ubiquitous and most of them impact property values in some tangential way—often in completely unanticipated ways. Treating them all as *per se* takings would transform government regulation into a luxury few governments could afford. By contrast, physical appropriations are relatively rare, easily identified, and usually represent a greater affront to individual property rights. "This case does not present the 'classic taking' in which the government directly appropriates private property for its own use; instead the interference with property rights "arises from some public program adjusting the benefits and burdens of economic life to promote the common good."

[P]etitioners . . . rely principally on our decision in *Lucas v. South Carolina Coastal Council,* to argue that the *Penn Central* framework is inapplicable here.

[I]t was Justice Holmes' opinion in *Pennsylvania Coal Co. v. Mahon,* that gave birth to our regulatory takings jurisprudence. In subsequent opinions we have repeatedly and consistently endorsed Holmes' observation that "if regulation goes too far it will be recognized as a taking." Justice Holmes did not provide a standard for determining when a regulation goes "too far," but he did reject the view expressed in Justice Brandeis' dissent that there could not be a taking because the property remained in the possession of the owner and had not been appropriated or used by the public. After *Mahon,* neither a physical appropriation nor a public use has ever been a necessary component of a "regulatory taking."

In the decades following that decision, we have "generally eschewed" any set formula for determining how far is too far, choosing instead to engage in "'essentially ad hoc, factual inquiries.' " Justice Brennan's opinion for the Court in *Penn Central* did, however, make it clear that even though multiple factors are relevant in the analysis of regulatory takings claims, in such cases we must focus on "the parcel as a whole."

■   ■   ■

Petitioners seek to bring this case under the rule announced in *Lucas* by arguing that we can effectively sever a 32-month segment from the remainder of each landowner's fee simple estate, and then ask whether that segment has been taken in its entirety by the moratoria. . . . With property so divided, every delay would become a total ban; the moratorium and the normal permit process alike would constitute categorical takings. Petitioners' . . . argument is unavailing because it ignores *Penn Central*'s admonition that in regulatory takings cases we must focus on "the parcel as a whole." . . . Thus, the District Court erred when it disaggregated petitioners' property into temporal segments corresponding to the regulations at issue and then analyzed whether petitioners were deprived of all economically viable use during each period. The starting point for the court's analysis should have been to ask whether there was a total taking of the entire parcel; if not, then *Penn Central* was the proper framework.

An interest in real property is defined by the metes and bounds that describe its geographic dimensions and the term of years that describes the temporal aspect of the owner's interest. Both dimensions must be considered if the interest is to be viewed in its entirety. Hence, a permanent deprivation of the owner's use of the entire area is a taking of "the parcel as a whole," whereas a temporary restriction that merely causes a diminution in value is not. Logically, a fee simple estate cannot be rendered valueless by a temporary prohibition on economic use, because the property will recover value as soon as the prohibition is lifted.

Neither *Lucas* nor any of our other regulatory takings cases compels us to accept petitioners' categorical submission. In fact, these cases make clear that the categorical rule in *Lucas* was carved out for the "extraordinary case" in which a regulation permanently deprives property of all value; the default rule remains that, in the regulatory taking context, we require a more fact specific inquiry. Nevertheless, we will consider whether the interest in protecting individual property owners from bearing public burdens "which, in all fairness and justice, should be borne by the public as a whole," justifies creating a new rule for these circumstances.

■   ■   ■

[F]or reasons set out at some length by Justice O'Connor in her concurring opinion in *Palazzolo v. Rhode Island,* we are persuaded that the better approach to claims that a regulation has effected a temporary taking "requires careful examination and weighing of all the relevant circumstances." Her comments on the "fairness and justice" inquiry are . . . instructive:

> Our polestar instead remains the principles set forth in *Penn Central* itself and our other cases. . . . Under these cases, interference with investment-backed expectations is one of a number of factors that a court must examine. . . .
>
> The Fifth Amendment forbids the taking of private property for public use without just compensation. We have recognized that this constitutional guarantee is "'designed to bar Government from forcing some people alone to bear public burdens which, in all fairness and justice, should be borne by the public as a whole.'" The concepts of 'fairness and justice' that underlie the Takings Clause, of course, are less than fully determinate. Accordingly, we have eschewed any "set formula" for determining when "justice and fairness" require that economic injuries caused by public action be compensated by the government, rather than remain disproportionately concentrated on a few persons." The outcome instead 'depends largely "upon the particular circumstances [in that] case."

In rejecting petitioners' *per se* rule, we do not hold that the temporary nature of a land-use restriction precludes finding that it effects a taking; we simply recognize that it should not be given exclusive significance one way or the other.

The interest in facilitating informed decision-making by regulatory agencies counsels against adopting a *per se* rule that would impose such severe costs on their deliberations. Otherwise, the financial constraints of compensating property owners during a moratorium may force officials to rush through the planning process or to abandon the practice altogether.

Accordingly, the judgment of the Court of Appeals is affirmed.

Case Questions

1. How does the Court usually decide when a government regulation "goes too far" and constitutes a "taking" under the Fifth Amendment?
2. Why does the Court reject the categorical or *per se* approach in this case?
3. If the Court had decided to apply the categorical or *per se* approach, what would have been the impact of such a decision on the numerous normal delays in obtaining building permits, changes in zoning ordinances, as well as to orders temporarily prohibiting access to crime scenes, businesses that violate health codes, or fire-damaged buildings?
4. Is the Court's answer to the question of whether a temporary moratorium effects a taking (a) "yes, always," (b) "no, never," or (c) "it depends upon the particular circumstances of the case"? Explain.
5. Does the Court's opinion increase or decrease the uncertainty and unpredictability in the area of takings law? Explain.

The Due Process Clause

The Due Process Clause, found in both the Fifth and Fourteenth Amendments, was originally intended to ensure procedural safeguards when life, liberty, or property were the subjects of governmental action. However, the Supreme Court has used the Due Process Clause to test the constitutional validity of legislation affecting life, liberty, or property.

Procedural Due Process

Due process traditionally means the procedure used in making decisions affecting life, liberty, or property. The procedure required to provide due process is a fair hearing. To be entitled to due process, someone must show that a governmental decision affects their life, their liberty, or their property. For example, a business claiming that it is entitled to a hearing before its operating license is revoked will have to show that it possesses a property interest in the license. What constitutes a property interest is a matter of state property law.

If a governmental action affects a person's life, liberty, or property, the due process requirement applies, and some form of hearing is required. The nature of the hearing depends on the interests involved, the nature of the governmental action, and the likelihood of error. The type of procedure required to provide procedural due process therefore varies with the situation. For example, greater procedural protections are required in a criminal trial than would be required in a license renewal hearing.

Substantive Due Process

Using the Due Process Clause to scrutinize the substance of legislation became known as the *substantive due process doctrine*. From 1890 until the 1930s the Supreme Court embarked on a path now considered to have been erroneous, in which it applied the Due Process Clause to invalidate a number of statutes dealing with social and economic matters.

Substantive due process hit its high-water mark with the case of *Lochner v. New York,* in which the Court invalidated a state statute setting a maximum work-week of 60 hours.[8] The Court reasoned that such a law restricted the liberty of an employer and an employee to contract to work more hours than the law allowed.

Justice Holmes's dissenting opinion in *Lochner* laid the foundation for future Court opinions. Holmes stated:

> I think that the word "liberty" in the Fourteenth Amendment is perverted when it is held to prevent the natural outcome of a dominant opinion, unless it can be said that a rational and fair man necessarily would admit that the statute proposed would infringe fundamental principles as they have been understood by the traditions of our people and our law.

The substantive due process doctrine fell into disfavor during the Great Depression, and the Court abandoned it with regard to economic legislation.

The Equal Protection Clause

The Equal Protection Clause of the Fourteenth Amendment commands that no state shall "deny to any person within its jurisdiction the equal protection of the laws." This clause essentially directs that all persons similarly situated should be treated alike. However, all legislative classifications discriminate. For example, a speed limit of 65 mph discriminates against those who would drive faster. The general rule is that social and economic legislation is presumed to be valid and will be sustained if the classification drawn by the statute is rationally related to a legitimate state interest. This is known as the *rational basis test of equal protection.* When social or economic legislation is at issue, the Supreme Court allows the states wide latitude. The Court has stated that the legislature need not address all social or economic problems in the same way, and that a legislature may phase in its programs. The Court presumes that erroneous decisions will eventually be corrected by the democratic process.

The general rule gives way, however, when a statute classifies by race, alienage, or national origin. These factors are seldom relevant to the achievement of any legitimate state interest. Laws based on these considerations reflect bigotry. For these reasons and because such discrimination is unlikely to soon be corrected by legislative means, these laws are subject to strict judicial scrutiny and are upheld only if they are designed to serve a compelling state interest by the least drastic means. This is known as the *strict scrutiny test of equal protection.* It is also applied when state laws impinge on personal rights protected by the Constitution.

The Supreme Court has decided that legislative classifications based on gender also call for a heightened judicial review—a middle level, between the rational basis test and the strict scrutiny test. Gender-based classifications generally provide no sensible ground for differences in treatment. They likely reflect outmoded notions of the relative abilities of men and women. Therefore, a gender-based legislative

---

[8] 198 U.S. 45 (1905).

classification fails unless it is substantially related to an important governmental interest. This is known as *heightened judicial review of equal protection.*

In sum, the level of judicial scrutiny of legislation under the Equal Protection Clause varies with the interest affected and the recognized invidiousness of the basis on which a classification is drawn. Social and economic legislation usually survives judicial review under the rational basis test.

In the following landmark decision, the Supreme Court considered whether a state law regulating the sale and fitting of eyeglasses was constitutional under the Due Process Clause and the Equal Protection Clause.

WILLIAMSON V. LEE OPTICAL OF OKLAHOMA, INC.
348 U.S. 483 (1955)

An Oklahoma statute made it illegal for anyone except a licensed optometrist or an ophthalmologist to fit lenses, and forbade opticians from fitting lenses without a prescription from an optometrist or an ophthalmologist. An optometrist examines eyes for refractive error, recognizes (but does not treat) diseases of the eye, and fills prescriptions for eyeglasses; an ophthalmologist is a licensed physician specializing in eye care; and an optician grinds lenses, fills prescriptions, and fits frames.

Lee Optical of Oklahoma, Inc., sued the state of Oklahoma in federal district court, and asked the court to declare the Oklahoma statute unconstitutional. Lee Optical argued that the statute violated the Due Process and Equal Protection Clauses of the Fourteenth Amendment. The district court held the statute unconstitutional, and Oklahoma appealed to the Supreme Court. The Supreme Court reversed the district court.

Justice Douglas

The effect of Section 2 is to forbid the optician from fitting or duplicating lenses without a prescription from an ophthalmologist or optometrist. In practical effect, it means that no optician can fit old glasses into new frames or supply a lens, whether it be a new lens or one to duplicate a lost or broken lens, without a prescription. The District Court . . . rebelled at the notion that a State could require a prescription from an optometrist or ophthalmologist "to take old lenses and place them in new frames and then fit the completed spectacles to the face of the eyeglass wearer." It

held such a requirement was not "reasonably and rationally related to the health and welfare of the people. . . ." It was, accordingly, the opinion of the court that this provision of the law violated the Due Process Clause by arbitrarily interfering with the optician's right to do business. . . .

The Oklahoma law may exact a needless, wasteful requirement in many cases. But it is for the legislature, not the courts, to balance the advantages and disadvantages of the new requirement. It appears that in many cases the optician can easily supply the new frames or new lenses without reference to the old written prescription. It also appears that many written prescriptions contain no directive data in regard to fitting spectacles to the face. But in some cases the directions contained in the prescription are essential, if the glasses are to be fitted so as to correct the particular defects of vision or alleviate the eye condition. The legislature might have concluded that the frequency of occasions when a prescription is necessary was sufficient to justify this regulation of the fitting of eyeglasses. . . . [T]he law need not be in every respect logically consistent with its aims to be constitutional. It is enough that there is an evil at hand for correction, and that it might be thought that the particular legislative measure was a rational way to correct it.

The day is gone when this Court uses the Due Process Clause of the Fourteenth Amendment to strike down state laws, regulatory of business and industrial conditions, because they may be unwise, improvident, or out of harmony with a particular school of thought. We emphasize again what Chief Justice Waite said in *Munn v. State of Illinois,* "For protection against abuses by legislatures the people must resort to the polls, not to the courts."

Secondly, the District Court held that it violated the Equal Protection Clause of the Fourteenth Amendment to subject opticians to this regulatory system and to exempt, as Section 3 of the Act does, all sellers of ready-to-wear glasses.

The problem of legislative classification is a perennial one, admitting to no doctrinaire definition. Evils in the same field may be of different dimensions and proportions, requiring different remedies. Or so the legislature may think. Or the reform may take one step at a time, addressing itself to the phase of the problem which seems most acute to the legislative mind. The legislature may select one phase of one field and apply a remedy there, neglecting the others. The prohibition of the Equal Protection Clause goes no further than the invidious discrimination. We cannot say that point has been reached here. For all this record shows, the ready-to-wear branch of this business may not loom large in Oklahoma or may present problems of regulation distinct from the other branch.

Case Questions

1. What did the Court decide with regard to the issue of the statute's validity under the Due Process Clause? Explain.

2. Which test did the Court use to determine the due process issue? Why?

3. What did the Court decide with regard to the issue of the statute's validity under the Equal Protection Clause? Explain.

4. Do you agree with the Court's limited review of economic legislation? Explain.

The First Amendment and the Freedom of Speech

The Supreme Court does not consider the First Amendment's guarantee of freedom of speech to be absolute. Justice Holmes said in *Schenck v. United States,* "The most stringent protection of free speech would not protect a man in falsely shouting fire in a theatre and causing panic."[9] What speech, then, is protected by the Constitution, and what speech may be prohibited or punished? These questions have not been easy ones for the Court. This discussion of the First Amendment focuses on freedom of speech in a commercial context.

---

[9] 249 U.S. 47 (1919).

> **The First Amendment of the Constitution**
> Congress shall make no law respecting an establishment of religion, or prohibiting the free exercise thereof; or abridging the freedom of speech, or of the press, or the right of the people peaceably to assemble, and to petition the Government for a redress of grievances.

Commercial Speech

The First Amendment to the Constitution protects freedom of speech and freedom of the press from infringement by the government. As the advertising industry expanded, courts faced the issue of whether these protections extended to advertising.

In 1942, the Supreme Court decided *Valentine v. Chrestensen.*[10] At issue was the constitutionality of an ordinance that forbade the distribution of commercial material, such as handbills, in the street. The Court sustained the constitutionality of the ordinance, holding that commercial speech was not entitled to First Amendment protection. This became known as the *commercial speech doctrine.* Under the commercial speech doctrine, advertisements, billboards, and other forms of commercial speech were not considered speech as that term is used in the First Amendment. Rather, such forms of expression were treated as commercial activity that could be regulated. The doctrine flowed from the Court's conclusion that the First Amendment was intended to protect political expression, which is necessary for a democracy to function, but not other forms of speech unrelated to the function of the public forum.

In *Virginia Pharmacy Board v. Virginia Citizens Consumer Council,* the Supreme Court confronted a claim that purely commercial speech was protected by the Constitution.[11] A Virginia statute prohibited licensed pharmacists from advertising their prices for prescription drugs. The Commercial Council, a consumer group, challenged the law's constitutionality. Noting that the advertiser's motivation was purely economic, the Court examined the interest of the parties to the advertisement. However, the Court focused on consumers' interests, which had not been represented before the Court in *Chrestensen* 24 years earlier. The Court recognized that the consumers' interest in the free flow of commercial information was at least as strong as the consumers' interest in political debates. Information about drug prices, the Court observed, facilitates the well-informed private economic decisions responsible for allocating resources in a predominantly free

---

[10] 316 U.S. 52 (1942).
[11] 425 U.S. 746 (1976).

enterprise economy. Consumers' interests, although not considered in *Chrestensen,* were also protected by the First Amendment. On that basis, the Supreme Court declared the Virginia statute unconstitutional. *Virginia Pharmacy* was the death knell for the commercial speech doctrine of *Valentine v. Chrestensen.*

However, the Court indicated, in *Virginia Pharmacy,* that reasonable restrictions on the time, place, and manner of commercial speech are permissible where such restrictions are justified by a significant governmental interest and where ample alternative channels of communication remain available. By this qualification, the Court in *Virginia Pharmacy* indicated that there was still life in the commercial speech doctrine.

In 1980, the Court set forth its approach in evaluating commercial speech regulations. In *Central Hudson Gas & Electric Corp. v. Public Service Commission of New York,* a utility company challenged a regulation forbidding advertising by private electrical utilities.[12] The Court held that commercial speech that was not misleading or illegal was entitled to constitutional protection. If the commercial speech at issue meets this initial test, government cannot regulate it unless its reason for doing so amounts to a substantial governmental interest, its regulation directly advances that interest, and its manner of regulation is not more extensive than necessary to serve the interest.

In *Posadas de Puerto Rico Associates v. Tourism Company,* the Supreme Court applied the *Central Hudson* analysis and upheld a law restricting advertising of a lawful activity.[13] In *Posadas,* a Puerto Rico law authorized gambling casinos but forbade casino operators from advertising their establishments on the island. They were permitted to run ads on the U.S. mainland. The Court held that the advertising ban directly advanced Puerto Rico's substantial governmental interest in the health, safety, and welfare of its citizens. The Court further found that the advertising restrictions were not more extensive than necessary to serve the government's interest since they did not affect advertising aimed at tourists, but applied only to advertising aimed at Puerto Rican residents. The Court stated that since a government can prohibit gambling, it is permissible for a government to take the less intrusive step of allowing gambling but reducing the demand through restrictions on advertising.

There is some question about the scope of the *Posadas* case. The case can be read to allow government to ban advertising of any lawful product to reduce demand for it, or it can be read as dealing only with a limited ban on ads aimed at a particularly vulnerable audience and promoting an activity that is generally unlawful.

The following case shows the level of protection that the Supreme Court has provided to commercial speech under the Constitution.

---

[12] 447 U.S. 557 (1980).
[13] 106 S. Ct. 2968 (1986).

Thompson v. Western States Medical Center
535 U.S. 357 (2002)

Drug compounding is where a pharmacist or doctor mixes or alters ingredients to create a medication tailored to the needs of an individual patient. Compounding is used to prepare medications that are not commercially available, such as medication for a patient who is allergic to an ingredient in a mass-produced product. The Food and Drug Administration (FDA) became concerned that some pharmacists might be manufacturing and selling drugs under the guise of compounding in order to avoid the requirements for new drug approvals under the Federal Food, Drug, and Cosmetic Act (FDCA). Enacted in 1997, 503A of the Food and Drug Administration Modernization Act of 1997 exempted compounded drugs from the FDCA's standard drug-approval requirements as long as the providers of such drugs refrained from advertising or promoting particular compounded drugs.

In a complaint filed in the United States District Court against the United States Secretary of Health and Human Services and the Commissioner of the FDA (Government), a group of licensed pharmacies that specialized in drug compounding (Respondents) alleged that 503A's speech-related provisions violated the free speech guarantee of the Federal Constitution's First Amendment. The District Court granted summary judgment for Respondents. The United States Court of Appeals affirmed. The United States Supreme Court affirmed.

Justice O'Connor

In *Virginia Bd. of Pharmacy v. Virginia Citizens Consumer Council, Inc.,* the first case in which we explicitly held that commercial speech receives First Amendment protection, we explained the reasons for this protection: "It is a matter of public interest that [economic] decisions, in the aggregate, be intelligent and well-informed. To this end, the free flow of commercial information is indispensable." Indeed, we recognized that a "particular consumer's interest in the free flow of commercial information . . . may be as keen, if not keener by far, than his interest in the day's most urgent political debate."

∎   ∎   ∎

Although commercial speech is protected by the First Amendment, not all regulation of such speech is unconstitutional. In *Central Hudson,* we articulated a test for determining whether a particular commercial speech regulation is constitutionally permissible. Under that test we ask as a threshold matter whether the commercial speech concerns unlawful activity or is misleading. If so, then the speech is not protected by the First Amendment. If the speech concerns lawful activity and is not misleading, however, we next ask "whether the asserted governmental interest is substantial." If it is, then we "determine whether the regulation directly advances the governmental interest asserted," and, finally, "whether it is not more extensive than is necessary to serve that interest." Each of these latter three inquiries must be answered in the affirmative for the regulation to be found constitutional.

The Government does not attempt to defend the FDAMA's speech-related provisions under the first prong of the *Central Hudson* test; *i.e.,* it does not argue that the prohibited advertisements would be about unlawful activity or would be misleading. Instead, the Government argues that the FDAMA satisfies the remaining three prongs of the *Central Hudson* test.

The Government asserts that three substantial interests underlie the FDAMA. The first is an interest in "preserving the effectiveness and integrity of the FDCA's new drug approval process and the protection of the public health that it provides." The second is an interest in "preserving the availability of compounded drugs for those individual patients who, for particularized medical reasons, cannot use commercially available products that have been approved by the FDA." Finally, the Government argues that "achieving the proper balance between those two independently compelling but competing interests is itself a substantial governmental interest."

Explaining these interests, the Government argues that the FDCA's new drug approval requirements are critical to the public health and safety. It claims that the FDA's experience with drug regulation demonstrates that proof of the safety and effectiveness of a new drug needs to be established by rigorous, scientifically valid clinical studies because impressions of individual doctors, who cannot themselves compile sufficient safety data, cannot be relied upon. The Government also argues that a premarket approval process, under which manufacturers are required to put their proposed drugs through tests of safety and effectiveness in order to obtain FDA approval to market the drugs, is the best way to guarantee drug safety and effectiveness.

While it praises the FDCA's new drug approval process, the Government also acknowledges that "because obtaining FDA approval for a new drug is a costly process, requiring FDA approval of all drug products compounded by pharmacies for the particular needs of an individual patient would, as a practical matter, eliminate the practice of compounding, and thereby eliminate availability of compounded drugs for those patients who have no alternative treatment." The Government argues that eliminating the practice of compounding drugs for individual patients would be undesirable because compounding is sometimes critical to the care of patients with drug allergies, patients who cannot tolerate particular drug delivery systems, and patients requiring special drug dosages.

Preserving the effectiveness and integrity of the FDCA's new drug approval process is clearly an important governmental interest, and the Government has every reason to want as many drugs as possible to be subject to that approval process. The Government also has an important interest, however, in permitting the continuation of the practice of compounding so that patients with particular needs may obtain medications suited to those needs. And it would not make sense to require compounded drugs created to meet the unique needs of individual patients to undergo the testing required for the new drug approval process. Pharmacists do not make enough money from small-scale compounding to make safety and efficacy testing of their compounded drugs economically feasible, so requiring such testing would force pharmacists to stop providing compounded drugs. Given this, the Government needs to be able to draw a line between small-scale compounding and large-scale drug manufacturing. That line must distinguish compounded drugs produced on such a small scale that they could not undergo safety and efficacy testing from drugs produced and sold on a large enough scale that they could undergo such testing and therefore must do so.

The Government argues that the FDAMA's speech-related provisions provide just such a line, *i.e.,* that, in the terms of *Central Hudson,* they "directly advance the governmental interests asserted." Those provisions use advertising as the trigger for requiring FDA approval—essentially, as long as pharmacists do not advertise particular compounded drugs, they may sell compounded drugs without first undergoing safety and efficacy testing and obtaining FDA approval. If they advertise their compounded drugs, however, FDA approval is required. The Government explains that traditional (or, in its view, desirable) compounding responds to a physician's prescription and an individual patient's particular medical situation, and that "advertising the particular products created in the provision of [such] service (as opposed to advertising the compounding service itself) is not necessary to . . . this type of responsive and customized service." The Government argues that advertising particular products is useful in a broad market but is not useful when particular products are designed in response to an individual's "often unique needs." The Government contends that, because of this, advertising is not typically associated with compounding for particular individuals. In contrast it is typically associated, the Government claims, with large-scale production of a drug for a substantial market. The Government argues that advertising, therefore, is "a fair proxy for actual or intended large-scale manufacturing," and that Congress' decision to limit the FDAMA's compounding exemption to pharmacies that do not engage in promotional activity was "rationally calculated" to avoid creating "'a loophole that would allow unregulated drug manufacturing to occur under the guise of pharmacy compounding.'"

The Government seems to believe that without advertising it would not be possible to market a drug on a large enough scale to make safety and efficacy testing economically feasible. The Government thus believes that conditioning an exemption from the FDA approval process on refraining from advertising is an ideal way to permit compounding and yet also guarantee that compounding is not conducted on such a scale as to undermine the FDA approval process. Assuming it is true that drugs cannot be marketed on a large scale without advertising, the FDAMA's prohibition on advertising compounded drugs might indeed "directly advance" the Government's interests. *Central Hudson*. Even assuming that it does, however, the Government has failed to demonstrate that the speech restrictions are "not more extensive than is necessary to serve [those] interests."

Several non-speech-related means of drawing a line between compounding and large-scale manufacturing might be possible here. First, it seems that the Government could use the very factors the FDA relied on to distinguish compounding from manufacturing in its 1992 Compliance Policy Guide. For example, the Government could ban the use of "commercial scale manufacturing or testing equipment for compounding drug products." Compliance Policy Guide. It could prohibit pharmacists from compounding more drugs in anticipation of receiving prescriptions than in response to prescriptions already received. It could prohibit pharmacists from "offering compounded drugs at wholesale to other state licensed persons or commercial entities for resale." Alternately, it could limit the amount of compounded drugs, either by volume or by numbers of prescriptions, that a given pharmacist or pharmacy sells out of State. Another possibility not suggested by the Compliance Policy Guide would be capping the amount of any particular compounded drug, either by drug volume, number of prescriptions, gross revenue, or profit that a pharmacist or pharmacy may make or sell in a given period of time. It might even be sufficient to rely solely on the non-speech-related provisions of the FDAMA, such as the requirement that compounding only be conducted in response to a prescription or a history of receiving a prescription, and the limitation on the percentage of a pharmacy's total sales that out-of-state sales of compounded drugs may represent.

The Government has not offered any reason why these possibilities, alone or in combination, would be insufficient to prevent compounding from occurring on such a scale as to undermine the new drug approval process. Indeed, there is no hint that the Government even considered these or any other alternatives. Nowhere in the legislative history of the FDAMA or petitioners' briefs is there any explanation of why the Government believed forbidding advertising was a necessary as opposed to merely convenient means of achieving its interests. . . . The Government simply has not provided sufficient justification here. If the First Amendment means anything, it means that regulating speech must be a last—not first—resort. Yet here it seems to have been the first strategy the Government thought to try.

Case Questions

1. What test does the Court apply for determining whether a particular commercial speech regulation is constitutional?

2. Under the test applied by the Court, what threshold question must be answered at the outset?

3. After the threshold question has been answered, what three additional requirements must be met for the regulation to be constitutional?

4. Why did the Court determine that the advertising restrictions were unconstitutional?

5. What is the impact of commercial speech on pharmacies? What is the interplay between the Supreme Court's commercial speech case law and the marketplace? Consider for example what would have been the impact on the following situations if the Court had decided the case opposite the way it did: (1) A pharmacist serving a children's hospital where many patients are unable to swallow pills wants to tell the children's doctors about a new development in compounding that allows the drug that was previously available only in pill form to be administered another way. (2) A pharmacist wants to post a notice informing customers that if their children refuse to take medications because of the taste, the pharmacist could change the flavor and giving examples of medications where flavoring is possible.

The Fourth Amendment

Government investigations often include administrative inspections. Inspection is an indispensable aspect of any agency's enforcement procedure. The Fourth Amendment, however, prohibits warrantless, unreasonable searches and seizures. This protection can apply to protect business against intrusive governmental investigations.

Ethical Dilemmas/Issues

Amanda Steward is the president of Top Broadcasting Company, which owns and operates the WSEE television station in New York City. As part of her duties, Steward prepares a daily editorial for WSEE that is broadcast just after the 6:00 P.M. local news. Steward had an appointment today with Shelli Triano, a representative of People Against the Sale of Tobacco (PAST). Triano asked Steward to join in PAST's lobbying campaign that is aimed at the enactment of a bill currently pending in Congress, which would outlaw all advertising of tobacco products, including advertising through newspapers, magazines, and billboards. Cigarette advertising via radio and television has been banned by Congress since 1971. Specifically, Triano asks for Steward to broadcast an editorial stating that WSEE supports enactment of the bill into law.

What are the ethical issues? What would you do?

The Fourth Amendment

The right of the people to be secure in their persons, houses, papers, and effects, against unreasonable searches and seizures, shall not be violated, and no Warrants shall issue, but upon probable cause, supported by Oath or affirmation, and particularly describing the place to be searched, and the persons or things to be seized.

In *See v. City of Seattle,* the Court recognized the constitutional right of a business premise to be free from an administrative inspection without a search warrant.[14] In 1970, the Court created an exception to the *See* warrant requirement, holding that it was not applicable to a closely regulated business, such as a liquor establishment.[15] In regulating such a business, the legislature may validly authorize warrantless inspection by relevant agencies. If the legislature is not restricted in the area of liquor regulation, it might be presumed that it is likewise unrestricted in other fields of economic activity subjected to pervasive regulation. However, in *Marshall v. Barlow's Inc.,* the Supreme Court refused to extend the exception to the *See* warrant requirement when the business premise involved is a pervasively regulated business, such as one subject to inspection by the federal Occupational Safety and Health Administration."[16]

The Fifth Amendment

The Fifth Amendment's self-incrimination clause prohibits compelling any person "in any criminal case to be a witness against himself." The Supreme Court has held that the privilege against self-incrimination is a personal right. It does not apply to corporations or other collective entities. This is known as the **collective entity doctrine.**

The Self-Incrimination Clause of the Fifth Amendment

Nor shall any person . . . be compelled in any criminal case to be a witness against himself. . .

Therefore, someone conducting his or her business as a sole proprietorship may invoke the privilege against self-incrimination. However, that same person operating his or her business as a corporation would be treated differently. As custodian of the corporation's records, he or she could not invoke the Fifth Amendment to refuse to turn over corporate records to government inspectors."[17]

---

[14] 387 U.S. 541 (1967).
[15] Colonnade Catering Corp. v. United States, 397 U.S. 72 (1970).
[16] 436 U.S. 307 (1978).
[17] Braswell v. United States, 108 S. Ct. Rptr. 2284 (1988).

Chapter Problems

1. Define the following terms:
   a. Separation of powers
   b. Doctrine of checks and balances
   c. Federalism
   d. Incorporation doctrine
   e. State action
   f. Affectation doctrine
   g. Police power
   h. Preemption doctrine
   i. Eminent domain
   j. Collective entity doctrine

2. In the Gun-Free School Zones Act of 1990, Congress made it a federal offense "for any individual knowingly to possess a firearm at a place that the individual knows, or has reasonable cause to believe, is a school zone." The term "school zone" is defined as "in, or on the grounds of, a public, parochial or private school" or "within a distance of 1,000 feet from the grounds of a public, parochial or private school." The Act neither regulates a commercial activity nor contains a requirement that the possession be connected in any way to interstate commerce. On March 10, 1992, Alfonso Lopez, Jr., who was then a 12th-grade student, arrived at Edison High School in San Antonio, Texas, carrying a concealed .38 caliber handgun and five bullets. Acting upon an anonymous tip, school authorities confronted Lopez, who admitted that he was carrying the weapon. He was arrested and federal agents charged him with violating the Gun-Free School Zones Act of 1990. Lopez moved to dismiss his federal indictment on the ground that the Gun-Free School Zones Act of 1990 "is unconstitutional as it is beyond the power of Congress to legislate control over our public schools." The District Court denied the motion, concluding that the Gun-Free School Zones Act of 1990 "is a constitutional exercise of Congress' well-defined power to regulate activities in and affecting commerce, and the 'business' of elementary, middle and high schools . . . affects interstate commerce." The District Court conducted a bench trial, found Lopez guilty of violating the Gun-Free School Zones Act of 1990, and sentenced him to six months' imprisonment and two years' supervised release. On appeal, Lopez challenged his conviction based on his claim that the Gun-Free School Zones Act of 1990 exceeded Congress' power to legislate under the Commerce Clause. Is the federal Gun-Free School Zones Act of 1990 a valid exercise of the federal government's commerce power? Explain. Suppose the statute is written as follows: "It shall be unlawful for any individual knowingly to possess a firearm that has moved in or that otherwise affects interstate or foreign commerce at a place that the individual knows or has reasonable cause to believe is a school zone." Would such statutory language be constitutional under the Commerce Clause? Explain.

3. Like many states, Iowa imposes a 60-foot length limit on trucks operating within the state. It allows 55-foot single-trailer trucks and 60-foot doubles (a tractor pulling two trailers). However, unlike other western and midwestern states, Iowa, by statute, prohibits the use of 65-foot doubles within state borders. Consolidated Freightways, a trucking company that carries commodities through Iowa on interstate highways, sued, alleging that the State of Iowa unconstitutionally burdened interstate commerce. Because Consolidated cannot use its 65-foot doubles to move through Iowa, it must use shorter truck units, detach the trailers of a 65-foot double, and shuttle each through Iowa separately, or divert 65-foot doubles around Iowa. Iowa defends the law as a reasonable safety measure, asserting that 65-foot doubles are more dangerous than 55-foot singles and that the law promotes safety and reduces road wear by diverting much truck traffic to other states. What should be the result, and why?

4. The state legislature is considering a bill that would ban the retail sale of milk in plastic nonreturnable, nonrefillable containers, but would permit such sale in nonreturnable, nonrefillable containers made of other materials, such as paperboard milk cartons. The bill's proponents argue that it will promote resource conservation, ease solid waste disposal problems, and conserve energy. Relying on the results of several studies, they stress the need to stop introduction of the plastic nonreturnable container before it becomes established in the market.

   You are the vice president of marketing for the Clover Leaf Creamery. If the bill is enacted into law, your company stands to lose a great deal of money because it is the only dairy in the state that is already marketing its milk in nonreturnable plastic containers. The company invested a large amount of capital in plastic container production. Studies conducted by the state Milk Producers Association, your industry trade association, present empirical evidence that the proposed legislation will not promote the goals asserted by its proponents, but will merely increase costs of retail milk products and prolong the use of ecologically undesirable paperboard milk cartons.

   Develop a strategy to respond to this legislative proposal. If the bill is enacted into law, which arguments can your company advance to challenge the legislation's constitutionality? Could your local United States congressional representative or senator be of any assistance to your company? If so, in what way? Explain.

5. As vice president for acquisitions for MITE Corporation, you have targeted the Chicago Rivet and Machine Co., an Illinois corporation, for acquisition. You and other members of MITE's management team decide to have MITE make a tender offer for all the outstanding shares of Chicago Rivet at a price that includes a premium over the market price per share. In this way you hope to entice Chicago Rivet shareholders into accepting your offer. You ask in-house counsel to advise you of any legal problems that might be encountered in the takeover bid. Counsel reports that MITE will need to comply with the federal Williams Act, which requires that certain disclosure forms be filed with the federal Securities and Exchange Commission.

Counsel also advises you of an Illinois statute that regulates corporate takeover bids through tender offers. The statute forbids the making of tender offers in the state until the offeror files a statement of intent with a state official and the target company, and agrees to participate in any hearings required by a state agency. Counsel warns that complying with the Illinois statute will involve delays that are not likely to be encountered with the Williams Act. These delays may jeopardize the success of the takeover if Chicago Rivet's management decides to resist the bid and compete with MITE for the stock of Chicago Rivet's shareholders.

Formulate a takeover strategy that takes into account what to do about the federal and state laws.

6. A New York statute provides that landlords must permit a cable television company (CATV) to install its facilities on their property and may not demand payment from any tenant or CATV company in excess of an amount determined by state commission to be reasonable. The purpose of the statute is to facilitate the installation of CATV facilities for tenants. The commission ruled that a onetime $1 payment was a reasonable fee.

After purchasing an apartment building, Jean Loretto discovered that Teleprompter Manhattan CATV Corp. had installed cables on the building. Loretto sued for damages and sought an injunction in a New York state court. She alleged that Teleprompter's installation was a trespass and, insofar as Teleprompter relied on the state law, a taking without compensation in violation of the Fifth and Fourteenth Amendments of the U.S. Constitution. Is Loretto correct? Explain.

7. Under New York City law, advance approval must be obtained from the New York City Landmarks Preservation Commission before exterior changes can be made on any property designated as a landmark. In 1967, the commission designated Grand Central Terminal as a landmark. The Penn Central Transportation Company, which owned the terminal, sought permission in 1968 to construct a 55-story office building above it. Penn Central submitted two plans—one requiring a cantilevered building resting on the terminal's roof, the other necessitating the destruction of the terminal's south facade. Both plans were rejected. New York City's law also provided owners of landmark sites additional opportunities to transfer development rights to adjacent parcels on the same city block. This is known in land-use planning as a transfer development rights program. Because of this program and because full development of the terminal site was prohibited, Penn Central was entitled to exceed zoning limits on the development of other parcels of land. Penn Central challenged the Landmarks Preservation Law, alleging that its property had been taken without just compensation in violation of the Fifth and Fourteenth Amendments. Is Penn Central correct? Explain.

8. Spam is out of the can and on the Internet, and getting the attention of state lawmakers. "Spamming" is the sending of unsolicited commercial e-mail. To sidestep filtering software, some spammers route their advertisements

through a third party's server without permission, and use misleading subject lines, like "Sorry I missed your call," when the e-mail is intended to advertise something for sale, such as a travel package.

California and Tennessee require spammers to label their e-mail by inserting "ADV" into the first four letters of the subject line. The State of Washington bans spam that is sent to Washington residents with an invalid return e-mail address or a misleading subject line.

Jason Heckel, of Salem, Oregon, and his company, Natural Instincts, were accused of violating the State of Washington's anti-spam law. Heckel was charged with sending bulk commercial email to Washington residents with a misleading subject line and an invalid return e-mail address in an effort to try to sell a booklet titled "How to Profit from the Internet."

Discuss the constitutional law issues with regard to the California, Tennessee and Washington statutes and the case brought by the State of Washington against Heckel and Natural Instincts.

9. In 1999, Massachusetts' attorney general promulgated comprehensive regulations governing the advertising and sale of cigarettes, smokeless tobacco, and cigars. Among other matters, these regulations (1) prohibited any outdoor advertising of such tobacco products within 1,000 feet of schools or playgrounds, (2) provided that tobacco product advertising could not be placed lower than 5 feet from the floor of any retail establishment located within a 1,000-foot radius of any school or playground, (3) barred the use of self-service displays of tobacco products, and (4) required that tobacco products be placed out of the reach of all consumers in a location accessible only to salespersons. The purpose of the regulations was to address the use of tobacco products by children under legal age and to prevent access to such products by underage consumers. Are the regulations constitutional? Explain.

10. The Occupational Safety and Health Act (OSHA) empowers agents of the secretary of labor to search the work area of any employment facility engaged in interstate commerce. The purpose of the search is to inspect for safety hazards and violations of OSHA regulations. No search warrant is expressly required under the law. One day an OSHA inspector entered the customer service area of Barlow's Inc., an electrical and plumbing installation business in Pocatello, Idaho. The president and general manager, Errol B. Barlow, was on hand. After showing his credentials, the OSHA inspector informed Barlow that he wished to search the working areas of the business. Barlow asked if a complaint had been received about his company. The inspector answered no, explaining that Barlow's Inc. had simply turned up in the agency's selection process. Barlow then asked to see a search warrant, but the inspector had none. Errol B. Barlow then pointed to the copy of the Bill of Rights that he kept posted on his office wall and told the OSHA inspector to go get a warrant, as required by the Fourth Amendment. Does the inspector need a warrant to inspect the work areas of Barlow's Inc.? Explain. Suppose the work area were visible from the customer area, and the inspector had a camera in his coat pocket. Does the inspector need a warrant to take a picture of the work area? Explain.

6 ADMINISTRATIVE LAW

Learning Objectives

After learning this chapter the student should be able to:

- Define an administrative agency and describe how it is created.
- Distinguish between executive and independent agencies.
- Describe the functions and powers of administrative agencies and be able to compare and contrast agency rulemaking procedures and agency adjudication.
- Describe how the three branches of government control administrative agencies.

Virtually every activity engaged in by organizations and individuals is subject to administrative regulation. Business managers must be particularly alert to the impact of administrative agencies on their lives and careers. This chapter focuses on administrative agencies and their creation, structure, and general procedures.

Creation of an Agency

An administrative agency is a government body other than a court or legislature; it takes action affecting the rights of private parties. Agencies may be called *boards, commissions, administrative departments,* or *divisions.* They may consist of single individuals, or they may be large bureaucratic structures employing hundreds of persons. Each administrative agency implements government policy in specifically defined fields.

In a complex technological society it is inefficient, and perhaps impossible, for Congress to immerse itself in the intricacies of each regulated activity. Congress has neither the time nor the expertise to do so. It therefore sets general goals and policies and delegates the task of applying them to administrative agencies composed of experts in the regulated areas.

Enabling Legislation

Congress creates an administrative agency by passing a statute. The statute, called the **enabling legislation,** specifies the name, composition, and powers of the agency. The Federal Trade Commission Act is an example of a typical enabling statute.

Federal Trade Commission Act (excerpts of sections)

Section 1: A commission is created and established, to be known as the Federal Trade Commission, which shall be composed of five commissioners, who shall be appointed by the President, by and with the advice and consent of the Senate.

Section 5: Unfair methods of competition in or affecting commerce, and unfair or deceptive acts or practices in or affecting commerce, are hereby declared unlawful.

Section 1 of the Federal Trade Commission Act creates the agency. Section 5 declares certain practices unlawful and empowers the agency to prohibit these practices. Section 5 also describes the hearing procedure (called *adjudication*) to be used by the agency in prohibiting illegal trade practices and provides for judicial review of agency orders in the federal courts of appeals. Another section of the Federal Trade Commission Act authorizes the agency to issue rules specifying practices that the agency interprets the statute to prohibit. This section also sets out the procedures (called *rulemaking*) to be followed by the agency in formulating these rules. Additionally, the section provides for judicial review of the agency's rulemaking in the federal courts of appeals, and establishes the standards applied by a court in the course of such review. Other sections of the Federal Trade Commission Act describe the agency's internal procedures and provide for such powers as those of conducting investigations and requiring reports from corporations.

Agency Type and Organization

Administrative agencies exist at all levels of government. State and local governments have agencies that perform strictly local functions, such as zoning boards and liquor control commissions. Some agencies on the state and local levels, such as state environmental protection agencies, are counterparts to federal agencies. This chapter concentrates primarily on federal administrative agencies.

Executive versus Independent Agencies

Many administrative agencies exist within the Executive Office of the President or within the executive department comprising the president's cabinet. These are called **executive agencies.** Congress has given the president general authority to delegate to subordinate officials functions vested in the office by law. Cabinet officials receive authority delegated to them by the president or by statutes that Congress enacts. These cabinet officials frequently redelegate such functions to agencies under their command. Other agencies are established by Congress to administer particular statutes. These are the **independent regulatory agencies.** Much of the administrative regulation businesses must deal with emanates from the independent regulatory agencies (see Table 6–1). An independent agency is usually headed by a board or commission, whose members are appointed for a term of years by the president with the advice and consent of the Senate. During their tenure these board members or commissioners may be removed by the president only for statutorily defined cause. Thus, independent agencies differ from executive agencies in that the president may appoint and remove the heads of executive agencies at will.

Agency Organization

An agency's organization varies with its functions and powers. Because all agencies have specialized functions, they develop bureaucratic hierarchies to implement and monitor regulations within their jurisdictions. Set forth in Figure 6–1, to provide a flavor of this bureaucracy, is the organizational structure of the Federal Trade

---

TABLE 6–1   Independent Agencies Affecting Business

Federal Trade Commission (FTC)
Consumer Product Safety Commission (CPSC)
National Labor Relations Board (NLRB)
Equal Employment Opportunity Commission (EEOC)
Securities and Exchange Commission (SEC)
Environmental Protection Agency (EPA)
Nuclear Regulatory Commission (NRC)

FIGURE 6-1 The Federal Trade Commission

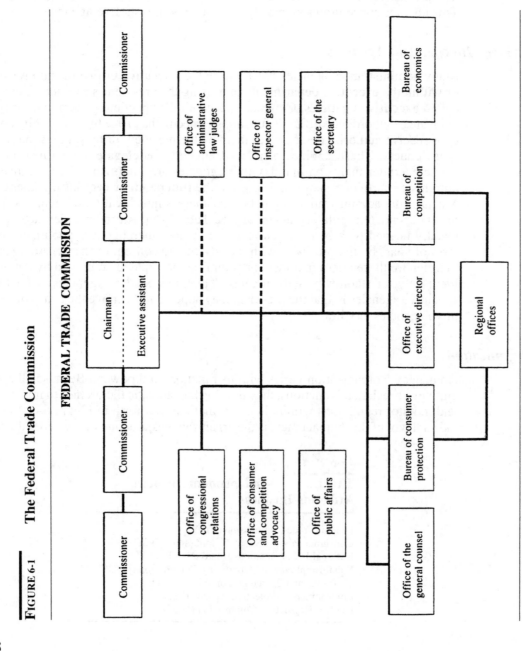

FEDERAL TRADE COMMISSION

SOURCE: *U.S. Government Manual 1992–1993* (Washington, D.C.: Office of the Federal Register (1992), p. 615.

Commission (FTC). The FTC was selected because it regulates many of the substantive areas covered in later chapters of this book. These include antitrust, advertising, consumer credit, and product safety.

The FTC consists of five commissioners appointed by the president, with the advice and consent of the Senate, for seven-year terms. The FTC staff is divided into three bureaus. The Bureau of Competition enforces the antitrust laws. The Bureau of Consumer Protection controls unfair and deceptive trade practices. The Bureau of Economics gathers data, conducts surveys, and provides expert support services for the other two bureaus.

Agency Functions and Powers

Most administrative activities are informal. Agencies undertake investigations, gather and analyze data, issue reports, administer grants-in-aid and other assistance programs, and provide advice to governments and private parties. The ability to give informal advice is one of the strongest powers of an agency. For example, if an inspector from the Occupational Safety and Health Administration suggests that a particular condition at a plant is unsafe, the employer, fearing a citation and fine, is very reluctant to ignore the suggestion.

Many agencies issue regulations that have the force and effect of law. This process is known as **rulemaking.** Agencies may also conduct administrative proceedings to determine whether a particular individual or corporation has violated a statute or regulation. This type of proceeding is called **adjudication**.

Rulemaking results in regulations of greater certainty and consistency and allows for broader public input. Adjudication, on the other hand, enables an agency to make law and policy on a case-by-case basis in much the same way as a court. Adjudication gives an agency considerable flexibility in developing an area of regulation.

An agency may use adjudication even where it wishes to announce new principles or to overturn prior decisions. The choice between rulemaking and adjudication is initially at the agency's discretion, and a court will overturn the agency's choice only if the agency has been arbitrary or capricious.

Standardizing Administrative Procedure

When engaging in rulemaking and adjudication, federal agencies must follow the procedures provided in their enabling legislation and in another federal statute, the Administrative Procedure Act (APA). The APA specifies the procedures agencies must follow and establishes standards and prerequisites for judicial review of agency action. The APA applies to all federal agencies; however, the APA does not supercede stricter procedural requirements imposed on an agency in its enabling legislation. If an agency's enabling legislation is silent as far as procedures are concerned, the APA applies.

Rulemaking

The APA defines a rule as "an agency statement of general or particular applicability and future effect designed to complement, interpret, or prescribe law or policy." Rulemaking is the process of issuing rules. In other words, rulemaking is the enactment of regulations that will be generally applicable in the future. All such regulations are compiled in the Code of Federal Regulations. The two types of administrative rules are interpretive and legislative rules.

Interpretive Rules

Interpretive rules are statements that express an agency's understanding of the statutes it administers. These rules are intended to advise the public of the agency's positions on particular issues. They are not legally binding on the agency, the courts, or the public. Nevertheless, when courts construe the underlying legislation, they frequently find such agency interpretations persuasive. Interpretive rules are exempt from the rulemaking requirements of the APA. The APA's requirements do apply, however, to legislative rules.

Legislative Rules

Legislative rules must be enacted in accordance with the APA. When such rules are consistent with the APA, the enabling legislation, and the Constitution, they have the force and effect of law. As such, they are binding on the agency, the courts, and the public.

The APA sets forth two methods for rulemaking: informal and formal (see Table 6–2). Most agencies use informal rulemaking. Formal rulemaking is used only when an agency's enabling legislation requires that its rulemaking be conducted on the record. Each method is considered in detail in the following sections.

Informal Rulemaking

Informal, or "notice and comment," rulemaking is begun when an agency publishes a notice of proposed rulemaking in the *Federal Register*. The notice must contain a statement of the time, place, and nature of the proceedings; the legal

---

TABLE 6–2   **APA Rulemaking Procedures**

Informal	*Formal*
Publication of notice of proposed rulemaking in the *Federal Register*.	Publication of notice of proposed rulemaking in the *Federal Register*.
Comment period: agency may limit parties to written comments.	Comment period: agency must conduct formal hearings.
Publication of final rule in the *Federal Register*.	Publication of formal findings and final rule in the *Federal Register*.

authority for the proposed rules (usually a citation to the enabling legislation); and either the terms of the proposed regulation or a description of the subjects or issues involved. The notice provides the public with sufficient information to participate in the proceedings. It need not parrot the language of the regulation eventually enacted; the agency need not even have any particular wording in mind. A simple, brief description of the subject matter is all that is usually required.

Following publication of the notice of proposed rulemaking, the agency gives interested parties time to submit written comments. The agency may hold public hearings, but it is not required to do so.

After the agency receives and considers the comments, it may publish the final version of the regulation in the *Federal Register* or discontinue proceedings. The agency must include a summary and discussion of the major comments received. However, it is not restricted to evidence produced in a formal manner. In addition to the comments received, it may consider information in its files, general knowledge in the field, material prepared by other agencies, and its own expertise. The regulation may take effect no sooner than 30 days following its publication.

The principal justification for using informal rulemaking is efficiency. The lack of required hearings minimizes opportunities for delay. But efficiency is obtained at a great cost: members of the public have minimal opportunity to be heard on the desirability of the proposed regulations. In the following case, several petroleum and chemical companies charged that the Environmental Protection Agency (EPA) failed to follow the Administrative Procedure Act's requirements for adequate notice and an opportunity to comment with regard to the EPA's hazardous waste regulations.

SHELL OIL COMPANY V. ENVIRONMENTAL PROTECTION AGENCY
950 F.2d 741 (D.C. Cir. 1991)

The Environmental Protection Agency (EPA) published a notice of proposed rulemaking defining hazardous waste by identifying nine characteristics of hazardous waste (i.e., toxicity). Because solid wastes that present a hazard but do not display one of the described characteristics remained subject to regulation by the EPA, the agency proposed to list certain wastes that it would treat as hazardous until a person managing the wastes petitioned the EPA to have the waste removed from the list by demonstrating to the EPA that the waste did not pose a hazard.

The final rules adopted by the EPA defined hazardous waste more broadly than did the proposed regulations, specifying a hazardous waste as any solid waste that was listed in the regulation or met any one of the nine characteristics. It further classified as a hazardous waste any mixture of a listed hazardous waste with any other solid waste (referred to as the "mixture" rule), and any residue (i.e., ash) derived from the treatment of hazardous waste (referred to as the "derived-from" rule). Neither definition was included in the proposed rule.

The Shell Oil Company and others (petitioners) sought review challenging the rules in the D.C. Circuit Court of Appeals. They argued that the EPA failed to provide adequate notice and opportunity to comment when it issued the mixture and the derived-from rules. The EPA argued that it had intended to treat waste mixtures containing hazardous wastes as hazardous, and that industry could have reasonably anticipated the final rules.

Per Curiam

In issuing regulations, the EPA must observe the notice-and-comment procedures of the Administrative Procedure Act. . . . The relationship between the proposed regulation and the final rule determines the adequacy of notice. A difference between the two will not invalidate the notice so long as the final rule is a "logical outgrowth" of the one proposed. If the deviation from the proposal is too sharp, the affected parties will not have had adequate notice and opportunity for comment. . . .

An agency, of course, may promulgate final rules that differ from the proposed regulations. To avoid the absurdity that the agency can learn from the comments on its proposals only at the peril of starting a new procedural round of commentary, we have held that final rules need only be a "logical outgrowth" of the proposed regulations. But an unexpressed intention cannot convert a final rule into a "logical outgrowth" that the public should have anticipated. Interested parties cannot be expected to divine the EPA's unspoken thoughts. . . .

Under the EPA's initial regulatory strategy, the EPA planned to identify and quantitatively define all of the characteristics of hazardous waste. . . . Generators would be required to assess their wastes in accordance with these characteristics and EPA would list hazardous wastes where it had data indicating the wastes exhibited one of the identified characteristics. As a consequence, listing was to "play [the] largely supplementary function" of increasing the "certainty" of the process. Listing was also to have relieved generators of listed wastes of the burden of testing for

characteristics "unless they wish to demonstrate that they are not subject" to . . . regulation. Thus, the proposed regulations imposed, as a generator's principal responsibility, the duty to test wastes for hazardous characteristics and suggested that if the required tests failed to reveal a hazard, the waste would not need to be managed as hazardous.

The final rules, however, place a heavy emphasis on listing. As a consequence, the final criteria for listing are "considerably expanded and more specific" than those proposed. . . .

Whatever the basis for this shift in strategy, it erodes the foundation of the EPA's argument that the mixture rule was implicit in the proposed regulations. A system that would rely primarily on lists of wastes and waste-producing processes might imply inclusion of a waste until it is formally removed from the list. The proposed regulations, however, did not suggest such a system. Rather, their emphasis on characteristics suggested that if a waste did not exhibit the nine characteristics originally proposed, it need not be regulated as hazardous. We conclude, therefore, that the mixture rule was neither implicit in nor a "logical outgrowth" of the proposed regulations.

Similarly . . . the derived-from rule . . . was not a logical outgrowth of the proposed regulations. The derived-from rule is not implicit in a system based upon testing wastes for specified hazardous characteristics—the system presented in the proposed regulations. To the contrary, the derived-from rule becomes counterintuitive as applied to processes designed to render wastes nonhazardous. Rather than presuming that these processes will achieve their goals, the derived-from rule assumes their failure.

Because the EPA has not provided adequate notice and opportunity for comment, we conclude that the mixture and derived-from rules must be set aside. . . .

Case Questions

1. Why did the court of appeals decide that the EPA had not provided adequate notice and opportunity to comment in adopting its final rule containing the definition of hazardous waste?
2. The requirement of notice of proposed rule-making allows businesses to determine if they will be affected by a rule and to submit comments to the agency concerning why the rule should not be adopted. One of the aims of requiring the agency to consider comments regarding a proposed rule is to allow the agency to make changes in the proposal to deal with problems identified by the comments. How far can an agency go in making changes to a proposed rule without violating the requirement of providing adequate notice of rulemaking? Explain.
3. If the EPA wishes to issue the rule that the court of appeals vacated, what must it do? Explain.

The opportunity to be heard is particularly important in legitimizing a regulation. Individuals who have that opportunity are less likely to view the regulation as being forced on them and, consequently, they are more likely to comply voluntarily with the rule. There is a much greater opportunity to be heard when an agency is required to use formal rulemaking.

Formal Rulemaking
Similar to informal rulemaking, formal or on-the-record rulemaking begins when the agency publishes a notice of proposed rulemaking in the *Federal Register*. The notice must set a date, time, and place for a public hearing. The agency must hold formal trial hearings where it presents all its evidence justifying the proposed regulation. Interested parties have the right to examine the agency's exhibits and to cross-examine its witnesses. They may also introduce their own exhibits and call their own witnesses. These exhibits and witnesses are subject to examination and cross-examination by the agency and all other interested parties. The agency must then make formal, written findings based on the evidence adduced at the hearings. The court of appeals for the appropriate circuit may review the findings and may set them aside if they are not supported by substantial evidence in the record.

The requirement of formal hearings enables parties that might be adversely affected by a proposed regulation to delay its implementation. Opportunities to do so exist at every stage of the rulemaking process. Such parties frequently flood the agency with issues they claim should be considered at the formal hearings. During prehearing conferences designed to simplify the issues, these parties can raise countless trivial procedural issues. Finally, they can drag the hearings out for years by cross-examining agency witnesses and by parading a seemingly endless supply of their own witnesses before the agency.

Ethical Dilemmas/Issues

Laura Cory is president of Fun Foods, Inc. One of Fun Foods' biggest sellers is its Play Time Peanut Butter. Cory recently learned that the Federal Food and Drug Administration was proposing to issue a rule requiring that peanut butter contain at least 90 percent peanuts.

Cory has consulted the company's vice president for finance, Anne Crowley, and learned that the rule will significantly increase Fun's production costs, because Play Time contains less than 90 percent peanuts. The vice president for marketing, Chrissy Snyder, informed Cory that Play Time's appeal lies in the fact that it is highly spreadable and does not stick to the roof of the mouth. Fun Foods accomplishes this by using several chemicals and by not using as much peanut content in its ingredients as compared to its competitors.

When Cory consulted with the company's attorney, Jennifer Blackburn, she was told that the FDA's proposal was reported in the Federal Register as a notice of proposed rulemaking, and that the FDA was following formal rulemaking procedures. Blackburn outlined a strategy that the company could take that would include participating in the FDA's formal rulemaking procedures. The participation would be designed to accomplish two objectives: (1) to convince the FDA that the appropriate amount of peanuts in peanut butter should be 87 percent, not 90 percent; and (2) to delay the rulemaking procedures as much as possible. To do this, Blackburn told Cory that the company could seek to participate in the rulemaking procedures, cross-examine the experts who would testify in the FDA's hearings, exhaust all appeals within the agency, and tie up the agency in litigation seeking judicial review of any rule the agency would issue. At the same time, Blackburn advised, the company could lobby Congress to put pressure on the FDA to drop its proposed rulemaking. When asked how long the process could be delayed through administrative procedures, Blackburn said it should be possible to delay the process for several years.

What are the ethical issues? What would you do?

Adjudication

The APA defines adjudication as any process, including licensing, that results in an order. An order is defined as a final disposition other than a regulation. From this cryptic definition, adjudication has developed as a primary means of enforcing agency statutes and regulation. An agency identifies and prosecutes an alleged violator and affords the violator a trial before it. Because the same agency serves as prosecutor and judge, there are obvious problems. The APA attempts to deal with these problems by requiring agencies to separate their prosecutorial and judicial functions.

Separation of Functions

The adjudicatory hearing is presided over by an agency employee known as an *administrative law judge* (ALJ). The APA prohibits ALJs from consulting ex parte (privately) with any person or party involved in the proceeding. It also requires that ALJs not be responsible to or subject to the supervision or direction of any persons in the prosecutorial or investigative divisions of the agency. The APA thus attempts to split the agency into somewhat autonomous judging and prosecutorial divisions. For example, in the chart in Figure 6–1 the FTC's administrative law judges are structurally separate from the enforcement sections of the Bureaus of Competition and Consumer Protection.

A Typical Adjudication

The National Labor Relations Board is fairly typical of an agency with adjudicatory enforcement powers. The board itself consists of five persons who serve staggered five-year terms after appointment by the president and confirmation by the Senate.

The board appoints administrative law judges. They may be removed only after a Civil Service Commission hearing, at which good cause for removal must be established.

The prosecutorial division of the NLRB is headed by the general counsel, who is appointed by the president. The general counsel has final authority over all prosecutions. The regional directors and their staffs are under the director's supervision.

To understand the adjudication process, consider the following example (see Figure 6–2). The XYZ Widget Corporation employed Harold Worker as a stock

---

FIGURE 6-2   **Adjucation: Flow a Case through an Administrative Agency**

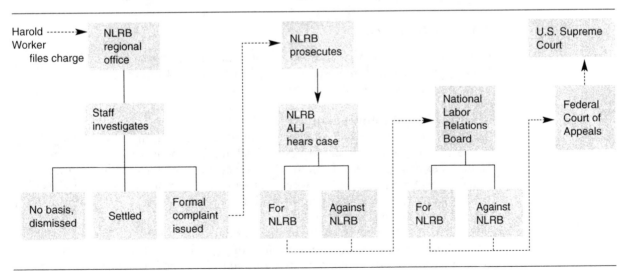

clerk. Worker had been very active in attempting to unionize the employees of XYZ. He had also been late for work on a few occasions, and once he called in sick when he was not ill. He was fired from his job. Section 8(a)(1) of the National Labor Relations Act prohibits employer restraint, interference, or coercion of employees exercising their rights to organize and bargain collectively. Worker believed that he had been fired because of his union activities, and thus his employer had violated section 8(a)(1).

If Worker wishes to prosecute the XYZ Widget Corporation, he must file a charge with the regional director, whose staff investigates the complaint. If the regional director finds reasonable cause to believe a violation has occurred, the regional director advises XYZ and tries to settle the matter informally. The settlements are entered in the form of consent decrees or consent orders. Frequently, they allow the respondent to deny the alleged violation while agreeing to take the action demanded by the agency. If a settlement is unattainable, the regional director must file a complaint with the board.

The complaint is served on XYZ, which may file an answer admitting or denying the allegations. The case is assigned to an administrative law judge (ALJ). Then there are prehearing proceedings, which are similar to pretrial court proceedings but less formal and with less extensive discovery.

The matter comes to trial before the ALJ. This sort of trial is less formal than a court trial. For example, the rules of evidence are relaxed, and hearsay and other types of evidence frequently not admissible in court are admissible before the ALJ.

The parties may present both written and oral arguments to the ALJ, who then examines the hearing transcript and prepares a decision that includes findings of fact, conclusions of law, and a recommended order. The losing party may appeal to the full board. After that, the losing party may appeal to a federal court of appeals (discussed in more detail later in the chapter).

Public Disclosure of Agency Information

Concern over secretive agency operations and the misuse of agency information led Congress to enact three statutes: the Freedom of Information Act, the Privacy Act, and the Government in the Sunshine Act.

The Freedom of Information Act (FOIA)

The FOIA requires all federal administrative agencies to make all agency documents publicly available on request unless the documents qualify for one of the statute's exemptions (see Table 6–3). The act provides for indexing certain documents, sets time limits and uniform fees for handling requests for documents, and subjects any agency employee to disciplinary action for arbitrarily refusing a request for a document.

The FOIA has been used by businesses to obtain sensitive information about competitors. This type of information is often found in agency files because of the numerous reports companies are required to file. The Supreme Court has ruled that companies cannot obtain court orders preventing FOIA disclosures to their

---

TABLE 6–3   **FOIA Exemptions**

The following items are exempt from the Freedom of Information Act's disclosure requirements:

1. Documents classified by the president in the interest of national security.

2. Documents related to an agency's internal personnel practices.

3. Documents whose disclosure is prohibited by other statutes.

4. Documents containing trade secrets or commercial and financial information.

5. Interagency and intra-agency memoranda that contain advisory opinions or recommendations or otherwise reflect the deliberative process of policy formulation.

6. Personnel, medical, and similar files if the disclosure "should constitute a clearly unwarranted invasion of privacy."

7. Records or information compiled for law enforcement purposes where disclosure would interfere with enforcement proceedings, jeopardize an individual's right to a fair trial, reveal a confidential source or investigative techniques, or endanger the lives of law enforcement personnel.

8. Documents regarding the operation of financial institutions.

9. Geological and geophysical maps and data.

---

competitors. Under the Court's interpretation, the statute's disclosure exemptions may be invoked only by an agency, and a company is protected only to the extent that an agency endorses its position.[1]

The Privacy Act

Although the FOIA seeks to protect access to agency files, the Privacy Act seeks to protect the confidentiality of certain information supplied to government agencies. The Privacy Act restricts agencies from gathering unnecessary information about individuals. However, it does not prevent agency officials from using agency records for official purposes. The Privacy Act provides individuals with a right of access to agency files maintained on them and a right to request a correction. Agencies must respond to these requests in 10 days, either by making the correction or by explaining why the correction was not made.

The Privacy Act forbids unwarranted disclosure of information that an agency maintains on someone. That is, the act forbids an agency from disclosing individual records to any other person or agency without the permission of the individual involved. However, the act provides that permission is not needed in certain situations (see Table 6–4).

The Government in the Sunshine Act

The Sunshine Act requires that all meetings of an independent agency be open to the public. The agency may close a meeting to the public if the meeting qualifies for one of several exemptions. These exemptions closely parallel those of the FOIA.

---

[1] Chrysler Corp. v. Brown, 441 U.S. 281 (1980).

TABLE 6–4   **Privacy Act Exemptions**

The Privacy Act provides that disclosure is allowed where it is:

1. To agency employees who need the record to perform their duties.
2. Required under the Freedom of Information Act.
3. The routine use of information.
4. To the Census Bureau.
5. To an individual for statistical research and the record is not individually identifiable.
6. To the National Archives.
7. To an agency for criminal and civil law enforcement.
8. To a person showing compelling circumstances affecting the health or safety of an individual.
9. To Congress.
10. To the General Accounting Office.
11. Pursuant to a court order.

Controlling Administrative Agencies

Businesses affected by administrative action may want to influence agency decision making. With regard to agency rulemaking and adjudication, this is done by participating, when possible, in the agency's procedures. Companies often belong to trade associations that alert their members of an agency's proposal to issue a rule. The trade association and its membership then communicate with the agency during the comment period or during any formal public hearings conducted by the agency. After an agency has issued a rule or after the agency has held a hearing and issued an order, businesses or others affected by the agency decision may wish to challenge that decision. To do so, they turn to Congress, the president, or the courts.

Congressional Control of Administrative Agencies

The control of agencies by Congress takes several forms. The Senate confirms agency appointments. Congress may amend enabling legislation or include restrictions in legislation appropriating funds to the agency. Each house of Congress has oversight committees that review the work of agencies, hold hearings, and propose action regarding appointments, amendments to the enabling statute, and appropriations.

Another method of congressional oversight is sunset legislation. Sunset legislation provides that an agency's authority shall expire on a given date unless Congress extends it.

Presidential Involvement in Agency Decision Making

Recent presidential administrations have sought to have an impact on administrative decision making beyond the usual influence of agency appointments. This involvement has taken place with regard to review of proposed regulations.

Two executive orders provide the Office of Management and Budget (OMB) with broad supervisory power over the rulemaking process of executive agencies. The executive orders do not apply to the independent agencies.

One executive order requires executive agencies to submit annually to OMB a Draft Regulatory Program listing all significant regulatory actions they plan to take during the coming year. OMB can ask the agencies to revise their proposals. Agencies can appeal disagreements with OMB to a cabinet-level body named by the president. However, once OMB publishes the plans for all agencies as the Administration's Regulatory Program, the agencies may not take actions not included in it unless they are legally required to or have obtained OMB's approval.

The other executive order requires all executive agencies to perform cost/benefit analyses of all proposed major regulations and to choose the least costly alternative. All proposed and final major regulations are submitted to the OMB, which reviews and analyzes them, subject to review by the president.

The executive orders reflect an attempt to modify agency rulemaking procedures. Their legality is debatable. Supporters of the presidential orders argue that they are valid exercises of executive authority to oversee the execution of the laws, and recommend amending the APA to extend the concepts embodied in the executive orders to the independent agencies. Critics argue that they violate the APA and encroach on the legislative prerogative in violation of the constitutional separation of powers principle.

Judicial Review of Administrative Action

The APA provides for judicial review of agency action. Although a few agency decisions are reviewed in the U.S. district courts, most agency decisions are reviewed in the circuit courts of appeal.

The Right to Judicial Review

Not all complaints about agency action receive judicial attention. To challenge agency action in court, a party seeking judicial review must take the initiative and meet the threshold requirements of reviewability, standing, and exhaustion of administrative remedies.

Reviewability.   The APA creates a strong presumption that final agency action is subject to judicial review. This presumption may be overcome if Congress specifies that a particular action shall be exempt from judicial review. This may require interpreting the enabling legislation to determine congressional intent. Congress must be clear and specific in indicating its intent to preclude judicial review. However, as the following case shows, there is a presumption against judicial review of agency decisions not to act.

HECKLER V. CHANEY
470 U.S. 821 (1985)

Chaney and several other prison inmates sentenced to death by lethal injection (respondents) complained to the Food & Drug Administration (FDA) (petitioner), alleging that the use of certain drugs for such a purpose violated the Food, Drug & Cosmetic Act (FDCA). The FDA refused Chaney's request, basing its refusal on its discretion to limit enforcement actions to situations where there is a serious danger to public health or a blatant scheme to defraud, neither of which the agency considered present. The U.S. Circuit Court of Appeals for the District of Columbia held that the FDA's refusal was both judicially reviewable and an abuse of discretion. The FDA appealed to the U.S. Supreme Court, which reversed the circuit court decision and ruled in favor of the FDA.

Justice Rehnquist

This Court has recognized on several occasions over many years that an agency's decision not to prosecute or enforce, whether through civil or criminal process, is a decision generally committed to an agency's absolute discretion. This recognition of the existence of discretion is attributable in no small part to the general unsuitability for judicial review of agency decisions to refuse enforcement.

The reasons for this general unsuitability are many. First, an agency decision not to enforce often involves a complicated balancing of a number of factors which are peculiarly within its expertise. Thus, the agency must not only assess whether a violation has occurred, but whether agency resources are best spent on the violation or another, whether the agency is likely to succeed if it acts, whether the particular enforcement action requested best fits the agency's overall policies, and indeed, whether the agency has enough resources to undertake the actions at all. An agency generally cannot act against each technical violation of the statute it is charged with enforcing. The agency is far better equipped than the courts to deal with the many variables involved in the proper ordering of its priorities.
. . .

In addition to these administrative concerns, we note that when an agency refuses to act it generally does not exercise its coercive power over an individual's liberty or property rights, and thus does not infringe upon areas that courts often are called upon to protect. Similarly, when an agency does act to enforce, that action itself provides a focus for judicial review, inasmuch as the agency must have exercised its power in some manner. The action at least can be reviewed to determine whether the agency exceeded its statutory powers. Finally, we recognize that an agency's refusal to institute proceedings shares to some extent the characteristics of the decision of a prosecutor in the Executive Branch not to indict—a decision which has long been regarded as the special province of the Executive Branch, inasmuch as it is the executive who is charged by the Constitution to "take care that the Laws be faithfully executed."

We of course only list the above concerns to facilitate understanding of our conclusion that an agency's decision not to take enforcement action should be presumed immune from judicial review under [the APA]. For good reasons, such a decision has traditionally been "committed to agency discretion," and we believe that the Congress enacting the APA did not intend to alter that tradition. . . . In so stating, we emphasize that the decision is only presumptively unreviewable; the presumption may be rebutted where the substantive statute has provided guidelines for the agency to follow in exercising its enforcement powers. . . .

[Justice Rehnquist then analyzed the language of the FDCA and found that it did not contain such guidelines.]

We therefore conclude that the presumption that agency decisions not to institute proceedings are unreviewable under . . . the APA is not overcome by the enforcement provisions of the FDCA. The FDA's decision not to take the enforcement actions requested by respondents is therefore not subject to judicial review under the APA. The general exception to reviewability provided by [the APA] for action "committed to agency discretion" remains a narrow one, but within that exception are included agency refusals to institute investigative or enforcement proceedings, unless Congress has indicated otherwise. In so holding, we essentially leave to Congress, and not to the courts, the decision as to whether an agency's refusal to institute proceedings should be judicially reviewable.

Case Questions

1. Why did the Court conclude that an agency's decision not to take action is presumed to be not reviewable by a court?

2. How can the presumption against judicial review of an agency's decision not to act be overcome?

3. How does the Court's decision with regard to agency decisions not to act differ from the rule with regard to judicial review of agency decisions to take action?

Standing.   Article III of the Constitution limits the jurisdiction of the federal courts to actual cases and controversies. Thus, a court case must be brought by a party that actually has a dispute with the defendant. Such a party is said to have **standing.**

A party challenging an agency action has standing if it has suffered (1) a resulting injury, economic or otherwise, that (2) falls within the zone of interests protected by the statute or the constitutional provision that the action is claimed to contravene. The first test for standing—the injury in fact requirement—derives from the Constitution's case and controversy requirement. The second test for standing—the zone of interests test (sometimes called *prudential standing*)—is statutory and asks whether Congress intended to allow parties in the plaintiff's position to obtain judicial review of the type of agency action challenged. In the following case, the court considered the requirements for standing.

CENTRAL ARIZONA WATER CONSERVATION DISTRICT V. ENVIRONMENTAL PROTECTION AGENCY
1993 U.S. App. LEXIS 5881 (9th Cir. 1993)

The Navajo Generating Station (NGS) is a power plant situated about 12 miles from the Grand Canyon near Page, Arizona. It is jointly owned by several utility companies and the U.S. Bureau of Reclamation (BOR).

The Environmental Protection Agency (EPA) issued a rule requiring a 90 percent reduction in sulfur dioxide emissions at NGS in order to improve the winter visibility of the Grand Canyon National Park. The estimated cost of the improvement is an initial capital cost of $430 million, with $89.6 million per year after that.

The Central Arizona Water Conservation District (CAWCD) and several water and irrigation districts (petitioners, or districts) obtained electricity to pump their water from NGS. They challenged the rule in the U.S. Court of Appeals for the Ninth Circuit. The EPA argued that the petitioners lacked standing to challenge the rule. The petitioners claimed an economic interest in the EPA rule. CAWCD claimed that it would be required to repay the major portion of the BOR's share of the costs due to a contractual relationship it had with the BOR. The Circuit Court concluded that the petitioners had standing, but (in part of the opinion omitted here) the EPA acted lawfully.

Circuit Judge Goodwin

A. Constitutional Standing

The Supreme Court recently outlined the three elements of the "irreducible constitutional minimum of standing" in *Lujan v. Defenders of Wildlife:*

> First, the plaintiff must have suffered an "injury in fact"—an invasion of a legally-protected interest which is (a) concrete and particularized, and (b) "actual or imminent, not 'conjectural' or 'hypothetical.'" Second, there must be a causal connection between the injury and the conduct complained of—the injury has to be "fairly . . . traceable to the challenged action of the defendant, and not . . . the result [of] the independent action of some third party not before the court." Third, it must be "likely," as opposed to merely "speculative," that the injury will be "redressed by a favorable decision. . . .

1. Injury in Fact

The Districts' claimed injury is an economic one: CAWCD claims it is contractually required to repay much of BOR's 24.3% share of the costs of installing and maintaining emission controls at NGS as required by the Final Rule. Pecuniary injury is clearly "a sufficient basis for standing." But while pecuniary or economic injury is generally a legally protected interest, the "injury in fact" test "'requires that the party seeking review be himself among the injured.'" That party's injury

must be (a) concrete and particularized, and (b) actual or imminent, and not conjectural or hypothetical.

■   ■   ■

We conclude that CAWCD's economic injury is sufficiently concrete and imminent to accord it standing to litigate this action. The Districts' claimed injury is by no means "a general or amorphous harm," nor is it a mere generalized grievance. While the extent of CAWCD's economic harm is not readily determinable, the record reveals that the Final Rule will likely cause Petitioners some amount of pecuniary harm given their obligation to repay BOR's share of the costs imposed by the Final Rule. [T]he possibility of passing on increased costs to consumers [does not] undermine the Districts' showing of the required "actual or threatened injury."

2. Causation and Redressability

In addition to the injury in fact requirement, the Districts must prove causation and redressability, i.e., that their alleged economic injury is fairly traceable to EPA's challenged action, and that the relief requested is likely to redress that injury. EPA argues that since the Districts' alleged economic injury flows from obligations under the BOR/CAWCD agreement, the injury is not caused by or fairly traceable to the challenged agency action. This argument misses the point. While CAWCD's contractual obligations may provide the basis for its economic liability for the increased costs imposed by the Final Rule, that hardly means that the Final Rule itself is not the direct cause of that liability. Further, the involvement of an intermediate third-party here does not undermine the Districts' causation argument since "the government's action [is] substantially likely to cause the petitioners' injury despite the presence of intermediary parties." Finally, the Districts' economic injury is likely to be redressed by a favorable decision since elimination of the Final Rule would necessarily eliminate the increased financial burden the rule causes.

B. Prudential Standing

In addition to the constitutional standing requirements, Petitioners must also prove that their asserted interest is "within the zone of interests protected by" the Clean Air Act. EPA contends that the Districts' economic injury is not within the zone of interests of the Act's visibility provisions, which are designed to "preserve, protect, and enhance the air quality in national parks." EPA's argument ignores the fact that "the zone of interest test is not meant to be particularly demanding."' As the Supreme Court in [*Clark v. Securities Indus. Ass'n.*] clarified:

> In cases where the plaintiff is not itself the subject of the contested regulatory action, the test denies a right of review if the plaintiff's interests are so marginally related to or inconsistent with the purposes implicit in the statute that it cannot rea-

sonably be assumed that Congress intended to permit the suit.

Under this permissive standard, the Districts' economic injury sufficiently falls within the "zone of interests" protected by the visibility provisions of the Act. [T]he Act requires the Administrator to consider "the costs of compliance" in setting standards to achieve reasonable progress towards the national visibility goal. As entities required to pay those costs of compliance, the Districts' interests cannot reasonably be described as "marginally related to or inconsistent with" the purposes of the Act.

We therefore conclude that Petitioners have standing to bring this challenge.

Case Questions

1. What requirements must a party meet to show it has standing to challenge agency action?
2. How did the petitioners satisfy the "injury in fact" test for standing? If the EPA withdrew its rule requiring reduction in sulfur dioxide emissions at NGS, would someone who had previously visited the Grand Canyon have standing to challenge the EPA action? Explain.
3. Why did the court reject the EPA's argument that CAWCD's economic injury was caused by its contract with the BOR and not the EPA's action?
4. Why did the court conclude that the districts' interests satisfied the "zone of interest" test of standing? Explain.

Exhaustion of Administrative Remedies. Congress creates administrative agencies when it believes that a particular activity must be regulated by an expert body. In reviewing agency action, therefore, courts generally defer to presumed agency expertise in technical matters. To ensure having the full benefit of agency expertise, courts require that an agency action be in final form before it is subjected to judicial review. Courts also require that a party seeking judicial review first exhaust the available administrative remedies.

The exhaustion requirement generally applies even though the complaining party contends that the agency has exceeded its authority. For example, Section 5 of the Federal Trade Commission Act empowers the FTC to order persons employing unfair or deceptive trade practices or unfair methods of competition to cease and desist using such practices, where such an order is in the public interest. If an FTC complaint counsel charges a party with violating Section 5, that party must file an answer, proceed to trial before an administrative law judge, and appeal to the full commission before the matter is subject to judicial review.

The Scope of Judicial Review

When a case meets the requirements of reviewability, standing, and exhaustion, a court may overturn an agency's action for any of the following reasons:

1. The agency failed to comply with the procedures detailed in its enabling legislation or the APA.
2. The agency's action exceeds the scope of its authority provided by its enabling legislation.
3. The agency's decision is premised on an erroneous interpretation of the law. Courts are never bound by an agency's legal interpretations. Nevertheless, courts defer greatly to an administrative agency's interpretation of its enabling legislation. This deferential attitude is captured in the especially strong language the Supreme Court used in *Chevron U.S.A. Inc. v. Natural Resources Defense Council, Inc.*[2] In *Chevron,* the Supreme Court reversed a D.C. Circuit Court decision that set aside a regulation of the Environmental Protection Agency. The regulation allowed businesses applying for permits under the Clean Air Act to avoid the elaborate review process whenever their increase in emissions of air pollutants was offset through reductions in emissions by a corresponding amount through modifications of the same plant. In rebuking the D.C. Circuit Court for setting aside the EPA regulation, the Supreme Court said:

   When a challenge to an agency construction of a statutory provision, fairly conceptualized, really centers on the wisdom of the agency's policy, rather than whether it is a reasonable choice within a gap left open by Congress, the challenge must fail. In such a case, federal judges—who have no constituency—have a duty to respect legitimate policy choices made by those who do. The responsibilities for assessing the wisdom of such policy choices and resolving the struggle between competing views of the public interest are not judicial ones: Our Constitution vests such responsibilities in the political branches.[3]

4. The agency's action conflicts with the Constitution. For example, a regulation prohibiting a certain type of advertising may violate the First Amendment's guarantee of free speech.
5. The agency erred in the substance of its action.

---

[2] 467 U.S. 837 (1984).
[3] Id. at 865–866.

The APA contains several standards that courts may apply in reviewing the substance of an agency's action: **de novo judicial review,** the **substantial evidence standard of judicial review,** and the **arbitrary and capricious standard of judicial review** (see Table 6–5). These standards vary in strictness and in the degree of discretion they afford the agency. The strictest standard employed by a court is de novo judicial review, which means examining anew the issue as if the agency had not made any decision. Here, the court is not bound by the agency's findings of fact, but instead holds an entirely new hearing and makes independent findings.

De novo judicial review is authorized by only a few statutes. In the U.S. district courts, it is provided for challenges of agency action under the Freedom of Information Act, the Privacy Act, and the Government in the Sunshine Act. A court also reviews an agency's findings de novo where the agency held an adjudicatory hearing but its fact-finding procedures were inadequate or where factual issues not considered by the agency are raised in court.

Enabling statutes frequently provide that agency findings of fact must be supported by substantial evidence on the record as a whole. In applying the substantial evidence standard, a reviewing court does not receive new evidence; instead, the court examines the record and weighs the evidence supporting an agency's findings against the evidence contradicting it. The finding is set aside only if the contradictory evidence substantially outweighs the supporting evidence. The Administrative Procedure Act requires courts to apply the substantial evidence standard to the review of formal rulemaking and adjudication.

The standard affording agencies the widest degree of discretion provides that agency findings not be set aside unless they are arbitrary and capricious. In applying this standard, a court must determine whether the agency considered all relevant factors and whether it made a clear error in judgment. The arbitrary and capricious standard of judicial review is applied to informal agency action, such as informal rulemaking.

TABLE 6–5   Judicial Standards for Reviewing the Substance of Agency Action

Type of Review	Approach	When Applied
De novo	Court decides issue anew.	Rarely (FOIA requests, Government in the Sunshine requests).
Substantial evidence	Court reviews the agency record and sets the agency decision aside only if substantial evidence supporting the agency decision does not exist.	Formal rulemaking and adjudication (because there is a record to review, a court can review the record to see if the decision is supported by substantial evidence).
Arbitrary and capricious	Court sets aside agency decision only if the agency failed to consider all relevant facts or did not provide a rational explanation for its decision.	Informal rulemaking (due to a lack of a formal record, a court defers to the agency, unless there is no rational connection between the facts found and the choice made by the agency).

The following is The Air Bag Case, in which the Supreme Court reviewed an agency decision to withdraw a rule.

MOTOR VEHICLE MANUFACTURERS ASSOCIATION V. STATE FARM MUTUAL AUTOMOBILE INSURANCE CO.
463 U.S. 29 (1983)

In 1967, the National Highway Transportation Safety Administration (NHTSA) (petitioner) issued Motor Vehicle Safety Standard 208, requiring the installation of seat belts in all automobiles. It soon became clear that the use of manual lap seat belts was too low to reduce traffic injuries to an acceptable level. In 1970, Standard 208 was changed to require installation of passive restraints—safety devices that do not depend on any action taken by the vehicle's occupants for their effectiveness. The 1970 standard required inflatable air bag crash restraints. In 1971, although NHTSA presumed that manufacturers would continue to meet the standard primarily by installing air bags, the agency revised the standard again to permit the use of automatic seat belts. An automatic seat belt is fastened to the inside of a car door and deploys automatically to protect the passenger when the door is closed. In 1977, after repeated delays in the implementation of the rule, NHTSA issued Modified Standard 208, which required that passive restraints be phased in by car size, starting in 1982.

By 1981, however, it became apparent that car manufacturers intended to comply with Standard 208 by installing detachable automatic seatbelts, rather than air bags, in virtually all new cars. The industry's plans led NHTSA to conclude that it could no longer reliably predict a significant increase in the use of passive restraints, and that only minimal safety benefits would result from application of Standard 208. The agency therefore rescinded the rule altogether. State Farm Mutual Automobile Insurance Company (respondent) sought review of the rescission of the rule in the U.S. Circuit Court of Appeals for the District of Columbia. That court held that NHTSA's rescission of Standard 208 was arbitrary and capricious. The Supreme Court affirmed the circuit court's judgment.

Justice White

[T]he Motor Vehicle Safety Act indicate[s] that motor vehicle safety standards are to be promulgated under the informal rulemaking procedures of the Administrative Procedure Act. The agency's action in promulgating such standards therefore may be set aside if found to be "arbitrary, capricious, and an abuse of discretion, or otherwise not in accordance with law." We

believe that the rescission or modification of an occupant protection standard is subject to the same test. Section 103(b) of the Motor Vehicle Safety Act states that the procedural and judicial review provisions of the Administrative Procedure Act "shall apply to all orders establishing, amending, or revoking a motor vehicle safety standard," and suggests no difference in the scope of judicial review depending upon the nature of the agency's actions. . . . [A]n agency changing its course by rescinding a rule is obligated to supply a reasoned analysis for the change beyond that which may be required when an agency does not act in the first instance . . . . The scope of review under the "arbitrary and capricious" standard is narrow and a court is not to substitute its judgment for that of the agency. Nevertheless, the agency must examine the relevant data and articulate a satisfactory explanation for its action including a "rational connection between the facts found and the choice made."

The ultimate question before us is whether NHTSA's rescission of the passive restraint requirement of Standard 208 was arbitrary and capricious. We conclude, as did the Court of Appeals, that it was. . . . The first and most obvious reason for finding the rescission arbitrary and capricious is that NHTSA apparently gave no consideration whatever to modifying the Standard to require that air bag technology be utilized.

Given the effectiveness ascribed to air bag technology by the agency, the mandate of the Safety Act to achieve traffic safety would suggest that the logical response to the faults of detachable seat belts would be to require the installation of air bags. At the very least this alternative way of achieving the objectives of the Act should have been addressed and adequate reasons given for its abandonment. But the agency not only did not require compliance through air bags, it did not even consider the possibility in its 1981 rulemaking. Not one sentence of its rulemaking statement discusses the air bags-only option. . . . We have frequently reiterated that an agency must cogently explain why it has exercised its discretion in a given manner.

[W]e also find that the agency was too quick to dismiss the safety benefits of automatic seat belts. NHTSA's critical finding was that, in light of the industry's plans to install readily detachable passive belts, it could not reliably predict "even a 5 percentage point increase as the minimum level of expected usage increase."

The agency also failed to articulate a basis for not requiring nondetachable belts under Standard 208. It is argued that the concern of the agency with the easy detachability of the currently favored design would be readily solved by a continuous passive belt, which allows the occupant to "spool out" the belt and create the necessary slack for easy extrication from the vehicle . . . . By failing to analyze the continuous seat belts in its own right, the agency has failed to offer the rational connection between facts and judgment required to pass muster under the arbitrary and capricious standard.

Case Questions

1. Which standard of review did the Court use in judging NHTSA's decision to rescind Standard 208? Why?
2. For an agency to meet the standard of judicial review used by the Court in *State Farm,* what must the agency do?
3. Why was the standard not met in *State Farm*?
4. Does the Court's decision mean that NHTSA's deregulation effort is completely aborted? Why or why not?
5. How far should a court go in deferring to an agency's decision to issue or withdraw a rule? Explain.

Damage Suits against the Government

With its many activities and millions of employees, the likelihood that government will inflict injury on private individuals and businesses is high. If an inspector from the Occupational Safety and Health Administration (OSHA) pushes over an expensive machine, damaging the equipment and injuring a nearby employee, the injured individual and company can be expected to bring a lawsuit seeking compensation for the inspector's negligence against the federal government.

Traditionally, governments cannot be sued. This immunity from liability is known as **sovereign immunity.** It originated during the days of the divine rights of kings, when a king could do no wrong. Today, many states and the federal government have passed laws waiving sovereign immunity for certain claims.

The Federal Torts Claims Act permits negligence claims to be brought against the federal government. Parties seeking compensation must first present their claims to the federal agency before going to court. In the example involving the OSHA inspector, the injured parties would first need to present their claims to OSHA, then, if their claims were denied, sue in federal court. The Federal Torts Claims Act does not permit lawsuits for the performance of a "discretionary function or duty on the part of a federal agency or an employee of the Government."

ADR and Administrative Law

The Administrative Dispute Resolution Act requires that each federal agency adopt a policy addressing the use of alternative dispute resolution (ADR) in connection with adjudication, rulemaking, enforcement actions, issuing permits and licenses, contract administration, and litigation. Each agency must designate a senior official dispute resolution specialist, who is responsible for implementing ADR and training agency employees in ADR techniques.

In using ADR, an agency may, if all the parties agree, use a neutral third party (i.e. arbitrator) to resolve the dispute. However, ADR cannot be used in matters likely to set a precedent, bear upon a significant policy question, or significantly affect persons or organizations who are not parties to the proceeding. The Act also requires confidentiality of agency ADR proceedings.

Chapter Problems

1. Define the following terms:
   a. Enabling legislation
   b. Executive agencies
   c. Independent regulatory agencies
   d. Rulemaking
   e. Adjudication
   f. Standing
   g. De novo judicial review
   h. Substantial evidence standard of judicial review
   i. Arbitrary and capricious standard of judicial review
   j. Sovereign immunity

2. A statute creates an Industrial Accident Commission (IAC), provides a comprehensive scheme to compensate employees for work-related injuries, and states that the IAC shall award such compensation after conducting hearings. The findings of the IAC are subject to judicial review and reversal only if the IAC acts outside its powers or if the award is not supported by substantial evidence on the record taken as a whole. What is the nature of the power exercised by the IAC in making awards?

3. You are the president of a restaurant trade association. The FTC issued a notice of proposed rulemaking stating that its studies found many restaurants misrepresented the food they served. Dishes described on menus and in advertising as veal often contained substantial amounts of beef and soy, hamburgers contained large percentages of soy and similar additives, and fresh vegetables were often frozen. The notice proposed regulations detailing specific requirements when these and similar terms were used on menus or in ads. The association's members oppose the proposed regulations. How will you respond to the notice?

4. You are the personnel manager for XYZ Corporation. The company president has given you a copy of a complaint served on the company by the regional director of the NLRB. The complaint charges that the company fired two employees because they were involved in union organizing activities. Your records show that both employees were active union organizers but that they were fired because each had 15 unexcused absences over the past year. Prepare a memorandum for the president outlining the procedures that the NLRB uses to process the complaint, and recommend a course of action.

5. Doe Corporation is a defense contractor. It is subject to periodic audits by the Defense Contract Audit Agency (DCAA), the accounting branch of the Department of Defense. In connection with a 1978 audit, an exchange of correspondence took place between the DCAA and Doe concerning the proper accounting treatment of certain costs. The government auditor, by letter, claimed the costs should have been charged to identifiable programs instead of a technical overhead account. About $4.7 million in 1977 costs were discussed. Doe, by letter, replied and defended its allocation. No further action regarding the allocation of those costs was taken by the DCAA or Doe during the next eight years.

   In 1985, the U.S. district attorney instituted an investigation into possible fraudulent practices by Doe. A subpoena was issued to Doe by a grand jury. It requested documents relating to the cost allocation question that was the subject of the 1978 correspondence. Doe then submitted to the DCAA a request under the Freedom of Information Act (FOIA) for any documents "that are related in any way to the subject matter" of the 1978 correspondence. The DCAA denied the request. Two days later the requested records were transferred to the Federal Bureau of Investigation (FBI). The corporation renewed its FOIA request but this time directed it to the FBI. The FBI denied the request. The corporation sued in federal district court, seeking review of the withholding of the requested documents. How should the court rule? Explain.

6. The secretary of the interior granted Walt Disney Enterprises a use permit to develop a ski resort in the Mineral King Valley of the Sequoia National Forest. The Sierra Club sought review of this decision in a federal court of appeals. The Sierra Club alleged that it was interested in preserving Mineral King in its undeveloped state, but the club did not allege that any of its members used Mineral King or would suffer any specific injury from the development of the ski resort. Does the Sierra Club have standing to challenge the secretary of the interior's decision? Explain.

7. The National Motor Vehicle Safety Act empowers the secretary of transportation to issue regulations establishing practicable standards that meet the need for motor vehicle safety. The secretary proposes a regulation requiring that all retread tires contain permanent labeling of tire size, inflatable pressure, ply rating, tubeless or tube type, and bias belted or radial construction. During the notice and comment period, tire retreaders seek modification of the proposal to eliminate the requirement of permanency. They claim that two thirds of all the tire casings they receive either lack labels or have labels that are obliterated during the retread process. They further argue that furnishing permanent labels will require the use of mold plates. Unlike a tire manufacturer who mass produces large batches of tires to the same specifications, retreaders deal with small batches of different sizes and construction. This means that the mold plates will have to be changed frequently by employees working with hand tools at temperatures up to 300° F. The retreaders produce a study showing that the labeling process is 80 percent effective and adds 30 percent to the cost of retreads. If the secretary promulgates the regulation, will it be sustained in court? Explain.

8. The Clean Air Act authorizes the Environmental Protection Agency (EPA) to regulate gasoline additives whose emissions "will endanger the public welfare." EPA promulgates regulations requiring a stepwise reduction of the lead content of gasoline. Scientific and clinical evidence shows that high concentrations of lead in the body are toxic, that lead can be absorbed from ambient air, and that 90 percent of the lead in the air comes from automobiles. However, air is only one of several sources of lead absorbed by the body. Furthermore, because all humans breathe the same air, it is impossible to conduct a controlled experiment. Consequently, it is impossible to identify the precise level of airborne lead that will endanger human health, and no single dispositive study fully supports the EPA's position. Will a court overturn the rule? Explain.

9. The Economic Development Administration (EDA) is empowered to award grants to communities with high unemployment for community projects designed to create jobs. To fund a project that competes with local private

businesses, EDA must find that there is sufficient demand to support the funded project as well as the local businesses. Relying on data from the Department of Labor showing 15 percent unemployment around Duluth, Minnesota, EDA makes a substantial grant to the City of Duluth for the operation of a ski resort at nearby Spirit Mountain. EDA projects future demand by using a formula based on an average of demand for the preceding five years. It, therefore, refuses to consider reports from the National Weather Service predicting an abnormally warm winter in the upper Great Lakes region. It also makes a mathematical error in applying its formula, resulting in an underestimation of the demand. If the competing private ski resorts sue EDA and the City of Duluth, would they succeed in having the grant set aside? Explain.

10. Kevan Berkovitz was a child who had been given an oral polio vaccine (Orimune), had contracted severe polio, and had become paralyzed. Kevan's parents sued the United States under the Federal Torts Claims Act. The claimed that the Division of Biologic Standards (DBS) had wrongfully licensed the manufacturer of the vaccine and also had wrongfully approved release to the public of the offending lot. The DBS issued a product license without first receiving data that the manufacturer must submit showing how the product, at various stages of the manufacturing process, matched up against regulatory safety standards. The statute and regulations under which the DBS operates require, as a precondition to licensing, that the DBS receive certain test data from the manufacturer relating to the product's compliance with regulatory standards. Although the regulations governing release of vaccine lots empower the DBS to examine any vaccine lot and prevent the distribution of a noncomplying lot, they do not require the DBS to take such action in all cases. The regulations generally allow the DBS to determine the appropriate manner in which to regulate the release of vaccine lots, rather than mandating certain kinds of agency action. Under the authority granted by the regulations, the DBS has adopted a policy of testing all vaccine lots for compliance with safety standards and preventing the distribution to the public of any lots that fail to comply. Will a federal court entertain the Berkovitz lawsuit? Explain.

III INTRODUCTION TO PRIVATE LAW AND THE REGULATORY ENVIRONMENT

Private law governs the interactions of individuals in society. Much is judge-made and has evolved through years of human experience. Private law provides a foundation for our public law-regulatory environment. Often government regulation is a response to the shortcomings of private law.

Contract, tort, and property law are private law topics treated in Part III. Product safety, truth in advertising regulation, and environmental law are regulatory topics that have evolved out of contract, tort, and property law. They are included as examples of areas of government regulation of business that have developed out of private law.

Chapter 7 covers contracts, the law governing rights that one party voluntarily confers on another and responsibilities that one party voluntarily undertakes. Chapter 8 covers torts, the law governing rights and responsibilities that the law imposes on individuals' conduct toward each other. The inadequate response of contract and tort law to consumer rights led to federal regulation designed to protect the consumer. This can be seen in Chapter 9, on product safety and truth in advertising. It illustrates the progression of two substantive areas of law from the common law of contracts and torts, to state and federal statutory protections, to government intervention and regulation.

Chapter 10 overviews the third foundation area of private law, the law of property. When thinking of business, it is only natural to think of property rights. Much of property law has come down through the centuries from a time when land was the dominant measure of wealth. Today, technological developments challenge old notions of what is property.

Chapter 11 discusses regulation of our environment. Regulation aimed at protecting the environment came about in response to the inability of the common law of contracts, torts, and property to provide the environmental protection society demanded. Today, several environmental laws are in place, each aimed at protecting an area of the nation's environment.

Chapters 7, 8, and 10 describe the common law of contracts, torts, and property, which serve as the private law foundations of much government regulation. Chapters 9 and 11 describe the federal regulatory response in the areas of consumer protection and environmental protection. This interaction between private law and government regulation should be kept in mind when reading the material in Parts IV through VI, dealing with government regulation of business organizations and finance, regulation of the employment relationship, and government regulation of the marketplace.

7 CONTRACTS

Learning Objectives

After learning this chapter the student should be able to:

- Determine whether a promise is legally enforceable.
- Determine whether particular promises require writings to be enforced and the legal significance of reducing a contract to writing.
- Evaluate whether particular promises are not enforceable because of a party's status or conduct or because of its substantive provisions.
- Evaluate the effects of unforeseen changes in circumstances on a party's duty to perform under a contract.
- Assess the remedies a court is likely to award for a breach of contract.

Most people associate the word *contract* with formal written documents, such as a contract to purchase real estate, a contract in a complex business transaction, or a professional athlete's employment agreement. The legal term *contract* is far broader than that, however; a contract is a promise that the law will enforce. The definition suggests that the law does not enforce every promise.

This chapter explores the factors that determine whether the law will enforce particular promises. Most contracts consist of exchanges of two or more promises. In the typical case, the *promisee,* that is, the party to whom one of the promises was made, is attempting to enforce that promise against the *promisor,* the party who made it.

Sources of Contract Law

The basic law of contracts is common law, that is, it is judge-made law. However, the National Commission on Uniform State Laws believed that some common-law rules did not serve the commercial community as well as they could, and tried to write new rules that more closely reflected how most people conducted business. These new rules were codified in the Uniform Commercial Code (UCC). The UCC consists of nine articles, governing such commercial transactions as security interests in property, checks, drafts and other commercial paper, and bulk transfers. The UCC has been enacted as a statute in 49 states and the District of Columbia. (Louisiana has enacted part of the UCC, but not Article II.)

Article I of the UCC contains general provisions. Article II governs contracts for the sale of goods. A *good,* as the term is used in the UCC, is a tangible commodity capable of being moved from place to place. Pens, books, desks, appliances, cars, factory equipment, and office supplies are examples of goods. Real estate, services, stocks, bonds and other securities, and intangible property—such as patents and copyrights—are not goods.

When a contract involves the sale of goods, the UCC applies. This chapter discusses the most significant changes introduced by the UCC. The UCC's influence on the law of contracts has not been limited to contracts for the sale of goods; at times, courts considering contracts outside the UCC view the UCC changes positively and adopt them into common law.

Intent to Contract—The Objective Theory of Contracts

Every day, people make promises they do not intend to carry legal consequences. Many of these are social obligations, such as a promise to meet for lunch or to study together; and family obligations, such as a promise to visit next month. Some promises are made in jest. Companies often sign nonbinding letters of intent, expressing their expectations that after negotiations, agreements will be reached, but providing that neither party will be obligated until an agreement is reached. If the parties do not intend to be legally bound, their promises are not legally enforceable.

Intent to contract does not refer to a party's subjective state of mind. Contractual intent is determined objectively by examining the parties' observable behavior—their words and conduct. The relevant legal inquiry thus becomes whether a reasonable person in the position of the promisee would conclude that the promisor intended to be legally bound.

For example, assume that Smith, a farmer, and Jones, the owner of a retail store, are enjoying a beer at their favorite tavern and discussing the low prices farmers are receiving for their crops. Jones says to Smith, "If you're fed up with farming, I'll buy your farm from you for $200,000." Smith thinks that Jones is joking and decides to play along. In a serious tone of voice he says, "You have a deal." Jones replies that he will need time to obtain financing. Smith still thinks the discussion is a joke, but discusses details of the transaction with Jones for a half hour and writes all the details on a piece of paper that Smith and Jones sign.

Subjectively, Smith did not intend to sell the farm to Jones—he thought the matter was a joke. Nevertheless, a reasonable person in Jones's position would conclude that Smith intended to sell. Therefore, Smith would be legally bound to sell the farm to Jones.

The Bargain Theory of Contracts

The law of contracts is the backbone of business. It enables parties to transact business with the knowledge that if one party fails to live up to the agreement the other party can seek redress from the courts. It is a primary guarantor of transactional integrity.

There are many reasons why parties would keep their promises even if the courts did not enforce them. For example, if a business developed a reputation for not abiding by its agreements, others would be very reluctant to do business with it.

As might be expected, there are costs to court enforcement of promises. These costs include the expenses of litigation and the cost to the promisor of being locked into the promise, regardless of the reasons for the breach. Therefore, courts weigh the costs and benefits of enforcing different types of promises.

The basic type of promise that a court enforces is one that is part of a bargained-for exchange. The elements of a bargained-for exchange are offer, acceptance, and consideration.

Offer

An **offer** is made by the *offeror* and gives the *offeree* the power to bind the offeror by accepting the offer. The objective theory is used to determine whether an offer has been made. The test is whether a reasonable person in the position of the offeree would interpret the offer as signifying the offeror's intent to be bound.

Offers must be distinguished from invitations to negotiate. Parties frequently send out announcements that they are seeking to do business and invite others to deal. These announcements may be contained in circulars, price quotes, catalogs, and advertisements. They are frequently indefinite concerning quantity and other terms. Most important, they usually do not identify the offeree. Some advertisements, however, are offers, as the following case illustrates.

IZADI V. MACHADO FORD, INC.
550 So.2d 1135 (Fla. App. 1989)

Machado Ford (defendant) ran an advertisement in the *Miami Herald*. The ad prominently invited customers to shop at the dealership and receive a trade-in of at least $3,000.00. Very small print at the bottom of the ad said that it applied only to the purchase of an Eddie Bauer Aerostar or Turbo T-Bird.

Izadi (plaintiff) sought to purchase a Ford Ranger Pickup, priced at $7,095, with $3,595 cash, a $500 factory rebate, and a trade-in. Machado refused and Izadi sued. The trial court dismissed the complaint. The Florida Court of Appeal reversed.

Chief Judge Schwartz

It is . . . well settled that an allegedly binding offer must be viewed as a whole. . . . We . . . believe that the complaint appropriately alleges that, objectively considered, the advertisement . . . contained just the unqualified $3,000 offer which was accepted by the plaintiff. . . . [T]he case thus is like many previous ones in which it has been held, contrary to what is perhaps the usual rule, that an enforceable contract arises from an offer contained in an advertisement. . . .

Of course, if an offer were indeed conveyed by an objective reading of the ad, it does not matter that the car dealer may subjectively have not intended for its chosen language to constitute a binding offer.

■   ■   ■

Machado—although it did not intend to adhere to the $3,000 trade-in representation—affirmatively, but wrongly sought to make the public believe that it would be honored; that, in other words, the offer was to be used as the "bait" to be followed by a "switch" to another deal when the

acceptance of that offer was refused. Indeed, it is difficult to offer any other explanation for the blanket representation of a $3,000 trade-in for any vehicle—which is then hedged in sub-microscopic print to apply only to two models which were not otherwise referred to in the ad. . . . This situation invokes the applicability of a line of persuasive authority that a binding offer may be implied from the very fact that deliberately misleading advertising intentionally leads the reader to the conclusion that one exists.

■   ■   ■

There is entirely too much disregard of law and truth in the business, social, and political world of today. . . . It is time to hold men to their primary engagements to tell the truth and observe the law of common honesty and fair dealing.

Case Questions

1. What was the offer made by Machado? What were its terms? How can you identify the offeree?

2. How was the offer accepted?
3. How did Machado's apparent bait-and-switch motive affect the court's analysis?
4. Chicago Medical School sent a prospective student a bulletin and an application. They stated that applicants would be evaluated based on undergraduate grades, MCAT scores, and letters of recommendation. A student completed the application and sent it along with the application fee. Chicago Medical School processed the application but rejected the student. Did the student and the school have a contract? Explain.
5. Manufacturer sent advertising circulars to retailers listing premiums that retailers could receive by ordering specified amounts of manufacturer's products. The circulars contained no discount or billing terms. Eastern Dealer ordered the appropriate amount of products to qualify for a new Audi 5000 car and 100 Polaroid Instant Cameras. Eastern's order specified a 5 percent truckload discount and 90-day billing, the terms of its prior orders with Manufacturer. If Manufacturer rejects the order, is Eastern entitled to the premiums? Why or why not?

An offer is not effective unless it is communicated to the offeree. For example, assume that John offers a $500 reward for the return of an antique watch he lost. Sarah, unaware of the offer, finds the watch and turns it over to the police, who return it to John. Sarah learns of the offer two days later. Sarah is not entitled to the reward because her acceptance, that is, her return of the watch, occurred before the offer was communicated to her.

Termination of an Offer

An offer may specify its expiration date. If it does not do so, the offer terminates after passage of a reasonable time. Death of the offeror also terminates an offer.

A rejection by the offeree terminates the offer. A counteroffer is both a rejection and a new offer. It terminates the original offer.

The most common method of terminating an offer is by **revocation.** A direct revocation occurs when the offeror advises the offeree that the offer is revoked. An indirect revocation occurs when the offeree receives truthful information from a reliable source that is inconsistent with the offer remaining open. For example, Susan offered to sell her house to James. The next day James learned from Carol that Susan had just sold her the same house. A sale to Carol is inconsistent with a possible sale to James. If the statement from Carol is truthful, the offer to James has been indirectly revoked.

Irrevocable Offers

If an offeror states that the offer will remain open until next Tuesday, the offeror usually can revoke prior to that time. Next Tuesday simply fixes the offer's expiration date. Even if the offeror promised not to revoke, the promise would be unenforceable unless the offeree gave *consideration* for it. If the offeree gives consideration, such as the payment of money, the offer would be part of an option contract and would be irrevocable.

Under the UCC, a merchant's firm offer is irrevocable. A merchant is a party who regularly deals in, or otherwise has expertise in, the goods involved in the transaction. A firm offer must be in writing and must be limited to a reasonable period of time, not to exceed 90 days.

Acceptance

An **acceptance** consists of words or actions by which an offeree signifies his or her intention to be bound by the offer. Acceptance binds the offeree and the offeror. Acceptance must occur before the offer is terminated.

An offer may only be accepted by the offeree. For example, assume that Ace Widget Co. writes Deuce Gizmo Co., offering to sell Deuce 100 widgets for $200. The president of King Gizmo Co., while visiting the president of Deuce, sees the offer on the desk. The King president writes to Ace, "We hereby accept your offer of 100 widgets for $200." There is no contract between King and Ace. Because King was not the offeree, King cannot accept the Ace offer. King's letter is merely an offer to Ace, which Ace is free to accept if it wishes to do so.

An acceptance must signify the offeree's clear intent to be bound. Ambiguous actions or statements, such as "Sounds like a good deal," are not acceptances. An offeror cannot declare that an ambiguous action will be treated as an acceptance. For example, assume Jack says to Jill, "I offer to sell you my car for $1,500. You may accept by taking the business law final exam next week." If Jill takes the final exam she will not have accepted Jack's offer because her action is ambiguous. She may be taking the final because she wishes to accept the offer, or she may be taking the final because it is required for the course.

Usually, silence by the offeree is ambiguous and cannot serve as an acceptance. Silence in the context of a prior course of dealings or silence plus acceptance of the benefits of the offer is not ambiguous and can serve as an acceptance.

The Mirror Image Rule and UCC 2–207

At common law, the acceptance must mirror the offer. If it adds new terms or changes any terms, it is not an acceptance but a counteroffer.

In commercial transactions, buyers and sellers frequently use printed forms with terms that do not agree. Under the mirror image rule, each form exchanged is a counteroffer, even though it is intended as an acceptance. The terms of the last form sent by either party govern the transaction because that counteroffer is accepted by the other party's shipment or acceptance of the goods.

Section 2–207 of the UCC changes this common-law rule. It provides that a document intended to be an acceptance is an acceptance even though it has terms different from or in addition to those in the offer. The acceptance creates a contract on the offeror's terms. The new terms found in the acceptance are proposals to add to the contract. Unless both parties are merchants, the new terms only become part of the contract when both parties expressly agree to them.

If both parties are merchants, the new terms automatically become part of the contract unless one of three conditions is met: (1) the offer expressly limited acceptance to the terms of the offer; (2) the offeror notifies the offeree of its objection to the new terms; or (3) the new terms materially change the contract.

For example, assume that Buyer sent Seller an offer to purchase 100 widgets for $200 on Buyer's printed order blank. The terms on the order blank included statements that full warranties apply and that the goods were to be delivered by Speedy Delivery Service. Seller responds with a printed acknowledgement form, promising to ship the widgets on the requested date. Seller's form specifies delivery via Quick Delivery Service and limits the warranty to replacement of defective widgets. Seller ships the widgets, Buyer accepts them, and two weeks later a defective widget causes $5,000 damage to Buyer's equipment. To determine the contents of the contract under the common law and the UCC, see Table 7–1.

Acceptance by Promise or Performance

Most offers contemplate contracts in which promises are exchanged for promises. For example, Owner offers to pay Roofer $1,500 for reroofing Owner's house. If

TABLE 7-1   The Mirror Image Rule and UCC 2–207

	Common Law	*UCC (At least 1 party is not a merchant)*	*UCC (Both parties are merchants)*
Buyer's order	Offer	Offer	Offer
Seller's acknowledgment	Counteroffer because of the delivery and warranty terms	Acceptance; changes in delivery company and limitation on warranty are proposals to change the contract	
Buyer accepts the goods	Acceptance of Seller's counteroffer	Irrelevant	Irrelevant
Change in name of delivery company	Part of contract as Buyer accepted Seller's counteroffer	Not part of contract as Buyer did not agree to it	Part of contract because Buyer did not specify in its offer that acceptance must be limited to the offer's terms, Buyer did not object to it, and it does not materially change the contract
Limitation on warranty	Part of contract as Buyer accepted Seller's counteroffer	Not part of contract as Buyer did not agree to it	Not part of contract as it materially changes the terms of the contract

Roofer accepts, the contract consists of Owner's promise to pay the money and Roofer's promise to do the work. This is often called a *bilateral contract.* Roofer may accept by promising to do the job or by actually starting. If Roofer begins performance, Roofer is impliedly promising to do the entire job.

Sometimes the offeror is not interested in the offeree's promise, but is only concerned with full performance. For example, if a company offers a reward for the return of some lost documents, it is not bargaining for someone to promise to search for the documents; the company is only interested in the documents. The offeree can accept only by producing the documents. This is often called a *unilateral contract.* Because the offeree makes no promise, the offeree is not obligated to perform; but if the offeree performs, the offeror is bound to perform.

After the offeree commences performance, but prior to completion of performance, the offeror might try to revoke the offer. Because only complete performance would bind the offeror, the offeree needs protection against revocation midway through performance. Therefore, when the offeree begins to perform, the offeror cannot revoke for a reasonable time in order to give the offeree a chance to complete.

Effective Date of Acceptance—The Mailbox Rule

The offeror is the master of the offer and can set any conditions on the acceptance. The offeror can expressly limit the means of communicating acceptance, for example, by specifying telegraph or overnight delivery, and can expressly provide that acceptance will be effective only on receipt.

If the offeror does not restrict the method of acceptance, the offeree may use any reasonable means to accept. If the offeror does not specify otherwise, acceptance is effective on dispatch by the offeree. This principle is frequently called the *mailbox rule,* as a mailed acceptance is effective on its deposit in the mailbox. The rule protects the offeree from unknown revocations. Because revocation is effective on receipt, an offeree who has not received a revocation can dispatch an acceptance knowing that a contract has been formed.

Consideration

Consideration refers to the requirement that a promise be part of a bargained-for exchange in order for it to be enforceable. Offer and acceptance are the bargaining process. Consideration refers to the bargain itself.

Consideration consists of two elements: (1) a legal detriment by the promisee that (2) is bargained for by the promisor. A legal detriment exists where the promisee does or promises to do something he or she was not previously obligated to do, or refrains from or promises not to do something he or she had a legal right to do. The detriment is bargained for if it is given in exchange for the promise. See Table 7–2 for an illustration of how consideration is present in a contract between Roofer and Owner to roof Owner's house for $1,500.

TABLE 7–2	**Consideration**		
Promise	*Consideration*	*Detriment*	*Bargained for*
Owner's promise to pay $1,500	Roofer's promise to roof the house	Roofer was under no prior obligation to do the job	Roofer's promise induced Owner's promise
Roofer's promise to roof the house	Owner's promise to pay $1,500	Owner was under no prior obligation to pay Roofer	Owner's promise induced Roofer's promise

Past Consideration

Past consideration is not bargained for and, therefore, cannot provide the consideration for a present promise. For example, assume that Employer says to Worker, "In consideration of your many years of service to this company, I promise to pay you a pension of $2,000 per month when you retire." Worker's past services were not given in exchange for the promise of a pension. Therefore, there is no consideration for the promise.

The Preexisting Duty Rule

A promise to perform or the performance of a preexisting legal duty is not a detriment and, therefore, is not consideration. For example, if Professor says to Student, "I promise to pay you $50 if you don't cheat on the final exam," the promise is unenforceable because Student is already under a legal duty not to cheat.

The preexisting duty rule has made modifications of existing contracts unenforceable. For example, assume that Owner and Builder contract for the construction of a swimming pool at a price of $5,000, with payment due on completion. After Builder starts work, Builder finds that due to unanticipated soil conditions the pool will cost $7,000 to build. Owner promises to pay Builder an extra $2,000 and Builder completes the job. Under the preexisting duty rule, Owner's promise of an additional $2,000 is unenforceable because the only consideration given by Builder was completion of the pool, something Builder was obligated to do by the original contract. However, if Builder also promised that Owner could pay for the pool 30 days after completion, Builder has given new consideration—30 days' credit.

Recently, a trend away from strict application of the preexisting duty rule has emerged. The *Restatement (Second) of Contracts* provides that for executory contracts, that is, those not fully performed on either side, a good faith modification in response to unanticipated conditions is enforceable without consideration.

Courts in a growing number of states are adopting this approach. UCC Section 2-209 provides that any good faith modification of a contract for the sale of goods is enforceable without consideration.

Mutuality of Obligation

When the consideration for a promise is another promise, the parties must be under mutual duties to perform. If one party's promise is illusory, such as a promise to perform "if I feel like it," mutuality is lacking and the other party's promise is unenforceable. This problem can arise where one party retains discretion over whether, and to what extent, he or she will perform. Courts frequently infer duties to use reasonable efforts to perform or to exercise the discretion in good faith to avoid interpreting such promises as illusory.

Statute of Frauds

Generally, oral contracts are enforceable, although their existence may be difficult to prove. Certain types of contracts, however, are not enforceable unless they are evidenced by a writing. The **Statute of Frauds** requires written evidence for promises:

- Made in consideration of marriage.
- For sales of goods priced $500 or more.
- For transfers of real property other than a lease of less than one year's duration.
- That cannot, by their terms, be performed within one year.
- To answer for the debt of another.

The first three promises are self-explanatory. Promises that by their terms cannot be performed within one year refer only to those promises that expressly call for more than a year's commitment. If the promise can be performed within one year, it does not fall within the Statute of Frauds even if a longer duration is contemplated. For example, if Worker promises Company to work for the next two years, the contract must be evidenced by a writing because it cannot be performed within one year. But if Worker promises Company to work until retirement, the Statute of Frauds does not apply because Worker can retire at any time. A writing is not required, even if Worker is 25 years old and intends to work for 40 more years.

Promises to answer for the debt of another come within the Statute of Frauds only if they are made to the creditor. A promise made to the debtor does not require a writing. Even where the promise is made to the creditor, a writing is not required if the promisor is also the debtor. For example, if Jill telephones the Ace Department Store and says, "Jack is coming over. Sell him a new suit and send me the bill," no writing is required. Jack never becomes indebted to Ace. When Jack makes a purchase, Jill becomes a debtor; thus, she has promised to pay her own debt rather than Jack's.

A promise to answer for the debt of another does not require a writing if the main purpose of the promise is to benefit the promisor. For example, assume that Big Bank holds a mortgage on David Debtor's home. Bank promises an insurance company that if Debtor fails to pay the premium for fire insurance, Bank will pay. Bank's main purpose is to protect its interest in the property, as the mortgage would be of little value if the property was destroyed by fire and was not insured.

Compliance with the Statute of Frauds

The Statute of Frauds does not require that the contract be in writing; it requires only that there be a written evidence of the contract signed by the party to be charged with enforcement of the contract. For example, a typical laundry ticket could be sufficient to satisfy the Statute of Frauds' requirement of a signed writing in a lawsuit against the laundry. Courts can also integrate several documents to arrive at the written evidence needed to satisfy the Statute of Frauds. For example, letters between parties or internal company memos can be integrated to show the existence of a contract.

The requirement of a signature is satisfied by any mark that is intended to authenticate a document. For example, a company's name on stationary letterhead would satisfy the signature requirement. A federal statute known as E-Sign was enacted to encourage the use of electronic signatures, such as those used in online transactions, in interstate commerce. E-Sign states that a contract may not be denied legal effect, validity, or enforceability solely because an electronic signature or electronic record was used in its formation.

In goods transactions between merchants, UCC 2–201 permits a written confirmation of a contract to satisfy the requirement of a signed writing if the party who receives the confirmation has reason to know its contents and does not send written notice of objection to the sender of the confirmation within 10 days after the confirmation is received. This allows the sender to enforce the contract against the recipient of the confirmation even though the recipient's signature is not on any writing. For example, if a merchant telephoned an order to a supplier for goods priced over $500, and the supplier sent an invoice to the buyer, who sees it and does not object to it within 10 days, the supplier can enforce the purchase agreement against the buyer even though the buyer did not sign anything. The written confirmation without written notice of objection substitutes for a signed writing in these circumstances.

Even where no writing exists at all, courts can enforce an oral contract where the parties have performed part of their obligation, and the performance is referable to the contract. That is, if the performance can be explained only on the basis of the existence of a contract, the performance serves as a substitute for a signed writing.

In the following case, the court discusses issues relating to the requirement of consideration and the Statute of Frauds' requirement of a writing.

DAVIES V. MARTEL LABORATORY SERVICES, INC.
545 N.E.2d 475 (Ill. App. 1989)

Janet Davies (Plaintiff) sued Martel Laboratory Services, Inc. (Defendant) for breach of an oral contract for permanent employment. The trial court dismissed Davies' complaint. Davies appealed, and the Appellate Court of Illinois reversed the trial court's dismissal and remanded the case for further proceedings. What follows is the appellate court's decision.

Presiding Justice Murray

Plaintiff Janet Davies appeals from an order of the circuit court of Cook County dismissing her . . . complaint for breach of an oral contract for permanent employment against defendant Martel Laboratory Services, Inc. She argues that the trial court erred in granting Martel's motion to dismiss her complaint based on its determination that she failed to establish consideration for an enforceable contract of permanent employment and that the court erred in granting Martel's motion based on its finding that her cause of action was barred by the Statute of Frauds. For the reasons set forth below, we reverse and remand the cause for further proceedings.

■   ■   ■

Davies . . . filed [a] . . . complaint in the trial court, the subject of this appeal, alleging that Martel hired her in April 1980 to perform oil analyses and mapping work until approximately March 1, 1983. During that time she was an employee at will. In the latter part of February 1983, however, she attended a dinner conference with Harold Flynn, Martel's president. At that time Flynn "made an offer [to her] to alter, change and modify the terms and conditions of [her] contract of employment." The terms and conditions were that she "would be made a Vice-President of MARTEL earning $40,000.00 per year" if she "would obtain an MBA Degree" and, if she accepted the offer then and there, "she would immediately be designated a permanent employee of MARTEL

and also appointed a member of the President's Council for which she would assume and become responsible for a policy making role for MARTEL." Flynn also promised that Martel would contribute one-half of her expenses incurred in obtaining her MBA, while she would be responsible for the other one-half. She immediately accepted the offer, thereby becoming a permanent employee. On March 1, one week later, she attended her first meeting as a member of the President's Council. In the fall of 1983, she enrolled at Northwestern University to begin an MBA program. Davies' complaint further alleged that she continued working, assuming additional duties and responsibilities as a "policy maker for MARTEL." On October 12, 1984, Martel terminated her employment without cause.

In response to Davies' complaint, Martel filed a motion to dismiss. On April 20, 1988, the trial court granted Martel's motions, finding that Davies failed to demonstrate consideration for Martel's oral promise of permanent employment and that her claim was also barred by the Statute of Frauds. A subsequent motion by Davies to amend her complaint was denied by the court, and this appeal followed.

To be enforceable, an oral contract for permanent employment, like any other contract, must be supported by sufficient consideration. It is also well settled that any act or promise which is of benefit to one party or a disadvantage to the other is a sufficient consideration to support a contract.

In the instant case, Martel contends that Davies suffered no disadvantage or detriment and therefore the trial court correctly ruled that her complaint was insufficient in law because it failed to allege sufficient consideration. Specifically, Martel contends that Davies' pursuit of an MBA degree was in fact a benefit to her, making her more marketable, and not a disadvantage or detriment. While this fact may be true, it is not necessarily legally so. The words "benefit" and "detriment" in contract cases involving consideration have technical meanings. "Detriment" as used in determining the sufficiency of consideration to support a contract means " 'legal detriment as distinguished from detriment in fact. It means giving up something which immediately prior thereto the promisee was privileged to retain, or doing or refraining from something which he was then privileged not to do, or not to refrain from doing.'" (*Hamilton Bancshares, Inc. v. Leroy* (1985), 131 Ill. App. 3d 907, 913, quoting 1 Williston, Contracts § 102A, at 380-82 (3d ed. 1957).) For example, a promise to give up smoking may be a benefit to the promisee's health, but a promise to give up smoking is also a legal detriment and sufficient consideration to support a contract.

In the present case, Davies did not have to obtain an MBA degree and expend her own time and money in doing so in order to continue as an at-will employee of Martel's; she could have continued to perform oil analyses and mapping work rather than enter the ivied walls of Northwestern. Nor does it appear that Davies was obligated to serve as a member on Martel's President's Council and to assume additional duties and responsibilities. In other words, Davies was privileged to refrain from serving on Martel's council and from pursuing an MBA degree. By giving up her privilege to refrain from so acting, Davies clearly could be said to have suffered a legal detriment, which would constitute sufficient consideration to support the alleged oral contract between the parties. Based on the foregoing, and in light of the fact that a motion to dismiss admits all facts well pleaded together with all reasonable inferences which can be drawn from those facts, we find that

Davies' amended complaint sufficiently alleged consideration in support of the contract at issue.

We also find, contrary to Martel's argument, that the trial court erroneously applied the Statute of Frauds to bar Davies' claim of breach of contract. The Statute of Frauds requires that any contract that cannot be performed within one year must be in writing. Martel contends that the alleged oral contract of permanent employment was incapable of being performed within one year, based on the fact that it was "contingent on plaintiff obtaining an MBA degree, that an MBA program at Northwestern University involves two years of study for full-time students and five years for part-time students, and that Davies did not even enroll in the program until the fall of 1983," more than six months after the oral contract.

Based on the foregoing, the oral contract would be unenforceable under the Statute of Frauds if in fact it was pleaded by Davies in her amended complaint that her permanent employment was contingent upon her obtaining an MBA degree. However, that is not the oral agreement pleaded by Davies. Rather, Davies pleaded that she would be immediately designated a permanent employee of Martel and also appointed a member of Martel's President's Council if she accepted the terms and conditions of the offer "then and there" (made a *commitment* to pursue an MBA degree and serve as a member of the President's Council), which she did do. On the other hand, the obvious inferences of the complaint unrebutted by anything in the record are that Davies' appointment as a vice-president of the company was predicated on her attaining the MBA, not the permanent employment promise. The fact that she could not complete the MBA program within one year might be a Statute of Frauds defense to that portion of the oral contract whereby Martel promised to make her a vice-president and pay her $40,000 annually. It is not a defense, however, to the promise to make her a permanent Martel employee, which she accepted immediately.

Moreover, we further observe that the Statute of Frauds has no application where there has been part performance by one of the contracting parties in reliance upon the agreement. Here, whether in fact Davies relied on Flynn's alleged oral promise and enrolled in the MBA program based on that promise, as she alleges in her amended complaint, is a question of fact that could not be decided on a motion to dismiss her amended complaint.

In light of the foregoing, the judgment of the circuit court of Cook County is reversed and the cause remanded for further proceedings.

Reversed and remanded.

Case Questions

1. Why did the appellate court find that Davies' complaint alleged sufficient consideration in support of the contract at issue in the case?

2. The appellate court stated that *[t]he words "benefit" and "detriment" in contract cases involving consideration use technical meanings.* What is the technical meaning of "detriment" for purposes of the doctrine of consideration?

3. Martel argued that the oral agreement between Martel and Davies was unenforce-able according to the provision of the Statute of Frauds that requires a contract that cannot be performed within one year to be in writing. Why was the appellate court not convinced by that argument?

4. If the oral agreement had been that Davies' permanent employment was contingent upon her obtaining an MBA degree, would the agreement have been enforceable? Explain. If not, what should Davies do under such circumstances? If you were in Davies' position, how difficult would it be for you to ask the president of the company to put his promise in writing? When you want someone to put their oral promises in writing, can you think of a way to express the request so that they might accede in the request? How would you politely respond if the other person were to say, "What's the matter, don't you trust me?"

5. What would be the effect of proof by Davies that she relied on Flynn's oral promise and enrolled in the MBA program based on that promise? Explain.

Alternatives to the Bargain Theory of Contracts

Alternatives to the bargain theory of contracts exist for courts to provide remedies in cases not meeting classical contract law's requirement of a bargained-for exchange. These alternative theories stem from an area of law known as the law of equity. Courts have drawn upon equity law to apply doctrines to do equity in a given case. The three alternative theories are: promissory estoppel, the doctrine of moral obligation, and the doctrine of quasi contract.

Promissory Estoppel or Reliance Theory

Under the doctrine of promissory estoppel, courts have enforced promises that lacked consideration and oral promises that would otherwise be unenforceable under the Statute of Frauds. Under the doctrine, a party is "estopped" to deny the existence of a promise. Three conditions must be met for the doctrine of promissory estoppel to apply:

1. There must be a *promise* from a promisor to a promisee.
2. There must be *reliance* by the promisee upon the promise.
3. The reliance must be to the promisee's *substantial economic detriment.*

The promise must be one that a reasonable promisor should foresee would induce reliance. The promisee's reliance must be reasonable. The requirement of substantial economic detriment means that an injustice can be avoided only by enforcing the promise.

For example, assume Employer promised Worker a pension "in consideration of" Worker's long years of service, and as a result Worker retired. Although there is no consideration for Employer's promise, it could be enforced under the doctrine of promissory estoppel. This is because Worker substantially relied on the promise by retiring. A reasonable employer should foresee that an employee would retire on being promised a pension. Worker's leaving the job would cause a substantial economic deteriment. The following case further illustrates the use of promissory estoppel.

ALLEN M. CAMPBELL CO., INC. v. VIRGINIA METAL INDUSTRIES, INC.
708 F.2d 930 (4th Cir. 1983)

Allen M. Campbell Co. (plaintiff) bid on a contract with the U.S. Navy to construct housing at Camp LeJeune, North Carolina. Approximately one half-hour before Campbell's bid was due, Virginia Metal Industries, Inc. (defendant) quoted plaintiff a price of $193,121 to supply doors and frames. Campbell used this quote in making its bid to the Navy. The Navy awarded Campbell the contract but Virginia Metals refused to supply the doors. Campbell sued and the trial court dismissed the claim. The Fourth Circuit Court of Appeals reversed.

Judge Murnaghan

In carrying out the functions of a judge, one comes to realize that there are very few cases indeed in which ultimately the facts do not control the outcome. Arguments impeccable in their abstract reliance upon broadly phrased principles of law tend to evaporate when the equities point to a different result. Purely linguistic considerations should not be permitted to outweigh substance.

■   ■   ■

As a consequence of the gigantic achievements in the field of contract law. . . , we have on rare occasions to confront situations posing some difficulty because they did not fit precisely into . . . the patterned concepts. . . . Nothing, not even the law of contracts, however, is altogether perfect.

We are not the first court to encounter the situation where there has been a promise unsupported by consideration which has occasioned reliance and change of position so that the promisor who backs away from his undertaking visits a real hardship on the promisee. An absence of consideration in such cases should not permit an unjust result. Rather, the law has developed the concept of promissory estoppel which allows recovery even in the absence of consideration where reliance and change of position to the detriment of the promisee make it unconscionable not to enforce the promise or to award damages for its breach.

■　　■　　■

At the present stage of the case, action in reliance on the promise to sell doors and frames for $193,121 plus taxes cannot be disputed. It was alleged in the amended complaint: "Plaintiff submitted its bid for the entire project to the Government in reliance upon defendant's quoted price for the hollow metal doors and frames."

In the case as pleaded by Campbell, the elements of a promissory estoppel are clearly present. Under the well-pleaded allegations of fact, even in the absence of consideration, there was a sufficiently binding promise by Virginia Metal.

Case Questions

1. What promise was Campbell seeking to enforce? Why was there no consideration for it?

2. Could Campbell have provided consideration? Explain.

3. Explain how Campbell met the requirements of promissory estoppel in this case. How does this case differ from the promise of a pension mentioned in the text?

4. Assume that after the Navy awarded Campbell the job, Campbell approached another supplier and asked it to undercut Virginia Metal's price quote. If the other supplier declined, could Campbell still enforce Virginia Metal's promise? If the other supplier did undercut Virginia Metal, could Virginia Metal sue Campbell? Explain.

Moral Obligation

Generally, a moral obligation to keep a promise is not sufficient to make the promise legally enforceable. However, if a promise becomes unenforceable by operation of law, a subsequent promise to keep the original promise is enforceable without new consideration. For example, assume John owes Mary $500, but because the statute of limitations period for bringing suit has expired, John's debt is uncollectible. If John promises to pay the $500 anyway, the promise is enforced without new consideration.

Quasi Contract

If a doctor finds a pedestrian unconscious on the street and treats the pedestrian, no contract has arisen between the two. An unconscious pedestrian cannot accept the doctor's offer.

However, where a party confers a benefit on another party with a reasonable expectation of payment, and the recipient of the benefit would be unjustly enriched if not required to pay for it, a court implies a contract as a matter of law. Under such a *quasi contract,* the doctor is able to recover the reasonable value of the services provided.

Policing the Bargain

Courts generally do not get involved in reviewing the fairness of particular contracts. If an agreement has been reached, a court cannot protect a party from a bad deal. In certain cases, however, courts refuse to enforce a promise because of a party's status. Courts protect particularly vulnerable parties deemed to lack the capacity to contract. In other cases, courts may rescind or reform a contract if a party's conduct produces a defect in the bargaining process. Finally, courts may refuse to enforce all or part of a contract if its substantive provisions are illegal or unconscionable.

Capacity

People so mentally infirm that they cannot understand the nature and consequences of their actions lack the capacity to contract. People who have not yet attained the age of majority—usually 18 but in some states 21—also lack contractual capacity. The overwhelming majority of capacity problems arise in contracts made by minors.

Minors have the right to disaffirm their contracts at any time prior to reaching the age of majority. On reaching the age of majority, a party may choose to disaffirm or ratify the contract. Ratification may be implied from the party's conduct or from the party's failure to disaffirm within a reasonable time after reaching the age of majority. An adult has no power to disaffirm. An adult is bound by a contract with a minor unless the minor disaffirms.

If a minor disaffirms, the law in most states only requires the minor to return to the adult any remaining consideration. It does not require the minor to make restitution.

For example, assume that Minor buys a car on credit from Dealer. After making only one payment and with an outstanding balance of $8,000, Minor is involved in an accident that totally destroys the car. In most states, if Minor disaffirms, Minor need only return the remaining wreck to Dealer and need not make restitution for the damage or the value of the use of the car.

Minors are responsible for their contracts for necessities, such as food, clothing, shelter, and medical care. A minor who disaffirms such a contract is liable in quasi contract for the reasonable value of the benefit received.

Defects in the Bargaining Process

Defects in the bargaining process may result in a court rescinding, or occasionally reforming, an agreement. A party's consent may have been obtained through misrepresentation or under duress or may be the result of a mistake.

Misrepresentation

Where a misrepresentation of a material fact is made and a party justifiably relies on the misrepresentation, the deceived party may rescind the transaction and receive restitution for any benefits conferred on the deceptive party. Misrepresentations need not be fraudulent (i.e., intentional), or even negligent, as long as they are material. A misrepresentation is material if it would likely influence the conduct of a reasonable person. A fraudulent misrepresentation is presumed to be material.

Only misrepresentations of fact are actionable. Misrepresentations of opinion are not actionable unless the deceived party is relying on the deceiver's expertise. Statements that an item is the "best buy" or a "superb value" usually are dismissed as puffing and nonactionable opinion. Similarly, predictions of future events are usually considered to be nonactionable opinion.

In certain circumstances, nondisclosure may amount to actionable misrepresentation. Deliberate concealment is actionable, as is deceptive partial disclosure. There is a duty to disclose latent defects and to correct misconceptions caused by the nondisclosing party. A duty to disclose also arises if the parties are in a fiduciary or other special relationship.

Nondisclosure or misrepresentation is actionable only if justifiably relied on. Reliance is not justified if the deceived party knows the representation is false or could discover it through a reasonable investigation.

Duress

Duress occurs when one party's wrongful act overcomes the free will of another party. If a party's agreement is obtained with threats of physical harm, the contract is void because of duress. The law considers the contract to have never been made. Duress can also result from economic pressure. Economic duress that results from a wrongful act renders a contract voidable. The victim of the duress may rescind the contract.

For example, assume that Repairer had a contract to repair a machine for Mechanic. Because the machine was indispensable to Mechanic's business, Repairer agreed to pick up the machine at the close of business on Friday and have it ready for Mechanic to pick up Monday morning. When Mechanic arrived on Monday, Repairer said that the machine was ready but would not be returned to Mechanic unless Mechanic promised to pay a debt that Mechanic's brother owed to Repairer and had refused to pay. Mechanic desperately needed the machine, so she promised to pay her brother's debt. Mechanic can rescind her promise because of duress.

Mistake

The parties may allocate the risk of mistake in their contract. The allocation may be expressed, or it may be implied from what a reasonable person would expect under the circumstances. For example, assume that Jack finds a gemstone and sells it to Jill for $50. Neither party knows what type of gem it is, but both assume that, although it is pretty, it is not very valuable. Under these circumstances, it is reasonable to imply that Jill is assuming the risk that the gem is worthless and Jack is assuming the risk that it is valuable. If the gem turns out to be a diamond worth $5,000, the mistake is not grounds for Jack to rescind the contract.

If the parties have not allocated the risk, a mutual mistake in a basic assumption allows either party to rescind the contract. If only one party is mistaken, rescission is allowed under some circumstances. Many courts allow rescission if the nonmistaken party knew or should have known of the other party's mistake. More liberal courts allow rescission if enforcement would be oppressive to the mistaken party and rescission would not impose a hardship on the nonmistaken party.

Sometimes the parties reach an oral agreement but make a mistake in reducing it to writing. In such a case, a court reforms the writing to conform to the original agreement.

Unconscionability

UCC Section 2–302 authorizes a court to deny or limit enforcement of a contract or part of a contract that it finds to be unconscionable. Unconscionability is determined as of the time the contract is made. Unconscionability exists where one party did not have a meaningful choice and where the terms are so one-sided as to be oppressive. Absence of meaningful choice has been found where there was a large disparity in bargaining power, the term was hidden in fine print, or the term was presented on a take-it-or-leave-it basis.

Courts have analogized to the UCC and applied the concept of unconscionability to contracts that did not involve sales of goods. Unconscionability is most commonly found in consumer transactions. As the following case illustrates, the concept may also apply in commercial transactions.

ART'S FLOWER SHOP, INC. V. C & P TELEPHONE CO.
413 S.E.2d 670 (W.Va. 1992)

Art's Flower Shop (plaintiff) contracted with C & P (defendant) to place an ad in C & P's Yellow Pages. C & P failed to run the ad and Art's sued. A clause in the contract limited C & P's liability to twice the price of the ad. The trial court held that Art's damages were so limited. The West Virginia Supreme Court reversed.

Justice Brotherton

[I]n many commercial transactions, some inequality of bargaining power exists. Since many of these situations may not revolve around an unconscionable contract despite that inequality, something more is required.

■   ■   ■

The end result of this analysis is that the liability clause in the 1978 contract between C & P and Art's Flower shop is void for unconscionability. The positions of C & P and Art's Flower Shop were grossly unequal: C & P had the only Yellow Pages directory in the area. As a monopoly, C &

P had the right to make the Yellow Pages an integral part of their regular white pages directory and the name recognition to make it successful. No evidence was presented of a comparable, meaningful alternative to a Yellow Page advertisement. . . . Art's Flower Shop . . . obviously was in no position to bargain for the contract.

The final element in the analysis is the determination of whether unfair contract terms exist. While the contract terms are valid in and of themselves, the limitation of out-of-pocket damages experienced as a result of C & P's omission of a contracted-for advertisement to twice the cost of the ad is unreasonably favorable to C & P. Under the terms of the liability clause in the contract,

C & P's negligent omission could cost a client its livelihood, yet C & P would be liable for only minimal costs, no matter how damaging its omission. Such a result cannot stand. Contrary to C & P's assertions, radio and TV advertisements, flyers and other methods of advertising Art's services are inadequate and costly compared to the Yellow Pages advertisements.

Case Questions

1. Was it significant that this was a commercial contract rather than a consumer contract? Explain.

2. What factors led the court to find that Art's had no meaningful choice but to agree to the damage limitation? Could Art's have advertised elsewhere? Should that matter?

3. What factors led the court to find the limitation oppressive? Could there be any commercially legitimate reasons for the damage limitation? Explain.

4. Jones, a welfare recipient, agreed to purchase on credit a freezer for $900 plus finance charges, property insurance, and credit life insurance. The total cost amounted to $1,439.69. The retail value of the freezer was $300. Was the contract unconscionable? Why or why not?

5. Williams purchased a chair from Walker-Thomas Furniture Co. for $54.67, on credit. In fine print on the reverse side of the credit agreement a clause provided that if Williams made additional credit purchases, all payments would be allocated pro rata to each purchase. In the event of default, Walker-Thomas retained the right to repossess the goods.

   Over the course of several years, Williams made numerous additional credit purchases from Walker-Thomas. She then defaulted on one payment. At the time of default Williams had paid $1,400 on a total debt of $1,800. However, because of the pro rata allocation of her payments she was not credited with fully paying for any items. Her outstanding balance on the first chair she had bought was 25 cents. If Walker-Thomas seeks to repossess all of the items will it succeed? Explain.

Ethical Dilemmas/Issues

You are the president of a large real estate rental company. Your standard residential lease has a clause that provides, "Tenant agrees that landlord shall not be liable for any personal injuries or property damage sustained by tenant on landlord's property or resulting from landlord's negligence." A recent decision from your state's supreme court held that a similar clause in another landlord's lease was unconscionable. The court refused to enforce the clause.

Several of your resident managers have advised you not to drop the clause from your leases. They reason that although a court would not enforce the clause, the tenants do not know that. In their experience, the clause deters tenants from pressing claims for minor injuries. As one resident manager explained, "If you take the clause out, every time someone slips and skins a knee, we'll see a claim." Your liability insurance company agrees and will raise your premiums if you do not retain the clause.

What are the ethical issues in this problem? What would you do? Explain.

Illegality

A contract is illegal if its formation or performance is tortious, forbidden by statute, or contrary to public policy. For example, contracts to bribe public officials, to embezzle money, to gamble in a state that prohibits gambling, and to sell cocaine are illegal.

The concept of public policy is difficult to define with precision but it enables courts to deny enforcement to contracts which they believe injure the public interest. One such contract that has received considerable judicial attention is the covenant not to compete. The following case illustrates the current approach to such promises.

WILEY v. ROYAL CUP, INC.
370 S.E.2d 744 (Ga. 1988)

Wiley (defendant) was district sales manager for Royal Cup (plaintiff). Wiley's employment contract provided that for one year after termination of employment, he would not disclose any of Royal Cup's business methods; sales, service, or distribution techniques; prices; or customer names and addresses. It also provided that for two years after termination, Wiley would not solicit business in 18 Georgia counties from anyone who had been a Royal Cup customer or who had been solicited by Royal Cup during the two years before termination. The trial court enjoined Wiley from breaching both provisions. The Georgia Supreme Court affirmed in part and reversed in part.

Justice Gregory

In a case involving a covenant not to compete, we held that territorial restrictions which relate to the territory in which the employee worked are generally enforceable. Those restrictions which relate to the territory in which the employer does business but the employee did not work will not be enforced absent a showing by the employer of the legitimate business interest sought to be protected.

It appears that the justification for this difference in treatment is that a court will accept as prima facie valid a covenant related to the territory where the employee was employed as a legitimate protection of the employer's investment in customer relations and good will. Thus a court will enforce an agreement prohibiting an employee from pirating his former employer's customers served by the employee during the employment, at the employer's direct or indirect expense. Conversely, a court will not accept as prima facie valid a covenant related to the territory where the employer does business where the only justification is that the employer wants to avoid competition by the employee in that area.

We apply this same requirement to a territorial restriction in a covenant not to solicit. In the case before us, the territorial restriction goes beyond the area in which Wiley served the customers of Royal Cup: Wiley is prohibited from soliciting customers in Bartow and Hall counties, counties in which Royal Cup does business, but where, it is undisputed, Wiley has never worked on behalf of Royal Cup. We conclude that the effect of this territorial restriction is not to protect the legitimate business interests of Royal Cup, but to prevent Wiley from competing against Royal Cup in these counties. As such, the territorial restriction is unreasonable and must fall.

■   ■   ■

[T]he entire covenant not to solicit is void. The trial court erred in holding it is enforceable against Wiley.

Wiley complains that the trial court erred in holding the covenant not to disclose is valid.

■   ■   ■

[I]n determining the reasonableness of a covenant not to disclose, the courts must consider "(1) whether the employer is attempting to protect confidential information relating to the business, such as . . . methods of operation, names of customers, personnel data . . . and (2) whether the restraint is reasonably related to the protection of the information." In this case the covenant specifically prohibits the disclosure of methods of operation and prices used by Royal Cup, as well as the names of Royal Cup's customers. Wiley has acknowledged in his employment contract that these items constitute confidential information. We hold that this restraint, imposed on Wiley for a period of one year may be enforced independently of a covenant not to compete whether it is in the same or distinct provisions of the employment agreement.

Justice Weltner
(Dissenting)

I respectfully dissent.

■   ■   ■

[A] covenant prohibiting solicitation of the employer's customers is less restrictive than a covenant prohibiting competition. . . ."

■   ■   ■

[W]e do not apply to such covenants all of the limitations that pertain to covenants not to compete.

Rather, the inquiry should be whether *in this case* it is unreasonable to require a district sales manager to covenant not to solicit his employer's customers in an 18 county area when, in twelve of those counties, Royal Cup had customers. Where Royal Cup had no customers, the restraint upon Wiley is almost illusory, as it prohibits the solicitation of "customers" that do not exist.

I suggest that this limitation is entirely reasonable. Wiley should be held to his covenants.

Case Questions

1. What is the difference between a covenant not to compete and a covenant not to solicit?
2. Why did the majority hold that the covenant not to solicit was void in this case? Why did Justice Weltner disagree?
3. The court voided the entire covenant not to solicit. Should it have enforced the covenant in the counties where Wiley had worked? Why or why not?
4. If the court refused to enforce any part of the covenant not to solicit, why did it enforce the covenant not to disclose confidential information?
5. Jackson was employed as a hairdresser for Hair Salon, Inc. Jackson's employment con-

tract prohibited Jackson from competing within a five-mile radius of the Hair Salon store for two years after leaving Hair Salon's employ. Is the covenant not to compete enforceable? Why or why not?

If a contract is illegal, usually a court will leave the parties where it finds them. There are several exceptions to this general rule. Courts enforce a contract that contravenes a statute if enforcement would be consistent with the purpose of the statute. For example, if a party does business without a required license and the license statute's purpose is to raise money rather than protect customers and clients, courts would enforce the unlicensed party's contracts. If the license is required for protection, courts would enforce the contracts on request of the customers or clients but not on the request of the unlicensed party.

Courts considering illegal contracts often inquire into whether the illegality involves *moral turpitude,* that is, serious misconduct. If the illegality does not involve moral turpitude and the parties are not *in pare delicto,* that is, not equally blameworthy, courts allow the more innocent party to recover in quasi contract for benefits conferred on the other party. If the illegality does not involve moral turpitude, a party who renounces the bargain and prevents the illegal act from taking place may recover in quasi contract.

Contract Interpretation

Frequently, contract disputes do not involve the existence or enforceability of a contract. Rather, they focus on what the contract's provisions mean. In interpreting contracts, courts inquire into how a reasonable person in the position of the parties would interpret the agreement. Often, courts look to the past practices of the industry. In written documents, ambiguities often are resolved against the drafter because that is the party responsible for the ambiguity.

The Parol Evidence Rule

The **parol evidence rule** provides that if a contract is reduced to writing and the parties intend the writing to be the final and complete evidence of the agreement, prior representations or agreements (i.e., parol evidence) may not be used to vary or contradict the writing. In such a case, the final writing is called an *integration.* Parties often specify that their writings are intended to be the final expressions of their agreements to the exclusion of all prior representations. Such clauses are called *integration, merger,* or *zipper clauses.*

Even if a writing is an integration, parol evidence may establish reasons for rescinding the contract, such as fraud, duress, mistake, or lack of capacity. Parol evidence may also explain the meaning of ambiguous terms contained in the writing. Finally, parol evidence may establish modifications agreed to after the original written contract.

Performance and Breach

A breach of contract occurs if a party has a duty to perform and fails to do so. A party may not have a duty to perform if conditions precedent to that duty have not been fulfilled. A party's duty to perform may be discharged by unforeseen subsequent events.

Conditions

The two types of conditions contained in contracts are express and constructive. **Express conditions** are those established by the parties themselves. For example, if George buys a $100,000 life insurance policy naming Sally as beneficiary, the insurance company has promised to pay Sally $100,000 if George dies. George's death is an express condition precedent to the insurance company's duty to pay Sally.

Express conditions must be literally fulfilled before a duty to perform arises. If George is seriously ill, the insurance company is not obligated to pay Sally; its obligation arises only if George dies.

Constructive conditions are implied as a matter of law from the order of performance contemplated by the parties. If one party is to perform first, that party's performance is a constructive condition precedent to the other party's duty to perform. If both parties are to perform at the same time, each party's performance is a constructive condition concurrent to the other party's duty to perform.

Constructive conditions need only be substantially fulfilled for a party's duty to perform to arise. For example, assume that Owner contracts with Builder to build a house according to stated specifications, with Owner to pay for the house on completion. Although the specifications call for using a certain brand of pipe for the plumbing, Builder uses a different brand that is identical in quality to the pipe specified.

Builder's completion of the house as specified is a constructive condition precedent to Owner's duty to pay. The condition has not been literally fulfilled because of the deviation from the specified brand of pipe. However, because the condition has been substantially fulfilled, Owner must pay.

Excuses for Nonperformance

The parties in their contract may expressly or impliedly allocate the risk of unforeseen changes in circumstances. Often, they fail to do so. Generally, if unforeseen events render performance impossible, the duty to perform is discharged. For example, if the subject matter of the contract is destroyed, the duty to perform is discharged. Similarly, supervening illegality discharges the duty to perform. Death of an individual who was to personally render services also discharges the duty to perform.

UCC Section 2–615 extends the doctrine of impossibility to cases of unforeseen impracticability. Courts in a few states have added this liberalization to their general law of contracts, but the majority of states have confined it to the sale of goods.

A related doctrine is the rule of frustration of purpose. It was first recognized in a 1903 English case.[1] The defendant agreed to pay the plaintiff £75 to use the plaintiff's apartment for two days to view the coronation of King Edward VII. The coronation was unexpectedly canceled due to the King's illness. Performance of the contract remained possible, but the purpose of the contract had been frustrated. Accordingly, the duty to perform was discharged.

Breach by Anticipatory Repudiation

Most breaches of contract occur at the time for performance. Sometimes, a party may declare prior to the time for performance that he or she has no intention of ever performing. In such a case, the other party may treat the anticipatory repudiation as a current breach of contract and sue immediately for relief. For example, assume that Seller agrees to sell Buyer 100 widgets a month for six months. After two months, Seller tells Buyer that it will not sell any more widgets. Although the time for performance of the next four months' supply of widgets has not yet arisen, Buyer may treat Seller's repudiation as an immediate breach.

Remedies

The basic remedy for breach of contract is an award of money damages. The basic measure of damages is lost expectation. **Expectation** damages are calculated to place the victim of the breach in the position he or she would have been in had the contract been performed. The two alternative measures of damages are reliance and restitution. **Reliance** damages are calculated to place the victim of the breach in the position he or she would have been in had the contract never been made. **Restitution** damages are designed to place the breaching party in the position he or she would have been in had the contract never been made.

To illustrate the differences among the three measures of damage, assume that Builder agreed to subdivide a lot and build two apartment buildings and Owner agreed to pay Builder $1 million. Builder completed the first building at a cost of

---

[1] Krell v. Henry, 2 K.B. 740 (1903).

$350,000. The building had a market value of $600,000. Before Builder started work on the second building, Owner repudiated the contract. It would cost Builder $300,000 to build the second building.

If the contract had been fully performed, Builder would have made a profit of $350,000. It will take $700,000 (the lost profit plus the $350,000 spent on the first building) to put Builder in the same position as if the contract had been fully performed. Thus, Builder's expectation damages are $700,000.

Builder spent $350,000 that it would not have spent if there had been no contract. It will take $350,000 to put Builder in the same position as if no contract had been made. Thus, Builder's reliance damages are $350,000.

Owner received a building worth $600,000 that Owner would not have had if there had been no contract. To place Owner in the same position as if no contract had been made, Owner must pay Builder $600,000. Thus, Builder's restitution damages are $600,000.

There are several limitations on the amount of damages. First, damages must be calculable with reasonable certainty. Uncertainty is frequently a problem when the damages requested include lost profits. A new business with no track record to use as a basis for calculating lost profits may be unable to recover them because they are too uncertain.

Second, damages must be reasonably foreseeable. This principle was established in an 1854 English case.[2] The plaintiffs mill was shut down because of a broken shaft. The defendant agreed to ship the shaft to a company that would make a new one. The defendant breached the contract by excessively delaying the shipment, thereby prolonging the period that the mill was closed. The plaintiff sought to recover the profit lost during the excessive closing, but the court denied recovery because the defendant had no way of knowing that the mill was shut down.

Third, the victim of the breach must make reasonable efforts to mitigate damages. For example, if a supplier breaches a contract to supply widgets to a manufacturer, the manufacturer must make a reasonable effort to obtain an alternate source of supply.

Sometimes the parties may specify the amount of damages in the contract. Such provisions are called *liquidated damages.* They are enforceable if they are intended as remedies rather than penalties, if actual damages would be difficult to calculate, and if they represent reasonable estimates of the damage done.

Sometimes a party wants a court to order the breaching party to actually perform the contract rather than pay damages. Orders of **specific performance** are available if money damages would not provide an adequate remedy. However, an award of specific performance is subject to the court's equitable discretion. A court would not order specific performance if the order would be difficult to enforce or overly harsh on one of the parties. The party requesting specific per-

---

[2] Hadley v. Baxendale, 156 Eng. Rep. 145 (1854).

formance must have acted promptly in asserting his or her rights and must be free of wrongdoing or bad faith.

Chapter Problems

1. Define the following terms:
   a. Offer
   b. Revocation
   c. Acceptance
   d. Consideration
   e. Statute of Frauds
   f. Promissory estoppel
   g. Parol evidence rule
   h. Express and constructive conditions
   i. Expectation, reliance, and restitution
   j. Specific performance

2. Sally Black sent an unsolicited recipe for fruit flavors to be used in making ice cream to General Foods Corporation, along with a letter asking General Foods to compensate her if the company should decide to use it. A vice president of General Foods replied with a letter thanking her for her suggestion, but added, "We shall be happy to examine your suggestion but only with understanding that our use of it and your compensation, if any, rest entirely at our discretion." Ms. Black did not reply to the letter. Six months later General Foods introduced a new product that followed Ms. Black's suggestion exactly. Is Ms. Black entitled to compensation? Explain.

3. First Colonial Bank ran an advertisement in a local newspaper which invited investors to "Deposit $14,000 for 3 1/2 years and receive an RCA 20″ color t.v. and $20,136.12 upon maturity. Rate shown is 8 3/4 percent. T.V. carries manufacturer's warranty; deposits are fully insured to $100,000 by FDIC. Substantial penalty for early withdrawal."

   The advertisement contained an error. To get $20,136.12, an investment of $14,000.00 earning 8 3/4 percent had to remain on deposit for four years. Pamphlets on display in the bank's lobby advised this.

   Sally Saver responded to the advertisement and deposited $14,000. She did not see the display. First Colonial gave her the advertised t.v. and a certificate of deposit (CD) redeemable in 3 1/2 years with interest at a rate of 8 3/4 percent. No one advised her of the mistake in the ad. Three and one-half years later, Sally liquidated the CD. She received $18,823.93, representing three and one-half years' interest at 8 3/4 percent. Is the bank liable for the remaining $1,312.19? Explain.

4. Architectural Glass & Metal Co. (AGM), an Indiana company, telephoned Falconer Glass Industries, a New York company, and ordered a special type

of glass manufactured by Falconer for use in a construction project in Indianapolis. Over the phone, the parties agreed on quantity, price, delivery, and payment terms. Falconer then mailed to AGM a form confirming the order. The form contained many preprinted terms, including one limiting Falconer's liability for defects in the product to replacement of the defective product or refund of the purchase price, and one requiring that any lawsuits arising out of the order be brought in New York. The product proved to be defective and the defects caused AGM $19,000 in damages. Is Falconer liable? If so, may AGM sue Falconer in Indiana, or must it sue in New York? Explain.

5. William Story made a promise to his nephew, William Story, 2d, that if he would refrain from drinking liquor, using tobacco, swearing, and playing cards or billiards for money until he became 21 years old, then he, William Story, would at that time pay William Story 2d, $5,000. William Story 2d fully performed his part of the agreement. William Story 2d had not been paid when William Story died. The executor of the estate of William Story would not allow the claim of William Story 2d for $5,000. Is William Story 2d's claim for the $5,000 enforceable? Explain.

6. Crabtree entered negotiations with Elizabeth Arden Sales Corp. concerning his employment as a sales manager. Ms. Arden, the corporation president, orally offered Crabtree a two-year contract starting at $40,000 per year, increasing to $45,000 after six months and $50,000 after one year, with an expense allowance of $5,000 per year. Crabtree replied, "Sounds interesting." Ms. Arden then had her secretary write a memo on a telephone order blank that happened to be at hand as follows:

EMPLOYMENT AGREEMENT WITH CRABTREE

Begin	$40,000
6 months	45,000
6 months	50,000
$5,000 per year expense money (2 years to make good)	

Two days later Crabtree telephoned his acceptance. On his first day at work, a payroll card was made up and signed by the company's general manager. It classified Crabtree as a sales manager and further stated:

First six months of employment	$40,000 per annum
Next six months of employment	$45,000 per annum
After one year of employment	$50,000 per annum

Crabtree received the first scheduled $5,000 pay raise but did not receive the second. When he inquired about it, Ms. Arden fired him. If Crabtree sues, will the contract be enforceable? Why or why not?

7. You own and operate a department store. For many years, you have rented space to Acme Furriers, Inc., to operate a fur concession in your store. Although Acme was a separate company, the appearance given the general public was that it was a department within your store. Unknown to you, Acme contracted with Fur Storage, Inc. (FSI) to provide cleaning and storage services to it. Acme accepted furs from customers in the spring and, for a fee, agreed to clean and store them until the late fall. Acme, in turn, paid FSI to clean and store the furs.

   Acme went bankrupt and closed. Acme's customers came to you to retrieve their furs. You approached Acme's president, who told you about FSI. You then asked FSI for the furs. FSI told you that Acme owed $1,500 for cleaning and storage of the furs. You offered to pay the $1,500, but FSI stated that Acme also owed it $4,500 for other services not involving your store. FSI demanded that you pay the entire $6,000 before it would release the furs. The customers are demanding their furs. The weather is getting colder by the day. What should you do? Explain.

8. Owner contracted with Red Roof Co. (RRC) for a new roof to be constructed on Owner's house for $2,000. The contract specified the type of shingles to be used and the color—asphalt gray. RRC completed the job, but ran out of asphalt gray shingles. It used three other colors—two other shades of gray and a dark blue. As a result, the roof is perfectly sound but Owner thinks it looks terrible. Must Owner pay RRC? Why or why not?

9. Gravel Contractors, Inc. (GCI) was the low bidder for a road construction contract and was awarded the contract by the state of Alaska. GCI's bid was so low because it owned a gravel pit near the site and intended to use gravel from that pit. After GCIs contract was announced, residents living near the gravel pit objected to GCIs hauling gravel from it. The local zoning board ruled that GCIs proposed use of the pit violated local zoning laws. GCI now has to purchase and haul gravel from a site 25 miles away and will incur an additional $20,000 in costs. Instead of making a $10,000 profit on the job, GCI will lose $10,000. Must GCI perform under the contract? Explain.

10. Al's Restaurant leased a storefront from Jane's Realty for three years. The lease provided that Al would pay a monthly rent of $1,000, maintain the premises in good repair, arrange for trash collection, and hold the restaurant open for business at least five days per week. The lease further provided that for any breach, Al's would be liable for $2,000 liquidated damages. Is this provision enforceable? Explain.

8   TORTS

Chapter Outline

Learning Objectives

After learning this chapter the student should be able to:

- Distinguish a tort from a breach of contract and a crime.
- Classify various torts under the appropriate headings: intentional, negligent, or strict liability.
- Recite the elements of a variety of torts, and apply them to factual situations involving business operations.

A **tort** is a civil wrong other than a breach of contract. The law recognizes the right of a victim of a tort to recover compensation in the form of money damages from the wrongdoer (tortfeasor).

A tort is not a crime, although many torts may also lead to criminal proceedings. In a tort action the victim sues to recover compensation from the tortfeasor

TABLE 8–1	**Classification of Torts**	
Intentional Torts	*Negligence*	*Strict Liability*
Intentional wrongdoing	Unreasonable conduct	Vicious animals Defective products Abnormally dangerous activities

for the injury that occurred. In contrast, in a criminal case the government brings charges seeking punishment (usually a fine or imprisonment) for the wrongdoer.

A breach of contract is not a tort. Contract duties arise by agreement of the parties. Tort duties, however, arise by operation of law and exist whether or not a person agrees to them. Tort law reflects society's determination of which injuries should be compensated, which interests protected, and which conduct deterred.

Tort law is important to business. Businesses harmed by the wrongful conduct of others may sue to recover damages. When businesses or their agents cause damage to others—whether they are customers, competitors, or strangers—liability may result. Insurance against possible damage awards is a necessary cost of doing business.

When an employee of a business commits a tort, the liability of the business is determined under the principle of vicarious liability or *respondeat superior* (let the master answer). Under this principle a business is liable for the torts of an employee who is acting within the scope of his or her employment. For example, if a pizza delivery driver causes an automobile accident while delivering a pizza, the driver's employer would be responsible for the damages inflicted on the other motorist.

The various types of torts can be divided into three categories: intentional torts, negligence, and strict liability torts (see Table 8–1).

Intentional Torts

Intentional torts are voluntary acts that invade a protected interest. In each of these torts, the tortfeasor intends to do the act that causes injury. The tortfeasor is liable for all reasonably foreseeable harm resulting from that intentional act.

Punitive Damages

Because a high degree of culpability attaches to intentional torts, the victim is entitled to punitive damages. These are damages intended to punish the offender, and further compensate the victim for wounded sensibilities. They are damages awarded above and beyond the compensatory damages. Compensatory damages included those for medical expenses, loss of wages, disability and pain and suffering. The amount of punitive damages to be awarded is normally within the province of the jury. Over the years large punitive damage awards have grabbed public attention. In the O.J. Simpson civil case the jury awarded punitives amounting to $25,000,000. The McDonalds' coffee cup spill case was first reported with a punitive damage award of $4 million. The United States Supreme Court made it clear in *BMW vs. Gore* that excessive punitive damage awards would be a denial of Due Process. The following U. S. Supreme Court case further defines the constitutional limits on the award of punitive damages.

BMW

STATE FARM MUTUAL AUTOMOBILE INSURANCE CO. VS. CAMPBELL
538 U.S. 408 (2003)

Curtis Campbell, while driving with his wife passed six vans travelling ahead of them on a two-way highway. Ospital, who was coming in the opposite direction swerved onto the shoulder, lost control of his car, and collided with another vehicle. Ospital was killed and the person in the other vehicle was rendered permanently disabled. The Campbells were not injured. Although investigators fixed the blame on Mr. Campbell, State Farm Insurance, the Campbell's insurance carrier refused offers to settle for the $50,000.00 policy limit. State Farm assured the Campbells that "their assets were safe, that they had no liability for the accident, that [State Farm] would represent their interests, and that they did not need to procure separate counsel." The jury determined that Mr. Campbell was at fault, and a judgment was rendered in the amount of $185,849.00.

At first State Farm refused to cover the excess liability in the amount of $135,849.00. The Campbells were told by State Farm's lawyer: "You may want to put for sale signs on your property to get things moving." State Farm refused to appeal the case.

The Campbells sued State Farm for bad faith refusal to settle, fraud and intentional infliction of emotional distress. (While that suit was pending State Farm paid the entire judgment.) The trial court granted State Farm's motion for summary judgment on the grounds that State Farm eventually paid the judgment. The trial court's decision was overturned by the Utah Court of Appeals. On remand the jury found that the refusal to settle was unreasonable because there was a substantial likelihood of an excess verdict. Evidence was admitted concerning State Farm's business practices for over 20 years in numerous states. The jury awarded the Campbells $2.6 million in compensatory damages and $145 million in punitive damages, which was reduced by the trial court to $1 million and $25 million respectively. Both parties appealed and the Utah Supreme Court reinstated the $145 million punitive damages award.

Justice Kennedy

. . . Compensatory damages "are intended to redress the concrete loss that the plaintiff has suffered by reason of the defendant's wrongful conduct." By contrast, punitive damages serve a broader function; they are aimed at deterrence and retribution. . . .

While States possess discretion over the imposition of punitive damages, it is well established that there are procedural and substantive constitutional limitations on these awards. The Due Process Clause of the Fourteenth Amendment prohibits the imposition of grossly excessive or arbitrary punishments on a tortfeasor. . . . The reason is that "[e]lementary notions of fairness enshrined in our constitutional jurisprudence dictate that a person receive fair notice not only of the conduct that will subject him to punishment, but also of the severity of the penalty that a State may impose." . . . To the extent an award is grossly excessive, it furthers no legitimate purpose and constitutes an arbitrary deprivation of property. . . .

■   ■   ■

In light of these concerns, in [*BMW of North America Inc. v. Gore*] we instructed courts reviewing punitive damages to consider three guideposts: (1) the degree of reprehensibility of the defendant's misconduct; (2) the disparity between the actual or potential harm suffered by the plaintiff and the punitive damages award; and (3) the difference between the punitive damages awarded by the jury and the civil penalties authorized or imposed in comparable cases. . . .

■   ■   ■

Under the principles outlined in *BMW of North America, Inc. v. Gore,* this case is neither close nor difficult. It was error to reinstate the jury's $145 million punitive damages award. We address each guidepost of *Gore* in some detail.

■   ■   ■

"[T]he most important indicium of the reasonableness of a punitive damages award is the degree of reprehensibility of the defendant's conduct." We have instructed courts to determine the reprehensibility of a defendant by considering whether: the harm caused was physical as opposed to economic; the tortious conduct evinced as indifference to or a reckless disregard of the health or safety of others; the target of the conduct had financial vulnerability; the conduct involved repeated actions or was an isolated incident; and the harm was the result of intentional malice, trickery, or deceit, or mere accident. . . . It should be presumed a plaintiff has been made whole for his injuries by compensatory damages, so punitive damages should only be awarded if the defendant's culpability, after having paid compensatory damages, is so reprehensible as to warrant the imposition of further sanctions to achieve punishment or deterrence.

Applying these factors in the instant case, we must acknowledge that State Farm's handling of the claims against the Campbells merits no praise. The trial court found that State Farm's employees altered the company's records to make Campbell appear less culpable. State Farm disregarded the overwhelming likelihood of liability and the near-certain probability that, by taking the case to trial, a judgment in excess of the policy limits would be awarded. State Farm amplified the harm by at first assuring the Campbells their assets would be safe from any verdict and by later telling them, postjudgment, to put a for-sale sign on their house. While we do not suggest there was error in awarding punitive damages based upon State Farm's conduct toward the Campbells, a more modest punishment for this reprehensible conduct could have satisfied the State's legitimate objectives, and the Utah courts should have gone no further.

The Campbells have identified scant evidence of repeated misconduct of the sort that injured them. Nor does our review of the Utah courts' decision convince us that State Farm was only punished for its actions toward the Campbells. Although evidence of other acts need not be identical to have relevance in the calculation of punitive damages, the Utah court erred here because evidence concerning reprehensibility was even more tangential. For example, the Utah Supreme Court criticized State Farm's investigation into the personal life of one of its employees and, in a broader approach, the manner in which State Farm's policies corrupted its employees.

■   ■   ■

Turning to the second *Gore* guidepost, we have been reluctant to identify concrete constitutional limits on the ratio between harm, or potential harm, to the plaintiff and the punitive damages award. . . . We decline to impose a bright-line ratio which a punitive damages award cannot exceed. Our jurisprudence and the principles it has now established demonstrate, however, that, in practice, few awards exceeding a single-digit ratio between punitive and compensatory damages, to a significant degree, will satisfy due process.

■   ■   ■

Nonetheless, because there are no rigid benchmarks that a punitive damages award may not surpass, ratios greater than those we have previously upheld may comport with due process where "a particularly egregious act has resulted in only a small amount of economic damages." . . . The converse is also true, however. When compensatory damages are substantial, then a lesser ratio, perhaps only equal to compensatory damages, can reach the outermost limit of the due process guarantee. The precise award in any case, of course, must be based upon the facts and circumstances of the defendant's conduct and the harm to the plaintiff.

In sum, courts must ensure that the measure of punishment is both reasonable and proportionate

to the amount of harm to the plaintiff and to the general damages recovered. In the context of this case, we have no doubt that there is a presumption against an award that has a 145-to-1 ratio. The compensatory award in this case was substantial; the Campbells were awarded $1 million for a year and a half of emotional distress. This was complete compensation. The harm arose from a transaction in the economic realm, not from some physical assault or trauma; there were no physical injuries; and State Farm paid the excess verdict before the complaint was filed, so the Campbells suffered only minor economic injuries for the 18-month period in which State Farm refused to resolve the claim against them.

■   ■   ■

The third guidepost in *Gore* is the disparity between the punitive damages award and the "civil penalties authorized or imposed in comparable cases." We note that, in the past, we have also looked to criminal penalties that could be imposed. . . . Punitive damages are not a substitute for the criminal process, and the remote possibility of a criminal sanction does not automatically sustain a punitive damages award.

. . . The most relevant civil sanction under Utah state law for the wrong done to the Campbells appears to be a $10,000 fine for an act of fraud, an amount dwarfed by the $145 million punitive damages award. The Supreme Court of Utah speculated about the loss of State Farm's business license, the disgorgement of profits, and possible imprisonment, but here again its references were to the broad fraudulent scheme drawn form evidence of out-of-state and dissimilar conduct. This analysis was insufficient to justify the award.

■   ■   ■

An application of the *Gore* guideposts to the facts of this case, especially in light of the substantial compensatory damages . . . likely would justify a punitive damages award at or near the amount of compensatory damages. The punitive award of $145 million, therefore, was neither reasonable nor proportionate to the wrong committed, and it was an irrational and arbitrary deprivation of the property of the defendant. The proper calculation of punitive damages under the principles we have discussed should be resolved, in the first instance, by the Utah courts.

The judgment of the Utah Supreme Court is reversed, and the case is remanded for proceedings not inconsistent with this opinion.

Case Questions

1. How should the Utah courts respond? What should be the award in order to be consistent with this opinion? Why?

2. What are the facts in this case that tend to mitigate the punitives? What are the facts that tend to aggravate the punitives?

3. Construct a scenario in which more than a single-digit multiple for punitives would pass constitutional muster.

4. How do you think that this case will impact future settlements involving punitive damages?

The following torts, although not exhaustive, are categorized as intentional torts. They include intentional torts against person, property, or both (see Table 8–2).

Battery and Assault

Battery is an unprivileged, unwanted touching of another. Any unwelcome contact, from a slap on the back to a punch in the face, constitutes a battery. Some possess a privilege to commit battery; for example, soldiers in war, and executioners lawfully charged with carrying out the death penalty.

Sexual harassment may be a battery. A woman or man who is touched in any manner against her or his will has been battered.

To be liable for a battery, the tortfeasor must intend to touch the other person, an article of clothing that person is wearing, or something the victim is carrying. A flick of another's hat or grabbing at an umbrella the victim is carrying constitutes a battery, although the injury here would ordinarily be slight.

TABLE 8–2   Classification of Intentional Torts

Against a Person	Against Property
Battery	Disparagement
Assault	Palming off
Intentional infliction of emotional distress	Interference with contract
False imprisonment	Trespass
Defamation: libel and slander	Nuisance
Deceit	
Invasion of privacy	**Against Property and Person**
	Wrongful discharge

Assault is causing another person to be apprehensive about a battery. Threatening to strike someone or advancing toward another with intent to sexually violate that person is deemed an assault.

Intentional Infliction of Emotional Distress

The tort of intentional infliction of emotional distress provides a remedy for conduct intended to unjustifiably upset the victim. Simple insults and indignities do not give rise to this tort. For the tort to occur, conduct must be outrageous; the perpetrator must intend to cause emotional distress.

To recover damages for intentional infliction of emotional distress the plaintiff must actually suffer severe mental distress. In the following case, the court considers whether an employer's termination of an employee amounts to intentional infliction of emotional distress.

DEBRA AGIS V. HOWARD JOHNSON COMPANY
355 N.E.2d 315 (Mass. 1976)

Debra Agis (plaintiff) sued the Howard Johnson Company and Roger Dionne, manager of the restaurant in which she was employed (defendants), to recover damages for mental anguish and emotional distress allegedly caused by her summary dismissal from such employment. The trial court dismissed Agis's claim. Agis appealed to the Supreme Judicial Court of Massachusetts, which reversed the trial court's dismissal and remanded the case for a trial.

Justice Quirico

Briefly, the allegations in the plaintiffs' complaint . . . are the following. Debra Agis was employed by the Howard Johnson Company as a waitress in a restaurant known as the Ground Round. On or about May 23, 1975, the defendant Dionne notified all waitresses that a meeting would be held at 3 P.M. that day. At the meeting, he informed the waitresses that "there was some stealing going on," but that the identity of the person or persons responsible was not known, and that, until the person or persons responsible were discovered, he would begin firing all the present waitresses in alphabetical order, starting with the letter "A." Dionne then fired Debra Agis.

The complaint alleges that, as a result of this incident, Mrs. Agis became greatly upset, began to cry, sustained emotional distress, mental anguish, and loss of wages and earnings. It further alleges that the actions of the defendants were reckless, extreme, outrageous and intended to cause emotional distress and anguish. In addition, the complaint states that the defendants knew or should have known that their actions would cause such distress.

■　　■　　■

[O]ne who, by extreme and outrageous conduct and without privilege, causes severe emotional distress to another is subject to liability for such emotional distress even though no bodily harm may result. However, in order for a plaintiff to prevail in a case for liability under this tort, four elements must be established. It must be shown (1) that the actor intended to inflict emotional distress or that he knew or should have known that emotional distress was the likely result of his conduct, (2) that the conduct was "extreme and outrageous," was "beyond all possible bounds of decency" and was "utterly intolerable in a civilized community," (3) that the actions of the defendant were the cause of the plaintiff's distress, and (4) that the emotional distress sustained by the plaintiff was "severe" and of a nature "that no reasonable man could be expected to endure it." These requirements are "aimed at limiting frivolous suits and avoiding litigation in situations where only bad manners and mere hurt feelings are involved," and we believe they are a "realistic safeguard against false claims. . . ."

Testing the plaintiff Debra Agis's complaint by the rules stated above, we hold that she makes out a cause of action and that her complaint is therefore legally sufficient. [W]e believe that the "[plaintiff] has alleged facts and circumstances which reasonably could lead the trier of fact to conclude that defendant's conduct was extreme and outrageous, having a severe and traumatic effect upon plaintiff's emotional tranquility." Because reasonable men could differ on these issues, we believe that "it is for the jury, subject to the control of the court," to determine whether there should be liability in this case. [T]he judgment must be reversed and the plaintiff Debra Agis must be given an opportunity to prove the allegations which she has made.

Case Questions

1. What are the requirements for the tort of intentional infliction of emotional distress?

2. Do you agree with the court that the defendants' alleged conduct was sufficiently extreme and outrageous?

3. What should a company do when conducting investigations into possible employee theft in order to avoid exposure to liability for the tort of intentional infliction of emotional distress?

4. ABC Company suspected that a manager of one of its stores was stealing from the company. As part of its investigation, ABC executives interviewed the manager, required the manager to take a polygraph (lie detector) test, and refused the manager's request that he be allowed to take his medication, which was Valium, a mood relaxant. As a result of its investigation, ABC concluded that the manager was guilty of theft and terminated the manager's employment. The manager went to see his psychiatrist, who admitted him to a mental institution. The manager sued ABC for intentional infliction of emotional distress. Should the manager win? Explain.

False Imprisonment

False imprisonment is interference with a victim's freedom of movement. A restraint that prevents a person from going where he or she pleases is considered false imprisonment, even if the restraint is accomplished nonviolently. It can take place on an open street or in a store. It is not necessary to actually harm the victim, the tort protects the victim's interest in freedom of movement. The victim of false imprisonment must be consciously aware of the restriction. Hence, an unconscious person or one who is sleeping may not be falsely imprisoned when in those states.

False imprisonment may arise when a merchant detains a suspected shoplifter. However, the law recognizes that merchants have a special interest in protecting themselves against shoplifting or theft. If a merchant reasonably believes that a person has taken goods without paying for them, the merchant is privileged to restrain the person for a reasonable period of time and in a reasonable manner. Restraint beyond what is reasonable to investigate the merchant's suspicions and summon the police, if necessary, destroys the privilege and leaves the merchant vulnerable to a successful suit.

Defamation: Libel and Slander

The tort of **defamation** protects a person's interest in his or her reputation and good name. Libel is written defamation, while slander is oral defamation. A person who attacks another's reputation or causes another to be held up to hatred, contempt, or ridicule, or to be avoided or shunned, may be liable for the tort of defamation. The tort of defamation requires proof that:

- The tortfeasor made a defamatory statement.
- The tortfeasor intended to communicate the defamatory statement.
- The defamatory statement identifies the victim to a reasonable reader or listener.
- The defamatory statement was communicated to a third party.
- The victim's reputation was damaged.

Because the First Amendment of the U.S. Constitution protects the right of free speech, defamation is more difficult to prove when the object of the statement is a public figure. In such cases, the public figure must prove that the tortfeasor knew the statement was false or made the statement in reckless disregard of the truth. In contrast, when the object of the statement is a private person, liability may exist where the tortfeasor negligently publishes a defamatory statement.

Another limitation on recovery for defamation in most states is the requirement that a victim of slander establish actual damage to his or her reputation. However, some statements that are clearly defamatory are presumed to cause damage. These statements are referred to as *slander per se*. The following statements fall under this category:

- A statement adversely reflecting on a person's business, trade, or profession.
- A statement that a person is afflicted with a loathsome, communicable disease.
- A statement that a person has committed a crime of moral turpitude.
- A statement imputing unchaste behavior to a person.

Slanderous statements falling outside the per se category require proof that the statements caused actual damage to reputation, such as loss of business or a contract. Many states afford a presumption of damages for libel.

In some situations, an individual is privileged to make an otherwise defamatory statement. This occurs when the communication serves an important public interest. For example, a former employer is privileged to tell a prospective employer about a job applicant's qualifications. However, the privilege can be lost if the statement is made in bad faith.

Truth is an absolute defense to the tort of defamation. The burden, however, is on the defendant to prove that the defamatory statements were in fact true.

Deceit

Deceit is a knowing and intentional misrepresentation of a material fact. To recover damages, the following elements must be established:

- A false representation of a material fact.
- Knowledge by the person making the representation that it is false.
- An intent to induce the listener to rely on the representation.
- Justifiable reliance on the representation by the listener.
- Damage to the duped party resulting from such reliance.

Deceit may take many forms. For example, a business's failure to disclose information relevant to a transaction may be considered deceitful if the business knows or should know that the other party does not have the same information and does not have the ability to obtain it. Similarly, a half-truth may be worse than silence, because it tends to mislead people or to lull them into complacency.

Clearly, the range of what can be considered fraud or misrepresentation is great; as the morals of the marketplace change, so does the definition of deceit. For example, in the past, negotiations between buyers and sellers were characterized by the notion of *caveat emptor,* or "let the buyer beware." This attitude has given way to an obligation on the part of a seller to inform a buyer of hidden defects. This is particularly true when dealing with consumers. In commercial transactions between parties on relatively equal bargaining levels, for example, a manufacturer and supplier, the obligation to disclose is not as strict. These parties can generally be expected to investigate and protect their own interests.

Invasion of Privacy

Most people assume that they have a right to privacy, but very few can describe the dimensions of this right. Tort law recognizes four distinct privacy rights: (1) intrusion, (2) public disclosure of private facts, (3) false light in the public eye, and (4) appropriation.

Intrusion into Seclusion

The more traditional notion of what the right of privacy protects is represented by an intrusion. Tortious intrusions include unauthorized physical entry or peering into someone's home or other private premises, eavesdropping, repeated or unwanted telephone calls, or unauthorized prying or access into someone's bank account or other personal affairs. Liability may occur if the nature of the intrusion is such that it would be objectionable or offensive to a reasonable person.

Questions arise as to whether drug testing in the work place constitutes an invasion of privacy. The following case illustrates the position of one court.

JANICE RUSHING V. HERSHEY CHOCOLATE—MEMPHIS
U.S. App. LEXIS 27392 (2000)

Janice Rushing, the plaintiff, was employed by Hershey, the defendant, for 17 years, in a non-sensitive safety job position. During her employment she consented to and took a urinalysis drug test as part of the mandatory company policy. Her test was inconclusive. Rushing refused to submit to additional urinalysis. She was terminated.

Rushing was never cited for deficiencies in her work and she never tested positive for drugs. She filed an action in wrongful discharge based upon a right to privacy, which she alleged was violated. Hershey moved for a dismissal, which the U.S. District Court granted. Rushing appealed to the United States Court of Appeals for the Sixth Circuit.

Circuit Judge Clay

Tennessee law recognizes the common law tort of invasion of privacy. Under Tennessee law, "'a person who unreasonably and seriously interferes with another's interest in not having his affairs known to others or his likeness exhibited to the public is liable to the other.'" Liability for invasion of privacy attaches only if (1) the defendant should have realized that his conduct would be offensive to persons of ordinary sensibilities; and, (2) the intrusion goes beyond the limits of decency.

An action for invasion of privacy may be asserted as one of four common law privacy torts: (1) intrusion into a person's seclusion, solitude or person affairs; (2) public disclosure; (3) false light; or (4) appropriation of one's likeness. Here Rushing has only asserted a claim for intrusion. One is liable for intrusion if he "'intentionally intrudes, physically or otherwise, upon the solitude or seclusion of another or his private affairs or concerns, . . . and the intrusion would be highly offensive to a reasonable person.'"

With these legal principles in mind, we conclude that Rushing's claim fails for two reasons: (1) there was no intrusion—physical or otherwise; and (2) Rushing's urinalysis test results were not a matter which she had a right to keep private in an employment setting.

In order for Rushing to state a claim for invasion of privacy based on intrusion upon her seclusion or solitude, she must allege that an intrusion took place. In *Baggs,* several of the plaintiffs asserted actions against their employer for invasion of privacy after they were terminated for refusing to submit to drug testing. The court held that those plaintiffs had no cause of action for invasion of privacy because "there was no intrusion" since the plaintiffs didn't actually take the test.

Baggs bears a striking resemblance to the case at bar. Here, as in *Baggs,* Rushing refused to submit to drug testing. Because Rushing refused to submit to the drug test, she cannot now complain that her privacy was invaded by that same test.

■   ■   ■

Because a claim for intrusion requires that an actual intrusion take place, and Rushing neither alleges that an intrusion took place nor provides a sufficient factual basis for this Court to infer that an intrusion took place, we conclude that Rushing's claim for invasion of privacy based upon intrusion must fail.

■   ■   ■

Furthermore, we conclude that Rushing's claim must fail because she did not allege facts that show that the drug tests implicated interests for which she had a right of privacy. Although there is no Tennessee case law specifically addressing the subject, Tennessee and other courts have indicated that employers may require an employee to take drug tests related to employment without committing an invasion of privacy.

■   ■   ■

Rushing attempts to argue she should not have been required to submit to a drug test because Hershey did not have particularized suspicion or probable cause to suspect that Rushing was under the influence of drugs while on the job. Rushing further argues that she should not have been required to submit to drug testing because she did not occupy a safety-sensitive position. This Court finds that these arguments are unpersuasive and unsupported by authority.

. . . Rushing attempts to attach to private employers standards [that] which have traditionally been applied to government action.

■   ■   ■

We therefore conclude that Rushing has failed to point to a privacy interest in the results of her urinalysis test, which presumably would reveal nothing more than whether she was under the influence of drugs while on the job. Moreover, we conclude that Hershey has a right to require its employees to submit to drug tests as long as they are not intrusive, i.e., the manner in which the program is conducted is not intrusive and the testing methods would not reveal private medical facts other than drug use.

Case Questions

1. What interest does Hershey have in keeping a drug free work place? Should it matter that Rushing was in a non-sensitive safety position and that her work was good? Explain.

2. Do you think the result would be different if the drug test required the extraction of blood? The taking of a swatch of hair? A saliva swab? Explain.

3. Draft a policy on drug testing in the work place that includes notice, procedure and consequences of non-compliance and test failure.

Public Disclosure of Private Facts
Another type of invasion of privacy, public disclosure of private facts, involves disclosing to the public the intimate facts of one's life. Information revealed to the public must not have been publicly known, and the disclosure must be offensive to a person of ordinary sensibility. Private facts that the courts have protected include the public disclosure of an unpaid debt, medical pictures of one's anatomy, and details of one's sexual relations.

False Light
The third form of interference with privacy involves placing someone in a false light in the public eye. A person has the right to be free from having false information publicly disseminated. Although similar to defamation, it is broader and

includes acts that would be objectionable to a reasonable person even though they are not necessarily defamatory. Examples of the tort are publicizing that a person is dead when he is in fact not, or that a person heroically rescued people from a burning building when this is untrue.

Appropriation

Tort law prohibits the appropriation or use of the plaintiff's name or likeness for financial benefit without consent. This was the earliest form of privacy protection recognized by the courts. The most common example is the use of the name or picture of a celebrity for business purposes without the celebrity's consent. However, private, unknown people are also protected.

Disparagement

False statements that injure a person's interest in property, as opposed to one's reputation, amount to disparagement. For example, assume that a patron accuses a butcher of selling spoiled meat. Because this statement tends to injure the butcher's reputation, it would be defamatory. Assume, however, that the patron falsely informs potential customers that the butcher went out of business. This does not directly injure the butcher's reputation; however, it injures the business by keeping potential buyers away from the butcher's business. This statement may constitute disparagement.

Disparagement is harder to prove than defamation. Plaintiffs must prove that the statements were false and malicious and that they resulted in monetary loss by, for example, causing certain customers to avoid dealing with them.

Palming Off

If an advertiser represents its goods in a way that deceives the average buyer into believing them to be the goods of a competitor, the advertiser is liable to that competitor for **palming off**. The misrepresentation may involve imitating the trademark, labels, containers, appearance of business, or any other distinctive characteristic of the competitor. Assume a local company that sells cheap wrist watches stamps the name Rolex (a watch of high quality) on the face of its watches and advertises them as such. This would amount to unlawful palming off—a practice that would injure Rolex in two ways. First, it would take away customers who would purchase the watches thinking that they were made by Rolex. Second, it would injure Rolex's image by associating the inferior watch with its name. Here, Rolex could obtain both an injunction restraining the company from misrepresenting its goods and damages for loss of business. (For a further discussion of palming off, see the Lanham Act discussion in Chapter 9.)

Palming off is not the only type of false advertising that injures competitors. Most often, false advertisements misrepresent the quality, price, or nature of the advertised goods. Some states, and a federal statute, give competitors an action against competitors who falsely advertise in this manner. These false advertisements harm competitors by taking customers away from them.

Interference with Contract

The intentional and wrongful interference with a contract is a tort. The origin of this tort can be traced to *Lumley v. Guy,* an English case decided in 1853.[1] In that case, an opera singer was obligated, pursuant to a contract, to sing at a theater. A competitor of the theater, aware of the contractual relationship, nevertheless persuaded the singer to break her contract. Liability was imposed against the competitor for interference with contract.

Tortious interference of contractual rights is not confined to existing contracts; it extends to potential contracts as well. Hence, it is a tort to prevent a person from obtaining employment, or to prevent a business from contracting with customers, or to dissuade a publisher from contracting with an author.

Trespass

The tort of trespass is really two torts: trespass to personal property (movables, such as merchandise), and trespass to real property (land).

A trespass to personal property is committed by interfering with someone's right to possess his or her personal property by, for example, taking merchandise for a short time, or harming the goods. The tortfeasor is liable for damages if the victim can prove:

- Interference with the owner's right of possession.
- Intent by the tortfeasor to do the act that constituted the interference.
- Interference caused damage to the owner's personal property.

If the interference with personal property is so great that it deprives the owner of its value, courts find that the tortfeasor converted the property and order the tortfeasor to pay the fair market value of the property to the owner. This constitutes another related tort, known as *conversion.* Common acts constituting conversion are the destruction of property, theft, receipt of stolen goods, and wrongful transfer or retention of property. The owner has the option of demanding the property back or receiving the fair market value at the time of conversion.

Trespass to real property is an unlawful interference with another's land. This tort action protects a landholder's interest in the exclusive possession of his or her properties. A person who physically intrudes on another's property commits a trespass. However, the intruder need not physically set foot on the property to be liable; he or she may be held liable for setting events in motion that cause the intrusion. For example, someone on his or her land creating pollutants that travel to a neighbor's land commits a trespass to real property. A trespass may be committed by a single act or by a continuing presence on the land.

---

[1] 118 Eng. Reprint 749.

Nuisance

A nuisance is a substantial and unreasonable interference with the use and enjoyment of an interest in land. A cause of action for nuisance thus protects landholders' interests in the use and enjoyment of their properties. In environmental litigation, nuisance includes interferences in the form of smoke, odor, noise, and vibration.

Trespass and nuisance are distinguishable. A trespass is an invasion of the right to exclusive possession of land, as by entry on it. A nuisance is an interference with the interest in the private use and enjoyment of land and does not require direct interference with possession. For example, the flooding of another's land constitutes a trespass because it interferes with the landholder's interest in possession. In contrast, a noxious odor spewing from a nearby factory smokestack might constitute a nuisance to the neighboring owners' use and enjoyment of their properties. Some courts do not differentiate between such subtleties; the label is not as important as the wrongful action and injury.

When determining whether a nuisance exists, the courts balance various factors—a practice referred to as *balancing the equities.* All landholders' rights to use and enjoy their properties are necessarily subject to the rights of other landholders to do the same. Consequently, the courts weigh the utility of the conduct of one landholder against the gravity of the harm caused to another. Generally, if the harm outweighs utility, the courts deem the conduct a nuisance. Other relevant considerations are the existence of practical means to avoid causing the harm and the location of the properties.

Wrongful Discharge

Employment relationships are based on contracts. Employees agree to perform services for their employers, who agree to compensate their employees. Most employees are hired for an indefinite period of time. Frequently nothing is said about when, how, or under what circumstances the contract may be terminated.

The traditional rule is that an employment contract of indefinite duration is terminable at the will of either party. If nothing is said about the length of employment, the employee is free to quit, and the employer is free to fire the employee at any time, for any reason, or for no reason at all.

This traditional employment-at-will doctrine is eroding. Courts in most states still agree that an employer has the power to discharge an at-will employee for any reason. Most states have decided that when an employer fires an employee in a manner that contravenes public policy, however, the employee may recover for the tort of abusive or **wrongful discharge**. These courts disagree over what constitutes public policy. However, most of the courts that recognize the tort of wrongful discharge require that the public policy be expressed by a constitutional provision or a statute. For example, in one case it was deemed a wrongful discharge for an employer to fire an employee when the employee refused to pump water out of the deck of a boat into the waterway because there was a statute that prohibited such pumping.[2] Some courts allow the public policy to be expressed in a state's common law. (See the discussion of wrongful discharge in Chapter 16.)

Defenses to Intentional Torts

Consent and privilege are two common defenses in intentional tort cases. A defendant can avoid liability by proving either that the plaintiff consented to the defendant's conduct or that the defendant was privileged to do what would otherwise be an intentional tort.

Whether a plaintiff has consented to the defendant's conduct is determined by the plaintiff's behavior under the circumstances, not by the plaintiff's actual feelings. Consent may be expressed. For example, it is common for hospitals to require patients to sign a consent form before undergoing medical procedures. Consent may also be implied by conduct, as, for example, where an employee engages voluntarily in an employer's drug testing program. Courts inquire into the reasonableness of the consent, and will declare consent ineffective if it is in violation of law or public policy.

Conduct that would otherwise be an intentional tort may nevertheless be privileged. For example, someone acting in self-defense can avoid liability for what would otherwise be a battery. When creating privileges, courts are deciding that the importance of certain conduct outweighs the risks of harm. A privilege is lost if the defendant acts in bad faith.

Negligence

Often damage is caused by unintentional or careless conduct. Under certain circumstances, the injured party can recover damages for the tort of **negligence**. Negligence is unintentional conduct that falls below the standard of care that is necessary to protect others against exposure to an unreasonable risk of a foreseeable injury.

Elements of Negligence

Negligence is conduct that is unreasonable under the circumstances. A plaintiff must prove the following elements to recover against a defendant for the tort of negligence:

- The existence of a duty to exercise the degree of care that a reasonable and prudent person would exercise under similar circumstances.
- A breach of that duty by a failure to adhere to the standard of reasonable conduct.

---

[2] Sabine Pilot Services v. Hauck, 687 S.W. 2d 734 (Tex. 1985).

- That the unreasonable conduct was the actual and proximate cause of the plaintiff's injury.
- Actual injury to the plaintiff.

Duty

Before liability for negligence is imposed, a court must first determine that the defendant was under a duty to protect the plaintiff from the injury that occurred. For example, suppose a passenger in the front seat of a van is injured when the van collides with a telephone pole. Could the passenger successfully sue the manufacturer of the van for negligence, claiming that the manufacturer had a duty to design the vehicle so that in collisions under 40 mph the passenger would not come into contact with the interior compartment of the van? Should the manufacturer be under a duty to design a crashworthy vehicle? In determining the existence of a duty, a court would weigh the nature and foreseeability of the risk of harm (here, the risk of collisions) against the social utility of the defendant's conduct (here, the social utility of a van) and the costs of taking precautions (here, the cost of redesigning the van).

In the example involving the van, a federal appellate court considered the foreseeability of automobile collisions, but found that it was outweighed by the burden of imposing precautions on the manufacturer, a burden that would require redesigning a van to the extent that it would no longer be useful for its intended purpose as a cargo carrier. The court also noted that imposing such a duty on the manufacturer would drastically increase the price of vans. The imposition of such a duty would, in the court's opinion, deprive society of a reasonably priced light-cargo carrier.[3] Thus, when determining the existence of a duty, courts determine as a matter of policy the social value of the parties' interests.

Breach of Duty

In the absence of a statute, the question of whether the defendant breached the duty of care is one that the jury determines (or the judge, if sitting without a jury). A standard of conduct, known as the *reasonable person standard,* is applied. Whether the defendant has breached a duty of care is determined by comparing the defendant's conduct to that of a reasonable and prudent person under the same or similar circumstances. When the defendant is a person with special training, such as a doctor, lawyer, or accountant, the standard takes into consideration the defendant's training. Thus, an accountant is held to the standard of a reasonably informed accountant; a certified public accountant would be held to the standard of a reasonably informed certified public accountant.

Actual and Proximate Cause

The plaintiff must also prove that the defendant's conduct was the actual and proximate cause of the injury. Determination of the existence of actual and proximate cause is a matter for the jury to decide (or the judge, if sitting without a jury).

---

[3] Dreisonstok v. Volkswagen of America, 489 F. 2d 1066 (4th Cir. 1974).

Actual cause refers to the direct causal connection between the defendant's conduct and the plaintiff's injury. The simplest way to determine whether an injury resulted from the defendant's conduct is to ascertain whether the plaintiff would have been injured *but for* the defendant's action. For example, a landlord's negligent failure to provide a fire escape could cause the death of someone who is thereby prevented from fleeing a fire. However, the absence of a fire escape would not cause the death of someone who suffocated in bed during the fire. When there are several causes of an injury or damage, each defendant whose conduct contributed to the injury can be held responsible for the damage if his or her conduct was a substantial factor causing the injury.

In addition to being the actual cause of the plaintiff's injury, the defendant's conduct must also be the **proximate cause**. A defendant is liable only for those injuries that are proximate, as opposed to injuries that are remote. Proximate cause, thus, has to do with the likelihood (foreseeability) of the injury. If the plaintiff's injury could not be reasonably foreseen by the defendant at the time of the defendant's act or omission, the defendant's conduct will not be considered the proximate cause of the injury. The element of proximate cause requires the plaintiff's injury to be the natural, probable, and foreseeable result of the defendant's conduct.

The following case, involving the placement of a telephone booth, illustrates the application of the negligence elements of duty and proximate cause.

BIGBEE V. PACIFIC TELEPHONE AND TELEGRAPH CO.
665 P. 2d 94 (Calif. 1983)

At approximately 12:20 A.M., Charles Bigbee was standing in a public telephone booth outside the Fortune Liquor Store on Century Boulevard in Inglewood, California. The phone booth in which Bigbee was standing was one of two booths in the parking lot of the store. They were close to the store's front wall, between the front door and the sidewalk bordering the boulevard, near an entrance to the parking lot. Bigbee occupied the booth nearer the street, 15 feet from the curb. Century Boulevard is a six-lane thoroughfare with a posted speed limit of 40 miles per hour.

At the same time Charles Bigbee was placing his phone call, an intoxicated Leona Roberts lost control of her car, veered off Century Boulevard into Fortune's parking lot, and crashed into the booth where Bigbee was standing. As Bigbee later told his story, he saw Roberts's car coming and attempted to get out of the booth but the door "jammed and stuck, trapping" him inside. Bigbee was severely injured as a result of the crash.

Bigbee sued Roberts and the companies allegedly responsible for serving her alcoholic beverages. A settlement was reached as to these defendants. In addition, Bigbee sued the companies he claimed were negligent in the design, location, installation, and maintenance of the telephone booth, which included Pacific Telephone and Telegraph Co. (defendant), the owner of the booth.

The companies filed a motion for summary judgment. In their motion, they argued that the facts demonstrated a lack of two elements essential to Bigbee's negligence claim: (1) the existence of a duty to protect Bigbee from the injuries he suffered, and (2) that their conduct could be found to be the proximate cause of Bigbee's injuries. The trial judge granted the companies' motion and entered judgment against Bigbee. Bigbee appealed to the Supreme Court of California, which reversed the summary judgment and ordered the trial judge to proceed with a trial.

Chief Justice Bird

Defendants contend that their duty to use due care in the location, installation, and maintenance of telephone booths does not extend to the risk encountered by plaintiff and that neither their alleged negligence in carrying out these activities nor any defect in the booth was a proximate cause of plaintiff's injuries. These contentions present the same issue in different guises. Each involves this question—was the risk that a car might crash into the phone booth and injure plaintiff reasonably foreseeable in this case?

Turning to the merits of this case, the question presented is a relatively simple one. Is there room for a reasonable difference of opinion as to whether the risk that a car might crash into the phone booth and injure an individual inside was reasonably foreseeable under the circumstances set forth above?

In pursuing this inquiry, it is well to remember that foreseeability is not to be measured by what is more probable than not, but, includes whatever is likely enough in the setting of modern life that a reasonabl[y] thoughtful [person] would take account of it in guiding practical conduct. One may be held accountable for creating even "the risk of a slight possibility of injury if a reasonabl[y] prudent [person] would not do so." Moreover, it is settled that what is required to be foreseeable is the general character of the event or harm—e.g., being struck by a car while standing in a phone booth—not its precise nature or manner of occurrence.

Here, defendants placed a telephone booth, which was difficult to exit, in a parking lot 15 feet from the side of a major thoroughfare and near a driveway. Under these circumstances, this court cannot conclude as a matter of law that it was unforeseeable that the booth might be struck by a car and cause serious injury to a person trapped within. A jury could reasonably conclude that this risk was foreseeable. This is particularly true where, as here, there is evidence that a booth at this same location had previously been struck.

Indeed, in light of the circumstances of modern life, it seems evident that a jury could reasonably find that defendants should have foreseen the possibility of the very accident which actually occurred here. Swift traffic on a major thoroughfare late at night is to be expected. Regrettably, so too are intoxicated drivers who lose control of their cars and crash into poles, buildings or whatever else may be standing alongside the road they travel—no matter how straight and level that road may be.

Where a telephone booth, which is difficult to exit, is placed 15 feet from such a thoroughfare, the risk that it might be struck by a car veering off the street, thereby causing injury to a person trapped within, cannot be said to be unforeseeable as a matter of law.

It is no consequence that the harm to plaintiff came about through the negligent or reckless acts of Roberts. If the likelihood that a third person may act in a particular manner is the hazard or one of the hazards which makes the actor negligent, such an act whether innocent, negligent, intentionally tortious, or criminal does not prevent the actor from being liable for harm caused thereby. Here, the risk that a car might hit the telephone booth could be found to constitute one of the hazards to which plaintiff was exposed.

Considering the case law and the circumstances of this case, this court cannot conclude as a matter of law that injury to plaintiff, inflicted by negligent or reckless third party drivers, was unforeseeable. Just as we may not rely upon our private judgment on this issue, so the trial court may not impose its private judgment upon a situation, such as this, in which reasonable minds may differ.

Justice Kroniger (Dissenting)

I respectfully disagree with this court's holding that the negligent siting theory of plaintiff's case should be submitted to the trier of fact.

To hold that defendants could be found liable for locating the booth where they did is tantamount to holding that one may be found negligent whenever he conducts everyday activities on or adjacent to the public sidewalk. It will go far toward making all roadside businesses insurers of safety for wayward travelers.

There is no suggestion of anything defendants might reasonably have done differently with respect to siting except simply not to maintain a telephone in the vicinity at all. Public telephones have, in fact, long been maintained adjacent to streets and highways for the convenience of the public, despite the obvious but remote risks.

Case Questions

1. Compare and contrast the majority and dissenting opinions.
2. Which facts does the court draw on to support its conclusion that the question of breach of duty and proximate cause are proper jury questions? Over the last century, the role of the American jury in negligence cases has enlarged. How do you think this trend affects business?
3. Assume that a vegetable stand's operating on the side of a country road results in a patron being injured by a reckless operator of an automobile. Under *Bigbee,* would the vegetable stand owner be liable? Explain. What about a particularly flashy billboard that results in auto accidents when drivers are distracted? Explain.
4. Are there any strategies that businesses might take to counter the result in *Bigbee?*

Injury

Generally, injury includes damage to property or person. A plaintiff who sustains physical injury is entitled to recover for damage, including medical expenses, loss of wages, and even pain and suffering. It may also include injury for loss of consortium (discussed in Chapter 3). The establishment of damages for injury usually requires the testimony of medical experts. The defendant often has its own medical experts to rebut the plaintiff's medical experts. Here is where the trier of the fact has to determine whose expert opinion to believe.

Procedural Doctrines

Two procedural doctrines help plaintiffs prove their case of negligence. The first one, the doctrine of *negligence per se,* employs a statute to establish negligence;

the second, the doctrine of *res ipsa loquitur,* employs reason to establish a presumption of negligence.

Negligence Per Se

Negligence may arise as a result of a violation of a statute or regulation. When enacting statutes or regulations, legislatures and agencies sometimes weigh the risk of harm resulting from certain conduct and the conduct's social utility. In many states the violation of such a statute or regulation in certain circumstances is considered **negligence per se**, which means that the violation, by itself, is considered unreasonable. For violation of a statute or regulation to qualify as negligence per se (1) the injured person must be within the class of persons the statute or regulation was designed to protect, and (2) the injury must be of a type that the statute or regulation was designed to prevent. Assume, for example, that a statute prohibits the mislabeling of any drug. From his local pharmacy Jack Plaintiff purchases a drug labeled aspirin; in reality it is a poisonous substance. If Plaintiff becomes violently ill as a result of ingesting the mislabeled drug, the manufacturer would be negligent per se. Plaintiff is a consumer, a person within the class the statute was designed to protect, and the statute is designed to prevent the very type of injury that occurred.

However, assume that a local health ordinance requires a restaurant to have smooth flooring for drainage and cleaning. One Star Restaurant violates the statute by having corrugated flooring. Jill Patron trips and injures herself when her high heel lodges within a riveted portion of the floor. Here, the violation of the statute would not constitute negligence per se. The statute is for sanitation purposes and is not designed to protect patrons against the injury that befell Jill.

Res Ipsa Loquitur

In some accidents it is not easy for the plaintiff to discover which act or omission led to the injury suffered; the plaintiff can find no direct evidence of negligence. For example, if a pedestrian is suddenly and unexpectedly struck by a falling brick while passing a construction site, the plaintiff may have difficulty knowing how or why the brick fell. To help deserving plaintiffs, courts have developed a rule of evidence referred to as **res ipsa loquitur** (the thing speaks for itself). Application of the doctrine of res ispa loquitur creates a presumption of negligence. The rule is applicable when the accident would not ordinarily occur without negligence. In addition, other causes—including conduct by the plaintiff—must be sufficiently eliminated by the evidence. As well, the instrumentality causing the injury must be within the defendant's control. Because of this rule, many plaintiffs are able to establish their cases without direct evidence of negligence. In the following case, the court considers the application of res ipsa loquitur in the context of "exclusive control" of a chair.

TRUJEQUE V. SERVICE MERCHANDISE CO.
872 P.2d 361 (N.M. 1994)

Carmen Trujegue was shopping at Service Merchandise, when she decided to sit down on a chair provided for shoppers' convenience. The chair broke as she sat upon it, and caused injury to her arm.

Trujeque sued Service Merchandise and at trial the court instructed the jury that "Trujegue had the burden of proving that the chair was under the 'exclusive control and management' of Service Merchandise," and further defined exclusive control as follows:

> In order to prove that the defendant had exclusive control and management over the instrumentality causing plaintiff's accident and injuries plaintiff must show from the evidence that others did not have an opportunity of equal access to the instrumentality.

The jury found for the defendant, and the Court of Appeals affirmed. The Supreme Court of New Mexico granted certiorari to review the case.

Justice Ransom

. . . The doctrine of res ipsa loquitur applies only when evidence establishes that in the ordinary course of events an injury would not occur except through negligence of the person in exclusive control and management of the injuring instrumentality. . . . Generally, cases in which the theory of res ipsa loquitur is presented fall into two categories: those in which the defendant directly uses an instrumentality so as to cause injury, and those in which the defendant is in charge of, created, or last controlled an instrumentality that inexplicably becomes dangerous and injures the victim outside of the defendant's presence. . . . The case at [hand] falls into the second category.

. . . In order to make a . . . case from which the jury may infer that the defendant is liable for the damages caused by the instrumentality outside of the defendant's presence, the plaintiff must provide evidence of the character of the occurrence and of the exclusive control of the defendant. The plaintiff's burden may vary according to the facts of the case. . . .

While the two "collapsing chair" cases in New Mexico . . . imply that a showing of ownership, management, and possession of chairs in a business establishment with many invitees is sufficient to establish exclusive control, they do not expressly state what the plaintiff's burden is in those cases. There are, however, many cases from other jurisdictions expressly holding that such a showing is sufficient. . . .

We are aware one jurisdiction holds that because chairs in use are under the control of the user, the exclusive control element cannot be met as a matter of law. This argument has been widely criticized as a ridiculous conclusion. . . . We believe that [this] theory . . . is an "overly rigid interpretation of the requirement of exclusive control," and that it is "artificial and ignores the purpose of the requirement that defendant have exclusive control."

That third parties may have had access to the chair did not preclude Service Merchandise from having exclusive control and management of the chair within the meaning of the doctrine of res ipsa loquitur, and did not preclude a reasonable inference that Service Merchandise was responsible for a danger within its use. Once Trujeque established that an accident occurred that normally does not occur absent negligence and that Service Merchandise owned, maintained, and provided the chair for use by its customers on the store's premises, she satisfied her burden of making a . . . case from which the jury could infer negligence. Service Merchandise could then choose to present no evidence or choose to rebut the inference by offering evidence that a latent manufacturing defect was the cause of the collapse or perhaps that some third party bore responsibility for the collapse of the chair. It has long been held that

> [a]ll that the plaintiff should be required to do in the first instance is to show that the defendant owned, operated, and maintained, or controlled and was responsible for the management and maintenance of, the thing doing the damage. . . . When he has done this, he has cast a burden on the defendant, who may then proceed to show that the accident was occasioned by . . . other causes for which he was not responsible.

"*[R]es ipsa loquitur* means that the facts of the occurrence warrant the inference of negligence, not that they compel such an inference; . . . that they call for explanation or rebuttal, not necessarily that they require it; that they make a case to be decided by the jury. . . ." Trujeque met her burden, and instructing the jury that she also had to prove that no other party had an opportunity of equal access to the chair was reversible error. We reverse and remand for a new trial.

Case Questions

1. Define res ipsa loquitur.
2. When is res ipsa loquitur applicable? Why was it applicable in this case?
3. What was the problem with the jury instructions?
4. What if a stack of chairs overhead (within the business establishment) fell, struck a patron and injured her? Would res ipsa loquitur be applicable?
5. Simpson was a paying guest at the Econo Lodge Motel in Durham, North Carolina. Simpson was given room number 27. After checking into the room, he went into the bathroom to take a shower in the combination bathtub-shower. He adjusted the hot and cold water control knobs to a comfortable temperature. He then pulled out the shower-bath control knob so that water came out of the shower head. After Simpson finished his shower, he pushed in the shower-bath control knob. The water from the shower head stopped, but moments later, a sudden burst of scalding hot water gushed out of the shower head hitting him. He jumped to get away from the hot water, slipped, lost his balance, and fell on the tile floor, sustaining injuries to his left leg and knee. Simpson sued Econo-Lodge, claiming that it was liable to him for negligence under the doctrine of res ipsa loquitur. Is Simpson correct? Explain.

Defenses to Negligence

Even when the plaintiff can successfully prove the elements constituting negligence, defenses may be raised to defeat recovery. Contributory negligence, comparative negligence and assumption of the risk are the more common defenses.

Contributory Negligence

In a few states the plaintiff's contribution to the injury, however slight, will bar plaintiff's recovery. Like negligence, the contributory negligence must be proximate, a contributing cause of the injury. In a few other states, for the bar to occur, the contribution must be substantial. The doctrine of contributory negligence has given way in the vast majority of the states to the doctrine of comparative negligence.

Comparative Negligence

Most states have adopted **comparative negligence** as a defense. Under this principle, recovery is reduced by the percentage that the plaintiff's negligence contributed to his or her injury. Assume, for example, that the defendant negligently designed a refuse bin so that it was unstable. The plaintiff purchased the bin and negligently placed it on an irregular and inclined surface. The plaintiff was injured when the bin overturned in a windstorm. If the jury determines that the plaintiff's damages are $40,000, that the defendant was 75 percent at fault, and that the plaintiff was 25 percent at fault, plaintiff's recovery would be reduced by 25 percent to $30,000. In a few states the plaintiff's contributory negligence in this example would prevent any recovery. In those states this would be true even if the defendant was more at fault than the plaintiff.

Assumption of the Risk

Assumption of the risk prevents a plaintiff from recovering against a negligent defendant, because the plaintiff is held to have assumed the risk of his or her injury. Assumption of the risk consists of a voluntary exposure to a known risk. It differs from comparative or contributory negligence in that contributory or comparative negligence is based on carelessness, whereas assumption of the risk is based on voluntariness—willful exposure to a known risk. A plaintiff who continues to drive an automobile with full knowledge that it has defective brakes is deemed to have assumed the risk of injury that is likely to result. If the plaintiff does not know about the defective brakes but really should, then he or she is guilty of comparative or contributory negligence.

Strict Liability

By emphasizing the factors of intent and reasonable conduct, the areas of intentional torts and negligence use a fault standard to determine liability. The third area of tort law, **strict liability**, does not emphasize fault. Liability is strictly imposed in certain situations even if the actor does not intend to do the act or exercises all reasonable care.

The areas in which strict liability apply are where injuries (1) are caused by a defective product that is unreasonably dangerous because of its defect (see Chapter 9), (2) result from the keeping of dangerous or vicious animals, or (3) result from abnormally dangerous activities, such as blasting operations.

Abnormally Dangerous Activities

Individuals or companies engaged in hazardous activities, such as oil drilling, are strictly liable for any injuries arising from those activities. It does not matter that the offender did not intend to cause injury or was exercising all reasonable care; nor does it matter that the victim may have failed to take reasonable precautions for his or her own protection. Since fault does not matter, liability is strictly imposed.

The theory of strict liability serves to reimburse victims harmed by abnormally dangerous activities carried on voluntarily. It treats the risk of injury as a cost of engaging in the activity. Under strict liability, those engaged in abnormally dangerous activities must pay for the damage they cause. Under negligence, the victim would not be compensated if reasonable care were undertaken in the performance of such dangerous activity. Negligence theory provides no recovery to the victims of dangerous yet reasonable activity; strict liability does.

Abnormally dangerous activities involve a serious risk of harm to people, land, or property. The risk is usually one that cannot be eliminated even if the actor exercises great care. Businesses engaged in abnormally dangerous activities bear responsibility for the injuries they cause despite any precautions taken to prevent them.

Activities are usually abnormally dangerous when they are out of place in their locality. Blasting operations and storage of large quantities of explosives or flammable gases are abnormally dangerous when conducted in cities. Such activities pose serious threats to human life and the integrity of property. In the following case, the court considers whether a fireworks display qualifies as an abnormally dangerous activity for purposes of imposing strict liability.

Ethical Dilemmas/Issues

Early one December morning, methyl isocyanate (a lethal gas) leaked from a fertilizer production plant in Bhopal, India. The plant was owned by Union Carbide of India, a subsidiary of Union Carbide, a U.S.-based corporation. The leakage resulted in the worst industrial disaster in history—more than 3,500 people were killed and more than 200,000 people were injured. Union Carbide had insurance of $200 million to cover such a disaster.

India does not provide for jury trials. Its discovery rules are more restrictive than those in the United States. Judgments are generally significantly less than they are in the United States, and the court system is much slower.

Union Carbide had a similar plant with the same design in West Virginia. What are the ethical issues? What would you do?

KLEIN V. PYRODYNE CORPORATION
810 P.2d 917 (Wash. 1991)

Danny and Marion Klein (plaintiffs) were injured when an aerial shell at a Fourth of July fireworks exhibition went astray and exploded near them. Pyrodyne Corporation (defendant) is a pyrotechnic company hired to set up and discharge the fireworks. The Kleins sued Pyrodyne in tort under the theory of strict liability. The trial court granted summary judgment in favor of the Kleins. Pyrodyne appealed to the Supreme Court of the State of Washington the trial court's holding that strict liability was the appropriate standard of liability. The Supreme Court of Washington affirmed the trial court decision favoring the Kleins.

Justice Guy

The Kleins contend that strict liability is the appropriate standard to determine the culpability of Pyrodyne because Pyrodyne was participating in an abnormally dangerous activity. . . .

The modern doctrine of strict liability for abnormally dangerous activities derives from *Rylands v. Fletcher* in which the defendant's reservoir flooded mine shafts on the plaintiff's adjoining land. *Rylands v. Fletcher* has come to stand for the rule that "the defendant will be liable when he damages another by a thing or activity unduly dangerous and inappropriate to the place where it is maintained, in the light of the character of that place and its surroundings."

The basic principle of *Rylands v. Fletcher* has been accepted by the Restatement (Second) of Torts (1977). Section 519 of the Restatement provides that any party carrying on an "abnormally dangerous activity" is strictly liable for ensuing damages. . . . The essential question is whether the risk created is so unusual, either because of its magnitude or because of the circumstances surrounding it, as to justify the imposition of strict liability for the harm that results from it, even though it is carried on with all reasonable care.

. . . Anytime a person ignites aerial shells or rockets with the intention of sending them aloft to explode in the presence of large crowds of people, a high risk of serious personal injury or property damage is created. That risk arises because of the possibility that a shell or rocket will malfunction or be misdirected. Furthermore, no matter how much care pyrotechnicians exercise, they cannot entirely eliminate the high risk inherent in setting off powerful explosives such as fireworks near crowds.

The dangerousness of fireworks displays is evidenced by the elaborate scheme of administrative regulations with which pyrotechnicians must comply. . . .

[R]elatively few persons conduct public fireworks displays. Therefore, presenting public fireworks displays is not a matter of common usage.

Pyrodyne argues that . . . fireworks are a common way to celebrate the Fourth of July. . . . Although fireworks are frequently and regularly enjoyed by the public, few persons set off special fireworks displays. Indeed, the general public is prohibited by statute from making public fireworks displays insofar as anyone wishing to do so must first obtain a license.

. . . In this case, the fireworks display was conducted at the Puyallup Fairgrounds. Although some locations—such as over water—may be safer, the Puyallup Fairgrounds is an appropriate place for a fireworks show because the audience can be seated at a reasonable distance from the display.

. . . This country has a long-standing tradition of fireworks on the Fourth of July. That tradition suggests that we as a society have decided that the value of fireworks on the day celebrating our national independence and unity outweighs the risks of injuries and damage.

In sum, we find that setting off public fireworks displays . . . is an activity that is not "of common usage" and that presents an ineliminably high risk of serious bodily injury or property damage. We therefore hold that conducting public fireworks displays is an abnormally dangerous activity justifying the imposition of strict liability.

■   ■   ■

Policy considerations also support imposing strict liability on pyrotechnicians for damages caused by their public fireworks displays, although such considerations are not alone sufficient to justify that conclusion. Most basic is the question as to who should bear the loss when an innocent person suffers injury through the nonculpable but abnormally dangerous activities of another. In the case of public fireworks displays, fairness weighs in favor of requiring the pyrotechnicians who present the displays to bear the loss rather than the unfortunate spectators who suffer the injuries.

In addition, the rule of strict liability rests not only upon the ultimate idea of rectifying a wrong and putting the burden where it should belong as a matter of abstract justice, that is, upon the one of the two innocent parties whose acts instigated or made the harm possible, but it also rests on problems of proof: One of these common features is that the person harmed would encounter a difficult problem of proof if some other standard of liability were applied. For example, the disasters caused by those who engage in abnormally dangerous or extra-hazardous activities frequently destroy all evidence of what in fact occurred, other than that the activity was being carried on. Certainly this is true with explosions of dynamite, large quantities of gasoline, or other explosives. In the present case, all evidence was destroyed as to what caused the misfire of the shell that injured the Kleins. Therefore, the problem of proof this case presents for the plaintiffs also supports imposing strict liability on Pyrodyne.

Case Questions

1. What is the principle of *Rylands v. Fletcher*?
2. What essentially determines whether strict liability for abnormally dangerous activities will be imposed?
3. What factors does the court weigh in determining whether an activity is one that qualifies for strict liability?
4. What are the policy reasons for imposing strict liability for abnormally dangerous activities?
5. The Tittles purchased land in the country and built a house there. Two years later, the IMAC Corporation began blasting operations in connection with strip mining on adjacent property approximately 300 feet from the Tittles' home. The Tittles claimed that the blasting has caused cracks in the foundation and the plasterboard of their house. If the Tittles sued IMAC Corp., under the tort theory of strict liability, should they win? Explain.

Chapter Problems

1. Define the following terms:
   a. Tort
   b. Intentional torts
   c. Punitive damages
   d. Defamation

e. Palming off
f. Wrongful discharge
g. Negligence
h. Negligence per se
i. Res ipsa loquitur
j. Comparative negligence
k. Assumption of the risk
l. Strict liability

2. Luella Davis was indebted to Public Finance Corporation. She informed Public Finance that she was no longer employed, was on public aid, and was unable to make payments on the indebtedness. Over an eight-month period, in attempts to collect the debt, employees of Public Finance called Mrs. Davis several times a week, sometimes more than once a day, and frequented her home weekly. On one occasion an agent of Public Finance telephoned Mrs. Davis at the hospital where she was visiting her sick daughter. On another occasion an employee of Public Finance persuaded Mrs. Davis to write a check on the promise that the check would not be cashed. The employee then informed an acquaintance of Mrs. Davis that she was writing bad checks. On still another occasion a Public Finance employee went to Mrs. Davis's home and took an inventory of her household furnishings, refusing to leave until Mrs. Davis's son entered the room. Public Finance was aware that Mrs. Davis suffered from hypertension and a nervous condition. Both of these ailments were aggravated as a result of Public Finance's conduct. Does Davis have any recourse against Public Finance? Explain.

3. Sally Serenade was a singer in Bismarck, North Dakota. She had a contract to sing at the Wild Moose, a tavern where she had a sizable local following. She took a vacation to New York where she met an old friend, Delbert D'Fram, who told her that she was too good to be singing at the Wild Moose and that in any case the owner of the Wild Moose was an idiot who could not differentiate between music and the noise of a chain saw; could not run a respectable business; and treated Sally scandalously. D'Fram introduced her to a journalist friend who wrote a story for *New York Today* repeating everything D'Fram had said about Sally Serenade, the Wild Moose, and its owner. The story also included rumors that the owner of the Wild Moose allowed prostitution in the tavern and that he was living with a prostitute. As a result of this story, Sally was offered a job singing at a New York nightclub. She never returned to North Dakota and never completed her contract to sing at the Wild Moose. Do the Wild Moose and its owner have any recourse under tort law? Explain.

4. Paul Luedtke and his brother Clarence were employed on Nabors Alaska Drilling, Inc.'s (Nabors) oil rigs. Paul supervised an oil rig crew. Nabors required him to undergo urinalysis as part of a physical exam conducted while off duty. He tested positive for use of marijuana. Consequently, he was suspended and told that he would have to pass two additional tests at

monthly intervals to be reinstated. He refused and was fired. Clarence Luedtke, Paul's brother, was fired when he refused to submit to the drug testing. Do Paul and Clarence Luedtke have any recourse against Nabors? Explain.

5. Continental Telephone Company of Vermont (Contel) ran a series of advertisements in Vermont Newspapers featuring certain of its employees. Cynthia Staruski, a sales and service representative at Contel's office in Springfield, Vermont, was featured in one such ad. The ad included a photograph of Mrs. Staruski smiling broadly. In large letters beside her photograph were the words "Hi, I'm Cindy Staruski." Accompanying this was text, attributed with quotation marks to Staruski, describing her job responsibilities and saying that "it has been exciting and reassuring to know that Continental continues to expand its equipment and services to meet its obligations to serve you." Upset by Contel's publication of her name and likeness in this manner, Staruski sued in tort for invasion of privacy. What should be the result and why?

6. The Atlantic Cement Co. operates a cement plant from which fine dust particles are constantly discharged into the air. The particles tend to stay in the air and have been proved to be hazardous to human health. The cement plant is a major source, but not the only source, of particulate contamination in the area. The cost of abating the pollution would be high. If ordered to abate, Atlantic would close the plant. The plant is a major employer in the community. If a group of neighboring landowners sue to enjoin Atlantic from polluting, will they succeed? Why or why not? Which strategies could Atlantic employ to reduce the tension?

7. Geary was employed as a salesperson for U.S. Steel Corporation. He discovered that one of U.S. Steel's products was defective. He complained to his supervisor, who told him to mind his own business. He then contacted the vice president in charge of marketing for the product, who investigated. The investigation led to the removal of the product from the market and a reprimand to Geary's supervisor. The supervisor fired Geary "for making me look bad." What cause of action, if any, does Geary have? Explain. What policy should U.S. Steel adopt to handle situations of this nature?

8. Hidell Corporation has offices in an isolated area with an unusually high crime rate. On several occasions, employees have been victims of robbery and other violent attacks. In December, Paul Peters was robbed and severely beaten in an unlit employee parking lot when getting in his car to go to an executive meeting scheduled for 7 P.M. The attacker, an unemployed drifter, was found. What causes of action would Paul Peters have and against whom? Explain. What if anything can Hiddell do to reduce potential liability for such episodes?

9. Hearn ran a classified advertisement in *Soldier of Fortune* magazine (SOF) that read "EX-MARINE—67–69 'NAM VET, EX-DI, weapons specialist—jungle warfare, pilot, M.E., high risk assignments, U.S. or overseas (404)

991–2684." After seeing the ad, Black called Hearn and proposed that Hearn kill Black's wife. Hearn did so. Black's mother-in-law and daughter sued SOF on the theory that SOF negligently published Hearn's classified ad. Analyze the suit under each of the elements of the tort of negligence. What is the result?

10. Hank Gathers played basketball in Los Angeles for Loyola Marymount University, which had an NCAA Division I basketball team. Gathers had a serious heart disorder and was under medication to normalize his heart rhythm. His doctor and coach knew of his medical condition. Nonetheless, Gathers insisted on playing. Because of Gathers's condition, the coach had a special medical device to revive him in the event he fell unconscious. On one occasion, Gathers passed out at the foul line during a game and was revived. During his final game, Gathers fell unconscious after a slam dunk. Efforts to revive him were of no avail and he died. Who is legally responsible for Gathers's death, if anyone? Explain. What should a college do under such circumstances?

11. Kathy Anderson sued Service Merchandise and Sylvania Lighting Services Corporation under the doctrine of res ipsa loquitur for injuries she suffered when an overhead light fixture fell and struck her as she stood in the checkout line of a Service Merchandise store. Service Merchandise has a maintenance contract with Sylvania, which had previously performed maintenance work on the lighting system. Notwithstanding this contract, Service Merchandise employees had occasionally changed light fixtures when they burned out.

    The trial court granted summary judgment for Service Merchandise and Sylvania. The trial judge ruled that the lighting system was not under the exclusive control of each defendant and therefore the doctrine of res ipsa loquitur did not apply. No other information indicated any specific negligence by Service Merchandise or Sylvania. For that reason, the trial court dismissed Anderson's action. Anderson appealed. What should be the result?

12. On December 3, 1971, a dam burst at a phosphate mine operated by Cities Service Company in Polk County, Florida. Approximately 1 billion gallons of phosphate slime retained in a settling pond escaped into Whidden Creek. The slime reached the Peace River, killing countless fish and inflicting other damage. What recourse do affected property owners have against Cities Service? Explain.

9 PRODUCT LIABILITY AND ADVERTISING

Chapter Outline

Learning Objectives

After learning this chapter the student should be able to:

- Determine when the elements of a strict product liability action are present.
- Distinguish among the three product warranties under the Uniform Commercial Code.
- List the major components of the Magnuson-Moss Warranty Act.
- Identify the circumstances under which the Consumer Product Safety Act applies.
- Recognize when it would be useful for a competitor to avail itself of the Lanham Act.
- Construct ways in which an advertiser may lawfully avoid FTC problems.

Hair dryers, microwave ovens, garage door openers, tools, blenders, snowblowers, and other household products make life more comfortable. They usually perform to the satisfaction of consumers. But when they are defective they may cause both inconvenience and injury.

Product manufacturers and distributors, in efforts to sell more of their products, engage in advertising. Product advertisements may provide useful information to consumers. But when advertisements contain false or misleading information, consumers suffer.

This chapter begins by surveying the area of product safety. After a brief review of common law liability, it focuses on state and federal warranty law related to products. Then the chapter examines the Consumer Product Safety Commission (CPSC) and its regulation of products. Finally, the chapter surveys the area of advertising with a view toward common law, statutory law, and administrative regulation of unfair and deceptive advertising.

Common Law Protections: Products

Consumers injured by defective products may institute suits against the responsible parties. A product liability action results when a plaintiff sues because of an injury caused by a defective product. Defects may occur in construction, design, or labeling of the product.

A construction defect results when a product falls short of the manufacturer's own established standards. Many household products are produced on assembly lines. Quality control becomes very important. Because of human frailty, an overly carbonized bottle or a defectively wired television set may go unnoticed—omissions that could result in injury to product users.

A design defect occurs when the product meets the manufacturer's standards but the standards are inferior. For example, a football helmet may conform to the manufacturer's specifications, yet its inability to absorb shock may invite injury.

A labeling defect occurs when the manufacturer fails to provide adequate warnings of the risk associated with product exposure or proper procedures for using a product. For example, failure to include a warning against a particular medicine's hazard to diabetics may constitute a labeling defect.

Under several common law theories of recovery, a plaintiff may proceed against the party responsible for a defective product that causes injury. The most common theories are negligence and strict liability, discussed next. (See also Chapter 8.)

Negligence

Negligence is the failure to exercise reasonable care in connection with the manufacture, maintenance, inspection, repair, labeling, or delivery of the product. The type of conduct considered reasonable may change with circumstances. In the early 1980s, several deaths and injuries occurred when Tylenol capsules were laced with cyanide. The packaging made it quite easy for this to happen. Since then federal laws have been enacted to require the use of tamperproof containers for certain drugs. Failure of a manufacturer or packager to use a tamperproof container now would be considered negligent conduct—a breach of reasonable care.

Plaintiffs injured by defective products may proceed in negligence, but they will have to prove that the defendant failed to use reasonable care. Even with the aid of res ipsa loquitur (discussed in Chapter 8), the plaintiff may find it virtually impossible to meet this burden, because the defendant may be in a position to convincingly explain away any presumption of negligence.

Strict Liability

The second area of common law product liability is strict liability in tort. This is the plaintiff's most popular legal action in product-related injury cases.

Although the concept of strict liability was developed as early as the 1930s, not until 1963 in *Greenman v. Yuba Power Products, Inc.* did it emerge as an independent tort.[1] In *Greenman,* the plaintiff was seriously injured while using a defective combination power tool. The Supreme Court of California imposed strict liability on the manufacturer without the necessity of proving it was negligent. In its opinion, the court said: "A manufacturer is strictly liable in tort when an article he places on the market, knowing that it is to be used without inspection for defects, proves to have a defect that causes injury to a human being. . . ."

The purpose of such liability is to ensure that the costs of injuries resulting from defective products are borne by the manufacturers that put such products on the market rather than by the injured persons who are powerless to protect themselves.

Since *Greenman,* courts have followed its lead in developing product liability law along the lines of strict liability. The strict liability standard has been set down in the Restatement (Second) of Torts §402A.[2]

Restatement (Second) of Torts 402A(1)

One who sells any product in a defective condition unreasonably dangerous to the user or consumer or to his property is subject to liability for physical harm thereby caused to the ultimate user or consumer, or to his property, if:

a. the seller is engaged in the business of selling such a product, and

b. it is expected to and does reach the user or consumer without substantial change in the condition in which it is sold.

---

[1] 50 Cal. 2d 57, 377 P.2d 897 (1963).

[2] The Restatement is a scholarly synthesis and summary of the law as perceived by the American Law Institute. It does not have the force of law, though courts often rely heavily on it and adopt its provisions as the law of their jurisdiction.

Strict liability applies only against those regularly engaged in selling the product; it is not intended to reach the person who makes an occasional sale. To recover under strict liability in most states, the plaintiff must prove that:

- The product was *defective.*
- The product left the defendant's *control* in a defective condition.
- The defect caused the product to be *unreasonably dangerous.*
- The defect was the *proximate cause* of injury.

Product Defect

Experts are often called on to determine whether a product is defective. An engineer may be needed to assess the stress potential of a lawn mower foot guard that breaks and causes injury. An expert may have to reconstruct an accident and render an opinion as to whether it was caused by the driver's negligence or defective brakes. Failure to warn a buyer of a product's hidden danger may also make the product defective. In absence of proof of a defect in the product, there can be no recovery under strict liability.

Product Control

Proving the condition of a product when it left the defendant's control is often difficult. Nonetheless, it can be established by circumstantial evidence. Assume, for example, that Wanda Consumer purchases a bottle of Liquid Drain Unstopper from the local hardware store. On her way home, the bottle leaks and the liquid burns her skin. An examination of the bottle shows that its safety cap was defective. In a suit against the manufacturer under strict liability, Wanda Consumer needs to trace the custody of the bottle from the store back through to the manufacturer. She must show that the cap was not tampered with after it left the manufacturer's control. Liability would not be limited to the manufacturer. Everyone in the distributive chain is liable, including the wholesaler and the retailer. Their liability, similar to the manufacturer's, is not dependent on their conduct. Even when a defective component is integrated into a larger product, any seller of the final product may still be strictly liable as long as it left the seller's control in a defective condition.

Product Danger

Additionally, the defect must make the product unreasonably dangerous. A defectively manufactured tire is a classic case for strict liability. It is reasonably foreseeable that a defect in a tire would cause the tire to be unduly dangerous. Tires support cars that travel at high speeds. When a tire blows because of a defective tread, there is a reasonable likelihood of injury to the car's occupants. Food, drugs, automobiles, power tools, water heaters, and gas stoves are just a few of the many products that are unreasonably dangerous if defective. In contrast, a defectively manufactured transistor radio would not normally present an unreasonably dangerous risk of injury to the user, and hence would not be the subject of strict liability. For the same reason paper clips, pens, window shades, and music boxes are not ordinarily the subject of strict liability.

A product danger may be created as a result of the absence of an appropriate design that would have avoided foreseeable injury. The following case examines a "clicking" heart valve implant to determine whether it is a defective product that is unreasonably dangerous.

BRAVMAN V. BAXTER HEALTHCARE CORPORATION
794 F. Supp. 96 (S.D.N.Y. 1992)

Bravman (plaintiff-appellant) underwent surgery to replace his natural mitral heart valve with an artificial Edwards-Duromedics Heart Valve. Without the surgery, Bravman's life expectancy would have been severely curtailed.

The clicking from the artificial valve is inordinately loud and can be heard 30 feet away. This causes Bravman much distress.

Bravman sued Baxter, the manufacturer of the valve, seeking recovery under strict product liability theory, contending the product is defective. The District Court Judge granted summary judgment in Baxter's favor.

Judge Sweet

[T]he Court assumes Bravman's . . . Heart Valve pulses with a [loud] jangle . . . . Bravman contends that, his Edwards-Duromedics Heart Valve is defective, and Baxter breached its duty to warn him of this potential defect. . . .

In New York, a manufacturer may be held strictly liable for a manufacturing defect, for a design defect, and for failing to adequately warn of a product's defects. Proving such a claim requires an unreasonably dangerous defect that leads to physical injury, . . . that is, "if the defect were known at the time of manufacture, a reasonable person would conclude that the utility of the product did not outweigh the risk inherent in marketing a product designed in that manner."

1. Design Defect

Bravman hints at a design defect claim by suggesting that one of the reasons the Edwards-Duromedics Heart Valve might be noisy is that its leaflets are twice as thick as those on a St. Jude Medical Valve. The primary purpose of the valve's design is to control the flow of blood, allowing its recipients to enjoy fuller and longer lives. As the overwhelming majority of the Edwards-Duromedics Heart Valves continue to meet this goal, it is reasonable to conclude as a matter of law that the utility of their design outweighs isolated instances of excessively noisy valves.

Of the approximately 18,364 Edwards-Duromedics Hearts Valves successfully installed, only the valves of Bravman and one other person emit extremely loud clicks. Although other recipients were troubled by noise, the number is not significant. The record further shows that the Edwards-Duromedics Heart Valve was less noisy than two other valves that were then available. Given the large number of persons whose lives were saved by the Edwards-Duromedics Heart Valve and the state of technology, Bravman has failed to establish that the Edwards-Duromedics Heart Valve was defectively designed.

2. Product Defect

Bravman contends that his Edwards-Duromedics Heart Valve is defective because it is noisy and has not performed as intended, thus injuring him. To prevail on a product defect claim, though, he must show that his heart valve has a legally cognizable defect and that that defect has caused him physical harm.

Section 402A of the Restatement allows a consumer to recover for physical harm caused by "a defective condition unreasonably dangerous to the user or consumer." A stone in a can of beans that causes someone to chip a tooth is such a condition. . . . So is a bottle that explodes, a ladder step that breaks, an accelerator pedal that sticks. . . . Each creates an unreasonably dangerous condition unexpected by the user. There are many other types of defects, however, that do not create such a condition and are not compensable as a tort. While the latter types of defects typically result in economic loss and are compensable . . . they also underscore the fact that the law often does not provide a remedy for every wrong.

Even if a noisy heart valve can be considered defective, there is no evidence showing that such a defect is unreasonably dangerous. Bravman has failed to show the clicking has placed him in harm's way. . . . While a product without an unreasonably dangerous defect can often be replaced, that option is likely to be unavailable to Bravman since he faces a much greater risk of death by undergoing surgery than by leaving the valve in place. Although the Court empathizes with the dilemma Bravman faces, he nevertheless has failed to show that the defect is unreasonably dangerous and that he has suffered any direct physical injury.

3. Failure to Warn

Bravman also contends that Baxter knew of the valve's noisy characteristic before he underwent surgery and was required to warn his surgeon of this potential.

A manufacturer is under a continuing obligation to warn of a product's potential dangers of which it knew or should have known. A manufacturer is generally in the best position to discern and correct dangerous product defects, justifying placing this responsibility on it. Nevertheless, a manufacturer is not under a duty to warn of each and every defect in a product—the law properly limits the duty to dangerous defects that are not obvious.

Bravman primarily relies on New York cases requiring drug manufacturers to notify the medical community of their products' side effects in making this argument. From this, he appears to imply that a heart valve is an unavoidably unsafe product . . . and that Baxter had an obligation to warn his surgeon of the noise potential. . . .

■   ■   ■

A product is unavoidably unsafe if it has the potential to inflict a physical harm. The insertion of a mechanical heart valve indeed can have such side effects, including stroke and myocardial infarction. The record shows, however, that Bravman's surgeon knew of these risks and discussed them fully with Bravman. The two also discussed the difference between porcine valves and mechanical valves, with the surgeon recommending the insertion of the more durable mechanical valve.

. . . A manufacturer is expected to warn about the possibility of danger so that doctors, as intermediaries, and others can make intelligent judgments concerning the risks associated with a product. A noisy prosthetic device, however, does not pose such a threat. There is no evidence showing that the Edwards-Duromedics Heart Valve has inflicted any physical harm on Bravman, nor that a failure to warn him of the noise has placed him in physical danger. . . . Indeed, the clicking indicates that the Edwards-Duromedics Heart Valve continues to regulate the flow of blood through Bravman's heart, as intended.

For the reasons set forth above, Baxter's motion for summary judgment is granted. . . .

Case Questions

1. What is the issue presented in this case?
2. Examine the facts under each of the elements of strict liability.
3. Do you agree that the product was not defective? Analyze.

4. Assume that the clicking was so loud as to interfere with Bravman's hearing and concentration and that as a result he became clinically depressed. Would there be a different result? Explain.

Ethical Dilemmas/Issues

General Motors (GM) produced a pickup truck from 1973–1987 that located the gas tanks on the underside of the vehicle outside of the truck's body frame. A number of side impact crashes involving these trucks have resulted in explosions, fires, and death or serious injury to the occupants.

In one suit against GM, based upon defective design of the sidesaddle fuel tank, the jury awarded the plaintiff $105.2 million. GM insists that the pickups are safe and that the design is not defective.

Recently, the company has been posting losses each quarter. Consumer organizations and at least one government agency are urging GM to recall the tens of thousands of pickups. The cost of such a recall would be so great that it would compound the financial troubles of the company, and probably result in a larger reduction in force, a drop in stock prices, and spiraling financial woes from there.

What are the ethical issues? What would you do?

Proximate Cause

Injury must proximately result from the defective product—the injury must be directly attributable to the defective product. Proximate cause (discussed in Chapter 8) is based on foreseeability. The question becomes whether it is foreseeable that this defective product would cause injury to a particular plaintiff. Recovery, then, is not limited to buyers. The trend has been to extend recovery to family members and those users and bystanders whose injury is reasonably foreseeable.

Defenses

Economics, not fault, is the basis for holding a manufacturer liable under strict liability. Hence, a plaintiff's contributory negligence does not affect recovery. Assumption of the risk, however, bars recovery in many states. A person who knows of a dangerous defect in a swimming pool slide but uses it nonetheless, assumes the risk of injuries caused by the defect. Akin to assumption of the risk is misuse of the product. Misuse of the product is a bar to recovery when it con-

TABLE 9–1	**Market Share Liability Example**				
Company	*Share of Market*		*Total Damages*		*Liability*
A	10%	×	$1,000,000	=	$100,000
B	15	×	1,000,000	=	150,000
C	25	×	1,000,000	=	250,000
D	50	×	1,000,000	=	500,000
	100%				$1,000,000

tributes to the plaintiff's injury. For example, a person who uses a power saw as a toenail clipper cannot recover for loss of a toe even if the saw was defective. This misuse cannot reasonably be foreseen by the seller.

Recently, questions have arisen as to whether a manufacturer can be held strictly liable for injury caused by a defective product that was not scientifically known to be defective at the time of manufacture. Although at least one court has rejected this state-of-the-art defense,[3] other courts have been very reluctant to follow.

Market Share Liability

Generally, an injured plaintiff must identify the specific defendant who caused injury. In some cases this is virtually impossible to do. For example, many pharmaceutical companies produced diethylstilbestrol (DES), a drug formerly prescribed for the prevention of miscarriages. Eventually, the drug proved to cause cervical and vaginal growths and cancer in the offspring of mothers who took the drug.

Plaintiffs who suffer from the effects of the drug sometimes 18 to 20 years after the drug was taken by their mothers are not in a position to identify which company produced the defective product that caused their injury. Where, as here, the whole industry has produced defective homogeneous products, some states shift the burden to the defendants to prove that they were not responsible for the injury; liability for damages is proportionally allocated according to the share of the market that each defendant enjoyed.

Assume, for example, that defendant A had a 10 percent share of the market, B had 15 percent, C had 25 percent, and D had 50 percent. Assume further that the damages to plaintiff as found by the jury are $1 million. The **market share liability** under these assumptions is calculated in Table 9–1.

In California, a defendant may avoid liability by proving that its product was not responsible for the specific injury. It may do this by proving, for example, that it did not sell to distributors in the geographical area where the plaintiff purchased the drug. In New York, however, defendants may only be exonerated if they can prove that they did not market the drug in the United States during the time in question.

---

[3] Beshada v. Johns-Manville Products Corp., 90 N.J. 191, 447 A 2d 539 (1982).

Statutory Law Protections: Products

States have enacted protections against defective products in the form of warranties. A warranty is a promise that a product will perform in a certain way. It is part of a contract. A plaintiff who proves that the defendant breached a warranty may recover damages. The plaintiff does not have to prove that the defendant was negligent, only that injury occurred because the product did not conform to the warranty.

In most states a party does not have to be in a contractual relationship with the warrantor in order to recover. In fact, some states extend the product warranty to family, household members, and guests of the buyer. Others include any person who might be reasonably expected to use or be affected by the product. Warranties may be expressly or impliedly made.

Express Warranty

Often, in an effort to make a product more attractive to the consumer, a seller makes explicit promises or representations about the product. For example, an energy conservation service may warrant that the homeowner will experience 40 percent energy savings by purchasing and installing a computerized rheostat to regulate a furnace. This is a warranty with respect to future performance, and the product will be expected to live up to the representations. A plaintiff who sustains injury as a result of a breach of the **express warranty** may recover damages against the warrantor. Warranties may also be based on representations regarding the nature or quality of the product. "This furnace is a new, gas-driven Ryan 5,000 BTU unit" is such a warranty.

A warranty need not be couched in formal language. Section 2–313 of the Uniform Commercial Code (UCC) recognizes that any statement of fact or promise that is part of the bargain creates an express warranty.

> **Uniform Commercial Code §2–313(1)(a)**
>
> Express warranties by the seller are created as follows: Any affirmation of fact or promise made by the seller to the buyer which relates to the goods and becomes part of the basis of the bargain creates an express warranty that the goods shall conform to the affirmation or promise.

A statement of opinion is not an express warranty or representation. A statement of the value of the goods or commendation of the goods does not create a warranty. It is to be expected by consumers that any merchant interested in selling a product is prone to make exaggerated claims about the product. A claim couched in terms of a general opinion, such as "This lawn mower is the safest on the market," normally is not the subject of a warranty. On the other hand, if more specific factual claims are made, such as "The blades in this lawn mower are built to last five years," then a failure of the blades in less than five years is a breach of that representation and may result in liability.

Implied Warranty

Under UCC §2–314, a seller of goods implicitly warrants that those goods are fit for ordinary purposes. This is known as the **implied warranty** of merchantability. In selling a hamburger, the seller impliedly warrants that it is fit for consumption. If the hamburger is rotten, the seller has breached the implied warranty of merchantability and is liable for resulting injury. This rule of law is consistent with the expectations of the consumer. It is only reasonable for a consumer to expect that a product on the market is safe for its intended use.

Uniform Commercial Code §2–314(1)

Unless excluded or modified . . . a warranty that the goods shall be merchantable is implied in a contract for their sale if the seller is a merchant. . . .

The implied warranty of merchantability applies only to merchants. A merchant is one who customarily deals in the goods that are the subject of the sale or who has a particular expertise regarding these goods. One who engages in an isolated sale of goods—for example, a homeowner who has a garage sale—is not a merchant. Such a seller would not normally be totally familiar with the mechanics of the products sold. Consequently, the buyer could not reasonably expect a nonmerchant to imply that the product sold is merchantable.

In addition to the implied warranty of merchantability, the UCC affords an injured plaintiff the protection of §2–315. This section grants the purchaser an implied warranty that goods are fit for a particular purpose.

Uniform Commercial Code §2–315

Where the seller at the time of contracting has reason to know any particular purpose for which the goods are required and that the buyer is relying on the seller's skill or judgment to select or furnish suitable goods, there is unless excluded or modified . . . an implied warranty that the goods shall be fit for such purpose.

The particular purpose warranty is more specific than the merchantability warranty. It involves situations in which the seller has been informed of a particular use as opposed to a customary use. The customary use of shoes would be for normal walking; a particular use would be for mountain climbing. If a customer asks for a pair of shoes suitable for mountain climbing and relies on the seller's recommendation, the implied warranty of fitness for a particular purpose comes into play. Similar to the implied warranty of merchantability, this type of warranty is applicable only to a seller who is a merchant.

Damages

Ordinarily, when a breach of warranty occurs, the injured person may recover damages—the difference between the value of the goods received and their value had they been as warranted. Buyers are also entitled to personal injury damages proximately resulting from any breach of warranty. Damages would include compensation for doctor and hospital expenses, loss of wages, disability, cosmetic disfigurement, and pain and suffering related to the injury. In most jurisdictions, family members injured as a result of the defective product could also recover their damages for personal injuries.

Warranty Limitations

Under the UCC, a merchant may exclude both express and implied warranties. Any disclaimer, however, must be clear and comply with the terms of the UCC. Ambiguities are resolved in favor of the consumer. Suppose that Crop Harvester, Inc. sold pesticide with a tag marked "safe for crop dusting," but that a contract covering the sale of that pesticide stated "no warranties." The conflict here would be resolved in favor of the existence of the warranty.

The UCC sets out the procedure for disclaiming implied warranties. To effectively disclaim an implied warranty of merchantability, the disclaimer must specifically mention merchantability and, if in writing, must be conspicuous. To disclaim an implied warranty of fitness, the disclaimer again must be by a conspicuous writing. A conspicuous writing is one for which a reasonable person would take notice. A written disclaimer should appear in larger letters than the surrounding print.

The UCC further specifies that all implied warranties may be excluded by expressions such as "as is," "with all faults," or other language that clearly communicates the intention of disclaiming implied warranties. A consumer who is aware of a defect in the product may not take advantage of an implied warranty. For example, a buyer who purchases a skateboard with an obvious crack in the platform may not claim the protection of an implied warranty. An injured purchaser who refuses the seller's request to inspect the goods may be without warranty protection.

Administrative Regulation: Products

State product liability law has not been totally effective in combatting product hazards and injury. One notable weakness is that it is not applicable until after injury occurs. The federal government, consequently, has intervened to prevent injury by passing laws to inform consumers about the products they buy and to impose safety standards on those products. Two noteworthy federal acts are the **Magnuson-Moss Warranty Act** and the **Consumer Product Safety Act**.

Magnuson-Moss Warranty Act

The Magnuson-Moss Warranty Act requires certain disclosures in connection with written warranties, imposes restrictions on disclaimers of implied warranties, and establishes a procedure through which consumers may more effectively enforce their warranty rights.

Magnuson-Moss is administered by the Federal Trade Commission (FTC). The act covers products normally used for personal, family, or household purposes and is applicable only when a seller offers a written warranty.

Disclosure

The act does not require the manufacturer or seller to make any warranties. A written warranty made in connection with a consumer product costing more than $15, however, must "fully and conspicuously disclose in simple and readily understandable language the terms and conditions of the warranty."[4]

The specific contents of disclosures under the act are entrusted to the scrutiny and regulation of the FTC. The FTC has the power to promulgate rules requiring that the writing clearly inform the purchaser of the terms of the warranty. For example, one FTC rule provides that any exclusion, such as a limitation of liability for personal injury or property damage, must be accompanied by the following statement: "Some states do not allow the exclusion or limitation of . . . damages, so the above limitation or exclusion may not apply to you."

Full and Limited Warranty

Magnuson-Moss also requires that any written warranty involving a product that costs more than $10 must clearly and conspicuously contain the tag "full" or "limited." The full tag is properly employed only if the warranty is consistent with at least the four federal standards contained in Table 9–2.

TABLE 9–2   Minimum Standards for Full Warranty Tags

- In case of a defect, malfunction, or failure to conform to the warranty, the warrantor must fix the product within a reasonable time without charge.
- The warrantor may not impose any limitation on the duration of an implied warranty on the product.
- The warrantor may not exclude or limit damages (including personal injury damages) for breach of warranty on the product unless the exclusion appears conspicuously on the face of the warranty.
- After a reasonable number of failed attempts to remedy the defects in the product, the warrantor must permit the customer to elect to receive a refund or replacement of the product without charge.

---

[4] Although the act authorizes the FTC to promulgate rules requiring disclosure on warranties pertaining to products that cost more than $5, the FTC requires disclosure only for products costing more than $15.

Any warranty that does not meet these federal standards must conspicuously be designated as limited.

Limitation of Disclaimer

A seller may disclaim implied warranties when the sale of that product is not connected with a written warranty or a service contract. Consequently, it is possible for a supplier to disclaim all implied warranties by selling "as is." However, a seller who extends a written warranty or a service contract may not *totally* disclaim implied warranties. A supplier may limit the duration of implied warranties to the duration of a written warranty, as long as the limitation is fair and conspicuously disclosed. An express warranty that restricts the duration of the implied warranty, however, must be designated as a "limited warranty."

Remedies

Consumers may sue warrantors who violate the Magnuson-Moss Warranty Act or otherwise breach express or implied warranties. A successful plaintiff may recover damages plus the costs of the suit, including an award of reasonable attorney fees.

The warrantor may establish an informal dispute resolution procedure that conforms to FTC rules and may include within the written warranty a requirement that the consumer use this procedure before pursuing legal action under the act. The consumer is bound by this provision. The Magnuson-Moss Warranty Act also requires that the warrantor be afforded a reasonable opportunity to rectify its failure to comply before a suit may be instituted.

The Consumer Product Safety Act

The National Commission on Product Safety was established to investigate the adequacy of consumer protection against unreasonable risks caused by hazardous household products. The commission took particular note of products notorious for presenting unreasonable hazards, including color TV sets, fireworks, glass bottles, infant furniture, lawn mowers, and unvented gas heaters. The commission believed that the industries producing these products were too profit-conscious to engage in self-regulation that would adequately protect consumers. It recommended the creation of a federal regulatory agency with broad authority to ensure the safety of consumer products by imposing mandatory safety standards. In response to these recommendations, Congress passed the Consumer Product Safety Act (CPSA), which established the **Consumer Product Safety Commission (CPSC)**.[5] The CPSC consists of five commissioners appointed by the president for seven-year terms (see Figure 9–1).

---

[5] The CPSA transferred to the CPSC the administration of several other acts related to consumer safety: the Federal Hazardous Substances Act, the Poison Prevention Packaging Act, the Flammable Fabrics Act, and the Refrigerator Safety Act.

FIGURE 9–1   **Consumer Product Safety Commission Organizational Chart**

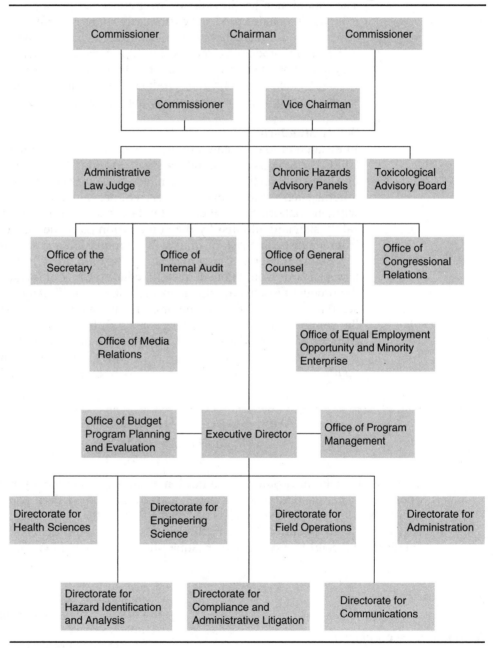

SOURCE: Michael R. Lemov, *Consumer Product Safety Commission*, Shepard's/McGraw-Hill, 1983.

Consumer Products

The commission has jurisdiction over consumer products, the definition of which is broad. It includes products customarily sold to consumers and used in the home, at school, or for recreation. A product need not be sold directly to a customer to be considered a product as long as it was produced or distributed for consumer use. Likewise, a product need not be intended for exclusive use or control by a consumer to be classified as a consumer product. For example, vending machines placed in schools, workplaces, or other public places are deemed consumer products.

Safety Standards

In its attempt to eliminate products that present unreasonable risks of injury, the CPSC issues **consumer product safety standards** in the form of performance or labeling specifications. A performance standard specifies minimum performance criteria, such as the number of pounds of pressure a glass window must withstand without shattering. A labeling standard may require warning labels. When no safety standard adopted by the commission could adequately protect the public from unreasonable risk of injury, the commission can seek to ban a product.

Before implementing a mandatory standard, the CPSC must find that voluntary standards would not adequately reduce the risk of injury. It must also find that the product presents an unreasonable risk of injury. Any standard must be "reasonably necessary" to mitigate or eliminate that risk. To make this determination the commission and courts engage in a cost/benefit analysis, weighing the effectiveness of the standard against its effects on the cost of the product. The following case concerning swimming pool slides offers some insight into a court's approach to determining whether a standard meets the "reasonably necessary" test.

AQUA SLIDE 'N' DIVE V. CPSC
569 F. 2d 831 (5th Cir. 1978)

The Consumer Product Safety Commission established standards for swimming pool slides. One standard requires that signs warning of the risk of paralysis from accidents in the use of the slide be placed on the steps of the ladder and in the water. Aqua Slide filed a petition in the Fifth Circuit Court of Appeals challenging the standard. The court found in favor of Aqua Slide and struck down the standard.

Judge Roney

Reasonable Necessity

Aqua Slide argues that substantial evidence does not support the Commission's conclusion, that this standard is "reasonably necessary," [since]

. . . the warning signs have not been tested, may not work, and may be so explicit as to deter slide use unnecessarily. . . .

The Act does not define the term "reasonably necessary," and apparently Congress intended the commission and the courts to work out a definition on a case-by-case basis. The legislative history, and the holdings of other cases decided under similar statutes, do discuss the meaning of "unreasonable risks," and indicate that term is interrelated with the "reasonably necessary" requirement. The necessity for the standard depends upon the nature of the risk, and the reasonableness of the risk is a function of the burden a standard would impose on a user of the product.

In this case, the severity of the risk is so terrible that virtually any standard which actually promised to reduce it would seem to be "reasonably necessary." [T]he Commission . . . concentrated [its] fact-gathering efforts on an attempt to identify the precise nature of the risk. After surveying slide accidents, and considering the result of scientific studies of slide dynamics, the Commission identified a risk of "quadriplegia and paraplegia resulting from users . . . sliding down the slide in a head first position and striking the bottom of the pool. . . ." Without question, paraplegia is a horrible injury.

The risk of paraplegia from swimming pool slides, however, is extremely remote. More than 350,000 slides are in use, yet the Commission could find no more than 11 instances of paraplegia over a six-year period. According to . . . figures, the risk, for slide users, is about one in 10 million, less than the risk an average person has of being killed by lightning . . . . Given the severity of the injury, however, and the precedent of other cases, it seems likely that a standard which actually promised to reduce the risk without unduly hampering the availability of the slides or decreasing their utility could render this risk "unreasonable." The question then is whether the specific provisions of the standard which Aqua Slide challenges have been shown to accomplish that task.

Given the infrequency of the risk, it was incumbent upon the . . . Commission to produce evidence that the standard actually promised to reduce the risk. Instead, . . . the Commission gave the matter short shrift. To begin with, the standard only applies to new slides. It does not affect slides

now in use, despite [a] . . . finding that "[t]here are many more slides in use than produced per year by a factor of ten to one." It is odd the Commission chose this limited method of addressing the risk rather than deciding to use its power to conduct a public education campaign, which could reach far more slide users.

Furthermore, the record contains only the most ambiguous of indications that the warning signs would actually be heeded by slide users. The Commission did not test the signs. . . .

In the preamble to the proposed standard, [the Commission] could do no more than say the signs "may achieve" a reduction in dangerous belly slides. Certainly the evidence of actual injuries bespeaks the kind of foolhardiness for which proper instructions would provide no cure. One accident victim had been drinking, and a jury apparently concluded he had hit a chair floating in a pool. Another dove through a hoop. Still a third went down a slide improperly installed in only three feet of water. Another went down on his knees, a position about which the proposed warning sign is silent.

In short, the Commission provided little evidence that the warning signs would benefit consumers. The risk is remote. The evidence that the signs would reduce the risk rests more on inference than it does on proof. In weighing the "reasonable necessity" for the signs, the crucial question, then, is whether the benefit has a reasonable relationship to the disadvantages the sign requirement imposes.

In this case, the prime disadvantage to which Aqua Slide points is the warning's effect on the availability of the slides. Because the Commission did not test the signs, it provided little evidence of whether the signs were explicit and shocking in their portrayal of the risk of paralysis as to constitute an unwarranted deterrent to the marketing of slides, and, hence, their availability to users. The record provides only scant assurance that purchasers would not be so alarmed by the warning signs that they would unnecessarily abstain. The signs do not indicate paralysis is a one in 10 million risk. The only evidence concerning the marketing impact the Commission's signs would have is a Commission staff report, based on [a research institute study]. The Commission report was developed to satisfy a required statutory finding concerning the economic impact of the standard. It was based on interviews with persons active in the industry; however, it did not test the reaction of slide buyers.

The Commission report indicated 20 percent of total sales would be lost over six years. . . . The Commission apparently thought that, because, absent the standard, the industry was expected to grow each year by 51 percent, the net effect would be merely to slow the industry's rate of growth and harm investment. . . . The Commission's economic report constitutes the only record evidence concerning the economic impact of the standard. As such it is the "basic data" upon which the Commission relied. . . .

Certainly, on this record, the economic finding is crucial. The only way to tell whether the relationship between the advantages of the signs is

reasonable is to know exactly what those disadvantages are. Yet the Commission's study of the standard's economic impact lacks the indicia of reliability. At the same time, the proof that signs will significantly reduce the risk is weak. We consequently hold that the Commission has failed to provide substantial evidence to demonstrate the reasonable necessity of the warning signs. We set aside the warning sign requirement. . . .

Case Questions

1. Which standard did the CPSC enact? Which risk was it designed to eliminate?
2. Why did the court determine that the agency failed to demonstrate that the warning signs were a reasonable necessity?
3. What could the agency have done to substantiate the need for the warning signs?
4. Which factors determine whether a risk of injury is unreasonable?
5. What does this case tell you about the power of administrative agencies?

Remedies

The CPSA authorizes various enforcement procedures, including product seizure and injunctions. Other remedies include civil and criminal penalties, private suits to enforce the act, and private damage actions.

Civil penalties may be assessed against a person who knowingly violates any CPSA provisions. Knowingly is not confined to actual knowledge; it includes knowledge that a reasonable person would possess by exercising reasonable diligence to discover truth. A manufacturer that knowingly sells banned products may be fined. A person who knowingly and willfully commits an act prohibited by the CPSA, after being notified by the commission of its prohibition, is subject to a criminal penalties of fine and imprisonment.

Any interested person may institute a private suit to enforce the CPSA. The individual must first notify the CPSC, the attorney general, and the alleged violator of the intention to sue. This notification affords the commission or the attorney general an opportunity to take appropriate civil or criminal action and gives the alleged offender an opportunity to resolve the complaint. If the commission or the Department of Justice files suit within 30 days, the individual is barred from suing.

An individual who has been injured as a result of a knowing or willful violation of a commission rule or order may seek damages in a federal district court when the amount in controversy exceeds $10,000. (Otherwise, the injured party is left solely to state remedies.) The aggrieved individual, if successful, may recover damages, the cost of the suit, and reasonable attorney fees.

Common Law Protections: Advertising

False advertising harms consumers by unfairly influencing them to buy goods and services they might otherwise avoid. Not surprisingly, both consumers and competitors have sought relief from false advertising.

Common law actions for false advertising exist for breach of contract and for the tort of deceit. Breach of contract is discussed in Chapter 7. It is a very limited remedy for consumers in relationship to advertising; normally, an advertisement is not considered an offer but only an invitation to the consumer to make an offer. Consequently, no contract exists even when the consumer accepts the terms of the advertisement.

Ethical Dilemmas/Issues

Joe Camel is a cartoon character (nicotoon) for Camel cigarettes. He appears on billboards, magazines, and T-shirts, he always refers to himself as a "smooth character," and he always has a cigarette—a Camel—hanging from his dromedary-like lip.

Since Joe Camel's advent on the advertising scene, the following has occurred:

- 98 percent of teens know who Joe Camel is, as compared to 68 percent of adults.
- 33 percent of smokers 18 and under smoke Camels, whereas before this advent only 1 percent smoked Camels.

The producers of Camel cigarettes deny that they are, in fact, targeting the youth; they contend that they are after the 38 million adult smokers who do not smoke Camels. Studies show that 400,000 people die a year from smoking-related diseases. Critics argue that the industry is targeting the young to replace these smokers.

The marketing director for a large competitor of Camel's is reviewing a report on her desk, conducted by a task force of the company. The report indicates that sales will rise by 10 percent more than otherwise expected if the company follows the "Joe Camel" model and adopts a cartoon mascot to accompany its advertisements.

What are the ethical issues? What would you do?

The tort of deceit is discussed in Chapter 8. It requires proof of (1) a misrepresentation of a material fact, (2) knowledge by the seller that the misrepresentation is false, (3) the seller's intent that the buyer rely on the misrepresentation, (4) the buyer's justified reliance on the misrepresentation, and (5) injury to the buyer. This tort gives consumers only limited protection because of the difficulty of proving these elements. For example, statements intended to induce a sale that express opinion, not fact, may not constitute deceit.

Statutory Law Protections: Advertising

Besides common law remedies for false advertising, a buyer may have a statutory remedy under the Uniform Commercial Code (UCC). As explained earlier, the UCC has been adopted by all states. Article 2 of the UCC governs sales of goods. Section 2–313 provides that any statement, sample, or model may constitute an express warranty if it is part of the basis of the bargain. Hence, a display depicting large pink grapefruits creates an express warranty that the grapefruits sold are of that variety.

Advertising terms may be express warranties. If the goods do not conform to the representation, the purchaser may sue for breach of warranty. However, courts require that the buyer reasonably rely on these terms; ordinary sales talk (puffing) does not create an express warranty under the UCC. Additionally, a seller may avoid liability by disclaiming express warranties in the sales contract. Thus, the puffing defense and disclaimer clauses have weakened the action for breach of warranty under the UCC.

The Lanham Trademark Act

Section 43(a) of the **Lanham Trademark Act** prohibits the use of "any false description or representation" in connection with any goods or services introduced into commerce. It provides a claim for any competitor likely to be damaged by false representation.

Lanham Act §43(a)

Any person who shall . . . use in connection with any goods or services . . . a false . . . description or representation . . . shall be liable. . . .

Section 43(a) enables one competitor to sue another for misrepresentation of a product. The following case, involving a renowned musical composer and performer, illustrates the application of the Lanham Act.

WAITS V. FRITO LAY, INC.
978 F.2d 1093 (9th Cir. 1992)

Tom Waits (plaintiff-appellee) is a professional singer, songwriter, and actor. He has a distinct raspy, gravelly singing voice. He has recorded more than 17 albums, traveled and performed extensively, and received top awards from *Rolling Stone* and *Spin* magazines. Additionally, he appeared on such shows as "Saturday Night Live" and "Late Night with David Letterman." Waits does not do commercials and is very emphatic about it, reasoning that commercials detract from artistic integrity.

Frito-Lay manufactures, distributes, and sells prepared and packaged food products, including Doritos brand corn chips. It hired an advertising firm to develop an advertising campaign to introduce a new Frito-Lay product, SalsaRio Doritos. The advertisement found inspiration from a Tom Waits hit song, "Step Right Up" (ironically a jazzy parody of commercial hucksterism), consisting of a succession of humorous advertising pitches. The final song echoed the rhyming word-play of the Waits song. It employed Stephen Carter, who impersonated Tom Waits' voice to near perfection. The commercial was broadcast on over 250 radio stations nationwide.

Waits sued the ad agency and Frito-Lay in the Federal District Court. One of his actions alleged false endorsement under the Lanham Act. The jury returned with an award of $100,000 and attorney fees on this claim in favor of Waits. Defendants appealed to the Ninth Circuit Court of Appeals, who affirmed in part.

Judge Boochever

Section 43(a) of the Lanham Act prohibits the use of false designations of origin, false descriptions, and false representations in the advertising and sale of goods and services. Waits' claim under §43(a) is premised on the theory that by using an imitation of his distinctive voice in an admitted parody of a Tom Waits song, the defendants misrepresented his association with and endorsement of SalsaRio Doritos. Before we address these contentions, however, we turn to the threshold issue of whether false endorsement claims are properly cognizable under §43(a) of the Lanham Act, a question of first impression in this circuit.

False Endorsement

At the time of the broadcast of the Doritos commercial, §43(a) provided in pertinent part:

Any person who shall affix, apply, or annex, or use in connection with any good or services . . . a false designation of origin, or any false designation or representation . . . shall be liable to a civil action . . . by any person who believes that he is or is likely to be damaged by the use of any such false designation or representation.

Courts in other jurisdictions have interpreted this language as authorizing claims for false endorsement. . . . Moreover, courts have recognized false endorsement claims brought by plaintiffs, including celebrities, where those attributes amount to an unregistered commercial "trademark."

The persuasiveness of this case law as the cognizability of Waits' Lanham Act claim is reinforced by the 1988 Lanham Act amendments. The legislative history states that the amendments to §43(a) codify previous judicial interpretation given this provision. Although these amendments did not take effect until November 1989, approximately a year after the broadcast of the defendants' Doritos commercial, as a codification of prior case law and in the absence of controlling precedent to the contrary, they properly inform our interpretation of the previous version of §43(a). Specifically, we read the amended language to codify case law interpreting §43(a) to encompass false endorsement claims. Section 43(a) now expressly prohibits . . . the use of any symbol or device which is likely to deceive consumers as to the association, sponsorship, or approval of goods or services by another person. Moreover, the legislative history of the 1988 amendments also makes clear that in retaining the statute's original terms, "symbol or device" in the definition of "trademark," Congress approved the broad judicial interpretation of these terms to include distinctive sounds and physical appearance. In light of persuasive judicial authority and the subsequent congressional approval of that authority, we conclude that false endorsement claims, including those premised on the unauthorized imitation of an entertainer's distinctive voice, are cognizable under §43(a).

Merits

The defendants next argue that Waits' false endorsement claim must fail on its merits because the Doritos commercial "did not represent that . . . [Waits] sponsored or endorsed their product." We disagree. The court correctly instructed the jury that in considering Waits' Lanham Act claim, it must determine whether "ordinary consumers . . . would be confused as to whether Tom Waits sang on the commercial . . . and whether he sponsors or endorses SalsaRio Doritos." The jury was told that in making this determination, it should consider the totality of the evidence, including the distinctiveness of Waits' voice and style, the evidence of actual confusion as to whether Waits actually sang on the commercial, and the defendants' intent to imitate Waits' voice. At trial, the jury listened to numerous Tom Waits recordings,

and to a recording of the Doritos commercial in which the Tom Waits impersonator delivered this "hip" endorsement of SalsaRio Doritos: "It's buffo, boffo, bravo, gung-ho, tally-ho, but never mellow . . . try 'em, buy 'em, get 'em, got 'em." The jury also heard evidence, relevant to the likelihood of consumer confusion, that the Doritos commercial was targeted to an audience which overlapped with Waits' audience, males between the ages of 18 to 35 who listened to the radio. Finally, there was evidence of actual consumer confusion: the testimony of numerous witnesses that they actually believed it was Tom Waits singing the words of endorsement.

This evidence was sufficient to support the jury's finding that consumers were likely to be misled by the commercial into believing that Waits endorsed SalsaRio Doritos. The jury's verdict on Waits' Lanham Act claim must therefore stand. [The court reversed the $100,000 damage award because it had already been awarded under another claim.]

Case Questions

1. What is the issue this case presents?
2. In what ways does a false endorsement claim differ from the standard Lanham Act violation?
3. What if there would have been an audible disclaimer stating "Not sung by the real Mr. Tom Waits?" Would there be a different result? Explain.
4. How would a court determine the damages in a case of this nature?
5. Assume that a company that manufactures health care supplements uses an Arnold Schwarzenegger "look alike" to endorse its products. Assume also that the commercial is in good taste, Schwarzenegger actually does use the product, and, unlike Tom Waits, is not against celebrity advertisements. Is this a violation of the Lanham Act? Explain.

Administrative Regulation: Advertising

The weakness of private remedies for false advertising has placed the burden of regulation on government agencies. Several federal agencies regulate advertising, including the Federal Communication Commission, the Food and Drug Administration, and the Federal Trade Commission (FTC). The FTC has been the most active.

Section 5 of the Federal Trade Commission Act empowers the FTC to initiate actions and, after hearings and findings, to order violators to stop engaging in "unfair methods of competition" and "unfair or deceptive practices."

Federal Trade Commission Act §5(a)(1)

Unfair methods of competition . . . and unfair or deceptive acts or practices . . . are hereby declared unlawful.

The act also gives the commission power to enact rules to prevent unfair and deceptive trade practices.

FTC Structure and Adjudicatory Procedure

The FTC consists of five commissioners appointed by the president and confirmed by the Senate for seven-year terms. The FTC's Bureau of Consumer Protection is responsible for controlling unfair and deceptive advertising. (See page 140 for the FTC organizational chart.)

When a deceptive advertisement is brought to the attention of the FTC, the staff investigates the alleged violation. After the investigation, if the bureau's director finds reasonable cause to believe a violation exists, the director attempts to negotiate a consent order with the alleged violator. A consent order is an agreement to cease activities that the government claims are illegal.

If the parties cannot agree to a consent order, the FTC complaint counsel may file a complaint against the alleged violator, who is now called the *respondent*. The case is tried before an administrative law judge (ALJ). The losing party may appeal the ALJ's decision to the full commission. If the commission finds against the respondent, the respondent may appeal to the appropriate U.S. court of appeals. The court of appeals reviews the decision to determine whether it is supported by substantial evidence on the record. (Administrative procedures are discussed in Chapter 6.)

Deceptive Price Advertising

Advertisements dealing with price were among the first to be scrutinized by the FTC. An ad offering free goods or services to customers who make purchases is lawful only if the goods to be bought are sold at the advertiser's regular price—

the price at which they were sold before the advertisement. They are deceptive if the advertiser recovers the cost of the free merchandise by marking up the price of the merchandise to be bought. Similarly, when ads offer "two for the price of one," the two units must be sold at the regular price of one unit before the ad was run.

Another deceptive advertising scheme similar to false price comparison is the **bait and switch.** Section 5 of the act is violated if one product is advertised to lure customers into a store to buy another, more expensive product, when the advertiser has no intention of selling the advertised product.

Testimonials and Mock-Ups

Testimonials and endorsements by well-known personalities sometimes violate the act. An advertisement is deceptive if it represents that a product is endorsed by a person who does not, in fact, use the product or prefer it. Advertisements are also deceptive if they imply falsely that the endorser has superior experience or training. For example, it is deceptive for an athlete to imply falsely that he or she is an expert in nutrition and praise the energy content of a cereal.

In television advertising, mock-ups are necessary because the medium cannot effectively transmit the real product. For example, on a black-and-white TV screen, white appears grey and coffee looks like mud. Advertisers often use mock-ups to counter the distortion or improve the effectiveness of their ads. If the viewing public is led to believe that it is seeing a real product or experiment, the advertisement violates the FTC act. The use of mock-ups must be disclosed, by clearly informing the viewer on the screen audibly or in print that the viewer is watching "a mock-up."

Quality Claims

Advertisers frequently make quality claims. Some of these are regarded as trade puffing and do not violate the act. Where quality claims exceed the bounds of permissible puffing, two issues frequently arise: (1) what claims did the advertiser make, and (2) were the claims false or deceptive?

Identifying Quality Claims

Quality claims may be expressly made in an advertisement, or they may be implied from its language. The FTC bears the burden of proving that a claim is implied in an ad. When the FTC interprets an advertisement to determine its meaning, it may rely on its own expertise in the area. If it chooses to do so, it simply views the ad and, aided by the arguments of counsel, draws its conclusions. The commission frequently supplements its expertise with testimony from doctors, psychologists, marketing specialists, and other experts, as well as with consumer surveys.

Deceptive Quality Claims

Once it has ascertained that a claim is made in an advertisement, the FTC must determine whether the claim is deceptive. The FTC considers an act or practice deceptive if it misleads reasonable consumers to their detriment.

Advertisers must possess adequate **substantiation** of their claims at the time they are made. It is deceptive advertising to make a product claim without substantiation. All quality claims imply that the advertiser has a reasonable basis, or substantiation, for making them. What constitutes a reasonable basis varies greatly with the type of product and the type of claim. The following case, involving an over-the-counter drug, illustrates the process of determining a deceptive quality claim.

AMERICAN HOME PRODUCTS CORP. V. F.T.C.
695 F.2d 681 (3rd Cir. 1982)

American Home Products (AHP) manufactures drugs. One drug, Anacin, is an over-the-counter (nonprescription) analgesic (painkiller). It contains two ingredients: aspirin and caffeine. Aspirin is Anacin's only pain-killing component. For years, AHP advertised its products through various news media, including magazines and television.

The FTC issued a complaint against AHP charging that AHP falsely advertised that Anacin (1) has a unique pain-killing formula, and (2) is proven to be superior to all other nonprescription analgesics. AHP denied that it made any false claims. An administrative law judge (ALJ) heard the case and ordered AHP to: (1) stop falsely representing that its nonprescription analgesics had been established as superior to competitors, and (2) not represent the superiority of its nonprescription analgesics unless supported with at least two well-controlled clinical studies. The FTC adopted these findings and the order of the ALJ. AHP appealed, but the court of appeals affirmed that portion of the commission's order.

Circuit Judge Adams

1. Were the Establishment Claims Made?

One advertisement which appeared in virtually identical form in several magazines is entitled "News about headache relief you probably missed (unless you read medical magazines)." Beneath what was designed to resemble a clipping from a medical journal, the body of the advertisement informed readers:

> In clinical tests on hundreds of headache sufferers, it has now been proven beyond a doubt that today's

Anacin delivers the same complete headache relief as the leading pain relief prescription. This advertisement in leading medical journals [i.e., the clipping] told the complete story. Doctors know Anacin contains more of the specific medication they recommend most for the pain than the leading aspirin, buffered aspirin, or extra-strength tablet. Is it any wonder that last year physicians and dentists distributed over 25 million packets of Anacin tablets to their patients?

Now you know that Anacin gives you the same complete headache relief as the leading pain relief prescription. Next headache, see how fast Anacin relieves your pain.

The advertisement . . . proclaims that Anacin has been clinically proven to be as effective as the leading prescription analgesic, and that Anacin is known by doctors to have more of the pain reliever they recommend most than do the other leading non-prescription analgesics. There is no explicit representation that Anacin has been clinically proven to be more effective than any other non-prescription analgesics. . . . [T]he fundamental objection to the advertisement is that consumers . . . will be likely to combine the claim of *proven* equivalence to the leading prescription drug, and the claim that doctors know that Anacin has more pain reliever than the other non-prescription products, into a claim that Anacin's superiority to the other non-prescription products has been proven.

The Commission, despite primary reliance on its own knowledge in interpreting the advertisements, weighed all the survey evidence in the record. Although AHP produced several types of empirical data, only one type—the Audience Studies, Inc. (ASI) tests—was relevant to determining the meaning of particular advertisements, as AHP's expert admitted. ASI had conducted tests on behalf of AHP's advertising agency to measure the effectiveness of some advertisements. These tests involved none of the print or radio advertisements but rather were limited to thirty of those that appeared on television. A sample of consumers was shown films . . . of the advertisements: Thirty or forty minutes later, the consumers wrote down what they recalled, and those responses were then tabulated and coded. AHP's expert, Dr. Smith, apparently found no consumers who thought that an "establishment" claim was made in the advertisements. The Commission, however, for a number of reasons discounted this result as being of limited usefulness. Dr. Smith's analysis was found to be flawed [for various technical reasons]. . . .

We cannot say that the Commission's appraisal of this evidence was unsupported. It is also significant that there was considerable record evidence of a widespread consumer belief in Anacin's superior efficacy. . . . In view of the inability of consumers to discriminate objectively between competing analgesics . . . the Commission was "convinced that the primary source of this consumer belief in Anacin's superiority is the advertising of the product. . . ." The Commission also concluded that consumers' belief in superiority, and their implicit belief in established superiority, would be likely to persist unless AHP carried out the directives of the Commission's order.

2. Were the Establishment Claims Deceptive?

Having upheld the Commission's determination that certain of AHP's advertisements should be read as making the "establishment" claim, we proceed to consider whether the Commission could have found that claim misleading. On this issue as well it is clear that the Commission must be sustained. Even though AHP's advertisements never disclosed the presence of aspirin in Anacin, the claim to superior effectiveness appears to be based on the belief that a somewhat larger dosage of aspirin, such as Anacin contains, is more effective in the relief of pain than "ordinary" aspirin.

The Commission carefully considered, and rejected, the evidence that Anacin's superiority had been established or proven. It found that there was "no real dispute as to the type of evidence scientists require before they regard it as having been proven (established) that one drug is more effective than another."

Quite apart from the argument that the word "established" is of uncertain meaning, AHP asserts that two studies performed for it by Dr. Gilbert McMahon meet the standard of two well-controlled clinical studies; but the Commission found numerous defects in these studies. The Commission objected that the results were not statistically significant; that the drug product tested against aspirin was not shown to be equivalent to commercially available Anacin; and that the studies failed to deal with headache pain, which

AHP's witness conceded to be different from other types of pain. The ALJ, in a closely reasoned analysis of the McMahon studies, made additional points, including that bias was introduced into the studies by the ongoing "peeking" at and evaluation of data by AHP. We are unable to hold that the commission acted unreasonably in refusing to assign to these studies the probative force that AHP wishes for them. . . .

Far from concluding that Anacin's superiority had been proven, the ALJ suggested that Anacin might be less effective than "ordinary" aspirin. The possibility that the caffeine in Anacin could actually heighten awareness of pain was not ruled out. Moreover, there was evidence that caffeine exacerbated aspirin's gastrointestinal side effects, and "in terms of chronic use, the record evidence strongly suggest[s] that more aspirin may be worse [in its side effects] than less aspirin."

Case Questions

1. Which explicit claims did AHP make about Anacin in its advertisement? Did the FTC contend these claims were false?

2. What impact do you think this advertisement would have on the average consumer? Do you agree with the court?

3. Why were Anacin's claims determined to be deceptive?

4. Is it unfair to require AHP to substantiate its claims with two clinical studies? What is wrong with one good study?

5. Assume that well-documented consumer surveys proved that the vast majority of people who had taken various over-the-counter pain killers believed Anacin to be superior. Would evidence of those surveys change the result in this case? Explain.

FTC Orders

The FTC is authorized to issue cease and desist orders to violators of Section 5. These orders instruct those who are engaged in unfair or deceptive acts or practices to stop using such methods.

The FTC also claims authority to order affirmative disclosures to dissipate the residual effects of an advertiser's deception. These disclosures are called **corrective advertising.** In one celebrated case, Warner-Lambert had been claiming for more than 50 years that its product, Listerine, relieved colds and sore throats. The FTC charged that these claims constituted a misrepresentation. The D.C. Court of Appeals, in addition to upholding an order requiring Warner-Lambert to stop its cold-fighting claims, required Warner-Lambert to append to its advertisements: "Listerine will not help prevent colds or sore throats or lessen their severity."

Truth in Labeling

The FTC and the Food and Drug Administration together administer the Truth in Packaging Act, which authorizes the agencies to establish and enforce standards concerning the labeling of various products. These products must contain such information as the name and place of the manufacturer and ingredients of the product. The FDA regulates food and drug products. A lack of specific regulation in this area, until recently, permitted advertisers to make grandiose claims about the nutritional and health aspects of their foods. And, until recently, there was a laxness about establishing standards and enforcing the act. However, more recently, there has been a flurry of consumer and governmental interest, which has led to more regulation. The Nutrition Labeling and Education Act of 1990 is designed to curb the abuses by requiring detailed, uniform labeling of food products. The FDA has placed uniform meaning to the following "claims" that were until recently only advertising jargon:

Low Cal	Less than 40 calories per serving
Sodium free	Less than 5 milligrams per serving
Sugar free	Less than .5 milligrams per serving
Reduced fat	No more than half the fat of an identifiable comparison item
High	Must contain at least 20 percent more than recommended daily intake

A few states, like California, also require extensive labeling along with warning requirements of any cancer-causing chemicals or additives contained in the food.

Chapter Problems

1. Define the following concepts and terms:
   a. Market share liability
   b. Express warranty
   c. Implied warranty
   d. Magnuson-Moss Warranty Act
   e. Consumer Product Safety Act
   f. Consumer product safety standards
   g. Lanham Trademark Act
   h. Bait and switch
   i. Substantiation
   j. Corrective advertising

2. Carolyn Miller was injured in a motorcycle accident while she was a passenger on a Suzuki motorcycle owned and operated by William Todd. Miller's right leg was crushed between the motorcycle and the ground when the cycle skidded on gravel and went out of control. The motorcycle was not equipped with rear passenger crash bars. Do you think the failure to equip the cycle with these crash bars was negligence? Explain. How would you analyze Suzuki's responsibility?

3. BIC Corporation manufactures BIC butane lighters. The lighters contain a warning, "KEEP OUT OF REACH OF CHILDREN." However, the particular lighter at issue does not have child-resistant features.

   Cory Todd, a young child, started a fire in her baby sister's bedroom with her parents' lighter. Her sister, Tiffany, perished in the fire. Is BIC liable on a strict liability theory? What could BIC have done to make the lighter safer?

4. Orange Electronics manufactures computers. A brochure accompanies the sale of an Orange computer. In big easy-to-read print, it includes the following language:

   • The manufacturer will remedy any defects within one year of the purchase. After three failed attempts the customer may elect a refund or replacement of the product without charge.
   • The manufacturer will not be liable for any personal injury sustained by the customer as a result of computer malfunction.
   • Before instituting suit against the manufacturer, the customer must submit to the arbitration procedure established by the manufacturer.

   May Orange Electronics include these terms without violating the Magnuson-Moss Warranty Act? If so, which type of warranty designation is proper?

5. The Consumer Product Safety Commission found that ureaformaldehyde foam (UFF) used to insulate residences posed a risk of injury from acute irritant effects and cancer. In arriving at this conclusion, the CPSC:
   a. Conducted a study of 1,164 homes; 827 of these homes contained occupants who complained of UFF-related health problems.
   b. Conducted a study on a number of commercial UFF products in wall panels, which simulated conditions of an unheated home without air conditioning.
   c. Exposed 240 rats to an average of 14.3 parts per millimeter of formaldehyde five days a week for six hours a day. After two years, 103 rats developed nasal cancer.

   Based on its findings, the CPSC seeks to ban UFF insulation. Which arguments might the industry make against the ban?

6. Kaiser Aluminum and Chemical Corporation manufactures aluminum branch-circuit wiring systems. These systems conduct electric current from fuses or circuit breakers to terminals within a residence, such as light fixtures and wall plug outlets. Kaiser sells the system to wholesalers, who then sell it to contractors for installation in residences. The Consumer Product Safety Commission, concerned about reports of electrical failures and overheating of the systems, commenced proceedings to adopt a consumer product safety standard regulating the system. How should Kaiser respond?

7. Bristol-Meyers ran TV commercials in which a model claimed that "in shampoo tests with over 900 women like me, Body on Tap got higher ratings than Prell for body. Higher than Flex for conditioning. Higher than Sassoon for strong, healthy-looking hair." Sassoon conducted a marketing study that showed that consumers interpreted the ad to mean that each of the 900 women had tried all of the mentioned products. The majority believed that the test showed Body on Tap to be superior to the other brands. In fact, the 900 women had been divided into groups of about 200, each group tested only one product, and the tests did not reveal a statisti-

cally significant difference between Body on Tap and Sassoon. Which cause of action may Sassoon have against Bristol-Myers? Explain.

8. Tropicana Products, Inc. aired a new television commercial for its Premium Pack orange juice. In it, American Olympic decathlon athlete Bruce Jenner squeezed an orange while saying, "It's pure, pasteurized juice as it comes from the orange." Jenner then pours the juice he squeezed into a Tropicana carton. The audio states, "It's the only leading brand not made with concentrate and water." Coca-Cola Co. (Coke), producer of Minute Maid orange juice, sued Tropicana for false advertising in violation of §43(a) of the Lanham Act. Coke claimed the commercial to be false because it represented that Premium Pack contains unprocessed, fresh-squeezed juice; in fact, the juice is heated and sometimes frozen before packaging. Coke sought an injunction to prevent Tropicana from continuing this advertisement. What is the result? Explain.

9. The Campbell Soup Company advertises its soups on television. In its commercials, Campbell's soups appear to be quite rich. This effect is achieved by adding marbles to the soups before showing them in the commercials. This ploy displaces the solid ingredients and gives the product a deceptively rich appearance. Campbell has been doing this for years. Should customers who relied on the apparently bounteous nature of the soup be informed of Campbell's past deception through corrective advertising? Explain.

10. Jack-in-the-Box sold hamburgers that contained E-coli bacteria. As a result, several people died from ingesting the hamburgers. One toddler died from the bacteria when he came into contact with another toddler who had eaten a hamburger infected with the bacteria. What should Jack-in-the-Box do product-wise and advertising-wise in order to minimize the damage?

10 PROPERTY

Learning Objectives

After learning this chapter the student should be able to:

- Define property.
- Categorize property as real or personal.
- Compare and contrast lost, stolen, and mislaid property.
- Identify the types of bailments.
- Identify a fixture by applying the appropriate tests.
- Compare and contrast patents, copyrights, and trademarks.
- Differentiate between those processes that are patentable and copyrightable from those that are not.

All around us we are surrounded by "things." From the smallest seed in the ground to the most distant star in the sky, these things occupy our existence. Things have certain properties. They are made up of molecular structures. However, property, in the legal sense, is concerned with relationships—the relationship between a thing and a person. This chapter deals with the law of property. It highlights the definition of property, and then focuses on personal property, real property, and intellectual property. The chapter concludes with an observation about property rights in other countries.

Definition of Property

Property can be thought of as a bundle of rights. This bundle of rights includes the right to possess, use, sell, donate, lease, improve, and destroy property. A distant star does not fit this definition; however, a house, a car, and a patent do.

Property may be real or personal. **Real property** is the land and anything that is permanently attached to land. In contrast, **personal property** is property that has no fixed site but is moveable. Personal property may be further divided into tangible and intangible property. Tangible personal property, such as clothing, frying pans, and doorknobs, may be touched. Intangible personal property has no physical being and, as such, may not be touched. It includes stocks, bonds, patent rights, and copyrights.

Personal Property

We are dependent upon personal property for our existence. The food we eat, the clothing we wear, and even the bed we sleep in are all personal property. Personal property may be acquired in a number of ways, and may be entrusted to another. The law regarding the acquisition and entrustment of personal property follows.

Acquiring Personal Property

The normal way of acquiring personal property is by purchase. The purchase may be by cash or by credit. However, some acquisitions do not involve an exchange of money. They occur as a matter of law, as, for example, when property is abandoned, lost, stolen, mislaid, or donated.

Abandoned Property

Abandonment occurs when the owner voluntarily and intentionally surrenders property. When this occurs the property is unowned. The next person to appropriate the property owns it. By example, assume that someone places a stuffed animal and papers with garbage to be picked up. The first person to retrieve them is the owner of this abandoned property.

Lost Property

Lost property is property that is involuntarily left somewhere. One who finds lost property has good title to the property against anyone in the world except the true owner. The finder, in fact, has an obligation to return the property to the known owner. Many states have statutes governing the disposition of lost property. Under these finder's statutes, the finder usually becomes the absolute owner of the property after the find is made public, a certain period of time elapses, and the owner fails to claim the property.

Stolen Property

Property that is stolen is ordinarily treated as lost property. The owner of the property has superior title to the world. A thief does not gain title to the property stolen. However, there is at least one instance where the Uniform Commercial Code (UCC) holds that one who acquires property from a thief becomes the absolute owner.

UCC § 2–403(2)

Any entrusting of possession of goods to a merchant who deals in goods of that kind gives him [or her] power to transfer all rights of the entruster to a buyer in ordinary course of business.

Assume that on Monday, Romeo and his girlfriend Juliet go to Badunov's Jewelry Store to size an engagement ring that was previously purchased by Romeo. Badunov tells them to come back in one week to pick up the ring. On Tuesday, Dick and Liz come into Badunov's in order that Dick may buy Liz a diamond to celebrate their engagement to be married. Badunov sells them Juliet's ring. It fits Liz's hand perfectly. Dick pays for the ring and takes it out of the store. Juliet and Liz, who have been friends since childhood, decide to go out for dinner Saturday night to celebrate their engagements. During dinner, Liz proudly displays her new engagement ring, and Juliet quickly discovers that Liz is wearing Juliet's ring. Between Juliet and Liz, who owns the ring?

Badunov is a thief, and, under common law, cannot convey good title to the ring. Normally, Juliet would be entitled to a return of her ring. However, under Uniform Commercial Code, section 2–403(2), which controls in cases involving the sale of goods, as here, Liz would be the owner of the ring. Naturally, Badunov would be subject to criminal liability, and civil liability to Juliet.

Note that this provision applies only to merchants—those who customarily deal in a particular type of good. The provision would not apply to the street vendor from whom one would buy a stolen watch. Consumers expect to obtain clear title to items they buy in a store. If a consumer could not have that expectation, retail sales could suffer greatly. The rights of the consumer have been balanced against the rights of the person entrusting goods to merchants. The balance is clearly in favor of the consumer knowing that he or she is getting good title when purchasing an item.

Mislaid Property

Mislaid property is property that is left somewhere and forgotten. The finder of mislaid property must surrender it to the owner of the premises where it is found. The reason for this requirement is that the owner of mislaid property will eventually remember where he or she left it and return to the premises. The owner of the premises then holds the property in trust for the true owner. Finding statutes, in some states, specify the rights and obligations of the true owner, the finder, and the owner of the premises.

The distinctions among abandoned, lost and mislaid property are examined in the next case in order to determine who was entitled to possession of old currency found in a motel room.

TERRY V. A.D. LOCK
343 Ark. 452, 37 S.W. 3d 202 (2001)

Joe Terry and Davis Stocks were stripping motel rooms at the Best Western Motel, in preparation for the renovation of the rooms. While removing some ceiling tiles in room 118 they found a cardboard box that was concealed on the top of the heating and air vent. The box contained $38,310.00 in old dusty currency.

Terry and Stocks, motel renovators, brought an action against the motel owners, seeking a determination that they were the rightful owners of the lost property. An Arkansas trial court held in favor of the motel owners. Terry and Stocks, the finders, appealed the case to the Supreme Court of Arkansas.

Justice Ray Thornton

Property is said to be "abandoned" when it is thrown away, or its possession is voluntarily forsaken by the owner, in which case it will become the property of the first occupant; or when it is involuntarily lost or left without the hope and expectation of again acquiring it, and then it becomes property of the finder, subject to the superior claim of the owner.

Lost Property

"Lost property" is property, which the owner has involuntarily parted with through neglect, carelessness, or inadvertence, that is, property which the owner had unwittingly suffered to pass out of his possession, and of whose whereabouts he has no knowledge. Property is deemed lost when it is unintentionally separated from the dominion of its owner. Popularly, property is lost when the owner does not know, and cannot ascertain, where it is[.] [T]he essential test of lost property is whether the owner parted with the possession of the property intentionally, casually or involuntarily; only in the latter contingency may it be lost property. Property is not "lost" unless the owner parts with it involuntarily and unintentionally, and does not, at any time thereafter, know where to find it. A loss is always involuntary; there can be no intent to part with the ownership of the property.

The finder of lost property does not acquire absolute ownership, but acquires such property interest or right as will enable him to keep it against the entire world but the rightful owner. This rule is not affected by the place of finding, as the finder of lost property has a right to possession of the article superior to that of the owner or occupant of the premises where it is found.

Mislaid Property

"Mislaid Property" is that which is intentionally put into a certain place and later forgotten. The place where money or property claimed as lost is found is an important factor in the determination of the question of whether it was lost or only mislaid. But where articles are accidentally dropped in any public place, public thoroughfare, or street, they are lost in the legal sense. In short, property will not be considered to have been lost unless the circumstances are such that, considering the place where, and the conditions under which, it is found there is an inference that it was left there unintentionally.

A finder of mislaid property acquires no ownership rights in it, and, where such property is found upon another's premises, he has no right to its possession, but is required to turn it over to the owner of the premises. This is true whether the finder is an employee or occupier of the premises on which the mislaid article is found or a customer of the owner or occupant. The right of possession, as against all except the true owner, is in the owner or occupant of the premises where the property is discovered, for the mislaid property is presumed to have been left in the custody of the owner or occupier of the premises upon which it is found. The result is that the proprietor of the premises is entitled to retain possession of the thing, pending a search by him to discover the owner, or during such time the owner may be considered to be engaged in trying to recover his property. . . .

The finder of the mislaid property must turn it . . . over to the owner or occupier of the premises where it was found; it is the latter's duty to keep mislaid property for the owner. . . . As against everyone but the true owner, the owner of such premises has the duty to defend his custody and possession of the mislaid property, and he is absolutely liable for a misdelivery.

■   ■   ■

. . . Appellant Stocks stated in his affidavit that "the box and its contents appeared to have been located at the site for very long time." Mr. Lock testifies that in 1988 a beam was replaced in room 118 and the box was not discovered at that time. Upon opening the box, a large amount of old, dusty currency was discovered. Neither appellants nor appellees claim to have concealed the property in the ceiling. It is apparent that the box was not lost. The circumstances suggest that it was either abandoned property . . . [or] mislaid property. . . . We hold that the trial court's findings that "the money in controversy was intentionally placed where it was found for its security, in order to shield it from unwelcome eyes . . ." and that the "money was mislaid [property]" were not clearly erroneous.

■   ■   ■

The natural assumption is that the person who concealed the bills in the case at bar was a guest of the hotel. Their considerable value, and the manner of their concealment, indicates that the person who concealed them did so for the purpose of security, and with the intention of reclaiming them. They were, therefore, to be classified not as lost, but as misplaced or forgotten property, and the defendant, as the occupier of the premises where they were found, had the right and duty to take them into his possession and to hold them . . . for the true owner.

■   ■   ■

Affirmed.

Case Questions:

1. Would there be a different result if the money had not been old and dusty? Explain.
2. Construct a scenario to explain how the money got where it was found. Is that important when characterizing it? Explain.
3. Should the money revert to the state rather than to the owner of the hotel? Why or why not?

4. Assume that a company, searching for sunken ships in the oceans, located a sunken ship and expended large sums of money to recover the silver and gold treasures from the ship. Who should own the treasure trove? What if 50 years ago an insurance company had paid money pursuant to an insurance policy issued to the owners of the trove? Would that make a difference?

Gifts

Property may also be acquired by gift. A gift occurs when one individual or entity gives something to another person or entity without any consideration. Gifts come in a variety of forms. An *inter vivos,* or living gift, is made by a person when the donor is alive and has no expectation of imminent death. When three necessary elements occur, the gift is completed, and irrevocable. First, the donor (or gift giver) must intend to make a gift to a donee (gift receiver). Second, that gift must be delivered to the donee or the donee's agent. Delivery must be either physical, by turning over control of the item to the donee, or may be achieved by giving the donee some evidence of title. For example, a gift of an automobile may be completed by handing over an endorsed certificate of title and the keys, even if the automobile is located elsewhere at the time. Unless the element of delivery is present, there is no gift. Finally, the donee must accept the gift.

A gift *causa mortis* is a gift in contemplation of death in the near future. In this type of gift, intent, delivery, and acceptance are still necessary. However, even when these three elements are present, the gift may still be revocable by the donor. Consider the situation where Carlos is to have major surgery, and has been told that he has only a 30 percent chance of recovering. Carlos gives his watch to his close friend Bruce, telling Bruce he wants him to have the watch if the surgery is unsuccessful and Carlos dies. If Carlos recovers, he can invalidate the gift. He can also revoke the gift for any reason before he dies, and the gift is invalid if the donee (in this case, Bruce) dies before the donor.

A gift may be complete subject to a condition. Under the common law, for instance, an engagement ring is a gift to the bride-elect, conditional upon the marriage taking place. Consequently, if the marriage does not occur because of the actions of the bride-elect, no gift occurs and the man gets the ring back. Because of a spate of litigation, many states have now adopted specific statutes that alter the common law rule regarding the status of gifts made in anticipation of marriage.

Entrusting Personal Property

The law governing the entrustment of personal property is known as the *law of bailments*. A **bailment** occurs when one person (the bailor) transfers personal property to another (the bailee) with instructions to return it or otherwise dispose of it. For example, assume that Freda takes her car to a mechanic to have it repaired. Here, a bailment is formed. After the repair, the mechanic is obligated to return the car to Freda. Title to property does not pass by a bailment.

Chapter 10 Property

269

Types of Bailments

Most bailments are voluntary. However, an involuntary bailment may arise as, for example, when someone finds property that is lost. The finder becomes an involuntary bailee. An involuntary bailee owes to the owner a slight duty of care, and is only liable for damages caused by intentional misconduct or gross negligence.

Another way of classifying bailments is by examining who benefits. Some bailments are solely for the benefit of the bailee. These bailments, sometimes referred to as *gratuitous bailments,* occur when, for example, one person lends a friend a car. Here, the bailee must return the car in the same condition and is liable for damages caused by even slight negligence. The duty here upon the bailee is to exercise extraordinary care. Other bailments are solely for the benefit of the bailor. These occur when a bailee takes possession of property without pay or benefit, but as an accommodation to the bailor, as, for example, when a friend agrees to temporarily store furniture. The bailee here will not be liable for damage to the property unless grossly negligent.

Finally, mutual benefit bailments are the most common. A mutual benefit bailment usually involves a contract for hire, for example, entrusting property to another for repair. Here, the bailor would benefit from having the item repaired, and the bailee would benefit by receiving compensation for the repair. The bailee will be liable for damages that result from a lack of ordinary care.

Rights and Duties

The rights and duties under a bailment may be part of a contract, express or implied. Any damages that occur as a result of a breach of the agreement may result in liability. However, bailees are often prone to include within the contract an exculpatory clause. An exculpatory clause limits or relieves liability for damages. Courts are apt to strike down such clauses when they are deemed to be against public policy—when there is an unequal bargaining position between the parties. For example, assume that Vera entrusts to Hank's Garage a car for the purpose of fixing the brakes. A clause within the contract states that Hank's is not liable for any damage to the car while in its possession. One of Hank's employees negligently rams the car into the gas pump island and damages the front end. Assume further that all the garages in the neighborhood have a similar exculpatory clause within their contracts. A court most likely would strike down the clause and hold Hank's Garage liable for the damage due to its employee's negligence.

Generally, in absence of specification, the bailee is entitled to reasonable compensation for the work done or for storage, and the bailor is entitled to a return of the goods in substantially the same condition as when first received. The following case considers the issue of a bailee's liability for the contents of bailed property.

HADFIELD V. GILCHRIST
343 S.C. 88, 538 S.E. 2d 268 (2000)

Mark Hadfield, a medical student, sought to retrieve his Lincoln Continental from a parking lot where his wife had left the car. Since the vehicle was parked in a private parking spot without the permission of the owner, it was towed to a storage facility. The facility, owned by Sam Gilchrist, maintained a chain link fence around the facility and there was an office employee on the lot 24 hours. Periodically, the employee would check on the storage facility. Hadfield went to the facility and paid fees. However, when he went to retrieve the car he found that vandals who had cut a hole in the fence had extensively damaged it. His radio/compact disc players were stolen, the car windows smashed, and the vehicle's computer mechanisms were permanently damaged.

Hadfield sued Gilchrist and a magistrate found Gilchrist liable for $4,035.00 in damages. Gilchrist appealed to the Circuit Court, which affirmed the magistrate's decision. Gilchrist prosecuted a further appeal to the Court of Appeals of South Carolina.

Judge Anderson

A bailment is created by the delivery of personal property by one person to another in trust for a specific purpose, pursuant to an express or implied contract to fulfill that trust.

Bailments are generally classified as being for (1) the sole benefit of the bailor, (2) the sole benefit of the bailee; or (3) the mutual benefit of both. Bailments, which benefit only one of the parties, the first and second classifications, are often described as gratuitous.

■   ■   ■

"A gratuitous bailment is, by definition, one in which the transfer of possession or use of the bailed property is without compensation." For instance, a gratuitous bailment arises if the bailment is undertaken as a personal favor or is involuntary.

A "gratuitous bailee" acts without expectation of reward or compensation. To show the bailment was for the sole benefit of the bailor, the bailee must establish that it was not expecting compensation. . . .

By contrast, a bailment for the mutual benefit of the parties arises when one party takes the personal property of another into his care or custody in exchange for payment or other benefit.

Although a bailment is ordinarily created by the agreement of the parties, the agreement of the parties may be implied or constructive, and the bailment may arise by operation of law. Such a constructive bailment arises when one person has lawfully acquired possession of another's personal property, other than by virtue of a bailment contract, and holds it under circumstances that the law imposes on the recipient of the property the obligation to keep it safely and redeliver it to the owner. A constructive bailment may occur even in absence of the voluntary delivery and acceptance of the property, which is usually necessary to create a bailment relationship.

Gilchrist argues he towed the vehicle pursuant to the Charleston Municipal Ordinances, and the ordinances are for the sole benefit of the vehicle owners. Accordingly, he contends, the relationship created a gratuitous bailment. We disagree. . . .

■   ■   ■

The vehicle owned by Hadfield was plucked by Gilchrist from . . . private property. . . . Gilchrist acted pursuant to and by virtue of the licensing authority under the city ordinance. Quintessentially, the factual scenario encapsulated in this case is a paradigm of a "constructive bailment." We conclude a constructive bailment, for the mutual benefit of Hadfield and Gilchrist, was created.

Although contractual in nature, and involving the conveyance of personal property, an action for breach of the duty of care by a bailor sounds in tort. . . . Concomitantly, after finding a bailment for mutual benefit exists in this case, we must determine whether Hadfield is entitled to damages. . . .

The degree of care required of a bailee for mutual benefit is defined as ordinary care, or due care, or the degree of care which would be exercised by a person of ordinary care in the protection of his own property. . . .

Under the decided cases in this state, liability of a bailee under a bailment for mutual benefit arises upon a showing that (1) the goods were delivered to the bailee in good condition, (2) they were lost or returned in a damaged condition, and (3) the loss or damage to the goods was due to the failure of the bailee to exercise ordinary care in the safekeeping of the property. The burden of proof in such cases, in the first instance, rests upon the bailor to make out a prima [facie] case. This has been done when the bailor proves that he delivered the goods to the bailee in good condition and their loss or return in a damaged condition. When the bailor has so proven, the burden is then shifted to the bailee to show that he has used ordinary care in the storage and safekeeping of the property.

The burden of proof in this case rests first upon the bailor, Hadfield, to prove the *prima facie case*. He must show: 1) the goods were delivered to the bailee in good condition, and 2) they were lost or returned in damaged condition. When the bailor, Hadfield, has so proven, the burden is then shifted to the bailee, Gilchrist, to show that he has used ordinary care in the good's storage and safekeeping.

Hadfield testified before the magistrate regarding the "nice" condition of the vehicle prior to being towed, and the damage to his vehicle, and the other vehicles on the lot. In addition, he introduced photographs depicting the damage. Thus, Hadfield made out his prima facie case. . . . The burden then shifted to Gilchrist to show that he used ordinary care in protecting the vehicle while in his care.

Gilchrist impounded the cars in a storage lot surrounded by a chain link fence. . . . The fact the guard was not on duty at the impound lot and, considering the only other security for the vehicles was the chain link fence, the lower court judge could have concluded that Gilchrist failed to exercise ordinary care. . . .

We rule that where a city ordinance is utilized as the legal justification for taking possession of a vehicle on private property the person or entity lawfully acquiring possession of the property under the ordinance becomes a constructive bailee as a matter of law. We find a constructive bailment, for the mutual benefit of Hadfield and Gilchrist, was created. Further, we hold an action for breach of duty of care by a bailor, although contractual in nature, sounds in tort. We conclude the burden of proof in a constructive bailment case rests first upon a bailor to prove a *prima facie* case and, once so proven, the burden shifts to the bailee to show use of ordinary care in the storage and safekeeping of the property. Accordingly, the order of the Circuit Court is

AFFIRMED.

Case Questions

1. Would the result have been different had the court found this to be a gratuitous bailment? Explain.

2. What specifically is the alleged negligent act or omission committed by Gilchrist that led to liability? Do you agree that this is sufficient?

3. Why is this a constructive bailment? What type of bailment does the court construct?

4. Assume that the owner of the vehicle left it to be fixed at a garage. Employees repaired it and left it parked outside with the keys in the car. The car was stolen and damaged. Would the garage owner be liable? Do you need additional facts? Explain.

Special Bailments

Innkeepers, common carriers, and warehousers are deemed professional bailees, and, in addition to the ordinary rules of bailment, are subject to special rules. Innkeepers operate inns, hotels, motels, and lodges. At the common law, innkeepers were strictly liable for the loss or damage to personal property of their guests. This rule has been modified in many states that place a limit on liability, for example, $1,000.

A common carrier is in the business of transporting goods. Common carriers must serve the public on a nondiscriminatory basis and are strictly liable for damage or loss of goods. The common carrier is, in that sense, an insurer of the property. There are some exceptions: acts of God, of war, or of public authorities; the bailor's negligence; or the natural spoilage or deterioration of the goods. Additionally, by clear terms in a contract, common carriers may limit their liability.

A warehouse company stores property for others. It is usually subject to extensive state and local fire, health, and safety regulations. Like the common carrier, it may limit its liability.

Real Property

Real property is comprised of land and every thing that is attached to land. As such, it consists of air, surface, and subsurface rights. The old theory was that a landowner owned from his or her property straight up to the heavens and straight down to the center of the earth. With the advent of air transportation and modern methods of excavation, this theory was not very pragmatic and, hence, fell into disuse, in favor of the reasonable use theory. The property owner owns everything above and below the land that he or she may reasonably use. This is an attempt to balance the competing interests of different members of society.

This section considers the law of fixtures (which is a way of determining whether an article is personal or part of the real estate), the law of estates and of concurrent interests in an estate.

Fixtures

A **fixture** is personal property that has been affixed to the realty in such a manner as to become part of the realty. For example, a kitchen sinktop is personal property when it is carried into the kitchen to be installed. After installation, it is considered a fixture and it is part of the real estate.

Fixtures pass with real estate by deed and are taxed as part of the real estate. It is important to distinguish between fixtures and personal property for purposes of insurance claims. For example, assume that an insured house burns to the ground. If the carpeting is a fixture, it will be covered for real property insurance purposes; but, if it is personal property, then it would not. Additionally, there may be a difference in taxing of the property, depending upon whether it is deemed personal or real.

The controlling test of whether an item is a fixture is the intent of the attacher. The law has three tests to determine this intent—annexation, adaptation, and relation tests.

Annexation
When an item is attached to the real estate in such a manner that it would cause damage to sever it or leave it in an unfinished condition, then it is probably a fixture. Built-in medicine cabinets, wall-to-wall carpeting, light fixtures, antennas, and permanent fences are examples. Throw rugs, davenports, and stacked timber do not meet this definition, and are probably personal property.

Adaptation
When an item that is not physically attached nonetheless is specifically adapted to the real estate, it is deemed a fixture. Hence, rugs that are not tacked down but are custom cut would be considered a fixture under the adaptation test. Custom-made storm windows or an air conditioner specially modified to accommodate a window meet the adaptation test and hence are fixtures. Consider the following case involving a posh estate and items in dispute that were consistent with its decor.

PAUL V. FIRST NATIONAL BANK
369 N.E.2d 488 (Ohio Common Pleas 1976)

The Longs died in an airplane crash. Among other things, they left a posh estate. Plaintiff, Paul, entered into a contract for $575,000 for the purchase of the estate—a 17-room, elegant stone house situated on a 97-acre picturesque estate of landscaped, rolling terraces, referred to as "Long Acres."

The purchase contract included all "fixtures." Before Paul took possession, heirs living in the house removed certain items. They included lighting fixtures, metal cranes and garden statues, an ornamental well housing, a statue of Mercury, and a walnut organ bench. Paul sued the estate representative, First National Bank, and the heirs of the estate for wrongful taking. The trial court found for the plaintiff.

Judge Black

In *Masheter v. Boehm . . . the* Supreme Court [of Ohio] designated . . . six "facts" to be considered in determining whether an item is a fixture:

1. The nature of the property;
2. The manner in which the property is annexed to the realty;
3. The purpose for which the annexation is made;
4. The intention of the annexing party to make the property a part of the realty;
5. The degree of difficulty and extent of any loss involved in removing the property from the realty; and
6. The damage to the severed property which such removal would cause.

. . . [T]he expression of "a comprehensive and generally applicable rule of law" about fixtures has bedeviled the courts for years and is complicated by the need for different definitions in those situations where the relationship between the parties is different. Nevertheless, the six considerations listed in *Masheter v. Boehm* are pertinent and applicable in the interpretation of "all fixtures relating to said real estate. . . ."

■   ■   ■

Using the Supreme Court's considerations, the light "fixtures" (there is no other available word) from the swimming pool, the stable apartment and the chapel are clearly fixtures in contemplation of law. . . . They are of a type universally recognized as fixtures. This is true even though the pool "fixtures" were hung on brackets and could be unplugged and simply lifted off the brackets. But they were designed and produced solely and only for the swimming pool, from the same design as was used for the light fixture in the porte cochere (which was not removed). Further, the poles from which they were taken are barren and incomplete without them.

The three metal cranes and the four garden statues also meet five of the six criteria, in the judg-ment of the court. The "nature" of these items is that they were a part of the total elegance of Long Acres. They are not the type of fixture which would be commonly found on other lawns or in other gardens, but they are an integral part of this sumptuous country estate. The cranes were "annexed" by being bolted or screwed into concrete foundations in a manner similar to the annexation of the marble table in the Great Hall, an item clearly admitted by all defendants to be a fixture passing with the real estate. The 4 garden statues . . . were not simply placed on top of their columns, but were held in place by 6-inch pipe protruding from the columns into the bases of the statues. The purpose of fixing these into position was to ensure their presence and preservation as part and parcel of the landscape and approach to Long Acres. These cranes and statues were not items moved about at the whim of the owner or according to the seasons: they were permanent emplacements, intended to be part of the continuing visual effect of the estate. While no great difficulty was encountered in removing any of them, their absence is a source of loss. The cranes were prominent in the approach to the front door, and that approach is damaged without them. . . . The removal of the statues leaves the columns on which they stood barren and incomplete; the columns appear to have been vandalized.

. . . [T]he ornamental well housing, the Mercury statue and the organ bench, were not attached in a permanent way. However, interpreting the contract from its four corners, in the light of all the facts and circumstances in evidence, the Court concludes that these items were "appurtenances" to the real estate, both in contemplation of law and in interpretation of this word as used in the purchase contract.

■   ■   ■

All three items . . . form a part of the character of Long Acres and enhance the style of its elegance. They are appurtenant to Long Acres in the sense that they are necessarily connected with the use and enjoyment of this country estate. They are incidental to the total value of this estate. The source of that value is not only the grand design but also all of the details whereby that design is executed: the location of the house on the property, the sweep of the driveway as it approaches the porte cochere, the spread-out location of the barns and other outbuildings, the majesty of the formal gardens, the spaciousness of the lawns on every side, and all the details of the exterior and interior of the mansion itself.

To allow the heirs to walk off with an organ bench, leaving the built-in organ behind would be plainly ridiculous. You cannot play an organ while standing up, and no ordinary bench will do.

The Mercury statue is pictured in two photographs included in the appraisal of Long Acres which was considered by plaintiff before purchase. It may have been moved from the pedestal from time to time by the Long family. . . . But interpreting the contract in the light of all facts and circumstances in evidence, the Court concludes that these items pass[ed] with the real estate.

■   ■   ■

[The court ordered damages due to the wrongful taking of the fixtures.]

Case Questions

1. What issue does this case present?
2. What do you think the intention of the Longs were regarding each item? Why?
3. Change the facts such that the items would not be considered fixtures.
4. How could the parties to the contract have clarified the sale, and reduced the possibility of a lawsuit?

Relation

In cases where it is difficult to come to a conclusion based upon the annexation and adaptation test, the relation test may tip the balance. Under the relation test, the law prefers purchasers over sellers and tenants over landlords. For example, consider an air conditioning unit, installed by the owner, that has been occupying a window for several years. Assume further, the owner sells the house. In favoring the buyer the law presumes that the intent of the seller when affixing the unit was that it be part of the house. The air conditioner, hence, would pass to the buyer by the deed, as it would be considered a fixture. However, in the event that a tenant installed the same air conditioner in an apartment, the law would favor the interpretation that the tenant did not intend for the air conditioner to become a fixture. As such, the tenant would be entitled to remove it after the termination of the lease.

Trade Fixtures

The law of fixtures relating to business use of property is different than it is for residences. Often, a business must make significant improvement to a property in order to be able to use that property effectively. A pizza parlor, for example, must install ovens, bolting them to the floor and venting them through the roof, creating a hole in the roof. A restaurant may install a walk-in cooler that attaches to the floor and/or walls. If the law of fixtures were to be applied in the same manner to both businesses and residences, businesses could be at a severe disadvantage in trying to do business, knowing that if they change location they lose all their business fixtures. Business fixtures are known as *trade fixtures,* and the business tenant is allowed to remove them prior to the expiration of the lease. The business tenant does have the obligation, however, to restore the property to its original condition once the personal property has been removed. For instance, the pizza parlor owner would have to repair the ceiling and roof once the pizza ovens were removed.

Estates and Interests

Estates are interests in real property. Some, like the fee simple absolute, fee tail, life estate, and leaseholds are possessory estates, while easements, profits and licenses are nonpossessory interests. Each is discussed.

Fee Simple Absolute

The fee simple absolute is the greatest quantum of interest that one may own in real property. The owner in fee simple may use the property as he or she sees fit, subject to local zoning laws, nuisance laws, and other laws of the municipality and state in which the property is located. One who owns a fee simple has the fullest interest in the bundle of rights, and, as such, has the power to sell, lease, improve, destroy, and pass the property to heirs. The fee owner may transfer less than the fee interest in the property to other entities without giving up the whole fee simple interest. For example, Tom purchases a parcel of property with a building on it. He gives the right to farm the land to his brother-in-law and he leases the building to Ichabod's Insurance Company for three years, but he still owns the fee. Most property today is owned in fee simple absolute.

Fee Tail

The fee tail passes the property from lineal generation to generation. It promotes family wealth, since the property is kept in the family. A transfer in fee tail is accomplished by transfer to the grantee and the heirs of his or her body. This would continue the property to the lineal descendants. The property is not very marketable as a result. Hence, most states have abolished the fee tail or have afforded ways where it may be converted to a fee simple absolute.

Old concept

Life Estate

A life estate is an interest in land. It is a right of use and enjoyment of land as measured by the life of that person or another person. At the death of the person whose life determines the length of the estate, the fee simple interest reverts to the grantor or to others, known as *remaindermen*. Holders of life estates may not do any act to damage or cause a decrease in the value of the land.

Leaseholds

A leasehold is an interest in land created by a contract called a *lease*. The tenant, or lessee, obtains the right to use the property for a specific purpose, usually for a specified period of time, in return for a periodic cash payment, known as *rent,* paid to the landlord, or lessor. A lease may apply to a residential unit or to commercial property. Lease provisions vary widely. For example, a residential lease may require the lessor to make all repairs and the lessee to pay a specified fee in dollars per month for rent. A commercial lease may provide that the tenant makes all repairs, and may further provide that the tenant pay a percentage of the real estate taxes on the leased property. In a commercial lease, other provisions may specify that the lessee must stay open for business a given number of hours each day, and that the lessee must pay a specified percentage of gross sales to the lessor.

Leases terminate at the expiration of the term. If no term is stated and rent is payable periodically, the lease is terminable upon giving one full period's notice. When the lease ends, possession of the property reverts to the owner.

Easements

An easement gives a right to use the land of another for a specified purpose, but not to possess the land. As an example, Paul may give Art an easement to drive across the back of Paul's paved parking lot so that Art may have access to another street. Easements may be bought or sold, or may be created at the time of transfer of the property from one owner to another. Easements can also be implied by law. Assume, for example, that Ginger sells half of her land to Fred, and that Fred's portion of the land has no access to a street. The law will imply an easement allowing Fred the right to gain access to the street by driving over Ginger's property.

Profits and Licenses

A profit gives one a right to remove something from another's land, such as trees or oil. While a profit is an interest in the land, a license is not. A license is a right to enter land for a particular purpose. For example, a license may grant an individual a right to play 18 holes of golf on the owner's course or to watch a movie in a theater.

Co-Ownership of Property

Ownership of real property is often shared by two or more individuals or other entities such as partnerships, corporations, or trusts. There are various methods of holding concurrently. They include tenancy-in-common, joint tenancy and tenancy by the entireties, community property, condominiums, and cooperatives. Each is discussed.

Tenancy-in-Common

In tenancy-in-common, each co-owner has an undivided fractional interest in the property. The potential interests need not be equal. Each tenant in common has a right to possess the property. One tenant-in-common may sell his or her share to another entity without affecting the existence of the tenancy-in-common.

Tenancies-in-common may also be used in time sharing agreements, where property is shared by a number of people, each having the right to use that property for a defined period each year. For example, 52 people may each have the right to use of an estate in Palm Beach, Florida, for one week each year. These people are tenants-in-common. They may sell their interests without disturbing the tenancy-in-common.

When a tenant-in-common dies, his or her share passes to heirs. If disputes arise as to the benefits from, or use of, the property among the co-tenants, a *partition* action may be undertaken in the courts. In such an action the court will either physically divide up the property among the co-tenants, or will order the sale of the property, with proceeds to be divided among the co-tenants according to their proportional share of ownership. If no particular type of relationship between co-tenants is specified in the deed, the law will ordinarily imply the existence of a tenancy-in-common.

Joint Tenancy and Tenancy by the Entireties
In a joint tenancy, upon the death of one joint tenant, his or her share passes to the other joint tenants. Each joint tenant owns an equal undivided share in the property. A joint tenancy will be terminated if one joint tenant conveys all or a part of his or her interest to another party, or if that interest is sold by a creditor to satisfy a debt. In either of those events, the remaining owners will then be tenants-in-common.

A form of joint tenancy, between husband and wife, called a *tenancy by the entireties,* is allowable in some states. This tenancy, like a joint tenancy, has a right of survivorship feature, so that when one spouse dies, the other immediately becomes sole owner of the property. Unlike the joint tenancy, however, neither party may sell his or her share without the consent of the other, nor may a creditor sever the tenancy to satisfy the debt of one of the spouses. Should the husband and wife sever the marriage relationship, the tenancy by the entireties ceases to exist. Because of a couple's ability to shield their real property from creditors through the tenancy by the entireties, many states have abolished this type of co-ownership.

Community Property
Some jurisdictions, including California, Texas, and a number of southern states, are community property states. Under this type of ownership, each spouse owns half of all property, real or personal, acquired by the efforts of either spouse during the marriage. Property owned by a spouse prior to marriage, or acquired with the proceeds of separate property owned by that spouse, remains the individual property of that spouse.

[handwritten note in margin: only in 9 states]

Condominiums
In a condominium, individuals own units of a larger parcel in fee simple, and are tenants-in-common with other owners in the parcel as to common areas such as elevators, swimming pools, and land. The individual owners also share the costs of maintaining the common areas. Since owners own their units in fee simple, they have the right to mortgage their property interests or the right to transfer title to their units.

The developer of the condominium records a Declaration of Condominium, which describes the land on which the condominium is to be developed, and includes rules for how the condominium is to operate. For example, the bylaws may provide that all owners must be at least 55 years of age, and that no individual under 18 years of age is allowed to live in the condominium more than a specified number of days each year. Once a certain number of units are sold, the unit owners form their own condominium association which governs the affairs of the condominium.

Co-Operative

A co-operative, or co-op, is usually established for an apartment or office building. The building in question is owned by one entity, such as a corporation. Individuals purchase shares in the corporation, which allows them the right to lease units in the co-operative. The bylaws of the corporation establish the rights and duties of tenants, and control the rights these shareholder-tenants have to either sublease their unit or transfer their share in the corporation to others. A share in the co-operative is not an ownership interest in land; consequently, the shareholders cannot obtain a mortgage loan to finance the purchase of their units.

Intellectual Property

Intellectual property deals with rights of individuals and businesses in applied ideas. For example, an author's idea may be translated into, and published as, a novel. The law of intellectual property does not protect the physical book itself. Stealing the book does not violate the author's intellectual property rights. Use of the plot and characters of the novel in a movie, however, does constitute misappropriation of the author's intellectual property.

Intellectual property is a form of intangible personal property. It includes several rather distinct areas of the law. Patents, copyrights, and trademarks are traditional areas of intellectual property rights. Each is discussed below.

Patents

> **U.S. Constitution, Art. I § 8**
>
> Congress shall have the power: "To promote the Progress of Science and useful Arts, by securing for limited Times to Authors and Inventors the exclusive Right to their respective Writings and Discoveries."

Patents are authorized by the U.S. Constitution. A patent is a limited monopoly to make, use, and sell an invention, granted by the government. To encourage innovation and technology, the government generally grants an inventor a 20-year monopoly on an invention, provided an application is filed, making public disclosure of the details of the invention.

[handwritten margin note: not necessarily → · excludes others from make, use and sell]

Patentable Subject Matter

Patents are obtainable on an invention that is novel and useful, and that falls under one or more classes listed in the statute. Specifically, the statute authorizes patents for any processes, machines, manufacture, composition of matter, or improvement on one of these classes. In addition, specific statutory provisions authorize patents on designs and asexually reproduced plants. The following case, involving genetically engineered bacteria, discusses and illustrates the breadth of the interpretation of the statutory subject matter.

DIAMOND V. CHAKRABARTY
447 US 303 (1980)

Chakrabarty, a microbiologist (respondent), filed an application for a patent relating to his invention of a human-made, genetically engineered bacteria capable of breaking down multiple components of crude oil. Because of this property, which is possessed by no naturally occurring bacteria, Chakrabarty's invention is believed to have significant value for the treatment of oil spills.

The United States Patent Office held that live, human-made micro-organisms were not patentable subject matter under the statute. The Court of Customs and Patent Appeals (now the Court of Appeals for the Federal Circuit) reversed, holding that the fact that the micro-organisms are alive is without significance for application of the law. The Supreme Court affirmed the Court of Customs and Patent Appeals.

Chief Justice Burger

The question before us in this case is a narrow one of statutory interpretation requiring us to construe 35 U.S.C. § 101, which provides: "Whoever invents or discovers any new and useful . . . manufacture, or composition of matter . . . may obtain a patent therefore. . . ."

■　　　■　　　■

. . . [T]his Court has read the term "manufacture" . . . in accordance with its dictionary definition to mean "the production of articles for use from raw or prepared materials by giving to these materials new forms, qualities, properties, or combinations, whether by hand-labor or by machinery. . . ." Similarly, "composition of matter" has been construed consistent with its common usage to include "all compositions of two or more substances and . . .

all composite articles, whether they be the results of gases, fluids, powders or solids. . . ." In choosing such expansive terms as "manufacture" and "composition of matter," modified by the comprehensive "any," Congress plainly contemplated that the patent laws would be given wide scope.

■　　　■　　　■

. . . The Committee Reports accompanying the 1952 Act inform us that Congress intended statutory subject matter to "include any thing under the sun that is made by man. . . ."

This is not to suggest that § 101 has no limits or that it embraces every discovery. The laws of nature, physical phenomena, and abstract ideas have been held not patentable. . . . Thus, a new mineral discovered in the earth or a new plant found in the wild is not patentable subject matter. Likewise, Einstein could not patent his celebrated law that $E = mc^2$; nor could Newton have patented the law of gravity. Such discoveries are "manifestations of . . . nature, free to all men and reserved exclusively to none."

Judged in this light, respondent's micro-organism plainly qualifies as patentable subject matter. His claim is not to a hitherto unknown natural phenomenon, but to a nonnaturally occurring manufacture or composition of matter . . . a new bacterium with markedly different characteristics from any found in nature and one having the potential for significant utility. His discovery is not nature's handiwork, but his own; accordingly it is patentable subject matter under § 101.

■   ■   ■

The petitioner's second argument is that micro-organisms cannot qualify as patentable subject matter until Congress expressly authorizes such protection. . . . The briefs present a gruesome parade of horribles. Scientists, among them Nobel laureates, are quoted suggesting that genetic research may pose a serious threat to the human race. . . .

It is argued that this Court should weigh these potential hazards in considering whether respondent's invention is patentable subject matter under § 101. We disagree. The grant or denial of patents on micro-organisms is not likely to put an end to genetic research or to its attendant risks. . . .

What is more important is that we are without competence to entertain these arguments—either to brush them aside as fantasies generated by fear of the unknown, or to act on them. . . . Congress is free to amend § 101 so as to exclude from patent protection organisms produced by genetic engi-

neering. . . . Or it may choose to craft a statute specifically designed for such living things. But, until Congress takes such action, this Court must construe the language of § 101 as it is. The language of that section fairly embraces respondent's invention.

Case Questions

1. The language of the patent statute quoted by the Court (". . . any new and useful . . . manufacture or composition of matter . . . ") was actually written in the first patent statute by Thomas Jefferson in 1793. Do you feel that Jefferson intended the language to cover a living micro-organism? Analyze.

2. Do you think the Court was unduly swayed by the obvious utility of the invention? Explain.

3. The Court dismisses the argument of scientists that genetic engineering could pose a serious threat to the human race. In authorizing patentability of genetically engineered micro-organisms, is the Court acting in the best interests of society? Discuss.

4. A researcher at a large pharmaceutical firm successfully isolated a biologically pure micro-organism believed to be extremely useful in producing a well-known antibiotic at significantly lower cost. Evidence was presented that while the micro-organism was known to exist in nature, it never existed in the biologically pure form. Can the researcher obtain a patent on this micro-organism? Analyze.

Procedure to Obtain a Patent

The process for obtaining a patent can be long and expensive. An inventor must prepare and file an application in the United States Patent Office. To comply with the Constitutional mandate, the application must fully describe the invention. The description must have sufficient detail such that upon expiration of the inventor's limited monopoly the invention may be reproduced by others.

The Patent Office examines the application to be sure that it is new and useful, and that it falls within one of the statutory classes. Not every development by an inventor rises to the level of an "invention." The Patent Office over the years has developed the objective test of **non-obviousness**. The question posed is, would the development described in the application have been obvious to the ordinarily skilled worker in the art at the time the "invention" was made? If it would have been obvious, the development is not patentable. Only those developments that represent a real step forward rise to the level of invention.

The Patent Office is an administrative agency under the Department of Commerce. An applicant dissatisfied with any decision by the patent examiner is entitled to an appeal within the agency to the Patent Office Board of Appeals, and, if dissatisfied with the decision of the board, may appeal to the Court of Appeals for the Federal Circuit, a special appellate level federal court that has jurisdiction in all patent matters.

Patent Owner's Rights

The patent statutes give the owner of a patent the exclusive right to make, use, and sell the invention. The application for a patent must be filed by the individual who made the invention. However, the inventor may assign (transfer ownership) all or any part of the patent rights to another individual or entity. Employees of a company, who work in technical areas, generally sign, at the time of employment, an agreement surrendering to their employer all rights to any inventions made during the course of their employment.

A license involves the transfer of rights under a patent, without transferring ownership. The owner of a patent may license one company to manufacture the patented product, while retaining the right to sell the product. Or, in the reverse, the inventor may manufacture the product and license someone else to sell the product.

Licenses may be either exclusive or nonexclusive. Under an exclusive license, only a single person or entity has the exclusive right; not even the inventor or patent owner retains a right to manufacture. A nonexclusive license, on the other hand, gives the patent holder the right to invest other entities with similar rights under the patent.

The owner of a patent may enforce patent rights through a suit for patent infringement filed in the federal courts. If successful, the patent owner is entitled to statutory damages, which include actual damages (at least in the amount of a reasonable royalty), which may be trebled, and attorney fees, as well as an injunction ordering the infringing party to stop the infringing activity.

Copyrights

A **copyright**, like a patent, is a limited monopoly that finds its origin in Article I, Section 8 of the U.S. Constitution. While the Constitution speaks in terms of writings and authors, copyright protection today covers a very broad span of business and the creative arts. Copyright law is governed exclusively by a federal statute.

The statute lists specific classes of copyrightable works, for example, literary works; musical works; dramatic works; choreographic works; pictorial, graphic, and sculptural works; motion pictures and other audiovisual works; sound recordings; and architectural works. At the same time, the statute expressly excludes copyright protection for any idea, procedure, system, method of operation, concept, principle, or discovery.

Procedure to Obtain a Copyright

The procedure for obtaining a copyright is very different from the procedure involved in patenting an invention. Copyright protection is obtained by publication of the work with the statutory notice, which is the word *copyright*, its abbreviation *copr.,* or the international copyright symbol ©, followed by the year of first publication, and the name of the owner of the copyright. The copyright is perfected by filing an application to register the copyright, along with copies of the work, in the copyright office in Washington, D.C.

Copyright Owner's Rights

The statute provides that the copyright owner has the exclusive right to do and to authorize reproduction of the copyrighted work, distribution of copies or phonorecords of the work to the public, and public performance or display of the work. The major limitation upon the exclusive rights is the doctrine of **fair use**, which permits use of the copyrighted work for purposes such as criticism, news reporting, teaching, or research. The fair use doctrine has been incorporated into the copyright statutes, and is discussed in the following case involving the electronic duplication and transfer of copyrighted musical recordings.

A & M RECORDS V. NAPSTER, INC.
239 F. 3d 1004 (9th Cir. 2001)

A & M Records, plaintiffs, are engaged in the commercial recording, distribution and sale of copyrighted musical compositions and sound recordings. Defendant, Napster, Inc., facilitates the transmission of audio musical recordings in an MP3 file format from one user to another, by electronic transfer and duplication. Through Napster's Musicshare software, available free from Napster's Internet site, network servers and server-side software users were able to engage in "peer-to-peer" file sharing. Napster also provides technical support for indexing, searching and chatting, all to assist the downloading and uploading of MP3 files.

Circuit Judge Beezer

The district court . . . determined that the plaintiff's exclusive rights under §106 were violated: "here the evidence establishes that a majority of Napster users use the services to download and upload copyrighted music. . . . And by doing that . . . the uses constitute direct infringement of the plaintiffs' musical composition, recordings." The district court also noted that "it is pretty much acknowledged . . . by Napster that this is infringement." We agree that plaintiffs have shown that Napster users infringe at least two of the copyright holders' exclusive rights: the rights of reproduction and distribution. Napster users who upload names to the search index for others to copy violate plaintiffs' distribution rights. Napster users who download files containing copyrighted music violate plaintiffs' reproduction rights.

■   ■   ■

Napster contends that its users do not directly infringe plaintiff's copyrights because the users are engaged in fair use of the material. Napster identifies three specific alleged fair uses: sampling, where users make temporary copies of a work before purchasing; space-shifting, where users access a sound recording through the Napster system that they already own in audio CD format; and permissive distribution of recordings by both the new and established artists.

The district court considered factors listed in 17 U.S.C. § 107, which guide a court's fair use determination. These factors are: (1) the purpose and character of the use; (2) the nature of the copyrighted work, (3) the "amount and substantiality of the portion used" in relation to the work as a whole; and (4) the effect of the use upon the potential market for the work or the value of the work. The district court first conducted a general analysis of Napster system uses under §107, and then applied its reasoning to the alleged fair uses identified by Napster. The district court concluded that Napster users are not fair users. We agree. We first address the court's overall fair use analysis.

1. Purpose and Character of the Use

The factor focuses on whether the new work merely replaces the object of the original creation or instead adds a further purpose or different character. In other words, this factor asks "whether and to what extent the new work is 'transformative.'"

The district court first concluded that downloading MP3 files does not transform the copyrighted work. This conclusion is supportable. Courts have been reluctant to find fair use when an original work is merely retransmitted in a different medium.

This "purpose and character" element also requires the district court to determine whether the allegedly infringing use is commercial or noncommercial. A commercial use weighs against finding a fair use but is not conclusive on the issue. The district court determined that Napster users engage in commercial use of the copyrighted materials largely because (1) "a host user sending a file cannot be said to engage in a personal use when distributing that file to an anonymous requester" and (2) "Napster users get for free something they would ordinarily have to buy." The district court's findings are not clearly erroneous.

Direct economic benefit is not required to demonstrate a commercial use. Rather, repeated and exploitative copying of copyrighted works, even if the copies are not offered for sale, may constitute a commercial use. In the record before us, commercial use is demonstrated by a showing that repeated and exploitative unauthorized copies of copyrighted works were made to save the expense of purchasing authorized copies. . . .

2. The Nature of the Use

Works that are creative in nature are "closer to the core of intended copyright protection" than are more fact-based works. The district court determined that plaintiffs' "copyrighted musical compositions and sound recordings are creative in nature . . . which cuts against a finding of fair use under the second factor." We find no error in the district court's conclusion.

3. The Portion Used

"While 'wholesale copying does not preclude fair use per se,' copying an entire work 'militates against a finding of fair use.' " The district court determined that Napster users engage in "whole-sale copying" of copyrighted work because file transfer necessarily "involves copying the entirety of the copyrighted work." We agree. We note, however, that under certain circumstances, a court will conclude that a use is fair even when the projected work is copied in its entirety.

4. Effect and Use on Market

"Fair use, when properly applied' is limited to copying by others which does not materially impair the marketability of the work which is copied." "[T]he importance of this [fourth] factor will vary, not only with the amount of harm, but also with the relative strength of the showing on the other factors." The proof required to demonstrate the present or future market harm varies with the purpose and character of the use. . . .

Addressing this factor, the district court concluded that Napster harms the market in "at least" two ways: it reduces audio CD sales among college students and it "raises barriers to the plaintiffs' entry into the market for the digital downloading of music." The district court relied on evidence plaintiffs submitted to show that Napster use harms the market for their copyrighted musical compositions and sound recordings. In a separate memorandum the order regarding the parties' objections to the expert reports, the district court examined each report, finding some more appropriate and probative than others. . . .

■　■　■

The district court cited both the Jay and Fine Reports in support of its finding that Napster use harms the market for plaintiffs' copyrighted musical compositions and sound recordings by reducing CD sales among college students. The district court cited the Teece Report to show the harm Napster use caused in raising barriers to plaintiffs' entry into the market for digital downloading of music. The district court's careful consideration

of defendant's objections to these reports and decision to rely on the reports for specific issues demonstrates proper exercise of discretion in addition to a correct application of the fair use doctrine. Defendant has failed to show any basis for disturbing the district court's findings.

We, therefore, conclude that the district court made sound findings related to Napster's deleterious effect on the present and future digital download market. Moreover, lack of harm to an established market cannot deprive the copyright holder of the right to develop alternative markets for the works. Here . . . the record supports the district court's finding that the "record company plaintiffs have already expended considerable funds and effort to commence Internet sales and licensing for digital downloads." Having digital downloads available for free on the Napster system necessarily harms the copyright holders' attempts to charge for the same downloads.

[The Court] did not abuse [its] discretion in reaching the above fair use conclusions, nor were the findings of fact with respect to fair use considerations clearly erroneous. . . .

■　■　■

Affirmed in part.

Case Questions

1. In what ways has Napster infringed on A & M Records copyrighted material? Explain.
2. What are the four factors to be considered when determining fair use?
3. MP3 format is a lesser quality than CDs. Would not the MP3s actually motivate users to purchase recordings that they would not otherwise purchase after listening to the MP3 recording, and thus increase the demand for the recordings? Explain.
4. What can Napster now do to avoid infringement while distributing music recordings electronically? Explain.

Licensing of copyrights is very much like assignment and licensing of patents. Like patents, the various rights granted by the statute may be divided up in licensing arrangements.

The copyright statute provides one major exception to the general rules of licensing. Specifically, if the owner of a music copyright permits a recording to be made and distributed, then anyone is free to make their own recording, provided the copier pays the royalty provided by statute. These are known as the *compulsory licensing provisions* of the copyright law.

The statutory remedies for copyright infringement include actual damages to the copyright holder, punitive damages, profits of the infringer, temporary and permanent injunctive relief, and impoundment and disposition (usually destruction) of the infringing articles.

Trademarks

While patents and copyrights have their origin in the U.S. Constitution, and are both the exclusive domain of federal statutory law, **trademarks** originate in the common law, and involve both federal and state law. Federal involvement with trademarks is limited to cases affecting "interstate commerce."

The federal law of trademarks is codified in the Lanham Act, which defines a trademark as ". . . any word, name, symbol, or device or any combination thereof adopted and used by a manufacturer or merchant to identify his goods and distinguish them from those manufactured or sold by others." For example, look at the following list of trademarks: Old Spice®, Kool Aid®, Tylenol®, Kleenex®, Q-Tips®, and Listerine®. These are immediately recognizable (see Table 10–1).

These trademarks are identifiable, and carry with them some concept of quality and performance. Even if people do not know the specific manufacturer, they buy the brand because of its known reputation for quality. Thus, the trademark is the basis for the purchase decision.

At the state level, trademark laws vary rather widely. Many states have adopted broad protection for trademarks, while other states offer more limited protection. Obviously, state protection is operative only within the bounds of a given state, and hence all but local companies opt for federal trademark protection. The balance of our discussion of trademarks will be limited to the Lanham Act and the federal law of trademarks.

TABLE 10–1   Trademarks

Trademark	Product	Owner
Old Spice®	Deodorant	Shulton
Kool Aid®	Powdered drink mix	General Foods
Tylenol®	Pain medication	McNeil PPC
Kleenex®	Facial tissues	Kimberly-Clark
Q-Tips®	Cotton-tipped swabs	Chesebrough
Listerine®	Mouthwash	Warner Lambert

Classification of Trademarks

Trademarks may be categorized in several ways. They may be classified by form (word marks, symbol or design marks, or composite marks), by use (use on a product, use on a service, or use as a certification), or by relative strength. It is this last classification that is most important to the businessperson in understanding the nature and scope of trademark protection.

A *generic* mark is one employing the common descriptive name for a product. For example, the term *carbonated* is the generic term for a beverage having carbonation. This is the weakest of marks. No one is permitted exclusive rights in a generic term.

A *descriptive* mark is one that merely describes the product or qualities of the product to which it is applied. For example, a bakery might employ the trademark "Oven-Fresh" on its goods. Because the term *oven-fresh* is simply descriptive of the qualities of baked goods, it would be unfair to permit any one merchant to develop exclusive rights in the mark. Thus, anyone in the bakery business is free to use this descriptive term. A merchant can use such a phrase as a trademark, but will be unable to develop any exclusive rights in the mark.

A *suggestive* mark is one that may suggest the product or the qualities of the product to which it is applied, but yet is not merely descriptive of that product. If a term requires imagination, thought, or perception to reach a conclusion as to the nature of the goods, it is "suggestive." For example, the Second Circuit Court of Appeals held that "Roach Motel" was a suggestive mark when used on an insect trap. Hence, suggestive marks are stronger than descriptive ones.

A trademark is considered *arbitrary* if it is a new word, or if it is a common word that has no relation whatsoever to the product to which it is applied. For example, the well-known trademark Kodak® is arbitrary. It is a combination of five letters that has no independent meaning at all. A more subtle example would be Ivory®. You can look in any dictionary and find a number of standard definitions for the word *ivory*. However, as applied to soap, the mark is considered "arbitrary." In the trademark sense, arbitrary trademarks are the strongest.

The statute provides that a mark that is not arbitrary may be registered only if it can be shown that ". . . the mark has become distinctive of applicant's goods in commerce." Such a showing is called **secondary meaning**. In reality, it means that through widespread, continuous, and exclusive use, a particular mark has developed a new or secondary meaning in which it serves to identify the specific goods of a particular merchant. The Qualitex case discussed below addresses "secondary meaning."

Federal Registration and Remedies

Under the common law, trademark rights were acquired by adopting a mark and applying it to goods sold in the trade. As originally codified in the Lanham Act, use of the mark in commerce was required before an application could be filed to register the mark.

The Lanham Act provides for registration of trademarks in the United States Patent Office. An application for registration is filed, and examined by the Patent

Office to be sure that all statutory conditions are met. Specifically, the Patent Office ensures that generic marks are not registered, and that nonarbitrary marks are registered only if an appropriate showing of secondary meaning is provided. The following case, involving the trademark of a color, is illustrative.

QUALITEX COMPANY V. JACOBSON PRODUCTS CO.
514 U.S. 159 (1995)

Plaintiff, Qualitex, used a special shade of green-gold color on pads that it manufactured and sold to dry cleaning firms for use on dry cleaning presses. Jacobson Products, defendant, a competitor, sold presses with similar colored pads. Qualitex registered the special green-gold color as a trademark.

Qualitex sued Jacobson for trademark infringement and unfair competition. The district court found in favor of Qualitex. The Ninth Circuit Court of Appeals set aside the trademark infringement claim on the basis that one cannot register a "color alone" as a trademark. The Circuit Courts of Appeals were split on this issue and the United States Supreme Court granted certiorari.

Justice Breyer

The question in this case is whether the Trademark Act . . . (Lanham Act) permits the registration of a trademark that consists, purely and simply, of a color. We conclude that, sometimes, a color will meet ordinary legal trademark requirements. And, when it does so, no special legal rule prevents color alone from serving as a trademark.

■   ■   ■

The Lanham Act gives a seller or producer the exclusive right to "register" a trademark, and to prevent his or her competitors from using that trademark. Both the language of the Act and the basic underlying principles of the trademark law would seem to include color within the universe of things that can qualify as a trademark. The language of the Lanham Act describes that universe in the broadest of terms. It says that trademarks "include any word, name, symbol, or device, or any combination thereof." Since human beings might use as a "symbol" or "device" almost anything at all that is capable of carrying meaning,

this language, read literally, is not restrictive. The courts and the Patent and Trademark Office have authorized for use as a mark a particular shape (of a Coca-Cola bottle), a particular sound (NBC's three chimes), and even a particular scent (of plumeria blossoms on sewing thread). If a shape, a sound, and a fragrance can act as symbols why one might ask, can a color not do the same?

A color is also capable of satisfying the more important part of the statutory definition of a trademark, which requires that a person "use" or "intend to use" the mark "to identify and distinguish his or her goods, including a unique product, from those manufactured or sold by others and to indicate the source of the goods, even if that source is unknown." True, a product's color is unlike "fanciful," "arbitrary," or "suggestive" words or designs, which almost *automatically* tell the customer that they refer to a brand. The imaginary word "Suntost," or the words "Suntost Marmalade," on the jar or orange jam immediately would signal a brand or a product "source"; the jam's color does not do so. But, over time, customers may come to treat a particular color on a product or its packaging (say, a color that in context seems unusual, such as pink on a firm's insulating material or red on the head of a large industrial bolt) as signifying a brand. And, if so, that color would have come to identify and distinguish the goods—*i.e.*, "to indicate" their "source"—much in the way that descriptive word on a product (say, "Trim" on nail clippers or "Car-Freshener" on deodorizer) can come to indicate a product's origin. In this circumstance, trademark law says that the word (*e.g.*, "Trim"), although not inherently distinctive has developed "secondary meaning." . . . Secondary meaning" is acquired when " in the minds of the public, the primary significance of a product feature . . . is to identify the source of the product rather than the product itself ". . . .

We cannot find in the basic objectives of trademark law any obvious theoretical objection to the use of color alone as a trademark, where that color has attained "secondary meaning" and therefore identifies and distinguishes a particular brand (and thus indicates its "source"). In principle, trademark law, by preventing others from copying the source-identifying mark, "reduce[s] the customer's costs of shopping and making purchasing decisions," for it quickly and easily assures a potential customer that *this* item—the item with the mark—is made by the same producer as other similarly marked items that he or she liked (or disliked) in the past. At the same time, the law helps assure a producer that it (and not an intimidating competitor) will reap the financial, reputation-related awards associated with a desirable product. The law thereby "encourage[s] the production of quality products," and simultaneously discourages those who hope to sell inferior products by capitalizing on a consumer's inability quickly to evaluate the quality of an item offered for sale. . . .

. . . Neither can we find a principled objection to use of color as a mark in the important "functionality" doctrine of trademark law.

. . . This court consequently has explained that, "in general terms, a product feature is functional,"

and cannot serve as a trademark, "if it is essential to the use or purpose of the article or if it affects the cost or quality of the article," that is, if exclusive use of the feature would put competitors at a significant non-reputation-related disadvantage. Although sometimes color plays an important role (unrelated to source identification) in making a product more desirable, sometimes it does not. And, this latter fact—the fact that sometimes color is not essential to a product's use or purpose and does not affect the cost or quality—indicates that the doctrine of "functionality" does not create an absolute bar to the use of color alone as a mark.

It would seem, then, that color alone, at least sometimes, can meet the basic legal requirements for use as a trademark. It can act as a symbol that distinguishes a firm's goods and identifies their source, without serving any other significant function. . . . Accordingly, unless there is some special reason that convincingly militates against the use of color alone as a trademark, trademark law would protect Qualitex's use of green-gold color on its press pads.

Respondent Jacobson Products says that there are four special reasons why the law should forbid the use of a color alone as a trademark. We shall explain, in turn, why we, ultimately, find them unpersuasive.

First, Jacobson says that, if the law permits the use of color as a trademark, it will produce uncertainty and irresolvable court disputes about the shades of a color a competitor may lawfully use. . . .

We do not believe, however, that color, in this respect, is special. Courts traditionally decide quite difficult questions about whether two words or phrases or symbols are sufficiently similar, in context, to confuse buyers. . . .

Second, Jacobson argues, as have others, that colors are in limited supply. Jacobson claims that, if one of many competitors can appropriate a particular color for use as a trademark, and each competitor then tries to do the same, the supply of competitors will soon be depleted. Put in its strongest form, this argument would concede that "hundreds of color pigments are manufactured and thousands of colors can be obtained by mixing." But, it would add that, in the context of a particular product, only some colors are usable. By the time one discards colors that, say, for reasons of customer appeal, are unstable, and adds the shades that competitors cannot use lest they risk infringement of a similar registered shade, then one is only left with a handful of possible colors. And, under these circumstances, to permit one, or a few, producers to use colors as trademarks will "deplete" the supply of usable colors to the point where a competitor's inability to find a suitable color will put that competitor at a significant disadvantage.

This argument is unpersuasive, however, largely because it relies on an occasional problem to justify a blanket prohibition. When a color serves as a mark, normally alternative colors will likely be available for similar use by others....

■   ■   ■

... *Third*, Jacobson points to many older cases—including Supreme Court cases—in support of its position. In 1878, this Court described the common-law definition of trademark rather broadly to "consist of any symbol, figure, letter, form, or device, if adopted and used by a manufacturer or merchant in order to designate the goods he manufactures or sells to distinguish the same from those manufactured or sold by another." Even though these statements amounted to dicta, lower courts interpreted them as forbidding protection for color alone.

These Supreme Court cases, however, interpreted trademark law as it existed *before* 1946, when Congress enacted the Lanham Act. The Lanham Act significantly changed and liberalized the common law to "dispense with mere technical prohibitions" most notably, by permitting trademark registration of descriptive words where they had acquired "secondary meaning." The Lanham Act extended protection to descriptive marks by making clear that (with certain explicit exceptions not relevant here) "nothing ... shall prevent the registration of a mark used by the applicant which has become distinctive of the applicant's goods in commerce." ...

■   ■   ■

Fourth, Jacobson argues that there is no need to permit color alone to function as a trademark because a firm already may use color as part of a trademark, say as a colored circle or colored letter or word.... The first part of this argument begs the question. One can understand why a firm might find it difficult to place a usable symbol or word on a product (say, a large industrial bolt that customers normally see from a distance); and, in such instances, a firm might want to use color, pure and simple, instead of color as part of the design....

Having determined that a color may sometimes meet the basic legal requirements for use as a trademark and that respondent Jacobson's arguments do not justify a special legal rule preventing color alone from serving as a trademark we conclude that the Ninth Circuit erred in barring Qualitex's use of color as a trademark. For these reasons, the judgment of the Ninth Circuit is

Reversed.

Case Questions:

1. The Lanham Act defines a trademark to include any "word, name, symbol, or design." Into which category did the court place "color"?

2. What is secondary meaning? How does it relate to color in this case? Explain.

3. What if a firm wanted to use a rainbow, consisting of all the colors in the spectrum, as a trademark? Would the Court have a problem with this?

4. The Yellow Transit Company, having painted its taxicabs "yellow" for more than 40 years, filed an application to register the trademark "yellow" for taxicabs. What action should be taken on the application by the patent office? Explain.

When the examiner is satisfied with the application, the mark is published for opposition. An official publication of the United States Patent Office lists all marks that have been passed by the trademark examiners, and anyone who may be damaged by registration of the mark is entitled to file an opposition. This is a contested administrative proceeding, adjudicated by the Patent Office. The amendments to the Lanham Act in 1988 provided for the first time an opportunity to register a mark based upon "intent to use." This provision had been widely sought by major corporations who wished to establish their trademark position prior to actually putting a product on the market with a new trademark.

Registration provides many major advantages to the trademark owner. First of all, it provides constructive notice throughout the entire country of the trademark user's claim to rights in the mark. In other words, if a small firm starts operations in the Pacific Northwest, registration will give the firm nationwide protection for its mark. Second, after six years of continuous use following registration, the mark becomes "incontestable." This incontestability gives the trademark owner significant procedural advantages to enforce rights in the mark. And finally, the statutory remedies become available in enforcement.

Under the Lanham Act, the trademark owner may bring an action for infringement seeking the statutory remedies of treble damages, attorney fees, and destruction of infringing labels. The fundamental issue in a trademark infringement action is likelihood of confusion. Where the marks are the same, and the goods on which they are used are the same, the issue is clear. However, when either the marks or the goods are different, the issue becomes much more difficult, and takes into account the strength of the mark, the similarity of the marks, the similarity of the goods upon which the marks are used, the similarity of the channels of distribution, and evidence, if any, of actual confusion. For example, Coca-Cola was able to stop a competitor from using the mark "LaCoq" on soft drinks. Even though the marks look different, they sound very similar, and Coke® is a very strong mark. The owner of the mark Johnny Walker® for whiskey was able to stop use of the identical mark on shoes. Again, the court found the mark to be very strong and accorded protection, even though the goods were very dissimilar.

International Property Rights

With the increase of multinational companies—those doing business in more than one country—there is a concomitant concern about protecting intellectual property. Patents, copyrights, and trademarks are afforded great protection in this country; however, not every country's laws are as protective. Some countries do have adequate protection. The United States does have patent, trademark, and copyright treaties with a number of nations. Some are nondiscrimination treaties. Others provide for limited protection, while others provide for protection upon registration. Still others give automatic protection without registration. Companies need to be wary of those nations that have a reputation for pirating intellectual works and either not deal in those nations when their property rights are at risk or take special precautions to protect those rights. Currently, serious problems exist with countries that are lax on enforcement of intellectual property laws. The United States has the power to impose trade restrictions on those nations.

Chapter Problems

1. Define the following terms and concepts:
   a. Personal property
   b. Bailment
   c. Real property
   d. Fixtures
   e. Patent
   f. Non-obviousness
   g. Copyright
   h. Fair use
   i. Trademark
   j. Secondary meaning

2. Karen Ray worked as a receptionist at Flower Hospital. One evening she noticed a soft-shell eyeglass case on the top of the information desk. It contained rings, earrings, and other jewelry. What should Ray do? Why?

3. Johnson played a round of golf at the Firestone Country Club. Prior to teeing off at the first hole, he took off his Rolex watch and placed it in the front compartment of the golf cart he had obtained from the club. At the end of the game one of the players drove the cart to the pro shop and dropped it off. About 20 minutes later, Johnson realized that he was not wearing his watch and remembered that he had left it in the cart. The watch was never found. What should Johnson do, and why?

4. The Premonstatensian Fathers (Fathers) owned a one-story building that was insured. The Fathers leased out the building to a tenant that used it as a supermarket. A major fire damaged the building. The insurer refused to pay for the damage to five Hussman walk-in coolers situated in the building, contending that they were personal property installed by the tenant. The construction of the coolers was as follows:
   a. The exterior walls of the cooler, in four instances, constituted the interior wall of another room.
   b. In the two meat coolers, a meat-hanging-and-tracking system was built into the coolers. These tracks were used to move large cuts of meat from the cooler area into the meat preparation areas, and were suspended from the steel girders of the building structure by means of large steel bolts. These bolts penetrated through the roof of the cooler supporting wooden beams, which, in turn, supported the tracking system. The tracking in the coolers was a part of a system of tracking throughout the rear portion of the supermarket.

   c. The coolers were attached to hardwood planks that were, in turn, attached to the concrete floor of the supermarket. The attachment of the planks to the floor was accomplished through the use of a ramsetting gun. The planks were laid on the floor, and the bolts were driven through them into the concrete floor, where they then exploded, firmly fixing the coolers into place. There was a material placed on the planks that served as both an adhesive and an insulation.

   d. The floor of the coolers was specially sloped during the construction of the building so that the slope would carry drainage into a specially constructed drain in the concrete. In addition, four of the coolers were coated with a protective coating to seal the floors. In the freezer, a special concrete buildup was constructed in the nature of a trough, the purpose of which was to carry away moisture as frozen chickens melted.

   e. A refrigeration unit was built into each cooler. The unit was suspended from the ceiling of the cooler, and tubing was run through the wall of the cooler to compressors located elsewhere in the store.

   f. Electric lights and power receptacles were built into each cooler and were connected by electrical wiring through the walls and the ceiling of the cooler to the store's electrical power supply.

   g. The walls of the cooler were interlocked and set into the splines, and the hardwood planks ramset into the concrete floor, in tongue-and-groove fashion.

    Are the Fathers entitled to be compensated for the damage to the coolers? Explain.

5. John, Mary, and James owned real estate in fee simple absolute as "joint tenants with the right of survivorship." John died, leaving Candy and Rollins as heirs. Then Mary sold her interest to Van. Who has what, and why?

6. John Moore was diagnosed with hairy-cell leukemia. Dr. David Golde, a physician attending Moore at the University of California-Los Angeles (UCLA) Medical Center, removed Moore's spleen to slow down the progress of the disease. Dr. Golde was aware of the scientific and commercial value of blood components from Mr. Moore as a result of his specific disease. In follow-up sessions, Dr. Golde withdrew blood and bodily fluids from which he was able to grow a culture to produce lymphokines on a continuous basis (cell line). Lymphokines are proteins that regulate the immune system, and they have particular therapeutic value. Dr. Golde and UCLA obtained a patent on the cell line.

    Genetics Institute has made Dr. Golde and UCLA an attractive financial offer for the exclusive access to the materials and research performed on the cell line and products derived from it. They are contemplating the offer.

    What are the ethical issues? What should the result be?

7. Universal (respondent) owned the copyrights on a variety of television programs that were broadcast over the public airwaves, and brought suit

against Sony (petitioner) for copyright infringement. Sony manufactured and sold the Betamax home video tape recorders, called at the time *VTRs*.

Universal argued that customers who had purchased the VTRs had used them to unlawfully record copyrighted programs, and that Sony, because of its marketing of the device, was liable for copyright infringement. Both parties conducted surveys that showed that the primary use of the machine for most owners was "time-shifting"—the practice of recording a program to view it once at a later time, and thereafter erasing it. Both surveys also showed, however, that a substantial number of interviewees had accumulated libraries of tapes. Has Sony infringed? Is the practice fair use? Explain.

8. Kinko photocopied excerpts of several copyrighted books, without permission and without payment, compiled them into course "packets," and sold them to college students. The owner of one of the copyrights sued for copyright infringement. Kinko defended by asserting that its copying was a "fair use" of the copyrighted material for educational purposes. Argue the case for the copyright owner. Who do you think should prevail, and why?

9. Professor of English I. B. Wright always dreamed of a career as a writer of fiction. His first attempt at a novel was generated on a word processor, and copies were sent to about a dozen publishers and several friends and acquaintances. None of the copies contained the copyright notice. Four years later, a new novel by an unknown author suddenly appeared on the bestseller list. To Wright's great surprise, it was his novel with a new title and the names of all the characters completely changed. Does Professor Wright have a claim against the publisher? Against the author? Explain.

10. Rolls Royce, a British company that has a worldwide reputation as a producer of luxury automobiles and jet engines, obtained a U.S. registration of the words "Rolls Royce" as a trademark for its products. Alexander Knockoff formed a small company and began producing a low-cost reproduction of a roll-top desk that he called "The Rolls Royce." What action, if any, would you recommend that Rolls Royce take? Explain.

11. Owings-Corning Fiberglass Corp (OCF) filed an application to register the color "pink" as a trademark for the company's fibrous glass residential insulation. It uses the color in advertising, employing the "Pink Panther" in a cartoon-type animation in connection with the rolling out of pink insulation.

Do you think that OCF will be able to obtain a trademark registration for the color pink? Explain.

12. Outline the steps you should take to ensure protection for intellectual property when exposing that property in other countries.

11 ENVIRONMENTAL LAW

Chapter Outline

Learning Objectives

After learning this chapter, the student should be able to:

- Describe the nature and contents of an environmental impact statement.
- Describe the activities of the Environmental Protection Agency.
- Identify the federal statutes aimed at controlling pollution and describe the requirements imposed on business by each statute.
- Explain federal policy regarding land use and resource management.
- Describe how environmental law affects international business operations.

Statistical evidence, substantiated by dramatic events, made American legislators of the 1960s and 1970s acutely aware of the nation's dependence on a protected environment. Evidence that emissions of sulfur dioxide increased from 22 million to 33 million tons annually between 1940 and 1970, for example, was punctuated by reports of deaths in Los Angeles caused by photochemically activated smog. Acid rain from fossil fuel combustion in the northeastern United States destroyed 200 lakes in the New York Adirondack Mountains alone; the fish in those lakes had been killed, and the aquatic vegetation had dwindled severely. Meanwhile, floating wastes in the Cuyahoga River self-ignited and Lake Erie was dying due to pollution.

Common law environmental protections serve to settle some individual disputes, but broader environmental policy concerns had to be addressed by statutes. During the 1970s, state and federal legislators responded to these hazards and other problems by enacting laws to protect the environment. Under common law, landholders can use a range of responses to keep their land free of encumbrances, their water free of obstructions, and their air free of debris. Depending on the interests they have at stake, landholders can sue under the tort theories of trespass, nuisance, negligence, or strict liability. (These tort theories are discussed in Chapter 8.) This chapter discusses national environmental policy, describes federal and state programs for pollution control, and concludes with a discussion of land use and resource management.

National Environmental Policy

The National Environmental Policy Act (NEPA) establishes the nation's environmental policy, sets goals, and provides means for carrying out the policy. NEPA declares a national policy of supporting harmony between humans and their environment. The goal of NEPA is to ensure that environmental information is made available to government officials and the public before decisions are reached or actions are taken. NEPA policies are carried out by means of the **environmental impact statement (EIS)**, a document disclosing the environmental effects of major federal actions.

Environmental Impact Statement (EIS)

NEPA requires federal agencies undertaking "major federal actions significantly affecting the quality of the human environment" to prepare a statement detailing the environmental impact of the proposed action and any alternative actions. Table 11–1 sets out the contents of the EIS. Copies of the EIS are to be distributed to federal agencies, state and local agencies, the president, and the public. The purpose of an EIS is to infuse national environmental policy into federal program planning. This is done by informing officials and the public of the environmental effects of federal action and by requiring the consideration of reasonable alternatives that reduce endangerment to the environment.

TABLE 11–1   **Contents of the Environmental Impact Statement**

NEPA requires that every EIS include the following items:

- The environmental impact of the proposed action.
- Any adverse environmental effects that would be unavoidable if the proposed action were taken.
- The relationship between local short-term uses of the environment and the maintenance or enhancement of long-term productivity.
- Irreversible commitments of resources that would be involved if the proposed action were taken.
- Alternatives to the proposed action.

Activities Requiting an EIS

An agency must prepare an EIS whenever it plans or engages in major federal actions significantly affecting the quality of the human environment. As NEPA has been interpreted, activities wholly undertaken by federal agencies are not the only federal actions subject to EIS preparation; activities also require an EIS if they are supported by federal funding. Private enterprise thus may be consulted on information for EIS preparation when it carries on business under federal contracts, grants, subsidies, or loans. Private companies may also become involved when they need federal leases, permits, licenses, or certificates to operate.

In the following case, the Supreme Court addressed the question of which environmental impacts or environmental effects of proposed federal action (the first and second items in Table 11–1) must be discussed in an EIS.

METROPOLITAN EDISON CO. v. PEOPLE AGAINST NUCLEAR ENERGY
460 U.S. 766 (1983)

Metropolitan Edison Company (petitioner) owns two licensed nuclear plants at Three Mile Island near Harrisburg, Pennsylvania. On a day when one plant (TMI–1) was shut down for refueling, the other plant (TMI–2) suffered a serious accident that damaged the reactor and caused widespread concern. The Nuclear Regulatory Commission (NRC) ordered Metropolitan to keep TMI–1 shut down until it determined whether the plant could be operated safely. The NRC invited interested parties to submit legal briefs on whether psychological harm or other direct effects of the accident or of renewed operation of TMI–1 should be considered. People Against Nuclear Energy (PANE) (respondent), an association of residents from the Harrisburg area opposed to further operation of either TMI reactor, submitted such a brief. After reviewing the briefs, the NRC decided not to include a discussion of the psychological effects in the EIS. PANE filed a petition for review in the Circuit Court of Appeals for the District of Columbia. The court held that the NRC had to consider whether the risk of an accident at TMI–1 might harm the psychological health and community well-being of residents around Three Mile Island. The Supreme Court reversed.

Justice Rehnquist

[W]here an agency significantly affects the quality of the human environment, the agency must evaluate the "environmental impact" and any unavoidable adverse environmental effects of its proposal. The theme of [NEPA] is sounded by the adjective "environmental": NEPA does not require the agency to assess every impact or effect of its proposed action, but only the impact or effect on the environment. If we were to seize the word "environmental" out of its context and give it the broadest possible definition, the words "adverse environmental effects" might embrace virtually any consequence of a governmental action that someone thought "adverse." But we think the context of the statute shows that Congress was talking about the physical environment—the world around us, so to speak. NEPA was designed to promote human welfare by alerting governmental actors to the effect of their proposed actions on the physical environment.

■   ■   ■

To determine whether [NEPA] requires consideration of a particular effect, we must look at the relationship between that effect and the change in the physical environment, caused by the major federal action at issue.

Our understanding of the congressional concerns that led to the enactment of NEPA suggests that the terms "environmental effect" and "environmental impact" in [NEPA] be read to include a requirement of a reasonably close causal relationship between a change in the physical environment and the effect at issue. . . .

■   ■   ■

The federal action that affects the environment in this case is permitting renewed operation of TMI–1. The direct effects on the environment of this action include release of low-level radiation, increased fog in the Harrisburg area (caused by operation of the plant's cooling towers), and the release of warm water into the Susquehanna River. The NRC has considered each of these effects in its EIS. . . . Another effect of renewed operation is a risk of a nuclear accident. The NRC has also considered this effect.

PANE argues that the psychological health damage it alleges "will flow directly from the risk of [a nuclear] accident." But a risk of an accident is not an effect on the physical world. In a causal chain from renewed operation of TMI–1 to psychological health damage, the element of risk and its perception by PANE's members are necessary middle links. We believe that the element of risk lengthens the causal chain beyond the reach of NEPA.

■   ■   ■

Time and resources are simply too limited for us to believe that Congress intended to extend NEPA as far as the Court of Appeals has taken it. The scope of the agency's inquiries must remain manageable if NEPA's goal of "ensur[ing] a fully informed and well considered decision" is to be accomplished.

If contentions of psychological health damage caused by risk were cognizable under NEPA, agencies would, at the very least, be obliged to expend considerable resources developing psychiatric expertise that is not otherwise relevant to their congressionally assigned functions. The available resources may be spread so thin that agencies are unable adequately to pursue protection of the physical environment and natural resources.

■   ■   ■

If a harm does not have sufficiently close connection to the physical environment, NEPA does not apply.

For these reasons, we hold that the NRC need not consider PANE's contentions.

Case Questions

1. Why did the Supreme Court support the NRC's reading of NEPA rather than that of the court of appeals?
2. How did the Supreme Court determine whether NEPA requires an agency to consider a particular effect in preparing an EIS?
3. Suppose that the Department of Health and Human Services were to implement extremely stringent requirements for hospitals and nursing homes receiving federal funds. Many perfectly adequate hospitals and nursing homes might be forced out of existence, and the remaining facilities might be so limited or expensive that many ill people would be unable to afford medical care and would suffer severe health damage. Would NEPA require the department to prepare an EIS evaluating that damage? Explain.

Pollution Control Measures

Federal antipollution measures are designed to eliminate or control the diffusion of waste particles through the air, water, and land.

Environmental Protection Agency (EPA)

The Environmental Protection Agency (EPA) oversees many of the federal pollution control programs. States have established similar agencies. The EPA is the largest regulatory agency in the United States today. It has an annual budget of $5.1 billion and employs over 17,000 people, who work in Washington D.C. and 10 regional offices and 26 research facilities located around the country.

The EPA was created to consolidate federal environmental pollution responsibilities. Its primary function is to establish and enforce standards, conduct research on pollution effects, monitor and analyze the environment, advise Congress of new policies to protect the environment from pollution, and assist state and local pollution control programs. Table 11–2 summarizes the major activities of the EPA discussed in this chapter.

The Clean Water Act (CWA)

The Clean Water Act (CWA) has two stated goals: to make the nation's water safe for swimming and fishing, and to eliminate the discharge of all pollutants into navigable waters. To accomplish these goals, the EPA is authorized to establish water quality criteria regulating the concentrations of pollutants that are permissible in a body of water, and **effluent limitations** regulating the amount of pollutants discharged from a particular source. To enforce these water quality criteria and effluent limitations, the CWA relies on a permit system, called the *National Pollutant Discharge Elimination System (NPDES)*. Companies must obtain permits to discharge pollutants into the navigable waters of the United

TABLE 11–2	**Major EPA Activities**

Water
Develops and enforces water quality criteria and effluent limitations.
Issues permits for point source discharges.
Administers cleanup of hazardous substances.

Air
Develops national ambient air quality standards.
Develops emission standards for new stationary sources.
Monitors enforcement of state implementation plans.

Solid Waste
Develops hazardous waste standards and regulations.
Identifies solid waste generators and monitors them.
Issues permits to waste storage, treatment, or disposal facilities.

Superfund
Administers federal cleanup of toxic substance spills.

Toxic Substances
Issues rules and orders relating to the use of toxic substances.

Pesticides
Monitors state certification of pesticide applicators.
Issues rules relating to the use and labeling of pesticides.
Establishes tolerance level for pesticides in food.

States. Although the CWA is ultimately administered by the EPA, the agency delegates actual enforcement to any state that requests such authority and agrees to meet EPA specifications.

National Permit System

The CWA makes it illegal to discharge any pollutant without a NPDES permit. Permits can be granted only by the EPA or authorized state agencies. Although the EPA delegates this authority to the states, it retains authority to veto a state permit or to step in and take enforcement action if a state fails to do so.

The permit specifies each pollutant that can be discharged and sets average and maximum daily limits, called *effluent limitations,* on each. The permits are designed to reflect the technological feasibility of particular methods of reducing pollution. Permit holders are required to monitor their discharges from point sources. A **point source** is defined as any discernible and confined conveyance, such as a pipe, ditch, well, or canal.

Nonpoint sources of water pollution include such things as overflows from irrigated agriculture, runoffs from mining activities, and runoffs from construction sites. Each state is required to submit for EPA approval a program for managing nonpoint sources of pollution. The plans must include the best management practices for controlling such pollution. However, the law lets the states decide whether to require landowners and managers to use such practices or to make them voluntary and rely on aid and education. The plans must include annual milestones for achieving nonpoint pollution control.

Publicly Owned Treatment Works
Discharges into publicly owned sewage treatment works, though also point source discharges, require no permit. Still, industrial users must meet certain pretreatment standards before they make their discharges. They must treat wastes to remove pollutants before discharging them into the system. Pretreatment standards are designed to ensure that the pollutants in industrial discharges are compatible with the treatment process used by the sewage treatment works. Sewage treatment works that receive federal grants must charge industrial users for their treatment services.

Hazardous Substances
The CWA forbids the discharge of hazardous substances in harmful quantities. Dischargers must report any leaking, spilling, pumping, or dumping, and are liable for cleanup costs. The EPA may clean up the spill, or authorize another agency to clean it up, and assess the discharger for the costs. The discharger is not liable if the spill results from (1) an act of God, (2) an act of war, (3) the negligence of the federal government, or (4) an act or omission of a third party.

Enforcement
The CWA authorizes the EPA to impose administrative civil penalties for permit violations through adjudicatory procedures. The EPA administrator may also bring a civil action to obtain an injunction or a civil penalty against a violator. The administrator may cause criminal proceedings to be instituted. In recent years, the EPA has increased its emphasis on criminal enforcement of the CWA.

   The statute also provides for **citizen suits.** Any citizen having standing may bring a civil action on his or her own behalf against a violator. The following decision by the Supreme Court shows when citizens may bring suit against violators of the Clean Water Act.

GWALTNEY OF SMITHFIELD V. CHESAPEAKE BAY FOUNDATION, INC.
484 U.S. 49 (1987)

Between 1981 and 1984, Gwaltney of Smithfield (petitioner) repeatedly violated the conditions of its NPDES permit by exceeding authorized effluent limitations. However, due to the installation of new equipment, Gwaltney's last reported violation occurred in May 1984. Nevertheless, in June 1984 the Chesapeake Bay Foundation, Inc. and the Natural Resources Defense Council (respondents) filed a citizen suit under Section 505(a) of the Clean Water Act, alleging that Gwaltney "has violated . . . [and] will continue to violate its NPDES permit." The federal district court denied Gwaltney's motion to dismiss, rejecting Gwaltney's argument that the Section 505(a)'s "alleged to be in violation" language required that the defendant be violating the act at the time of suit. The district court further decided that respondents satisfied Section 505(a)'s requirements because their complaint alleged in good faith that Gwaltney was continuing to violate its permit at the time the suit was filed. The circuit court of appeals affirmed. The Supreme Court reversed.

Justice Marshall

The holder of a state NPDES permit is subject to both federal and state enforcement action for failure to comply. In the absence of federal or state enforcement, private citizens may commence civil actions against any person "alleged to be in violation of" the conditions of either a federal or state NPDES permit.

■   ■   ■

The Court of Appeals concluded that the "to be in violation" language of Section 505 is ambiguous, whereas petitioner asserts that it plainly precludes the construction adopted below. We must agree with the Court of Appeals that Section 505 is not a provision in which Congress' limpid prose puts an end to all dispute. But to acknowledge ambiguity is not to conclude that all interpretations are equally plausible. The most natural reading of "to be in violation" is a requirement that citizen plaintiffs allege a state of either continuous or intermittent violation—that is, a reasonable likelihood that a past polluter will continue to pollute in the future. Congress could have phrased its requirement in language that looked to the past ("to have violated"), but it did not choose this readily available option.

■   ■   ■

Respondents seek to counter this reasoning by observing that Congress also used the phrase "is in violation" in Section 309(a) of the Act, which authorizes the Administrator of EPA to issue compliance orders. . . . Because it is little questioned that the Administrator may bring enforcement actions to recover civil penalties for wholly past violations, respondents contend, the parallel language of Section 309(a) and Section 505(a) must mean that citizens, too, may maintain such actions.

. . .

This Court recently has recognized that Section 309(d) constitutes a separate grant of enforcement authority. . . . A comparison of Section 309 and Section 505 . . . supports rather than refutes our conclusion that citizens, unlike the Administrator, may seek civil penalties only in a suit brought to enjoin or otherwise abate an ongoing violation.

■   ■   ■

Permitting citizen suits for wholly past violations of the Act could undermine the supplementary role envisioned for the citizen suit. This danger is best illustrated by an example. Suppose that the Administrator identified a violator of the Act and issued a compliance order under Section 309(a). Suppose further that the Administrator agreed not to assess or otherwise seek civil penalties on the condition that the violator take some extreme corrective action, such as to install particularly effective but expensive machinery, that it otherwise would not be obliged to take. If citizens could file suit, months or years later, in order to seek the civil penalties that the Administrator chose to forgo, then the Administrator's discretion to enforce the Act in the public interest would be curtailed considerably. The same might be said of the discretion of state enforcement authorities. Respondents' interpretation of the scope of the citizen suit would change the nature of the citizens' role from interstitial to potentially intrusive. We cannot agree that Congress intended such a result.

■   ■   ■

Our conclusion that Section 505 does not permit citizen suits for wholly past violations does not necessarily dispose of this lawsuit, as both lower courts recognized. The District Court found persuasive the fact that "[respondents'] allegation in the complaint, that Gwaltney was continuing to violate its NPDES permit when plaintiffs filed suit[,] appears to have been made fully in good faith." On this basis, the District Court explicitly held . . . that "even if Gwaltney were correct that a district court has no jurisdiction over citizen suits based entirely on unlawful conduct that occurred entirely in the past, the Court would still have jurisdiction here."

. . . Because we agree that Section 505 confers jurisdiction over citizen suits when the citizen-plaintiffs make a good-faith allegation of continuous or intermittent violation, we remand the case . . . for further consideration.

Case Questions

1. Does the Clean Water Act allow citizens to bring suit against companies for wholly past violations of the Act? Explain.
2. Does the Clean Water Act allow citizens to bring suit against companies for continuous or intermittent ongoing noncompliance? Explain.
3. Who has authority to bring suit against companies for wholly past violations of the Clean Water Act?
4. In your opinion, what will be the effect of *Gwaltney* on company compliance with the Clean Water Act?

The Clean Air Act (CAA)

The Clean Air Act (CAA) encourages states to control local sources of harmful airborne particles, classified as carbon monoxide, particulates, sulfur oxides, hydrocarbons, and nitrogen oxides.

The Clean Air Act authorizes the EPA to determine concentrations of various particles that would be consistent with human health. The EPA has set standards for common pollutants such as dust, carbon monoxide, and ozone. The standards are called the *National Ambient[1] Air Quality Standards (NAAQS).*

State Implementation Plans (SIP)

Once the EPA sets the NAAQS, states are responsible for controlling and cleaning up areas that do not comply with them. States have to detail the measures they would use to achieve the standards, and submit their plans to the EPA. If a state's implementation plan is inadequate, the EPA can withhold federal funds, prohibit the construction of new air pollution sources, or intercede with its own measures. All SIPs must include **emission limitations** and measures that will be taken to uphold air standards. Emission limitations are specific rules that operators of pollutant sources must follow to reduce emission from mobile sources of pollution.

---

[1] The term *ambient* refers to atmospheric air, as opposed to air inside of buildings.

Nonattainment Areas

Nonattainment areas are those areas that have failed to meet the NAAQS. The Clean Air Act provides that SIPS require nearly all major sources of air pollution in a nonattainment area to obtain an operating permit. The permits set forth detailed requirements governing emission limits, as well as monitoring and reporting requirements. A company that is in compliance with its permit cannot be found in violation of any provision of the Clean Air Act that is addressed in the permit. (This is called the *permit shield*.)

Enforcement

Enforcement of the Clean Air Act is accomplished through administrative penalties, criminal prosecution, and citizen suits.

The Resource Conservation and Recovery Act (RCRA)

The Resource Conservation and Recovery Act (RCRA) addresses the special problems of hazardous waste sites. Under the RCRA, handlers of hazardous wastes must conform to specified standards. Handlers include those who generate, transport, treat, or store hazardous wastes. Hazardous wastes are those wastes that contribute significantly to serious, irreversible illnesses or pose hazards to human health when improperly managed.

Generators and Transporters

Generators and transporters of hazardous wastes must notify the EPA of the location and general description of their activities. They must also specify which wastes they are handling. The EPA issues identification numbers to each handler.

Generators of waste must keep records on their hazardous wastes. If waste generators transport the wastes off the site of their manufacture, they must package and label the wastes and ship the packages with a manifest. The manifest identifies the persons originating, carrying, and receiving the wastes and states the nature and quantity of the wastes. If a generator does not receive a signed copy of the manifest from the intended receiver within 45 days of the time it transports its wastes, it must report to the EPA regional administrator. In any event, generators must report to the regional administrator yearly.

Transporters must comply with the terms of the manifests they receive from generators and must keep a copy of each manifest. If waste discharge occurs during carriage, transporters must take appropriate immediate action to protect human health and the environment. They may have to clean up the discharge or notify authorities, depending on the action officially approved for them.

Owners or Operators

Owners or operators of a hazardous waste treatment, storage, or disposal facility (TSDF) have to apply for permits allowing them to dispose of their hazardous wastes. Owners and operators of hazardous waste landfills are required to submit, with their permit applications, information about the potential for public exposure to hazardous substances in connection with the facility. Permits are not issued for TSDFs unless certain performance standards are met. Owners or operators of TSDFs must obtain identification numbers from the EPA. In running their facilities, they must analyze representative samples of waste before storing or treating them. They must also provide training for personnel and inspect facilities to discover malfunctions. Where discharges occur, they must take necessary remedial action.

Enforcement

EPA employees are authorized to enter facilities at reasonable times. They may inspect and obtain samples, and they may copy records. If violations of the hazardous waste provisions are not corrected, violators may ultimately be liable for a civil penalty. Knowingly making a false statement in required documents is a crime punishable by fine. The RCRA's ban on open dumping of hazardous wastes is enforceable by citizen suits.

The Superfund Law

Superfund, formally known as the *Comprehensive Environmental Response, Compensation, and Liability Act (CERCLA),* deals with the uncontrolled releases of hazardous wastes. CERCLA creates a fund (Superfund) that can be tapped by the EPA and state and local governments to clean up hazardous waste sites listed by the EPA on the National Priorities List (NPL). Sites are listed on the NPL if the risk they present is high enough on the EPA's Hazard Ranking System (HRS). Cleanup of sites must be consistent with the EPA's National Contingency Plan (NCP).

Notice Requirement

Persons in charge of a vessel or a facility that has released a hazardous substance must immediately notify the National Response Center. Notice must also be provided to potentially injured parties by publication in local newspapers. Failure to comply with these notice requirements subjects the person in charge to a fine and/or to imprisonment.

Obligations of Industry

Generators and transporters of hazardous substances, as well as past and present owners and operators of hazardous waste sites, are strictly liable for the costs of cleanup of that waste. They are referred to as **potentially responsible parties (PRPs)** for what are called *response costs*. Where PRPs can be identified, they can be ordered to perform cleanups under enforcement actions, can be sued for response costs after the federal or state government has performed a cleanup, or can enter into voluntary settlements with the government concerning their liability for cleanup costs. The existence of the Superfund enables the government to go ahead with cleanups where PRPs are not willing to undertake the work, are not available, or are insolvent.

Superfund provides an alternative dispute resolution (ADR) procedure that facilitates private settlements between PRPs and the EPA. The procedure calls for the EPA to provide PRPs with information about a site, and allows a 60-day grace period for negotiations. The information that the EPA provides consists of its investigative record and remedial decision, which the EPA can either carry out itself with resources from the Superfund or order the PRP to carry out. PRPs have 60 days from receipt of the EPA information to make a proposal to the EPA for voluntarily undertaking or refunding the cleanup under a consent agreement. The law requires the EPA to consider the input of state and public groups, who must receive notice of any consent agreement. PRPs have an incentive to settle with the EPA, because court challenges of EPA action under the Superfund law are limited to claims that the EPA's conduct was arbitrary and capricious.

Although the statute makes owners and operators strictly liable for cleanup costs, the act contains certain liability limitations. Liability is not imposed where the release results from an act of God, an act of war, or the act or omission of a third party.

Innocent landowners who acquire property without knowledge of contamination, and who had no reason to know of it, are not liable for response costs under Superfund. Thus an innocent landowner who exercises due diligence in acquiring property is not liable under Superfund.

Public Right to Know Provisions under Superfund

Superfund's **right to know provision** requires owners and occupiers of facilities that produce, use, and store hazardous chemicals to file with local and state officials a material safety data sheet (MSDS) for each hazardous chemical. The MSDS provides government officials with information regarding the use of hazardous chemicals in their communities. The statute provides limited protection for trade secrets. Trade secret information can be withheld from the MSDS, but the company must submit the withheld information with an explanation to the EPA.

Enforcement

In addition to EPA enforcement of Superfund, states can also sue PRPs for removal costs if such efforts are not inconsistent with the National Contingency Plan. The statute also authorizes citizen suits. Superfund does not impose liability for injuries to private individuals. However, the statute does not supersede any state or common law remedies available to private individuals.

In the following case, the court considers several issues involving the application of Superfund. The case shows the potential liability of businesses and their owners and operators under the law.

NEW YORK V. SHORE REALTY CORP.
759 F.2d 1032 (2nd Cir. 1985)

The State of New York (plaintiff) sued Shore Realty Corp. (Shore) and Donald LeoGrande, its officer and stockholder (defendants), under CERCLA in federal district court to recover response costs involved in the cleanup of a hazardous waste disposal site at One Shore Road, Glenwood Landing, New York. Shore had acquired this property to develop a waterfront condominium. At the time of the acquisition, LeoGrande knew there were 700,000 gallons of hazardous waste stored on the site and the cleanup would be expensive. Although neither Shore nor LeoGrande had placed hazardous waste on the premises, some additional 90,000 gallons of the waste were deposited on the premises after they took title and before the tenant responsible for the accumulation of the waste was evicted from the premises. The district court granted summary judgment for the State, finding the defendants liable for the State's response costs. The defendants appealed to the United States Court of Appeals for the Second Circuit. The circuit court of appeals affirmed the district court judgment against the defendants.

Circuit Judge Oakes

CERCLA . . . applies "primarily to the cleanup of leaking inactive or abandoned sites and to emergency responses to spills." [I]t distinguishes between two kinds of response: remedial actions—generally long-term or permanent containment or disposal programs—and removal efforts—typically short-term cleanup arrangements.

■ ■ ■

Liability for Response Costs under CERCLA

CERCLA holds liable . . . (1) the owner and operator of a . . . facility. . . .

Shore argues that [CERCLA] should be interpreted as requiring a showing of causation. We agree with the State, however, that CERCLA unequivocally imposes strict liability on the current owner of a facility from which there is a release or threat of release, without regard to causation.

■ ■ ■

Shore's causation argument is . . . at odds with the structure of the statute. Interpreting [CERCLA] as including a causation requirement makes superfluous the affirmative defenses provided in [CERCLA], each of which carves out from liability an exception based on causation. Without a clear congressional command otherwise, we will not construe a statute in any way that makes some of its provisions surplusage.

■ ■ ■

Furthermore, as the State points out, accepting Shore's arguments would open a huge loophole in CERCLA's coverage. It is quite clear that if the current owner of a site could avoid liability merely by having purchased the site after chemical dumping had ceased, waste sites certainly would be sold, following the cessation of dumping, to new owners who could avoid the liability otherwise required by CERCLA. Congress had well in mind that persons who dump or store hazardous waste sometimes cannot be located or may be deceased or judgment-proof. We will not interpret [CERCLA] in any way that apparently frustrates the statute's goals, in the absence of a specific congressional intention otherwise.

■ ■ ■

Shore also argues that because the Shore Road site is not on the NPL, the State's action is inconsistent with the NCP and thus Shore cannot be found liable under [CERCLA]. This argument is not frivolous. Section 9007(a)(4)(A) states that polluters are liable for response costs "not inconsistent with the national contingency plan." And section 9605, which directs EPA to outline the NCP, includes a provision that requires EPA to publish the NPL. Nevertheless, we hold that inclusion on the NPL is not a requirement for the State to recover its response costs.

■   ■   ■

We see the NPL as a limitation on remedial, or long-term, actions—as opposed to removal, or short-term actions—particularly federally funded remedial actions. The provisions requiring the establishment of NPL criteria and listing appear to limit their own application to remedial actions.

■   ■   ■

Moreover, limiting the scope of NPL listing as a requirement for response action is consistent with the purpose of CERCLA. The NPL is a relatively short list when compared with the huge number of hazardous waste facilities Congress sought to clean up. And it makes sense for the federal government to limit only those long-term remedial efforts that are federally funded. We hold that Congress intended that, while federally funded remedial efforts be focused solely on those sites on the NPL, states have more flexibility when acting on their own.

■   ■   ■

LeoGrande's Personal Liability

We hold LeoGrande liable as an "operator" under CERCLA, for the State's response costs. Under CERCLA "owner or operator" is defined to mean "any person owning or operating" an onshore facility, and "person" includes individuals as well as corporations. More important, the definition of "owner or operator" excludes "a person, who, without participating in the management of a . . . facility, holds indicia of ownership primarily to protect his security interest in the facility." The use of this exception implies that an owning stockholder who manages the corporation, such as LeoGrande, is liable under CERCLA as an "owner or operator."

Case Questions

1. Why did the court hold that it was not necessary to show that Shore caused the hazardous waste site for it to be liable for the cleanup costs?

2. Why did the court hold that inclusion of the Shore Road property on the NPL was not a requirement for liability under Superfund?

3. Why did the court hold LeoGrande personally liable for the cleanup costs of the Shore Road property?

4. What could Shore Realty and LeoGrande have done to reduce the risk of liability for cleanup costs under Superfund? Which policies and practices should purchasers of real estate employ to reduce the risk of liability under Superfund? Explain. What are the implications of *Shore Realty* and Superfund with regard to parties to mergers and acquisitions? Explain.

5. Suppose that a bank held a mortgage to the Shore Road property—would it be liable for the cleanup costs under Superfund? Explain. Suppose the bank were to obtain title to the property as a result of foreclosing on that mortgage. Would the bank be liable now? Explain. Which policies should lending institutions employ when taking mortgages on industrial properties? Explain.

The Oil Pollution Control Act

Congress passed the Oil Pollution Control Act in response to the Exxon *Valdez* oil spill off the Alaska shore in March 1989. The statute provides that a party responsible for a vessel or a facility that has discharged oil upon the navigable waters or adjoining shoreline is liable for the removal costs and damages that result from the incident. Defenses exist for acts of God, acts of war, and acts or omissions of a third party. The statute establishes a fund, paid for by a tax on oil, to provide the money for federal cleanup efforts.

The Toxic Substances Control Act (TSCA)

The Toxic Substances Control Act (TSCA) regulates hazardous chemical substances and mixtures. The EPA maintains an inventory of all chemical substances and mixtures handled in the United States. All persons seeking to manufacture any new substance or to process a present substance for a significant new use have to notify the EPA of their intention.

The EPA administrator is empowered to make rules necessary to protect personal health and the environment against unreasonable risks posed by all substances and mixtures. The administrator must apply the least burdensome rule that will be effective, but the possible rules range from requiring notice of the unreasonable risk of injury to prohibiting entirely the manufacture of the substance or mixture. Intermediate options include limiting its scope of distribution or its concentration for certain uses. The EPA may also mandate that adequate warnings or instructions be given or that continuous testing and record-keeping be done. TSCA also established an Interagency Testing Committee, whose function is to inform the administrator of substances and mixtures that should be tested immediately in order to propose rules.

The administrator may issue rules on review of a premanufacturing notice. If the information the proposed manufacturer has given is sufficient for the administrator to evaluate the risk of harm posed by the substance to be manufactured, the administrator may propose an order prohibiting its manufacture. The administrator would then go to court only if the manufacturer or processor filed an objection to the proposed order. Where threatened with the imminent production of a substance hazardous to the public, however, the administrator may directly seek an injunction in a U.S. district court to stop the manufacturing process.

The Federal Environmental Pesticide Control Act (FEPCA)

Pesticides are regulated by the Federal Environmental Pesticide Control Act (FEPCA). That act provides that pesticides in interstate shipments be adequately labeled and unadulterated. The statute also extends to interstate manufacturing and actual misuse of pesticides.

Pesticides are classified for general or restricted use. Restricted pesticides may be applied only by persons certified to use them. States certify pesticide applicators under the approval of the EPA.

Ethical Dilemmas/Issues

Chrissy Snyder is the recently hired manager of Waste Transport's division in Columbus, Ohio. Waste Transport specializes in transporting industrial waste products to waste treatment facilities. Waste Transport has been doing business in Columbus for 20 years. Its Licking County facility has been in existence for three years, and is 20 miles east of Columbus. Licking County is a rural county with a high unemployment rate.

The nearby residents, approximately 20 farm families, are unhappy about having Waste Transport as a neighbor. They have complained to the company and to the local county government about the noise Waste Transport's trucks make as they arrive and leave the facility. Waste Transport's trucks arrive and leave the facility around the clock, seven days a week. The residents have also complained about a shrill whistle used at the plant to announce shift changes and employee work breaks. Furthermore, the residents have complained about the bright lights the company shines on its property to illuminate the facility. Their complaints to the Licking County government have not resulted in a favorable response, because the company employs many local workers and adds to the county's tax revenue.

On joining Waste Transport's Columbus facility, Snyder learned that employees have been cleaning the company trucks in the facility in a manner violating company policy. According to employee accounts, the drivers have used water hoses at the facility to wash out their tanker trucks, letting the water drain out of the trucks and onto the ground.

Snyder is concerned that contaminants in the drained water could have seeped into the ground water, which is the source of water for the wells on the farms throughout the county. Because the nearby residents have not complained about this practice, Snyder assumes that they are unaware of it.

What are the ethical issues? What would you do?

The use of any registered pesticide in any way inconsistent with its labeling instructions is prohibited. Conviction of knowing violations of FEPCA's provisions by farmers or private applicators may result in fine or imprisonment.

Pesticide manufacturing plants must register with the EPA. The plants must report annually on types and amounts of pesticides produced and sold. EPA agents may inspect the plants and take samples.

When a pesticide violates FEPCA provisions, the EPA administrator may issue an order to stop its sale or use. Pesticides violating the law may also be seized.

Land Use and Resource Management

Energy demands in the highly industrialized United States have prompted strip mining, wetlands filling, and other activities that destroy virgin lands and spoil scenic places. Animals displaced by these activities rarely survive. State and federal laws allow development to continue in critical areas such as virgin lands and scenic places, while minimizing environmental damage. Critical areas include parks, forests, tidelands, wetlands, and continental shelves.

Approximately one third of the land area in the United States is owned by the federal government, which preserves part of its critical areas for natural beauty and develops part of them through permits granted to private industry. The U.S. government regulates both federal and state lands when licensing nuclear power plants. Federal regulations cover both nuclear power plant operations and nuclear by-products that pose waste storage problems for the entire country.

Nuclear Power Development

The Nuclear Regulatory Commission (NRC) oversees the private construction, ownership, and operation of commercial nuclear power reactors.

Nuclear Plant Licensing

Persons seeking to build a nuclear power plant must apply to the NRC for a construction permit. If a construction permit is issued, the initial application to build is carried over to the operational licensing stage. The application is adjusted to include new facts that emerge during the course of construction. Unless good cause can be shown as to why an operating license should not be issued, the license is awarded when the facility has been completed.

NRC Criteria for Plant Siting

The suitability of an applicant's site is determined by comparing the design and operating characteristics of the proposed reactor with the physical characteristics of the site. The human environment of the site is also considered, with particular regard for population density in the surrounding area. Otherwise unacceptable sites can become acceptable if compensating engineering safeguards are included in reactor designs.

The Price-Anderson Act

The Price-Anderson Act protects a nuclear licensee from the risks of liability resulting from a nuclear incident. Under the Price-Anderson Act, a nuclear licensee is required to carry $60 million in financial protection (insurance) to cover liability claims. The licensee then must enter into a $500 million indemnity agreement with the NRC. This agreement serves to indemnify (reimburse) and hold harmless the licensee or any other person who might be liable as a result of a nuclear incident. Finally, the act places a ceiling on total liability at $560 million. If public liability for a nuclear incident exceeds this amount, the appropriate bankruptcy court is required to apportion the $560 million fund among the claimants. As a result of the Price-Anderson Act, the nuclear industry is insulated from any possible liability not covered by insurance and the indemnity arrangement.

The Nuclear Waste Policy Act

The Nuclear Waste Policy Act establishes a national plan for the disposal of highly radioactive nuclear waste. The statute sets into motion a process for locating and constructing two temporary repositories (storage facilities) for high-level nuclear fuel until permanent repositories are built.

The Endangered Species Act

The Endangered Species Act protects many species from activities that would harm them or their habitats. The act makes it a federal offense to buy, sell, possess, export, or import any species listed by the Interior Department as endangered or threatened, or any product made from such a species. Federal agencies must ensure that their projects do not jeopardize a listed species or adversely affect its habitat. Agencies must obtain a permit by consulting with the Interior Department for land-based species or the Commerce Department for marine species.

Environmental Crimes and Environmental Audits

In recent years, criminal prosecutions of corporations and their officers for environmental violations have increased. Emphasis on criminal enforcement of environmental laws reflects an enforcement policy that is based on penalties. However, the federal government also encourages businesses to police themselves by undertaking voluntary environmental audits, corrective action, and self-disclosure.

The EPA encourages companies to undertake **environmental audits** on the basis that such proactive environmental corporate policy is less costly than reacting to environmental crises and agency investigations. The EPA has included environmental audits in its negotiated consent decrees. An environmental audit is a report of a company's environmental practices with regard to compliance with environmental laws.

In deciding whether to criminally prosecute someone, the Department of Justice's prosecutorial guidelines state that the department will take into account the following factors: whether the company made a prompt and timely voluntary disclosure of noncompliance, whether the company cooperated with the government's investigation, and whether the company already had in place an environmental compliance program with preventative measures. Under the federal Sentencing Commission's guidelines, a company's fine for violating environmental laws may be reduced "if the offense occurred despite an effective program to prevent and detect violations of the law." Participation by a high-level executive in an environmental violation, however, creates a presumption that the business did not have an effective program.

As a result of these enforcement policies, companies are increasingly developing environmental audit policies. Companies sometimes contract with outside consultants to undertake environmental audits and report the findings to the company's chief executive officer (CEO). Some companies use the company attorney to direct the company's compliance program.

ADR and Environmental Disputes

The use of alternative dispute resolution (ADR) techniques in the environmental field is new and likely to increase. Environmentalists, businesses, and enforcement agencies increasingly realize that litigation is costly. For companies, rational business planning is difficult under the circumstances of uncertainty and delay that are inherent in litigation.

As was discussed in the section on Superfund, the Superfund law incorporates the concept of ADR by requiring the EPA and responsible parties to attempt to negotiate settlements of a remedial action.

The EPA also promotes ADR of other environmental disputes. An EPA policy guideline defines various methods of ADR, explains how to choose a case for resolution by ADR, and how to select a neutral third party. An enforcement dispute with the EPA may be submitted to ADR only with EPA approval.

ADR organizations exist that will help parties solve their hazardous waste problems. These organizations usually include specialists from business, environmental groups, and universities. Use of ADR in these cases usually focuses on the allocation of cleanup costs.

International Environmental Law

The problems of pollution do not stop at a nation's borders. As a result, there is a growing internationalization of environmental law. A large number of international treaties (called *conventions*) exist among nations. One example of such a treaty is the **Montreal Protocol,** which is an international agreement to reduce reliance on air emissions that deplete the stratospheric ozone layer.

In Europe, the European Community's (EC) *Single Europe Act* gives the EC the power to legislate in environmental matters. The most common form of EC legislation in the environmental field has been the directive. A directive is addressed to member states (countries) and not individuals. It is binding as to the results to be achieved and deadlines, but national authorities may choose the form and method of implementation. For example, Britain has implemented the EC's directives on water and air pollution in Britain's Environmental Protection Act, and Britain has implemented the EC's directive requiring environmental impact assessments through regulations.

When interpreting national law, courts and agencies in EC member countries must interpret it in accordance with EC law. Thus, when doing business in Europe (the EC), in order to ascertain the full extent of a company's rights and responsibilities in respect to the environment, it is necessary to check to see if there is any EC legislation on the topic. This is so even where there is national legislation in force that apparently defines those rights and duties.

Chapter Problems

1. Define the following terms:
   a. Environmental impact statement (EIS)
   b. Effluent limitation
   c. Point source
   d. Citizen suits
   e. Emission limitation
   f. Nonattainment area
   g. Potentially responsible party (PRP)
   h. Right to know provision
   i. Environmental audit
   j. Montreal Protocol

2. In November 1974, the secretary of defense announced 111 actions involving realignment of units and closures of army bases. One of these actions affected the Lexington-Bluegrass Army Depot (LBAD) in Lexington, Kentucky. The action was to eliminate 18 military jobs and 2,630 civilian jobs in the Lexington area, with personnel transferred to depots in California and Pennsylvania. The army prepared an environmental assessment, which concluded that because there would be no significant effect on the human environment, a formal environmental impact statement was not required. A nongovernmental research institution studied the possible socioeconomic impact of the action and concluded that the Lexington area would suffer only minimal short-term unemployment as a result of the partial closure. In August 1975, four Kentucky congressmen, two U.S. senators, two county judges, the city of Richmond, the Lexington-Fayette Urban County Government, the Greater Lexington Chamber of Commerce, three property and business owners in the vicinity of LBAD, and four civilian employees of LBAD all sued to block the proposed action. They claimed that an environmental impact statement was required before action by the army could be undertaken. Do you agree? Explain.

3. Pinole Point Steel Company purchased a tract of land from Bethlehem Steel Corporation in 1979. From 1965 to 1975, Bethlehem had released hazardous substances into a pond on the land. Pinole Point discovered the existence of hazardous substances and began cleanup operations at the pond. Pinole Point then sued Bethlehem, alleging that Bethlehem was liable under Superfund to Pinole Point for the cleanup costs. Will Pinole Point succeed in holding Bethlehem liable under Superfund? Explain. Does Pinole Point have any other liability theories that it can assert against Bethlehem?

4. Roy Cauffman owned and operated a hazardous waste site under the name Cauffman's Clean Acres. A fire and explosion occurred on the night of July 4, 1987, causing the release of hazardous substances into the environment. The fire and explosion were of undetermined origin. The EPA incurred substantial costs in cleaning up the site and nearby property and sought to recover these costs from Roy Cauffman. Cauffman claimed that he did not cause the fire at the facility; therefore, he should not be held liable for the cleanup costs. Is Cauffman correct? Explain.

5. On November 20, 1975, Marathon Pipe Line Co. was notified by local police that a pipeline it owned had ruptured and was discharging crude oil into the Kaskaskia River in southern Illinois. The company immediately took steps to contain the spill and reported the occurrence to the Environmental Protection Agency. In all, 19,992 gallons of crude oil were discharged from the pipeline and 10,920 gallons were recovered or burned, so approximately 9,072 gallons escaped downriver. Subsequent investigation by the company revealed that a bulldozer had struck the buried four-inch pipe in June or July of 1975 while digging an irrigation ditch for the owners of the land. The bulldozer operator reported the damage to the landowners, but since they thought the pipeline was no longer in use, neither ever reported the damage to Marathon. The location of the pipeline was a matter of public record, the easement having been duly recorded with the local recorder's office, and the pipeline was marked in accordance with all federal regulations. What liability does Marathon Pipe Lines Co. have to neighboring property owners on whose land the oil spilled? Explain. What is Marathon's liability to property owners located downriver from the spill with regard to property damage? Explain. If the Environmental Protection Agency cleans up the 9,072 gallons that Marathon was unable to recover or burn, what recourse does the EPA have against Marathon? Explain.

6. Ohio has been found to produce twice as much sulfur dioxide as all the New England States combined. The EPA administrator attempted to implement a plan to clean up Ohio's air when Ohio could not produce a satisfactory state implementation plan to achieve national clean air standards. The administrator found that the EPA was without sufficient money or political power to control the local situation effectively. By what authority could the administrator provide a plan for Ohio? Which alternative actions could the administrator have taken, and how effective were those actions likely to be?

7. The Blozis Widget Factory wishes to expand its plant operations in Cincinnati, Ohio. However, if it carries out its expansion plan, Blozis will increase its output of air pollution. Installation of the required air pollution control technology would be quite expensive. Across the street from the Blozis factory is Ace Smelting Factory, which currently contributes more air pollution than will be produced by the Blozis factory expansion. Because Ace Smelting is currently undergoing serious financial difficulties, the owner is considering closing its Cincinnati operations. The price of buying the Ace Smelting plant and closing it down would be less than the price of installing and maintaining the latest air pollution technology on the Blozis expansion. What should the management of Blozis consider doing under these circumstances? Explain.

8. Donegal's Power Company is planning to build a nuclear power plant along the Pacific Ocean. Donegal's scientists have determined that earthquake activity is not significant in the area in which they want to build, but that tremors in the region may produce vibrations sufficient to cause occasional flooding. Will Donegal's be able to build its plant in the place the scientists have chosen? Explain.

9. The core of Nuclear Power Plant XIII melted down, releasing radioactive wastes, water, and air at 50 times acceptable levels as far as 20 miles away. The countryside for 10 miles was thoroughly poisoned, and vegetation for 15 miles has become wilted or diseased. Increased levels of cancer have been detected among populations formerly located near the plant. Losses by farmers in land, livestock, and private residences have already been estimated at $500 million. If the farmers sue immediately, would victims of radiation poisoning or cancer suing later have to split the remaining $60 million available under Price-Anderson's liability limit? Explain.

10. The design of Commons Nuclear Power Plant proves to be faulty. Water used in cooling the power plant becomes contaminated and seeps into water holes used by grazing animals in nearby low-population zones. How much of its own money would the utility company have to pay out to livestock owners? What is the company's maximum responsibility?

IV BUSINESS ORGANIZATIONS AND FINANCIAL MARKETS

Ours is a money-oriented society. We live in a world of finance, where material demands are fueled by the opportunities to raise money. Chapter 12, on business associations, examines the basic forms and structures through which businesses operate in the financial world; it concentrates on the law of agency, partnerships, and corporations.

Businesses need to raise money to function. Normally they can use available cash and assets to meet their needs; however, a new enterprise needs start-up capital. Before expanding or undertaking a special project, an existing business must raise money. The sale of stocks, bonds, and other securities is a prime method for raising capital. Investors purchase these securities with hopes of earning a profit or deriving some other benefit. Once these securities are in the hands of investors, the original investors may resell them to other investors. Chapter 13 is about the laws that govern the issuance and resale of securities. The Great Depression of the 1930s undermined public confidence in the securities markets. Federal securities laws were enacted to restore that confidence. They are administered and enforced by the Securities and Exchange Commission (SEC). The basic federal securities laws discussed in detail in Chapter 13 consist of the Securities Act of 1933 and the Securities Exchange Act of 1934.

Chapter 14, which deals with special topics in corporate law, expands the treatment of the corporate environment of business to encompass the competing corporate interests of profitability and responsibility. Current activities resulting from this conflict include business crimes, fiduciary duties of corporate directors, the treatment of minority shareholders, and the strategies of corporate mergers and takeovers. Finally, Chapter 14 treats corporate social responsibility. A corporation's long-term survival may well turn on its ability to develop markets by developing the communities where the corporation does business. The corporation is a positive engine for social change with a vested interest in raising living standards and fostering social justice.

The need for money is not limited to business enterprises, as Chapter 15, on debtor-creditor relations, illustrates. Consumers are also in the market to raise money to realize their demands. Borrowing is the consumer's predominate vehicle to accomplish this end. Until the 1960s, most regulation of consumer transactions occurred at the state level. During the ensuing era of consumerism, federal legislation was enacted in response to growing abuses in the credit industry. These pieces of federal legislation are treated in Chapter 15.

12 BUSINESS ASSOCIATIONS

Learning Objectives

After learning this chapter the student should be able to:

- Compare and contrast the relationships among principals, agents, and third parties.
- Identify the advantages and disadvantages of the major types of business organizations.
- Compare and contrast the partnership and the corporation in the areas of creation, operation, and termination.
- Compare the dissolution and winding-up process for partnerships and the dissolution process for corporations.
- Define the corporate structure and the interrelationship of the corporation's directors, officers, and shareholders.

Businesses are organized under a variety of legal structures. The dilemma faced by a new business is what organizational structure to embrace. The three most common organizational forms are the sole proprietorship, the partnership, and the corporation, although there are variants of these forms. Types of business organizations are compared in Table 12–1.

The sole proprietorship is the simplest form of business organization. It involves one person who owns and operates a business. Although this structure is discussed briefly, the chapter's main focus is on more complex business organizations—the partnership and the corporation. Both of these business forms are examined in terms of creation, operation, and termination.

These organizations—the partnership and the corporation—engage in a variety of activities to carry on business. To do this, they involve agents who act on behalf of the enterprises. Hence, before the discussion of partnerships and corporations begins, it is necessary to examine the law of agency.

Agency

An agent acts on behalf of another. The party for whom an agent acts is the **principal**. Every business organization, whether it be a sole proprietorship, partnership, or corporation, employs agents. Agents ordinarily have authority to bind their principals, and may enter into contracts on behalf of their principals. As well, principals are liable to third parties for the tortious acts committed by agents within the scope of their agency. And, the agent is liable to the principal for entering into unauthorized contracts and for the agent's torts.

TABLE 12–1   Business Organizations Compared

Organization	Ownership	Management Control	Liability Exposure	Duration	Tax-Paying Entity
Sole proprietorship	Self	Self	Unlimited	Limited	Yes
Joint venture	Venturers	Venturers	Unlimited	Limited	No
Partnership	Partners	Partners	Unlimited	Limited	No
Limited partnership	Limited partners	General partners	Limited for limited partners	Limited	No
Corporation	Shareholders	Board of directors	Limited	Perpetual	Yes
Subchapter S corporation	Shareholders	Board of directors	Limited	Year to year	No
Limited liability company	Partners	Partners	Limited	Perpetual	No

---

Creation of Agency Relationship

Agency relationships usually arise by mutual consent. For example, a national tire manufacturer may contract with a distributor of wholesale tires to be its exclusive agent within a local geographical area. This creates an agency relationship by contractual agreement.

Not every agency, however, is created so formally. All that is really necessary is assent to an agency relationship. Assume, for example, that Fred asks a neighbor to buy some baseball cards the next time he is at the baseball card store. The neighbor consents. No contract results because the agreement lacks consideration (discussed in Chapter 7). Nonetheless, the neighbor is Fred's agent by consent.

An agent's authority is derived from the principal. That authority may be express, implied, apparent, or result from a ratification.

Express Authority

Many agencies are created by express direction. For example, a power of attorney is a written instrument that authorizes another to act as one's agent (see Form 12–1).

Many agency agreements are created orally, and they are just as effective as written agency agreements. One of the more common agencies created orally is the employer-employee relationship. Here, the employee acts as an agent of the employer.

FORM 12–1   **Power of Attorney**

I, Henry Hansome, of sound mind, and over the age of eighteen years, do hereby invest in my attorney in fact, Elma Nichol, the following powers:

1. To deposit and withdraw funds from my savings and checking accounts and to sign all checks, deposit slips, and any other instruments necessary to perform such.
2. To sell securities that I presently own and deposit the proceeds from such in my savings account, and to sign all instruments to accomplish such.
3. To manage my real estate; pay taxes, insurance, and mortgage payments; and sign all instruments to accomplish such.
4. To make all medical decisions on my behalf and in my stead, should I become incompetent to do so, including a decision that no extraordinary medical procedures be used to prolong my life when there is no reasonable prognosis for recovery from a comatose or vegetative state.

_____   _____
Witness   Henry Hansome

_____
Witness

On February 12, 2004, Henry Hansome appeared before me and acknowledged his signature.

                                         _____
                                                          Notary Public

---

Implied Authority

Agency relationships may arise by implication. Usually agency authority by implication arises as a natural addition to express authority. For example, assume that an agent is hired to manage a swimming pool. This express authorization gives rise to the agent's implied authority to do all things reasonable and necessary to perform the managerial tasks. The agent could enter into contracts for the supply of chemicals to purify the water, repair the filtration system, and replace unsafe diving boards. This implied authority is derived from the express authorization.

Apparent Authority

In certain cases, a principal is estopped, or prevented, from denying that he or she authorized an agent's act. This occurs when the principal clothes an agent with **apparent authority,** thereby giving third parties the impression that the agent is empowered to act. The following case details the principles involving apparent authority.

HAMILTON HAULING INC. V. GAF CORPORATION

719 S.W. 2d 841 (Mo. App. 1986)

Bajt was a purchasing agent for GAF. His duties included the purchase of raw materials necessary for day-to-day plant production, including wood chips. Bajt entered into a 10-year contract with Hamilton Hauling for the purchase of $6 million worth of wood chips. This was the only long-term contract Bajt had ever entered into on behalf of the company, although he had purchased wood chips before by purchase order. Company policy required approval at corporate headquarters for long-term contracts. Bajt never sought approval, nor did he inform anyone at corporate headquarters of the contract.

When GAF found out about the contract, the company refused to honor it, maintaining that Bajt lacked agency authority. Hamilton Hauling maintained that Bajt possessed apparent authority. Hamilton Hauling sued GAF. At the trial, a jury found in favor of GAF. The Missouri Court of Appeals affirmed the trial court decision.

Judge Dixon

It is generally held that when a principal "holds out" another as possessing certain authority, thereby inducing others reasonable to believe that authority exists, the agent has apparent authority to act even though as between himself and the principal, such authority has not been granted. Apparent authority differs from actual authority in that the principal communicates directly with a third person to create apparent authority; to create actual authority, the principal communicates directly with the agent.

When a principal has by his voluntary act placed an agent in such a situation that a person of ordinary prudence, conversant with business usages and the nature of the particular business, is justified in persuming that such an agent has authority to perform a particular act on behalf of his principal, the principal is estopped . . . from denying the agent's authority to perform the act.

It must be emphasized that the third party must reasonably rely on the authority held out by the principal. . . . Apparent authority is that which a reasonably prudent man, using diligence and discretion, in view of the principal's conduct would suppose the agent to possess.

Establishment of apparent authority by direct, express statements is obvious. The other methods of creating apparent authority by "position" and by "prior acts" have both been recognized. . . .

Wynn v. McMahon Ford Co. exemplifies the apparent authority that may be generated by an agent's position. In *Wynn,* defendant's agent [was] designated as used car sales manager, [and] was placed by defendant in a managerial position. The court found that persons dealing with the agent could reasonably believe that he had authority to conclude transactions. . . .

Apparent authority may result from a prior relation of agent and principal. The principal by allowing an agent to carry out prior similar transactions may create an appearance of authority of the agent to carry out such acts.

There was no evidence to show that GAF knowingly permitted Bajt to enter into the contract in question. Bajt had never entered into a long-term contract before. Bajt admitted he did not send a copy of the contract to corporate headquarters and no one at GAF seemed to know about the contract. Clearly, the contract was made in violation of internal corporate policy and nothing was presented to show that GAF generally "ignored" its policy in making long-term multi-million dollar contracts. . . .

Hamilton Hauling claims Bajt's authority came from his position[.] [H]owever, there was no evidence of any sort in this case as to the usual authority of purchasing agents generally. There was nothing to support an inference that a vendor dealing with a purchasing agent expects that agent to have the power to make a contract like the long-term agreement in evidence. . . . There was no evidence that Bajt had ever entered into a long-term contract on behalf of GAF; in fact, Bajt admitted that in all his years at GAF, he had not made any other such contract. Bajt was not clothed with apparent authority by virtue of his position. Moreover, there was no evidence to support Hamilton's claim that he reasonably relied on Bajt's authority. Hamilton admitted that the contracts he had entered into with other corporations were signed at corporate headquarters, not locally. . . .

The judgment favoring GAF is affirmed.

Case Questions

1. What is the issue this case presents?
2. Why did the court hold that apparent authority was absent?
3. What could Hamilton Hauling have done to avoid the problem? Explain. What should Bajt insist on in order to avoid the problem in the future?
4. Assume that Bajt entered into a similar contract for five years. Would the result be different? What about one year?

Ratification

A principal may ratify, or approve, unauthorized action taken by an agent. When ratification occurs, the principal is fully responsible for the agent's action. For ratification to be effective, the principal must have full knowledge of the transaction; the fact of the existence of a principal must have been disclosed to the third party at the time of the unauthorized act.

Assume, for example, that Doakes's auto breaks down and she leaves it at Main Standard gas station, where she is known by the owner. The owner of the gas station mistakenly, without authorization, acts as agent for Doakes and agrees to sell Doakes's auto for $400 to an interested customer. When Doakes learns of the mistake she is at first upset, but thereafter accepts payment. The acceptance of payment is an act ratifying the transaction. Her ratification creates an enforceable contract.

Principal and Agent Relationship

Once an agency relationship exists, the law imposes certain duties and obligations on the parties to that relationship. The agent has certain responsibilities to the principal, and the principal, in turn, owes certain duties to the agent.

Duties of Agent to Principal

Agents are characterized as fiduciaries. A fiduciary holds a position of trust and is held to the highest standard in the law. As fiduciaries, such persons owe to their principals the duties of obedience, care, loyalty, and accounting. An agent who breaches any of these duties is liable for damages to the principal and forfeits any compensation.

Obedience.   An agent owes a duty to obey the principal's instructions. For example, an agent may not bid higher on an item at an auction than the principal's instructions dictate. Or, if the principal instructs the agent not to purchase a particular brand of goods, the agent must comply.

Blind obedience, however, is not required. The agent is under no obligation to act contrary to law. Additionally, where a change of circumstances occurs that would jeopardize the principal's interest, the agent may deviate from the principal's instruction. For example, an agent is not required to comply with a principal's direction to store bales of hay at a particular location when a fire has rendered that location unsafe.

Care.   The agent must exercise proper skill and care in carrying out agency responsibilities. Anything less than reasonable care subjects the agent to liability for negligence. As is explained later in the chapter, the principal may also be liable to third parties for injury negligently caused by the agent.

Loyalty.   The agent owes a duty of loyalty to the principal. The agent may not act against the principal's interest, or in any way engage in self-dealing. A real estate agent may not, for example, secretly purchase the very property he or she is selling for a principal. Moreover, the agent may not represent both parties to a transaction—the buyer and seller—without fully disclosing this representation to each party. Neither may agents take advantage of a business opportunity without sharing that advantage with the principal. (See *Meinard v. Salmon* on page 325.)

Accounting.   Agents owe a duty to the principal to account for all monies generated by the agency. This should be done by accounting statements at agreed-on intervals.

Agents must not commingle their personal funds with those of their principals. Professionals, such as lawyers, accountants, brokers, and others, seriously jeopardize their licenses if they do. Separate trust accounts must be maintained.

Duties of Principal to Agent

The principal owes certain duties to the agent. They include the duty to comply with the contract and to reimburse the agent for expenses and losses incurred as a result of the agency.

Contract Compliance.   A principal has the power to breach a contract, but does not have the right to do so. Any breach results in liability to the agent. Assume, for example, that Tri-State Company lists its property with XYZ Realty under an exclusive listing. This means that Tri-State agrees to authorize only its agent to sell the property and collect a commission. Tri-State would breach the exclusive agency contract by selling the property through another agent. If this occurred, XYZ Realty would still be entitled to the commission.

Reimbursement.   The agent is entitled to reimbursement (or indemnification) for all expenses incurred as a result of duties performed within the scope of agency authority. Hence, a pilot hired to fly corporate passengers from New York to Atlanta would be entitled to reimbursement for fuel for the trip.

The agent is also entitled to indemnification for any losses incurred while operating within the scope of the agency. For example, assume that an agent is hired to dump a company's wastes at a particular site. The agent is then fined by the city for dumping without a license. The company is required to compensate the agent for the amount of the fine.

Principal and Third-Party Relationship

An agent acts on behalf of a principal. The principal is normally responsible for the acts of his or her agent. Acts engaged in by agents may involve (1) contracts, (2) torts, and (3) crimes. This section examines the principal's legal liability for each of these agency acts.

Contracts

Normally, a principal is liable for contracts entered into by his or her agent. This is true as long as the agent has authority—express, implied, or apparent—to enter into the contract. If, however, the third party is on notice or should reasonably know that the agent lacks authority, the principal would not be bound.

Assume that Dax, on behalf of his employer, Pixie Fish Market, enters into a contract with Fisher whereby Fisher is to sell, and Pixie is to buy, all the salmon Fisher catches. Pixie and Fisher are bound by contract. Assume, however, that before Dax entered into the contract Pixie informed Fisher that Dax was no longer authorized to enter into contracts for Pixie. Any contract after this notification would not bind Pixie.

Torts

The principal is normally liable for the tortious acts committed by the agent within the scope of the agency. In the employer-employee context, this doctrine is known as *respondeat superior* (let the master respond).

Questions often arise as to whether the employee was operating within the scope of employment when the tort was committed. Assume that Hank, a truck driver, is to make a delivery for his employer. Instead of making the delivery, Hank deviates from the course, drives to a bar, and crashes the truck into the bar's plate glass window. Hank's employer would not be liable for the damages because it occurred outside of the scope of his employment, while Hank was on a frolic of his own.

Principals are not ordinarily liable for the acts of independent contractors. An **independent contractor**, a type of agent, must be distinguished from an employee. The employer possesses control over the physical conduct of the employee, and may dictate the means and method by which the employee accomplishes the employer's work. This is not the case with an independent contractor. Here, the principal may not dictate the means and methods of performance, but only the result. For example, assume that Frank hires Louise, a taxicab driver, to take him downtown. Louise is an independent contractor because Frank does not have the authority to control the specifics of the travel, such as the speed and route. Ordinarily, Frank could only dictate the destination. Consequently, Frank, the passenger-principal, would not be liable to a pedestrian whom Louise negligently injured.

Crimes

Generally, the principal is not liable for the crimes of an agent. Of course, a principal who directs the agent to perform an illegal act is criminally liable. And if the agent's act is committed in the scope of an illegal business, the principal is liable.

Some states impose criminal liability on business owners for violating certain laws designed to protect the health and safety of the public. For example, in those states a grocery store owner may be held criminally liable should an employee sell adulterated meat, even without the owner's knowledge.

Agent and Third-Party Relationship

The general rule is that an agent is not a party to a contract entered into with a third party on behalf of a principal. This general rule holds true, however, only if the specific identity of the principal is disclosed to the third party. If the principal is only partially disclosed, the agent also becomes a party to the contract. A partially disclosed agency occurs when the, fact that the agent is acting for a principal is disclosed, but the identity of the principal is not (see Table 12–2).

Liability of Principals and Agents for Contracts

Agents who enter into written contracts must clearly designate their authority to avoid liability. The designation, "H. B. Corporation, by J. Adams, agent," for

TABLE 12–2	**Liability of Principals and Agents for Contracts**		
	Disclosed	*Partially Disclosed*	*Undisclosed*
Agent liability		X	X
Principal liability	X	X	X

example, is sufficient to inform the third party that J. Adams is acting only as an agent for an identified principal.

Agents are liable to third parties for their torts. Under the doctrine of respondeat superior, the principal is liable for the torts of the agent committed within the scope of the agency. Hence, both the agent and the principal may be liable to a third party for the agent's wrongs. Their liability is termed *joint and several*. This means that the third party may collect an entire judgment against either the principal or the agent, or a share of the judgment against each.

Termination of the Agency Relationship

A principal-agency relationship may terminate in any number of ways. For example, it may terminate under the terms of the agency contract. Clauses stating, "This agency shall terminate in two years," or "This agency shall end when the sale of the building is complete," specify the moment of termination. Even absent a specific provision for termination in the contract, the parties may always terminate the agency relationship by mutual consent.

At times, a change in circumstances can cause an agency to end. Changes in circumstances resulting in termination of the agency include death of the principal or agent, impossibility of performance, and destruction of the subject matter of the agency.

The agency relationship may also terminate on the unilateral action of either party. Either party has the power to terminate the relationship, even if he or she does not have the right. Simply stated, the law does not force a party to continue in a personal service relationship against his or her will. Unilateral termination, however, may constitute a breach of contract, in which case the nonbreaching party may have an action for damages.

The principal has a duty to notify third parties of the termination of the agency relationship. Actual notice must be given to those who have extended credit or contracted with the principal through the agent. Absent such notice, the agent may still possess apparent authority and continue to bind the principal. Constructive notice of the termination should be given to all other third parties. Constructive notice may be accomplished by publishing the fact of termination in a newspaper that is designed to reach third parties with whom the agent has had contact. Notice is not required when the termination is due to death, insanity, or bankruptcy.

Sole Proprietorship

A sole proprietorship is owned by a single person. This organization is normally a small business, such as the corner grocery.

The principal advantage of the sole proprietorship is that the owner has exclusive control over its operations. The proprietor may make managerial decisions without accounting to board members, partners, or stockholders. Sole proprietors may hire employees to act as agents for the proprietor. This relationship is governed by the law of agency just discussed.

This form of business also has disadvantages. First, the owner is exposed to unlimited liability. That means the owner is personally liable for all debts of the business. These debts may be incurred as a result of a contract obligation or tort liability. Second, the sole proprietorship is normally not in the best position to raise large sums of money. This is true because its ability to repay loans is limited by the assets of the individual proprietor.

Partnership

The partnership form of organization involves two or more persons and, as such, is more complex than the sole proprietorship. In all states but Louisiana, partnership law is governed by the Uniform Partnership Act (UPA).[1] Partnership law employs the principles of agency law previously discussed.

Definition of Partnership

The UPA defines a partnership as "an association of two or more persons to carry on as co-owners a business for profit." To determine whether a partnership exists, each of the elements of the definition must carefully be examined.

An association implies voluntariness. Two or more persons may associate to form a partnership. Thus, a partnership is consensual and ordinarily formed by a contract.

The association is treated as a distinct entity for some purposes and as an aggregate of persons for others. For example, under the UPA the partnership may own, buy, and sell property in its own name. The partnership files a federal income tax return for information purposes. Each partner is an agent of the partnership. These characteristics make the partnership look like a distinct entity.

On the other hand, the partnership does not pay income taxes; rather, the individual partners pay taxes on respective portions of what the partnership earns. Also, a partnership dissolves on the death or departure of a partner. These characteristics make the partnership appear to be composed of an aggregate of persons.

---

[1] The UPA was originally proposed and adopted in 1914 by the National Conference of Commissioners on Uniform State Law.

The UPA requires that a partnership consist of "two or more persons." *Person* is defined broadly to include individuals, partnerships, corporations, and other associations.

A fundamental element of a partnership is that the persons must "carry on as co-owners." Evidence of co-ownership of the business includes sharing profits and jointly owning property, contributing capital, and jointly participating in managerial decision making.

Finally, the UPA specifies that the business must be for profit. This would exclude ventures formed for religious, charitable, or fraternal purposes.

Formation of Partnership

Under most circumstances, the creation of a partnership does not require a formal written agreement. Partnerships may be formed informally, by handshake, or may arise by implication, as when, for example, the parties share profits and co-manage the business.

Nonetheless, it is desirable to have an agreement in writing, referred to as *articles of partnership.* The existence of such an agreement often helps to avoid conflict by clarifying the rights and responsibilities of the parties. The normal partnership writing covers the matters found in Table 12–3.

In the absence of an agreement, the UPA controls. For example, the UPA states that absent an agreement, partners shall share profits and losses equally.

Rights of Partners

The partnership agreement should be consulted to determine the rights of partners as to each other. In the absence of an agreement covering the specific issue in question, the UPA governs. Rights concerning partnership property, profit sharing, and management participation are discussed next.

TABLE 12–3   Matters Covered in a Typical Partnership Agreement

---

Names of the partners.
Name of the partnership.
Location of the partnership.
Purposes of the partnership.
Duration of the partnership.
Allocation of profits and losses among partners.
Capital contributions by partners.
Partners' rights and responsibilities.
Dissolution procedures.
Buyout provisions for death or withdrawal.

Partnership Property

Each partner has a right to possess partnership property in furtherance of the partnership business. The partners have an equal right to use or possess the property for this purpose. Hence, each partners' right in partnership property is indivisible: each has a full right to the whole.

Ordinarily, the initial contributions made by the partners, referred to as *capital contributions,* constitute partnership property. Any additional property acquired by the partnership is also deemed partnership property. Of course, the intent of the parties controls whether an item is owned by a partner personally or by the partnership. Offering some help in this area, the UPA states: "Unless the contrary intention appears, property acquired with partnership funds is partnership property."

Profit Sharing

The UPA provides that the partners share profits and losses equally. This may be altered by agreement. For example, partners may agree to share profits in proportion to their capital contributions. Assume that X contributed $20,000, Y contributed $30,000, and Z contributed $50,000. Under such an agreement, X would receive 20 percent ($20,000/$100,000) of the profits; Y would receive 30 percent ($30,000/$100,000); and Z would receive 50 percent ($50,000/$100,000). The parties similarly could designate the same or a different ratio for loss sharing. Failure to do so would result in the same ratio of loss distribution as that specified for the profit sharing.

Partners are not entitled to salaries, absent an agreement to the contrary. This is true even if one partner does the bulk of the work, or even all of the work. A partner is, however, entitled to reasonable compensation for services rendered for winding up the partnership affairs (as discussed later in this chapter).

Management Participation

Each partner has an equal right to participate in the management of the partnership. As with profit sharing, this may be altered by agreement.

On ordinary decisions, the vote of the majority controls unless the partnership agreement specifies otherwise. Any decision on extraordinary matters, however, requires unanimous consent. Extraordinary matters include a change of the partnership purpose, admission of a new partner, or a decision to relocate the business.

Additional rights enjoyed by partners include reimbursement, inspection, accounting, and assignment. Partners are entitled to *reimbursement* for payments made in connection with the ordinary conduct of the business. This includes, for example, the purchase of office supplies or the payment of taxes on partnership property. Partners are also entitled to be indemnified for personal liability resulting from conducting the partnership business.

Every partner has the right to *inspect* and copy any part of the partnership books. The books contain financial information, minutes of meetings, and other information germane to the conduct of the business.

The UPA grants a partner the right to an accounting. An accounting is a detailed statement of the financial affairs and condition of the business. Partners may derive an accounting when, for example, they have been wrongfully excluded from the partnership business.

Finally, any partner has the right to assign (sell or give away) his or her monetary interest in the partnership. This may be accomplished without the other partners' consent. However, the assignee (the one to whom the property is assigned) does not become a partner unless all partners consent. Hence, the assignee does not obtain any nonfinancial rights in the partnership, such as, for example, the right to management participation. The assignee is entitled only to the respective share of the profits and any other financial rights.

Obligations of Partners

Each partner stands in a fiduciary relationship to each other partner. (This relationship was discussed in the section on agency.) The partner, as fiduciary, owes certain obligations to the partnership, among which is the duty of loyalty. This duty exists between partners and is illustrated in the next case.

MEINHARD V. SALMON
164 N.E. 545 (N.Y. 1928)

Gerry leased to Salmon the Hotel Bristol at the corner of 42d Street and Fifth Avenue in New York City. The lease was for 20 years. Salmon undertook to change the hotel building for use as shops and offices.

Salmon entered into a venture with Meinhard to obtain the funds to finance the improvements. Under the terms of the venture, Meinhard was to pay to Salmon half of the cost to reconstruct, manage, and operate the property. (This relationship is referred to as a *joint venture*. A joint venture is formed for a single purpose and terminates automatically on completion of the purpose. In most respects, a joint venture is like a partnership, and some view joint ventures as a type of partnership.)

Salmon was to pay Meinhard 40 percent of the profits from the first five years of the lease and 50 percent for the remaining years. Each was to bear the losses equally. Salmon was to have sole power to manage the building.

When the lease was coming to a conclusion, Gerry sold the property to a relative also bearing the name Gerry, who became the lessor-owner. With fewer than four months remaining on the lease, this new owner approached Salmon with a new lease, including the Bristol property. Salmon entered into the lease through Midpoint Realty Company, which he owned and controlled. Salmon did not tell Meinhard about the lease. When Meinhard found out about it, he demanded that the new lease be held in trust as an asset of the venture. Salmon refused that demand.

Meinhard sued. The lower court and intermediate appellate court found in favor of Meinhard. Salmon appealed to New York's highest appeals court, which affirmed the decision.

Chief Judge Cardozo

The two were co-adventurers, subject to fiduciary duties. . . . As to this we are all agreed. The heavier weight of duty rested, however, upon Salmon. He was a coadventurer with Meinhard, but he was manager as well. During the early years of the enterprise, the building, as reconstructed, operated at a loss. If the relation had then ended, Meinhard as well as Salmon would have carried a heavy burden. Later the profits became large with the result that for each of the investors there came a rich return. For each the venture had its phases of fair weather and of foul. The two were in it jointly, for better or for worse.

Joint adventurers . . . owe to one another, while the enterprise continues the duty of the finest loyalty. Many forms of conduct permissible in a workaday world for those acting at arm's length, are forbidden to those bound by fiduciary ties. A trustee is held to something stricter than the morals of the marketplace. Not honesty alone, but the punctilio of an honor the most sensitive, is then the standard of behaviour. As to this there has developed a tradition that is unbending and inveterate. Uncompromising rigidity has been the attitude of courts of equity when petitioned to undermine the rule of undivided loyalty by the "disintegrating erosion" of particular exceptions. Only thus has the level of the conduct for fiduciaries been kept at a level higher than that trodden by the crowd. It will not consciously be lowered by any judgment of this court.

The owner . . . Mr. Gerry . . . had vainly striven to find a tenant who would favor his ambitious scheme of demolition and construction. Baffled in the search, he turned to the defendant Salmon in possession of the Bristol, the keystone of the project. He figured to himself beyond a doubt that the man in possession would prove a likely customer. To the eye of an observer, Salmon held the lease as owner in his own right, for himself and no one else. In fact he held it as a fiduciary, for himself and another, sharers in a common venture. . . . The . . . opportunity, that was thus an incident of the enterprise, Salmon appropriated to himself in secrecy and silence.

The trouble about his conduct is that he excluded his coadventurer from any chance to compete, from any chance to enjoy the opportunity for benefit that had come to him alone by virtue of his agency.

We have no thought to hold that Salmon was guilty of a conscious purpose to fraud. Very likely he assumed in all good faith that with the approaching end of the venture he might ignore his coadventurer and take the extension for himself. He had given to the enterprise time and labor as well as money. He had made it a success. Meinhard, who had given money, but neither time nor labor, had already been richly paid. . . . [But] [f]or [Salmon] and those like him the rule of undivided loyalty is relentless and supreme. A different question would be here if there were lacking any nexus of relation between the business conducted by the manager and the opportunity brought to him as an incident of management. For this problem, as for most, there are distinctions of degree.

A question remains as to the form and extent of the equitable interest to be allotted to the plaintiff. . . . [A]n equal division of the shares might . . . take away from Salmon the power of control and management which under the plan of the joint venture he was to have from first to last. . . . To that end an extra share should be added to his half.

[Judgment affirmed]

Case Questions

1. Which fiduciary duty did Salmon breach? Under the circumstances of this case, what does the law require Salmon to do?
2. Would the result have been different had Salmon entered into a new lease with Gerry for property that did not include the Bristol property? Explain.
3. Assume that Salmon had entered into a new lease with Gerry (including the Bristol property) after the expiration of the old lease and the venture. Would there be a different result? Explain.

Relationship to Third Parties

A partnership creates a principal-agent relationship. The partnership is the principal. Partners are agents of the partnership. As such, the previously discussed agency principles are applicable.

Partners are jointly liable on the contracts of the partnership. Joint liability requires that all partners be sued on the contract obligation. The individual partners, however, would not be held liable unless all the partnership assets were first used up to satisfy the indebtedness.

Unlike contractual liability, partners are jointly and severally liable for torts. That means that all partners need not be sued at once. For example, one partner may be sued for the whole amount. Additionally, the release of one partner does not release other partners from liability. As well, partnership assets do not have to be used up first to satisfy the judgment; the partners are personally liable. Any partner, however, who is required to pay on the judgment and who did not personally commit the tort, may recover against the partner(s) who committed the tort.

In some cases, partner and partnership liability to third parties may arise by estoppel, or **apparent partnership**. This may occur under two circumstances. First, a person (apparent partner) may represent that he or she is a partner when in fact this is not true, and the partnership has no knowledge of the representation. If a third party, in reliance on this representation, extends credit to the partnership, the apparent partner would be liable for any injury the third party sustains.

Second, a partner may have knowledge that a nonpartner is misrepresenting himself or herself as a partner. Any partner with such knowledge who consents to the misrepresentation is liable to third parties who sustain injury as a result of reliance on the representation.

Termination of Partnership

Termination of a partnership is a legal process that involves two stages: dissolution and winding up.

Dissolution

The UPA defines dissolution as a "change in the relation of the partners caused by any partner ceasing to be associated in the carrying on . . . of the business." Some dissolutions are merely technical. They occur, for example, when a partner dies or retires. These events result in a dissolution because there is a change in the relation of the partners. However, in most of these cases, the surviving partners wish to continue the business; the dissolution is only a bookkeeping entry whereby a new partnership is formed. In the absence of agreement, the UPA provides that a retiring partner or the estate of a deceased partner is entitled to the value of his or her share in the partnership plus interest or, in lieu of interest, profits.

The partnership agreement may designate a date for termination, or the partners may at any time mutually agree to dissolve the partnership. In either case, dissolution occurs and the liquidation process begins.

A partner may seek to dissolve the partnership by obtaining a court decree. A court issues the decree if a partner is judicially declared to be insane or is otherwise incapable of performing the partnership duties; a partner is guilty of impairing the ability of the business to continue; or where it is impractical to continue the business, as when the partners are constantly unable to cooperate and make decisions.

When a partnership dissolves for any reason other than illegality or bankruptcy, notice must be given to third parties. Specific notice must be given to those creditors with whom the business has dealt. Constructive notice, by publication in a newspaper distributed in the area of the business, must be given to all other third parties. Failure to give proper notice may result in liability for unauthorized contracts and debts.

Winding Up

The winding-up process involves the liquidation of assets and distribution of its proceeds. The UPA establishes the rules for distribution of assets in the following order: (1) to creditors other than partners; (2) to partners who are creditors; (3) to partners to repay capital contributions; and (4) to partners for profits. In the event of insufficient partnership assets to pay creditors, the partners must contribute the amount necessary to satisfy the liabilities.

Difficulties may arise when assets are insufficient to satisfy partnership debts and when the partners are indebted to personal creditors. The general rule is that partnership creditors have first priority on partnership property and personal creditors have first priority on partners' property.

Limited Partnership

The basic disadvantage of the general partnership is that it subjects all partners to unlimited personal liability. However, most states have adopted legislation affording an alternative to the general partnership limiting the liability of some partners.

This alternative is called **limited partnership** and is governed in these states by the Revised Uniform Limited Partnership Act (RULPA).[2] Under this uniform act, the partnership consists of general and limited partners. General partners manage and control the partnership and they are liable without limit. Limited partners enjoy limited liability, as long as they do not participate in the management or control of the partnership and as long as they comply with state law. Limited partnerships may be formed only by compliance with the state statute. This requires the filing of a certificate of limited partnership with a state agency, often the secretary of state. The certificate contains the name of the partnership, its purpose, and its location; the names of partners; and other information.

Limited partnerships are usually formed for investment purposes. The limited partners are the investors. The partnership may be formed for the purpose of, for example, erecting an outlet mall or drilling for oil. As members of a partnership, the partners enjoy tax advantages.

The limited partnership involves passive investors who are like shareholders in a corporation. Consequently, this form of business ownership, like the corporate form, creates securities questions (treated in Chapter 13).

Corporations

The corporate form of business has existed in some form as far back as the days of the Code of Hammurabi (about 1750 B.C.). Its early usage, however, was restricted to the government and the church. Later, the sovereign, through special legislation, chartered private corporations to perform trade. In the United States, corporations were introduced in the 18th century and since then have been growing in numbers and popularity. Today, corporations are a dominant institution in our economy, accounting for about 90 percent of the gross national income.

Characteristics of Corporations

Corporations are distinct from sole proprietorships and general partnerships in several respects (see Table 12–1). First, a corporation is a separate legal entity for all purposes. It is an artificial being created by legislation. As such, a corporation can purchase, hold, and sell property in its own name. It enters into contracts in its own name. It can be sued and can sue in its own name. It is a tax-paying entity.

Second, a corporation is not mortal; theoretically, it has a perpetual existence. A partnership certainly terminates at the death of the last partner. A corporation, in contrast, is not dependent on the life of particular individuals for existence. Corporations continue until dissolved, merged, or otherwise terminated.

---

[2] About one half of the states have adopted the Revised Uniform Limited Partnership Act (RULPA) proposed in 1976. RULPA underwent revisions in 1983 and 1985.

A third distinct characteristic of the corporation is that the owners of the corporation, called *shareholders,* enjoy limited liability. This is a prime feature of the corporation that makes it attractive to investors. Unlike general partners, a shareholder can lose only what he or she invests. Creditors cannot, under ordinary circumstances, reach the personal assets of the shareholder to satisfy debt. In this respect, shareholders resemble limited partners.

A fourth important characteristic of the corporation is the ease of transferring ownership interests. Sale of a partnership normally involves a detailed process of valuation and an interruption of the affairs of the partnership. A corporation's ownership, represented by shares of stock, may be bought and sold freely without business interruption.

A fifth characteristic of the corporate form is the separation of ownership from management. Shareholders always own the corporation but often do not manage

Ethical Dilemmas/Issues

As a successful tire salesperson for Swift Wholesale Tire, Inc., Louis Rosenmund called on Warren Hubbard, manager of the King Tire Store. On one visit, Rosenmund told Hubbard that the owner of the Tough Tire Store in Westerville wanted to sell his store due to a lack of business. Hubbard replied: "Louis, with your sales ability and my business judgment, we could turn that business around. I'll put up the money to buy the business, if you will manage the daily operations. You can take a monthly salary of $3,500, and the rest of the profits will be ploughed back into the business. We can split the profits later. Since we'll have to act quickly, I'll go ahead and buy the property. The incorporation papers will be filed as soon as possible after the purchase."

Rosenmund quit his $40,000-per-year position with Swift and started working at the Tough Tire Store. Hubbard purchased the store and named himself owner on the title. Rosenmund had business cards and newspaper advertising printed that included both his name and Hubbard's under the name of the business. Three months later, the Tough Tire Store was a success.

Whenever Hubbard visited the store, Rosenmund asked about the corporation papers. Hubbard's response was vague. Finally, Hubbard told Rosenmund to meet him at the office of Richard Stone, an attorney, who opined that Rosenmund was an employee and that Hubbard had no additional obligation to him.

When Rosenmund arrived, Stone introduced himself as Hubbard's attorney. He told Rosenmund that his services as an employee of Tough Tire were no longer required.

What are the ethical issues? What would you do?

it. This separation in functions between investment and management makes corporations subject to the securities laws (discussed in Chapter 13).

Sixth, and perhaps an undesirable aspect of the corporation, is that it pays taxes on its earnings. Then, when it distributes dividends to its stockholders, they pay taxes on those earnings. This results in double taxation, which has led many small corporations to elect the form of subchapter S status.

A subchapter S corporation is a creation of the tax laws. It is treated as a partnership for purposes of taxation. Hence, only the shareholders are taxed on earnings, not the corporation. This type of election is available only to corporations that have 35 or fewer shareholders, and all shareholders must elect the subchapter S status. To qualify for favorable subchapter S treatment, a corporation must strictly adhere to IRS filing guidelines.

Finally, the corporate form requires compliance with an array of formalized procedures. Incorporation can be very costly as a result. Also, government more closely supervises corporations than partnerships or sole proprietorships. Each state has detailed statutes covering the regulation of corporations.[3]

Creation of Corporations

The formation of a corporation is controlled by state statutory law. Normally, promoters come together to form a corporation. They handle the plans for financing the corporation and draw up the corporate charter, referred to in many states as the *certificate,* or *articles, of incorporation* (see Form 12–2).

Promoters involve themselves in the sale of stock subscriptions and in contracting for loans, goods, and supplies. The promoters are normally personally liable for these contracts because the corporation is not in existence during this state of formation. After the corporation forms, however, it may adopt the promoters' actions and agree to indemnify them.

The next step is to file the articles of incorporation with the designated state office, usually with the secretary of state. This is accomplished by incorporators, who may be the same persons as the promoters. Articles of incorporation normally include the name of the corporation, principal place of business of the corporation, purpose of the corporation, powers of the corporation, names of incorporators, amount and types of authorized stock, and designation of an agent of the corporation who is to receive all official papers.

After the state receives the filing and issues a charter, the first shareholders' meeting occurs. At that meeting stockholders participate in three events: They (1) receive stock certificates, (2) elect a board of directors of the corporation, and (3) adopt a set of bylaws to govern the operation of the corporation. The next meeting is that of the newly elected board of directors. The board elects officers and covers any other matters necessary to begin business.

---

[3] Some states have adopted the Model Business Corporation Act (MBCA) as approved by the National Conference of Commissioners on Uniform State Law (NCCUSL) and the House of Delegates of the American Bar Association (ABA). More than half of the states have adopted the MBCA or a 1994 revision of that act, in whole or in part.

After all of the procedures for formation of the corporation have been completed, a de jure corporation exists. Neither the state nor other parties may challenge its existence. At times, although the incorporators make a good-faith attempt to comply with the statute, they fail. In these cases, a court may find that a de facto corporation exists, that is, even though there has not been full compliance, nonetheless it is treated as a corporation. This may occur if, for example, the incorporators failed to pay the filing fee.

To exist, a de facto corporation must act as a corporation. A de facto corporation may not be challenged by any parties except the state. Shareholders in a de facto corporation enjoy limited liability.

When an organization substantially deviates from the statutory mandated procedure, it is neither a de jure nor a de facto corporation. Many states require the

---

FORM 12–2   Certificate of Incorporation

The undersigned, desiring to form a corporation for profit do hereby certify:

First.   The name of the corporation shall be TransAir Mobile, Inc.
Second.   The principal place of business will be in City, State.
Third.   The purposes for which said corporation is formed are

1. Manufacturing air mobiles for use as public transportation within cities.
2. Marketing the concept of air mobiles as a more efficient form of public transportation.
3. Lobbying cities, counties, and other governmental agencies in attempts to influence them to adopt air mobiles as a major form of city transportation.
4. Doing all things necessary and lawful to accomplish these purposes.

Fourth.   The following persons shall serve as interim directors until the first meeting called to elect a board of directors:

_____
Dr. Angela Moore

_____
Laura Williams

_____
Nelson Odis

Fifth.   The corporation shall be authorized to issue 1 million shares of no par value common stock.

In witness whereof, we, the incorporators subscribe our names this 5th day of January, 2005.

_____
Ruth Anne Hills

_____
Constance Rivers

_____
Howard Randal

filing of articles of incorporation before a corporation comes into being. Even here, however, it is still possible for a court to treat a business which has not filed its articles as a corporation under estoppel principles. For example, a business that holds itself out as a corporation and incurs debts as a corporation but is not a corporation is not allowed to deny its corporate existence for purposes of avoiding repayment of the debt.

Sometimes a corporation is used for the exclusive purpose of hiding the assets of shareholders, and thereby shielding them from personal liability. Often, these organizations do not act like corporations but are only such in name. They are merely the alter ego of the shareholders. For example, in one case, the owners of a taxicab company incorporated the operation of each taxicab. They did not have board of directors' meetings, keep any minutes of the "corporations," or even keep separate financial books for each "corporation." The scheme was a sham to protect the assets of the taxicab company from creditors. In such cases, creditors are able to **pierce the corporate veil** and hold shareholders personally liable for the business's debt. The next case, involving a bar, an uninsured motorist, and injured plaintiffs, discusses the parameters of piercing the corporate veil.

BAATZ V. ARROW BAR
452 N.W. 2d 138 (S.D. 1990)

Kenny and Peggy Baatz (appellants) were injured while riding a motorcycle; they were struck by Roland McBride, who crossed the center line of the street with his automobile. McBride was uninsured.

The Baatzes allege that Arrow Bar (appellee) served alcoholic beverages to McBride while he was already intoxicated, before the accident. Arrow Bar was incorporated and Edmond and LaVella Neuroth were shareholders of the corporation. Arrow Bar did not have insurance. The Baatzes sought to pierce the corporate veil and to hold the Neuroths liable. The trial court entered summary judgment in favor of the Arrow Bar and the Neuroths. The Supreme Court of South Dakota affirmed.

Justice Sabers

Baatz claims that . . . the corporate veil should be pierced, leaving the Neuroths, as the shareholders of the corporation, individually liable. A corporation shall be considered a separate legal entity until there is sufficient reason to the contrary. When continued recognition of a corporation as a separate legal entity would "produce injustices and inequitable consequences," then a court has sufficient reason to pierce the corporate veil. Factors that indicate injustices and inequitable consequences and allow a court to pierce the corporate veil are:

1. fraudulent representation by corporation directors;
2. undercapitalization;
3. failure to observe corporate formalities;
4. absence of corporate records;

5. payment by the corporation of individual obligations; or

6. use of the corporation to promote fraud, injustice or illegalities.

When the court deems it appropriate to pierce the corporate veil, the corporation and its stockholders will be treated identically.

Baatz advances several arguments to support his claim that the corporate veil of Arrow Bar, Inc. should be pierced, but fails to support them with facts, or misconstrues the facts.

First, Baatz claims that since Edmond and LaVella personally guaranteed corporate obligations, they should also be personally liable to Baatz. However, the personal guarantee of a loan is a contractual agreement and cannot be enlarged to impose tort liability. . . . Baatz also argues that the corporation is simply the alter ego of the Neuroths, and . . . the corporate veil should be pierced. Baatz' discussion of the law is adequate, but he fails to present evidence that would support a decision in his favor in accordance with that law. When an individual treats a corporation "as an instrumentality, through which he [is] conducting his personal business," a court may disregard the corporate entity. Baatz fails to demonstrate how the Neuroths were transacting personal business through the corporation. In fact, the evidence indicated the Neuroths treated the corporation separately from their individual affairs.

Baatz next argues that the corporation is undercapitalized. Shareholders must equip a corporation with a reasonable amount of capital for the nature of the business involved. Baatz claims the corporation was started with only $5,000 in borrowed capital, but does not explain how that amount failed to equip the corporation with a reasonable amount of capital. . . .

Finally, Baatz argues that Arrow Bar, Inc. failed to observe corporate formalities because none of the business signs or advertising indicated that the business was a corporation. Baatz cites [a South Dakota statute] as requiring the name of any corporation to contain the word corporation,

company, incorporated, or limited or an abbreviation for such a word.

. . . [T]he "mere failure upon occasion to follow all the forms prescribed by law for the conduct of corporate activities will not justify" disregarding the corporate entity. . . .

Therefore, we affirm summary judgment dismissing the Neuroths as individual defendants.

Justice Henderson *(Dissenting)*

This corporation has no separate existence. It is the instrumentality of shareholders, officers, and employees. Here, the corporate fiction should be disregarded. . . .

Peggy Baatz, a young mother, lost her left leg; she wears an artificial limb. Kenny Baatz, a young father, has had most of his left foot amputated; he has been unable to work since this tragic accident. Peggy uses a cane. Kenny uses crutches. Years have gone by since they were injured and their lives have been torn asunder.

Are the Neuroths subject to personal liability? It is undisputed by the record that the dismissed defendants (Neuroths) are immediate family and stockholders of Arrow Bar. By pleadings . . . it is expressed that the dismissed defendants are employees of Arrow Bar. Seller of the Arrow Bar would not accept Arrow Bar, Inc., as buyer. Seller insisted that the individual incorporators, in their individual capacity[,] be equally responsible for the selling price. Thus, the individuals are the real party in interest and the corporate entity, Arrow Bar, Inc., is being used to justify any wrongs perpetrated by the incorporators in their individual capacity. Conclusion: Fraud is perpetrated upon the public. At a deposition of Edmond Neuroth (filed in this record), this "President" of "the corporation" was asked why the Neuroth family incorporated. His answer: "Upon the advice of counsel, as a shield against individual liability." . . .

Therefore, I respectfully dissent.

Case Questions

1. What are the circumstances under which a corporate veil may be pierced?

2. Why do the majority and dissent arrive at different conclusions on the issue of whether the corporate veil should be pierced? Should the difference make it clear that reasonable minds can differ and, hence, summary judgment is inappropriate? Explain.

3. What is undercapitalization? Is there an objective way to measure it? Do you favor a statute that would establish minimum levels of capitalization? Explain.

4. Do you favor a law requiring bars to be fully insured in order to be licensed to sell alcoholic beverages? Explain.

Types of Corporations

Corporations may be classified in a number of ways (see Table 12–4). Some corporations are domestic. A corporation is considered domestic within the state in which it is incorporated. It is considered foreign when transacting business in any other state. Transacting business does not include merely maintaining bank accounts, holding directors' or shareholders' meetings, or borrowing money. Each state regulates foreign corporations doing business within the state. States usually require that the corporation register in the state and obtain a certificate of authority from the secretary of state. Failure to do so may result in criminal penalties and limitations on the corporation's right to enforce its contracts.

Public corporations are established by the government. For example, a local municipality may incorporate to form itself, thus forming a municipal corporation. The U.S. Postal Service is an example of a federal public corporation.

Quasi-public corporations are public service companies, such as public utilities. Although they are private, the high degree of government regulation and protection makes them public in nature.

Private corporations are those established for private interests and include the bulk of existing corporations. Private corporations may further be divided between nonprofit and profit. Nonprofit corporations are formed for charitable or religious purposes. Profit corporations are usually formed to carry out business.

Private corporations for profit may be further subdivided into closely held corporations and publicly held corporations. A corporation owned by one or a few shareholders (who normally have family or other close ties and also manage the business) is termed a *closely held corporation.* These corporations do not publicly offer their stock. Ninety percent of all private-profit corporations fall in this category. The *publicly held corporation,* in contrast, has a number of unrelated shareholders who are passive investors; they do not actively manage the company. The shares of stock are traded freely on stock exchanges.

Some corporations, however, do not fall in either group. They are too small to be publicly held and yet they are larger than closely held corporations.

The professional corporation has been legalized by every state. Until the 1960s, lawyers, doctors, accountants, and other professionals could not incorporate. They

---
TABLE 12–4   **Types of Corporations**

Public   Quasi public   Private

| Nonprofit | Profit |

| Professional | Closely held | Publicly held |

---

could not take advantage of certain corporate tax breaks and pension benefits. Professional corporation statutes now allow them to do so; however, these professionals are still personally liable for their wrongful acts.

Corporate Management

Shareholders elect a board of directors to manage the corporation. The board, in turn, delegates the day-to-day operations to officers. The directors and the officers comprise the management of the corporation.

Directors

The articles of incorporation normally list the initial board of directors that serves until the first shareholders' meeting. At that meeting, shareholders elect a new board or, as often is the case, reelect the same board.

State statutes, the articles of incorporation, and bylaws may establish eligibility requirements for board membership. For example, the corporation's bylaws may require that a board member own stock in the company or be a resident of the state of incorporation. In the absence of such restrictions, anyone is eligible to be elected to the board of directors.

Ordinarily, board members serve one-year terms. This, however, is also governed by the bylaws. Although boards normally consist of at least three members, some states permit as few as one board member.

Directors must meet regularly. Some boards meet only once a year, others monthly, and still others more frequently. A quorum of board members must be present to hold a meeting. The number necessary for the quorum—normally a majority—is designated in the bylaws. Bylaw provisions may permit the board to make decisions by telephone or by writings through the mail.

The board of directors establishes the policy of the company and is responsible for guiding the company in a manner consistent with that policy. Other decisions made by the board include declaring dividends, proposing amendments to articles of incorporation and bylaws, proposing candidates for the board, and removing officers.

Commonly, some boards delegate some of their powers to executive committees. Executive committees may be composed of board members, officers, and others. They normally relieve the boards of detail work by studying alternatives and making suggestions. For example, the board may decide to implement a pension/profit-sharing plan and ask the executive committee to research alternatives and come up with a proposal.

Directors stand in a fiduciary relationship to the corporation. They must act with loyalty and due care in their actions and decision making. They may not act in their own self-interest; in all business relationships with the corporation they must make full and fair disclosure. Where a conflict of interest arises, a director may not vote on the issue that is the subject of conflict.

Board members are protected in their decision making by the **business judgment rule**. The business judgment rule, when applicable, affords board members great latitude in their decision making. This rule is designed to encourage board members to freely make difficult decisions, free from the fear of liability, even should those decisions, in hindsight, turn out to be harmful to the corporation. In effect, courts recognize their limitations in reviewing business decisions and defer to the company directors who are presumed to act in the best interests of the company.

For the business judgment rule to be applicable, the board must have made an informed and rational decision, free from conflicts of interests. Consider these qualifications when reading the next case, involving a board's decision to sell the company.

SMITH V. VAN GORKOM
488 A.2d 858 (Del. 1985)

Trans Union was a publicly traded corporation in the railcar leasing business. Van Gorkom was the chief executive officer and chairman of the board of directors. He owned 75,000 shares of company stock out of 20 million outstanding shares.

Van Gorkom located a social acquaintance, Pritzker, who offered to purchase the company at a price of $55 a share. The stock was selling for about $38 a share on the open market. Van Gorkom called a meeting of the board and made a 20 minute presentation to the board concerning the proposal. After two hours, the board approved the Pritzker proposal.

Shareholders sued Van Gorkom and the company directors. The Delaware Court of Chancery held that the defendants were protected under the business judgment rule. The plaintiffs appealed the judgment, and the Supreme Court of Delaware reversed.

Judge Horsey

Under Delaware law, the business judgment rule is the offspring of the fundamental principle that the business and affairs of a . . . corporation are managed by or under its board of directors. . . . The business judgement rule exists to protect and promote the full and free exercise of the managerial power granted to Delaware directors. The rule itself "is a presumption that in making a business decision, the directors of a corporation acted on an informed basis, in good faith and in the honest belief that the action taken was in the best interest of the company."

The determination of whether a business judgment is an informed one turns on whether the directors have informed themselves "prior to making a business decision, of all material information reasonably available to them."

■   ■   ■

Under the business judgment rule there is no protection for directors who have made "an unintelligent or unadvised judgment." A director's duty to inform himself in preparation for a decision derives from the fiduciary capacity in which he serves the corporation and its stockholders. Since a director is vested with the responsibility for the management of the affairs of the corporation, he must execute that duty with the recognition that he acts on behalf of others. Such obligation does not tolerate faithlessness or self-dealing. But fulfillment of the fiduciary function requires more than the mere absence of bad faith or fraud. Representation of the financial interests of others imposes on a director an affirmative duty to protect those interests and to proceed with a critical eye in assessing information of the type and under the circumstances present here.

■   ■   ■

On the record before us, we must conclude that the Board of Directors did not reach an informed business judgment . . . in voting to "sell" the Company for $55 per share pursuant to the Pritzker cash-out . . . proposal. Our reasons, in summary, are as follows:

The directors (1) did not adequately inform themselves as to Van Gorkom's role in forcing the "sale" of the Company and in establishing the per share purchase price; (2) were uninformed as to the intrinsic value of the Company; and (3) given these circumstances, at a minimum, were grossly negligent in approving the "sale" of the Company upon two hours' consideration, without prior notice, and without the exigency of a crisis or emergency.

Without any documents before them concerning the proposed transaction, the members of the Board were required to rely entirely upon Van Gorkom's 20-minute oral presentation of the proposal. No written summary of the terms . . . was presented; the directors were given no documentation to support the adequacy of [a] $55 price per share for sale of the Company; and the Board had before it nothing more than Van Gorkom's statement of his understanding of the substance of an agreement which he admittedly had never read, nor which any member of the Board had ever seen.

■   ■   ■

A substantial premium (difference between stock price and sales price) may provide one reason to recommend [the proposal], but in the absence of other sound valuation information, the fact of a premium alone does not provide an adequate basis upon which to assess the fairness of an offering price. . . .

The record is clear that Van Gorkom and other members of Trans Union's Board knew that the market had consistently undervalued the worth of Trans Union's stock, despite steady increase in the Company's operating income in the seven years preceding. . . .

■   ■   ■

. . . [T]here was no call by the Board . . . for any valuation study or documentation of the $55 price per share as a measure of the fair value of the Company in a cash-out context. It is undisputed that the major asset of Trans Union was its cash flow. Yet, at no time did the Board call for a valuation study taking into account that highly significant element of the Company's assets.

■   ■   ■

The record also establishes that the Board accepted without scrutiny Van Gorkom's representation as to the fairness of the $55 price per share for sale of the Company—a subject that the Board had never previously considered. The Board thereby failed to discover that Van Gorkom had suggested the $55 price to Pritzker. . . .

■   ■   ■

None of the directors . . . were investment brokers or financial analysts. Yet the Board did not consider recessing the meeting until a later hour that day (or requesting an extension . . .) to give it time to elicit more information as to the sufficiency of the offer, either from inside Management or from Trans Union's own investment banker, Salomon Brothers, whose Chicago specialist in merger and acquisitions was known to the Board and familiar with Trans Union's affairs.

■   ■   ■

We conclude that Trans Union's Board was grossly negligent in that it failed to act with informed reasonable deliberation in agreeing to the Pritzker . . . proposal. . . .

■   ■   ■

We hold, therefore, that the Trial Court committed reversible error in applying the business judgment rule in favor of the director defendants in this case.

REVERSED and REMANDED for proceedings consistent herewith.

Case Questions

1. What issue does this case present?
2. For what reasons did the court find that the Board was not protected by the business judgment rule?
3. Why is the market price not necessarily a fair price?
4. What questions would you as a board member want to ask before making a decision?
5. Assume that after the board entered into an agreement with Pritzker, another "suitor" came along and offered $75/share for the buyout. What should the board do, and why?

Officers

Officers of the corporation are appointed by the board of directors pursuant to the bylaws. They are responsible for implementing the policies of the board and for the oversight of the day-to-day operations of the business. Officers include a president, vice president, secretary, and treasurer. Large corporations may have a number of vice presidents, including such specialized officers as vice president-marketing, comptroller, and financial secretary.

Officers are agents of the corporation, and, as such, may bind the corporation. Like directors, officers owe fiduciary duties to the corporation.

Shareholders

The publicly held corporation is usually financed by issuing securities to investors, known as *shareholders* (as discussed in Chapter 13). Of the various classifications of shareholders, the most common distinction is between common stockholders and preferred stockholders. A primary difference between the two is that, ordinarily, preferred stockholders are entitled to receive their dividends before common stockholders and, on dissolution, preferred stockholders are entitled to distributions of assets before common stockholders.

Voting

Some stockholders have voting rights. Other stockholders may lack those rights or only be entitled to vote on extraordinary matters.

At the annual shareholders' meeting, the voting members elect directors and vote on other matters of corporate concern. There are two principal methods for voting for directors: straight and cumulative.

Under the straight method, each shareholder is entitled to one vote per share per director's position. Each vacant director's position is voted on at a time. The second method, cumulative, affords each shareholder one vote times the number of shares owned times the number of directors' vacancies to be filled. The election for all board members takes place at one time. For example, assume five vacant board positions must be filled. Harriet owns 1,000 shares of stock. She has 5,000 votes (1 x 1,000 x 5). She may vote the entire 5,000 shares for one candidate, or she may split her votes in any combination among several candidates. Cumulative voting gives minority shareholders the chance to elect some members(s) to the board.

Dividends

Dividends are portions of corporate earnings distributed to shareholders. They are declared by the board of directors. A board maintains almost absolute discretion to declare or not declare dividends. It may not, however, declare dividends if the corporation is insolvent. Additionally, it may not refuse to declare dividends in bad faith—for example, to squeeze out minority shareholders.

Dividends may be in the form of cash or stock. Cash dividends are the most common type of dividend. They increase the wealth of the stockholder and are taxable to the receiver. Stock dividends may be declared by the board of directors. For example, a 10 percent increase in stock may be declared and distributed. In such a case, a shareholder who owns 100 shares would receive 10 additional shares. This does not change shareholders' percentages of ownership of the company; although a stockholder's net worth may be increased, there is no immediate taxable gain.

The stock split is sometimes confused with a stock dividend. In a stock split, the existing shares are divided, for example, two for one. A shareholder receives two shares for every one he or she owns. Again, this does not give the shareholder any additional interest or even theoretically increase net worth. If the stock is selling for $100 a share, in a two-for-one split the value of a share is theoretically reduced in half to $50 a share (although in reality the market value is usually a little higher). The prime reason for issuing a stock split is to make the stock more affordable to more people, thereby stimulating a flow of capital into the corporation.

Preemption

Shareholders may be granted **preemptive rights** by the articles of incorporation. Preemptive rights ensure that existing shareholders may maintain their proportionate interest in the company. They require the corporation to offer new shares to existing shareholders before offering them to the public. Assume that Phil owns 100,000 shares in a corporation that has 1 million shares outstanding. Phil owns 10 percent of the company. Now assume that the company desires to raise more capital and does so by issuing 1 million new shares. If Phil does not have a first right to buy a proportional number of shares, his interest in the company could be diluted to 5 percent. If, however, Phil has preemptive rights, he would be entitled to purchase 100,000 shares and thus preserve his percentage of the relative ownership interest (10 percent). Of course, preemptive rights do not help Phil if he cannot afford to purchase the shares.

Inspection

Stockholders have the right to inspect the books and records of the corporation; this includes the shareholders list, the minutes of meetings, and financial records. The one qualification on this right is that the shareholder must show a proper purpose. The purpose must be related to the status of a shareholder. It would not be a proper purpose if the shareholders list is to be used to buttress the mailing list for one shareholder's personal business. It would be proper, however, if the shareholder's purpose is to gain control of the company by soliciting proxies.

Suits

Shareholders may sue the corporation individually or on behalf of the corporation. A shareholder who has been injured by wrongful corporate acts may sue the corporation. These acts may include a refusal to permit inspection of the shareholders list and illegal inside trading (discussed in Chapter 13).

Derivative actions to recover monies on behalf of the corporation may be filed by individual shareholders when the board of directors refuses to act. Assume one of the directors has illegally absconded with company monies. Should the majority of the board refuse to sue to recover, any shareholder would have the right to sue on behalf of the corporation. Any recovery would directly inure to the benefit of the corporation.

Dissolution

In theory, a corporation can live forever, although it can and does expire under various circumstances. The termination of corporate existence is referred to as *dissolution*. Dissolution may occur voluntarily or involuntarily.

Voluntary dissolution occurs when the corporation files a certificate of dissolution with the secretary of state. This normally requires both board of directors' and shareholders' approval. The main reason for voluntary dissolution is unprofitability of the company. Some profitable corporations, however, voluntarily dissolve to fend off hostile takeovers.

Involuntary corporate dissolutions are accomplished by administrative or judicial process. A corporation's failure to comply with certain administrative requirements, such as filing of forms, payment of taxes, and maintaining a statutory agent, may result in an action by the state attorney general to dissolve the corporation. Additionally, shareholders may file suit seeking dissolution of the corporation under circumstances where, for example, there is gross mismanagement or unfair treatment of shareholders.

On dissolution, the board of directors, or in some cases a court-appointed trustee, must wind up the affairs of the corporation. This entails liquidating the corporate assets and distributing the proceeds, first to creditors, and then to the shareholders.

Limited Liability Company

The newest type of organization on the business scene is the **limited liability company (LLC)**. It is a creature of legislation in ~~about one half~~ all the states in the United States, and that number is expected to grow rapidly. The LLC is a hybrid of the partnership and the subchapter S corporation, selecting the best characteristics of each. Like the subchapter S corporation, its owners enjoy limited liability, without, however, the restriction of number of owners and the necessity of electing the status annually. Like the partnership, the LLC avoids double taxation, and unlike the limited partnership there is no restriction on control and management of the business.

There are, however, some practical limitations. First, some states place restrictions on the transfer of interests, requiring unanimous agreement for the transferee to have management input. Additionally, jurisdictions that do not have LLC statutes may not recognize the limited liability aspects of an LLC transacting business in that jurisdiction.

Chapter Problems

1. Define the following concepts and terms:
   a. Principal
   b. Apparent authority
   c. Independent contractors

    d. Apparent partnership

    e. Limited partnership

    f. Pierce the corporate veil

    g. Private corporations

    h. Business judgment rule

    i. Preemptive rights

    j. Limited liability company (LLC)

2. Wheeler spoke with Stewart, an agent of Stewart Insurance, an independent insurance agency, about obtaining insurance for his mobile home. Wheeler filled out an application for insurance on a Puritan Insurance Company form and made partial payment. Stewart informed Wheeler, "As quick as I write this receipt out and accept your money, you will be covered by Puritan." Stewart failed to send Wheeler's application to Puritan and to obtain insurance protection for Wheeler.

   Stewart did not have any express authorization from Puritan to bind the company. Puritan considered each application on arrival. Fire destroyed Wheeler's mobile home. Stewart informed Wheeler that the loss was not covered by Puritan. Do you agree? Explain. Would Wheeler have any other alternatives to recovery? Explain.

3. Loehr's is a used car dealer. One of its salespeople misrepresented the mileage of a used car in a sale to a customer. Under agency principles, is Loehr's liable for the damages due to the misrepresentation? What additional information, if any, do you need to answer the question? Explain. What can the owners of car dealerships do to minimize the risk of such misrepresentation occurring?

4. Lancaster was a mechanic in the locomotive shop at Norfolk and Western Railway Co. Lachrone, a hot-tempered foreman, lost his temper and approached Lancaster with a broom in a menacing manner. Lancaster developed a severe mental disorder as a result. Is Norfolk and Western Railway Co. liable for Lancaster's injury under agency principles? Explain.

5. Harris and Zajac worked together in a salvage operation business. They bought wrecked cars and rebuilt them or sold them for salvage. Zajac had a controlling voice in the management of the business. There was no written partnership agreement; neither did the business file a partnership tax return. Harris used his own money to buy cars, as did Zajac. The parties split the profits on the sales from time to time. Zajac withheld federal withholding and social security taxes on Harris's share of the profit. Is this a partnership? Why or why not?

6. Able, Baker, and Carter formed ABC Partnership. Able contributed $5,000, Baker $10,000, and Carter $15,000. During the term of the partnership, Baker loaned ABC $5,000 and Able loaned ABC $6,000. The partnership is

winding up its affairs after a voluntary dissolution. It owes creditors $100,000. Assume ABC has assets in the amount of $150,000 to distribute. How will Able, Baker, and Carter divide the profits or losses? What if ABC had $132,000 to distribute?

7. Dr. Bennet signed articles of incorporation for Aero-Fabb Co. Because these articles were not in accord with the state statutes, the secretary of state did not issue a certificate of incorporation. Timberline leased equipment to Aero-Fabb Co. Aero-Fabb refused to pay. May Timberline enforce payment against the corporation? Explain.

8. Gries Sports Enterprises, Inc. (GSE) and Gries own 43 percent of the outstanding stock of the Cleveland Browns Football Co., Inc. (Browns), a Delaware corporation. Gries is a director and officer of the Browns. Modell owns 53 percent of the stock in the Browns and is a director, president, and chief executive officer of the Browns. Other board members include Modell's wife; Bailey, general counsel of the Browns; Berick, outside legal counsel; Wallack, a full-time employee; and Cole.

   Modell formed Cleveland Stadium Corporation (CSC). CSC leased the Cleveland Municipal Stadium from the city and subleased it to the Browns. Modell owned 80 percent of the stock in CSC. Berick, Bailey, Cole, Wallack, and Gries also owned stock in CSC.

   Modell had an outstanding personal indebtedness of $4 million. In an effort to retire that debt, he set about to sell CSC to the Browns for $6 million. Since he owned 80 percent of the shares in CSC, that would net him sufficient funds to pay off his $4 million debt. A brokerage and investment firm rendered an opinion that CSC would be worth from $6.2 million to $6.9 million if acquired by the Browns.

   At the Browns meeting of the directors, Gries objected to the acquisition. By a four-to-one vote the board approved the acquisition. The Modells abstained.

   Gries and GSE filed suit seeking to set aside the transaction, contending that the transaction was "intrinsically unfair." The Browns defended by contending that the board's decision was protected by the business judgment rule. What additional information would you want to present to support the Browns' contention?

9. Mesa Petroleum owned 13 percent of Unocal's stock. It attempted to gain control of Unocal's stock by a cash offer for outstanding shares. It offered to purchase 64 million shares for $54 per share. It then intended to eliminate the remaining shares by exchanging Mesa stock for Unocal stock. Unocal's board is unanimously against accepting and recommending to its shareholders Mesa's offer. Assuming that Mesa's offer is fair and that the offering price is above the market price, what are some alternatives for the board to consider?

10. Home Owners Warranty Corp. (HOW) administers a homeowner's program for the benefit of member-builders. Two shareholders demand to inspect the books, records, and membership lists of HOW and its subsidiaries. Under which circumstances, and for what purpose, would HOW shareholders be entitled to such inspection?

13   SECURITIES REGULATION AND SARBANES-OXLEY

Chapter Outline

Learning Objectives

After learning this chapter the student should be able to:

- Identify a security by the economic reality and common characteristic tests.
- State what is prohibited and what is permissible during stages of the registration process.
- Construct a securities offering so that it is exempt from registration.
- Identify the various transactions subject to Exchange Act compliance.
- Distinguish between lawful trading on information and impermissible trading on inside information.
- Identify the corporate governance implications of the Sarbanes-Oxley Act.

Securities are different from most of the merchandise bought by the average person. A consumer who purchases a loaf of bread can touch and smell the bread and evaluate its worth by comparing it with other brands on the shelf. This is not the case with securities where the worth of a share of stock depends on the worth of the enterprise that issued it. Evaluating this worth is complex. It requires full knowledge of that enterprise's finances, present and projected information ordinarily beyond the investor's reach. An alternative is to rely on the issuer's claims about the enterprise. In the past, this means of ascertaining value often tempted those issuing and trading stocks and other securities to exaggerate the financial status and future prospects of the enterprise. Unsuspecting investors were enticed with fanciful promises of "pie in the blue sky."[1] This practice made legislators aware of the need for investor protection. At the turn of the 20th century, a few states enacted laws designed to protect investors. By 1933, virtually every state had some type of securities regulation.[2]

State regulation proved inadequate to protect investors, mainly because state laws lacked uniformity. Opportunists preyed on consumers in the states that had permissive securities laws. In addition, it was often possible to avoid state securities laws altogether by operating on a purely interstate basis or by falling under liberal state exemptions.

Many Americans lost their life savings in the 1929 stock market crash, and billions of dollars were lost due to the flotation of worthless securities. The securities industry was blamed for the debacle; many securities dealers had made alluring promises of easy wealth without informing investors of the facts necessary to accurately assess the value of the security.

Recognizing that federal intervention was needed to restore public confidence in securities and their markets, Congress passed the Securities Act of 1933 (Securities Act), the first of several federal laws to regulate securities. Congress next passed the Securities Exchange Act of 1934 to regulate the securities markets and persons who conduct business in securities (see Figure 13–1).

This chapter begins with a brief look at the Securities Exchange Commission (SEC), the federal agency responsible for administering the securities laws. It then focuses on the Securities Act of 1933 and the laws governing the issuing of securities. Identifying a security and registering a security under that act are topics treated, along with exemptions from the registration process and violations under the act. The chapter then examines the Securities Exchange Act of 1934 and the regulation of securities traded in secondary markets and transactions affecting such trading. Antifraud provisions under the act are also discussed.

---

[1] The term *blue sky laws* refers to state securities regulations intended to protect investors from "speculative schemes which have no more basis than so many feet of blue sky." [Hall v. Geiger Jones, Co., 242 U.S. 539 (1971).]

[2] Nevada was the sole exception.

FIGURE 13–1   **Primary and Secondary Sale of Securities**

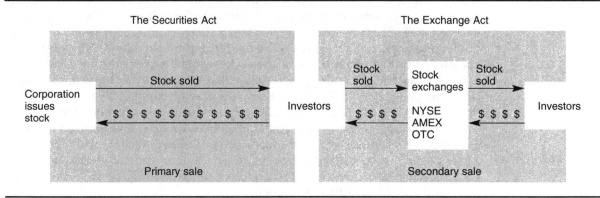

The Securities and Exchange Commission

Congress created the SEC to administer the securities laws. Its five members, appointed by the president, serve five-year terms. Most of the commission's staff are located in Washington, D.C., and the remainder are situated in nine regional and eight branch offices in key cities throughout the country.

The SEC has broad rulemaking powers, and its rules have the force of law. Informal SEC releases define the attitudes and policies of the agency, although they do not have the effect of law. In addition, the SEC responds to specific questions by advising inquirers of its opinion on proposed transactions. These responses are sometimes referred to as *no-action letters.* They often state that the SEC will take no action against the inquirer based on the given facts and the intended action outlined in the inquirer's letter.

Identifying a Security

The Securities Act contains an expansive definition of a security, which includes notes, stocks, bonds, investment contracts, and other interests "commonly known as a security."

Definition of a Security §2(1)

[U]nless the context otherwise requires . . . the term "**security**" [boldface added] means any note, stock, . . . bond, debenture, evidence of indebtedness, certificate of interest or participation in any profit-sharing agreement, . . . transferable share, investment contract . . . certificate of deposit for a security, fractional undivided interest in oil, gas or other mineral rights . . . or, in general, any interest or instrument commonly known as a "security. . . .

In *SEC v. Howey Co.,* the Supreme Court established the general test for an investment contract which is expressly deemed a security under the act.[3] In this case, the W. J. Howey Company (Howey), which owned 500 acres of citrus groves in Florida, offered 250 acres to the public. The company sold each purchaser a narrow strip of the grove (one sale, for example, consisted of two thirds of an acre) on a land installment contract, with the deed to be delivered to the buyer when the last installment was paid. Howey also offered a service contract for maintaining the acreage. This contract required pooling the proceeds of the whole crop and distributing those proceeds pro rata to individual investors. The Supreme Court held that the combination of the land contract, service contract, and deed as a package constituted an investment contract, which is specifically denoted as a security under the Securities Act definition. In arriving at its findings, the Court listed the following three characteristics of an investment contract: (1) a contract, transaction, or scheme whereby a person invests money in a common enterprise; (2) whose investors have reasonable expectation of profit; and (3) whose profits are derived from the efforts of persons other than the investors. However, as the following U.S. Supreme Court case expresses, Howey is not a generic test for all securities; there is a different test for a "note."

REVES V. ERNST & YOUNG
494 U.S. 56 (1990)

In order to raise funds for their business, The Farmers Cooperative of Arkansas and Oklahoma (Co-Op) sold promissory notes that were payable on demand. The notes were not secured by any collateral, nor were they insured; they paid a variable interest rate higher than the financial institutes.

Farmer's Co-Op filed for bankruptcy. Petitioners, holders of the notes, filed suit against the Co-Op's auditor, alleging a violation of the antifraud provisions of the Securities Exchange Act (the Act), due to their failure to follow generally accepted accounting principles that would have revealed the Co-op's financial problems.

The Court of Appeals reversed a $6.1 million trial decision in favor of petitioners. The U.S. Supreme Court reversed.

Justice Marshall

This case presents the question whether certain demand notes issued by the . . . Co-Op are "securities" within the meaning of . . . (the Act). We conclude that they are.

■   ■   ■

The term 'security' means any note . . . but shall not include . . . any note . . . which has a maturity at the time of issuance of not exceeding nine months. . . .

■   ■   ■

Some instruments are obviously within the class Congress intended to regulate because they

---

[3] 328 U.S. 293 (1946).

are by their nature investments. In *Landreth Timber Co. v. Landreth,* we held that an instrument bearing the name "stock" that, among other things, is negotiable, offers the possibility of capital appreciation, and carries the right to dividends contingent on the profits of a business enterprise is plainly within the class of instruments Congress intended the securities laws to cover. Landreth Timber does not signify a lack of concern with economic reality; rather, it signals a recognition that stock is, as a practical matter, always an investment if it has the economic characteristics traditionally associated with stock. . . .

■   ■   ■

We made clear . . . that stock was a special case, explicitly limiting our holding to that sort of instrument. Although we refused finally to rule out a similar per se rule for notes, we intimated that such a rule would be unjustified. Unlike "stock," we said, "'note' may . . . be viewed as a relatively broad term that encompasses instruments with widely varying characteristics, depending on whether issued in a consumer context, as commercial paper, or in some other investment context." While common stock is the quintessence of a security and investors therefore justifiably assume that a sale of stock is covered by the Securities Acts, the same simply cannot be said of notes, which are used in a variety of settings, not all of which involve investments. Thus, the phrase "any note" should not be interpreted to mean literally "any note," but must be understood against the backdrop of what Congress was attempting to accomplish in enacting the Securities Acts.

Because the Landreth Timber formula cannot sensibly be applied to notes, some other principle must be developed to define the term "note. . . . "

The Second Circuit's "family resemblance" approach begins with a presumption that any note with a term of more than nine months is a "security." Recognizing that not all notes are securities, however, the Second Circuit has also devised a list

of notes that it has decided are obviously not securities. Accordingly, the "family resemblance" test permits an issuer to rebut the presumption that a note is a security if it can show that the note in question "bear[s] a strong family resemblance" to an item on the judicially crafted list of exceptions, or convinces the court to add a new instrument to the list.

■   ■   ■

[T]he Second Circuit has identified a list of instruments commonly denominated "notes" that nonetheless fall [outside] the "security" category. Types of notes that are not "securities" include "the note delivered in consumer financing, the note secured by a mortgage on a home, the short-term note secured by a lien on a small business or some of its assets, the note evidencing a 'character' loan to a bank customer, short-term notes secured by an assignment of accounts receivable, or a note which simply formalizes an open-account debt incurred in the ordinary course of business."

. . . It is impossible to make any meaningful inquiry into whether an instrument bears a "resemblance" to one of the instruments identified by the Second Circuit without specifying what it is about those instruments that makes them non-"securities. . . ."

. . . First, we examine the transaction to assess the motivations that would prompt a reasonable seller and buyer to enter into it. If the seller's purpose is to raise money for the general use of a business enterprise or to finance substantial investments and the buyer is interested primarily in the profit the note is expected to generate, the instrument is likely to be a "security." If the note is exchanged to facilitate the purchase and sale of a minor asset or consumer good, to correct for the seller's cash-flow difficulties, or to advance some other commercial or consumer purpose, on the other hand, the note is less sensibly described as a "security." Second, we examine the "plan of distribution" of the instrument, to determine whether it is an instrument in which there is "common trading for speculation or investment[.]" Third, we examine the reasonable expectations of the investing public. . . . Finally, we examine whether some factor such as the existence of another regulatory scheme significantly reduces the risk of the instrument, thereby rendering application of the Securities Acts unnecessary.

■   ■   ■

Applying the family resemblance approach to this case, we have little difficulty in concluding that the notes at issue here are "securities." Ernst & Young admits that "a demand note does not closely resemble any of the Second Circuit's family resemblance examples. . . ." The Co-Op sold the notes in an effort to raise capital for its general business operations, and purchasers bought them in order to earn a profit in the form of interest. Indeed, one of the primary inducements offered purchasers was an interest rate constantly revised to keep it slightly above the rate paid by local banks and savings and loans. From both sides, then, the transaction is most naturally conceived as an investment in a business enterprise rather than as a purely commercial or consumer transaction.

As to the plan of distribution, the Co-Op offered the notes over an extended period to its 23,000 members, as well as to nonmembers, and more than 1,600 people held notes when the Co-Op filed for bankruptcy. To be sure, the notes were not traded on an exchange. They were, however, offered and sold to a broad segment of the public, and that is all we have held to be necessary to establish the requisite "common trading" in an instrument.

The third factor—the public's reasonable perceptions—also supports a finding that the notes in this case are "securities." We have consistently identified the fundamental essence of a "security" to be its character as an "investment." The advertisements for the notes here characterized them as "investments," and there were no countervailing factors that would have led a reasonable person to question this characterization. . . .

Finally, we find no risk-reducing factor to suggest that these instruments are not in fact securities. The notes are uncollateralized and uninsured. . . .

■   ■   ■

For the foregoing reasons, we conclude that the demand notes at issue here fall under the "note" category of instruments that are "securities. . . ." [The court found that the notes did not fall under the nine-month exclusion exception.] Accordingly, we reverse the judgment of the Court of Appeals and remand the case for further proceedings consistent with this opinion.

Case Questions

1. What is the issue in this case?
2. What is the family resemblance test? How does it differ from the Howey test?
3. Craft an argument that demand notes mature within nine months, and thus fall under the exclusion exception. What are the counterarguments?
4. Are you surprised that this case arose to the U.S. Supreme Court on the interpretation of "note," a term that seems clearly within the statute? Explain.

Registering a Security

All securities must be registered with the SEC unless they are exempt. In fact, a security may not be offered for sale until a registration statement is filed and becomes effective. The registration statement is designed to assure that a person

> **Securities Registration**
>
> Unless a registration statement is in effect . . . it shall be unlawful for any person . . . to . . . use . . . any means . . . of . . . interstate commerce or . . . the mails to sell [a] security. . . .

who sells securities discloses all material information related to the sale. Material information is the type that makes a difference to prudent investors. Investors may use the information contained in the registration statement to make an informed decision.

The SEC examines the statement for disclosure about the company and the securities it intends to offer for sale. As long as the statement is complete, the commission cannot deny the registration. The commission, however, does not vouch for the financial condition of the company or the fairness of the terms of the securities offering. Neither does the commission guarantee the accuracy of the information the registration statement contains. Criminal laws, however, make it illegal for a registrant to make false or misleading representations, under pain of fine and imprisonment. In addition, an investor who suffers financial injury due to a material misrepresentation in the registration statement may pursue civil remedies discussed later in this chapter.

The registration statement offers detailed information about the registrant's business and properties; the management, control, and operation of the business; the securities to be offered for sale; and the company's financial condition. This information is available for public inspection. Additionally, a **prospectus** must be given to each person to whom a security is offered for sale. A prospectus is a pamphlet that summarizes the information contained in the registration statement. Preparation of these documents is very costly because the work involves lawyers, accountants, financial analysts, management specialists, and other experts.

The registration process may be divided into the prefiling, waiting, and posteffective periods, summarized in the following sections and in Table 13–1.

TABLE 13–1   The Registration Process

	Prefiling	*Waiting*	*Posteffective*
Prohibited:	Offers to buy or sell	Sales	Written offers or confirmation of sale unless accompanied by prospectus
Permitted:	Establish distribution network Release of limited news of proposed offering	Oral offers Red herring prospectus Tombstone ads	Offer and sale of securities

Prefiling Period

The prefiling period is the time before a registration statement is filed. The Securities Act prohibits offers to buy or sell during that time, although it does not prohibit preliminary negotiations or agreements between issuers and underwriters. Thus, during this prefiling stage the issuer may begin to set up its network for distribution of the securities in anticipation of its eventual offering.

Offers are not confined to formal proposals. The SEC considers unusual publicity about the proposed securities or the issuer's business to be part of a sales effort to condition the public. Offers disguised as speeches or writings are considered "gun jumping," which is prohibited by the act during this stage. An SEC rule does permit an issuer to release news of a proposed offering that contains only the name of the issuer and the purpose and terms of a proposed issue.

Waiting Period

The interlude between filing and the time when the registration becomes effective is called the *waiting period*. During this time, the SEC examines the registration to ensure its completeness. Sales are not permitted during this period. Oral offers can be made, but written offers are expressly prohibited unless they conform to SEC requirements.

The most common form of compliance is a preliminary prospectus that summarizes the information contained in the registration statement. This prospectus is commonly referred to as a *red herring prospectus,* because it requires a special legend printed in red. This legend states that the securities may not be sold and offers to buy may not be accepted before the registration statement becomes effective. The SEC further requires that copies of the preliminary prospectus be distributed to persons intending to solicit customers and to any customers requesting a copy.

During the waiting period, the SEC also permits the distribution of notices that include identifying information and legends specifying that they are not an offer to sell or a solicitation of an offer to buy the securities. These notices appear in newspapers. Because they are often bordered in black, they are termed *tombstone ads.*

Posteffective Period

The registration becomes effective 20 days after filing unless the registration process is accelerated or postponed by the commission. On that date, underwriters and dealers are free to offer and sell the securities. Before a registration becomes effective, the original registration statement, including the preliminary prospectus, must be amended to include prices and other information that may have been omitted. A prospectus must accompany a written offer to sell a security or a confirmation of its sale.

The SEC has adopted a rule that permits issuers to delay the effective registration period for up to two years. Under this **shelf registration** procedure, the issuer, is in a better position to time an offering with the market conditions. The issuing firm may file a single registration with the SEC and place designated securities on the shelf to be issued at a later date. Then, when the market conditions are favorable for issuance, the firm can enter the market, taking the securities off the shelf. The issuer need not publish a new registration statement or detailed prospectus. Shelf registration is available only to large companies. Studies have shown that the primary benefit of shelf registration is the substantial cost savings to registrants.

Exemptions

For many businesses, cost considerations tend to discourage the issuance of securities as a means of raising capital, unless they can be issued under an exemption. Some exemptions are made for securities issued by the government or charitable institutions. However, qualifying under an exemption does not relieve the issuer from the antifraud provisions of the securities laws (discussed later in this chapter). The exemptions most relevant to the businessperson are **private placements**, limited offerings, and intrastate offerings.

Private Placements

The Securities Act, under Section 4(2), exempts "transactions by an issuer not involving any public offering." To qualify for this preferred exempt status, an offering must be confined to selected purchasers that have access to the same type of information provided by registration. These purchasers also must be sophisticated enough to evaluate the merits of the offering. This category includes insurance companies, pension funds, and other institutional investors meeting the access and sophistication criteria. Sales to these investors pose no threat to the public and are routinely honored as legitimate private placement exemptions by the SEC. In fact, these institutional investors are normally able to command more information from the issuer than is required for registration.

In *SEC v. Ralston Purina Co.* the Supreme Court announced that the validity of a private offering exemption is determined by whether the offerees need the protection of the Securities Act.[4] If they have sufficient information, knowledge, and skill to fend for themselves, they do not need the disclosures registration provides.

Under Section 4(2) and the cases interpreting that section, no magic formula ensures the exempt status of a promotional offering. The following case, involving limited partnership interests in cable television systems, illustrates the restrictiveness of the private placement exemption under Section 4(2).

---

[4] 346 U.S. 119 (1953).

SECURITIES AND EXCHANGE COMMISSION V. MURPHY
626 F. 2d 633 (9th Cir. 1980)

Stephen Murphy (appellant) organized and controlled Intertie. In connection with the International Securities Corporation (ISC), a securities brokerage firm, Intertie promoted about 30 limited partnerships to which it sold cable television systems.

Intertie would first buy a cable television system. It would make a cash down payment on the system and finance the remainder. Then it would sell the system to one of the limited partnerships for a cash down payment and notes promising to repay the balance. Finally, Intertie would lease the system back from the partnership. Neither Intertie nor ISC registered the limited partnership interest as securities. They relied on the private offering exemption of Section 4(2) of the Securities Act. The SEC brought suit, charging Murphy with fraud and failure to register a security. The district court granted summary judgment in favor of the SEC and granted an injunction against Murphy. The court of appeals affirmed the district court's decision.

Judge Ferguson

Courts have developed flexible tests for the private offering exemption, focusing upon: (1) the number of offerees; (2) the sophistication of the offerees; (3) the size and manner of the offering; and (4) the relationship of the offerees to the issuer. . . . The party claiming the exemption must show that it is met not only with respect to each purchaser, but also with respect to each offeree.

1. The Number of Offerees

The *Ralston Purina* decision made it clear that there was no rigid limit to the number of offerees to whom an issuer could make a private offering. Nonetheless, while the number of offerees, itself, is not decisive, "the more offerees, the more likelihood that the offering is public." Murphy introduced no evidence below to suggest that the number of offerees was small or that there was even any attempt to monitor the number of offerees at all.

The SEC introduced Murphy's deposition, in which he stated that offering memoranda were not numbered. Apparently, then, no one knows how many offerees ISC contacted on any of the part-

nership offerings. Once the SEC provided evidence that there was no control placed on the number of offerees, it was incumbent upon Murphy . . . to rebut that evidence. . . .

When we look at the number of purchasers in the aggregate, as we must, their number—400—clearly suggests a public offering rather than a private placement.

2. The Sophistication of the Offerees

It was also incumbent upon Murphy to introduce evidence to rebut the inferences of lack of investor sophistication that the court could have drawn from Murphy's deposition testimony. His statement that 60 percent of the investors used offeree representatives suggests at least that the majority of the purchasers, if not the majority of the offerees, lacked the sort of business acumen necessary to qualify as sophisticated investors. Moreover, Murphy's admission that offeree representatives who were also salesmen and general partners in the cable systems did not disclose this relationship to prospective investors suggests the inadequacy of the representatives. His further testimony that some of the offeree representatives whom he met were incompetent reveals both that the investors needed the protection of the Act and that Murphy and Intertie were not concerned about investor sophistication. Intertie did not obtain information about the investors in the limited partnerships, nor did it insist that ISC do so. Murphy merely stated that Intertie relied on ISC to qualify the investors, but he did not produce evidence suggesting that ISC actually took any such steps.

3. The Size and Manner of the Offering

If an offering is small and is made directly to the offerees "rather than through the facilities of public distribution such as investment bankers or the securities exchange," a court is more likely to find that it is private. The SEC's evidence shows that the amounts invested in individual systems varied, but that the purchase price for several of the systems was more than $1 million each. Viewed individually, these offerings cannot automatically be labeled small; and there is reason to believe that they should not be viewed individually in any case. When we consider the placements as one integrated offering, we are confronted with a sale of $7.5 million in securities. Without question, that is a sizeable offering, and it is one that we are inclined to consider as public, absent a significant showing that the investors did not need the protection of the Act. . . .

4. The Relationship between the Issuer and the Offeree

A court may only conclude that the investors do not need the protection of the Act if all the offerees have relationships with the issuer affording them access to or disclosure of the sort of information about the issuer that registration reveals. As

with the other requirements discussed, after the SEC demonstrated that the requisite relationship did not exist, it was incumbent upon the defendant to produce evidence that the offerees had available the necessary information. . . . Included in [the required] information is the use of investor funds, the amount of direct and indirect commissions, and accurate financial statements. Intertie supplied almost none of this required information. In addition, there were a number of general facts of enormous importance regarding Intertie's operation that were omitted. Operating memoranda purported to show cash flow projections for individual systems but did not reveal that no system would be self-sustaining; thus, offerees did not know that because of Intertie's large short-term debt obligations, the continued viability of Intertie depended upon a consistent influx of new capital. . . .

Thus, other considerations aside, because the offerees clearly lacked access to financial information about Intertie, we would have to sustain the court's entry of summary judgment on this ground alone.

The judgment of the district court is AFFIRMED.

Case Questions

1. Describe the arrangement between Intertie and its investors. How did that benefit Intertie? What was the benefit to investors?
2. Which factors are relevant in determining whether an offering is exempt under Section 4(2)?
3. Why did the offering fail to qualify as a private exempt offering? Explain.
4. Which precautions could Murphy, Intertie, and ICS have taken to ensure private offering status?

Limited Offerings

Certain small issues are exempt from full registration. Section 3(b) of the Securities Act authorizes the SEC to exempt offerings not exceeding $5 million when "by reason of the small amount involved or the limited character of the public offering" registration is not necessary.

Regulation A

Regulation A affords a limited exemption for issues not exceeding a total amount of $5 million within a one-year period. The exemption is not available to those who have been convicted of securities offenses.

Regulation A provides a faster and less expensive procedure than full registration (see Table 13–2). Instead of filing a registration statement with the SEC in Washington, an issuer files a notice and an offering circular at a regional office. The offering circular is a miniregistration form containing unaudited financial statements. The offering circular must be given to every offeree.

Regulation D

The SEC also has enacted Regulation D, which contains various rules simplifying exemptions for limited offerings. These exemptions are designed to make it easier for small businesses to qualify for exemptions and hence raise capital to meet their needs. One rule under Regulation D permits a sale of up to $1 million of securities to any number of purchasers, without requiring the issuer to furnish information. Another rule is more liberal and permits an unlimited amount of securities to be sold to accredited investors, without supplying information. Accredited investors include banks, insurance companies, directors, and officers of the issuer, persons whose net worth exceeds $1 million, persons with an annual income exceeding $200,000 and those who, with their spouse, have a joint annual income of $300,000 or more. These accredited investors do not need the full protection of registration. In many instances, they are in a position to obtain more information than registration requires. Table 13–3 summarizes the various Regulation D rules.

Regulation D includes a good-faith defense. Under this standard, failure to comply with a Regulation D requirement does not result in a loss of the registration exemption if it can be shown that (1) the term violated was not intended to protect the particular individual or entity involved; (2) the failure to comply was insignificant to the offering as a whole; and (3) the issuer made a good-faith and reasonable attempt to comply with all of the Regulation D requirements.

The good-faith defense only applies in suits by private parties. It does not apply to attacks by the SEC.

TABLE 13–2   Regulation A Exemption: Comparison

	Regulation A Securities	*Nonexempt Securities*
Amount	$5 million	Unlimited
Filing statement	Miniregistration	Full-blown registration
Filing place	Regional office	Washington, D.C.
Delivered to purchaser	Offering circular	Prospectus
Contents of filing	Uncertified financial statements	Certified financial statements

TABLE 13–3	**Regulation D Exemptions: Comparisons**		
	Rule 504	*Rule 505*	*Rule 506*
Amount	$1 million	$5 million	Unlimited
Number of purchasers	Unlimited	Accredited: unlimited Nonaccredited:35	Accredited: unlimited Nonaccredited:35
Disclosure requirements	None	Full disclosure if any nonaccredited purchasers	Full disclosure if any nonaccredited purchasers and must reasonably believe purchasers or their agents are capable of evaluating merits and risks
Manner of offering	No general solicitation	No general solicitation	No general solicitation

Intrastate Offerings

The Securities Act provides an exemption for any security offered and sold only to residents within a single state or territory. To qualify, the issuer of the security must be a resident and doing business within the state or territory. The exemption is quite narrow, as the SEC and the courts have been very strict in their interpretation of "doing business within the state." To take advantage of this exemption, the issuer must do substantial business in the state. In addition, each offeree of the securities must be a resident of the same state; offering the security to a single nonresident invalidates the exemption for the whole issue. This virtually precludes the use of general advertising in the offering because of the possibility of communicating the offer to an out-of-state resident. This exemption was designed for purely local financing for local businesses accomplished by local investment.

Violations

Persons who violate the Securities Act are subject to public remedies, which include injunctions and criminal penalties. Conviction for an offense carries stiff fines and imprisonment.

In addition to public remedies, the Securities Act imposes private remedies against specified persons who violate the act. These sections offer injured investors certain civil remedies in the form of damages for injury. One section makes it unlawful to fail to file a registration statement; another makes misrepresentations in connection with the sale of a security illegal.

Section 11 of the Securities Act imposes liability on certain persons if the registration statement contains material untruths or omissions. The omission or untrue statement must concern a material fact. Such facts include impending litigation or new acquisitions, customers' delinquencies, proposed government controls that would affect the company, and loans to corporate officials.

Persons Liable

The act imposes absolute liability on an issuer for violation of its provisions.[5] In addition, the following persons also may be liable:

- Every person who signed the registration statement.
- Every director of the issuer at the time of registration.
- Every person who consented to being named as a director or a future director.
- Every accountant, appraiser, attorney, or other expert whose statement was used in the preparation of the registration statement.
- Every underwriter.

Defenses

Several defenses are available to defendants. An action predicated on allegations of material untruths or omissions in the registration statement must be brought within one year after discovery has been made by the exercise of reasonable diligence. In no event may an action be brought more than three years from the date of the original offer.

When a defendant can prove that the plaintiff knew of the untruth or omission, the plaintiff's claim fails. In addition, before liability attaches, the plaintiff must establish a relationship between the decline in value of the security and the material untruth or omission. If the two events are wholly unrelated and the defendant can demonstrate that the reduced value of the security resulted from other causes, such as economic trends, the claim would be defeated.

The most popular defense is the **due diligence defense**, available to all persons other than the issuer. Basically, the due diligence defense requires defendants to prove that they exercised ordinary prudence and, nonetheless, were unaware of a material misrepresentation contained in the registration statement. To satisfy the exercise of the due diligence requirement, defendants must conduct independent investigations of portions of the statement not prepared by experts. However, defendants may rely on portions of the statement prepared by experts, such as accountants, as long as they do not have knowledge that the statements are false (see Table 13–4).

---

[5] The Securities Act imposes vicarious liability on "[e]very person who, by or through stock ownership, agency, or otherwise, . . . controls any person liable under section [11] . . . unless the controlling person had no knowledge or reasonable grounds to believe in the existence of the facts by reason of which the liability of the controlled person is alleged to exist." [15 U.S.C. §77(0)(1982).]

TABLE 13–4	**Due Diligence Defense**
Reliance on Registration Statement	*Due Diligence*
Nonexpert	Conduct a reasonable investigation
Expert	Conduct a reasonable investigation only if there is reason to believe information is false

Securities Exchange Act

As previously discussed, the Securities Act of 1933 regulates the offering of original securities by requiring that they be registered. The Federal Trade Commission was responsible for the act's enforcement until Congress passed the Securities Exchange Act of 1934 (Exchange Act). That act created the Securities and Exchange Commission (SEC) to administer federal securities laws. The Exchange Act regulates the secondary trading of securities (as opposed to their original sale) by regulating those involved in the securities industry (see Figure 13–1). This section explores several specific areas regulated by the Exchange Act, including:

- Registration of securities traded in secondary markets
- The use of proxies
- Attempts to take over corporate control
- Corporate insiders
- Fraudulent activities
- Remedies for violations

Registration and Reporting

The Exchange Act requires that, unless exempt, any equity or debt security must be registered to be traded on a national securities exchange. An equity security is any stock or similar security that evidences an ownership interest to the equity security holder in the issuing company. A debt security is any bond or similar security that makes the issuing company a debtor to the security holder. The issuer of these securities must file a registration statement with the exchange where listed and with the SEC.

The Exchange Act also requires the registration with the SEC of any equity security that will not be traded on an exchange but will be traded in the over-the-counter market, if the issuer (1) is engaged in a business that affects interstate commerce or uses interstate facilities for trading in the security; (2) has more than $3 million in assets; and (3) has at least 500 shareholders. A security registered under the Securities Act must still be registered under the Exchange Act if it is to be traded in a secondary market. The Securities Act registration permits the initial sale of the security. The Exchange Act registration permits the security to be resold in secondary markets.

Periodic Disclosure

The Exchange Act was designed to ensure the continuing availability of adequate information about publicly traded securities, since trading is ongoing. To further that design, the registrant must update its registration with the annual, quarterly, and as-needed reports summarized in Table 13–5. Generally, SEC Form **10-K** must be filed within 90 days after the end of the fiscal period. It includes current audited financial statements and information regarding the operations of the business and the status of its securities. Form 10-Q must be filed quarterly. It includes an unaudited summary of the financial changes that have occurred in the registrant's finances, management, and securities since the preceding report was made. Much of the information to be included in forms 10-K and 10-Q may incorporate by reference the company's annual and quarterly shareholders' report. Form 8-K must be filed to disclose materially important events, such as a change in the control of the registrant, a change in the registrant's certifying accountants, bankruptcy, or the resignation of a director.

Integration of Disclosure

Disclosure requirements for the Securities Act and the Exchange Act have been integrated by standardizing the disclosure forms required under each act. Companies issuing securities and having reported under the Exchange Act for at least three years are permitted to incorporate information from their Exchange Act filings by reference to their periodic reports or their annual reports to shareholders. This saves them time and money

Proxy Rules

Most shareholders do not attend the shareholders' meeting; in fact, only a very small proportion do. The nonattending shareholders delegate their voting rights to others who attend. This is called *voting by proxy*. Proxy voting is the principal

TABLE 13–5   Reporting Requirements

Form	Frequency	Contents
10-K	Annually	Audited financial statements; information about operation of business
10-Q	Quarterly	Unaudited financial summary
8-K	As needed	Disclosure of materially important events

method of voting corporate shares in the United States. A proxy is a document that grants an agent authority to vote for a shareholder. The Exchange Act and the commission's rules regulate proxy solicitation to prevent management and others from obtaining or maintaining corporate control through deception or inadequate disclosure. The Exchange Act also requires management to make certain disclosures to shareholders even if it solicits no proxies.

Proxy Statements

Under the commission's rules, no proxies may be solicited unless the solicitor furnishes prescribed information to the shareholders in the form of **proxy statements**. Some of the information is general, for example, the names of the persons making the solicitation, the interest of the solicitors regarding the matters to be considered at the shareholders' meeting, and the vote required on specific matters. Other required disclosure concerns specific proposals, such as information about nominees and directors when an election of board members is on the agenda of the shareholders' meeting.

Proxy contests necessitate the filing of additional information, and special procedures govern the fight for management control. The opponents to management must file a proxy statement and information about those participating in the fight. Management must provide its opponents with a list of the shareholders or mail the proxy material to the shareholders at the opponents' expense. It is unlawful to solicit proxies by means of a proxy statement that is false or misleading with respect to a material fact.

Information Statements

Corporations with securities registered under the Exchange Act are required to make disclosures to their shareholders even if they are soliciting no proxies. These disclosures are made in an information statement. The statement includes a notice of the date, time, and place of the shareholders' meeting and states that proxies are not being solicited. It also discloses the interest of certain persons involved in any matter to be voted on and presents the proposals of security holders.

When a proxy or information statement relates to voting for directors, stockholders must be supplied with annual reports containing financial statements for the last two years. An agenda of the proposals expected to be considered at the shareholders' meeting must also be included in the statement, along with a place for the shareholders' approval or disapproval for each proposal.

Shareholder Proposals

The Exchange Act gives each shareholder the right to make a proposal at the shareholders' meeting. The shareholder must notify management of the proposal, and management must include the proposal in the proxy statement and give the shareholders the right to vote on it. If management opposes the proposal, the shareholder is entitled to include a written rationale for the proposal in the proxy statement. Management may exclude a proposal from consideration if it violates the law; is a personal, political, or social grievance not related to the corporation's business; relates to ordinary business operations; relates to elections; or is identical or similar to a recent proposal that was defeated by a wide margin.

Takeover Bid

Various techniques may be used to acquire a controlling interest in a company. A proxy contest may divest current management of its control, but such contests are expensive and usually unsuccessful. An alternate strategy involves publicly offering cash or securities to stockholders in return for their stock. This action is called a **takeover bid**, or *tender offer*. The subject of a takeover attempt is called the *target company*. The company attempting the takeover is referred to as the *tender offeror*.

Courted with inflated purchase offers for their stock, shareholders are often the pawns in takeover contests. The tender offeror may or may not be interested in the welfare of the target company. If the target company has fallen prey to the tender offeror because of its own mismanagement, however, the takeover could benefit the target company's shareholders and its market. In any case, market manipulation, coercion, and confusion are natural by-products of takeover contests.

A tender offeror that attempts to take over a company by making a public offer to exchange its own securities for the stock of the target company is governed by the Securities Act and must comply with its registration requirements. The Williams Act, an amendment to the Exchange Act, also regulates tender offers.

Under the Williams Act, a person or group that acquires more than 5 percent of a class of securities registered under the Exchange Act is required to file a statement with the SEC and the issuer of the securities. The act also stipulates that no one may make a tender offer for more than 5 percent of a class of securities without first filing a statement with the SEC. In both cases the statement must include the background of the person or entity; the number of shares owned; the source of the funds for the acquisition; the purpose of the acquisition; the tender offeror's plans for the target company; and information regarding agreements between the tender offeror and any person related to the target company. The target company that is attempting to ward off its attacker must also comply with the same filing and disclosure provisions.

Under the Williams Act it is unlawful to omit any material facts; to make any untrue or misleading statements of such facts; or to engage in "fraudulent, deceptive, or manipulative acts or practices" in extending or opposing a tender offer.

Control of Corporate Insiders

Registration of a security under the Exchange Act also subjects certain corporate insiders to requirements and to liability for short-swing profits. By definition, insiders are directors, officers, and 10 percent owners of an issuer with equity securities registered under the Exchange Act. Officers include the president, chief executive officer, financial officers, vice presidents in charge of business units, and any other person who makes policy decisions for the company.

Because of their positions, insiders within a corporation may acquire information that, when made public, affects the value of the corporation's securities. To realize profits, insiders familiar with the ultimate market impact of the information might trade before the information is publicly circulated. For example, as a result of attending a board meeting, a corporate director may learn that the company has just made a valuable mineral ore find. By purchasing that stock before the information becomes public, the director would realize profits.

The Exchange Act seeks to prevent such uses of inside information. Under the act, an insider is liable for any profits made on the sale or purchase of equity securities within a six-month period. These short-swing profits are conclusively presumed to be a direct result of inside advantage. The fact that they did not result from inside information is no defense.

It is very unlikely that an insider would voluntarily surrender short-swing profits. However, the corporation can recover those profits by suing the insider, or shareholders can also sue on behalf of the corporation to recover inside profits. To facilitate the enforcement by or on behalf of the corporation, directors, officers, and 10 percent owners are required to register with the SEC and file periodic reports disclosing their portfolio of corporate holdings, and changes in ownership of securities.

Short-swing profits are calculated by matching the lowest purchase price for a class of securities against the highest sale price. This yields the highest possible profit. Insiders may not offset their losses (see Figure 13–2).

FIGURE 13–2   Calculation of Short-Swing Profits

On February 1, Insider purchased 200 shares of Megaton stock at $30 a share.
On March 1, Insider sold 200 shares of Megaton stock at $20 a share.
On April 1, Insider purchased 200 shares of Megaton stock at $40 a share.
On May 1, Insider sold 200 shares of Megaton stock at $50 a share.

Sold 200 shares at $50 a share	$10,000
Purchased 200 shares at $30 a share	6,000
Profit	4,000
Sold 200 shares at $20 a share	$ 4,000
Purchased 200 shares at $40 a share	8,000
Loss	$ (4,000)

Because losses are not taken into consideration, Insider is liable for $4,000 short-swing profits, even though he broke even on the transactions.

Fraudulent Activities

The Exchange Act includes various provisions that prohibit securities fraud. The act authorizes the SEC to enact rules and regulations to combat fraud in connection with the purchase or sale of securities. Under that authority, the commission adopted **Rule 10b-5** prohibiting fraud during the purchase or sale of a security.

Securities and Exchange Commission Rule 10b-5

It shall be unlawful for any person, directly or indirectly, by the use of any means or instrumentality of interstate commerce, or of the mails, or of any facility of any national securities exchange,

1. To employ any device, or scheme, or artifice to defraud,
2. To make any untrue statement of a material fact or to omit to state a material fact necessary in order to make the statements made, in the light of the circumstances under which they were made, not misleading, or
3. To engage in any act, practice, or course of business which operates or would operate as a fraud or deceit upon any person, in connection with the purchase or sale of any security.

Rule 10b-5 applies to fraud in connection with any sale or purchase of securities, including exchanges of stock and mergers.[6] The rule has been invoked to impose liability on deceptive tender offerors and target companies. Rule 10b-5 has also been applied to the area of **inside trading**. In the landmark case of *SEC v. Texas Gulf Sulphur,* officers and employees of the company purchased stock after learning that exploratory drilling on the company's property gave evidence of a significant ore discovery.[7] They failed to disclose this information to the sellers of the stock and were found in violation of Rule 10b-5.

Originally, the scope of insider liability for nondisclosure was confined to officers and directors of corporations who traded their securities on inside nonpublic information. Now it has evolved to encompass others who gain access to and trade on material nonpublic information without making disclosure. The concept is far broader than the class of insiders subject to the short-swing profit regulations previously discussed. It recently has been applied to Wall Street financiers and large stock brokerage firms.

The expansion is designed to promote the federal regulatory policy of ensuring that everyone has equal access to material information necessary for informed decision making. The broad application of Rule 10b-5 manifests a concern for fairness in the marketplace. Private investors are less inclined to participate in market trading if they believe that others have a strategic advantage because of access

---

[6] In the 1960s and 1970s the rule was interpreted to include liability for negligent conduct. That line of cases has since been reversed. [Ernst & Ernst v. Hochfelder, 425 U.S. 185 (1976).]

[7] 401 F. 2d 833 (2d Cir. 1968).

to information generally unavailable. When this happens, the market's integrity is undermined.

In *Shapiro v. Merrill Lynch, Pierce, Fenner & Smith, Inc.,* the stock brokerage firm, while preparing an offering of stock for Douglas Aircraft Company, learned from some Douglas officers, directors, and employees about unfavorable conditions that would affect Douglas's earnings.[8]

The information was not yet public. Merrill Lynch disclosed the information to some of its customers. These customers sold their holdings in Douglas, or otherwise improved their positions, without disclosing the information to the purchasers. The court held that both Merrill Lynch, the tipper, and the favored customers, the tippees, were liable to the specific purchasers of the shares sold on the basis of Merrill Lynch's information. They were also liable to all those who purchased Douglas stock without benefit of the material information in the defendants' hands. *Shapiro* sounds a warning not only to nontrading tippers but also to trading tippees, who trade on information they know or have reason to know is not public and was wrongfully obtained.

Ethical Dilemmas/Issues

Henry Schum is a sales representative for Intercontinental Business Computer, Inc., a U.S. corporation. His sales territory includes Germany; thus, although he is a U.S. citizen, Henry Schum lives in Germany.

While calling on an executive at the Deutschland Wunderkind, a toy manufacturer in Germany, Schum learns that Wunderkind is planning to merge with a large Hong Kong toy company. The resulting firm could virtually dominate the European and Asian toy markets. Schum's contact has assured him that his information is accurate and, as yet, not public. Deutschland Wunderkind's stock is traded on the German Stock Exchange.

Hong Kong has repealed its prohibitions against trading on inside information. Germany relies on voluntary inside trading guidelines; the practice is proscribed but not illegal. These guidelines are enforced through employment contracts. It is the firm's choice whether to enforce the contract. Deutschland Wunderkind's contract includes a prohibition against insider trading by its employees, but it has never fired an employee or sued to enforce this provision in its employment contract. If Henry Schum makes a large purchase of Deutschland Wunderkind stock, he stands to make a large profit when he sells the stock after the merger.

What are the ethical issues? What would you do?

---

[8] 495 F. 2d 228 (2d Cir. 1974).

Dirks v. SEC established the parameters of tippee liability. Dirks was an officer of a broker-dealer firm. He received information from a former officer of Equity Funding about fraudulent corporate activities. Dirks investigated the activities and spread the news of the fraud.

The SEC censured Dirks for violating Rule 10b-5 by repeating the fraud allegations to people who later sold their stock in Equity Funding before the information became public, and the stock prices fell. The U.S. Supreme Court overturned the censure, reasoning that Dirks did not receive the information from an insider who breached a fiduciary duty to the shareholders. This is true because the tipper did not stand to benefit financially or otherwise by the revelation; and

> absent a breach by the insider there is no derivative . . . [duty by the tippee].
>
> [A] tippee assumes a fiduciary duty to the shareholders of a corporation not to trade on material nonpublic information only when the insider has breached his fiduciary duty to the shareholders by disclosing the information to the tippee and the tippee knows or should know that there has been a breach. . . .
>
> [T]he test is whether the insider personally will benefit, directly, or indirectly, from his disclosure. Absent some personal gain, there has been no breach of duty to stockholders. And absent a breach by the insider there is no derivative [duty by the tippee]. . . .
>
> [W]e believe that there must be a breach of the insider's fiduciary duty before the tippee inherits the duty to disclose or abstain.[9]

The following case involving a Wall Street reporter who took advantage of a securities column he wrote and was charged with securities fraud applies the 10b-5 principles derived from Dirks.

UNITED STATES V. CARPENTER
791 F. 2d 1024 (1986)

Winans, a reporter for *The Wall Street Journal,* wrote its Heard on the Street (Heard) column. Carpenter worked as a news clerk at the *Journal.* Felis and Brant were stockbrokers at the brokerage firm of Kidder Peabody. The Heard column discussed stocks, giving information about those stocks and expressing an opinion respecting investment in those stocks.

The Wall Street Journal had a company policy that all news gleaned during the scope of employment was confidential. Winans and Carpenter were aware of this policy. Nonetheless, they participated in a scheme whereby Winans agreed to provide Felis and Brant with securities information scheduled to appear in the Heard columns. Based on that information, the two brokers would buy or sell the securities. Carpenter acted as a messenger among Winans, Felis, and Brant. The scheme netted profits amounting to about $690,000.

---

[9] 463 U.S. 646 (1983).

Winans and Felis (appellants) were charged with and convicted of securities fraud for misappropriating material nonpublic information in connection with the purchase and sale of securities. Carpenter (appellant) was convicted of aiding and abetting in the fraud. They appealed to the United States Court of Appeals for the Second Circuit, which affirmed securities fraud convictions.

Judge Pierce

This case requires us to decide principally whether a newspaper reporter, a former newspaper clerk, and a stockbroker, acting in concert, criminally violated or conspired to violate or aided and abetted in the violation of federal securities laws by misappropriating material, nonpublic information in the form of the timing and the content of *The Wall Street Journal*'s confidential schedule of columns . . . in contravention of the established policy of the newspaper, for their own profit in connection with the purchase and sale of securities.

Although the facts render the securities fraud issue herein one of first impression, we do not write on a clean slate in assessing whether this case falls within the purview of the "misappropriation" theory of section 10(b) and Rule 10b-5 thereunder. . . . It is clear that defendant Winans, an employee of *The Wall Street Journal,* breached a duty of confidentiality to his employer by misappropriating from the *Journal* confidential pre-publication information, regarding the timing and content of certain newspaper columns, about which he learned in the course of his employment. We are presented with the question of whether that unlawful conduct may serve as the predicate for the securities fraud charges hereon.

The core of appellants' argument is that . . . the misappropriation theory may be applied only where the information is misappropriated by corporate insiders or so-called quasi-insiders . . . who owe to the corporation and its shareholders a fiduciary duty of abstention or disclosure. Thus, appellants would have us hold that it was not enough that Winans breached a duty of confidentiality to his employer, *The Wall Street Journal,* in misappropriating and trading on material non-public information; he would have to have breached a duty to the corporations or shareholders thereof whose stock they purchased or sold on the basis of that information.

Although *Dirks* disapproved of certain trading by insiders or quasi-insiders who owe a fiduciary duty to investors, courts are not thereby constrained from recognizing other misconduct. . . . As the district court correctly stated, "[i]t is not accurate to say that *Dirks* wrote the book on insider or outsider trading; it wrote one chapter with respect to one type of fraudulent trading. . . ."

The legislative intent of the 1934 Act is . . . broad reaching. As this Court has noted in applying the misappropriation theory, "the antifraud provision was intended to be broad in scope, encompassing all 'manipulative and deceptive practices which have been demonstrated to fulfill no useful function.'" We perceive nothing "useful" about defendants' scheme. Nor, in our view, could any purported function of the scheme be considered protected given Congress' stated concern for the perception of fairness and integrity in the securities markets and the potential costs of forsaking such legislated concerns, including fewer market participants and greater reliance on fraud as a means of competing in the market. . . .

Obviously, one may gain a competitive advantage in the marketplace through conduct constituting skill, foresight, industry and the like. Certainly this is as true in securities law as in antitrust, patent, trademark, copyright and other fields. But one may not gain such advantage by conduct constituting secreting, stealing, purloining or otherwise misappropriating material nonpublic information in breach of an employer-imposed fiduciary duty of confidentiality. Such conduct constitutes chicanery, not competition; foul play, not fair play. Indeed, underlying section 10(b) and the major securities laws generally is the fundamental promotion of " 'the highest ethical standards' . . . in every facet of the securities industry. . . ."

The information misappropriated here was the *Journal*'s own confidential schedule of forthcoming publications. It was the advance knowledge of the timing and content of these publications, upon which appellants, acting secretively, reasonably expected to and did realize profits in securities transactions. Since section 10(b) has been found to provide fraudulent trading by insiders or outsiders, such conduct constituted fraud and deceit, as it would had Winans stolen material nonpublic information from traditional corporate insiders or quasi-insiders. Felis' liability as a tippee derives from Winans' liability given the district court's finding of the requisite scienter on Felis' part.

Nor is there any doubt that this "fraud and deceit" was perpetrated "upon a[ny] person" under section 10(b) and Rule 10b-5. It is sufficient that the fraud was committed upon Winans' employer. Appellants Winans, and Felis and Carpenter by their complicity, perpetrated their fraud "upon" *The Wall Street Journal,* sullying its reputation and thereby defrauding it "as surely as if they took [its] money."

Thus, because of his duty of confidentiality to the *Journal,* defendant Winans—and Felis and Carpenter, who knowingly participated with him—had a corollary duty, which they breached under section 10(b) and Rule 10b-5, to abstain from trading in securities on the basis of the misappropriated information or to do so only upon making adequate disclosure to those with whom they traded.

[The case was reviewed by the United States Supreme Court, which was evenly divided on the issue of securities convictions. For that reason the court of appeals' judgment was affirmed.]

Case Questions

1. What is the misappropriation theory? What argument did appellants make as to why the misappropriation theory was not applicable in this case?

2. Which information was misappropriated? Against whom was the fraud perpetuated? How did it injure the victim? How could appellants have lawfully traded on the information?

3. Could *The Wall Street Journal* trade on the information before its public release without running afoul of Rule 10b-5? Explain. What if the *Journal* did not have a policy regarding confidentiality? Could the appellants then have done what they did without violating securities fraud laws?

4. The court speaks about fairness and integrity in the securities market. Is it fair that this case was one of first impression and it resulted in criminal convictions being upheld? Explain.

5. How can this case be distinguished from *Dirks*?

Remedies

The Exchange Act imposes liability on violators. It also imposes liability on everyone who controls a person who violates the act.[10] A controlling person may avoid

---

[10] *Controlling person* is defined in footnote 5.

liability if he or she acted in good faith and did not induce the acts constituting the violation.

Willful violations of most provisions of the Exchange Act carry criminal penalties of stiff fines and imprisonment. Civil liabilities imposed under the Exchange Act are of two kinds. First, the Securities and Exchange Commission may enforce the act by taking administrative action or by instituting an action in a federal district court to compel compliance or enjoin violations. Second, purchasers or sellers of securities that have been injured as a result of an Exchange Act violation may bring suit in the federal courts. The complaint may demand relief in the form of an injunction to prevent or stop the prohibited conduct. The plaintiff may also seek damages for injury. These private civil remedies are predicated on the antifraud provisions in the Exchange Act and SEC rules.

The Insider Trading Sanctions Act creates an additional remedy against inside traders. Under this act, the SEC may seek a civil penalty up to "three times the profit gained or loss avoided as a result of such unlawful purchase or sale." Private parties may not seek relief under the act—only the SEC.

Antifraud provisions may create an express or implied cause of action. Several sections in the Securities Exchange Act provide for express civil remedies. We have already examined liability of an insider who acquires a short-swing profit. In addition, another section of the Exchange Act prohibits the manipulation of security prices. It provides an express remedy for the sellers and purchasers against the manipulator. These remedies have short statutes of limitations; in addition, plaintiffs invoking them find it difficult to prove that the violation caused the price change in the security. Consequently, express remedies are not often used by private parties.

Implied remedies do not have the same shortcomings as express remedies. The basis of an implied remedy is a finding that a legislative act that does not recognize an express right nonetheless implies a cause of action in favor of an injured party. A great majority of securities cases involving implied causes of actions are brought under Rule 10b-5. Although this rule does not expressly provide for private remedies, nonetheless the SEC and the courts have interpreted the rule to afford injured parties a remedy.

The Uniform Securities Act adopted by some states incorporates the wording of Rule 10b-5. Even states that have not adopted the act have a general antifraud provision authorizing criminal sanctions against violators and granting government officials the power to enjoin fraudulent activities. Violation of a state's antifraud provision may also be a basis for civil remedies by injured parties.

The Sarbanes-Oxley Act

The Sarbanes-Oxley Act of 2002 (SOX) provides for government regulation of public accounting firms, independent director oversight of the audit process, executive accountability for the financial reporting process, and increased corporate responsibility for governance. A violation of the act is treated as a violation of the Securities and Exchange Act.

The Public Company Accounting Oversight Board

The statute establishes the Public Company Accounting Oversight Board (Oversight Board) to oversee the audit of public companies that are subject to the federal securities laws. This oversight is to protect the interests of investors and further the public interest in the preparation of informative, accurate and independent audit reports for public companies.

SOX provides for the registration of public accounting firms. Only registered public accounting firms may prepare or issue audit reports for a public reporting company. Public accounting firms must apply for registration with the Oversight Board. The law forbids a registered accounting firm that performs an audit for a public company to provide at the same time non-auditing services. Non-auditing services include bookkeeping, designing and implementing financial information systems, appraisals, actuarial services, internal audit outsourcing, management or human resources functions, investment advising, legal services, and expert services related to the audit.

The Oversight Board adopts auditing standards, periodically inspects accounting firms, conducts investigations and disciplinary proceedings, and enforces compliance with SOX. It conducts annual quality reviews for public accounting firms that audit more than 100 public companies, and every three years for other accounting firms.

The Oversight Board may investigate firms and associated persons for violations of SOX, the Oversight Board's rules, or the federal securities laws. It may sanction an accounting firm if the firm fails to reasonably supervise any associated person with regard to auditing or quality control standards. Sanctions include suspension of registration, civil monetary penalties, and training. The Oversight Board findings and sanctions are subject to review by the Securities and Exchange Commission (SEC).

Public Company Audit Committees

SOX effectively requires that public companies have an audit committee created from their board of directors. An audit committee is established from the board of directors of a public company to oversee the accounting and financial reporting processes of the company and to audit the company's financial statements. A company cannot avoid audit committee responsibilities by not having an audit company. If there is not an audit committee of the independent directors designated by the board, the statute designates the entire board of directors as the audit committee.

The audit committee is responsible for hiring, firing and compensating the auditors. It oversees the auditor's work and resolves disagreements with management. It must establish procedures for receiving complaints, including anonymous submissions by employees. It also engages independent legal counsel and other advisers funded by the company. Audit committee members must be independent, meaning that they cannot accept any consulting, advisory, or other compensatory fee from the company or be an affiliated person of the company or its subsidiary.

The company must disclose whether it has at least one audit committee financial expert serving on its audit committee, and if so, the name of the expert and whether the expert is independent of management. A company that does not have an audit committee financial expert must disclose this fact and explain why not.

Under SOX, the audit committee must pre-approve all services provided by the company's auditors. SOX requires that the company's auditors report to the audit committee all critical accounting policies and practices used and alternative treatments as well as the treatment preferred by the accounting firm. The auditors must report to the audit committee any disagreements with management. Other written material communications between the auditors and management must also be reported to the audit committee.

The statute requires the company attorney to report to the audit committee in certain situations. If the attorney has evidence of violations of the securities laws or breach of fiduciary duty, the attorney must inform the chief legal counsel of the CEO of the company of the violation. If the legal counsel or the CEO does not respond by adopting remedial measures, the attorney must report the evidence to the audit committee.

The audit committee must receive complaints received by the company regarding accounting, internal accounting controls, or auditing matters, including anonymous submissions by employees. As a result of this requirement, most public companies have a company hot line for anonymous reporting to the audit committee.

Corporate Governance and Disclosure Requirements

SOX establishes corporate leadership responsibility for financial reports. The company's chief executive officer (CEO) and the chief financial officer (CFO) must certify the company's periodic financial reports to the SEC. With each form 10-Q and 10-K, among others, the CEO and CFO must certify:

- They reviewed the report
- The accuracy and completeness of the financial report
- The report fairly presents the company's financial condition
- They are responsible for the company's internal controls
- They have evaluated within the last 90 days the effectiveness of the company's internal controls
- They have reported deficiencies in the financial reports to the audit committee and the auditors

It is unlawful for an officer or director of the company to fraudulently influence, coerce, manipulate or mislead any auditor for the purpose of rendering financial statements materially misleading. This also includes any person acting under the direction of a company officer or director.

Under SOX, public company financial reports must reflect all material correcting adjustments identified by the company's auditors. Each annual and quarterly report must disclose all material off-balance sheet transactions, arrangements and obligations. Pro forma information must be presented so as to not contain an untrue statement or omit a material fact. Pro forma financial statements include projections into the future—they are found often in business plans and financial reports of potential mergers and acquisitions.

SOX requires company management report on internal controls in each annual report. The auditors must attest to and report on management's assertions regarding the internal controls.

Company insiders (directors, officers and 10% shareholders) must report transactions in the company's securities by the end of the second business day following the transaction.

SOX also requires real-time disclosure of certain company information. Companies must disclose additional information concerning material changes in their financial condition or operations on a rapid and current basis. This real-time disclosure must be in plain English.

SOX requires each public company disclose whether it has adopted a code of ethics for senior financial officers and the content of the code. There are immediate disclosure requirements through filing a Form 8-K with the SEC, or by the internet, for any change in, or waiver of, the company's code of ethics.

SOX prohibits personal loans to executives. It is unlawful for a public company to extend credit to any director or executive officer.

Enforcement and Penalties

The SEC is directed by SOX to review financial statements and disclosures of public companies on a regular and systematic basis. The minimum review period is every three years. More frequent review can occur based on the statute's review criteria.

TABLE 13–6   **Some Key Provisions of the Sarbanes-Oxley Act (SOX)**

- Requires securities exchanges not list any security of a company not in compliance with requirements regarding company audit committees.
- Requires a company's chief executive officer (CEO) and chief financial officer (CFO) certify the company's financial reports.
- Requires reports filed with the SEC reflect material correcting adjustments identified by the company's accounting firm, disclose material off-balance sheet transactions, and present financial information in a manner that is not misleading.
- Requires a company's management establish and maintain adequate internal financial controls and procedures for financial reporting.
- Requires the company disclose in annual reports whether it has adopted a code of ethics for senior financial officers and, if not, the reasons why.
- Requires real-time reporting of the company's financial condition and operation in plain English.
- Protects employees who report security law violations by their employer.

If a restatement of a financial report is required, SOX requires the CEO and the CFO reimburse the company for incentive-based or equity-based compensation and any profits realized from the sale of the company's securities within the last year. The SEC can also prohibit a person who is found "unfit" because of a violation of the federal securities laws from serving as an officer or director of a public company.

Violations of the requirements regarding the CEO and CFO certifications are subject to criminal penalties of up to five million dollars in fines and imprisonment of up to 20 years.

The SEC requires a public accountant who conducts an audit to maintain all audit or review work papers for seven years. It is a felony for anyone to destroy documents or create documents to impede, obstruct or influence an investigation.

It is also a felony to retaliate against whistleblowers.

International Securities Regulation

Most countries' securities laws are not as comprehensive and stringent as U.S. securities laws. Hence, firms may be enticed to relocate by lax securities laws in other countries. For this reason, the United States has desired to see a globalization of securities laws, with the United States as a model. This has not happened; however, the International Securities Enforcement and Cooperation Act (ISECA) is a step closer.

The ISECA seeks bilateral cooperation between the SEC and other countries. The act empowers the SEC to provide officials of a foreign country with information on securities violations when that country has agreed to reciprocate. In addition, the ISECA authorizes the SEC to investigate securities violations in other countries and impose sanctions against securities professionals who violate foreign securities laws.

The ISECA is based upon mutual cooperation and reciprocity. Its values will be directly proportional to the degree to which other nations see the need for stricter securities laws and enforcement.

Chapter Problems

1. Define the following concepts and terms:
   a. Security
   b. Prospectus
   c. Shelf registration
   d. Private placement
   e. Due diligence defense
   f. Form 10-K
   g. Proxy statements

     h. Takeover bid

     i. Rule 10b-5

     j. Inside trading

2. Koscot Interplanetary, Inc. has set up a multilevel network of independent distributors engaged in selling a line of cosmetics. The beauty advisor is at the lowest level. Beauty advisors may purchase products from Koscot at a 45 percent discount. At the second level is a beauty supervisor. For a $1,000 investment, the supervisor receives a 55 percent discount on products. A supervisor receives $600 for introducing a prospect who buys into the program at the beauty supervisor level. At the top of the program is a beauty distributor. For an investment of $5,000, the distributor may purchase products at 65 percent discount. The distributor is also entitled to $600 or $3,000, respectively, for bringing in prospects who later buy a supervisor's or distributor's position.

     Those who have invested in the Koscot plan bring prospects to opportunity meetings, where they are introduced to the program. At that meeting, Koscot employees sell the prospects on the program, and investors sometimes participate directly in the sales pitch. They are required to follow a Koscot manual that instructs them to drive to the meetings in expensive cars, dress fashionably, and flaunt large sums of money. Those who do not follow the manual verbatim can be dismissed from participation.

     Analyze the scheme and explain why Koscot is offering a security. How could Koscot structure the offering to avoid registration?

3. Hocking was interested in purchasing a condominium in Hawaii as an investment. Dubois, a real estate broker, found a suitable unit located in a resort complex. The complex had been developed by Aetna Life Insurance Company (Aetna) and managed by the Hawaii Corporation of the Pacific (HCP). Aetna and HCP offered those who purchased units participation in a rental pool agreement, whereby all those within the pool would divide the income pro rata regardless of whether their unit rented. Hocking purchased the unit and entered into the rental pool agreement. Is Dubois subject to the antifraud requirements of the securities laws? Explain.

4. The Bangor Punta Corporation was contemplating issuing a block of securities. Bangor prepared to file a registration statement covering the proposed distribution under the Securities Act. Before filing, Bangor issued a press release announcing its intention to issue the securities. The release also stated that "in the judgment of the First Boston Corporation, each share of Bangor stock has a value of not less than $80." Did Bangor's press release violate Section the Securities Act? Explain.

5. Truckee Showboat, Inc. was organized in the state of California. All of its directors and officers are residents of California. It does 90 percent of its business in that state.

     Truckee placed an ad in the *Los Angeles Times* offering to sell 4,080 shares of its stock at $1,000 per share exclusively to bona fide residents of

California. The proceeds from the sales were to be used to purchase, improve, and operate the El Cortez Hotel in Las Vegas, Nevada. Truckee Showboat received a permit to issue the securities from the Commissioner of Corporations of California. No stock was actually purchased. May Truckee take advantage of the intrastate offering exemption? Explain.

6. Winter & Hirsch, Inc. (WH), a consumer finance company, issued short-term promissory notes amounting to $1,612,500. Forty-two investors purchased these notes through John Nuveen & Co., an underwriting firm. Nuveen prepared commercial paper reports on the WH paper and distributed them to investors.

   WH issued fraudulent financial statements. They overstated the accounts receivable by $14 million and omitted $750,000 of indebtedness. The registration statement filed by WH reflected these misrepresentations and omissions. Nuveen was not aware of the fraud. Its commercial paper reports reflected the false WH financial statements.

   WH defaulted on the notes. The buyers of the notes now seek a return of the purchase price. Discuss the possible remedies against WH and Nuveen.

7. On May 23, 1972, Designcraft made a public offering of 300,000 shares of its common stock. The total outstanding common stock of Designcraft, including the 300,000 newly issued shares, was 817,500 shares. William Norton and Company, a broker-dealer in securities, was co-underwriter of the public offering, distributing 250,000 shares itself. The underwriting agreement required Norton to buy the shares from Designcraft and to resell them to the public, a process completed within a few days. At all material times Designcraft was registered pursuant to the Exchange Act. There was no relevant connection between Norton and Designcraft before the underwriting transaction took place. H. Perine, a stockholder of Designcraft, brought an action against Norton under the Exchange Act to recover the short-swing profits earned by Norton in its underwriting of the distribution. Is Norton liable for short-swing profits? Explain.

8. Fred Lowenschuss was a shareholder of Great Atlantic & Pacific Tea Co., Inc. (A&P). He tendered A&P shares to Gulf & Western Industries, Inc. (G&W) in response to G&W's tender offer. The tender offer announced that G&W was willing to purchase up to 3,750,000 shares of A&P common stock (15 percent of its outstanding shares) at $20 per share. G&W held extensive investments in other food processors and distributors, and its acquisition of A&P stock would probably result in a violation of the antitrust laws. Furthermore, evidence indicated that G&W intended to acquire a controlling position in A&P or at least to exercise influence over A&P's management and policies. Neither G&W's holdings nor its intentions regarding control over A&P were disclosed in the tender offer. Devise a strategy that does not violate the Exchange Act to prevent G&W from gaining control of A&P.

9. Basic was a publicly traded corporation engaged in the business of manufacturing chemical refractories for the steel industry. Because Combustion desired to acquire Basic, they engaged in merger negotiations. Basic, however, denied thrice that it was engaged in merger negotiations. Thereafter, a merger by tender offer occurred. Stockholders who changed their position before the merger when the denial occurred brought an action against Basic asserting that the denials were false and misleading under Rule 10b-5 and Section 10(b). What should be the test to determine whether Basic has violated Rule 10b-5? Does it matter whether the misrepresentation is material? How do you define *material*?

10. Because of the sensitivity of tender offer information, tender offerors omit information from printed documents that might identify a target company until the last possible moment. Anthony Materia worked for Bowne, a financial printing firm, as a proofreader. Bowne attempted diligently to communicate the need for secrecy to its employees. Materia was able to determine the identities of four tender offer targets. Within hours of each discovery he bought stocks and then sold them after the tender offer, making profits. Has Materia violated 10b-5? Has Bowne? Explain.

14 SPECIAL TOPICS IN CORPORATE LAW

Learning Objectives

After learning this chapter the student should be able to:

- Identify the most common business crimes.
- Identify the fiduciary duties imposed by law on corporate directors.
- Recognize corporate takeover tactics and defensive techniques.
- Contrast minority squeeze outs and defenses to squeeze outs.
- Recognize issues dealing with corporate social responsibility.

Corporations entrust to corporate directors and officers the power to make policy decisions. It is true that these corporate officials may be strategically situated to breach their trust and commit crimes of greed. Nonetheless, corporate officials are expected to uphold the public trust and conduct themselves as law-abiding citizens.

Directors and officers are required to exercise care and loyalty and to refrain from misappropriating corporate opportunities. Their responsibilities also extend to shareholders and the way in which they treat minority shareholders.

The world of corporate activity has changed drastically over the last few decades. Not only must corporate officials concern themselves with internal corporate affairs but they must also watch their backs to protect the corporation from hostile takeovers. This external threat is accompanied by added responsibilities.

Finally, the legal environment of business is demanding more corporate social awareness. Consequently, corporate officials must anticipate the trend and practice sound social responsibility. All of these topics are treated in this chapter.

Business Crimes

Sometimes referred to as *white-collar crimes,* business crimes are associated with some type of business activity. The nature of business activities may provide particular temptations and opportunities to commit crime. For example, a real estate broker is in a strategic position to wrongfully take clients' monies; an accountant for a business firm is in a position to cheat on income tax returns for the business; a lobbyist who works for a trade association has potential opportunities to bribe public officials.

Business crimes have several features distinguishing them from other crimes. First, these crimes are often particularly difficult to detect because their methods of commission are heavily interconnected with proper commercial practices. Additionally, the crimes may consist of a very complex series of transactional steps difficult for law enforcement to unravel. Hiding illegal funds in foreign bank accounts makes detection even more difficult. For these reasons, business crimes challenge the investigatory and enforcement apparatus of the legal system. Second, business crimes, in contrast to other crimes, more often involve individuals who are economically successful and appear to be upright, law-abiding citizens. Third, the power and political influence of those who commit business crimes often enable them to muster strong legal defenses. Prosecutors overburdened with large caseloads are sometimes forced to forgo lengthy trials; instead, they plea bargain corporate crimes for lesser offenses.

Business crimes come in endless variety. Securities fraud and antitrust violations are treated elsewhere in this book. Discussions of embezzlement, bribery, racketeering, and computer and regulatory crimes follow.

Embezzlement

Embezzlement occurs when a person wrongfully appropriates property entrusted to him or her. This crime is different from ordinary theft, usually referred to as *larceny.* Larceny is the wrongful taking of another's property. For embezzlement to occur, the wrongdoer must first come into lawful possession of the property, whereas, with larceny, the wrongdoer is never in lawful possession of the property.

For example, assume that a janitor of a stock brokerage firm opens the firm's safe and takes $500. This is larceny. However, assume that a stock broker in that firm receives $500 from a customer to deposit in the customer's account and, instead, the broker takes the money. This is embezzlement. In the first case the janitor never lawfully possessed the monies; in the second case the broker lawfully possessed the $500 before the unlawful taking occurred.

Persons in a position to commit embezzlement usually occupy places of high trust. This means that the crime is most often committed by professionals or people in the higher echelons of management.

Estimates of losses due to embezzlement run well into the billions of dollars annually. Each state has laws making embezzlement a crime. Because the crime involves a breach of trust, it usually carries greater penalties than larceny. However, most crimes of embezzlement committed against corporate enterprises never are elevated to the level of a criminal prosecution. To avoid embarrassment and unwanted publicity, the company often settles for firing the employee and/or working out a repayment plan.

Bribery

Bribery is the offering or receiving of anything of value to influence official action. Commercial bribery occurs when bribery is used to acquire sensitive information from a competitor, such as customer lists, new product lines, unpatented secrets, or expansion plans.

Bribing federal officials is a federal crime. In addition, state laws make it a crime to bribe anyone. In the 1970s, widespread bribery of public officials came to light when the Watergate Special Prosecution Force uncovered numerous illegal campaign contributions. Additionally, Abscam, a sting operation, used decoys to film transactions of federal legislators taking bribes. This resulted in passage of federal and state laws known as *anticorrupt practice acts.* These acts typically not only limit the amount of campaign contributions but also require strict reporting and disclosure.

In some foreign countries bribing local officials is an accepted way of doing business. Without such bribes, business slows or comes to a halt. For example, a typical case might involve a large highly competitive project. The size of the project is such that the bribe may be buried in the price of the bid without obvious detection. Until 1977, companies doing business in foreign countries were basically free from domestic prosecution for bribery. In that year, however, Congress passed the **Foreign Corrupt Practices Act**, making it a crime to bribe an official of another country.

The Foreign Corrupt Practices Act establishes accounting procedures making it virtually impossible for companies to attempt to disguise bribes. Violation of the law carries a penalty for companies of up to $2 million and stiff fines and imprisonment for individuals.

"Grease" payments to foreign officials to speed up the governmental process (as opposed to influencing officials to decide favorably) are legal. This includes fees given to low-level bureaucrats to process licenses and stamp documents.

Racketeering and Organized Crime

Organized crime and racketeering involve a structure of individuals who provide illegally obtained goods and services. These individuals use the profits from their activities to expand to other legal and illegal enterprises. Often, they seek to corrupt political officials for the purpose of protecting or furthering their illegal activities.

To combat organized crime, in 1970 Congress enacted the Racketeer Influenced and Corrupt Organizations Act (**RICO**). The primary thrust of the act was the removal of organized Mafia crime from the business community. Its application has been extended, however, to reach beyond organized criminal activity, to businesses of more conventional kinds.

RICO makes it a crime to acquire or operate an enterprise by a pattern of racketeering. The enterprise includes partnerships, corporations, or an informal association of persons who are economically motivated. It may be a legal or illegal enterprise. Private businesses, foreign and domestic corporations, labor organizations, government agencies, drug dealers, and pornographers have all been found to satisfy the enterprise aspect. The offender must additionally be involved in a pattern of racketeering. One act does not create a pattern; the statute requires at least two acts within 10 years. The acts are mentioned within the statute and include such crimes as murder, arson, bribery, extortion, illegal drug dealing, embezzlement, fraud, and securities violations (see Table 14–1).

TABLE 14–1	RICO Predicate Acts	
• Murder	• Drug trafficking
• Kidnapping	• Securities fraud
• Prostitution	• Mail or wire fraud
• Robbery	• Gambling
• Arson	• Extortion
• Bribery	• Pornography
• Counterfeiting	• Obstruction of justice
• Money laundering	• Interstate transportation of stolen property

The following case, involving alleged bribery of administrative agency officials, defines the term *pattern of racketeering.*

H.J. Inc. v. Northwestern Bell Telephone Co.
492 U.S. 229 (1989)

Petitioners are customers of Northwestern Bell Telephone Co. (respondent). They filed a class action against Northwestern Bell seeking injunctive and damage remedies under RICO's civil liability provisions. They alleged that Northwestern Bell bribed members of the Minnesota Public Utilities Commission (MPUC) and caused them to approve rates for the company in excess of a fair and reasonable amount. They alleged that Northwestern Bell derived income from a pattern of racketeering activity involving this bribery and that it used the income to engage in its business as an interstate enterprise.

The District Court dismissed petitioner's complaint on the basis that there was no pattern of racketeering activity. The Court of Appeals for the Eighth Circuit affirmed the dismissal. The U.S. Supreme Court granted certiorari and reversed.

Justice Brennan

The Racketeer Influenced and Corrupt Organizations Act (RICO or the Act) . . . imposes criminal and civil liability upon those who engage in certain "prohibited activities." Each prohibited activity is defined . . . to include, as one necessary element, proof either of "a pattern of racketeering activity" or of "collection of an unlawful debt." "Racketeering activity" is defined in RICO to mean "any act or threat involving" specified state-law crimes, any "act" indictable under various specified federal statutes and certain federal "offenses," . . . but of the term "pattern" the statute says only that it "requires at least two acts of racketeering activity" within a 10-year period. . . . We are called upon in this civil case to consider what conduct meets RICO's pattern requirement.

RICO renders criminally and civilly liable "any person" who uses or invests income derived "from a pattern of racketeering activity" to acquire an interest in or to operate an enterprise engaged in

interstate commerce . . . who acquires or maintains an interest in or control of such an enterprise "through a pattern of racketeering activity." . . . RICO provides for drastic remedies: conviction for a violation of RICO carries severe criminal penalties and forfeiture of illegal proceeds . . . and a person found in a private civil action to have violated RICO is liable for treble damages, costs, and attorney's fees. . . .

■   ■   ■

In *Sedima* this Court rejected a restrictive interpretation that would have made it a condition for maintaining a civil RICO action both that the defendant had already been convicted of a predicate racketeering act or of a RICO violation, and that plaintiff show a special racketeering injury. . . .

■   ■   ■

The legislative history, which we discussed in *Sedima,* shows that Congress indeed has a fairly flexible concept of a pattern in mind. A pattern is not formed by "sporadic activity," and a person cannot "be subjected to the sanctions . . . simply for committing two widely separated and isolated criminal offenses. . . . Instead, "[t]he term 'pattern' itself requires the showing of a relationship" between the predicates, and of "'the threat of continuing activity.'" . . . "It is this factor of *continuity plus relationship* which combines to produce a pattern." RICO's legislative history reveals Congress' intent that to prove a pattern of racketeering activity a plaintiff or prosecutor must show that the racketeering predicates are related, *and* that they amount to or pose a threat of continued criminal activity. . . .

■   ■   ■

RICO's legislative history tells us, however, that the relatedness of racketeering activities is not alone enough to satisfy [the] pattern element. To establish a RICO pattern it must also be shown that the predicates themselves amount to, or that they otherwise constitute a threat of, *continuing* racketeering activity. . . .

■   ■   ■

It is argued that Congress' purpose in enacting RICO, as revealed in the Act's title . . . and in the legislative history, was to combat organized crime; and that RICO's broad language should be read narrowly so that the Act's scope is coextensive with this purpose. We cannot accept this argument for a narrowing construction of the Act's expansive terms.

■   ■   ■

Congress drafted RICO broadly enough to encompass a wide range of criminal activity, taking many different forms and likely to attract a broad array of perpetrators operating in many different ways. It would be counterproductive and a mismeasure of congressional intent now to adopt a narrow construction of the statute's pattern element that would require proof of an organized crime nexus.

■   ■   ■

Petitioners' complaint alleges that at different times over the course of at least a 6-year period the noncommissioner respondents gave five members of the MPUC numerous bribes, in several different forms, with the objective—in which they were allegedly successful—of causing these Commissioners to approve unfair and unreasonable rates for Northwestern Bell. RICO defines bribery as a "racketeering activity," so petitioners have alleged multiple predicate acts.

Under the analysis we have set forth above, and consistent with the allegations in their complaint, petitioners may be able to prove that the multiple . . . [acts] constitute "a pattern of racketeering activity," in that they satisfy the requirements of relationship and continuity. The acts of bribery alleged are said to be related by a common purpose, to influence Commissioners in carrying out their duties in order to win approval of unfairly and unreasonably high rates for Northwestern Bell. Furthermore, petitioners claim that the racketeering predicates occurred with some frequency over at least a 6-year period, which may be sufficient to satisfy the continuity requirement. Alternatively, a threat of continuity of racketeering activity might be established at trial by showing that the alleged bribes were a regular way of conducting Northwestern Bell's ongoing business, or a regular way of conducting or participating in the conduct of the alleged and ongoing RICO enterprise, the MPUC.

The Court of Appeals thus erred in affirming the District Court's dismissal of petitioners' complaint for failure to plead "a pattern of racketeering activity." The judgment is reversed and the case is remanded for further proceedings consistent with this opinion.

Case Questions

1. How does RICO define a pattern of racketeering? How did the court interpret that definition?

2. Assume that on behalf of your legitimate enterprise you are called on to lobby the Congress to amend RICO to apply only to organized crime. What are your arguments?

3. A hoodlum sells insurance to a neighborhood's storekeepers to cover them against breakage of their windows, telling his victims he would be reappearing each month to collect the premium that would continue their coverage. Does this meet the pattern of racketeering requirement? Explain.

Criminal RICO prosecutions may result in seizure and forfeiture of property related to the RICO crimes, forced divestiture of the enterprise, a large fine, and up to 20 years imprisonment for the offender. Civil RICO results in triple damage awards, and attorney fees.

Critics of RICO say that the courts have gone too far in applying what was intended to be a statute to curb organized crime. Its use for securities and commercial fraud, and other "predicate" acts, has reached epidemic proportions. Plaintiffs' attorneys have been quite creative in applying it in the civil sphere as a kind of "federal tort law" that enables plaintiffs to win treble damage awards. While the scholarly literature is in agreement concerning the overbreadth of application of RICO, there does not seem to be a very serious move by Congress to amend the law.

Computer Crime

Computer technology has revolutionized major segments of our society, not the least of which is the business world. With the advent of computers and computerized data base systems, a new crime has emerged—computer crime. A computer crime is any illegal act requiring knowledge of computer technology, or involving use of a computer. Most computer crimes are committed for economic gain.

There are two distinct classes of computer crimes. First, the computer may be used as the tool of a crime, as in the cases of embezzlement and fraud. In one case involving an insurance fraud, employees of an insurance company manufactured insurance policies issued to fictitious insured persons so that the company could resell the policies and avert a cash flow problem. Before the scam was uncovered, stockholders in the company sustained monumental losses. Several company officials responsible for the crime served jail terms.

The second class of computer crimes are those where the computer is the object of a crime. Massive quantities of computer information can be stored on microchips the size of pinheads. Many companies now store customer accounts, product codes, inventory data, and other financial data on computer. Similar to other property, the data is subject to sabotage and destruction. This may occur when, for example, a computer virus is introduced into a computer system. A computer virus occurs when someone mischievously introduces into a computer system a computer program that destroys existing data.

Additionally, magnetic tapes and disks containing company data may be the real object of theft. Theft occurs when there is unauthorized entry into a computer system by use of an illegally obtained password. Employees who access their computers at work for personal use without authorization commit a crime tantamount to theft. This computer time has been deemed to be valuable property and is analogous to the unauthorized use of another's automobile.

Many statutes not written specifically to cover computer crimes may be interpreted nonetheless to apply to such crimes. More and more states are adopting legislation shaped specifically to prohibit computer-related wrongdoing.

Regulatory Crime

Corporations, being legal entities, are responsible for their wrongful acts. The criminal wrongdoing of directors, officers, and employees may be imputed to the corporation.

When a corporation is charged with a crime, much of the procedural process is inapplicable. For example, the corporation is not arrested, nor is it sentenced to jail time if convicted. Fines, or in an extreme case, divestiture, are the normal punishment. As discussed in Chapter 5, the corporation does not have a privilege against self-incrimination; it must surrender its books and records pursuant to subpoena, regardless of how damaging the information may prove to the corporation.

Some industries are highly regulated; for example, the securities field discussed in Chapter 13 and the antitrust area discussed in Chapters 19 through 21. Criminal violations of the antitrust and securities laws are business crimes that may be committed by corporations, their directors, and employees.

Other regulated areas include the sale of liquor, drugs, and guns. How culpable must a person be before violating the law against mislabeling drugs, selling liquor to intoxicated persons, or guns to convicted felons? The following case, involving a chief executive officer's violation of the Pure Food and Drug Act, explores this question of the guilty mind.

UNITED STATES V. PARK
421 U.S. 658 (1975)

Park (respondent), the president of a large national food store chain, was convicted of causing the adulteration of food transported in interstate commerce and held for sale in violation of the federal Pure Food and Drug Act. He was fined $250. He appealed, and the court of appeals reversed the conviction. The Supreme Court reversed the court of appeals.

Chief Justice Burger

Acme Markets, Inc., is a national retail food chain with approximately 36,000 employees, 874 retail outlets, 12 general warehouses, and four special warehouses. Its headquarters, including the office of the president, respondent Park, who is chief executive officer of the corporation, is located in Philadelphia, Pennsylvania. . . . [T]he Government alleged that the defendants had received food that had been shipped in interstate commerce and that, while the food was being held for sale in Acme's Baltimore warehouse . . . they caused it to be held in a building accessible to rodents and to be exposed to contamination by rodents.

Acme pleaded guilty to each count of the information. Respondent pleaded not guilty. The evidence at trial demonstrated that in April 1970 the Food and Drug Administration (FDA) advised respondent by letter of insanitary conditions in Acme's Philadelphia warehouse. In 1971 FDA found that similar conditions existed in the firm's Baltimore warehouse. An FDA consumer safety officer testified concerning evidence of rodent infestation and of the insanitary conditions discovered during a 12-day inspection of the Baltimore warehouse in November and December 1971. He also related that a second inspection of the warehouse had been conducted in March 1972. On that occasion the inspectors found that there had been improvement in the sanitary conditions, but that "there was still evidence of rodent activity in the building and in the warehouse and we found some rodent-contaminated lots of food items." . . .

■   ■   ■

Respondent was the only defense witness. . . . He identified those individuals responsible for sanitation and related that upon receipt of the . . . FDA letter, he had conferred with the vice president for legal affairs, who informed him that the Baltimore division vice president "was investigating the situation immediately and would be taking corrective action and would be preparing a summary of the corrective action to reply to the letter." Respondent stated that he did not "believe there was anything [he] could have done more constructively than what [he] found was being done."

The rule that corporate employees who have "a responsible share in the furtherance of the transaction which the statute outlaws" are subject to the criminal provisions of the Act was not formulated in a vacuum. . . . Cases under the Federal Food and Drugs Act of 1906 reflected the view both that knowledge or intent were not required to be proved in prosecutions under its criminal provisions, and that responsible corporate agents could be subjected to the liability thereby imposed. . . . Moreover, the principle had been recognized that a corporate agent, through whose act, default, or omission the corporation committed a crime, was himself guilty individually of that crime. The principle had been applied whether or not the crime required "consciousness of wrongdoing," and it had been applied not only to those corporate agents who themselves committed the criminal act, but also to those who by virtue of their managerial positions or other similar relation to the actor could be deemed responsible for its commission.

In the latter class of cases, the liability of managerial officers did not depend on their knowledge of, or personal participation in, the act made criminal by the statute. Rather, where the statute under which they were prosecuted dispensed with "consciousness of wrongdoing," an omission or failure to act was deemed a sufficient basis for a responsible corporate agent's liability. It was enough in such cases that by virtue of the relationship he bore to the corporation, the agent had the power to have prevented the act complained of. . . .

■   ■   ■

Thus . . . the cases . . . reveal that in providing sanctions which reach and touch the individuals who execute the corporate mission—and this is by no means necessarily confined to a single corporate agent or employee—the Act imposes not only a positive duty to seek out and remedy violations when they occur but also, and primarily, a duty to implement measures that will insure that violations will not occur. The requirements of foresight and vigilance imposed on responsible corporate agents are beyond question demanding, and perhaps onerous, but they are no more stringent than the public has a right to expect of those who voluntarily assume positions of authority in business enterprises whose services and products affect the health and well-being of the public that supports them. . . .

The Act does not . . . make criminal liability turn on "awareness of some wrongdoing" or "conscious fraud." The duty imposed by Congress on responsible corporate agents is, we emphasize, one that requires the highest standard of foresight and vigilance, but the Act, in its criminal aspect, does not require that which is objectively impossible. The theory upon which responsible corporate agents are held criminally accountable for "causing" violations of the Act permits a claim that a defendant was "powerless" to prevent or correct the violation to "be raised defensively at a trial on the merits." If such a claim is made, the defendant has the burden of coming forward with evidence but this does not alter the Government's ultimate burden of proving beyond a reasonable doubt the defendant's guilt, including his power, in light of the duty imposed by the Act, to prevent or correct the prohibited condition. . . .

[The court of appeals is reversed].

Case Questions

1. Was Park found guilty simply because he was the chief executive officer of Acme? Explain.

2. Which actions did Park take to alleviate the problem at the Baltimore warehouse? What should he have done? What are the lessons and implications of the *Park* decision for organizational communication, structures, and decision-making processes?

3. Do you think the penalty imposed is a sufficient deterrent? Explain.

4. You are an inspector employed by Acme. On two visits to the Baltimore warehouse you notice the presence of rat infestation. You advise the vice president for the Baltimore division of the problem. The vice president does nothing. Are you obligated to advise the president? To inform the FDA? Explain.

Fiduciary Duties of Corporate Officials

Corporate directors and officers possess broad managerial powers that include establishing policy, charting the course of the corporation, and making decisions that place the corporation at risk. Because of these broad powers, corporate directors owe a high degree of fidelity to the corporation. In this special relationship of trust, they are sometimes referred to as fiduciaries.

Fiduciary duties owed by a director and officer to the corporation may be divided into (1) a duty of care, (2) a duty of loyalty, and (3) a duty not to personally appropriate the firm's business opportunities.

Duty of Care

Directors and officers are required to exercise proper care in the management of the corporation. This is the degree of care "which ordinary prudent men would exercise under similar circumstances in their personal business affairs."[1]

In practicality, corporate officials have broad managerial discretion in making corporate decisions. As long as there is an exercise of good faith and prudent care in a manner the official honestly believes is in the interests of the corporation, the director is safe from liability. This is true even when the decision, in hindsight, turns out to be disastrous. This principle is illustrated in Chapter 12, where the business judgment rule is examined. However, even the business judgment rule does not shield officers or directors from wrongdoing. Where, for example, a director authorizes an improper use of the corporation's credit or knowingly diverts funds, the director is personally liable. Directors may also be personally liable for breach of their fiduciary duty of care even when a wrongful act is absent. For example, directors who fail to exercise diligence in examining financial statements may be liable if such examination would have revealed unauthorized diversion of corporate funds by managers. Failure to keep reasonably informed on corporate matters may result in personal liability for consequent losses.

Corporate officials are entitled to rely in good faith on reports, statements, and opinions prepared by professionals. For example, directors may rely on financial statements prepared by an accountant. Directors who do so are safe even if the statements turn out to be misleading. However, neither a director nor the officers may ignore that which he or she knows to be false.

Duty of Loyalty

As a fiduciary standing in a relationship of trust to the corporation, a director may not engage in self-dealing. Self-dealing breaches a duty of loyalty. The expression "one cannot serve two masters" is true in the corporate sector. A director may not serve self and corporation. Classical examples of self-dealing include a corporation making interest-free loans to directors and selling corporate property to directors at less than market prices. The evil here is that the corporation may not be treated fairly. Consequently, shareholders may be injured.

Some self-dealing transactions are fair. For example, directors may extend loans to corporations at better interest rates than exist in the marketplace. For this reason not all dealings between directors and corporations are struck down when there is a conflict of interest—only those transactions that take advantage of the corporation.

Duty to Preserve Corporate Opportunity

Corporate officials owe a duty to avoid appropriation of business opportunities belonging to the corporation. When an opportunity is presented to the corporation, a director or officer may not personally take advantage of it.

---

[1] Selheimer v. Manganese, 244 A. 2d 634 (Pa. 1966).

A two-part test determines whether a corporate official has personally misappropriated a **corporate opportunity**. First, the line of business test compares the closeness of the business opportunity to the corporation's line of business. The closer the opportunity is to the business the corporation conducts, the more suspect the transaction. For example, assume that Faraday, Inc. is in the business of printing. It is looking to expand its operations. In searching for an opportunity to expand, a corporate director gains information that Handy Print, Inc. desires to sell its operations. The director personally purchases Handy Print. Under the line of business test, the director has clearly breached a fiduciary duty. Factors relevant to considering the closeness of the opportunity to the business include: (1) the closeness of the type of business the corporation conducts and the opportunity; (2) whether the opportunity arose out of negotiations with the corporation; (3) whether the director learned of the opportunity as a result of the relationship with the corporation; (4) the extent to which the director used corporate facilities to discover and take advantage of the opportunity.

The fairness test is the second test. Under this test, courts scrutinize the transaction to determine its lawfulness even when the line of business test has not been met. Corporations may pass on a business opportunity and thus voluntarily decide not to take advantage of it. The reasons for such deferral vary. The corporation may determine that taking advantage of the opportunity would be contrary to law or to the corporate charter. Or, perhaps, it is not financially feasible for the corporation to pursue the opportunity. Even here the opportunity must be disclosed and presented to the corporation for its consideration.

Minority Shareholders

Corporate fiduciaries must be fair in their dealings with minority shareholders. They may not oppress or otherwise take advantage of the minority shareholders to advance their own interests. Additionally, directors must treat each class of stock evenhandedly, so as not to unduly enhance the value of one class of stock at the expense of another.

Corporate officials must take care to ensure that shareholders are given full and complete information so that they may make informed decisions with respect to their options. This is the most important aspect of determining whether minority shareholders have been treated fairly—whether they have been given all of the information necessary to make informed decisions.

In some instances directors elected by a majority of shareholders desire to eliminate the minority shareholders. There are legitimate ways of squeezing out these shareholders as well as defensive tactics designed to anticipate and avoid such a squeeze out, both discussed in the following sections.

Squeeze Outs

A **squeeze out** (or freeze out) involves the elimination of minority shareholders. The classical squeeze out involves a merger. For example, a parent corporation and its subsidiary merge; the majority shareholders receive stock and the minority stockholders receive cash. This type of freeze out may occur in a publicly held corporation where the controlling shareholders desire to go private by eliminating minority shareholders. This has the effect of forcing out unwanted shareholders. In many instances, the minority shareholders are entitled to vote on the merger, but because they are a minority, their vote means little.

Many states have adopted a short form merger, where minority shareholders are summarily squeezed out without a vote. In such cases minority shareholders are entitled to a specified amount of cash.

Minority shareholders unhappy with the cash allotted are generally afforded **appraisal rights**. The appraisal remedy must be pursued through the courts. It is ordinarily governed by state statute. The statute normally requires that the minority shareholder first file a written notice of dissent at the shareholders' meeting. Negotiations may then proceed between the corporate officers and dissenting shareholders for the price of the minority shares. If there is a failure to settle, a court appraises the value of the shares.

Squeeze out strategies are varied. Directors may choose not to issue dividends and thus discourage minority shareholders from continuing to hold onto their stock. They may eliminate minority shareholders from company employment and instead employ majority shareholders at high compensation. They may issue stock and thus further dilute minority shareholders' interests.

Various tests have been applied to determine whether a squeeze out of minority shareholders is lawful. Illustrated in the next case involving a major league football team are the business purpose test and the intrinsic fairness test.

COGGINS V. NEW ENGLAND PATRIOTS FOOTBALL CLUB
492 N.E. 2d 1112 (Mass. 1986)

In 1959 Williams H. Sullivan, Jr., purchased an American Football League (AFL) franchise for $25,000. He organized a corporation called the American League Professional Football Team of Boston, Inc. Nine other people contributed $25,000 each. The 10 investors, including Sullivan, received 10,000 shares of voting stock in the corporation. The corporation sold an additional 120,000 shares of nonvoting stock at $5 a share to the public.

Sullivan lost control of the corporation in 1974. He succeeded in regaining control by obtaining ownership or control of 100 percent of the voting shares of the stock of the corporation renamed the New England Patriots Football Club, Inc. (Old Patriots). To finance the transaction necessary to regain control, Sullivan borrowed over $5 million from banks. To convert the personal debt to a corporate debt, Sullivan was required to eliminate the interest of the nonvoting shares of which he now owned a substantial number. He organized a new corporation called the New Patriots Football Club, Inc. (New Patriots). The boards of directors of the Old Patriots and the New Patriots entered into a merger agreement providing that after the merger the voting stock of the Old Patriots would be extinguished and the nonvoting stock would be exchanged for cash at $15 per share. Sullivan, as part of the plan, gave the New Patriots his voting shares in the Old Patriots in return for 100 percent of the New Patriots' stock. The merger was approved by the voting and nonvoting classes of stock and the merger was accomplished.

Coggins owned 10 shares of nonvoting stock in the Old Patriots. He prided himself in the fact that he was a part owner of the team he faithfully followed. He voted against the merger and then sued on behalf of the stockholders who believed the merger to be unfair. The trial court found in favor of Coggins and his class and held that the plaintiffs were entitled to damages as of the date of the merger. The Supreme Judicial Court of Massachusetts affirmed in part and remanded the case to the trial court for calculation of the damages.

Judge Liacos

In deciding this case, we address an important corporate law question: What approach will a Massachusetts court reviewing a cash freeze-out merger employ? This question has been considered by courts in a number of other States.

■   ■   ■

Judicial scrutiny should begin with recognition of the basic principle that the duty of a corporate director must be to further the legitimate goals of the corporation. The result of a freeze-out merger is the elimination of public ownership in the corporation. The controlling faction increases its equity from a majority to 100 percent, using corporate processes and corporate assets. The corporate directors who benefit from this transfer of ownership must demonstrate how the legitimate goals of the corporation are furthered. A director of a corporation violates his fiduciary duty when he uses the corporation for . . . personal benefit in a manner detrimental to the corporation. Because the danger of abuse of fiduciary duty is especially great in a freeze-out merger, the court must be satisfied that the freeze-out was for the advancement of a legitimate corporate purpose. If satisfied that elimination of public ownership is in furtherance of a business purpose, the court should then pro-

ceed to determine if the transaction was fair by examining the totality of the circumstances.

The plaintiffs here adequately alleged that the merger of the Old Patriots and New Patriots was a freeze-out merger undertaken for no legitimate business purpose, but merely for the personal benefit of Sullivan. While we have recognized the right to "selfish ownership" in a corporation, such a right must be balanced against the concept of the majority stockholder's fiduciary obligation to the minority stockholders. Consequently, the defendants bear the burden of proving, first, that the merger was for a legitimate business purpose, and second, that, considering totality of circumstances, it was fair to the minority. . . .

". . . It . . . appears that the sole reason for the merger was to effectuate a restructuring of top Patriots that would enable the repayment of the [personal] indebtedness incurred by Sullivan. . . ." The trial judge considered the defendants' claims that the policy of the National Football League (NFL) requiring majority ownership by a single individual or family made it necessary to eliminate public ownership. He found that "the stock ownership of the Patriots as it existed just prior to the merger fully satisfied the rationale underlying the policy as expressed by NFL Commissioner Pete Rozelle. Having acquired 100% control of the voting common stock of the

Patriots, Sullivan possessed unquestionable authority to act on behalf of the franchise at League meetings and effectively foreclosed the possible recurrence of the internal management disputes that had existed. . . . Moreover . . . the Old Patriots were under no legal compulsion to eliminate public ownership." Likewise, the defendants did not succeed in showing a conflict between the interests of the league owners and the Old Patriots' stockholders. . . . Under the approach we set forth above, there is no need to consider further the elements of fairness of a transaction that is not related to a valid corporate purpose. . . .

■   ■   ■

We do not think it appropriate, however, to award damages based on a 1976 appraisal value. To do so would make this suit a nullity, leaving the plaintiffs with no positive remedy except appraisal, a position we have already rejected. . . . [D]amages must be determined based on the present value of the Patriots, that is, what the stockholders would have if the merger were rescinded.

The case is remanded to the Superior Court for further proceedings consistent with this opinion.

Case Questions

1. Describe the freeze-out merger in this case. What is the business purpose test? What is the fairness test? Which one did the court indicate was applicable to a cash-out merger transaction? Explain.
2. Why did Sullivan engage in a freeze-out merger? Was this deemed a valid business purpose? Explain.
3. What damages did the lower court order? What damages did the appeals court order?
4. If you had been in Coggins's place, would you be satisfied with the result? Why or why not?

Avoiding Squeeze Outs

The best way to avoid being squeezed out of a corporation is to plan ahead. Most squeeze outs occur in closely held corporations. Because the shareholders may know each other, when they form a partnership or corporation, they enter into an arrangement of mutual trust. However, a business relationship built on trust may dissipate. Provisions should be made for contingencies.

Each shareholder should be represented by an attorney when entering into a close corporation and when significant events occur, such as the drafting of bylaws, a shareholders' agreement, or contractual arrangements. These events affect corporate control; a naive shareholder may quickly find that his or her corporate interest has seriously changed.

Buy-out provisions should be determined in advance before shareholders retire, become disabled, or die. Provisions for dispute resolution should be made in the bylaws or by the shareholders' agreement. Conflicts do occur and making provision for their resolution is smart. Dispute resolution may take the form of mediation, arbitration, or some other alternative to litigation.

A most frequently used tactic for avoiding a minority squeeze out is the shareholders' agreement. Provisions that may be contained within it to protect minority shareholders include employing the shareholder at a specified salary, not to be diminished; power to veto specific corporate decisions; requirement of payment of dividends under defined financial thresholds; and prohibition of selling shares to outsiders before first offering them to existing shareholders. Other devices include long-term employment contracts between minority shareholders and the corporation; and bylaw provisions requiring a higher than majority vote for shareholder and director actions.

Corporate Takeovers

Mergers, via hostile takeovers, have injected a great degree of uncertainty into the corporate world. In the typical **hostile takeover**, an aggressor corporation makes a tender offer to the shareholders of a target corporation. The tender offer may consist of a cash offer substantially above the market price of the stock; or, it may consist of an offer to exchange the aggressor's stock for the target's stock. After the tender offer, the aggressor might approach the management of the target company in an attempt to convert the unfriendly takeover to a friendly merger. This combined strategy is referred to as a *bear hug* in Wall Street lingo.

In such a scenario, corporate directors are called on to exercise their judgment in the best interest of the company. Their decision is protected by the business judgment rule, discussed in Chapter 12. These transactions are governed by certain federal securities disclosure requirements, discussed in Chapter 13. In addition, they are governed by the antifraud requirements of Rule 10b-5 of the Securities Exchange Act, also discussed in Chapter 13.

The board of directors of the corporation may determine that it is in the best interests of the corporation to engage in a friendly merger. In some instances, however, the board determines that it is in the best interest of the corporation to fight the takeover.

Defensive Tactics

Takeover attempts may result in bitter contests between the tender offeror and the target company. Corporate officials often resist takeovers for fear of losing their jobs if the takeover is successful.

A target company faced with the threat of a takeover may deploy a number of defensive tactics to neutralize the outside threat. Shareholders can be warned of the takeover attempt and solicited not to sell their shares. The target company may buy up its own shares on the open market or issue additional shares to management and its allies. It might also declare a dividend increase or a stock split to boost the stock's market price. This would make the takeover more expensive, and perhaps prohibitive, for the tender offeror. To escape the clutches of an unfriendly merger, targets sometimes merge with friendly companies called white knights. On a few occasion targets have responded with the PAC-man defense, whereby the target retaliates by taking over the attacker.

Most recently, several innovative defensive techniques have been employed to ward off suitors. They include the use of shark repellents, poison pills, and greenmail. Shark repellents are provisions inserted in the company's corporate documents to discourage takeover attempts. A provision requiring greater than shareholder majority to approve a merger is an example. Poison pills make a takeover undesirable by making the costs or risk prohibitive. For example, the target could acquire a firm that would cause the attacker antitrust problems should a merger occur. Greenmail is payment of money by a target to an attacker to dissuade the attacker from taking over the target.

Defensive tactics are scrutinized for disclosure and deception under the securities laws discussed in Chapter 13 and under the business judgment rule discussed in Chapter 12.

Executive Compensation

Directors and officers of corporations are often compensated for their service. The board of directors may establish the compensation or senior management may do so. Because of the appearance of self-dealing and impropriety in establishing directors' salaries, some companies have compensation committees comprised of outside directors to monitor compensation amounts.

Courts use a fairness test to determine whether compensation is excessive. Under this test, there must be a relationship between the services rendered and the compensation. Otherwise, the payments constitute corporate waste.

Director and officer compensation is not limited to present payments; it may include stock options, severance pay, and bonuses. Because of the possibility of mergers, hostile and friendly, job security is always a question. To reduce the anxiety of job insecurity and attract competent directors and officers, lucrative compensation clauses are often offered. These clauses, called **golden parachutes**, often grant liberal benefits to directors and officers in the event the executive is terminated after a takeover. These contractual clauses are scrutinized for fairness by courts. The following case involving a negotiated friendly takeover describes the legal limitations of golden parachutes.

GAILLARD V. NOTAMAS CO.
256 Cal. Rptr. 702 (Cal. App. 1989)

Natomas was a publicly held corporation engaged in petroleum and geothermal exploration and production. Its board of directors consisted of 12 outside directors and 5 inside directors who were officers of the corporation.

Diamond attempted to take over Natomas by a hostile tender offer. The two companies' executives met and agreed on a plan for a friendly takeover.

As a result of their existing employment contracts, two of the inside directors were entitled to golden parachute benefits in the event of a takeover. On the recommendation of a compensation committee that included Flom, an outside counsel and a specialist in corporate takeovers and mergers, the terms of the parachutes were amended. The amended agreement gave the directors the right to terminate their employment within six months following the merger "for good reason," or for any reason following the six-month period and receive up to a sum equal to five times their total annual compensation.

Golden parachutes were also approved for the other inside directors. The five inside directors abstained from voting on the golden parachute package. Diamond approved of the golden parachutes.

Four of the executives terminated their employment with Natomas shortly after the merger. They were paid approximately $10 million under the golden parachute provisions. The fifth executive, Seaton, was entitled to $250,000 annually under a consulting agreement, for which he provided minimal services.

Shareholders challenged the golden parachute agreements in court. The case was dismissed. On appeal to the California Appellate Court the judgment was reversed.

Judge Strankman

A. Liability of Inside Directors . . .

■   ■   ■

The record discloses issues of fact on appellants' claims of . . . breach of fiduciary duty . . . as to the five inside directors, which cannot be resolved as a matter of law on the basis of the record before us. As to Seaton, the record is unclear as to the nature and extent of his participation in the events which led to the proposal of the consulting agreement. Although the record shows that the consulting agreement, on its face, served a valid corporate purpose, and the outside directors are immune from liability as to this particular agreement . . . the record is inadequate to determine as a matter of law that Seaton's conduct incident to the adoption of the agreement comported with his fiduciary duties. Although the fairness of the agreement to the corporation must be judged at the time of its adoption, the fact that Seaton provided, at the most, minimal services in return for his annual $250,000 salary raises at least the inference that the agreement was not in the best interests of Natomas at the time of its adoption. Summary judgment as to all five inside directors therefore must be reversed.

B. Liability of Outside Directors

We next look to whether the conduct of the outside directors in approving these benefits can withstand judicial scrutiny as a matter of law. . . .

Our inquiry . . . is whether the record discloses controverted issues of fact as to whether the outside directors acted in a manner they believed to be in the best interests of Natomas, and with such care, including reasonable inquiry, as an ordinarily prudent person in a like position would use under similar circumstances; and whether, in relying upon various sources, they made reasonable inquiry if the need therefor was indicated by the circumstances. We reach a different conclusion as to the directors' approval of the golden parachutes than we reach as to their approval of Seaton's consulting agreement.

■   ■   ■

We find that with the evidence before us, we cannot say as a matter of law that the [outside directors who were] compensation committee members were justified in relying to the extent that they did upon Flom in approving the golden parachutes, or that the circumstances did not warrant further reasonable inquiry. . . . We so conclude for the following reasons.

First, the golden parachutes, by their terms, would not serve the recognized valid functions of golden parachutes. . . . Because they were discussed after the terms of the merger had been negotiated and agreed upon, the function of executive objectivity would not be served. . . . In addition, because they were provided to existing executives, the function of attracting top-level management obviously was not served. Significantly, the existing employment agreements for [two executives], of which the committee members should have been aware, already provided golden parachutes which served the desirable functions of these forms of compensation. . . .

■   ■   ■

Second, the golden parachutes [purportedly] served the purpose of ensuring continuity of management. Certain respondents at one point therefore refer to the benefits as "golden handcuffs," rather than golden parachutes. The very terms of the amended agreements, however, indicate that the opposite purpose would be served, and that they in fact would encourage the executives to leave Natomas within the six-month period following the merger or shortly thereafter. . . .

■   ■   ■

Third, the golden parachutes payable . . . exceeded the three-year annual salary lump-excessive for tax purposes under current law. Although these tax provisions, effective in 1984, apparently were not applicable to the 1983 merger, the compensation committee members arguably should have been aware of the pendency of such legislation affecting matters within their purview, and that the lump-sum payments in question would be excessive under the new tax laws.

■   ■   ■

We reach a different conclusion as to the approval of the consulting agreement. The record indicates the compensation committee members themselves raised the issue of the need for the consulting agreement, and perceived that such agreement would serve a valid and necessary purpose for Natomas. Whether Seaton ultimately rendered $250,000 worth of services per year is irrelevant. . . . We therefore conclude the compensation committee members are not liable as a matter of law for their recommendations to approve the consulting agreement.

We finally turn to the conduct of the outside directors who were not on the compensation committee. . . . [T]hese directors were entitled to rely on the compensation committee, which they believed "to merit confidence" and were not required to initiate their own independent investigation. However, in this case, the nature of these particular golden parachute agreements and the timing of their proposal create a triable issue of fact as to whether *some* further inquiry should have been made by the board members who were not on the compensation committee. . . . The proposal of the golden parachutes here under somewhat suspicious circumstances, i.e., *after* the tender offer and in the midst of merger discussions, raises the question of whether these directors should have examined the golden parachutes more attentively.

■   ■   ■

[The judgment of the lower court is reversed.]

Case Questions

1. What are the legitimate purposes of golden parachutes?
2. What made this golden parachute agreement suspect?
3. What is the difference between the liability of the inside versus the outside directors?
4. Develop a scenario that would have clearly validated the golden parachute agreements.

Antitakeover Statutes

During the 1960s and 1970s, most states enacted **antitakeover statutes**. These statutes were worded to favor the interests of incumbent management, facing a takeover threat. They required more disclosure than required by federal securities laws and imposed a waiting period between the time of the announcement of the tender offer and the commencement of the tender offer. Some of the statutes required a hearing before state administrative agencies to determine the fairness of the takeover. These statutes were ultimately held unconstitutional by the U.S. Supreme Court as an undue burden on interstate commerce.[2]

More recently, second generation state antitakeover statutes have arisen. They tend to regulate the voting rights of persons who acquire outstanding stock. This type of statute, which permits disinterested shareholders to determine whether an acquirer of controlling shares of a target may have voting privileges, was upheld as constitutional by the U.S. Supreme Court.[3]

Corporate Social Responsibility

Corporations, by definition, are thought by many to be socially irresponsible. This is not entirely true. Many corporations are extremely conscious of their responsibility to society and to the components of the corporation.

Socially responsible corporations may take an affirmative stand by their gifts to charities, minority business loans and programs, job training, and local community assistance. Additionally, social responsibility may be expressed by firms refraining from doing things that cause harm, such as polluting the environment or engaging in activities that result in the destruction of the rain forests.

Some assert that a corporation's sole responsibility is to maximize earnings, provided the corporation abides by the law. They argue that the corporation cannot be separated from the shareholders who own it. All nonprofit activities in which the corporation engages and all opportunities for profit that the corporation forgoes represent diminutions in corporate profits that would otherwise become the property of the shareholders. Thus, the use of corporate resources for any activity other than profit maximization may be viewed by some as forcing the shareholder to subsidize the ideals of corporate management.

Historically, the corporation has not always been regarded as a profit maximizer. During the late 19th century, however, the corporation came to be viewed as an institution operated solely for the benefit of its shareholders. Thus, profit maximization was its only function. This change in attitude coincided with a period of major industrial expansion and economic development spearheaded by corporations. Consequently, corporations devoted exclusively to profit maximization were perceived as consistent with the national interest.

---

[2] Edgar v. MITE Corp., 457 U.S. 6245 (1982).
[3] See CTS Corp. v. Dynamics Corp., 481 U.S. 69 (1987).

Ethical Dilemmas/Issues

Hazardous Industries Technologies (HIT) is a private corporation located in Arkansas. It is a wholly owned subsidiary of Banc Roll, a Monaco-based company. The board of directors desire to establish a hazardous waste incineration plant at a five-acre site in Any City, which it purchased for $5 million. They have a proper state and federal permit to do so. HIT would insure against any spills or accidents, and comply with all state and federal regulations.

The economy in Any City is poor and depressed. It has been a landfill site for hazardous wastes for years. The site is located within 250 yards of an elementary school and within 1/2 mile of the most populous portion of the community. A recent state law prohibits the establishment of any hazardous waste incineration plant within two miles of a school. However, HIT is exempt from this law since it obtained its permit before the law went into effect. In addition, a recent epidemiological study indicates that the dioxins produced by the incineration of the combination of chemicals to be burned will result in 40 more cancers a year per 1 million population than otherwise.

The five-member board has determined that it will take $140 million dollars to build the plant and make it operational over the next five years. Its studies have shown that there is a tremendous market for such an incineration program; it already has entered into contingent contracts with major companies. HIT prognoses that its return on investment will be a healthy 20 percent per year. The local community is against the plant, and has voted to fight it "by any legal means necessary."

What are the ethical issues? What would you do?

In recent decades, many people have come to believe that the corporation must serve not only the interest of its shareholders but also the well-being of employees, consumers, suppliers, creditors, and the community. The law has changed to accommodate the changing view of the role of the corporation in society. Many states have amended their corporation statutes to authorize nonprofit activities. In these states, such activities of management are shielded from shareholders' attacks unless the activities are arbitrary or in bad faith.

On closer examination, profit and social responsibility do not necessarily conflict; the two may complement each other. First, the goodwill or image of a corporation is important for long-run return. Corporations who fail to engage in the acceptable social graces expected by society may ultimately alienate their customers. Second, industries that ignore social responsibility run the risk of heaping increased government regulation on the industry. Third, intangible detriments occur when companies disregard the internal social atmosphere. Employee morale and management's motivation all suffer, and productivity and profitability consequently wane.

Proposals to facilitate advances in corporate social responsibility have been developed. They include institutionalizing ethics of the corporation, altering the corporate structure by permitting a wider base of representatives on the corporation's board, and a change in the reporting of a corporation, which would include social disclosure. Each is discussed below.

Codes of Ethics

Many professional organizations operate under ethical standards. The National Association of REALTORS® (NAR) has an elaborate set of ethical standards. A member who violates the standards is subject to expulsion. The American Institute of Certified Public Accountants, the American Bar Association, the American Psychological Association, the American Medical Association, the American Institute of Architects, and many other national, state, and local associations have adopted professional codes of conduct designed to promote ethical behavior.

There have been proposals regarding the formulation and the adoption of a Code of Business Ethics. Such a code of ethics could include standards and directions regarding company layoffs, pensions, safety, lockouts, and takeovers. To date the idea is still in the discussion stages.

Nothing excludes a company from formulating its own code of conduct; a number of firms have done this by including such matters in their handbooks of company policies. There is an incentive for companies to establish ethical codes of conduct. The federal **sentencing guidelines** hold companies liable when one or more employees are convicted of certain criminal offenses. The companies face mandatory fines that reach into the hundreds of millions of dollars for a broad range of crimes. However, a company's criminal fines will be drastically reduced if corporate compliance programs designed to discover violations are in place. As a result, over 90 percent of Fortune 500 companies have a code of ethics in place, and about half have ethics or compliance officers. Many are holding regular ethics workshops and seminars.

There are a number of factors that judge the efficacy of a compliance program designed to prevent and detect employee misconduct. (See Table 14–2) Other

---

TABLE 14–2   **Minimum Guidelines for Effective Compliance Program**

- Standards reasonably capable of reducing criminal conduct.
- Oversight of program by high-level personnel.
- Due care to prevent assigning discretionary authority to unqualified individuals.
- Effective communication of standards to employees.
- Use of compliance mechanisms, such as reporting and auditing systems for violations.
- Consistent discipline for violations of standards.
- Effective response to offenses by modifying the program to detect similar wrongdoing.

mitigation factors involve reporting criminal violations, cooperating with prose-cutors, and accepting responsibility for misconduct.

Altering the Corporate Structure

The need for greater social sensitivity in decision making demands that the corporate structure change in response to this need. The traditional structure enlists a board of successful businesspeople who are bottom-line oriented. Many have recognized a need to break out of the traditional mold and broaden the mix of corporate directors. Large companies have established ethics committees charged with giving input on the social and ethical impact of corporate decisions. Corporate social advocates seated on boards of directors can give another side to the corporate focus and represent the social concerns of society and the corporate environment.

Corporate social responsibility may be furthered by including additional inputs into the corporate decision-making process. For example, employees could be represented on the board of directors. In 1979, the Chrylser-United Auto Workers (UAW) collective bargaining contract provided for the inclusion of the UAW president on the Chrysler board of directors. Only in Europe is there a legal requirement for employee representation on corporate boards. Changing the corporate structure need not be confined to placing workers on corporate boards; some have argued that consumers and community members should also be represented.

Social Disclosure

The disclosure of corporate social responsibility undertakings has been suggested as a way of institutionalizing corporate social performance. So far, several corporations in the United States have voluntarily instituted social reports. Only in France, however, is social reporting required in the form of a legislatively mandated social balance sheet.

A social balance sheet provides a system of reporting that is comparable from one year to the next. For example, one entry could be the number of plant accidents per reporting period. Other entries might include the average salaries of employees, benefits, health and safety violations, number of minority workers, training programs, and investment practices. The information, however, does not have to be confined to the internal environment; it could be expanded to include the amount of pollution emitted, the number of product liability suits and customer complaints, and the extent of community involvement.

The information derived from the social balance sheet serves as an informational tool for the various components of the corporation and the community at large. Investors may make investment decisions based on it. As well, employees may make employment decisions. It might also serve as a basis for negotiating a collective bargaining contract. In addition, the balance sheet can serve as a basis for corporate social planning.

Chapter Problems

1. Define the following terms:
   a. Foreign Corrupt Practices Act
   b. RICO
   c. Fiduciary duties
   d. Corporate opportunity
   e. Squeeze out
   f. Appraisal rights
   g. Hostile takeover
   h. Golden parachutes
   i. Antitakeover statutes
   j. Sentencing guidelines

2. B&O is a railroad that owns two subsidiaries, WMR and WMG. Approximately 98.5 percent of the outstanding shares of B&O stock is owned by C&O, a wholly owned subsidiary of CSX. CSX set out to rid itself of B&O's minority shareholders by merging B&O with C&O. It froze out minority shareholders in the two B&O subsidiaries, WMR and WMC. It directed B&O's board of directors to approve the sale of B&O's controlling interest in WMR to C&O at a price below fair value. CSX froze out WMC minority stockholders in the same way. In each case, the stockholders were unknowingly given false information that undervalued their interest as shareholders. Finally, CSX rid itself of B&O's minority shareholders by merging B&O with C&O.

   The state statute did not require shareholder approval where, as here, one entity owned more than 90 percent of the stock. In connection with the merger, CSX made several false representations as to the value of B&O assets to induce shareholders to accept less than the fair value of their stock.

   Are the necessary elements present to justify a RICO action? Explain. Are there any other actions that the minority shareholders may have? Detail.

3. BP operates company-owned gas stations. There are also noncompany-owned gas stations, whereby the company enters into a lease and franchise agreement with an entrepreneur who runs the station. Company auditors have discovered a lot of theft and embezzlement from the company by the managers of both the company- and noncompany-owned gas stations. What policy should the company adopt regarding managers who embezzle company funds? Should there be a different policy regarding company-owned stations than noncompany-owned stations? Explain.

4. Mrs. Pritchard was a director of Pritchard & Baird, a reinsurance brokerage firm. While she was a director, fraudulent loans were extended to Mrs. Pritchard's sons by Pritchard and Baird. Mrs. Pritchard was unaware of the fraudulent transfer of money. No corporate resolution authorized the loans and no note evidenced the debt. The loans were reflected on financial

statements prepared annually. As a result of the size of the interest-free loans that were not repaid, the company was forced into bankruptcy.

Mrs. Pritchard was not active in the business and knew very little about its corporate affairs. She did not attempt to educate herself. She never read the annual financial statements. She did not participate in corporate decisions or policymaking. She was a heavy drinker. Do these factors exonerate Mrs. Pritchard for liability for the fraudulent loans? Explain.

5. Klinicki (plaintiff) and Lundgren (defendant) entered the air transportation business by incorporating Berlinair. Each man was a director and each owned 33 percent of the stock of the company. Plaintiff and defendant, on behalf of the corporation, met with BFR, a consortium of Berlin travel agents that contracted to take tourists to summer climates. Plaintiff and defendant hoped to enter into a contract with BFR where Berlinair would be BFR's carrier.

Lundgren separately formed a new company called Air Berlin Charter Co. (ABC). He entered into a contract on behalf of ABC with BFR. Lundgren concealed his separate negotiations with plaintiff, Klinicki. Berlinair probably would have been financially unable to pursue the opportunity. Was Lundgren's conduct appropriate?

6. Roberts and his partner Graves were the founders and sole shareholders of Publicorp, Inc., a small corporation. During the 1960s, when stock prices were generally high, each sold some of their stock publicly at $15 per share. The stock rose to $20 per share, and Roberts sold additional shares. Approximately 18 percent of the stock of Publicorp is held by outsiders.

Recently, the stock market has been depressed and Publicorp has dropped to $3 per share. Many of the outside shareholders voiced concern about this at the company's annual meeting. The company's bylaws provide for cumulative voting, and the outsiders narrowly missed electing one of their people to the board of directors. Roberts is concerned that next year they will succeed.

Roberts has tried to repurchase some Publicorp stock on the open market and has succeeded in obtaining 8 percent by offering to pay $4.50 per share. The remaining 10 percent is owned by five individuals who refused to sell because they believed the stock had bottomed out and would be rising soon.

Graves has suggested the following plan to freeze out the remaining outsiders. Roberts and Graves will form Privatecorp, Inc., a new corporation, and then sell their shares in Publicorp to Privatecorp. Publicorp would thus be a 90 percent-owned subsidiary of Privatecorp.

A state statute permits a parent corporation to merge with a subsidiary at least 90 percent of whose stock it owns and to eliminate the equity interests of the outside shareholders. (The outsiders' sole remedy is an independent appraisal of the value of their stock and payment of that value in cash.) The procedure would enable Roberts and Graves to regain complete control of the company. Should they use it? What are the considerations?

7. In response to a takeover threat, Union Commerce Corporation (UCC) executed a golden parachute contract with Worth, an executive officer in a subsidiary of UCC. The contract stated that in the event of a change of control of UCC, Worth would be entitled to resign within two years and receive specified economic benefits if he in good faith believed that his status had diminished following the takeover. The benefits included twice his annual salary for two years, medical coverage for two years, country club dues for two years, and a lump-sum cash payment for purchase of an annuity. Huntington Bancshares, Inc. acquired UCC and there was a change of control.

    Which factors determine whether Worth's resignation was in good faith? Explain. Suggest a scenario where his resignation would clearly be considered in good faith. What are some bad-faith reasons why he might desire to resign?

8. Signal is a diversified company operating through its subsidiaries. Its stock is publicly traded. It acquired a majority of the shares of stock in Universal Oil Products (UOP), a diversified industrial company. Therefore, Signal conducted a feasibility study to determine whether it would be a good investment to acquire the remaining 49.5 percent shares of UOP stock. Two Signal directors conducted the study. They were also corporate directors of UOP. They determined that it would be a good investment to acquire the remaining UOP shares at a price up to $24 per share. Signal's executive committee has scheduled a meeting to finalize any proposal. Which steps should they take to ensure fairness to UOP's minority shareholders?

9. Diversified Distributors, Inc. (DDI) is a megacorporation listed on a major stock exchange. It conducts extensive business in South Africa and is involved heavily in exporting tobacco and baby formula to Third World countries. The company has consistently turned a profit, has a high return on earnings, and has been growing at the rate of 20 percent per year. DDI has 10 directors on its board. They are long-time employees of the corporation and have very liberal stock option plans. As a result, they together possess the controlling interest in the stock of the corporation. These directors have vowed to resist enlisting outside directors on their board. They have a very autocratic style of corporate governance and staunchly refuse to delegate any authority to executive committees made up of outsiders or to listen to the outcry of minority stockholders who have begun to criticize the company's lack of social and moral consciousness. Which possible legal problems are facing DDI? Which ethical problems is it facing?

10. Hugh Hefner is the chairman of the board and chief executive officer of Playboy Enterprises, Inc. He owns about 72 percent of the company's stock. The company maintains the Chicago Mansion, which consists of two buildings. The principal building has four stories, 54 rooms, and contains 11 apartments. It has a swimming pool, underwater bar, and sauna. The second building has 20 rooms, which include an office for Hefner. Hefner's accommodations in the mansion include a "Roman Bath," an elaborate bathing/sleeping area.

Playboy Mansion West is a 30-room, Tudor-style stone structure on 5 1/2 wooded acres. The main floor consists of a two-story hall, living room, library, dining room, breakfast room, and kitchen/servant's dining area. The master bedroom suite includes a bedroom that contains an extensive array of audio/visual equipment. On the grounds are a lighted tennis court, a barbecue area, swimming pool with a bathhouse/cabana/sauna, an animal shelter, and a greenhouse/aviary. The grotto, a cavern with underwater access and multiple sitting area, contains individualized Jacuzzi systems and a stereophonic sound system.

Playboy spent about $20 million for operating costs for the mansions over seven years. It also engaged in renovations of the mansions totaling over $1 million for Hefner's living quarters alone.

Personal guests of Hefner stay at the Mansions for extended periods. Out of 21,049 overnight guest stays at the Mansions, 6,020 were personal to Hefner. Hefner maintains that the lifestyle is important to the corporate strategy of promoting the Playboy image. Comment on the propriety of Hefner's position.

15 DEBTOR-CREDITOR RELATIONS

Learning Objectives

After learning this chapter the student should be able to:

- List and summarize the federal consumer credit laws.
- Identify the various transactions requiring compliance with the federal consumer credit laws.
- Determine which form of bankruptcy is applicable under a particular set of circumstances.
- Calculate the consequences of a chapter 7 liquidation given the relevant financial information.

TABLE 15–1 **Federal Consumer Credit Laws**

Law	Description
Truth in Lending Act	Encourages informed use of credit
Equal Credit Opportunity Act	Promotes nondiscrimination in the extension of credit
Fair Credit Reporting Act	Regulates the content and use of credit reports
Fair Credit Billing Act	Sets out procedures for the resolution of billing errors
Electronic Funds Transfer Act	Clarifies the rights and liabilities of electronic funds transfer users
Fair Debt Collection Practices Act	Limits deceptive and abusive conduct of bill collectors
Title III Restrictions on Garnishment	Places restrictions on garnishment of wages

Americans have purchased installment goods on credit since colonial times. However, only beginning in the 20th century has the widespread use of consumer credit become a major economic force. The extension of credit creates a debtor-creditor relationship. The debtor is the person who owes money; the creditor is the person to whom money is owed.

The increased use of credit has been spurred in part by the growing number of high-tech products available on the market. A walk through the local department store stirs the demand for computers, software, compact discs, DVDs, and many more state-of-the-art items. Also, the ease of obtaining credit cards, such as VISA, MasterCard, and Discover, facilitates the use of credit. As a result, consumer credit has grown exponentially since World War II. Consumer debt, including home mortgage debt, is up to 13 digits. Today, on average, consumers allot one half of their paychecks to repay debt.

The debtor-creditor relationship involves such activities as credit extension, billing, and debt collection. The Consumer Credit Protection Act covers areas listed in Table 15–1. These laws directly affect business. As such, they demand the attention of business managers and those responsible for regulatory compliance.

In addition, debtor financial failure is on the rise not only among individuals and small business but also among large corporations. Thus, it is appropriate in this chapter to cover the Bankruptcy Reform Act (and its most recent amendments), federal legislation designed to relieve debtor failures.

The Truth in Lending Act

The Truth in Lending Act (**TILA**) ensures that consumers have adequate information about the cost of credit. Lenders are required to disclose certain credit terms in a standard way. TILA does not dictate credit terms. Rather, it requires creditors to disclose and express credit terms uniformly when involved in consumer credit transactions.

The Federal Reserve Board (FRB) is authorized to adopt regulations implementing TILA. FRB has issued Regulation Z specifying the rules creditors must follow when making decisions. Various administrative authorities enforce TILA.

The Federal Trade Commission enforces the act with respect to all transactions not specifically covered by any other agency. This is the enforcement scheme of many of the consumer protection statutes treated in this chapter.

Under TILA, creditors are required to make certain disclosures to consumers. A creditor is one who (1) regularly extends consumer credit, (2) requires a finance charge or repayment in more than four installments, and (3) is the person to whom repayment is required.

Consumer credit is extended primarily for personal, family, or household purposes. Credit extended to corporations does not qualify as consumer credit; neither does credit extended primarily for business, commercial, or agricultural purposes. Most credit transactions, other than home financing, are exempt when the total amount to be financed exceeds $25,000.

Disclosure

The specific type of disclosure required under TILA is applicable to both open-end and closed-end credit transactions. Open-end credit involves accounts such as MasterCard and VISA; the customer may enter into a series of credit transactions and may choose to pay the balance in installments. Closed-end credit involves transactions such as loans, where a specific amount of credit is extended for a definite time. In closed-end transactions, the borrower agrees to repay the amount in predetermined installments with the balance due by a specific date.

Both open-end and closed-end transactions require disclosures. However, TILA requires large merchants in open-end credit transactions to make ongoing disclosure in the form of periodic statements detailing each transaction.

In both open-end and closed-end transactions, a creditor must conspicuously disclose to the consumer the key terms of the transaction. These generally include the total amount financed, the finance charges, schedule of payments, penalty charges, and the annual percentage rate of interest (APR). The APR is determined by computing the annualized interest paid on the amount of money actually used during a given time. The finance charges used to compute the APR consist of the total of all charges for the loan. These charges include interest, service charges, and loan fees. Since lenders must quote the cost of loans in APR terms, consumers can more easily compare prices among lending institutions. Consumers presumably benefit from the competition that arises from more informed credit shopping.

The board of governors of the Federal Reserve System provides model disclosure forms. The forms use nontechnical language to help borrowers understand the transactions. Creditors need not use these forms, but doing so ensures compliance. Figure 15–1 is an example of a model form.

TILA also applies to credit advertising. An advertisement that lists any credit terms must also include other significant terms, including the APR and terms of repayment. Consumers are inundated with solicitations through the mail, the internet and the phone, offering a temporary APR on balance transfers from other accounts, money advances, and other types of credit extensions. TILA now requires that the advertiser prominently use the term, "Introductory" to identify these offers. The advertiser must also disclose the duration of the period the introductory rate

---

FIGURE 15–1   **Model Truth in Lending Disclosure Form**

Friendly Bank & Trust Co.
700 East Street
Little Creek, USA

Lisa Stone
22–4859–22
300 Maple Avenue
Little Creek, USA

ANNUAL PERCENTAGE RATE The cost of your credit as a yearly rate.	FINANCE CHARGE The dollar amount the credit will cost you.	AMOUNT FINANCED The amount of credit provided to you or on your behalf.	TOTAL OF PAYMENTS The amount you will have paid after you have made all payments as scheduled.
12 %	$ 675.31	$ 5000–	$ 5675.31

You have the right to receive at this time an itemization of the Amount Financed.

☐ I want an itemization.   ☒ I do not want an itemization.

Your payment schedule will be:

Number of Payments	Amount of Payments	When Payments Are Due
1	$262.03^e	6/1/91
23	$235.36	monthly beginning 7/1/91

Late Charge: If a payment is late, you will be charged $5 or 10% of the payment, whichever is less.

Prepayment: If you pay off early, you ☒ may ☐ will not have to pay a penalty.

Required Deposit: The annual percentage rate does not take into account your required deposit.

See your contract documents for any additional information about nonpayment, default, any required repayment in full before the scheduled date, and prepayment refund and penalties.

e means an estimate.

SOURCE: See Regulation Z Truth in Lending; 12 CFR 226, Appendix H (1991).

will apply, and the rate that will apply after the period ends. Consumers should scrutinize other required disclosures in connection with these offers, including the consequence of late payments, failure to pay the minimum monthly amount, and balance transfer fees. Leases are also covered under TILA which requires disclosure of the details of the terms of the lease.

Cancellation of Credit Agreements

Under certain circumstances a debtor may cancel a credit transaction. When a person's home is used as security for a loan, the borrower may cancel the transaction within three business days, although this right does not apply to a first mortgage given to secure the financing of a home. Because of the owner's right to cancel the credit agreement, contractors normally wait three days after an agreement to begin work or supply goods. However, the homeowner may waive the right to cancel by notifying the contractor in writing that there is a real emergency and credit is needed immediately to finance repairs. In that event, the contractor may start the work or supply goods immediately without fear of cancellation.

Credit Cards

More than 1 billion credit cardholders in North America have a total of $750 billion in debt. More than 75 million credit cards are reported lost or stolen each year, and thousands of cards are used fraudulently each day. The credit card industry estimates it is losing billions of dollars each year as a result of credit card misuse.

TILA regulates the issuance and use of credit cards. It provides that no credit cards may be issued without a request by the consumer.

TILA also limits the cardholders' liability to $50 if another person uses the credit card without authorization. This could happen, for example, if the card were lost or stolen. The cardholder can, however, avoid all liability by notifying the issuer of the card's loss or theft before the unauthorized use occurs.

Penalties

TILA provides both criminal and civil liability for violation of its disclosure provisions. Willful violations of the act carry a fine and imprisonment. A creditor who fails to disclose required information may also be civilly liable to a consumer. The liability is limited to twice the amount of the finance charge. In the case of a lease, the maximum liability is $1,000. In the case of violations connected to closed-end loans secured by real estate, the statutory damage maximum is $2000.00. Successful debtors are also entitled to actual damages, reasonable attorney fees, and court costs.

Creditors may avoid liability for errors by correcting them within 60 days after discovery. They may also escape liability by showing that the violation was unintentional and resulted from a good-faith error. An example of a good-faith error would be one resulting from a computer malfunction.

Anyone who uses a counterfeit, altered, forged, lost, stolen, or fraudulently obtained credit card may incur criminal liability under TILA. A violation carries a fine and imprisonment of up to 10 years. State laws also provide criminal penalties.

The Equal Credit Opportunity Act

The Equal Credit Opportunity Act (**ECOA**) prohibits discrimination in credit extension transactions on the basis of sex, race, color, religion, national origin, marital status, age, public assistance income, or a good-faith exercise of a right under the act. The Act covers consumer and commercial credit transactions.

The act forbids creditors from asking credit applicants certain questions. For example, a creditor may not ask whether any of the income listed in the application is derived from alimony or child support. Neither may a creditor ask the race, color, religion, or national origin of an applicant (except for statistical monitoring purposes).

ECOA prohibits disguised forms of discrimination that may injure a protected class. One act that may result in a violation is redlining. Redlining is the practice of denying mortgage loans to finance property located in specific neighborhoods.

TABLE 15–2	Actions Not Constituting Adverse Action

- Change in terms of account expressly agreed to by applicant.
- Action taken on an account as a result of inactivity, default, or delinquency.
- Refusal to authorize an account transaction at a point of sale or loan (with some exceptions).
- Refusal to extend credit because applicable law prohibits such extension.
- Refusal to extend credit because the type of credit requested is not offered.

Since neighborhoods often follow ethnic and racial patterns, redlining may amount to discrimination due to race or national origin.

A creditor must notify the applicant of its loan decision within 30 days of the application. When the decision is adverse, the applicant is entitled to a statement of the specific reasons. Adverse action includes a denial or revocation of credit or an undesirable change in the terms of the existing credit arrangement. Legitimate reasons in support of adverse action may include insufficient income, excessive debt, and irregular employment. Table 15–2 contains a listing of actions not deemed to constitute adverse action.

Penalties

Violators of ECOA are liable to credit applicants for actual and punitive damages, up to $10,000.00. Where members of a discriminated group bring a class action suit against a creditor, recovery is limited to the lesser of $500,000 or 1 percent of the net worth of the creditor. Costs and reasonable attorney fees are added to the damage award. In some cases, the court grants an injunction prohibiting the creditor from further acts of discrimination.

The Fair Credit Reporting Act

The Fair Credit Reporting Act (**FCRA**) regulates consumer reporting agencies. These agencies assemble and evaluate consumer credit information for the purpose of furnishing consumer reports to users who request them. A business may avoid the regulation of the act if it assembles credit information for its own use as opposed to use by another.

Under the act, a consumer reporting agency may furnish consumer reports in response to a valid court order; on the written request of a consumer to whom it relates; and for use in determining a consumer's eligibility for credit, insurance, employment, or other legitimate business purposes.

Every consumer reporting agency is required to maintain reasonable procedures to avoid violations of the act. The reporting agency must take measures to ensure that those requesting information identify themselves and certify the intended use of the information. The reporting agency must also maintain reasonable procedures to ensure the accuracy of its consumer reports and the completeness of public information reported. It is required to purge information that is older than seven years (ten years for bankruptcies). Medical information is sharply curtailed and may ordinarily only be released pursuant to the consumer's consent.

Consumers are entitled to disclosure of the information about them contained in the files of the reporting agency. Generally, consumers are also entitled to the names of those to whom the agency supplied consumer reports. They have the right to obtain one free credit report annually, including credit scores. Under the U.S. Patriot Act, the FBI has liberal access to consumer credit information.

Investigative Consumer Reports

Consumer reporting agencies often accumulate information about a consumer's character, reputation, or mode of living. This information, gathered through personal interviews with neighbors, friends, associates, or others, is called an **investigative consumer report**. Upon proper request those reports are supplied to employers, insurance companies, and landlords.

Under the FCRA, no unfavorable private information based on an investigative report that is at least three months old may be included in a consumer report unless reverified. The consumer must be informed when an investigative consumer report is requested or prepared. The consumer has a right to an accurate disclosure of the nature and scope of the investigation if a written report has been requested. This right does not, however, apply, if the investigative report is to be used to consider the consumer's suitability for a job for which the consumer did not specifically apply, as, for example, when one is sought after by a "head-hunter"—a type of employment broker.

Dispute Resolution

A consumer may dispute the accuracy of information in the reporting agency's files. In such a case, the reporting agency may be required to reinvestigate the accuracy of the data. If the reinvestigation fails to confirm its validity, the reporting agency must delete the information from its files. If the reinvestigation fails to resolve the dispute, the consumer is permitted to file a brief written rebuttal. On all future reports containing the information, the agency must point out that the facts are disputed and supply the consumer's statement or an abstract of it. The consumer may also insist that any deleted or disputed information be brought to the attention of persons who previously received a report.

Requirements on Users of Reports

An unfavorable consumer report may result in denial of credit, insurance, or employment, or in higher finance charges or insurance premiums. In such cases, the user of the report is required to advise the consumer of the name and address of the consumer reporting agency that supplied the report. Sometimes consumer credit is denied or the charge for consumer credit is increased because of information received from a source other than a consumer reporting agency. When this occurs, on written request, the user of the information must inform the applicant of the nature of the information that resulted in the unfavorable action.

Remedies

The act also provides for criminal penalties, for example, against persons who obtain information about a consumer from a consumer reporting agency under false pretenses. Violators may be fined and imprisoned.

Civil liability under the act is divided into two categories. First, any consumer reporting agency or user that willfully violates the act is liable to the consumer for actual damages, punitive damages, court costs, and reasonable attorney's fees. Second, a reporting agency or user of information that negligently fails to comply with the act is liable to the consumer for the actual damages, court costs, and reasonable attorney's fees.

The following case establishes some boundaries on the issue of reasonable investigation and procedures.

LLOYD SARVER V. EXPERIAN INFORMATION SOLUTIONS
390 F.3d 969 (7th Cir. 2004)

Experian Information Solutions (Experian), a national credit reporting agency, reported inaccurate information on Lloyd Sarver's credit report, causing a bank to deny him credit, on August 2, 2002. The credit report, which Sarver received before the denial of credit, showed falsely that Sarver was involved in a bankruptcy. On August 29, 2002 Sarver wrote Experian, requesting that the bankruptcy inaccuracy be corrected. Experian responded by letter of September 11, 2002, requesting further identifying information, before it would begin an investigation. Sarver responded by filing suit against Experian. The District Court granted summary judgment in favor of Experian. Sarver appealed, and the court of appeals affirmed.

Judge Terrence T. Evans

Section 1681i requires a credit reporting agency to reinvestigate items on a credit report when a consumer disputes the validity of those items. . . . We do not need to decide whether Sarver's failure to provide the information Experian requested rendered his complaint frivolous; his claim . . . fails for another reason, a lack of evidence of damages. . . .

Without a causal relation between the violation of the statute and the loss of credit, or some other harm, a plaintiff cannot obtain an award of "actual damages."

On this point the district court concluded that there were no damages. . . .

Sarver, however, disagrees and claims that he suffered damages when he was denied credit by [the Bank]. This letter cannot be a basis for his damage claim, however, because as of August 2, Experian had no notice of any inaccuracies in the report. . . . Experian must be notified of an error before it is required to reinvestigate. As we have made clear the FCRA is not a strict liability statute. . . . Finally, to obtain statutory damages under FCRA section sign 1681n(a), Sarver must show that Experian willfully violated the Act. There is similarly no evidence of willfulness. . . .

We turn to Sarver's claim . . . which requires that a credit reporting agency follow "reasonable procedures to assure maximum possible accuracy" when it prepares a credit report. The reasonableness of a reporting agency's procedures is normally a question for trial unless the reasonableness or unreasonableness of the procedures is beyond question. However, to state a claim under the statute,

> a consumer must sufficiently allege "that a credit reporting agency prepared a report containing 'inaccurate' information." However, the credit reporting agency is not automatically liable even if the consumer proves that it prepared an inaccurate credit report because FCRA "does not make reporting agencies strictly liable for all inaccuracies." A credit reporting agency is not liable under the FCRA if it followed "reasonable procedures to assure maximum possible accuracy," but nonetheless reported inaccurate information in the consumer's credit report.

The Commentary to the Federal Trade Commission to the FCRA states that the section does not hold a reporting agency responsible where an item of information, received from a source that it reasonably believes is reputable, turns out to be inaccurate unless the agency receives notice of systemic problems with its procedures.

Experian has provided an account of its procedures. The affidavit of David Browne, Experian's compliance manager, explains that the company gathers credit information originated by approximately 40,000 sources. The information is stored in a complex system of national databases, containing approximately 200 million names and addresses and some 2.6 billion trade lines, which include information about consumer accounts, judgments, etc. The company processes over 50 million updates to trade information each day. Lenders report millions of accounts to Experian daily; they provide identifying information, including address, social security number, and date of birth. The identifying information is used to link the credit items to the appropriate consumer. Mr. Browne also notes that Experian's computer system does not store complete credit reports, but rather stores the individual items of credit information linked to identifying information. The credit report is generated at the time an inquiry for it is received.

One can easily see how, even with safeguards in place, mistakes can happen. But given the complexity of the system and the volume of information involved, a mistake does not render the procedures unreasonable. In his attempt to show that Experian's procedures are unreasonable, Sarver argues that someone should have noticed that only [the Bank] . . . accounts were shown to have been involved in bankruptcy. That anomaly should have alerted Experian, Sarver says, to the fact that the report was inaccurate. What Sarver is asking, then, is that each computer-generated report be examined for anomalous information and, if it is found, an investigation is launched. In the absence of notice of prevalent unreliable information from a reporting lender, which would put Experian on notice that problems exists, we cannot find that such a requirement to investigate would be reasonable given the enormous volume of information Experian processes daily.

We found in *Henson* that a consumer reporting agency was not liable, as a matter of law, for reporting information from a judgment docket unless there was prior notice from the consumer that the information might be inaccurate. We said that a

> contrary rule of law would require credit reporting agencies to go beyond the face of numerous court records to determine whether they correctly report the outcome of the underlying action. Such a rule would also require credit reporting agencies to engage in background research which would

substantially increase the cost of their services. In turn, they would be forced to pass on the increased costs to their customers and ultimately to the individual consumer.

The same could be said for records from financial institutions. As we said, in his affidavit Mr. Browne proclaims, and there is nothing in the record to make us doubt his statement, that lenders report many millions of accounts to Experian daily. Sarver's report . . . contains entries from six different lenders. The increased cost to Experian to examine each of these entries individually would be enormous. We find that as a matter of law there is nothing in this record to show that Experian's procedures are unreasonable.

Accordingly, we AFFIRM the judgment of the district court.

Case Questions

1. Why was Experian not required to reinvestigate? Explain.
2. Explain what the court means when it says that FCRA is not a strict liability statute.
3. What argument does Sarver make regarding Experian's "unreasonable procedures."? Why does the court reject the argument?
4. List the factors that you think are most relevant when determining whether a credit reporting agency's procedures are reasonable.
5. The San Antonio Retail Merchants Association (SARMA), a computerized credit reporting agency, provides service to local business subscribers. These subscribers feed credit information into SARMA's computers and have access to SARMA's credit information files. To obtain information about a consumer, a subscriber must feed identifying information from its own computer terminal into SARMA's central computer. SARMA's computer displays on the subscriber's terminal the history file of the consumer who most nearly matches the identifying information. If

the subscriber accepts the file as that of the particular consumer, SARMA's computer automatically captures any information from the subscriber's terminal that it did not already have.

William Daniel Thompson, Jr., opened an account with Gordon's Jewelers (Gordon's) in November 1974. He listed his social security number as 457–68–5778, his address as 132 Baxter, marital status as single, and his occupation as a truck loader. He charged $77.25 at Gordon's, which he failed to pay. Gordon's reported the debt to SARMA, which placed the information and a bad credit rating in file number 5867114. It failed to include any social security number.

William Douglas Thompson III (plaintiff) applied for credit in early 1978 with Gulf and with Ward's in San Antonio. He gave his social security number as 407–86–4065, his address as 6929 Timber-Creek, his wife as Deborah C., and his occupation as groundskeeper. Gulf's terminal operator mistakenly accepted file number 5867114 as the plaintiff's, and SARMA's computer automatically loaded information about William Douglas Thompson III into file number 5867114. That information included plaintiff's social security number. The original file on William Daniel Thompson, Jr. became an amalgam of information on both William Daniel Thompson, Jr. and the plaintiff. It included plaintiff's social security number.

When Ward's ran a check on plaintiff, the terminal operator was given the garbled data and accepted file number 5867114 as that of the plaintiff. It contained adverse information about Gordon's delinquent account. Ward's denied credit to the plaintiff. In May 1979, plaintiff applied again and was rejected.

Gulf requested a revision of file number 5867114 in February 1978. SARMA apparently contacted Gordon's to verify the credit information but failed to check the social security number of Gordon's delinquent customer. The adverse information stayed in the file under plaintiff's social security number, and Gulf denied him credit. Plaintiff sued

SARMA under the FCRA for failing to employ reasonable care in reporting credit information. Did SARMA fail to employ reasonable standards? Explain.

Identity Theft

Identity theft occurs when an unauthorized person appropriates information of a consumer and runs up debt. The growing concern has resulted in new tools to combat the devastating results of identity theft. Victims are entitled to place fraud alerts in their credit files and block information caused by theft or fraud. Credit agencies notify the consumer when there appears to be suspicious additions or deletions to their record. They must employ reasonable procedures to prevent re-dissemination of information that is the subject to identity theft. What is reasonable is determined by the totality of the facts and circumstances. Nonetheless, the agency must reinvestigate information based upon alleged identity theft when on notice.

The Fair Credit Billing Act

The Fair Credit Billing Act regulates procedures for resolving billing errors. It applies to creditors that issue credit cards, that regularly extend credit payable in more than four installments, and that assess a finance charge. These creditors must advise consumers of their rights and responsibilities when an account is opened, and at semiannual intervals thereafter. They also must disclose, on the periodic billing statement, where to address billing inquiries.

Any creditor that receives written notice of a billing error must respond in writing. When the creditor agrees that an error exists, it must adjust the account and notify the consumer. If the creditor concludes that the billing statement is correct, it must give the consumer reasons supporting its conclusion. The creditor must include documentary evidence of the debt if the consumer requests it.

The creditor may not institute any action to collect the debt until it makes the proper response. However, the creditor may continue to send periodic statements reflecting the disputed amount. The creditor may not close or restrict the consumer's account before it responds, but it may use the amount of the dispute to determine whether the consumer has exceeded credit limits.

A creditor may not give a bad credit report concerning the disputed amount until at least 10 days after the creditor informs the consumer of its belief in the accuracy of its bill. This allows the consumer time to respond. If the consumer continues to dispute the billing statement, the creditor must indicate that dispute on future reports. A creditor that violates the act forfeits the right to collect the disputed amount and finance charges not to exceed $50 for each disputed item.

The Electronic Funds Transfer Act

The Electronic Funds Transfer Act (EFTA) establishes the rights and responsibilities of consumers and financial institutions involved in electronic funds transfers. An electronic fund transfer is any transfer of funds (other than by paper instruments) initiated through electronic means that authorizes a financial institution to debit or credit an account. Electronic funds transfers occur through the use of ATMs, electronic deposits, internet banking and telephone payment services.

Under the act, financial institutions must disclose to customers the terms and conditions of EFT service. The disclosure must include the consumer's liability for unauthorized fund transfers, who to notify in the event of an unauthorized transfer, any charges for electronic funds transfers, and the procedure necessary to stop payment.

The act requires that users be given receipts for each transaction. Periodic statements identifying each transaction are also required.

Error Resolution

Under the act, financial institutions are required to investigate all consumer allegations of errors (including unauthorized use) and notify the consumer of its findings in writing within 10 business days. The institution may extend the investigation to 45 days if it credits the consumer's account pending the outcome of the investigation. On examination, if the institution determines that there is an error, it must reverse the error within one business day. Failure to comply with the error-resolution procedure may result in treble damages against the noncomplying institution.

Remedies

Under the act, consumers may be liable if their EFT card is used without authorization. Liability, however, is limited to $50 as long as the consumer gives prompt notification of the unauthorized use to the institution. Financial institutions are liable to consumers for all damages resulting from the institution's failure to make an electronic funds transfer ordered by the consumer. There are certain specified exceptions, for example, when the transfer would exceed an established credit line. The institution is also liable for damages caused by a failure to stop payment when properly instructed to do so by the consumer. For wilful failure to follow the error resolution procedures the consumer is entitled to three times the actual damages. Financial institutions are liable to the consumer for failure to otherwise comply with the act for actual damages plus additional damages not exceeding $1,000, costs of the action, and reasonable attorney fees.

Debt Collection

When a debtor defaults, the creditor naturally attempts to collect the debt. The initial attempt usually takes the form of letters and phone calls; sometimes these communications are extremely harsh and threatening. If these efforts fail, the creditor may employ a third party to collect the debt. Professional collection agencies often invoke creative techniques to force payment, but they cannot go beyond certain defined permissible limits in pursuing the debtor.

In the past, a creditor's conduct was governed only by the common law. Because of the inadequate protection provided by the common law against abusive collection tactics, Congress responded with legislation that regulates creditors' collection activities.

The Fair Debt Collection Practices Act

The Fair Debt Collection Practices Act (FDCPA) regulates debt collectors in the business of collecting consumer debts for others. The act also applies to those who process their own debts when they do so under other names. It does, however, not apply to creditors who collect their own debts in their own names.

Communications

Under the act, a covered debt collector may contact a person other than the debtor, the debtor's spouse, or the debtor's parents (if the debtor is a minor) only for the purpose of obtaining location information. Location information includes the debtor's home telephone number, place of residence, and place of employment.

When talking to a third party, the debt collector cannot volunteer the nature of his or her business. That information may be supplied only if it is expressly requested. Even then, the collector is not permitted to inform the third party that a debt is owed. The debt collector cannot communicate with the same third party more than once unless the party so requests or the collector reasonably believes that the information received from that party was erroneous or incomplete.

The debt collector may not contact the debtor at a time or place which should be known to be inconvenient. In the absence of knowledge as to convenient times or places, the act specifies as convenient the hours between 8:00 A.M. and 9:00 P.M. Any other hours are considered inconvenient. The debt collector may not contact the consumer on the job if the collector is aware that the employer prohibits such communications.

As soon as the collector becomes aware that the debtor is represented by an attorney, further contacts with the debtor must cease. Contacts with the debtor must also cease if the debtor communicates, in writing, a refusal to pay or a request that the contacts end. This communication often leads to the creditor suing the debtor.

Prohibitions

The collector may not harass, oppress, or abuse any person in connection with the collection of a debt. For example, a debt collector may not make repeated or obscene phone calls to the debtor or advertise the debt for sale.

TABLE 15–3   **Prohibitions Under the FDCPA**

A debt collector may not:

- Contact a debtor at any unusual or inconvenient time or place.
- Contact a debtor if represented by a responsive attorney.
- Contact a debtor at place of employment if collector knows this is forbidden by the employer.
- Contact a third party to obtain other than location information.
- Use obscene language in connection with debt collection.
- Call debtor with intent to annoy, abuse, or harass.
- Attempt to collect more than is due.
- Threaten to take action the collector may not lawfully take.
- Make any false representations in connection with the debt collection.
- Use language on any envelope identifying that the sender is a debt collector.

Debt collectors cannot make false or misleading statements in collection efforts. They cannot, for example, falsely claim to be attorneys or government officials. Collectors also may not threaten to take action that they cannot legally take or do not intend to take. For example, a creditor may not ordinarily take a debtor's property without legal process; any threat to do so violates the act. In addition, collectors cannot engage in unfair practices. Attempting to collect a debt that is not authorized by law and concealing charges for collection are examples of unfair practices. Prohibitions under the FDCPA are listed in Table 15–3.

Validation of Debts

Under the act, the debt collector is required to give the consumer written notice not only of the details of the debt but also that the consumer has a right to dispute it in writing. On receipt of a writing disputing the debt, the creditor must cease collection efforts and verify the debt.

The following case illustrates the application of the validation requirements and other aspects under the FDCPA.

SWANSON V. SOUTHERN OREGON CREDIT SERVICE, INC.
869 F.2d 1222 (9th Cir. 1989)

Swanson owed $262.20 to Cascade Community Hospital. The debt was referred to Southern Oregon Credit Service for collection. Southern Oregon sent various notices to Swanson and made telephone calls to collect the debt.

Swanson sued Southern Oregon alleging violations of the Fair Debt Collection Practices Act. The U.S. District Court entered summary judgment in favor of Southern Oregon. Swanson appealed to the U.S. Court of Appeals which reversed the district court's judgment, in part.

Per Curiam

Swanson argues that the first notice that Southern Oregon sent to him (initial communication) violates the validation of debts provision contained in . . . section 1692g(a) [of the act]. That section provides that debt collectors must send consumers written notice containing certain information regarding the alleged debt and advising them . . . that it will be assumed to be valid unless the consumer contests its accuracy or validity within thirty days. . . .

■   ■   ■

Congress designed the Federal Act to "eliminate the recurring problem of debt collectors dunning the wrong person or attempting to collect debts which the consumer has already paid. . . ." In this circuit, the impact of language alleged to violate section 1692g is judged under the "least sophisticated debtor" standard. That is, if we find that the least sophisticated debtor would likely be misled by the notice which Swanson received from Southern Oregon, we must hold that the credit service has violated the Act.

Swanson admits that the initial communication from South Oregon contained the basic language required by section 16928, but argues that its message was contradicted and "overshadowed" by the balance of the notice. The notice Southern Oregon sent Swanson contained, in bold faced type several times larger than the debt validation notice required by section 16928, the following message:

> "IF THIS ACCOUNT IS PAID WITHIN THE NEXT 10 DAYS IT WILL NOT BE RECORDED IN OUR MASTER FILE AS AN UNPAID COLLECTION ITEM. *A GOOD CREDIT RATING— IS YOUR MOST VALUABLE ASSET."*

Beneath this language, in small standard-face type, was the notice required by the statute. Swanson argued to the district court, and contends again here, that the "visual effect" of the large type language overshadowed the debt validation notice,

and that its language and tone constituted an impermissible threat of harm to his credit rating if he should avail himself of the Act's 30 day validation period.

The magistrate, whose findings were adopted without revision or comment by the district court, termed Swanson's argument "frivolous," concluding that "[n]othing in the notice can reasonably be construed as threatening [Swanson] with adverse consequences." This conclusion is patently at odds with the tenor and text of the notice itself. The reference to the undefined "master file," juxtaposed with the admonition that Swanson's credit rating was his "most valuable asset," cannot reasonably be interpreted as anything but a threat: if Swanson did not pay within 10 days, his name would be placed in Southern Oregon's "master file" and as a result he would lose his "most valuable asset."

■   ■   ■

Congress designed section 1692g to provide alleged debtors with 30 days to question and respond to the initial communication of a collection agency. The form used by Southern Oregon in this case invokes a shorter response period, promising harm to the debtor who waits beyond 10 days. . . .

Accordingly, we hold that Southern Oregon's initial communication with Swanson violated section 1692g of the Federal Act.

Swanson also attacks the second notice that Southern Oregon sent him which stated: "Unless payment in full on definite arrangements are made on your account(s) within 48 hours a complete investigation will begin concerning your employment and assets." . . .

Section 1692e(5) bars a debt collector from making a threat "to take any action that cannot legally be taken." Section 1692c(b) prohibits a debt collector from "communicating" with most third parties, including a debtor's employer. Section 1692a(2) defines a "communication" as "the conveying of information regarding a debt directly or indirectly to any person through any medium."

■ ■ ■

Under the least sophisticated debtor standard, we hold that Southern Oregon's threat to make a "complete investigation concerning your employment" violates section 1692e(5). Because section 1692c(b) prohibits such unconsented and unauthorized communication with a debtor's employer concerning the debt, the threat constitutes a "threat to take any action that cannot legally be taken."

To the least sophisticated debtor, the notice threatens that which Southern Oregon legally could not do. Thus, Southern Oregon violated section 1692e(5), and summary judgment in its favor on that issue should not have been granted.

Circuit Judge Wallace (Concurring and dissenting)

I conclude that the fact that the debt validation notice is clearly printed on the same page and is in ordinary typesize, . . . that even the least sophisticated debtor would understand his debt validation rights. Moreover . . . I do not believe that the least sophisticated debtor would understand that some grave consequence would follow from the master file threat in this case. . . . I conclude that

the debt validation clause in the initial communication is not so overshadowed by the master file statement that the least sophisticated debtor would fail to recognize his section 1692g right. Thus, I would affirm the district court's entry of summary judgment on this issue.

Case Questions

1. What is the least sophisticated debtor standard? Why did the majority believe it was satisfied? Why did the dissent not believe it was satisfied?

2. Is the "least sophisticated debtor" standard an objective one? How do you determine the identity of the least sophisticated debtor? Does the fact that the majority and dissent disagree on the standard's application mean that summary judgment is not proper? Explain.

3. Was there a violation of the section prohibiting taking action that cannot legally be taken? Explain.

4. How would you redraft Southern Oregon's "validation notice" and its second letter to come into clear compliance with the act?

Penalties and Enforcement

Any debt collector who violates the act is liable to the debtor for actual damages. Actual damages might occur if an employer fires the debtor after learning of the debt. The debt collector may be assessed additional damages of up to $1,000. Reasonable attorney's fees and court costs are also recoverable.

Postjudgment Collection

When private debt collection attempts are unsuccessful, a creditor might resort to a court to aid in the collection process. Even if a creditor receives a court judgment, the debtor might still refuse to pay. A court judgment is reflected by an entry signed by a judge acknowledging the amount awarded to the winning party. If the debtor is judgment-proof, that is, has no assets, the court entry does not help the creditor. However, judgments are good for many years, depending on state law. If the uncooperative debtor has property, or eventually acquires property, the creditor may attach it. Under attachment, a sheriff seizes the property, the property is sold, and the proceeds are distributed to the creditor to the extent necessary to satisfy the judgment and related expenses. Any excess funds derived from the sale are returned to the debtor.

Garnishment is another remedy available to a judgment creditor. Garnishment enables creditors to reach debtors' property that is held by third parties. Bank accounts and wages are the most commonly garnisheed property. (Under certain circumstances, a creditor may attach or garnishee a debtor's property before a judgment; many states permit this when it appears that the debtor intends to leave the jurisdiction to avoid creditors.) Each state has enacted its own statute to regulate a creditor's right to garnishee a debtor's wages.

To curb the impact of unrestricted garnishment of earnings and discharge because of garnishment, Congress passed Title III of the Consumer Credit Protection Act. Title III does not supplant state garnishment statutes but merely places limitations on them.

A state statute providing for garnishment procedure must be at least as restrictive as Title III. The act limits the percentage of a debtor's disposable earnings subject to garnishment. Disposable earnings are the wages that an employee receives after certain amounts required by law are deducted. These withholdings include federal, state, and local taxes; social security payments; and deductions for pension plans required by state law for government employees. Under the act, the maximum amount that may be garnisheed for any workweek is generally either (1) 25 percent of an employee's disposable earnings for the week; or (2) the amount that the disposable earnings for the week exceeds 30 times the federal minimum hourly wage, whichever is less. However, the allowable amount for garnishment for spousal or child support is greater, up to 65% of the worker's disposable income, depending on the specific circumstances.

The act also places restrictions on discharge from employment by reason of garnishment. An employer may not discharge an employee whose earnings have been subjected to garnishment for any one indebtedness. An employer who violates this provision may be fined and imprisoned.

The Bankruptcy Reform Act

The failure of a business means loss of jobs for its employees and a financial loss to its creditors. Shareholders and others who have an interest in the business may lose their investment, and customers may lose a supplier. Whatever the reason for the failure, there is a need for debtor relief to lighten the burden. Those affected must be treated fairly. Debtors can seek relief not only through state statutes but also through the federal Bankruptcy Reform Act, which most recently underwent a substantial overhaul in 2005 via the Bankruptcy Abuse Prevention and Consumer Protection Act. The recent amendments seek to prevent some of the abuse that occurred when debtors with reckless abandon took advantage of the bankruptcy laws, even though they may have been potentially financially sound. For example, it is no longer possible to build up credit card debt on the eve of bankruptcy and expect a discharge of that debt. Additionally, debtors must produce an itemized statement of income, other financial evidences of income and expenses, and their tax returns. They must be current on their tax filings in order to avail themselves of the bankruptcy laws.

Before declaring bankruptcy a debtor must now first undergo credit counseling. The counseling is for the purpose of apprizing the debtor of various options as alternatives to bankruptcy. It may be accomplished through the internet or even by telephone. Before being discharged in bankruptcy the debtor must complete an approved personal financial management course. This is intended to impart financial management skills in hopes of preventing further financial failure.

This section discusses three types of debtor relief under bankruptcy law: liquidation (chapter 7 of the act), reorganization (chapter 11), and adjustment of the debts of an individual (chapter 13) (see Table 15–4).

Liquidation

A debtor may not file for a Chapter 7 liquidation if one was filed within the last eight years.

Liquidation is sometimes referred to as *straight bankruptcy* or as a *chapter 7 proceeding*. Generally, a liquidation involves the sale of the debtor's assets, distribution of the proceeds to creditors, and the discharge of the debtor's remaining liabilities. Liquidation is consistent with the philosophy of allowing an honest debtor to get a fresh start. Individuals, partnerships, or corporations that are insolvent may be the subjects of liquidations.

TABLE 15–4   Comparison of Forms of Bankruptcy

Chapter	Type	Eligibility	Exceptions	Description
7	Liquidation	• Corporations • Partnerships • Individuals	• Banking Institutions • Railroads • Credit unions • Insurance companies	Nonexempt assets are sold and distributed to creditors.
11	Reorganization	• Corporations • Partnerships • Individuals • Unincorporated associations • Railroads	• Stockbrokers • Commodities brokers • Banks • Savings & loans • Credit unions • Insurance companies	Debtor continues in possession and a plan of reorganization is formulated.
13	Adjustment of debts for individuals	• Individuals	• Stockbrokers • Commodities brokers • Unsecured debts exceed $250,000 or secured debts exceed $750,000	Individual continues in possession and a plan for adjusting debts is formulated.

Insolvency for the purpose of liquidation means that the debtor cannot meet financial obligations as they become due. This differs from the ordinary balance sheet concept of insolvency, under which liabilities exceed assets. It is not uncommon for a debtor to possess assets in excess of liabilities, yet still be unable to meet the liabilities as they mature. The assets might be in the form of unmarketable securities, slow-moving inventory, or real property. The nonliquid state of these assets might prevent the debtor from meeting day-to-day debts. Under the recent amendments, debtors whose average income is higher than the median incomes for their state may not be eligible to file a Chapter 7 petition. They will be required to calculate their expenses based upon an IRS expense table. In the event that after deducting the expenses there remains at least $6,000 over 60 months, debtors will be disqualified from Chapter 7 and will need to look at Chapter 13, discussed below.

Petitions

Liquidation may be voluntary or involuntary. In a voluntary liquidation, the debtor files a bankruptcy petition. The petition acts as an order for relief and gives the court jurisdiction to administer the liquidation. Railroads, governmental units, banks, savings and loan associations, and insurance companies may not initiate voluntary petitions in bankruptcy. These industries are subject to rigid supervision and control by regulatory agencies.

A debtor may be forced into liquidation by creditors. To force a debtor into liquidation, the creditors must file an involuntary petition. If the debtor has 12 or more creditors, at least 3 must join in filing the petition. If there are fewer than 12 creditors, at least 1 creditor must file the petition. In either case, the petitioning creditor(s) must have unsecured claims totaling at least $12,300. The petitioning creditors are granted an order for relief if they can prove that (1) the debtor is insolvent, or (2) someone was appointed to take possession of the debtor's property within 120 days before the petition was filed. Farmers and charitable corporations may not be targets of involuntary liquidations.

Both voluntary and involuntary debtors are required to file lists of their creditors, schedules of assets and liabilities, and statements of financial affairs. Each creditor and other interested parties receive notice of the filing of the petition.

Automatic Stay

The filing of a petition in bankruptcy causes an automatic stay (suspension) of most attempts by creditors to collect on their indebtedness. Government agencies acting to enforce their regulatory powers are exempt from the stay, as are landlords seeking to enforce an eviction judgment, and creditors pursing alimony or child support. In fact a debtor must pay domestic support obligations since the date of the filing of the petition in order to secure a discharge in bankruptcy.

In some cases creditors that are not exempt from the stay may be granted relief on application to the bankruptcy court. If the creditor can show that an interest in specific property held as collateral on a debt is jeopardized by the stay, the court relieves the creditor from the stay unless adequate protection can otherwise be afforded by the debtor. (Adequate protection is discussed in the next section.)

Trustees

After an order for relief is granted, an interim trustee is appointed to take over the debtor's property. The takeover is not usually physical at this stage, although the interim trustee does possess the legal rights of ownership. The interim trustee conducts a first meeting of creditors. The debtor appears at the meeting and is questioned by the creditors and the trustee about assets and other matters. At this stage, creditors are generally most concerned about the whereabouts of property in which they have or might have an interest.

The creditors may elect a permanent trustee; otherwise the interim trustee continues to serve. The debtor's property passes to the trustee, who converts it to cash to the extent necessary to pay creditors.

The debtor's estate includes all property in which the debtor has an interest. Anyone holding estate property must turn it over to the trustee. That includes anyone having an interest in the property, such as a secured creditor. A secured creditor possesses a security interest in specific property as collateral for a debt. This creditor is entitled to be paid out of the proceeds of the sale of the secured property. A secured creditor has a strong interest in protecting the secured property. Consequently, a secured creditor may insist upon adequate protection from the trustee before surrendering possession. The trustee may provide such a creditor with adequate protection by, for example, agreeing to make cash payments to the creditor in an amount equal to the periodic depreciation of the secured property.

The trustee has broad discretionary powers over the debtor's property. One such grant is the power to abandon the debtor's property. This is often done when the property has no value or, for example, when the cost of storage exceeds the value of the property. However, a trustee may not abandon hazardous wastes or property that may cause injury to public health or safety when the abandonment is against state law or public policy.[1]

Exemptions

An individual debtor is entitled to exempt certain property from distribution to creditors. The debtor may elect to take exemptions provided by either state or federal law. State law, however, may restrict the debtor to state exemptions, as most states have done. Federal exemptions are more liberal than those granted in most states. Consequently, debtors usually choose the federal exemptions where state law does not prohibit them from doing so (see Table 15–5).

Preferential and Fraudulent Transfer

The trustee has the power to void a **preferential transfer** of property made by the debtor. A preferential transfer is (1) a transfer of property made for the benefit of a creditor, (2) to pay a preexisting debt, (3) when the debtor is insolvent under a balance sheet test, and (4) made during the 90-day period before the petition is

---

[1] Midlantic National Bank v. New Jersey Dept. of Environmental Protection, 474 U.S. 494 (1986).

TABLE 15–5   Federal Bankruptcy Exemptions

- Equity in a residential home not exceeding $18,450.00 (homestead exemption).
- Equity in a motor vehicle not exceeding $2,950.00.
- Household items, wearing apparel, and other property for personal use, up to $9,850.00 (up to $475.00 per item).
- Jewelry not exceeding $1,225.00.
- Property selected by a debtor of up to $975 in value in addition to up to $9,250.00 of any unused portion of the homestead exemption mentioned earlier.
- Trade tools not exceeding $1,850 in value.
- Interests in life insurance policies up to $9,850.00.
- Health aids.
- State and federal benefits, such as social security, unemployment, alimony, and pensions, to the extent reasonably necessary for support.
- Awards and payments arising from certain actions, including personal injury, life insurance policies, wrongful death, and victims' reparation laws.

---

filed, (5) which gives a creditor a greater percentage of the debt than would have been received under the distribution provision of the act. (See Example 15-1).

Under these circumstances, trustees also may void transfers to an insider if the transfers were made within one year before the filing of the petition and the insider reasonably believed that the debtor was insolvent. An insider here is one who is in a close relationship to the debtor, such as a spouse, relative, partner, corporate officer, or director.

Some types of transactions cannot be voided by the trustee even if they appear to be preferential. The trustee cannot, for example, set aside the payment of a debt incurred within the ordinary course of the debtor's business.

The trustee may set aside certain fraudulent transfers that were made within two years before the filing of the petition. Fraudulent transfers include those intended to hinder, delay, or otherwise defraud creditors.

EXAMPLE 15–1   Preferential Transfer

Assume that Ham owes his creditors the following amounts: Round, $500; Square, $1,000; and Pentagon, $2,500. The total owed is $4,000. Ham's total assets equal $3,000, making him insolvent under a balance sheet test because his liabilities exceed his assets. On February 1, Ham pays Square $750. Sixty days later he files bankruptcy, listing assets of $3,000 and exemptions amounting to $1,000. Because the transfer was preferential, the trustee in bankruptcy may recover the $750 transfer to Square and include it in Ham's bankruptcy estate.

The first four criteria of a preferential transfer are easy to see in this case. Square also received a greater percentage of the debt than he would be entitled to under bankruptcy law. The transfer gave Square 75 percent of the amount due. However, under the act Square would be entitled only to 25 percent of the indebtedness since that is the percentage the amount due him ($1,000) bears to the amount due all the creditors ($4,000).

Ethical Dilemmas/Issues

Susan McGonigle is the owner of the Happy Health Spa, Inc., an exercise and health club. The club has 1,300 members. Nonrefundable membership fees are $300 per year per member. Despite this, the spa is in financial difficulties. Last week, McGonigle started a life membership sale designed to generate revenues to solve the club's current financial crisis. Although the sale is to last 30 days, it has become apparent that the sales will not be sufficient to turn around the spa's financial situation. After one week, only 120 new memberships were sold; McGonigle had planned to sell twice that number.

McGonigle met with her attorney, who advised her to file bankruptcy as soon as possible and to try to sell the business premises. A buyer has been located, and a purchase contract has been entered into. Possession of the premises is to be transferred to the buyer in 90 days. The buyer will not be continuing the health spa business. McGonigle's attorney has started preparing the bankruptcy petition. The attorney plans to file the bankruptcy petition in 90 days, when possession of the premises is transferred to the new buyer.

The sales personnel at the Happy Health Spa are unaware that McGonigle has sold the premises and plans to declare bankruptcy. People continue to inquire into the purchase of memberships.

What are the ethical issues? What would you do?

Distribution and Priority

The trustee is charged with distributing the cash realized from the liquidation to satisfy the allowed claims of creditors. The three classes of creditors are secured creditors, priority creditors, and general creditors. Secured creditors are paid out of the proceeds of the sale of the collateral in which they have an interest. If those proceeds are insufficient to satisfy the debt, the secured creditor is a general creditor for the balance due.

Certain unsecured claims are entitled to priority in distribution. These claims are paid before the claims of other unsecured creditors. They include the following:

- Domestic support obligations.
- Administrative expenses, including court costs and trustee and attorney fees.
- Claims of up to $4,000 per employee for wages earned within 90 days before the petition is filed.
- Claims of up to $1,800 per claimant for deposits on consumer goods or services that were never received.
- Claims for federal, state, and local taxes.

After the claims of the priority creditors have been satisfied, any remaining nonexempt assets are distributed among the general (unsecured) creditors. Any assets remaining after distribution of the general creditors are delivered to the debtor. (See Example 15–2).

Discharge

A debtor may be afforded a discharge in bankruptcy. A discharge excuses the debtor from the obligation to pay the remaining dischargeable unpaid debts. Unpaid creditors may contest the discharge in bankruptcy on any one of several grounds, including the following: concealment of assets, commission of a bankruptcy crime, and a prior discharge in bankruptcy within the last six years.

Certain claims are nondischargeable. They must ultimately be paid by the debtor. These include, for example, domestic support obligations (child support and spousal obligations), certain taxes; debts not listed by the debtor in the schedule of debts; debts arising from court awards due to drunken operation of automobiles or boats, illegal evictions, and wilful and malicious actions; and certain debts incurred for the purchase of luxuries, and as the next case illustrates claims for student loans unless repayment would cause undue hardship.

EXAMPLE 15–2   Distribution to Creditors

Assume John Jefferson, doing business as Jefferson Meat Market, files for bankruptcy under chapter 7. Jefferson incurs administrative expenses for the filing in the amount of $2,000. He owes three employees: Adams, $500; Hanks, $300; and Robins, $100. He owes $1,200 in federal taxes, $600 in state taxes, and $300 in local taxes. He has nine unsecured creditors as follows:

Creditor	Amount
A	$ 2,000
B	4,000
C	6,000
D	8,000
E	1,000
F	3,000
G	9,000
H	5,000
I	7,000
	$45,000

Assume that Jefferson's nonexempt assets available for distribution amount to $27,500. The assets would be distributed as follows:

Funds available for distribution	$27,500
Administrative expenses	–2,000
	25,500
Wages	–900
	24,600
Taxes	–2,100
	$22,500

The $22,500 is available for distribution to the nine unsecured creditors. Each creditor would receive one half of the amount owed them ($22,500/$45,0000 = ½).

IN RE DYKSTRA
362 B.R. 221 (D. Md. 2007)

Suzanne Dykstra is a 51 year old single woman and has no dependents. She graduated from college with a B.S. in bio-engineering, and then joined the U.S. army reserves and pursued a medical degree. Due to psychological and medical problems she did not complete her studies. Thereafter, she went back to school and entered a doctorate program which she failed to complete. During the course of her educational pursuits she incurred student loans amounting to $180,000, and pays $10.00 per month on this debt when she can.

Ms. Dykstra works 13-30 hours per week on a flexible work schedule doing telephone surveying for medical offices, and earns about $1,150.00 per month. Her expenses are about $1460.00, per month. Her basement apartment (with no working stove) is $575.00 per month. She drives a nine year old Saturn which consistently fails emission control tests. She lives very modestly.

Ms. Dykstra has been treated over the last 25 years for severe anxiety and depression, panic disorder, borderline personality disorder, urinary tract infections, irritable bowel syndrome and sinus and thyroid problems. She also suffers from ulcerative colitis, recurrent herpes viral infections and obesity. After a negative experience with a psychiatrist she ceased psychiatric care.

Ms. Dykstra filed a complaint in bankruptcy court seeking a determination that her student loans were dischargeable in bankruptcy.

Bankruptcy Judge Wendelin I. Lipp

The Debtor seeks determination that her student loan debt is dischargeable as an undue hardship. . . .

■　　■　　■

The test in the Fourth Circuit for "undue hardship" is a stringent one. The debtor must establish that: (1) she cannot maintain, based on current income and expenses, a "minimal" standard of living for herself and any dependents if she is forced to repay the loan; (2) additional circumstances show that her inability to pay the loan is likely to persist for a significant portion of the repayment period of the student loans; and (3) the Debtor has made good faith efforts to repay the loans. The Debtor must prove all three factors by a preponderance of the evidence. Mere inability to repay the loan is not sufficient; if that were the case, all

debtors would be able to prove undue hardship. The debtor must show that the unique or extraordinary circumstances which created her hardship make it unlikely that she will ever be able to honor her obligations.

In order to determine whether or not the Debtor can maintain a minimal standard of living, the Court must evaluate, at the very least, whether her monthly expenses exceed her income. This does not mean subsistence at the poverty level but is reviewed on a case-by-case inquiry into the Debtor's situation. As to the second factor, the Debtor must show that her circumstances are likely to persist for a significant portion of the repayment period on her loans. The Court also evaluates a variety of "additional circumstances," including: (1) whether or not there are any dependents in the Debtor's care; (2) the Debtor's level of education and the quality of that education; (3) the Debtor's lack of marketable job skills; (4) age or other factors that would prevent retraining or relocation in order to increase her income; (5) lack of assets; (6) underemployment; (7) number of years remaining in the Debtor's work life to allow repayment of the loan; (8)maximum income potential in the Debtor's chosen educational field; and (9) illness or incapacity. Importantly, discharge based on medical disability requires corroborating evidence to substantiate "what would otherwise be merely self-supporting testimony by the debtor." The third factor requires the Debtor to show that she has made an effort to obtain employment, maximize her income, minimize expenses and make payments when she can.

The Court finds that the Debtor has satisfied her burden with respect to all three factors of the Brunner Test. As discussed, the Debtor earns about $1,150.00 per month and her monthly expenses total about $1,463.57. The parties did not dispute these amounts or that her minimal expenses exceed her income. The Debtor established at trial that she is on the edge, financially, physically and mentally. Although she is not employed commensurately with her education and abilities, this is not the Debtor's desire; it is necessitated by her condition. She cannot work full time and her current employment is probably the best economically, considering her need for a flexible work schedule. Dr. Hertzberg testified that while she may have contributed to the exacerbation of her psychological problems due to her unwillingness to seek psychiatric treatment, the damage has been done and her situation is not likely to improve. He further testified that it was highly unlikely that the Debtor would have the capacity to work in a better or more advanced job even with medical care and a healthier lifestyle.

There is no dispute that the debtor has tried to repay her loans, through consolidation through the contingent income program and on her own. She has established that, despite a college education and some doctorate work, she will never be a doctor and she is unlikely to improve her employment opportunities. All of these facts, together with the evidence presented about her age, physical and mental condition leads this Court to conclude that the Debtor is probably earning as much as she can and there is very little prospect for change in the future.

For the foregoing reasons, the Court finds that the student loan debt imposes an undue hardship on the Debtor and . . . the debt will be discharged.

Case Questions

1. Justify the decision of the court by applying each of the three Bruner tests.
2. To what extent could the failure to pursue psychiatric treatment have contributed to Ms. Dykstra's woeful condition? Should that make a difference?
3. Under the Brunner test, what if Ms. Dykstra was unable to pay any amount on the student loans and made no attempt to repay because of her medical and psychological circumstances? Would the court have ruled differently?
4. Would you favor a "totality of the circumstances test" in place of the Brunner test that would look at all of the factors? Is that really what this court is doing? Explain.
5. Amy Smithson earned an undergraduate degree in International Studies and a law degree. She incurred student loan debt in the amount of $200,000.00. Shortly after graduating from law school she married Michael who had a 2 year old boy from a previous spouse who died of a rare cancer. Michael owned an old home in the inner city, and had about a $30,000.00 mortgage on the home, and another $30,000.00 in credit card debt. Michael was diagnosed with an incurable cancer after three months into the marriage. He died on their first wedding anniversary. Michael's hospitalizations and treatment for his illness amounted to $300,000 which Amy was required to assume in order for him to get the treatment. They did not have health insurance.

   Amy has taken the bar examination three times and has been unable to pass it. She is working in a job that pays $45,000.00 per year, with expectations that it will double should she pass the bar examination. Her expenses are $60,000.00 per year with the bulk of it being the student loan and medical debt.

What additional information do you need to determine whether Amy's student loan repayment presents a hardship, and thus is dischargeable in bankruptcy?

Reaffirmation

A debtor may agree to pay an obligation that has been discharged through bankruptcy. This reaffirmation may be done so that the creditor can continue to deal with the debtor, or so that the creditor does not take secured property to satisfy the debt. Because creditors are in a position to exert undue influence on unsuspecting debtors, the act affords the debtor certain procedural safeguards in connection with reaffirmation agreements, for example, the requirement that the court approve the reaffirmation. Under the recent amendments, courts will scrutinize the reaffirmation agreements closely and deny them if they are not affordable.

Reorganization

The purpose of **reorganization** is to allow a financially disturbed business to continue while arrangements for the adjustment of debts are made with creditors of the business. Most individuals and entities eligible for chapter 7 liquidation treatment are also eligible for chapter 11 reorganization.

Reorganizations may be voluntary or involuntary. Generally, the same rules that apply to liquidation cases apply to reorganization, including trustee powers, exemptions, preferential transfers, and discharges.

After issuing the order for relief, the court appoints creditors' and stockholders' committees. The committees represent their respective interest groups. The committees also investigate the financial condition and activities of the debtor as well as participate in the formulation of a reorganization plan. They may also request the appointment of a trustee to replace the debtor in possession, if no trustee was previously appointed.

When no trustee has been appointed, the debtor has the exclusive right to submit a reorganization plan for the first 120 days after the order for relief. If a trustee has been appointed or if the debtor fails to submit a plan accepted by each class of creditors, any interested party may submit a proposed plan for reorganization. Interested parties include the debtor, the trustee, and the committees.

Creditors are afforded an opportunity to accept or reject reorganization plans. A class of creditors accepts a plan when it is approved by a majority of the creditors within the class that represents at least two thirds of the allowed claims. A class of stockholders accepts a plan when it is approved by shareholders who represent at least two thirds of the shares.

The court confirms a plan accepted by the various classes of creditors and stockholders as long as the plan is fair and reasonable. Even if a class has failed to accept the plan, the court may still confirm the plan if the plan treats the nonaccepting class fairly and equitably. A confirmed plan is binding on all interest holders and discharges all debts not provided for under the plan.

Under certain circumstances, a debtor may convert a reorganization into a liquidation. Additionally, the court may, at its own option, convert a reorganization into a liquidation or dismiss the case in the best interest of the creditors.

Adjustment of Debts for Individuals

As long as a debtor has not filed a Chapter 13 within the last six years, most individuals with regular incomes may file a voluntary petition to adjust their debts. This includes wage earners and individuals engaged in business. To qualify for chapter 13 status, a debtor's unsecured debts must be less than $307,675.00 and his or her secured debts must be less than $922,975.00. A chapter 13 resembles a reorganization, except it may be sought only by individuals. Unlike the debtor in a liquidation, a chapter 13 debtor does not surrender assets. Creditors may not force a debtor into a chapter 13 proceeding. As long as the debtor is complying with the plan, creditors may not compel the conversion of a chapter 13 into a chapter 7.

The chapter 13 debtor files a plan for repaying creditors. It may be a **composition plan** or an **extension plan**. In a composition plan, the creditors receive a percentage of the indebtedness and the debtor is discharged of the remaining obligation. Under an extension plan, the creditors receive the entire indebtedness, but the payments extend past the due date. Both plans provide for completion within three to five years.

The court appoints a trustee to administer the plan. The debtor normally pays a monthly sum to the trustee directly or by payroll deduction. The trustee then apportions the payment to creditors in accordance with the plan.

At the completion of the plan, a chapter 13 debtor receives a discharge from all debts covered by the plan. Even when the debtor has not completed the payments within the prescribed period, the court may still grant a discharge, as long as the failure was due to circumstances beyond the debtor's control.

Table 15–6   **Factors to Be Considered to Accommodate Foreign Bankruptcy Proceedings**

- Just treatment of all claimants of the estate.
- Protection of U.S. claimholders against prejudice and inconvenience in processing of claims in foreign proceedings.
- Prevention of preferential or fraudulent dispositions.
- Distribution of proceeds of such estate substantially in accord with the order prescribed in the U.S. Bankruptcy Code.
- Comity—the recognition of foreign law.
- Provision of an opportunity for a fresh start for the debtor.

International Bankruptcy

Virtually every civilized nation has a bankruptcy law to relieve honest debtors and protect legitimate creditors. However, the laws of the various nations differ, and few international bankruptcy treaties exist. This poses potentially serious problems, as when, for example, a multinational firm seeks bankruptcy protection in one country with some of its assets and creditors in other countries.

The United States Bankruptcy Code section 304 is an attempt to provide some solution to the multinational bankruptcy problem. This section permits a foreign trustee to seek help in the U.S. to administer the bankruptcy case in accord with the foreign jurisdiction's laws. Section 304 attempts to achieve the goals of promoting an expeditious administration of foreign bankruptcies, while protecting the rights of U.S. creditors. In determining how to accommodate foreign bankruptcy proceedings, the domestic court must take into consideration the six factors listed in Table 15–6. Under Section 304, the U.S. court has the power to enjoin creditor actions, order the turnover of property, and order other appropriate relief.

Section 304 is a good beginning, but not the panacea for the problem of multinational bankruptcies. As a result, various proposals for model insolvency acts, treaties, and other approaches are being considered.

Chapter Problems

1. Define the following terms:
   a. TILA
   b. ECOA
   c. FCRA
   d. Investigative consumer report
   e. EFTA
   f. Garnishment
   g. Preferential transfer
   h. Reorganization
   i. Composition plan
   j. Extension plan

2. Linda Glaire purchased a seven-year membership in a health club owned and operated by LaLanne. The price of the membership was $408, regardless of whether the sum was paid in cash at the outset or over a two-year period in monthly installments of $17 each. Glaire elected to pay over time, as do most of LaLanne's customers. She entered into a standard contract that stated that no finance charge would be assessed for the extension of credit. In accordance with its usual practice, LaLanne then sold Glaire's contract to Universal Guardian Acceptance Corporation at a discount of 37.5 percent. LaLanne thus immediately received $255 in cash. Glaire became obligated to Universal for the full $408, payable over two years. LaLanne and Universal are interlocking corporations with common owner-

ship and control. Universal regularly assists LaLanne in its financing by accepting contracts at a discount. On learning of the arrangement between LaLanne and Universal, Glaire filed suit against LaLanne. She alleged violations of the Truth in Lending Act.

Is the act applicable to LaLanne? Explain. Has LaLanne violated the act? Who, if anyone, is required to make TILA disclosures to Glaire?

3. Robert Cragin and his wife submitted a written application for a $2,000 property improvement loan to First Federal Savings. Mr. and Mrs. Cragin signed the application as joint applicants. The loan was approved by First Federal and the Cragins were informed of the approval in a letter from Arthur Barnett, a loan manager of the bank.

Thereafter, Barnett informed Cragin that several documents would have to be signed by both he and his wife, and then notarized. Cragin informed Barnett that it would be extremely inconvenient for his wife to sign the documents before a notary since she took care of two small children and could not get away from the house. When Barnett insisted that this procedure be followed, Cragin asked if he could apply for the loan in his own name. Barnett responded by saying, "You will have to submit a new application in writing as required by the bank's procedure." Cragin refused and sued First Federal, alleging a violation of the Equal Credit Opportunity Act based on sex and marital status discrimination. Who will prevail? Why?

4. Vincent Palmiotto applied to the Bank of New York for a line of credit. The bank informed him by letter that the extension of credit was denied because of information contained in a credit report. Later, by letter, Palmiotto was informed that the reason for denial was that there had been excessive inquiries on the credit report. Was the Bank of New York in violation of ECOA? Explain.

5. Joe T. Morris (plaintiff) was denied credit on several occasions because of an unfavorable credit report communicated by the Credit Bureau of Cincinnati. The bad credit rating was based on a bankruptcy and two unpaid department store accounts. The delinquent accounts belonged to his wife, who had filed for bankruptcy before they were married. They erroneously wound up in Joe Morris's credit file.

After Morris personally informed the credit bureau of the mistake, they purged his file of the inaccurate information. Thereafter, another inquiry was made about the plaintiff's credit history in the name of Joseph T. Morris (instead of Joe T. Morris). The credit bureau opened up a new file on Joseph T. Morris and the same inaccurate information regarding the bad accounts and bankruptcy turned up in the file. Morris was again denied credit on the basis of that information. Morris sought damages under the Fair Credit Reporting Act for injury to his reputation, his family, his work, and his sense of well-being.

Has the credit bureau violated the act? Explain. What can the credit bureau do in the future to minimize the repetition of this type of incident?

6. Glen Wood, an executive vice president of SAR Manufacturing Company, checked into the Holiday Inn in Phenix City, Alabama, and tendered a Gulf Oil Company credit card to pay for his room. After an imprint of the card was made, it was returned to Wood. Gulf Oil Company monitors the accounts of its cardholders on an ongoing basis and cancels a customer's credit if it determines that he or she cannot afford to pay. Gulf furnishes National Data Corporation with a list of all credit cancellations and authorizes it to disburse credit information to inquirers authorized to extend credit to Gulf cardholders.

   Gulf noticed that Wood had been charging large amounts in comparison to his income. (Gulf was unaware that Wood had been using the card to charge business expenses.) Although Wood's account was not in arrears, Gulf canceled his credit and directed National Data Corporation to give the following report to those seeking approval of his credit card use:

   Pick up travel card. Do not extend further credit. Send card to billing office for reward.

   When the night auditor at Holiday Inn checked with National Data Corporation he received the above communication. The auditor then went to Wood's room at 5:00 A.M. and awakened him on the pretense that he needed Wood's credit card because the imprinting had not taken. Wood inquired at the front desk when the credit card was not returned. He was told that the card had been seized upon the authority of National Data. Wood left the motel, but his anger over the incident caused a heart attack.

   Wood sued Gulf, alleging that it negligently failed to comply with the Fair Credit Reporting Act as a consumer reporting agency. He also sued National Data Corporation and Holiday Inn, alleging that they negligently failed to comply with the Fair Credit Reporting Act as users of a consumer report. Do you agree with Wood? Explain. Should Gulf alter its policy regarding credit card practices? If so, in what way?

7. Ken Baker owed money to two oil companies. These past-due accounts were given to G. C. Services Corp. (G.C.) for collection. G.C. sent three form letters in an effort to collect the money owed. One letter stated:

   It is our policy to attempt to settle these matters out of court before making any decision whether to refer them to an attorney for collection. . . . Unless we receive your check or money order, we will proceed with collection procedures.

   • • •

   Verification of this debt, a copy of judgment, or the name and address of the original creditor, if different from the current creditor, will be provided if requested in writing within 30 days. Otherwise the debt will be assumed to be valid.

   Does the letter sent by G. C. Services violate the Fair Debt Collection Practices Act? Explain.

8. Assume that Rocky Hound receives a court judgment against Ron Debtor in the amount of $500. Ron Debtor, a business law professor, earns $400 each

week. Assume that the federal minimum hourly wage is $4.25. Deductions from Debtor's pay each week amount to: taxes, $100; social security, $50; credit union, $10; Blue Cross-Blue Shield, $20; and alimony, $50. What is the maximum weekly amount subject to garnishment?

9. Assume that Ham owes his creditors the following amounts: Round, $5,000; Square, $6,000; Pentagon, $9,000. Ham's total assets equal $5,000, making him insolvent under a balance sheet test because his liabilities exceed his assets. On January 1, 1991, Ham pays Square $3,000. Eighty days later he files bankruptcy, listing assets of $5,000 and exemptions amounting to $1,000. Was the transfer preferential? Explain. What are the consequences?

10. Johns-Manville (debtor), a successful Fortune 500 company, shocked the business community when it filed for reorganization under the bankruptcy code. Johns-Manville's sole reason for filing was the number of health suits brought against it. These suits were a result of exposure to Johns-Manville's products containing asbestos, a lethal substance. As of the date of the filing under the bankruptcy code, about 16,000 such suits were pending, and it was estimated that over the next 20 to 30 years many more asbestos health claims would be filed. Johns-Manville's total liability as a result of these asbestos claims was estimated at $1.9 billion. Name some possible proposals in a plan for reorganization that would deal with the massive number of asbestos claimants.

V   BUSINESS AND ITS EMPLOYEES

The United States is a nation of employees who work for various reasons. For most, employment is the means by which they generate income to pay for life's necessities and luxuries. Employment also provides a sense of self-identity, and frequently serves many social functions. Thus, losing a job is one of the most stressful experiences an individual can encounter.

The employment relationship has changed considerably in American history. Between the Civil War and World War I, the United States was transformed from a nation of farmers, individual merchants, and artisans into a nation of urban-based wage earners and capitalists. Urbanization transformed the nature of the employment relationship. Due to a dramatic increase in capital investment, the personal employer-employee relationship that had existed in smaller enterprises gave way to an impersonal worker-management relationship. Workers previously employed by individuals became part of large, impersonal organizations. Employers dealt with these workers as groups rather than as individuals. An adversarial relationship developed between employers and employees.

Initially, the law was unresponsive to changing social conditions and the emergence of an organized labor movement. The common law developed a rule that most employment relationships were terminable at the will of either party. The power to fire employees without any reasons often gave employers absolute control over their workers.

In response to the common law's shortcomings, Congress and state legislatures have enacted social legislation designed to provide minimum labor standards and safety for the American worker. This legislation has come in four waves.

The first wave occurred during the 1920s, when most states enacted workers' compensation laws. The second wave of regulation came during the New Deal administration of Franklin D. Roosevelt. New Deal legislation was a reaction to the Great Depression, and included the National Labor Relations Act, the Fair Labor Standards Act, the Social Security Act, and the Federal Unemployment Act. The common theme of these statutes was to spread income across a broad segment of the population, thereby maintaining consumer buying power and avoiding another economic depression.

For almost 30 years, the law depended on collective bargaining to regulate terms and conditions of employment. The civil rights movement made the country aware that collective bargaining had not solved the problem of racial discrimination in employment and, in some cases, had contributed to the problem.

Consequently, a third wave of legislation occurred during the civil rights era of the 1960s and 1970s. The cornerstone of the period was the Civil Rights Act of 1964. This period also saw Congress enact the Equal Pay Act, the Age Discrimination in Employment Act, the Rehabilitation Act, the Occupational Safety and Health Act, and the Employment Retirement Income Security Act.

The current wave of regulation, which began in the mid-1980s, features legislation directly specifying terms and conditions of employment. Congress has enacted the Employment Polygraph Protection Act and the Family and Medical Leave Act.

Recently, courts have reassessed the common law view that employment may be terminated at will. Businesses and workers attempting to deal with each other on a day-to-day basis must do so in a workplace dominated by government regulation. The next three chapters consider that regulation in detail.

16 THE EMPLOYMENT RELATIONSHIP

Learning Objectives

After learning this chapter the student should be able to:

- Evaluate the likelihood of liability for firing employees under particular circumstances.
- Determine whether notice of a forthcoming reduction in force is legally required.
- Understand the requirements of the Family and Medical Leave Act.
- Analyze compensation policies for compliance with the Fair Labor Standards Act.
- Determine whether an employee who leaves the work force will be eligible for income security benefits and, if so, under which programs.
- Evaluate personnel actions that could expose the employer to intentional tort liability.

Today's manager must be prepared to deal with a complex maze of statutory, administrative, and judicial regulation of the basic terms and conditions of employment. This chapter analyzes the basic common law and federal statutory limitations on employer power (except for the employment discrimination laws and the National Labor Relations Act, treated in the next two chapters).

Job Security

Most employers link wages and fringe benefits, in part, to length of service on the job. Employees generally advance to higher pay classifications, and qualify for greater vacation and other fringe benefits the longer they remain with their employers. Loss of a job involves more than the immediate loss of income; it also means that on finding a job with a new employer, the employee must begin anew with no seniority credit.

Three threats to job security are discharge, reduction in force (RIF), and changes in an employee's personal life requiring time off from work. Statutes prohibit discharge, or other discrimination, on certain bases, such as race, sex, religion, national origin, or age. Traditionally, courts have allowed employers to fire employees at will as long as the reason was not prohibited by statute. Recently, courts have begun to erode the at will rule. The Worker Adjustment and Retraining Notification (WARN) Act regulates RIFs, and the Family and Medical Leave Act provides for necessary time off.

Development and Erosion of the At Will Rule

Before the Industrial Revolution, most employees were domestic agricultural workers. The law regarded employment as a relationship based on the status of master and servant. The status of master or servant had certain responsibilities comparable to the status of husband and wife or parent and child.

The mutual responsibilities of master and servant resulted in a rule that presumed employment would last a year. This rule prevented a servant from taking employment during the winter and then abandoning the master when needed most during planting and harvesting seasons. It also prevented the master from accepting the servant's work during planting and harvest and abandoning the servant during the winter.

The Industrial Revolution changed the personal nature of employment. Courts came to view employment not as a status relationship but as a contract. Receptive to employers' claimed need to control their workforces, courts held employment contracts to be **terminable at will**. This meant that employers could discharge employees without any cause.

Recently, courts have begun to reexamine the at will rule. Many have recognized a cause of action in tort where a discharge violates public policy. Many courts have also reconsidered their dogmatic view that all employment contracts, except those for a stated period of time, are terminable at will. The following case illustrates the relationship between contract and tort.

FOLEY V. INTERACTIVE DATA CORP.
47 Cal. 3d 654, 765 P.2d 373 (1988)

Daniel Foley (plaintiff) worked for Interactive Data Corp, (defendant) for almost seven years. During that period, plaintiff received pay raises, promotions, awards, superior performance evaluations, and bonuses. He alleged that defendant's officers repeatedly assured him of job security and had a series of termination guidelines. Plaintiff claimed he was fired because he accurately reported to the defendant that the FBI was investigating for embezzlement a person the defendant had hired to be his boss.

Foley sued in tort and contract. The trial court dismissed Foley's claim. The California Court of Appeal affirmed. The California Supreme Court affirmed in part and reversed in part.

Chief Justice Lucas

We turn first to plaintiff's cause of action alleging he was discharged in violation of public policy. . . . [T]he employer's right to discharge an "at will" employee is still subject to limits imposed by public policy, since otherwise the threat of discharge could be used to coerce employees into committing crimes, concealing wrongdoing, or taking other action harmful to the public weal.

■   ■   ■

In the present case, plaintiff alleges that defendant discharged him in "sharp derogation" of a substantial public policy that imposes a legal duty on employees to report relevant business information to management. . . . Plaintiff asserts, if he discovered information that might lead his employer to conclude that an employee was an embezzler, and should not be retained, plaintiff had a duty to communicate that information to his principal.

■   ■   ■

Whether or not there is a statutory duty requiring an employee to report information relevant to his employer's interest, we do not find a substantial public policy prohibiting an employer from discharging an employee for performing that duty.

Past decisions recognizing a tort action for discharge in violation of public policy seek to protect the public, by protecting the employee who refuses to commit a crime, who reports criminal activity to proper authorities, or who discloses other illegal, unethical, or unsafe practices. No equivalent public interest bars the discharge of the present plaintiff. When the duty of an employee to disclose information to his employer serves only the private interest of the employer, the rationale underlying the . . . cause of action is not implicated.

■   ■   ■

Plaintiff's second cause of action alleged that over the course of his nearly seven years of employment with defendant, the company's own conduct and personnel policies gave rise to an "oral contract" not to fire him without good cause.

■   ■   ■

Defendant contends that courts should not enforce employment security agreements in the absence of evidence of independent consideration and an express manifestation of mutual assent. Although . . . there may be some historical basis for imposing such limitations, any such basis has been eroded by the development of modern contract law and, accordingly, we conclude that defendant's suggested limitations are inappropriate in the modern employment context. We discern no basis for departing from otherwise applicable general contract principles.

■　　■　　■

[A] rule imposing a requirement of separate consideration as a substantive limitation on an enforceable employee security agreement would be "contrary to the general contract principle that courts should not inquire into the adequacy of consideration. Thus there is no analytical reason why an employee's promise to render services, or his actual rendition of services over time, may not support an employer's promise both to pay a particular wage . . . and to refrain from arbitrary dismissal."

■　　■　　■

In the employment context, factors apart from consideration and express terms may be used to ascertain the existence and content of an employment agreement, including "the personnel policies or practices of the employer, the employee's longevity of service, actions or communications by the employer reflecting assurances of continued employment, and the practices of the industry in which the employee is engaged."

■　　■　　■

Finally, we do not agree with the Court of Appeal that employment security agreements are so inherently harmful or unfair to employers, who do not receive equivalent guaranties of continued service, as to merit treatment different from that accorded other contracts. On the contrary, employers may benefit from the increased loyalty and productivity that such agreements may inspire. Permitting proof of and reliance on implied-in-fact contract terms does not nullify the at-will rule, it merely treats such contracts in a manner in keeping with general contract law. . . .

Defendant's remaining argument is that even if a promise to discharge "for good cause only" could be implied in fact, the evidentiary factors . . .

relied on by plaintiff, are inadequate as a matter of law. This contention fails on several grounds.

First, defendant overemphasizes the fact that plaintiff was employed for "only" six years and nine months. Length of employment is a relevant consideration but six years and nine months is sufficient time for conduct to occur on which a trier of fact could find the existence of an implied contract. . . . Agreement may be "shown by the acts and conduct of the parties, interpreted in the light of the subject matter and of the surrounding circumstances." Plaintiff here alleged repeated oral assurances of job security and consistent promotions, salary increases and bonuses during the term of his employment contributing to his reasonable expectation that he would not be discharged except for good cause.

Second, an allegation of breach of written "Termination Guidelines" implying self-imposed limitations on the employer's power to discharge at will may be sufficient to state a cause of action for breach of an employment contract. . . .

In sum . . . plaintiff has pleaded an implied-in-fact contract and its breach, and is entitled to his opportunity to prove those allegations.

Case Questions

1. Why did the court conclude that Foley did not have a tort cause of action?

2. If Foley had been fired for reporting embezzlement by a co-worker to the employer, would he have a cause of action? Would he have a claim if he had been fired for reporting embezzlement to the FBI? Explain.

3. Would Foley have had a claim if he had worked for Interactive Data for three years? If he had received average performance evaluations? Explain.

4. Assume that Foley signed this statement on his first day on the job: "I acknowledge that I am an at will employee and can be terminated without cause." What effect would this have had on Foley's claim?

The Worker Adjustment and Retraining Notification Act (WARN)

WARN covers employers with 10 or more workers. WARN requires 60 days' notice to: 100

- Workers or their unions
- State and local government

of

- Shutdown of a site or facility closing idling at least 50 workers.
- Layoff of at least 500 workers, or at least 50 workers amounting to one third or more of the workforce.

WARN does not apply to layoffs or shutdowns resulting from natural disasters, strikes, lockouts, or unforeseen circumstances. Notice is not required if it would disrupt an employer's active pursuit of capital or business that would avoid the shutdown.

Employers who violate the statute may be liable to affected employees for up to 60 days' back pay and lost fringe benefits. Violators who fail to offer such payments to employees within three weeks after ordering the closing or layoff and who fail to notify the affected unit of local government may be liable for a court penalty of up to $500 per day of violation. Violators also may be liable for court costs and attorney fees. A court may reduce a violator's liability if the violator proves it had a good-faith, reasonable belief it was not violating the act.

The Family and Medical Leave Act (FMLA)

The Family and Medical Leave Act of 1993 (FMLA) covers employers with 50   50 or more employees, and employees who have worked at least 1,250 hours in the prior year. Under the act, employers:

- Must allow employees to take up to 12 weeks of leave without pay in any year for the birth or adoption of a child or a serious medical condition of the employee or an immediate family member.
- May require workers to use accumulated sick leave or vacation during the leave.
- Must maintain health insurance for an employee on leave and must reinstate the employee to the same or equivalent job upon return.
- May deny leave to their 10 percent most highly paid employees if the leave would cause "substantial and grievous economic injury" to the business.

Prior to the FMLA, many states required employers to provide family leave. One such state was Wisconsin.

KELLEY CO. V. MARQUARDT
493 N.W.2d 68 (1992)

Elizabeth Marquardt (appellant) was a credit manager for Kelley Co. (appellee). She supervised four employees, provided customer service, and oversaw credit rating investigations, budgeting, financial risk evaluations, collection agencies, and accounts receivable.

Marquardt took leave for the birth of her child. While she was on leave, Kelley reorganized its Finance Division, eliminating Marquardt's position. Marquardt returned to a new position that was 25 percent clerical work, involved no customer contact, and supervised only one employee. The job paid the same and had the same hours as her prior job. The Wisconsin Department of Industry held that Kelley violated the Wisconsin FMLA by not returning Marquardt to a job equivalent to the one she held before her leave. The lower courts reversed, but the Wisconsin Supreme Court reversed the lower courts.

Justice Weller

The primary issue before this court is whether Kelley Company violated the FMLA, by failing to place Marquardt in an equivalent employment position when she returned from family leave.

■   ■   ■

Marquardt asserts that her new position was not an equivalent employment position because her authority and responsibility were greatly reduced in the new position. We agree.

■   ■   ■

The FMLA is designed to protect employees' jobs and benefits while on leave to care for their families or their own medical needs. The FMLA accomplishes this by ensuring that an employee who takes a family or medical leave must be returned to the same position he or she held before taking leave or if that position is not vacant, an equivalent employment position. An equivalent employment position must have equivalent compensation, benefits, working shift, hours of employment and other terms and conditions of employment. We conclude that the legislature

included the language "other terms and conditions of employment" to protect the employee's status, responsibility and authority while on leave. There is a deterrent factor in taking leave if all that is protected is an employee's salary, hours, and benefits. It is punitive in nature for an employee to have job responsibility and authority stripped while on leave. This forces an employee to choose between their family or health and job which is exactly what the legislature intended to prevent by adopting the FMLA.

■   ■   ■

Kelley Company asserts that it would be poor public policy to require employers to hold jobs open while employees are on family or medical leave. We agree. An employer is not stopped from reorganizing departments or making changes in job positions for legitimate business reasons during the time an employee is away on family or medical leave as long as the same position or an equivalent employment position is available for the employee upon return from leave. This makes sense from a public policy perspective. On one hand, businesses are not curtailed from making legitimate business decisions and changes, and on the other hand, an employee may take family or medical leave without the fear of losing his or her position in the work place which includes status, authority, and responsibility. The legislature determined that it is important to protect employees' jobs while they are on family or medical leave. An employer can make changes in job positions while an employee is on leave as long as the employee is placed in an equivalent employment position upon return from leave.

■   ■   ■

Kelley Company argues that before she took leave, Marquardt had no right to prevent Kelley Company from reorganizing the Finance Division and she had no guarantee that she would remain in the same job with similar duties. This is true and the fact that Kelley Company reorganized Marquardt's department and gave her new job duties is not a violation of the FMLA. Kelley Company violated the FMLA by giving Marquardt job duties that were not equivalent in significance to those she performed before taking leave. The fact that Marquardt's new job involved 25% clerical work and less supervisory duties indicates that her status, responsibility and authority were greatly reduced in violation of the FMLA.

. . . Kelley Company maintains that Marquardt's reassignment to a position that eliminated customer contact was inevitable whether she took family leave or not. While this may be true, the FMLA required Kelley Company to place Marquardt in an equivalent employment position upon her return from family leave. The equivalent position upon return from leave need not include the same job duties, but it must be equivalent in status, responsibility and authority.

Case Questions

1. If Kelley had reorganized the Finance Division prior to Marquardt's leave would Marquardt have had a claim? Why or why not?
2. Did Kelley intend to punish Marquardt for taking leave? Explain.
3. What is the basis for the court's finding that Marquardt's new job was not equivalent to her old one?
4. Does the decision preclude an employee from reorganizing a department while an employee is on leave? Explain.

Wages and Hours

The Fair Labor Standards Act (FLSA) regulates minimum wages and maximum hours. It also prohibits employment of children under age 14, allows employment of 14- and 15-year-olds only in certain approved jobs and within certain time limits, and limits employment of 16- and 17-year-olds to nonhazardous occupations.

The Labor Department's Wage and Hour Division administers the FLSA. The Labor Department and private individuals can sue employers for FLSA violations. They can recover unpaid minimum wage and overtime compensation, as well as double damages for willful violations. The most important provisions of the FLSA regulate wages and hours.

Minimum Wage

In 1938, the FLSA set a minimum hourly wage of 25 cents. It has increased many times since. Since 1991, it has been $4.25. FLSA permits employers to credit against the minimum wage some of the tips of employees who regularly receive them and the reasonable cost of board, lodging, or other facilities furnished to employees. The facilities provided must be for the benefit of the employees rather than for the convenience of the employer. For example, an employer may apply the reasonable cost of the meals it regularly provides waiters and waitresses toward their wages. Other deductions, however, may result in violations if they reduce the employee's compensation below the minimum wage. For example, a retail store that reduces a cashier's wages by the amount of cash register shortages, regardless of their cause, violates the FLSA if the effect is to bring the cashier's pay below the minimum wage.

Overtime Compensation

Overtime compensation of "time and one half" must be paid when an employee works more than 40 hours in a workweek. The number of hours worked in any given day is not relevant. If the employer is a federal contractor, however, the Walsh-Healey Act requires that overtime be paid when an employee works more than eight hours in one day.

A frequent issue that arises is how to determine how many hours an employee worked. Employees who are "on call" must be paid if they are "engaged to be waiting" but not if they are "waiting to be engaged." The key concern is the degree of control the employer has over the employee's activities while on call.

Exemptions

Congress has explicitly exempted various occupations from some or all of FLSA's provisions. The most common exemptions that managers must deal with are those governing executive, administrative, and professional personnel. To qualify for these **white-collar exemptions**, employees must have certain job characteristics and be paid the minimum salary specified in Labor Department regulations. The salary must be paid regardless of the number of hours worked in a given week as long as the employee is ready, willing, and able to work. The minimum amount must be paid free and clear of the value of lodging, meals, or other facilities provided by the employer and of unreimbursed expenses that the employer requires the employee to incur. Hourly employees do not qualify.

Income Security

Many events can threaten an employee's income security. Chief among these are injuries, disability, retirement, major medical expenses, death, and unemployment. Employees receive protection from job-related injuries through workers' compensation. Social Security benefits cushion employees' income from the effects of disability and retirement. Employers frequently further provide for retirement through pension plans and provide employees with medical and life insurance. These fringe benefits are regulated by the Employee Retirement Income Security Act (ERISA). Unemployment compensation helps cushion the financial blow of loss of a job.

Workers' Compensation

Workers' compensation statutes establish a basic trade-off between employees and employers. Employees and their dependents are entitled to benefits regardless of fault or their employers' tort liability. In return, employers are immune from most tort liability to their workers for injuries covered by the compensation act.

Injured employees still can sue parties other than their employers in tort. For example, an employee injured by a defective machine can sue the manufacturer of the machine. In this case, the employer or the state workers' compensation insurance fund is entitled to be reimbursed out of the employee's tort recovery for benefits provided.

Benefits

Although compensation benefits vary from state to state, they normally include payment for hospital and medical expenses, including artificial limbs and rehabilitation services. They also include compensation for lost wages. The amounts vary from one half to two thirds of the employee's average weekly wage. Some states require that an employee be out of work for a specified period of time, such as a week, before qualifying for lost-income benefits. Most states also pay death awards to a deceased employee's dependents or survivors.

Funding

State workers' compensation statutes generally use one of three methods for funding compensation benefits: private insurance, self-insurance, and payment into a state fund. The amount paid by the employer is determined by various factors, including the type of industry and prior accident experience. Most states have official rating systems for determining the premiums necessary to pay all accepted claims. Many states have a merit rating system whereby an employer with a history of fewer claims pays a reduced premium.

Compensable Injuries

An injury is compensable if it arises out of the employment and happens in the course of the employment. An injury arises out of the employment if it results from a risk or hazard peculiar to the type of work the employee performs. For example, a bulldozer operator injured when the bulldozer overturns on an embankment has obviously sustained injury as a result of a risk peculiar to the job. If a bulldozer operator is struck and killed by a crashing plane, there is a serious question of whether the death arose out of the employment. The risks created by the plane appear to be no greater to the bulldozer operator than to the public at large. Many states grant recovery in such a case, however, reasoning that but for the particular employment the injury would not have occurred because the worker would not have been in the plane's path.

A compensable injury must have occurred in the course of the employment. Here, courts examine the time, location, and circumstances of the accident in relationship to the employment.

Among the most common employment problems are those that involve the **going and coming rule**. Under this rule, employees with a fixed time and place of employment are not generally compensated while commuting to or from work.

Most courts apply the premises rule. Under the premises rule, an employee injured while on the employer's premises may recover even if he or she was only going to or coming from the work site.

Injuries that occur going to or coming from work are compensable if the employee is engaged in a work-related activity for the employer's convenience. For example, an employee asked to mail letters on the way home is covered for injuries sustained while walking to the mailbox. On the other hand, an accountant who, for personal convenience, takes home files to work on is not covered for injuries sustained by slipping on the icy steps at home.

Employees whose work entails travel away from the employer's premises do not fit easily under the going and coming rule. Most jurisdictions find such employees to be continuously within the course of employment during a trip, except where a distinct deviation from the course of employment occurs. Issues involved in the going and coming rule are explored in the following case.

ROBINSON V. INDUSTRIAL COMMISSION
449 N.E. 2d 106 (Ill. 1983)

Robinson (decedent) was a marketing director for a real estate developer (respondent). His job involved traveling between his office and real estate development sites. On December 23, 1976, Robinson left his office to visit the Red Haw development and to take his son Christmas shopping. He apparently planned to take the most direct route to accomplish both tasks; go first to his home to pick up his son, then to Red Haw, and then to the shopping mall. This was not the most direct route between his office and Red Haw. Robinson was killed in a traffic accident between his office and home.

Mrs. Robinson (petitioner) appealed the Industrial Commission's denial of compensation for the death of her husband. The Illinois Supreme Court reversed.

Justice Goldenhersh

This court has on many occasions been required to consider the question whether accidental injuries sustained by an employee while away from his place of employment are compensable. In *Ace Pest Control, Inc. v. Industrial Com.* the court said:

The Workmen's Compensation Act was not intended to insure employees against all accidental injuries but only those which arise out of acts which the employee is instructed to perform by his employer; acts which he has a common law or statutory duty to perform while performing duties for his employer; or acts which the employee might be reasonably expected to perform incident to his assigned duties.

■   ■   ■

In *Ace Pest Control* a termite control operator was killed by a passing automobile while assisting a stranded motorist. In holding that his death arose out of and in the course of his employment the court said that the activities in which he was engaged at the time of his death "were such as might have been reasonably expected or foreseen by his employer. . . ."

The testimony shows that the least circuitous route to follow in accomplishing decedent's objective of picking up his son, visiting the houses at Red Haw and then taking his son to a shopping mall was to go first to his home, then to Red Haw and then to the mall. . . . [D]ecedent's supervisor testified that his action in stopping to pick up his son on the way to the job site did not violate any of the respondent's rules. . . . [T]he extent of the deviation which resulted from his first going to his home rather than directly to Red Haw . . . appears to be insubstantial. Had the accident occurred while the decedent was en route from his office directly to Red Haw there would be no question of compensability, and recovery should not be denied because he performed the reasonable and foreseeable act of stopping on the way to pick up his son.

■   ■   ■

We hold that the decision of the Industrial Commission is contrary to the manifest weight of the evidence. . . . The judgment is therefore reversed . . . and the cause is remanded to the Industrial Commission with directions to award workmen's compensation in the appropriate amount.

Justice Moran (Dissenting)

I disagree with the majority's conclusion that because decedent's trip to his home to pick up his son was reasonable it therefore arose out of and in the course of his employment. The mere fact that one is an outside employee does not ipso facto[1] bring all of his reasonable activities within the course of employment. "Employees whose work entails travel away from the employer's premises are held in the majority of jurisdiction [sic] to be within the course of their employment continuously during the trip, except when a distinct departure on a personal errand is shown."

Picking up his son to go Christmas shopping was not in the course of the decedent's business; rather, it was part of his own personal affairs. "When an employee deviates from his business route by taking a side-trip that is clearly identifiable as such, he is unquestionably beyond the course of his employment while going away from the business route and toward the personal objective. . . ."

The evidence showed . . . decedent had turned off the closest, direct route to Red Haw and headed toward his home. As such, decedent was on a personal side-trip at the time of his accident and was therefore not in the course of his employment. For this reason, I would affirm the denial of compensation.

Case Questions

1. Which standard does Justice Goldenhersh apply to the decedent's conduct? Which standard does Justice Moran apply?

2. Is it significant that the employer's rules permitted decedent to pick up his son on the way to Red Haw? Why or why not?

3. Assume that decedent's home had been located on the most direct route between his

---

[1] By the mere fact itself. Author.

office and Red Haw. What effect would this have had on the case?

4. How would Justice Moran reconcile his dissent in this case with the result in the *Ace Pest Control* case?

5. Metropolitan Maintenance Company allows all employees working an eight-hour shift a half-hour lunch break. Employees must punch out on the time clock for lunch and punch in when they return. The company has a cafeteria but employees are not required to eat there.

Smith, an employee, punched out for lunch and went to a nearby restaurant where she purchased a sandwich to go. As she left the restaurant she was robbed and shot. Are her injuries compensable? Explain.

Social Security

The Social Security Act creates a federal social insurance system designed to prevent the severe financial hardship that many elderly persons suffer on retirement. Under the system, employees are compelled to pay a certain percentage of their annual income to the government during their entire working lifetimes. On attaining retirement age, the contributors become eligible to receive various benefit payments from the general social security fund.

Old-Age, Survivors, and Disability Insurance

In common usage, when people refer to social security, they are talking about Old-Age, Survivors, and Disability Insurance (OASDI). All except a very few working Americans contribute to, and are covered by, OASDI.

Taxes paid into the social security fund are governed by the provisions of the Federal Insurance Contributions Act (FICA). Workers and their employers each pay half the tax.

Benefit Eligibility

Eligibility for benefits is based on the number of quarters of coverage an individual has been credited with during employment. One quarter of credit is earned for each calendar quarter in which at least $50 in income was earned ($100 for self-employed individuals). Table 16–1 summarizes the eligibility rules.

Disability Benefits

Eligible workers may receive disability benefits under OASDI. In addition to having attained insured status, a beneficiary must be incapable of any substantial

TABLE 16–1   OASDI Benefits

Status	Benefits	Quarters Required
Fully insured	All benefits	Equal to number of years since 1950 or since age 21
Currently insured	Survivor benefits	6 of last 13 quarters
Disability insured	Disability benefits	20 of last 40 quarters

TABLE 16–2   **Differences between Workers' Compensation and Social Security Disability**

Workers' Compensation	Social Security
Coverage immediately on employment.	Coverage on attaining insured status.
Injury must arise out of and occur in the course of employment.	Impairment need not be work related.
Benefits available for temporary and partial as well as permanent and total disabilities.	Disability must be total and last at least 12 months.
Benefits cover medical expenses and rehabilitation services and lost earning capacity.	Benefits only replace earning capacity.

gainful activity due to a medically determinable physical or mental impairment. The impairment must be expected either to prove fatal or to last for at least 12 months. Mere inability to continue doing one's job does not necessarily qualify a worker for social security disability payments. If an individual has remedial capacity to do other jobs that exist in significant numbers in the national economy, that person is not entitled to benefits—even if there are few or no vacancies for those jobs.

Social security disability benefits should not be confused with workers' compensation benefits. Although they may overlap in some cases, there are several significant differences. These are highlighted in Table 16–2.

Medicare

Medicare coverage consists of two distinct insurance plans. The first, Hospital Insurance (HI), provides hospital and related benefits to all persons at least 65 years old who are entitled to receive OASDI or Railroad Retirement benefits. The second Medicare plan is Supplementary Medical Insurance (SMI), which covers all persons over age 65 and all disabled persons covered by HI. This plan provides benefits for physicians' services and related medical services. SMI coverage is provided only on a voluntary basis. Unlike HI and OASDI benefits, which are provided as a matter of entitlement once eligibility is established, SMI coverage must be elected by its beneficiaries, who pay a premium in partial financial support of the plan. SMI closely resembles private health insurance plans, but the coverage is partly subsidized by the government.

Private Employee Benefit Plans

The Employee Retirement Income Security Act (ERISA) regulates private employee benefit plans. ERISA's coverage includes medical, disability, and other welfare plans and pensions. Its major requirements are explored in the following sections.

Reporting and Disclosure

All employee benefit plans covered by ERISA are subject to its reporting and disclosure requirements. The plan administrator must file with the Labor Department a description of the plan, a **summary plan description**, a statement of any material modifications to the plan, annual reports including certified financial statements, and terminal and supplementary reports if the plan is to be terminated. On request, the plan administrator must also supply copies of any documents relating to the plan and any other information necessary to carry out the purposes of the act.

Plan administrators must automatically provide plan participants with summary plan descriptions, summaries of material modifications, periodic updated summary plan descriptions that incorporate these modifications, and annual report summaries. On request, the plan administrator must make available for inspection, and provide at reasonable charge, copies of all plan documents. Additionally, the administrator must furnish, on the request of any plan participant or beneficiary, a statement of the status of his or her benefits. If the administrator does not provide information within 30 days of the request, the plan is liable for damages of $100 per day of delay.

Fiduciary Duties

ERISA imposes fiduciary responsibility on all individuals who have discretionary authority over benefit plan management, administration, or handling of assets and on all paid investment advisers. ERISA requires that these individuals:

- Act solely in the interest of the plan participants and beneficiaries.
- Act with the skill and care of a prudent person qualified to act in such matters.
- Diversify plan assets to minimize the risk of large losses.

ERISA also specifically prohibits certain transactions, such as those involving dealings between the plan and its fiduciaries or other conflicting interests.

Discrimination

ERISA prohibits employers from discharging or otherwise discriminating against benefit plan participants or beneficiaries for the purpose of interfering with their rights under the act or the plan. The reach of this provision is explored in the following case.

MCGANN V. H. & H. MUSIC CO.

946 F.2d 401 (5th Cir. 1991), *cert. denied*, 113 S. Ct. 462 (1992)

H & H Music Co. (defendant-appellee) provided health insurance for its employees with a lifetime maximum benefit of $1 million. John McGann (plaintiff-appellant), an H & H employee, discovered he had AIDS in December 1987 and began submitting claims for treatment. In July 1988, H & H changed the medical insurance by limiting AIDS-related claims to a lifetime maximum of $5,000. McGann sued, claiming that the change violated ERISA by retaliating against him for exercising his rights under the medical insurance plan. The trial court granted summary judgment to H & H. The Fifth Circuit Court of Appeals affirmed.

Circuit Judge Garwood

Although we assume there was a connection between the benefits reduction and either McGann's filing of claims or his revelations about his illness, there is nothing in the record to suggest that defendants' motivation was other than as they asserted, namely to avoid the expense of paying for AIDS treatment (if not, indeed, also for other treatment), no more for McGann than for any other present or future plan beneficiary who might suffer from AIDS. McGann . . . does not challenge defendants' assertion that their purpose in reducing AIDS benefits was to reduce costs.

Furthermore, McGann has failed to adduce evidence of the existence of "any right to which [he] may become entitled under the plan. . . ."

McGann's allegations show no promised benefit, for there is nothing to indicate that defendants ever promised that the $1,000,000 coverage limit was permanent. . . .

. . . AIDS was the only catastrophic illness to which the $5,000 limit was applied and . . . McGann was the only employee known to have AIDS. He contends that if defendants reduced AIDS coverage because they learned of McGann's illness through his exercising of his rights under the plan by filing claims, the coverage reduction therefore could be "retaliation" for McGann's filing of the claims. Under McGann's theory, any reduction in employee benefits would be impermissibly discriminatory if motivated by a desire to avoid the anticipated costs of continuing to provide coverage for a particular beneficiary. McGann would find an implied promise not to discriminate for this purpose; it is the breaking of this promise that McGann appears to contend constitutes interference with a future entitlement.

McGann's claim cannot be reconciled with the well-settled principle that Congress did not intend that ERISA circumscribe employers' control over the content of benefits plans they offered to their employees. McGann interprets section 510 to prevent an employer from reducing or eliminating coverage for a particular illness in response to the escalating costs of covering an employee suffering from that illness. Such an interpretation would, in effect, change the terms of H & H Music's plan. Instead of making the $1,000,000 limit available for medical expenses on an as-incurred basis only as long as the limit remained in effect, the policy would make the limit permanently available for all medical expenses as they might thereafter be incurred because of a single event, such as the contracting of AIDS. Under McGann's theory, defendants would be effectively proscribed from reducing coverage for AIDS once McGann had contracted that illness and filed claims for AIDS-related expenses. If a federal court could prevent an employer from reducing an employee's coverage limits for AIDS treatment once that employee contracted AIDS, the boundaries of judicial involvement in the creation, alteration or termination of ERISA plans would be sorely tested.

Case Questions

1. Why did H & H reduce its coverage for AIDS? Why was this not an ERISA violation?

2. What interpretation of ERISA did McGann urge? Why did the court reject it?

3. Could H & H's "Use it and lose it" approach affect employee exercise of remaining health benefits? Should this matter?

■   ■   ■

4. You are director of human resources for Capable Computers Company (CCC). CCC has a defined benefit pension plan. Employees are fully vested after five years of service. Then retirement benefits are based on age and salary at retirement and length of service. There are substantial increases in pensions after service of 10, 20, and 30 years.

Wendy Worker has been a CCC employee for 29 years. Recently, her supervisor caught her borrowing CCC computer equipment.

Worker would take the equipment home at night and return it the next morning. A CCC rule permits employees to use CCC equipment in the office for personal matters, but forbids borrowing equipment. The rule has been enforced sporadically.

Worker's supervisor wants to fire her but has heard that to do so might violate ERISA. The supervisor has sought your advice. How will you respond?

Pension Plans

Although ERISA covers employee benefit plans generally, its primary concern is private pension plans. Most pension plans are either **defined contribution** or **defined benefit plans**. In a defined contribution plan, an employer and/or employee contribute a specified percentage of the employee's salary to a retirement account, where it accumulates earnings. On retirement, the employee receives a pension based on the amount in the account. In a defined benefit plan, an employee receives a retirement benefit based on length of service, age, and salary.

Pension plans are subject to minimum ERISA standards for participation, vesting, and funding. Employee participation may not be delayed beyond the date on which the employee attains age 25 and has rendered one year of service. One year of service is defined as a 12-month period in which the employee works at least 1,000 hours. If an employee immediately becomes 100 percent vested, participation may be delayed until age 25 and completion of three years of service.

An employee's pension benefits are **vested** when the employee is entitled to those benefits even if he or she leaves the employer before retirement. ERISA establishes minimum vesting requirements. Employers must meet either one of two standards: (1) employees are 100 percent vested after no more than five years of service, or (2) employees are 20 percent vested after no more than three years of service and receive an additional 20 percent for each additional year until they are 100 percent vested after seven years. ERISA also requires that employers who have defined benefit plans meet minimum funding requirements to ensure that the plan has sufficient assets to pay all benefits. To ensure payment of vested benefits, ERISA provides that an employee's right to benefits is nonforfeitable on attaining normal retirement age.

ERISA established the Pension Benefit Guaranty Corporation (PBGC) within the Department of Labor. All defined benefit pension plans that qualify for favorable tax treatment must pay for termination insurance provided by the PBGC. Plan administrators must notify the PBGC of plan terminations. The PBGC guarantees to beneficiaries of terminated plans payment of nonforfeitable vested benefits. Employers that contribute to or otherwise maintain such plans may be liable to the PBGC to the extent that the plan's assets are insufficient to meet its guaranteed benefits. However, an employer is not liable to the PBGC if it paid contingent liability insurance premiums for each of the five plan years immediately preceding plan termination.

Unemployment Compensation

Unemployment insurance (UI) is funded by federal and state payroll taxes. **Experience-rating provisions** adjust an employer's UI tax rate based on UI claims filed by its employees. An employer with a good record can substantially reduce the tax, while an employer with a bad rating may have to pay the entire tax.

To be eligible for UI benefits, an employee must have earned a specified, average minimum income during a base period, usually 52 weeks. Eligible workers must also be available for work and actively looking for work. Workers may be disqualified from receiving benefits if they refuse to accept suitable employment, although they need not accept work drastically different from their former jobs. Disqualification may also result from voluntarily quitting employment without good cause, discharge for serious misconduct, or loss of employment due to a labor dispute.

Occupational Safety and Health Protection

The Occupational Safety and Health Act (OSH Act) covers all employers except those regulated by other occupational safety acts, employers of domestic household employees, and religious organizations whose employees are engaged in religious activities. The OSH Act established three federal administrative agencies: the National Institute of Occupational Safety and Health (NIOSH), the Occupational Safety and Health Administration (OSHA), and the Occupational Safety and Health Review Commission (OSHRC).

NIOSH is housed in the Department of Health and Human Services. It conducts research into health-related problems in the workplace. OSHA is housed in the Labor Department and enforces the OSH Act. **OSHRC** is an independent agency that adjudicates contested cases of OSH Act violations.

Duties

The OSH Act imposes on employers a general duty to provide a place of employment free from "recognized hazards causing or likely to cause death or serious physical harm to employees" and a duty to comply with all OSHA health and safety standards. Employees must also comply with all OSHA rules.

The General Duty
A hazard must meet four criteria to trigger the general duty under the OSH Act:

- The hazard must arise from employment.

- The hazard must be generally recognized in the industry as a hazard about which the employer knows or should know.
- The hazard must cause or be likely to cause death or serious physical harm. This includes hazards that result in temporary disablement requiring hospitalization. It does not include hazards that result in dizziness or minor abrasions.
- The hazard must be preventable in the course of business.

If these criteria are met, the employer has an absolute duty to remove the hazard.

Specific Standards

The OSH Act further requires employers to comply with specific occupational safety and health standards promulgated under the act. Safety standards are designed to prevent accidents. They usually specify what an employer must do. For example, they may require that an employer provide guard rails or safety nets for employees working at a certain height.

Health standards are designed to prevent occupational diseases. They set maximum levels of exposure to toxic substances, noise, and other harmful matter. They often leave it to employers to decide how to achieve compliance.

An employer who needs time to comply with a standard may obtain a temporary variance but must show that all necessary steps will be taken to protect the employees until compliance has been attained. A permanent variance may be granted to an employer only if it is shown that under the variance the employer will provide an environment as safe as would have been obtained if the standard were followed.

Excuses for Noncompliance

Isolated incidents of employer noncompliance may be excused. The isolated-incident defense has been successful in cases where the alleged violation resulted exclusively from an employee's misconduct that was in breach of the employer's express safety rules. For this defense to be successful, the employer must have provided an adequate safety and training program for the employees, must have actually enforced the safety rules, and must have been ignorant of the employee's noncompliance.

In rare cases, complying with an OSHA safety standard may be more hazardous than not complying. In these cases compliance is excused. Similarly, if the nature of the physical plant or of the work makes it impossible to comply with a standard, compliance may be excused.

Right to Know

Employers frequently ask employees to handle chemicals and other toxic substances that may be harmful to their health. Until recently, employees could be required to work with such substances without knowing of the potential dangers.

To remedy this situation, OSHA adopted an employee **hazard communication standard**.

The standard requires chemical manufacturers and importers to evaluate the hazards of all chemicals they produce or import and develop Material Safety Data Sheets for each chemical. All employers are required to ensure that every container holding chemicals is labeled with information concerning the chemical and its hazards. All employers are also required to develop a hazard communication program to advise their employees on the hazards involved and the safe handling of chemicals.

Record-Keeping, Notification, and Posting Requirements

Employers with 11 or more employees must maintain a detailed log of all recordable incidents and enter each incident in the log no later than six workdays after learning of it. Recordable incidents include occupational injuries or illnesses resulting in fatalities, lost workdays, job transfers, job termination, medical treatment other than first aid, loss of consciousness, and restriction of work or motion. In addition, each establishment must complete an annual summary of all injuries and illnesses within one month after the close of the calendar year. All employers, regardless of size, must report within 48 hours any accident that results in a death or in hospitalization of more than four employees.

Enforcement

OSHA enforcement begins when an OSHA compliance officer presents his or her official credentials to the employer and requests permission to inspect the premises. In most instances, advance notice of an inspection is prohibited. If an employer denies permission, the inspector must obtain a search warrant. To obtain a warrant, OSHA must demonstrate a reasonable basis for selecting the workplace in question for inspection. Employee complaints, high accident rates, a history of employer noncompliance with the OSH Act, a large number of employees in a large business place, and the passage of a long interval since the last inspection may all be neutral criteria that constitute the necessary reasonable basis for obtaining an administrative search warrant.

The employer or a designated representative is entitled to accompany the inspector during the walk-around, and a representative authorized by the employees may also be present. After the walk-around, there is a closing conference between the inspector and the employer or the designated representative to "informally advise [the employer] of any apparent safety or health violations disclosed by the inspection."

If OSHA finds a violation, it issues a citation to the employer. The citation describes the violation and provides a reasonable time for its abatement. Penalties range from a notice without a formal citation for de minimus violations to a mandatory penalty of up to a $10,000 fine and six months in jail for a willful violation that results in a worker's death.

An employer who wishes to contest a citation must file a notice of contest within 15 days with OSHRC. The employer's contest is assigned to an administrative law judge. The ALJ conducts a hearing and issues a recommended decision. The parties may file exceptions to the ALJ's decision with OSHRC. OSHRC decisions may be appealed to the U.S. Courts of Appeals.

Employer Retaliation

The OSH Act forbids discharge or any other discrimination against an employee who exercises rights under the act. Victims of discrimination may complain to the secretary of labor; and the secretary may seek relief in a U.S. district court. In the following case, the secretary sought appropriate relief under the OSH Act on behalf of two employees who were suspended when they refused to work under conditions that posed an imminent threat to their safety.

WHIRLPOOL CORP. V. MARSHALL
445 U.S. 1 (1980)

Secretary of Labor Marshall (respondent) filed suit against Whirlpool (petitioner), alleging that Whirlpool's act of reprimanding and suspending two employees for refusing to work under what they believed were unsafe conditions violated a regulation promulgated under the Occupational Safety and Health Act. The incident arose when the employees refused to perform maintenance work on a wire mesh guard screen, 20 feet above the floor, at petitioner's manufacturing plant. A few weeks before the incident, another employee was killed when he fell through the screen. Although petitioner had repaired the screen and changed maintenance procedures, the two employees believed that the screen remained unsafe.

The district court denied the claim, holding that the secretary's regulation was inconsistent with the act. The court of appeals reversed. The U.S. Supreme Court affirmed the court of appeals.

Justice Stewart

The Secretary is obviously correct when he acknowledges in his regulation that, "as a general matter, there is no right afforded by the Act which would entitle employees to walk off the job because of potential unsafe conditions at the workplace." By providing for prompt notice to the employer of an inspector's intention to seek an injunction against an imminently dangerous condition, the legislation obviously contemplates that the employer will normally respond by voluntarily and speedily eliminating the danger. And in the few instances where this does not occur, the leg-

islative provisions authorizing prompt judicial action are designed to give employees full protection in most situations from the risk of injury or death resulting from an imminently dangerous condition at the worksite.

As this case illustrates, however, circumstances may sometimes exist in which the employee justifiably believes that the express statutory arrangement does not sufficiently protect him from death or serious injury. Such circumstances will probably not often occur, but such a situation may arise when (1) the employee is ordered by his employer to work under conditions that the employee reasonably believes pose an imminent risk of death or serious bodily injury, and (2) the employee has reason to believe that there is not sufficient time or opportunity either to seek effective redress from his employer or to apprise OSHA of the danger.

Nothing in the Act suggested that those few employees who have to face this dilemma must rely exclusively on the remedies expressly set forth in the Act at the risk of their own safety. But nothing in the Act explicitly provides otherwise. Against this background of legislative silence, the Secretary has exercised his rulemaking power . . . and has determined that, when an employee in good faith finds himself in such a predicament, he may refuse to expose himself to the dangerous condition, without being subjected to "subsequent discrimination" by the employer.

■   ■   ■

The regulation clearly conforms to the fundamental objective of the Act—to prevent occupational deaths and serious injuries. . . .

To accomplish this basic purpose, the legislation's remedial orientation is prophylactic in nature. The Act does not wait for an employee to die or become injured. It authorizes the promulgation of health and safety standards and the issuance of citations in the hope that these will act to prevent deaths or injuries from ever occurring. It would seem anomalous to construe an Act so directed and constructed as prohibiting an employee, with no other reasonable alternative, the freedom to withdraw from a workplace environment that he reasonably believes is highly dangerous.

Moreover, the Secretary's regulation can be viewed as an appropriate aid to the full effectuation of the Act's "general duty" clause. That clause provides that "[e]ach employer . . . shall furnish to each of his employees employment and a place of employment which are free from recognized hazards that are causing or are likely to cause death or serious physical harm to his employees. . . ." Since OSHA inspectors cannot be present around the clock in every workplace, the Secretary's regulation ensures that employees will in all circumstances enjoy the rights afforded them by the "general duty" clause.

The regulation thus on its face appears to further the overriding purpose of the Act, and rationally to complement its remedial scheme.

. . . [T]he Secretary's regulation must, therefore, be upheld, particularly when it is remembered that safety legislation is to be liberally construed to effectuate the congressional purpose.

Case Questions

1. Under what authority did the secretary promulgate the regulation relied on by the two employees? Is the regulation derived from any express provisions of the act? Is it implied? How?

2. Aside from the secretary's regulation, what else did Whirlpool violate?

3. Which conditions must be present to justify an employee's refusal to work?

4. Will this decision result in many employees walking off their jobs and, consequently, increase work stoppages? What should management do to ensure that this does not happen?

5. As a result of *Whirlpool,* could a firefighter refuse to enter a burning building because of the unsafe conditions and successfully seek the protection of the secretary's regulation? Explain.

Protection of Employees' Personal Integrity

The interests of employees in their personal integrity often clash with the employer's interests in managing the workplace. For example, employees may be offended by being required to take tests purporting to measure their honesty, while employers may view the tests as needed to cope with problems of employee theft. Employees' interests in protecting their reputations may conflict with employers' needs to provide and receive references. Generally, courts have balanced the conflicting interests of employers and employees through the common law of tort. However, in 1988 Congress enacted legislation regulating employers' use of lie detectors.

The Employee Polygraph Protection Act

The Employee Polygraph Protection Act of 1988 prohibits employers from requiring, suggesting, or causing employees or prospective employees to take lie detector tests. It also forbids discharging, disciplining, discriminating against, refusing to promote or hire, or threatening to take any action against employees or applicants because they refuse to take lie detector tests or because of the results of lie detector tests. Employers are also prohibited from retaliating against employees or applicants for exercising or aiding others in exercising their rights under the act.

Violators are subject to court penalties of up to $10,000 and may be liable for reinstatement, promotion, back pay, and lost benefits. The act does not apply to government employers and FBI contractors. It contains exceptions for security employees, employees with access to controlled substances, and investigations of a specific employer's economic loss, such as a theft or embezzlement, if the employee had access to the property and the employer has a reasonable suspicion of the employee's involvement. Even where the exceptions apply, the employee has the right to refuse to take the test, to terminate the test at any time, to consult with counsel or an employee representative, and to receive a written statement of his or her rights and of the nature, date, time, and location of the test. In giving a test, the examiner may not ask the employee's belief about religion, politics, racial matters, labor unions, or any question relating to sexual behavior. The examiner may not ask any question that was not presented in writing to the employee before the test.

Intentional Torts

Many of the intentional torts discussed in Chapter 8 apply to protect employees' personal integrity in the workplace. For example, review the *Staruski* case involving the tort of invasion of privacy in the workplace.

Generally, courts recognize legitimate employer interests in protecting their businesses. They balance employer and employee interests by allowing employers a qualified privilege to act in an otherwise tortious way. However, where an employer's actions exceed that which is reasonably necessary to protect its interests, it may lose the privilege and be liable to the employee.

For example, in one case, a court held a retailer liable to one of its cashiers for intentional infliction of emotional distress. A customer had accused the cashier of theft. The retailer's manager publicly accused the cashier, searched her cash

---

Ethical Dilemmas/Issues

Carol Mehling is employed as a marketing manager by Conglomerate Computer Company. She has consistently received excellent performance appraisals and full merit raises from her supervisor, Roger Wilko. She has been dating Terry Recker. Recker was a financial analyst for Conglomerate when they met, but left Conglomerate to work for a competitor, Intercontinental Computer Company.

Wilko called Mehling into his office one day. Wilko asked, "Are you dating Terry Recker?"

"Yes," Mehling replied, "but what difference does it make if I am?"

Wilko said, "I think we have a conflict of interest, or the appearance of a conflict of interest here."

Mehling said, "Well, gee, Roger, you've pointed out to me that there are no problems in the office, and I don't really understand why that would have any pertinency to my job. You said I'm doing an OK job. I just got a raise."

"I'll tell you what," Wilko answered. "I'll give you a week to think it over."

Mehling asked, "Think what over?"

Wilko answered, "You either stop dating Terry Recker or I'm going to take you out of your management job."

What are the ethical issues? What would you do?

---

drawer several times, and subjected her to a strip search under the customer's observation.[2] One area of frequent employer concern is liability for defamation when evaluating current or former employees. The following case illustrates one approach to this problem.

LEWIS V. EQUITABLE LIFE ASSURANCE SOCIETY OF THE UNITED STATES
389 N.W. 2d 876 (Minn. 1986)

Carole Lewis and three other dental claims processors (plaintiffs) were fired by Equitable Life Assurance Society of the United States (defendant) for gross insubordination when they refused to obey a supervisor's instructions to alter their employee expense vouchers to reflect lower overall expenses. The employees maintained that they had honestly and accurately completed the vouchers.

---

[2] Bodewig v. Kmart Inc., 54 Or. App. 480, 635 P.2d 657 (1981).

In seeking new employment, the plaintiffs were asked by prospective employers to disclose their reasons for leaving Equitable Life. Each was refused employment when she stated that she had been terminated for gross insubordination. Equitable Life never communicated to any prospective employer that the plaintiffs had been terminated for gross insubordination. Its policy was to give only the dates of employment and the final job title of a former employee unless specifically authorized to release additional information.

The plaintiffs sued Equitable Life for defamation, claiming that to explain to prospective employers their reason for leaving Equitable Life, they were forced to repeat a slander. Equitable Life argued that the only publication of the alleged defamation was made by the plaintiffs, and that the company was protected against liability by a qualified privilege.

The trial jury found in favor of the plaintiffs and awarded $515,000 in damages, and the trial judge further ordered that the reason for the plaintiffs' termination be removed from their personnel files.

Equitable Life appealed to the Supreme Court of Minnesota, which ruled in favor of the plaintiffs and upheld the trial court decision.

Chief Justice Amdahl

[T]he company argues that the trial court's conclusion of liability on the part of the company was erroneous because: the only publications of the allegedly defamatory statement were made by plaintiffs; and . . . the company was qualifiedly privileged to make the statement.

Publication

In order for a statement to be considered defamatory, it must be communicated to someone other than the plaintiff, it must be false, and it must tend to harm the plaintiff's reputation and to lower him or her in the estimation of the community. Generally, there is no publication where a defendant communicates a statement directly to a plaintiff, who then communicates it to a third person. . . .

Courts . . . have recognized a narrow exception to the general rule that communication of a defamatory statement to a third person by the person defamed is not actionable. . . . [I]f a defamed person was in some way compelled to communicate the defamatory statement to a third person, and if it was foreseeable to the defendant that the defamed person would be so compelled, then the defendant could be held liable for the defamation.

■   ■   ■

The trend of modern authority persuades us that Minnesota law should recognize the doctrine of compelled self-publication. . . . The concept of compelled self-publication does no more than hold the originator of the defamatory statement liable for damages caused by the statement where the originator knows, or should know, of circumstances whereby the defamed person has no reasonable means of avoiding publication of the statement or avoiding the resulting damages; in other words, in cases where the defamed person was compelled to publish the statement. In such circumstances, the damages are fairly viewed as the direct result of the originator's actions.

■   ■   ■

In the present action, the record indicates that plaintiffs were compelled to repeat the allegedly defamatory statement to prospective employers and that the company knew plaintiffs would be so compelled. The St. Paul office manager admitted that it was foreseeable that plaintiffs would be asked by prospective employers to identify the reason that they were discharged. Their only choice would be to tell them "gross insubordination" or to lie. Fabrication, however, is an unacceptable alternative.

Qualified Privilege

Even though an untrue defamatory statement has been published, the originator of the statement will not be held liable if the statement is published under circumstances that make it conditionally privileged and if privilege is not abused. . . .

The doctrine of privileged communication rests upon public policy considerations. . . . In the context of employment recommendations, the law generally recognizes a qualified privilege between former and prospective employers as long as the statements are made in good faith and for a legitimate purpose.

■   ■   ■

A qualified privilege may be lost if it is abused. The burden is on the plaintiff to show that the privilege has been abused. While the initial determination of whether a communication is privileged is a question of law for the court to decide, the question of whether the privilege was abused is a jury question.

■   ■   ■

A qualified privilege is abused and therefore lost if the plaintiff demonstrates that the defendant acted with actual malice. The jury instructions correctly placed the burden of demonstrating malice on the plaintiff. [T]he jury . . . found the actual malice which negates the company's entitlement to the privilege. . . .

We . . . find no error in the jury instructions.

Justice Kelley
(Dissenting)

Even though I concede that it is not difficult to conclude that the terminations of these four employees was done in a shoddy, callous, and perhaps even deceiving manner, I feel constrained to dissent with today's court opinion.

■   ■   ■

I suggest that today's ruling substantially expands the scope of the defamation action. Now, the only way an employer can avoid litigation and the possible liability for substantial damages, is to cease communicating the reason it felt justified the termination, not only to third persons, but even to the employee himself or herself.

For these reasons, I would reverse.

Case Questions

1. What are the essential elements for defamation?

2. What is the doctrine of compelled self-publication that the Minnesota Supreme Court adopts? How does this doctrine modify the general requirements for the tort of defamation? Under which circumstances does the doctrine apply? Is the doctrine recognized in most states? Explain.

3. Why did the dissenting justice disagree with the majority opinion's recognition of the doctrine of compelled self-publication? With which opinion do you agree? Explain.

4. Ordinarily, an employer has a qualified privilege with regard to communications to prospective employers of former employees. In light of the existence of such a privilege, why was Equitable Life held liable for defamation to its former employees?

Chapter Problems

1. Define the following terms:
   - *a.* Terminable at will
   - *b.* White-collar exemptions
   - *e.* Defined contribution plan
   - *c.* Going and coming rule
   - *d.* Summary plan description
   - *h.* Experience-rating provision

    f. Defined benefit plan   *i.* OSHRC

    g. Vesting   *j.* Hazard communication standard

2. Computer Consultants, Inc. (CCI) has 25 employees. Leslie Leader is a project manager. She is the fourth highest-paid CCI worker. CCI hired her six months ago to supervise a project revamping a large hotel chain's centralized reservations computer system. Leader and three other employees work full-time on the project.

   Two weeks ago, Leader's child was in a serious accident and hospitalized. The child is expected to be released next week and will need another four weeks at home to recuperate. Leader has requested a four-week leave of absence. CCI is reluctant to grant the leave because Leader's project is at a critical stage of development. Does the FMLA require CCI to grant the leave? Explain.

3. Houston Medical Center, a hospital, employs Harold Bright as an equipment technician. Bright works a standard 40-hour week. When not on duty, he is required to wear a pager. When paged, he must report to the hospital within 30 minutes and be ready to repair complicated medical equipment. When called in, the hospital pays Bright time and a half for the hours he actually works. Must it pay him time and a half for the time he is "on call" but not actually working? Explain.

4. Two workers were on a scaffold when the supporting cables broke. One fell to his death, but the other landed safely on the roof of an adjacent building. Thereafter he was unable to work in high places and suffered from a nervous disorder evidenced by temporary paralysis, troubled sleep, nightmares, eyelid tremors, and other symptoms. He filed a workers' compensation claim for loss of wages as well as medical and psychiatric expenses. Should he recover compensation? Is he eligible for Social Security disability payments?

5. James Adams is a chronic alcoholic. He consumes two pints of alcohol on an average day. His drinking has caused him to suffer seizures. Doctors have prescribed medication and told Adams to stop drinking to control his seizures. Adams responded with increased drinking. He refuses to take his medication, choosing to drink instead. Due to his seizures, Adams is unable to work. Assuming he has worked a sufficient period of time to be eligible for OASDI, is Adams entitled to Social Security disability benefits? Explain.

6. A plumber residing in the Detroit, Michigan, area was laid off due to lack of work. The plumber was unable to find work in the Detroit area, but found a job in Cincinnati, Ohio, 270 miles away. He lived in Cincinnati during the week, returning home on the weekends. After one month, he found that he was having transportation problems and that the weekend commuting was straining his family life and himself. He quit the Cincinnati job and applied for unemployment compensation in Detroit. Is he eligible? Explain.

7. Reliable Lumber Co. suspected that one or more employees on the midnight to 8 A.M. shift was stealing material. Reliable required all five employees

who worked that shift to take lie detector tests. Three employees passed. Two refused to take the test and were fired. Discuss Reliable's liability to the five employees. May the two who were fired collect unemployment compensation? Explain.

8. Acme Manufacturers has a defined benefit pension plan that is fully funded in compliance with ERISA. Employees' benefits are 100 percent vested after three years. The plan also provides that any employee terminated for dishonesty or for being convicted of a felony that occurred while on duty shall be disqualified from receiving benefits. Is this provision legal? Why or why not?

9. All employees of the Grumman Corporation participate in the company pension plan. The plan's three trustees are also officers of Grumman. The LTV Corporation recently announced a tender offer of $45 per share for up to 70 percent of Grumman stock, conditioned on obtaining at least 50.01 percent of all shares. Prior to the announcement, the stock had been selling at $25 a share.

   The Grumman board of directors passed a resolution to fight the LTV takeover attempt. The pension plan currently owns 525,000 shares of Grumman stock. It has the opportunity to purchase an additional 1,258,000 shares at an average price of $37 a share. The plan administrator has asked the trustees to decide whether to purchase additional Grumman stock, to tender the existing 525,000 shares to LTV, or to do nothing. What should the trustees do? Explain.

10. Old Bridge Chemical, Inc. (Old Bridge) was charged with a serious OSHA violation for failing to abide by a safety standard and for failing to adequately train employees engaged in the rescue of other employees from a railroad tank car. An employee had been assigned to collect chemical samples from the bottom of a railroad tank car. He passed out after being manually lowered through a hatch at the top of the car. A second employee jumped in to rescue the first and was also overcome by fumes. A third employee, lowered into the tank in an attempt to rescue the second, also succumbed to fumes. The employees had never been instructed in the hazards of confined entry space and emergency rescue procedures. The employer had admonished its employees not to enter the tank without authorization.

   An OSHA standard requires that employers provide rescuers with air respirators. Old Bridge failed to do this on the ground that air respirators were not needed because the chemical in the tank did not form a vapor, dust, or fumes. Was Old Bridge in violation? Explain. Would the result be different if the employees received safety instruction procedures but ignored them? What if the employees were provided with air respirators but refused to use them? What should employers do to ensure employees' compliance with health and safety instructions?

17   EQUAL EMPLOYMENT OPPORTUNITY

Learning Objectives

After learning this chapter the student should be able to:

- Recognize employment decisions having a high risk of disparate treatment liability.
- Determine the likelihood that an employment practice would result in disparate impact liability.
- Apply the bona fide seniority system, bona fide occupational qualification, and bona fide employee benefit plan exceptions to different problems.
- Evaluate the likelihood that an affirmative action plan is lawful.
- Determine when harassment amounts to illegal discrimination.
- Determine when to accommodate an employee's religious practices or physical or mental disability.

During the Reconstruction period, Congress passed several civil rights acts to protect the newly freed slaves. These acts were soon ignored, as segregation and discrimination became widespread within America's social institutions. Although many Americans worked against segregation in the late 19th and early 20th centuries, it was not until the 1950s that the civil rights movement began to gain momentum. The movement achieved its most significant legislative victory with the passage of the Civil Rights Act of 1964, a comprehensive assault on discriminatory practices in America. Title VII of the Civil Rights Act prohibits discrimination in employment on the basis of race, color, religion, national origin, or sex. It is the broadest federal statute regulating employment practices. Today, it is one of several major sources of federal equal employment regulation.

These regulations weave a tangled legal web that can snare today's employers. They establish the following categories of illegal discrimination: race, sex, religion, national origin, age, and disability. Each of these categories is known as a *protected class.* The federal equal employment opportunity laws contain different provisions concerning coverage of protected classes, defenses, and enforcement. They are summarized in Table 17–1.

The Concept of Discrimination

Regardless of which protected class or statute is involved, the concept of discrimination is basically the same. Discrimination in any employment decision is illegal. This includes hiring, firing, promotion, job assignments, training programs, compensation, and similar decisions. The law does not require an employer to hire, promote, or retain anyone; it simply prohibits an employer from using membership in a protected class as a basis for an employment decision. The two types of illegal discrimination are:

- Disparate treatment of a member of a protected class.
- Disparate impact of an employment practice on a protected class.

The disparate treatment and disparate impact approaches were first developed by the courts in cases interpreting Title VII. They have also been applied in cases involving other federal equal employment opportunity laws.

Disparate Treatment

Disparate treatment results when an employer, union, or employment agency treats one employee less favorably than another because of race, sex, religion, national origin, age, or disability. Thus, disparate treatment is intentional discrimination. In a disparate treatment case, the focus is on the defendant's motive.

A plaintiff may prove disparate treatment with direct evidence of discriminatory motive. For example, an employer may have sent a rejection letter to a female applicant stating, "You are certainly well qualified, but this is a man's job.

TABLE 17–1   **Federal EEO Laws**

Law	Coverage	Protected Class(es)	Defenses	Enforcement
Title VII, 1964 Civil Rights Act	Employers with at least 15 employees; unions; employment agencies	Race, sex, religion, national origin	Seniority systems, ability tests, bona fide occupational qualifications (except race)	EEOC or private lawsuit after using EEOC remedies
Equal Pay Act	Similar to FLSA coverage	Sex (equal pay for equal work)	Seniority system, factors other than sex, quantity or quality of output	EEOC or private lawsuit
Age Discrimination in Employment Act	Employers with at least 20 employees; unions; employment agencies	Age (40 or older)	Seniority system, bona fide occupational qualification, reasonable factors other than age, employee benefit plan	EEOC or private lawsuit after using EEOC remedies
Americans with Disabilities Act	Employers with 15 or more employees	Disability, including a duty to accommodate	Undue hardship	Same as Title VII
§§503, 504, Rehabilitation Act of 1973	Federal contractors and recipients of federal financial assistance	Handicap, including a duty to accommodate		Private lawsuit, debarment from federal contracts
1866 Civil Rights Act Executive Orders	Employers; unions Federal contractors	Race, national origin Affirmative action re women and racial and ethnic minorities		Private lawsuit Debarment from federal contracts

Usually, direct evidence of discriminatory motive is not available. Motive, therefore, must be inferred from a defendant's conduct in view of the surrounding circumstances. A plaintiff may raise an inference of discrimination by showing that he or she (1) belonged to a protected class, (2) applied and was qualified for a job for which the employer was seeking applicants, and (3) was rejected, after which the position remained open and the employer continued seeking applicants with similar qualifications. A plaintiff who accomplishes this is said to have established a prima facie case of disparate treatment, or intentional discrimination. This approach may be adapted to establish a prima facie case of disparate treatment with regard to matters other than initial hire.

When a prima facie case of disparate treatment has been established, the defendant must provide a legitimate, nondiscriminatory explanation for the employment decision. The defendant is not required to prove that it did not discriminate, nor must it prove the factual validity of its explanation. However, a demonstration that an employment practice is required by business necessity may not be used as a defense against a claim of intentional discrimination.

Once the defendant provides an explanation, the plaintiff must prove that the explanation is really a pretext for discrimination. To do so, the plaintiff may attempt to show that the defendant's rationale lacks credibility, that the rationale was not uniformly applied, or that statistics indicate a general practice of discrimination by the defendant. The ultimate issue is a factual one: is the defendant's apparently valid reason really a cover-up for intentional discrimination?

Strong circumstantial evidence of intentional discrimination is provided by a statistical comparison between the percentage of minorities in the employer's workforce and the percentage of minorities in the relevant labor market. Employers are not required to hire a specified percentage of minorities, but the minority composition of the employer's workforce may suggest that the employer has discriminated.

For example, assume that an employer has 1,000 qualified applicants for 10 openings, and that 500 applicants are black and 500 are white. If the employer hires randomly, one would expect 50 blacks and 50 whites to be hired. Fifty is said to be the "expected value." If the employer hires 47 blacks, it is still very likely that the selection is random and that the deviation from the expected value occurred by chance rather than by design. If only 10 blacks were hired, one may suspect discrimination. If no blacks are hired, it is almost certain that the employer discriminated. One cannot be absolutely certain, because it is possible to randomly select 100 whites. Nevertheless, the greater the deviation from the expected value, the less likely it is that the result occurred by chance.

If the frequency of all possible random outcomes is plotted on a graph, the result is a bell curve, as illustrated in Figure 17–1. A statistical measure, known as **standard deviation**, is derived from the bell curve. It measures the probabil-

FIGURE 17–1   **Bell Curve**

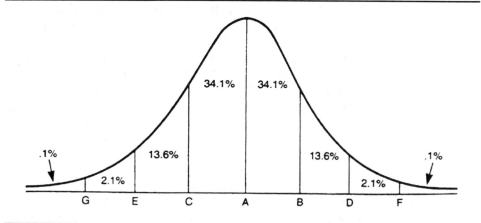

ity that a given result occurred by chance. On the curve below, point A is the expected value. Points B and C are equal distances away from point A. We expect to find 68 percent of all results between points B and C; and 34 percent between A and C. Points D and E are equidistant from points B and C, respectively. Between points D and E, we expect to find 96 percent of all results. The distance between each point and its closest neighboring point is one standard deviation. Thus, when the minority or sexual composition of an employer's workforce is two to three standard deviations less than the expected value, we are 96 percent to 98.8 percent sure that the hiring did not occur randomly. Under these circumstances, a court infers that the employer has committed intentional discrimination.

An employer faced with statistical proof of intentional discrimination may attempt to rebut the inference in several ways. The employer may argue that the statistical comparison is not valid because the plaintiff failed to select the appropriate relevant labor market. The appropriate relevant labor market depends on the skill required for the job. If the job requires little specialized skill, general population figures would provide an appropriate basis of comparison. If the job is highly specialized, the relevant labor market must be restricted to those who are qualified. For example, the workforce of an employer charged with discrimination in hiring messengers may be compared to the general population, whereas the workforce of an employer charged with discriminating in hiring certified public accountants must be compared to CPAs generally.

The employer's location may also influence the composition of the relevant labor market. Commuting patterns in a given metropolitan area may be significant in determining the relevant market of an employer located in the central city or in a suburb.

Besides attacking the validity of the statistical comparison, the defendant may also attack its probative value. For example, the employer might show that its workforce has experienced little turnover and little expansion since the effective date of Title VII. The employer might also offer nondiscriminatory explanations for statistical disparities.

In some cases, the evidence may show that both discriminatory and legitimate reasons contributed to the defendant's actions. These cases are called **mixed motive cases**. The defendant may claim that it would have taken the same action even if the plaintiff had not been a member of a protected class. As long as the plaintiff proves that membership in a protected class was a motivating factor in the decision, the defendant is liable, even though other factors also motivated the practice. The defendant may avoid the remedies of damages, reinstatement, hiring, promotion, and back pay, however, by proving that it would have reached the same decision without considering the plaintiff's protected class status. The available remedies would be only declarative relief, certain types of injunctive relief, attorney fees and costs.

Disparate treatment can take many forms. For example, an employer that segregates its workforce for fringe benefits purposes engages in illegal disparate treatment. Thus, an employer may not offer male employees lower life insurance benefits or higher pension benefits than similarly situated female employees even though women, as a group, live longer than men.

Another type of disparate treatment occurs when an employer uses a double standard for members of a protected class. This conduct is illegal, even if the employer does not otherwise discriminate. For example, an employer whose work-force is predominantly female acts illegally if it refuses to hire women with preschool children but hires men with preschool children. Such a policy is often called *sex plus discrimination.*

Disparate Impact

Employers often impose requirements for particular jobs. For example, employers might require security guards to be at least six feet tall. On its face this requirement does not appear to disqualify any job applicant because of sex or national origin. However, if scrutinized, it may prove to disqualify a larger percentage of women, Latinos, and Asians than nonminority males. Because, on average, they are shorter than white males, these groups may be systematically excluded from consideration for the security guard jobs. The employment discrimination laws do not prohibit the use of such facially neutral criteria. When the criteria systematically exclude members of a protected class from job opportunities, the employer must justify their use or it will be liable for **disparate impact**.

In a disparate impact case, the plaintiff must prove that the challenged practice disqualifies a protected class at a significantly greater rate than the majority class. The defendant may avoid liability by proving that the practice is job related and consistent with business necessity. The defendant may still be liable if the plaintiff can prove that there was a less discriminatory practice available to meet the defendant's needs.

In the following case, the Supreme Court applies the disparate impact approach to a case brought under the Age Discrimination in Employment Act (the ADEA). Note that the application of the disparate impact approach is narrower in cases involving the ADEA than in cases brought under Title VII. This is because of differences in the text of the two federal laws. The ADEA contains a separate provision not found in Title VII. The ADEA includes a defense for "reasonable factors other than age" (the RFOA).

SMITH V. CITY OF JACKSON, MISSISSIPPI
125 S. Ct. 1536 (2005)

In revising its employee pay plan, the City of Jackson, Mississippi (Respondent) granted raises to all police officers and police dispatchers in an attempt to bring their starting salaries up to the regional average. Officers with less than five years' service received proportionately greater raises than those with more seniority, and most officers over 40 had more than five years of service. A group of older officers (Petitioners) filed suit under the Age Discrimination in Employment Act (ADEA), claiming that they were adversely affected by the plan because of their age. The District Court granted the City summary judgment. The Court of Appeals affirmed, ruling that disparate-impact claims are unavailable under the ADEA. The Supreme Court of the United States affirmed. The following is the Supreme Court's decision.

Justice Stevens

We . . . hold that the ADEA does authorize recovery in "disparate-impact" cases. . . . Because, however, we conclude that petitioners have not set forth a valid disparate-impact claim, we affirm.

■   ■   ■

In determining whether the ADEA authorizes disparate-impact claims, we begin with the premise that when Congress uses the same language in two statutes having similar purposes, . . . it is appropriate to presume that Congress intended that text to have the same meaning in both statutes. . . .

In *Grigges [vs. Duke Power Co.]*, a case decided four years after the enactment of the ADEA, we considered whether §703 of Title VII prohibited an employer "from requiring a high school education or passing of a standardized general intelligence test as a condition of employment in or transfer to jobs when (a) neither standard is shown to be significantly related to successful job performance, (b) both requirements operate to disqualify Negroes at a substantially higher rate than white applicants, and (c) the jobs in question formerly had been filled only by white employees as part of longstanding practice of giving preference to whites." Accepting the Court of Appeals' conclusion that the employer had adopted the diploma and test requirements without any intent to discriminate, we held that good faith "does not redeem employment procedures or testing mechanisms that operate as 'built-in headwinds' for minority groups and are unrelated to measuring job capability."

We explained that Congress had "directed the thrust of the Act to the *consequences* of employment practices, not simply the motivation." We relied on the fact that history is "filled with examples of men and women who rendered highly effective performance without the conventional badges of accomplishment in terms of certificates, diplomas or degrees. Diplomas and tests are useful servants, but Congress has mandated the commonsense proposition that they are not to become masters of reality." And we noted that the Equal Employment Opportunity Commission (EEOC), which had enforcement responsibility, had issued guidelines that accorded with our view. We thus squarely held that §703(a)(2) of Title VII did not require a showing of discriminatory intent.

■   ■   ■

Griggs, which interpreted the identical text at issue here, thus strongly suggests that a disparate-impact theory should be cognizable under the ADEA. . . .

[T]extual differences between the ADEA and Title VII make it clear that even though both statutes authorize recovery on a disparate-impact theory, the scope of disparate-impact liability under ADEA is narrower than under Title VII. The first is the RFOA provision . . . *[The RFOA provision provides that it shall not be unlawful for an employer "to take any action otherwise prohibited . . . where the differentiation is based on reasonable factors other than age."]*

Turning to the case before us, . . . the disparate impact is attributable to the City's decision to give raises based on seniority and position. Reliance on seniority and rank is unquestionably reasonable given the City's goal of raising employees' salaries to match those in surrounding communities. In sum, we hold that the City's decision to grant a larger raise to lower echelon employees for the purpose of bringing salaries in line with that of surrounding police forces was a decision based on a "reasonable factor other than age" that responded to the City's legitimate goal of retaining police officers. While there may have been other reasonable ways for the City to achieve its goals, the one selected was not unreasonable. Unlike the business necessity test, which asks whether there are other ways for the employer to achieve its goals that do not result in a disparate impact on a protected class, the reasonableness inquiry includes no such requirement.

Accordingly, while we do not agree with the Court of Appeals' holding that that the disparate-impact theory of recovery is never available under the ADEA, we affirm its judgment.

Case Questions

1. Describe the disparate impact approach to determining the existence of illegal job discrimination and how that approach differs from the disparate treatment approach.

2. In which types of cases will the disparate impact approach and the disparate treatment approach be applied?

3. How is the disparate impact approach different in cases brought under ADEA and cases brought under Title VII of the Civil Rights Act? Is the protection against disparate impact discrimination as strong under the ADEA as it is under Title VII? Why or why not? Which is easier to prove: that an employer's policy or practice is necessary or that it is reasonable? Under Title VII an employer charged with disparate impact discrimination must justify the practice as a business necessity to avoid liability, but under the ADEA, when an employer is charged with disparate impact discrimination, it must only show that the practice was reasonable.

4. Is it enough to avoid liability under either Title VII or the ADEA that the employer can prove that its policy or decision is not motivated by discrimination?

5. What are the practical implications of *Smith vs. City of Jackson, Mississippi?* Suppose an employer's hiring criteria can be shown to statistically have a negative impact on employees over age forty. What must the employer be able to prove to avoid liability?

Exceptions

The federal laws contain a variety of exceptions to their prohibitions against discrimination. The three most common exceptions are:

- Bona fide occupational qualifications.
- Professionally developed ability tests.
- Bona fide seniority systems.

The Bona Fide Occupational Qualification

The **bona fide occupational qualification** (BFOQ) is a statutory exception to employment practices that might otherwise violate Title VII or the Age Discrimination in Employment Act. This exception allows an employer to discriminate in its hiring where religion, national origin, sex, or age is a bona fide occupational qualification reasonably necessary to the normal operation of the business. The exception does not apply to racial discrimination. To establish a BFOQ, the employer must show that employees of a given sex, religion, national origin, or age are a business necessity because any other groups would undermine the essence of the business operation. This may be done by showing that certain qualifications possessed by persons of a given sex, religion, national origin, or age are essential to the employer's business and that it is impracticable to find members of the excluded class who possess these qualifications.

The BFOQ is interpreted narrowly, and the employer bears a heavy burden of proof. The employer must prove that the discrimination is necessary, not merely convenient. The following case illustrates how courts evaluate the BFOQ.

UNITED AUTO WORKERS v. JOHNSON CONTROLS, INC.
499 U.S. 187 (1991)

Johnson Controls (respondent) manufactured automobile batteries. It prohibited fertile women from working in jobs where they would be exposed to lead. It imposed the ban after eight employees became pregnant and had blood lead levels that could endanger their fetuses.

The United Auto Workers (petitioners) sued respondent for violating Title VII. The trial court granted summary judgment for respondent. The Seventh Circuit Court of Appeals affirmed. The Supreme Court reversed.

Justice Blackmun

The bias in Johnson Controls' policy is obvious. Fertile men, but not fertile women, are given a choice as to whether they wish to risk their reproductive health for a particular job. . . . The policy excludes women with childbearing capacity from lead-exposed jobs and so creates a facial classification based on gender. . . .

■   ■   ■

We therefore turn to the question whether Johnson Controls' fetal-protection policy is one of those "certain instances" that come within the BFOQ exception.

The BFOQ defense is written narrowly, and this Court has read it narrowly. . . . Johnson Con-

trols argues that its fetal-protection policy falls within the so-called safety exceptions to the BFOQ. . . .

■   ■   ■

Our case law . . . makes clear that the safety exception is limited to instances in which sex or pregnancy actually interferes with the employee's ability to perform the job. This approach is consistent with the language of the BFOQ provision itself, for it suggests that permissible distinctions based on sex must relate to ability to perform the duties of the job. Johnson Controls suggests, however, that we expand the exception to allow fetal-protection policies that mandate particular standards for pregnant or fertile women. We decline to do so. Such an expansion contradicts not only the language of the BFOQ and the narrowness of its exception but the plain language and history of the Pregnancy Discrimination Act.

■   ■   ■

We have no difficulty concluding that Johnson Controls cannot establish a BFOQ. Fertile women, as far as appears in the record, participate in the manufacture of batteries as efficiently as anyone else. Johnson Controls' professed moral and ethical concerns about the welfare of the next generation do not suffice to establish a BFOQ of female sterility. Decisions about the welfare of future children must be left to the parents who conceive, bear, support, and raise them rather than to the employers who hire those parents. Congress has mandated this choice through Title VII, as amended by the Pregnancy Discrimination Act. Johnson Controls has attempted to exclude women because of their reproductive capacity. Title VII and the PDA simply do not allow a woman's dismissal because of her failure to submit to sterilization.

Case Questions

1. What was Johnson Controls' motivation for excluding fertile women from jobs involving exposure to lead?

2. What must an employer prove to establish a BFOQ?

3. Do you think that removing the ban on fertile women will result in large numbers of women taking jobs involving exposure to lead? Why or why not?

4. An employer requires that its director of Latin American marketing be male. The position involves extensive travel to Latin America to deal with present and potential customers. Business meetings are often held in hotel rooms. Many Latin American customers would find conducting business with a woman in a hotel room offensive to their cultural customs and mores. They generally prefer to do business with men and would probably switch to a competitor if the employer's Latin American marketing director were female. Does the employer's refusal to consider females for the position violate Title VII? Why or why not?

Professionally Developed Ability Tests

Title VII permits the use of any professionally developed ability test, provided that the test is not designed or used to discriminate. The EEOC has issued guidelines detailing the **validation** processes it approves for establishing the job relatedness of any selection procedure that has an adverse impact on a protected group. Under the guidelines, a test is considered discriminatory if it results in a selection rate for one race, sex, religion, or national origin that is less than four fifths of the selection rate for another. The burden then shifts to the user of the test to validate the test by one of three methods: criterion validity, content validity, or construct validity.

Criterion validity establishes a statistical relationship between performance on the test and an objective indicator of job performance. Criterion validity is established by a study comparing test scores to the specified measure of performance. For example, if a study showed that a statistically significant correlation existed between GMAT scores and grades in an MBA program, the GMAT exam would be criterion valid.

Content validity establishes that the test representatively samples a function of the job. A word processing test for a word processor is content valid.

Construct validity establishes that the test indicates a psychological trait required for the job. A test indicating leadership ability is construct valid for a police commander.

Seniority Systems

Title VII, the ADEA, and the Equal Pay Act permit employers to apply different standards of employment pursuant to **bona fide seniority systems** that are not the result of an intention to discriminate. In *Teamsters v. United States,* the Supreme Court held that a seniority system can be bona fide even though it perpetuates the effects of pre-act discrimination.[1] The Court further held that a seniority system is bona fide where it applies equally to all employees regardless of membership in a protected class, was not established or maintained for the purpose of discriminating, and operates rationally in accord with practices in the industry.

Special Problems Involving Equal Employment Opportunity

In addition to the basic types of discrimination, employers face special problems when dealing with affirmative action and workplace harassment. Employers also must handle issues that are peculiar to sex, religion, national origin, age, and handicap discrimination.

Affirmative Action

Affirmative action issues arise in two settings. First, employers might voluntarily adopt affirmative action plans that give preference to minority employees. Second, after finding that an employer has discriminated against minorities, a court might require the employer to take affirmative action. In either case, whites or males may argue that the voluntary plan or the court order illegally discriminates against them.

Employers adopt voluntary affirmative action plans for a variety of reasons. One reason an employer might do so is to be eligible for contracts with the federal government. Executive Order 11246, administered by the Office of Federal Contract Compliance Programs (OFCCP), requires that government contractors take affirmative action to ensure that their employees are hired and promoted on a nondiscriminatory basis.

To supplement the affirmative action programs required of all government contractors, the OFCCP issued Revised Order No. 4, which requires that an accept-

---

[1] 431 U.S. 324 (1977).

able affirmative action plan with realistic goals and timetables be prepared by each employer with 50 or more employees and a contract or subcontract of $50,000 or more. The employer must first perform a utilization analysis, including evaluation of the size of the minority and female population and labor force in the area, the requisite skills among minorities and women in the area, and the available training programs and facilities. Having completed this analysis, the employer must identify the deficiencies in its workforce, and must then establish attainable goals for correcting and eliminating those deficiencies, along with timetables and methods for achieving the goals. An employer is not in violation of its plan if it fails to meet its goals provided that the employer has made good-faith efforts to do so. This is the principal difference between goals and quotas: if a contractor is required by law to meet the goals, they become quotas.

Whites and males have often challenged affirmative action programs as illegally discriminating against them. *United Steelworkers v. Weber* (reprinted in Chapter 3) was the first major affirmative action decision of the Supreme Court. Review it again at this point.

Harassment

Harassment does not per se violate Title VII. Harassment that is discriminatory can violate Title VII. For example, an employee who is required to have sexual relations with a supervisor to secure, maintain, or advance in employment is subjected to conditions that are not imposed on employees of the opposite sex. An employee who is promoted as a reward for having sexual relations with a supervisor is given an opportunity that employees of the opposite sex do not have.

Sexual harassment is unwelcome sexual conduct that is a term or condition of employment. There are two types of sexual harassment: (1) quid pro quo harassment and (2) hostile environment harassment. Quid pro quo harassment is where job benefits are exchanged for sexual favors. ("Date me or lose your job.") Hostile environment harassment is where unwelcome sexual conduct creates an intimidating, hostile, or offensive environment. In the following case, the Supreme Court sets the standard for determining when there is hostile environment sexual harassment.

HARRIS V. FORKLIFT SYSTEMS, INC.
510 U.S. 117 (1993)

Teresa Harris worked as a manager at Forklift Systems. Charles Hardy was Forklift's president. Throughout Harris' time at Forklift, Hardy often insulted her because of her gender and often made her the target of unwanted sexual innuendos. Hardy told Harris on several occasions, in the presence of other employees, "You're a woman, what do you know" and "We need a man as the rental manager."

Hardy occasionally asked Harris and other female employees to get coins from his front pants pocket. He threw objects on the ground in front of Harris and other women, and asked them to pick the objects up. He made sexual innuendos about Harris' and other women's clothing.

When Harris complained to Hardy about his conduct, Hardy said he was surprised that Harris was offended, claimed he was only joking, and apologized. He also promised he would stop, and based on this assurance Harris stayed on the job. But a month later, Hardy began anew: While Harris was arranging a deal with one of Forkift's customers, he asked her, again in front of other employees, "What did you do, promise the guy . . . some [sex] Saturday night?" Harris collected her next paycheck and quit.

Harris then sued Forklift, claiming that Hardy's conduct had created an abusive work environment for her because of her gender. The district court held that Hardy's conduct did not create an abusive environment. The court found that Hardy's comments "were not" so severe as to be expected to seriously affect [Harris's] psychological well being. The court of appeals affirmed, and Harris appealed to the Supreme Court of the United States, which reversed. The following is the Supreme Court's opinion.

Justice O'Connor

Title VII of the Civil Rights Act of 1964 makes it "an unlawful employment practice for an employer . . . to discriminate against any individual with respect to his compensation, terms, conditions , or privileges of employment, because of such individual's race, color, religion, sex, or national origin." As we made clear in *Meritor Savings Bank*v. *Vinson,* this language "is not limited to 'economic' or 'tangible' discrimination. The phrase 'terms, conditions, or privileges of employment' evinces a congressional intent 'to strike at the entire spectrum of disparate treatment of men and women in employment,'" which includes requiring people to work in a discriminatorily hostile or abusive environment. When the workplace is permeated with "discriminatory intimidation, ridicule, and insult," that is "sufficiently severe or pervasive to alter the conditions of the victim's employment and create an abusive working environment," Title VII is violated.

This standard, which we reaffirm today, takes a middle path between making actionable any conduct that is merely offensive and requiring the conduct to cause a tangible psychological injury. As we pointed out in *Meritor,* "mere utterance of an . . . epithet which engenders offensive feelings in an employee," does not sufficiently affect the conditions of employment to implicate Title VII. Conduct that is not severe or pervasive enough to create an objectively hostile or abusive work environment—an environment that a reasonable person would find hostile or abusive—is beyond Title VII's purview. Likewise, if the victim does not subjectively perceive the environment to be abusive, the conduct has not actually altered the conditions of the victim's employment, and there is no Title VII violation.

But Title VII comes into play before the harassing conduct leads to a nervous breakdown. A discriminatorily abusive work environment, even one that does not seriously affect employees' psychological well being, can and often will detract from employees' job performance, discourage employees from remaining on the job or keep them from advancing in their careers. Moreover, even without regard to these tangible effects, the very fact that the discriminatory conduct was so severe or pervasive that it created a work environment abusive to employees because of their race, gender, religion, or national origin offends Title VII's broad rule of workplace equality. . . .

We therefore believe the District Court erred in relying on whether the conduct "seriously affect[ed] plaintiff's psychological well being" or led her to "suffe[r] injury." Such an inquiry may needlessly focus the factfinder's attention on concrete psychological harm, an element Title VII does not require. Certainly Title VII bars conduct that would seriously affect a reasonable person's psychological well being, but the statute is not limited to such conduct. So long as the environment would reasonably be perceived, and is perceived, as hostile or abusive, there is no need for it also to be psychologically injurious.

This is not, and by its nature cannot be, a mathematically precise test. We need not answer today all the potential questions it raises, nor specifically address the EEOC's new regulations on this subject. But we can say that whether an environment is "hostile" or "abusive" can be determined only by looking at all the circumstances. These may include the frequency of the discriminatory conduct; its severity; whether it is physically threatening or humiliating, or a mere offensive utterance; and whether it unreasonably interferes with an employee's work performance. The effect on the employee's psychological well being is, of course, relevant to determining whether the plaintiff actually found the environment abusive. But while psychological harm, like any other relevant factor, may be taken into account, no single factor is required.

■   ■   ■

We therefore reverse the judgment of the Court of Appeals, and remand the case for further proceedings consistent with this opinion.

Case Questions

1. What kind of harassment was involved in this case: quid pro quo or hostile environment? Explain. What is the difference between the two types of sexual harassment?

2. What standard does the Court apply in determining whether there is illegal sexual harassment?

3. What factors does the Court say should be considered in determining whether an environment is hostile or abusive? Suppose an employee complained to you about sexual harassment. What questions should you ask the employee?

4. Does the Court's opinion provide greater clarity or confusion as to when there will be illegal sexual harassment? Explain. Will the opinion likely lead to more or less litigation? Explain. What should an employer do to reduce the likelihood of charges of sexual harassment?

5. Suppose an employee complains of harassment based on race, religion, national origin, age, or disability. Does the approach taken by the Court reach those forms of harassment? Explain.

Sex

Sexual discrimination in employment is not a new phenomenon. The concepts of men's work and women's work have been ingrained in society since civilization began. Today, sex roles in our society are changing, yet the notion of gender-based jobs remains a threat to the freedom to work, regardless of sex.

Ethical Dilemmas/Issues

Frieda Rosenmund is a financial analyst for Stevedore Pants Company. Her supervisor is Gus Goyert. As the company's controller, Goyert hires the secretaries in the controller's office. Applications for secretarial positions are screened by Goyert. Selected applicants are then interviewed by Goyert and all the other employees in the controller's office. After conferring with the other employees, Goyert decides whom to hire.

Several applications have been sent to Goyert for an open secretarial position. Among the applicants is a male. Goyert looks over the man's application in Rosenmund's presence and announces with an air of finality, "Don't interview this one. I'm not going to hire any man as my secretary. He's probably gay, and I don't want any AIDS epidemic at Stevedore Pants."

What are the ethical issues? What would you do?

Pregnancy

Only women can become pregnant, but not all women choose to do so. Title VII, as amended by the Pregnancy Discrimination Act of 1978 (PDA), equates discrimination on the basis of pregnancy, childbirth, or related medical conditions with sex discrimination.

An employer must treat pregnancy in the same manner as any other medical condition. It may not exclude pregnancy coverage from the medical insurance it provides for employees' spouses. To do so discriminates against male employees. The PDA, however, does not prohibit an employer from providing special pregnancy benefits, such as special maternity leave, that it does not provide to employees generally.

Compensation

Sex discrimination in compensation violates Title VII. It may also violate the Equal Pay Act of 1963 (EPA).

The EPA prohibits differences in pay between the sexes for employees who are performing work that requires "equal skill, effort, and responsibility" and is "performed under similar working conditions." If even one worker is paid at a higher rate than members of the opposite sex who are doing equal work, a violation of the act may be found.

The term *equal* does not require that the work of men and women employees be identical, but only that it be substantially equal, to justify equal pay. Thus, small differences in job description do not make jobs so unequal as to justify a higher pay scale for one sex.

In writing the EPA, Congress referred to equality of "skill," "effort," and "responsibility" exercised "under similar working conditions" because these are criteria by which industry evaluates jobs for classification purposes. For example, in *Corning Glass v. Brennan,* the Supreme Court considered whether the differences between the day and night shifts were sufficient to justify paying male night-shift employees more than female day-shift employees.[2] The Court rejected the employer's argument that different shifts constituted different working conditions, noting that in the glass industry working conditions did not usually refer to the time of day during which work was performed.

Several exceptions to the equal work-equal pay standard are:

- Bona fide seniority and merit systems.
- Earnings based on quantity or quality of output.
- Factors other than sex.

Pay differentials based on seniority or on performance evaluations are justified, provided that the policy is uniformly applied. Systems in which employees are paid according to an individual production piece rate are immunized from liability by the quantity or quality of output exception.

Exceptions for factors other than sex immunize other legitimate bases for wage disparities. For example, although a shift differential results in unequal pay for equal work under similar conditions, the inequity may be justified because it arises from a factor other than sex.

An EPA violation does not exist where a wage disparity arises out of a bona fide management training program that rotates employees of one sex through all departments, thereby requiring them to work temporarily with members of the opposite sex who receive a lower rate than the trainees. However, courts scrutinize training programs that involve employees of only one sex to determine whether they are, in fact, bona fide exceptions. If the programs are informal, do not regularly result in promotion to the position being trained for, and appear to be geared more to the employer's needs than to actual training, they are not likely to survive scrutiny.

Title VII has been interpreted to implicitly incorporate the EPA's affirmative defenses in compensation discrimination cases. However, intentional sexual discrimination in pay violates Title VII even though the employees do not perform equal work. Thus, an employer who pays truck drivers more than secretaries because the truck drivers are male and the secretaries are female does not violate the EPA but may violate Title VII.

Religion

The term *religion* encompasses such traditional religions as Judaism, Catholicism, Protestantism, and Islam, but is far broader. It includes all moral or ethical beliefs that are sincerely held with the strength of traditional religious views. Atheism and agnosticism are considered religions for Title VII purposes.

---

[2] 417 U.S. 188 (1974).

The Duty to Accommodate Religion

Title VII requires an employer to make reasonable accommodations to employees' religious beliefs and practices unless accommodation would work an undue hardship on the business. The most frequent charges of religious discrimination dealt with by the courts and the EEOC involve not raw prejudice, but instances in which an employer's work rule, innocent in intent, conflicts with an employee's religious belief. Such conditions trigger the employer's duty to accommodate the employee's religious beliefs.

An employer need not accommodate an employee's religious beliefs if to do so would impose more than a *de minimis* cost. For example, an employer need not give an employee the day off for his or her religious Sabbath if this would require the employer to pay another employee at an overtime rate to fill in.

An employer fulfills its duty under Title VII when it offers a reasonable accommodation to the employee. The employer is not obligated to agree to the accommodation requested by the employee even if it would cost the employer nothing.

National Origin

National origin refers to the country from which an individual or the individual's ancestors came. It also includes persons with characteristics generally identified with particular national groups.

Citizenship

Although Title VII prohibits national origin discrimination, it does not forbid discrimination on the basis of American citizenship. This does not mean that aliens have no Title VII rights; they are entitled to the same protection from discrimination on the basis of national origin as citizens. Thus, Mexican citizens residing in the United States cannot claim illegal national origin discrimination against employers who require American citizenship for a job, but they can press claims against employers who refuse to hire persons of Mexican ancestry.

The Immigration Reform Act prohibits employers from hiring illegal aliens. The act also requires employers to verify the residence or citizenship status of every employee.

Under the act, an employer who hires an illegal alien is subject to a cease and desist order, with civil penalties ranging from $250 to $10,000. An employer who is found guilty of a pattern or practice of violations faces fines of up to $3,000 for each illegal alien, prison for up to six months, or both.

The act also forbids an employer to discriminate against a person who is not an illegal alien because of his or her national origin or citizenship status with regard to hiring for employment or discharge.

Age

The Age Discrimination in Employment Act covers employers with 20 or more employees, employment agencies, and unions with 25 or more members or who operate hiring halls. The ADEA prohibits age discrimination against persons age 40 or older.

The ADEA contains BFOQ and bona fide seniority system exceptions. It also excepts employment decisions based on reasonable factors other than age and discharges for cause. These two exceptions are essentially denials of, rather than justifications for, age discrimination. They have been interpreted as codifying the employer's burden of rebutting a prima facie case of disparate treatment with legitimate, nondiscriminatory reasons for its actions.

The ADEA excepts **bona fide employee benefit plans** that are not subterfuges to avoid the act. This exception applies only where employers reduce benefits to older workers to offset the increased costs of those benefits as employees age. For example, employers may reduce life insurance benefits based on age. Often it may be difficult to distinguish between age and other characteristics correlated with age.

Employers should be particularly sensitive to ADEA liability when terminating older employees. More than 90 percent of the cases brought under the ADEA have involved terminations. This is particularly true during economic recessions, when many companies lay off or terminate large numbers of workers.

In the following case, the Supreme Court considers whether younger employees can bring reverse age discrimination cases against their employer.

GENERAL DYNAMICS LAND SYSTEMS, INC., V. CLINE
540 U.S. 581 (2004)

General Dynamics (petitioner) and the United Auto Workers negotiated a new collective bargaining agreement that provided retiree health benefits only to those employees who were at least fifty years old at the time of the new agreement. A group of employees who were in their forties (collectively, Cline) sued, claiming that the terms of the new agreement violated the ADEA. The district court dismissed their complaint. The court of appeals reversed the district court's decision. General Dynamics appealed to the Supreme Court of the United States, which reversed the court of appeals and reinstated the district court's dismissal of the complaint. What follows is the Supreme Court's opinion.

Justice Souter   ■   ■   ■

The Age Discrimination in Employment Act of 1967 (ADEA) or Act forbids discriminatory preference for the young over the old. The question in this case is whether it also prohibits favoring the old over the young. We hold it does not.

Congress chose not to include age within discrimination forbidden by Title VII of the Civil Rights Acts of 1964, being aware that there were legitimate reasons as well as invidious ones for making employment decisions on age. Instead it called for a study of the issue by the Secretary of

Labor, who concluded that age discrimination was a serious problem, but one different in kind from discrimination on account of race. . . .

Congress then asked for a specific proposal, which the Secretary provided in January 1967. . . .

The testimony at both hearings dwelled on unjustified assumptions about the effect of age on ability to work. . . . The record . . . reflects the common facts that an individual's chances to find and keep a job get worse over time; as between any two people, the younger is in the stronger position, the older more apt to be tagged with demeaning stereotype. Not surprisingly, from the voluminous records of the hearings, we have found . . . nothing suggesting that any workers were registering complaints about discrimination in favor of their seniors.

Nor is there any such suggestion in the introductory provisions of the ADEA, which begins with statements of purpose and findings . . . (The findings stress the impediments suffered by "older workers . . . in their efforts to retain . . . and especially to regain employment,"); "the [burdens] of arbitrary age limits regardless of potential for job performance,"; the costs of "otherwise desirable practices [that] may work to the disadvantage of older persons,"; and "the incidence of unemployment, especially long-term unemployment [which] is, relative to the younger ages, high among older workers." The statutory objects were "to promote employment of older persons based on their ability rather than age; to prohibit arbitrary age discrimination in employment; [and] to help employers and workers find ways of meeting problems arising from the impact of age on employment.

■   ■   ■

Such is the setting of the ADEA's core substantive provision prohibiting employers and certain others from "discriminat[ion] . . . because of [an] individual's age" whenever . . . the individual is "at least forty years of age . . . The prefatory provisions and their legislative history make a case that we think is beyond reasonable doubt, that the ADEA was concerned to protect a relatively old worker from discrimination that works to the advantage of the relatively young.

Nor is it remarkable that the record is devoid of any evidence that younger workers were suffering at the expense of their elders, let alone that a social problem required a federal statute to place a younger worker in parity with an older one. Common experience is to the contrary, and the testimony, reports, and congressional findings simply confirm that Congress used the phrase "discriminat[ion] . . . because of [an] individual's age" the same way that ordinary people in common usage might speak of age discrimination any day of the week. One commoplace conception of American society in recent decades is its character as a "youth culture," and in a world where younger is better, talk about discrimination because of age is naturally understood to refer to discrimination against the older.

This same, idiomatic sense of the statutory phrase is confirmed by the statute's restriction of the protected class to those 40 and above. If Congress had been worrying about protecting the younger against the older, it would not likely have ignored everyone under 40. The youthful deficiencies of inexperience and unsteadiness invite stereotypical and discriminatory thinking about those a lot younger than 40, and prejudice suffered by a 40-year-old is not typically owing to youth, as 40-year-olds sadly tend to find out. The enemy of 40 is 30, not 50. ("[T]estimony indicated [40] to be the age at which age discrimination in employment becomes evident"). Even so, the 40-year threshold was adopted over the objection that some discrimination against older people begins at an even younger age; female flight attendants were not fired at 32 because they were too young. Thus, the 40-year threshold makes sense as identifying a class requiring protection against preference for their juniors, not as defining a class that might be threatened by favoritism toward seniors.

■   ■   ■

We see the text, structure, purpose, and history of the ADEA . . . as showing that the statute does not mean to stop an employer from favoring an older employee over a younger one. The judgment of the Court of Appeals is reversed.

Case Questions

1. Does the Court's decision allow employers to grant preferential treatment to older workers? Explain. Why or why not? Explain.

2. Have you observed employment discrimination against younger workers? If so, what is your reaction to it? Do you think that the law should prohibit discrimination against younger as well as older workers? (Some state statutes prohibit age discrimination directed against both younger as well as older workers.)

3. What are the practical implications of the Court's decision with regard to employee benefits? If you were in senior management at General Dynamics, what might you have done regarding the company's health care benefits if the Court had decided in favor of the younger workers?

4. Suppose an employer wishes to reduce its workforce. Can it offer an early retirement incentive program that offers a lump-sum payment of a year of pay for anyone over a certain age who wishes to retire? Explain.

5. Do you agree with the Court's decision to allow employment practices and policies that benefit older workers even if the policies adversely impact younger workers? Explain.

Disability

The Americans with Disabilities Act (ADA) prohibits discrimination against otherwise qualified persons with disabilities. A person with a covered disability is someone who has a physical or mental impairment that substantially limits one or more of life's major activities, has a record or history of such an impairment, or is regarded as having such an impairment. Impairments may result from diseases such as tuberculosis or AIDS.

The ADA is modeled on the Vocational Rehabilitation Act of 1973, which covered recipients of federal funds. Both apply to any job that, with reasonable accommodation, a worker can perform at the minimum level of productivity expected of a normal person in that job. However, they do not require an employer to hire an unqualified person to do the job.

A reasonable accommodation may include modifying facilities, equipment, examinations, or other job requirements or working conditions. The duty to accommodate may involve providing readers or interpreters, or restructuring jobs. An accommodation poses an undue hardship if it involves significant difficulty or expense, considering the employer's type of operation; the nature and cost of the accommodation; or the size, type, and financial resources of the employer and of the facility where the accommodation would take place.

The ADA prohibits using qualifications, standards, or tests that tend to screen out individuals with disabilities, unless the practice is job related and consistent with business necessity. The ADA prohibits employers from requiring medical examinations before a job offer is made. Employers may condition a job offer on passing a medical examination if it is job related and consistent with business necessity and is required of all employees regardless of disability.

In the following case, the Supreme Court addresses the queston of when someone is disabled under the ADA.

TOYOTA MOTOR MANUFACTURING, KENTUCKY, INC., V. WILLIAMS
534 U.S. 184 (2002)

Ella Williams (respondent) began working at Toyota's (petitioner) automobile manufacturing plant in Georgetown, Kentucky, in August 1990. She was soon placed on an engine fabrication assembly line, where her duties included work with pneumatic tools. Use of these tools eventually caused pain in her hands, wrists, and arms. She sought treatment at Toyota's in-house medical service, where she was diagnosed with bilateral carpal tunnel syndrome and bilateral tendonitis. Williams consulted a personal physician who placed her on permanent work restrictions that precluded her from lifting more than 20 pounds or from "frequently lifting or carrying of objects weighing up to 10 pounds," engaging in "constant repetitive . . . flexion or extension of [her] wrists or elbows," performing "overhead work," or using "vibratory or pneumatic tools."

In light of these restrictions, for the next two years Toyota assigned Williams to various modified duty jobs. Williams missed some work for medical leave, and eventually returned to work.

On December 6, 1996, the last day Williams worked at Toyota's plant, she was placed under a no-work-of-any-kind restriction by her treating physicians. On January 27, 1997, Williams received a letter from Toyota that terminated her employment, citing her poor attendance record.

Claiming to be disabled from performing her automobile assembly line job by carpal tunnel syndrome and related impairments, Williams sued Toyota for failing to provide her with a reasonable accommodation as required by the Americans with Disabilities Act. The district court granted Toyota summary judgment. The circuit court of appeals reversed. Toyota appealed to the Supreme Court of the United States. The Supreme Court reversed the circuit court. What follows is the Supreme Court opinion.

Justice O'Connor

The Court of Appeals held that in order for respondent to demonstrate that she was disabled due to a substantial limitation in the ability to perform manual tasks at the time of her accommodation request, she had to "show that her manual disability involved a 'class' of manual activities affecting the ability to perform tasks at work." Respondent satisfied this test, according to the Court of Appeals, because her ailments "prevented her from doing the tasks associated with certain types of manual assembly line jobs, manual product handling jobs and manual building trade jobs (painting, plumbing, roofing, etc.) that require the gripping of tools and repetitive work with hands and arms extended at or above shoulder levels for extended periods of time." In reaching this conclusion, the court disregarded evidence that respondent could "tend to her personal hygiene [and] carry out personal or household chores," finding that such evidence "does not affect a determination that her impairment substantially limited her ability to perform the range of manual tasks associated with an assembly line job," . . .

The ADA requires covered entities, including private employers, to provide "reasonable accommodations to the known physical or mental limitations of an otherwise qualified individual with a disability who is an applicant or employee, unless such covered entity can demonstrate that the accommodation would impose an undue hardship." The Act defines a "qualified individual with a disability" as "an individual with a disability who, with or without reasonable accommodation, can perform the essential functions of the employment position that such individual holds or desires." In turn, a "disability" is:

"(A) a physical or mental impairment that substantially limits one or more of the major life activities of such individual;

"(B) a record of such impairment; or

"(C) being regarded as having such an impairment."

■   ■   ■

The question presented by this case is whether the [Court of Appeals] properly determined that respondent was disabled under subsection (A) of the ADA's disability definition at the time that she sought an accommodation from petitioner. The parties do not dispute that respondent's medical conditions, which include carpal tunnel syndrome, myotendinitis, and thoracic outlet compression, amount to physical impairments. The relevant question therefore, is whether the [Court of Appeals] correctly analyzed whether these impairments substantially limited respondent in the major life activity of performing manual tasks. . . .

Our consideration of this issue is guided first and foremost by the words of the disability definition itself. "Substantially" in the phrase "substantially limits" suggests "considerable" or "to a large degree." The word "substantial" thus clearly precludes impairments that interfere in only a minor way with the performance of manual tasks from qualifying as disabilities.

"Major" in the phrase "major life activities" means important. "Major life activities" thus refers to those activities that are of central importance to daily life. In order for performing manual tasks to fit into this category—a category that includes such basic abilities as walking, seeing, and hearing—the manual tasks in question must be central to daily life. If each of the tasks included in the major life activity of performing manual tasks does not independently qualify as a major life activity, then together they must do so.

■   ■   ■

We therefore hold that to be substantially limited in performing manual tasks, an individual must have an impairment that prevents or severely restricts the individual from doing activities that are of central importance to most people's daily lives. The impairment's impact must also be permanent or long-term.

It is insufficient for individuals attempting to prove disability status under this test to merely submit evidence of a medical diagnosis of an impairment. Instead, the ADA requires those "claiming the Act's protection . . . to prove a disability by offering evidence that the extent of the limitation [caused by their impairment] in terms of their own experience . . . is substantial. That the Act defines "disability" with respect to an individual," makes clear that Congress intended the existence of a disability to be determined in such a case-by-case manner.

An individualized assessment of the effect of an impairment is particularly necessary when the impairment is one whose symptoms vary widely from person to person. Carpal tunnel syndrome, one of respondent's impairments, is just such a condition. While cases of severe carpal tunnel syndrome are characterized by muscle atrophy and extreme sensory deficits, mild cases generally do not have either of these effects and create only intermittent symptoms of numbness and tingling. Given these large potential differences in the severity and duration of the effects of carpal tunnel syndrome, an individual's carpal tunnel syndrome diagnosis, on its own, does not indicate whether the individual has a disability within the meaning of the ADA.

■   ■   ■

While the Court of Appeals in this case addressed the different major life activity of performing manual tasks, its analysis . . . focus[ed] on respondent's inability to perform manual tasks associated only with her job. This was error. When addressing the major life activity of performing manual tasks, the central inquiry must be whether the claimant is unable to perform the variety of tasks central to most people's daily lives, not whether the claimant is unable to perform the tasks associated with her specific job. . . .

■   ■   ■

[T]he manual tasks unique to any particular job are not necessarily important parts of most people's lives. As a result, occupation-specific tasks may have only limited relevance to the manual task inquiry. In this case, "repetitive work with hands and arms extended at or above shoulder levels for extended periods of time," the manual task on which the Court of Appeals relied, is not an important part of most people's daily lives. The court, therefore, should not have considered respondent's inability to do such manual work in her specialized assembly line job as sufficient proof that she was substantially limited in performing manual tasks.

At the same time, the Court of Appeals appears to have disregarded the very type of evidence that it should have focused upon. It treated as irrelevant "the fact that [respondent] can . . . tend to her personal hygiene [and] carry out personal or household chores." Yet household chores, bathing, and brushing one's teeth are among the types of manual tasks of central importance to people's daily lives, and should have been part of the assessment of whether respondent was substantially limited in performing manual tasks.

. . . [A]ccording to respondent's deposition testimony, even after her condition worsened, she could still brush her teeth, wash her face, bathe, tend her flower garden, fix breakfast, do laundry and pick up around the house. The record also indicates that her medical conditions caused her to avoid sweeping, to quit dancing, to occasionally seek help dressing, and to reduce how often she plays with her children, gardens, and drives long distances. But these changes in her life did not amount to such severe restrictions in the activities that are of central importance to most people's daily lives that they establish a manual-task disability as a matter of law. On this record, it was therefore inappropriate for the Court of Appeals to grant partial summary judgment to respondent on the issue of whether she was substantially limited in performing manual tasks, and its decision to do so must be reversed.

Case Questions

1. What must an applicant or employee demonstrate to establish a substantial limitation in a specific major life activity of performing manual tasks?

2. How relevant are occupation-specific tasks to the inquiry of whether a person is substantially limited in a major life activity?

3. How relevant is the performance of household chores, bathing, and brushing one's teeth as manual tasks in the inquiry of whether a person is substantially limited in a major life activity?

4. Why did the Court not conclude that Williams was substantially limited in the performance of a major life activity?

5. As a result of this case, how difficult will it be for an employee with job-specific limitations to obtain protection under the ADA? Explain. For example, will an employee who is unable to work around work-place chemicals be considered "disabled" under the ADA? Explain. Does *Toyota v. Williams* mean that employers do not have to reasonably accommodate employees under any circumstances? Explain.

Enforcement of Equal Employment Opportunity Laws

Table 17–2 summarizes the enforcement scheme of the major civil rights laws.

Title VII, the ADA, and the ADEA have similar enforcement provisions. All require victims to file charges of violations with the EEOC and their state employment discrimination agencies if they exist. The EEOC is allowed time to investigate the charges and to try informally to resolve the dispute. The EEOC or the individual victims can sue to correct the violations.

Title VII, the ADA, and the ADEA differ in their timing of the enforcement process. Under Title VII, and the ADA, the charge must be filed with the EEOC within 180 days following the discriminatory act if it arises in a state that does not have an antidiscrimination agency. If the state has an antidiscrimination agency, the charge must be filed first with the state agency. The charge may be filed with the EEOC after the state agency has had it for 60 days or has terminated proceedings, whichever occurs first. The charge must be filed within 300 days following the discriminatory act.

Individuals cannot file Title VII or ADA lawsuits until the EEOC notifies them of their right to sue. This EEOC notice is called a **right-to-sue letter**. If the EEOC's investigation of the charge discloses no reasonable cause to believe a Title VII violation occurred, the EEOC dismisses the charge and issues a right-to-sue letter. The EEOC's dismissal does not prohibit the charging party from suing.

TABLE 17–2   **EEO Enforcement**

Law	Who Enforces	Jury Trial	Punitive Damages
ADA, Title VII	EEOC and private plaintiffs	Yes	Yes, for actual malice or reckless disregard for victim's rights; maximum recovery $50,000–$200,000, depending on size of employer
ADEA, EPA	EEOC and private plaintiffs	Yes	Double damages for willful violations
1866 Civil Rights Act	Private plaintiffs	Yes	Yes, with no monetary limits
E.O. 11246	Federal agencies	No	No

If the EEOC finds reasonable cause, it issues a determination letter. The EEOC attempts to conciliate the dispute. If conciliation efforts fail, it issues a right-to-sue letter. In all cases, suit must be filed within 90 days after receipt of the right-to-sue letter.

Under the ADEA, the charging party can file charges with the state antidiscrimination agency and the EEOC in any order. The charging party is not required to file with the state first. The 180- and 300-day time limits for filing with the EEOC apply to the ADEA. The charging party need not receive a right-to-sue letter to file suit. He or she can sue anytime after the EEOC has had the charge for 60 days. ADEA lawsuits must be filed within 90 days following a right-to-sue letter.

Chapter Problems

1. Define the following terms:
   a. Disparate treatment
   b. Disparate impact
   c. Mixed motive cases
   d. Standard deviation
   e. Bona fide occupational qualification
   f. Validation
   g. Bona fide seniority system
   h. Hostile work environment
   i. Bona fide employee benefit plan
   j. Right-to-sue letter

2. An insurance company has found that black people are more likely to buy insurance if approached by a black agent, while white people are more receptive to a white agent. The company plans to assign its black agents to offices in predominantly black neighborhoods and its white agents to offices in predominantly white neighborhoods. Is the practice legal? Why or why not?

3. The Vita Company has a job opening for a financial analyst. It advertizes its position as requiring that the applicant possess an accounting undergraduate degree. Three applicants apply. Bob Bender, an African-American male, possesses an undergraduate business degree from a large state university, with an accounting major. Wilma Wood, a white female, possesses an undergraduate degree from a small private college, with three years of job experience. Joe Goodbar, a white male, possesses an MBA from an Ivy League college and an undergraduate accounting degree from a state university.

   All three candidates are interviewed by members of the management team at Vita Company. Each member of the management team fills out an evaluation form. One management team member responds that "Wilma is cute but dumb." Another states that Bob "won't be able to get into the right clubs." All of the team members agree that Joe is preferable because his MBA provides flexibility for future promotions and work assignments beyond the financial analyst job. Who should be hired? Why?

4. Smith Sporting Goods is a chain of 15 retail sporting goods and apparel shops. Each store is run by a general manager. Smith had an opening for a general manager and advertised the position as follows: "Sporting goods store general manager; must have five years' retail sporting goods sales experience and business degree; MBA preferred; prefer former varsity football or basketball player." Smith has narrowed the candidates to Joyce Jones and Brian Baker. Jones has 10 years of sporting goods sales experience, including two as an assistant general manager, and an MBA. She played varsity tennis in high school. Baker has seven years' experience, none in management, a bachelor's degree in business, and was a star quarterback for a local college football team. All of the other 14 Smith stores are run by former collegiate football or basketball players. Twelve are male and two are female. Smith often used its general managers' intercollegiate sports experience in its advertising. For this reason, Smith wishes to hire Baker. What risks of liability to Jones, if any, will Smith incur? Explain.

5. An employer requires all of its entry-level managers to complete a six-month training program. The employer gives a test to all applicants for entry-level management positions. The passing rate is 75 percent for whites and 45 percent for blacks. The test measures several skills needed to succeed in the training program but not necessarily needed to perform the entry-level managerial jobs. Are the tests lawful? Explain.

6. A real estate management company manages an office building and employs a receptionist in the building lobby. The company requires the receptionist to wear a uniform that is a low-cut, tight-fitting body suit. The top of the receptionist's breasts are visible. Her legs and thighs are covered only by black fishnet stockings. Every day various people entering the building have whistled and stared at her and made cat calls, and a few have pinched her or put their arms around her. Does Title VII require the company to change the uniform? Explain.

7. You are the vice president for human resources of XYZ Corp. You have a recommendation from your manager of quality control to discharge John Jones, an 18-year XYZ employee. Jones is 57 years old. The manager, who is 35, has told you that he caught Jones falsifying quality control reports. The manager has also cited Jones's attitude and said that "he has been knocked around a bit over the years. He is getting old and forgetful. Although he does well for an old goat, his productivity has fallen considerably behind his younger co-workers." Should you fire Jones? Explain.

8. You are vice president for human resources for a large company. Your director of employee benefits has proposed offering an early retirement plan for all managers. The plan would save a large sum of money because senior

older managers who accept early retirement could be replaced by younger managers receiving lower salaries. It would also open up promotional opportunities and improve morale among the younger employees.

Under the proposal, any employee age 55 or older who has worked for the company at least 10 years would be eligible. In addition to their regular pensions, employees would receive payment for a percentage of their accumulated sick days at their base salary for the past year. The percentage depends on age as follows:

55–58	50%
59	60
60–64	80
65–70	45

In addition, managers who retire between ages 55 and 64 would continue to be covered by the company's group health, life, dental, and vision insurances until age 70. Evaluate the legality of this proposal.

9. A school has a salary scale for its teachers which sets each teacher's level of pay based on educational level and years of teaching experience. The school has to fill a position for band director. For budgetary reasons the school has decided that it cannot afford to pay more than the salary for a teacher with a bachelor's degree and six years of teaching experience. An otherwise qualified 60 year old applicant has 32 years of teaching experience, which would place her at a point on the salary scale $11,000.00 above what the school can afford to pay. If the school rejects the applicant, will it violate the ADEA? Explain.

10. An employer employs several mail clerks. Mail clerks lift 70-pound mail bags, dump out the mail, sort it, and distribute it. An applicant for one such job has a physical disability that impairs her ability to walk, bend, and lift heavy objects. May the employer reject her because she cannot lift 70-pound mail bags? Explain.

18 LABOR-MANAGEMENT RELATIONS

Learning Objectives

After learning this chapter the student
should be able to:

- Determine whether proposed
  responses to union organizing
  activities are lawful.
- Determine whether proposed
  bargaining units are appropriate.
- Determine whether and to what
  extent a firm must negotiate with a
  union before taking particular
  action.
- Determine whether particular
  complaints by employees or unions
  must be arbitrated.
- Determine how to respond lawfully
  to union economic pressure such as
  job actions, boycotts, and picketing.

The interests of businesses and their workers frequently conflict. Workers want higher wages and better working conditions, but meeting these demands can lower corporate profits. Businesses sometimes wish to change their operating methods in ways that threaten workers' job security. Most individual workers have little bargaining power when dealing with their employers. Consequently, they often group together in labor unions to deal collectively with employers. Employers frequently resist unionization because it tends to reduce their power over their workers.

This chapter explores federal laws regulating the union-employer relationship. Before doing so, however, it is necessary to understand the National Labor Relations Board's (NLRB) structure and the scope of the National Labor Relations Act's (NLRA) coverage.

An Overview of the National Labor Relations Act

The heart of the NLRA is Section 7.

National Labor Relations Act, Section 7

Employees shall have the right to self-organization, to form, join, or assist labor organizations, to bargain collectively through representatives of their own choosing, and to engage in other concerted activities for the purpose of collective bargaining or other **mutual aid or protection**, and shall also have the right to refrain from any or all of such activities except to the extent that such right may be affected by an agreement requiring membership in a labor organization as a condition of employment as authorized in Section 8(a)(3).

The NLRA safeguards employees' Section 7 rights by prohibiting certain employer conduct known as **unfair labor practices**. Therefore, a frequent threshold issue when an employer is charged with committing an unfair labor practice is whether the employee's conduct is protected by Section 7. An activity by employees need not involve a formal labor union to qualify for Section 7 protection. For example, if several employees walk off the job to protest unsafe working conditions, they are protected under Section 7. However, the activity must be for mutual aid and protection and it must be concerted. Action by a single employee complaining about personal grievances is not protected.

Usually at least two employees must be involved for activity to be concerted. The following case explores the narrow circumstances in which action by a single individual may qualify for Section 7 protection.

NLRB v. CITY DISPOSAL SYSTEMS, INC.
465 U.S. 822 (1984)

City Disposal Systems, Inc. (respondent), a garbage collection firm, had a collective-bargaining agreement with Teamsters Local 247. The agreement prohibited respondent from requiring employees to operate unsafe trucks and permitted employees to refuse to operate them. Respondent fired an employee who refused to drive a truck that he believed had defective brakes. The NLRB (petitioner) held that the employee's conduct was protected by Section 7. The Sixth Circuit Court of Appeals reversed, reasoning that because the employee acted alone, his refusal to drive the truck was not concerted. The Supreme Court reversed the Sixth Circuit.

Justice Brennan

The term "concerted activity" is not defined in the Act but it clearly enough embraces the activities of employees who have joined together in order to achieve common goals. What is not self-evident from the language of the Act, however, and what we must elucidate, is the precise manner in which particular actions of an individual employee must be linked to the actions of fellow employees in order to permit it to be said that the individual is engaged in concerted activity.

The invocation of a right rooted in a collective-bargaining agreement is unquestionably an integral part of the process that gave rise to the agreement. That process—beginning with the organization of a union, continuing into the negotiation of a collective-bargaining agreement—is a single, collective activity. Obviously, an employee could not invoke a right grounded in a collective-bargaining agreement were it not for the prior negotiating activities of his fellow employees. Nor would it make sense for a union to negotiate a collective-bargaining agreement if individual employees could not invoke the rights thereby created against their employer. Moreover, when an employee invokes a right grounded in the collective-bargaining agreement, he does not stand alone. Instead, he brings to bear on his employer the power and resolve of all his fellow employees. When, for instance, James Brown refused to drive a truck he believed to be unsafe, he was in effect reminding his employer that he and his fellow employees, at the time their collective-bargaining agreement was signed, had extracted a promise from City Disposal that they would not be asked to drive unsafe trucks. He was also reminding his employer that if it persisted in ordering him to drive an unsafe truck, he could reharness the power of that group to ensure the enforcement of that promise. It was just as though James Brown was reassembling his fellow union members to reenact their decision not to drive unsafe trucks. A lone employee's invocation of a right grounded in his collective-bargaining agreement is, therefore, a concerted activity in a very real sense.

Furthermore, the acts of joining and assisting a labor organization which §7 explicitly recognizes as concerted, are related to collective action in essentially the same way that the invocation of a collectively bargained right is related to collective action. When an employee joins or assists a labor organization, his actions may be divorced in time, and in location as well, from the actions of fellow employees. Because of the integral relationship among the employees' actions, however, Congress viewed each employee as engaged in concerted activity. The lone employee could not join or assist a labor organization were it not for the related organizing activities of his fellow employees. Conversely, there would be limited utility in forming a labor organization if other employees could not join or assist the organization once it is formed.

Thus, the formation of a labor organization is integrally related to the activity of joining or assisting such an organization in the same sense that the negotiation of a collective-bargaining agreement is integrally related to the invocation of a right provided for in the agreement. In each case, neither the individual activity nor the group activity would be complete without the other.

In enacting §7 of the NLRA, Congress sought generally to equalize the bargaining power of the employee with that of his employer by allowing employees to band together in confronting an employer regarding the terms and conditions of their employment. There is no indication that Congress intended to limit this protection to situations in which an employee's activity and that of his fellow employees combine with one another in any particular way. Nor, more specifically, does it appear that Congress intended to have this general protection withdrawn in situations in which a single employee, acting alone, participates in an integral aspect of a collective process. Instead, what emerges from the general background of §7 . . . is a congressional intent to create an equality in bargaining power between the employee and the employer throughout the entire process of labor organization, collective-bargaining, and enforcement of collective-bargaining agreements.

Case Questions

1. If the employee acted alone, why did the Supreme Court conclude that his actions were concerted?

2. Should it matter whether the employee simply stated, "This truck's brakes are bad, I won't drive it," or added, "The contract says I don't have to drive it"? Explain.

3. An employer's employees were not unionized. One employee was injured on the job and filed a claim for workers' compensation. The employer retaliated by firing the employee. Was the filing of the compensation claim protected under Section 7? Why or why not?

4. Assume that the employees in City Disposal were not unionized. Would Brown's conduct have been protected? Would it matter if other employees had complained about unsafe trucks? Explain.

5. An employer's employees are unionized, and their collective-bargaining agreement prohibits discharge or discipline without just cause. The employer attempts to interview an employee as part of its investigation of a theft. The employee refuses to be interviewed unless his shop steward is allowed to be present. Is the refusal protected under Section 7? Would it be protected if the employees were not unionized and the employee demanded that a co-worker be present? Explain.

Section 8 sets forth the NLRA's prohibitions in the form of unfair labor practices. Section 8(a) establishes five unfair labor practices by employers (see Table 18–1). Section 8(b) establishes seven unfair labor practices by unions (see Table 18–2).

Section 9 establishes procedures for holding elections to enable employees to choose to have a union represent them or to discontinue an incumbent union's representation. When a majority of employees voting in an NLRB-conducted election choose to have a union represent them, the union is certified as their exclusive bargaining representative.

TABLE 18–1   Unfair Labor Practices/Employer

NLRA Section	Employer
Interfere, restrain, or coerce employees' exercise of Section 7 rights	8(a)(1)
Dominate, interfere, or support labor organization	8(a)(2)
Discriminate to encourage or discourage union membership	8(a)(3)
Retaliate against employees who file charges or testify under the act	8(a)(4)
Refuse to bargain in good faith	8(a)(5)

TABLE 18–2   Unfair Labor Practices/Union

Union	NLRA Section
Restrain or coerce employees' exercise of Section 7 rights or employers' choice of bargaining representative	8(b)(1)
Force employer to discriminate to encourage or discourage union membership	8(b)(2)
Refuse to bargain in good faith	8(b)(3)
Engage in secondary boycotts or picketing in a work assignment dispute	8(b)(4)
Require excessive dues in a union shop	8(b)(5)
Require employer to pay for services not performed or not to be performed (featherbedding)	8(b)(6)
Picket for recognition under certain circumstances	8(b)(7)

The National Labor Relations Board

The NLRA is administered and enforced by the National Labor Relations Board (NLRB), an independent regulatory agency. The NLRB has two principal functions:

- To prevent and remedy unfair labor practices.
- To conduct secret ballot elections in which employees decide whether unions will represent them in collective bargaining.

Board Organization

The NLRB is headed by a five-member board, appointed to staggered five-year terms by the president and confirmed by the Senate. Under the board are administrative law judges (ALJs), who conduct trials and make recommended rulings that may be appealed to the board.

Independent of the board members is the general counsel (GC), who is also appointed by the president and confirmed by the Senate. The GC operates through regional offices. A regional director heads each regional office. Through the regional directors and their staffs, the GC evaluates unfair labor practice charges and issues and prosecutes unfair labor practice complaints.

Board Procedure

The NLRB can act only when it is formally requested to do so by employers, unions, or employees. Two types of requests may be filed with the NLRB: representation petitions and unfair labor practice charges. Each is filed in the appropriate regional office. Figures 18–1 and 18–2 illustrate the procedures these cases follow.

Coverage of the National Labor Relations Act

Congress extended the NLRA's coverage to the full limit of its constitutional powers under the commerce clause; those powers are discussed in detail in Chapter 5. However, Congress specifically excluded certain classes of employers and employees and gave the NLRB discretion to further limit its jurisdiction.

FIGURE 18–1   Representation Procedures

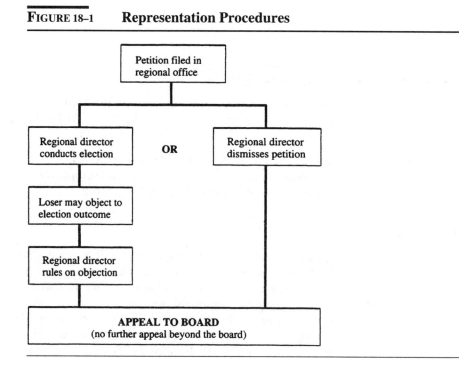

FIGURE 18–2   ULP Procedures

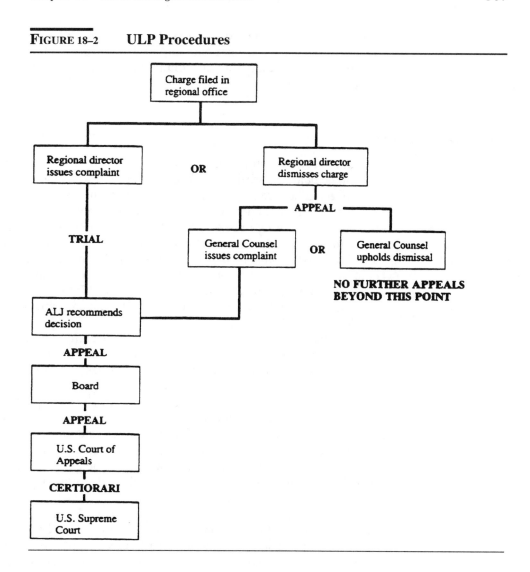

Excluded Employers

The NLRA does not cover the railroad and airline industries, which are subject to the Railway Labor Act. It also excludes government entities and wholly owned government corporations. The statute does cover the U.S. Postal Service.

The NLRB may decline to assert jurisdiction over companies so small that their labor disputes do not have a substantial effect on commerce. The board has adopted certain requirements for exercising its jurisdiction, called *jurisdictional standards.* These standards are based on the yearly amount of business done by an enterprise or on the yearly amount of its sales or purchases. An enterprise that exceeds the total annual dollar volume of business listed in the standard is covered by the NLRA.

Excluded Employees

Certain classes of employees are not covered by the NLRA and, thus, are not within the board's jurisdiction. These are agricultural laborers, domestic servants, employees of a parent or spouse, government employees, employees of railroads and airlines, independent contractors, and supervisors. There has been frequent litigation concerning the exclusions for independent contractors and supervisors.

Independent contractor status generally depends on the degree of supervision and the right to control the process. In an employment relationship, the employer controls the end to be achieved and the means used by the employee to achieve that end. In an independent contractor relationship, the party receiving the service may specify the end to be achieved, but the means are controlled by the independent contractor.

For example, assume that a company hires an individual to clean its offices. If the company specifies only what cleaning should be done nightly, weekly, and monthly and the individual agrees to perform these services for a stated price, the individual is an independent contractor. The company controls the end to be achieved, cleaning at specified intervals, but the individual controls the means of achieving that end, including the number of hours to be worked, the order in which the tasks are performed, the taking of breaks, and similar matters. If, however, the company hires an individual as an office cleaner, specifies the hours that the individual must work, assigns specific tasks to be performed, and otherwise controls how the individual achieves the end of cleaning at specified intervals, the individual is an employee.

Whether an individual is a supervisor depends on his or her authority over employees and not merely on his or her job title. A supervisor must have authority to hire, fire, discipline, lay off, recall, promote, transfer, reward, adjust grievances, or direct the work of employees, or effectively recommend such action. The supervisor must use independent judgment in carrying out this authority and must act in the interests of the employer.

In addition, the board has excluded managers. Managers are employees who formulate or effectuate their firms' policies. They exercise independent discretion in planning and carrying out high-level policies. Supervisors and managers are excluded from the act to ensure their single-minded loyalty to the employer by not involving them in a conflict of interest between the employer and the union.

Employer Responses to Union Organizing

When a group of employees believe that their working conditions are inadequate, they may seek a union to represent them in bargaining with their employer. They usually begin by approaching an existing union, which sends a union organizer to talk with the employees who wish to unionize. The organizer attempts to convince these employees of the advantages of joining the union. If they are convinced, the employees form an organizing committee to work with the union organizer to convince the rest of the work force of the need to unionize.

On learning of the organizing campaign, an employer might react instinctively. The employer might call employees into the personnel office and interrogate them about the union, fire the union activist, forbid employees from discussing the union on company property, or grant new benefits with the hope that the employees will reject the union. These reactions may constitute unfair labor practices, which can occur at any time, but most commonly arise during union organizing campaigns.

Employer Interference, Restraint, or Coercion

Section 8(a)(1) of the NLRA prohibits employer interference, restraint, or coercion of employees exercising their Section 7 rights. All other employer unfair labor practices also violate Section 8(a)(1). Additionally, several Section 8(a)(1) violations do not violate other provisions of the act.

The NLRA does not prohibit employer activities that tend to obstruct organizational efforts but do not amount to interference, restraint, or coercion. The act attempts to balance the self-organization rights of employees with the property rights of their employer. Section 8(c) provides that the mere "expressing of any views, argument or opinion . . . shall not constitute an unfair labor practice . . . if such expression contains no threat of reprisal or force, or promise of benefit." Section 8(c) is known as the *employer free speech provision.*

No-Solicitation Rules

Employees organizing a union may want to solicit their co-workers' support while at work. Many employers, however, have rules prohibiting solicitation. No-solicitation rules protect the employer's interests in running the enterprise. The law recognizes these managerial interests as legitimate. As long as the rules apply to all solicitation, not just union solicitation, the employer may ban such activity during working time or in work areas. However, during nonworking time, such as breaks, in nonworking areas, such as lunchrooms and parking lots, the employees' rights to organize are stronger than the employer's managerial interests. Thus, Section 8(a)(1) prohibits banning solicitation under those circumstances.

Often the organizer trying to solicit the employees on employer property is not an employee of the firm. That occurred in the following case.

LECHMERE, INC. v. NLRB
112 S. Ct. 841 (1992)

Lechmere, Inc. (petitioner) owned a retail store in Newington, Connecticut. In June 1987, the United Food and Commercial Workers Union tried to organize Lechmere's employees. It placed an ad in a local newspaper that drew little response. Nonemployee organizers entered Lechmere's parking lot and placed handbills on cars parked in an area used by employees. Lechmere removed the handbills and told the union that it prohibited all solicitors on its property. The union picketed on a public grassy strip located between a major highway and the parking lot. By copying license plates of cars in the parking lot, the union secured the names and addresses of 20 percent of the store's employees, and sent mailings to them. For its efforts the union secured one signed authorization card.

The NLRB (respondent) held that Lechmere violated Section 8(a)(1). The Second Circuit Court of Appeals enforced the Board's order. The Supreme Court reversed.

Justice Thomas

By its plain terms, the NLRA confers rights only on employees, not on unions or their nonemployee organizers. . . . [I]nsofar as the employees' right of self-organization depends in some measure on their ability to learn the advantages of self-organization from others, §7 of the NLRA may, in certain limited circumstances, restrict an employer's right to exclude nonemployee union organizers from his property. It is the nature of those circumstances that we explore today.

■   ■   ■

In cases involving employee activities . . . the Board "balance[s] the conflicting interests of employees to receive information on self-organization on the company's property from fellow employees during nonworking time, with the employer's right to control the use of his property." In cases involving nonemployee activities . . . however, the Board [is] not permitted to engage in that same balancing. . . . Section 7 simply does not protect nonemployee union organizers except in the rare case where "the inaccessibility of employees makes ineffective the reasonable attempts by nonemployees to communicate with them through the usual channels. . . ." [U]nions need not engage in extraordinary feats to communicate with inaccessible employees. . . . Where reasonable alternative means of access exist, §7's guarantees do not authorize trespasses by nonemployee organizers, even under . . . reasonable regulations established by the Board.

■   ■   ■

The threshold inquiry in this case, then, is whether the facts here justify application of [the] inaccessiblity exception. . . .

■   ■   ■

[T]he exception . . . is a narrow one. It does not apply wherever nontrespassory access to employees may be cumbersome or less-than-ideally effective, but only where the location of a plant and the living quarters of the employees place the employees beyond the reach of reasonable union efforts to communicate with them. Classic examples include logging camps, mining camps, and mountain resort hotels. [The] exception . . . protects] the §7 rights to those employees who, by virtue of their employment, are isolated from the ordinary flow of information that characterizes our society. The union's burden of establishing such isolation is . . . "a heavy one," and one not satisfied by mere conjecture or the expression of doubts concerning the effectiveness of nontrespassory means of communication.

The Board's conclusion in this case that the union had no reasonable means short of trespass to make Lechmere's employees aware of its organizational efforts is based on a misunderstanding of the limited scope of this exception. Because the employees do not reside on Lechmere's property, they are presumptively not "beyond the reach," of the union's message. Although the employees live in a large metropolitan area (Greater Hartford), that fact does not in itself render them "inaccessible. . . ." Their accessibility is suggested by the union's success in contacting a substantial percentage of them directly. . . . Such direct contact, of course, is not a necessary element of "reasonably effective" communication; signs or advertising also may suffice. . . . Access to employees, not success in winning them over, is the critical issue—although success, or lack thereof, may be relevant in determining whether reasonable access exists. Because the union in this case failed to establish the existence of any unique obstacles that frustrated access to Lechmere's employees, the Board erred in concluding that Lechmere committed an unfair labor practice by barring the non-employee organizers from its property.

Case Questions

1. Why does the court treat nonemployee organizers different from employees?

2. Why did the union want to place handbills on the cars in Lechmere's parking lot if it was able to reach employees through other means? What were these means?

3. If the union's efforts netted only one authorization card, why does the court conclude that they were reasonable methods of communication?

4. An oil company owns a drilling concession in a remote area of Alaska. Employees live on the premises in a barracks. They work seven days a week, twelve hours per day for four weeks and then get two weeks off. The only way to get to the area is by company plane from Anchorage. Bad weather often delays flights for days at a time. The camp receives one newspaper. Radio reception is sporadic. The company provides the employees with unedited videotaped television programs. The Oil Workers Union has asked the company to allow an organizer to come onto the property to solicit employees during nonworking time in the barracks. How should the company respond? Explain.

5. A company runs two shifts. May it prohibit an employee on the first shift from returning to the plant to solicit co-workers during the second shift's lunch break? Why or why not?

Speeches to Employees

Employers may wish to violate their own no-solicitation rules by using company property and time to address employees and distribute antiunion literature. In determining whether such employer efforts constitute employer free speech under Section 8(c) or an unfair labor practice under Section 8(a)(1), the board considers the enormous economic power employers have over their employees. Thus, the employer may not make any statement threatening union supporters or promising benefits to those who do not support the union. An employer's predictions of adverse economic consequences following unionization are considered coercive unless they are based on objective facts over which the employer has no control.

Although an employer has a captive audience when addressing employees on company property and time, the employer need not offer the union an equal opportunity to respond, so long as the employer's speech is not coercive. However, the board forbids even noncoercive speeches to captive audiences during the 24-hour period before a representation election. This election eve rule does not ban speeches where attendance is voluntary and on the employees' own time.

Granting or Withholding Benefits

An employer's natural reaction to a union organizing drive is to find out why the employees are unhappy and remedy the situation. For example, if the workers believe they are underpaid, the employer might raise their wages. If the employer improves employee wages, benefits, or working conditions in an effort to influence the outcome of a representation election, the employer violates Section 8(a)(1). The Supreme Court has called an increase in wages or benefits "a fist inside the velvet glove."[1] The benefit increase emphasizes the employer's control over wages and benefits and suggests that benefits may be reduced if the employees vote for the union.

The NLRB may infer that a grant of benefits shortly before an election was intended to influence the vote. An employer may rebut this inference by showing objective reasons why the benefit was not related to the election. For example, the employer might show a pattern of granting wage increases at the same time over the past five years.

On the other hand, an employer who withholds a planned wage or benefit increase because of a pending representation election is punishing its employees for exercising their right to organize a union. An employer who regularly grants pay raises on June 1 might be tempted to withhold a planned raise until after a pending election to have more room in bargaining if the union wins. The NLRB would probably find that such action violates Section 8(a)(1). The general rule is that the employer should act as it would have acted if no election were pending.

Interrogation and Polling

Sometimes an employer wants to gauge the union's strength by interrogating employees. An employer's questioning of employees would be evaluated by the NLRB in the context of the whole campaign and the particular circumstances of the questioning. If an employer desires to determine how many employees support the union, a secret poll of the employees may be conducted, provided the employer observes the following safeguards:

- The poll's purpose is to test the validity of a union's claim of majority support.

---

[1] NLRB v. Exchange Parts Co., 375 U.S. 405 (1964).

- The purpose is communicated to the employees.
- Assurances against reprisals are given.
- The employer has neither committed prior unfair labor practices nor created a coercive atmosphere.

Company Unions

Before enactment of the NLRA, many employers fought independent unions by organizing company unions, which they dominated and required all employees to join. Section 8(a)(2) of the NLRA was designed to outlaw company unions.

Section 8(a)(2) prohibits employer domination, interference, and financial or other support of a labor organization. An employer violates Section 8(a)(2) by taking an active part in organizing a union or committee to represent its employees, bringing pressure on employees to join a particular union, or playing favorites with one of two or more competing unions. An employer who voluntarily recognizes a union that is not supported by a majority of the employees violates Section 8(a)(2), even if the employer in good faith believes that the union has majority support.

The prohibition of employer domination, interference, or support goes beyond unions and encompasses labor organizations. The NLRA defines a labor organization as any organization or plan "in which employees participate and which exists for the purpose, in whole or in part, of dealing with employers concerning grievances, labor disputes, wages, rates of pay, hours of employment, or conditions of work." Today, many employers are experimenting with employee quality circles and other participative management programs. Such programs may potentially violate Section 8(a)(2). To avoid violations, they either must be free from employer domination or interference, or they must not represent employees in dealing with the employer concerning grievances or working conditions.

Employee participation plans are not labor organizations if their purpose is not to represent the employees collectively or if they exercise managerial or adjudicative functions delegated to them. Even if the plans are labor organizations, they are not illegal if they maintain their existence independent of the employer. Where, however, the employer creates them or appoints their members, they exist only as long as the employer approves. Such employer domination is illegal.

Employer Discrimination Based on Union Membership

Section 8(a)(3) forbids employers to discriminate against employees for the purpose of encouraging or discouraging membership in any labor organization. For example, an employer cannot demote or discharge an employee for urging co-workers to join or organize a union. The employer may discipline a union activist for poor job performance or misconduct. The question is always what was the motive for the action.

Illegal employer discrimination is not limited to dealings with individual employees. Employers may not relocate or close part of their operations simply because the employees have selected a union. However, they may do so for economic reasons and can go out of business altogether, regardless of motive.

Ethical Dilemmas/Issues

You are plant manager for ABC Company. A union has begun organizing at your plant. You know of three employees who are leading the organizing drive. They are very good workers who have become frustrated over their low pay and poor fringe benefits.

ABC's vice president for employee relations met with you and said confidentially: "I want you to find out who the organizers are and then I want you to get something on them, even if you have to fake it, and fire them."

When you protested that this was illegal, the vice president replied, "Don't worry. Even if they complain to the NLRB, we'll deny that they were fired for being union organizers. Come to think of it, you should probably fire a few other workers to make it look good.

"Anyway, we'll give the NLRB some good reasons and our lawyers will delay the hearing for months. If we lose before the ALJ, we'll appeal to the board and if we lose there, we'll take it to court. Meanwhile, they'll be out of work. As their money dries up and their bills mount, they'll be willing to drop their claims for reinstatement in exchange for a lump-sum cash settlement. They'll never go back to the plant and the rest of the workers will learn that you can't join the union and expect to stay here. Even if they fight us all the way and we lose, the money we spend on lawyers and back pay will be a lot less than what we'd have to spend on the pay raise a union could force us to give.

"So, find out who they are and give me some good reasons to fire them. And be assured that if you don't do it, I'll find someone who will. You have two weeks. Your job could depend on it."

Most empirical studies confirm the accuracy of the vice president's predictions. Most victims of discriminatory discharges are never reinstated. Those who are, often are fired again or harassed into quitting. Even when they fight and win, companies frequently find it costs less in back pay and attorney fees than it would have cost if the company had recognized the union.

What are the ethical issues? What should you do?

The Representation Process

A union may file a representation petition if it can show that at least 30 percent of the employees desire that union's representation. A union usually shows this with cards signed by the employees authorizing the union to represent them. These cards are called **authorization cards**. Figure 18–3 is an example of an authorization card.

When a majority of the employees have signed authorization cards, the union usually advises the employer of this fact and demands recognition. The employer may ignore the demand or file a representation petition with the NLRB. The employer and union might also agree to have an independent third party check the authorization cards against the payroll list to verify the union's claim of majority support. If the claim is verified, the employer must recognize the union.

Employees currently represented by a union may file petitions to decertify that union. Decertification petitions must be supported by at least 30 percent of the employees.

When a petition is filed, the regional staff investigates it and, if necessary, conducts a hearing. If the regional director finds that a question of representation exists, he or she directs an election by secret ballot. The election results may be

---

FIGURE 18–3   Authorization Card

AUTHORIZATION FOR REPRESENTATION

I authorize the International Brotherhood of Electrical Workers,

to represent me in collective bargaining with my employer.

Name ....

(Please Print)

Address ....Phone ....

City ....State .... Zip ....

Employer ....

Department ....Shift: 1st ☐ 2nd ☐ 3rd ☐

Classification ....

Date ....Signed ....

FORM 141   445 challenged. The regional director rules on the objections and either orders a new election or certifies the results.

Appropriate Bargaining Units

For purposes of collective bargaining, employees are grouped into **bargaining units**. A bargaining unit may consist of all the employer's employees, a defined portion of the employer's employees or, in appropriate cases, the employees of several employers.

When filing a representation petition, a union must designate the bargaining unit in which it seeks to represent employees. The employer may challenge that unit. An employer challenging the union's choice must show that it is inappropriate, not simply that a different unit would be more appropriate. In resolving these challenges, the NLRB determines whether the employees share a "community of interest" in wages, hours, and working conditions.

For example, assume that an appliance retailer has six stores in a given city. Each store employs approximately 75 workers as cashiers, stock clerks, and sales representatives. The union has authorization cards from 60 workers in one store and petitions the NLRB to hold an election for a bargaining unit of employees in that store only.

The employer would prefer that the bargaining unit consist of all six stores because it will be more difficult for the union to organize all six stores at the same time. The employer has to convince the NLRB that a unit limited to one store is inappropriate; merely showing that a unit of six stores is more appropriate is not sufficient.

An employer who shows only that the employees at all six stores work for the same company, perform the same tasks, and are paid the same wage rate would probably lose. This shows that a unit of six stores is appropriate but does not show that a unit of one is inappropriate. However, if management shows that hiring, assignment, evaluation, and discipline of employees is centrally managed for all six stores and that there are frequent transfers among the stores, the employer will establish that a one store unit is inappropriate.

Protection of Laboratory Conditions

Before the election, the union and the employer wage campaigns to win the workers over to their positions. The board has stated that elections must be conducted under **laboratory conditions**; that is, the election proceedings must be conducted under conditions that make it possible to determine the uninhibited wishes of the employees.

Actions that would otherwise be legal may destroy laboratory conditions. That is why employers may not hold captive-audience meetings of employees within 24 hours before the election. Similarly, an employer normally need not furnish a union with a list of employees' names and addresses. However, when an election is ordered, the employer must provide such a list to the NLRB regional director for use by the union.

The board's policy regarding misrepresentations in election campaign propaganda has wavered in recent years. In 1962, it ruled that an election would be set aside if substantial misstatements were made and the opponent did not have time to respond. Since then it has changed its position three times. In 1982, the board ruled that it would not set aside elections because of misleading statements in the campaign.

The controversy centers over regulatory philosophy. Proponents of close scrutiny of election statements argue that employees require protection from misrepresentations. Opponents contend that employees are sophisticated enough to assess the validity of campaign propaganda, that regulation of speech should be kept to a minimum, and that close scrutiny encourages frivolous challenges to elections interposed only for delay.

Laboratory conditions may also be violated by emotional appeals. For example, appeals to racial prejudice may result in the setting aside of an election.

Unfair labor practices automatically destroy laboratory conditions. When the NLRB finds that a union committed unfair labor practices during an election, it sets aside any union victory in the election, orders the union to cease and desist its illegal activity, and orders other affirmative relief. When the NLRB finds that an employer committed unfair labor practices during an election, it sets aside any union defeat, orders the employer to cease and desist its illegal conduct, and orders other affirmative relief. If it finds employer interference with employee choice so serious that a fair election cannot be conducted, the board may order the employer to bargain with the union even when the union has lost the election.

Negotiation of the Collective Bargaining Agreement

Once the union has been certified, the employer must recognize and bargain with it as the exclusive representative of the employees. The employer may not negotiate individual contracts with individual employees. The certification binds all members of the bargaining unit to the act's policy of majority rule. The union must fairly represent all of the employees in the bargaining unit and both the union and the employer must bargain in good faith.

Because a newly elected union needs time to establish itself and implement its programs, it is immune to attack for one calendar year after certification. During this year, the union is presumed to represent a majority of the employees and an employer cannot refuse to bargain, even if the employees no longer want the union as their representative.

After a year, there remains a continuing presumption that the union has majority status. The employer may rebut this presumption and refuse to continue bargaining with the union if the employer has objective evidence that a majority of the employees does not wish to be represented by the union. The following case considers which type of evidence suffices.

NLRB v. Curtin Matheson Scientific, Inc.
494 U.S. 775 (1990)

Teamsters Local 968 represented 27 employees of Curtin Matheson Scientific, Inc. (respondent). On May 21, 1979, their collective bargaining agreement expired. Respondent offered a new contract; the union rejected the offer and struck. Five employees crossed the picket line, and respondent hired 29 permanent replacements. These 34 employees and the 22 strikers comprised the bargaining unit.

The union ended the strike, and offered to return to work and accept respondent's contract proposal. Respondent rejected this and withdrew its recognition of the union. The union filed unfair labor practice charges. The NLRB (petitioner) held that respondent did not have sufficient objective evidence that the union had lost majority support and ordered respondent to bargain with the union and execute a contract. The Fifth Circuit Court of Appeals reversed. The Supreme Court reversed the Fifth Circuit.

Justice Marshall

[T]he starting point for the Board's analysis is the basic presumption that the union is supported by a majority of bargaining-unit employees. The employer bears the burden of rebutting that presumption . . . either by showing that the union in fact lacks majority support or by demonstrating a sufficient objective basis for doubting the union's majority status. Respondent here urges that in evaluating an employer's claim of a good-faith doubt, the Board must adopt a second, subsidiary presumption—that replacement employees oppose the union. . . . The presumption of the replacements' opposition to the union would, in effect, override the presumption of continuing majority status. In contrast . . . the Board "take[s] into account the particular circumstances surrounding each strike and the hiring of replacements, while retaining the long-standing requirement that the employer must come forth with some objective evidence to substantiate his doubt of continuing majority status."

We find the Board's no-presumption approach rational as an empirical matter. . . . Although replacements often may not favor the incumbent union, the Board reasonably concluded, in light of its long experience in addressing these issues, that replacements may in some circumstances desire union representation despite their willingness to cross the picket line. Economic concerns, for instance, may force a replacement employee to work for a struck employer even though he otherwise supports the union and wants the benefits of union representation. In this sense the replacement worker is no different from a striker who, feeling the financial heat of the strike on herself and her family, is forced to abandon the picket line and go back to work. . . . In addition, a replacement, like a nonstriker or a strike crossover, may disagree with the purpose or strategy of the particular strike and refuse to support that strike, while still wanting that union's representation at the bargaining table.

Respondent insists that the interests of strikers and replacements are diametrically opposed and that unions inevitably side with the strikers. . . . [U]nions often negotiate with employers for strike settlements that would return the strikers to their jobs, thereby displacing some or all of the replacements. Respondent asserts that replacements, aware of the union's loyalty to the strikers, most likely would not support the union. . . .

These arguments do not persuade us that the Board's position is irrational. Unions do not inevitably demand displacement of all strike replacements. . . .

The extent to which a union demands displacement of permanent replacement workers logically will depend on the union's bargaining power. . . . [A]n employer is not required to discharge permanent replacements at the conclusion of an economic strike to make room for returning strikers; rather, the employer must only reinstate strikers as vacancies arise. The strikers' only chance for immediate reinstatement, then, lies in the union's ability to force the employer to discharge the replacements as a condition for the union's ending the strike. Unions' leverage to compel such a strike settlement will vary greatly from strike to strike. If, for example, the jobs at issue do not require highly trained workers and the replacements perform as well as the strikers did, the employer will have little incentive to hire back the strikers and fire the replacements; consequently, the union will have little bargaining power. . . . A union with little bargaining leverage is unlikely to press the employer . . . to discharge the replacements and reinstate all the strikers. Cognizant of the union's weak position, many if not all of the replacements justifiably may not fear that they will lose their jobs at the end of the strike. . . .

The Board's refusal to adopt an antiunion presumption is also consistent with the Act's "overriding policy" of achieving "industrial peace. . . ."

The Board's approach . . . limits employers' ability to oust a union without adducing any evidence of the employees' union sentiments and encourages negotiated solutions to strikes. It was reasonable for the Board to conclude that the antiunion presumption, in contrast, could allow an employer to eliminate the union merely by hiring a sufficient number of replacement employees. That rule thus might encourage the employer to avoid good-faith bargaining over a strike settlement, and instead to use the strike as a means of removing the union altogether.

Case Questions

1. What must an employer show to justify withdrawing recognition from a union?
2. Why did the NLRB refuse to presume that strike replacements oppose the union?
3. Assume that two of the replacements found the tires on their cars slashed. Would this justify the employer in withdrawing recognition?
4. Should the employer be allowed to take a secret ballot poll of the replacements to determine whether they support the union? Why or why not?

The Duty to Bargain in Good Faith

Section 8(d) defines the type of collective bargaining that is required.

> **National Labor Relations Act, Section 8(d)**
>
> [T]he performance of the mutual obligation of the employer and the representative of the employees to meet at reasonable times and confer in good faith with respect to wages, hours, and other terms and conditions of employment . . . . [b]ut such obligation does not compel either party to agree to a proposal or require the making of a concession.

Collective bargaining usually begins with the union making a request for a meeting. Section 8(d) requires that the meeting be "at reasonable times" for both parties. The act contains no precise requirements regarding the time and place of negotiations, but a reasonableness standard is used. Excessive delays are not allowed.

It is an unfair labor practice for either party to refuse to bargain in good faith. The board uses two standards to assess the bargaining faith of parties: the totality of the circumstances approach, and the per se violations approach. Some practices are viewed as evidencing bad faith but are considered in light of other practices to see whether the total circumstances add up to bad-faith bargaining. The act does not require the parties to reach an agreement, but it prohibits bad-faith bargaining designed to avoid a contract.

Some practices are so inconsistent with good-faith bargaining that they are per se violations. These include:

- Refusing to bargain at all.
- Insisting on an illegal provision in the contract.
- Refusing to execute a written contract.
- For an employer, unilaterally changing some aspect of wages, hours, and working conditions, unless the employer has bargained to an impasse with the union.
- For either party, refusing to supply the other with relevant information.

A party's duty to provide the other side with information is determined by balancing the information's relevance against the interests served by keeping it secret. For example, generally an employer need not let the union see its books. Although this information is relevant to bargaining, its proprietary nature should be protected. However, if an employer raises the issue of its financial health during negotiations, the books take on a heightened relevance and the union has a right to inspect them.

Subjects of Bargaining

There are three categories of bargaining subjects: mandatory subjects, permissive subjects, and prohibited subjects. If either party makes a proposal on a **mandatory subject** during negotiations, the other party cannot refuse to bargain on the proposal. Section 8(d) requires bargaining on "wages, hours, and. other terms and conditions of employment," but the NLRA does not define which subjects can be classified as falling under these headings. However, by its decisions the board has developed what may be described as an exhaustive list of mandatory subjects. These include retirement benefits, vacations, rest periods, and work assignments.

Permissive subjects are those that either party may refuse to bargain on without committing an unfair labor practice. Among permissive subjects are corporate organization, the size of the supervisory force, and the location of plants.

While the classifications seem fairly straightforward, the following case reveals their complexity.

FIRST NATIONAL MAINTENANCE CORP. V. NLRB
452 U.S. 666 (1981)

First National Maintenance Corp. (petitioner) provided maintenance services to commercial establishments. Petitioner's employees were represented by the National Union of Hospital and Health Care Employees. One of the petitioner's customers was Greenpark Care Center nursing home. Greenpark and First National had a stormy relationship for some time. After a dispute over petitioner's fee, petitioner decided to terminate its contract with Greenpark and discharge those of its employees who had been assigned to the Greenpark work. Petitioner refused to bargain with the union over the decision to terminate the Greenpark contract.

The NLRB (respondent) held that the petitioner had a duty to bargain over the decision to terminate the Greenpark contract, and found petitioner guilty of violating Section 8(a)(5). The court of appeals enforced the NLRB's order. The Supreme Court reversed.

Justice Blackmun

Some management decisions, such as choice of advertising and promotion, product type and design, and financing arrangements, have only an indirect and attenuated impact on the employment relationship. Other management decisions, such as the order of succession of layoffs and recalls, production quotas, and work rules, are almost exclusively "an aspect of the relationship" between employer and employee. The present case concerns a third type of management decision, one that had a direct impact on employment, since jobs were inexorably eliminated by the termination, but had as its focus only the economic profitability of the contract with Greenpark, a concern under these facts wholly apart from the employment relationship. This decision, involving a change in the scope and direction of the enterprise, is akin to the decision whether to be in business at all, "not in [itself] primarily about conditions of employment, though the effect of the decision may be necessarily to terminate employ-

ment. . . ." At the same time, this decision touches on a matter of central and pressing concern to the union and its member employees: the possibility of continued employment and the retention of the employees' very jobs. . . .

The aim of labeling a matter a mandatory subject of bargaining, rather than simply permitting, but not requiring, bargaining, is to "promote the fundamental purpose of the Act by bringing a problem of vital concern to labor and management within the framework established by Congress as most conducive to industrial peace. . . ." The concept of mandatory bargaining is premised on the belief that collective discussions backed by the parties' economic weapons will result in decisions that are better for both management and labor and for society as a whole. This will be true, however, only if the subject proposed for discussion is amenable to resolution through the bargaining process. Management must be free from the constraints of the bargaining process to the extent essential for the running of a profitable business. It also must have some degree of certainty beforehand as to when it may proceed to reach decisions without fear of later evaluations labeling its conduct an unfair labor practice. Congress did not explicitly state what issues of mutual concern to union and management it intended to exclude from mandatory bargaining. Nonetheless, in view of an employer's need for unencumbered decision making, bargaining over management decisions that have a substantial impact on the continued availability of employment should be required only if the benefit, for labor-management relations and the collective-bargaining process, outweighs the burden placed on the conduct of business.

■   ■   ■

A union's interest in participating in the decision to close a particular facility or part of an employer's operations springs from its legitimate concern over job security. The union's practical purpose in participating, however, will be largely uniform: it will seek to delay or halt the closing. No doubt it will be impelled, in seeking these ends, to offer concessions, information, and alternatives that might be helpful to management or forestall or prevent the termination of jobs. It is unlikely, however, that requiring bargaining over the decision itself, as well as its effects, will augment this flow of information and suggestions. There is no dispute that the union must be given a significant opportunity to bargain about these matters of job security as part of the "effects" bargaining mandated by §8(a)(5). And, under §8(a)(5), bargaining over the effects of a decision must be conducted in a meaningful manner and at a meaningful time, and the Board may impose sanctions to insure its adequacy. A union, by pursuing such bargaining rights, may achieve valuable concessions from an employer engaged in a partial closing. It also may secure in contract negotiations provisions implementing rights to notice, information, and fair bargaining.

Management's interest in whether it should discuss a decision of this kind is much more complex and varies with the particular circumstances. If labor costs are an important factor in a failing operation and the decision to close, management will have an incentive to confer voluntarily with the union to seek concessions that may make continuing the business profitable. At other times, management may have a great need for speed, flexibility, and secrecy in meeting business opportunities and exigencies. It may face significant tax or securities consequences that hinge on confidentiality, the timing of a plant closing, or a reorganization of the corporate structure. The publicity incident to the normal process of bargaining may injure the possibility of a successful transition or increase the economic damage to business. The employer also may have no feasible alternative to the closing, and even good-faith bargaining over it may both be futile and cause the employer additional loss.

There is an important difference, also, between permitted bargaining and mandated bargaining. Labeling this type of decision mandatory could afford a union a powerful tool for achieving delay, a power that might be used to thwart management's intentions in a manner unrelated to any feasible solution the union might propose.

We conclude that the harm likely to be done to an employer's need to operate freely in deciding whether to shut down part of its business purely for economic reasons outweighs the incremental benefit that might be gained through the union's participation in making the decision, and we hold that the decision itself is not part of §8(d)'s "terms and conditions," over which Congress has mandated bargaining.

Case Questions

1. Which factors led the Court to conclude that a decision to terminate part of a business is not a mandatory subject of bargaining?

2. What is the difference between decision bargaining and effects bargaining? Can there be meaningful effects bargaining without decision bargaining?

3. Is an employer prohibited from bargaining over its decision to close part of the business?

4. A company that employs five janitors decides that the work could be done less expensively if it fires the janitors and hires an outside contractor to perform janitorial services. Must the company bargain with the janitors' union about the decision? Why or why not?

5. A restaurant chain has always made fried shrimp by purchasing raw shrimp and having its employees process it into frozen breaded shrimp, which is then delivered to the chain's outlets. The chain is concerned with the erratic quality of raw shrimp and the high cost of processing. It wants to stop processing shrimp and purchase frozen breaded shrimp from an independent supplier. Must it bargain with the union about the decision? Explain.

Administering the Collective Bargaining Agreement

Although many issues affecting employment may be resolved in the collective bargaining contract, controversies continue to arise after the parties have entered into the contract. The parties are obligated to bargain in good faith over contract interpretation. The settlement of contract interpretation disputes is often left to an arbitrator.

Arbitration

Arbitration is a process in which the parties submit issues for decision by a mutually agreed-on third party. It differs from mediation, a process in which the third party attempts to persuade the parties to reach an agreement. Most contracts contain grievance procedures that provide for the union and employer to discuss disputes over contract interpretation and application at successively higher levels within their hierarchies. If they cannot reach agreement, the dispute may be referred to arbitration.

The arbitrator's authority is based on the contract's arbitration clause. Most contracts contain broad arbitration clauses, authorizing the arbitrator to decide all disputes regarding the interpretation and application of the contract. If a controversy arises over whether a dispute is arbitrable, it must be decided by a court. The presumption is that the dispute is arbitrable. If the parties do not wish to have particular disputes decided by arbitration, they must explicitly state so in their arbitration clause.

Usually, in exchange for a grievance and arbitration procedure, unions agree not to strike for the duration of the collective-bargaining agreement. If the union strikes in breach of a no-strike clause and the underlying dispute is arbitrable, a federal district court can enjoin the strike and order the parties to arbitration.

The arbitrator's authority is confined to deciding disputes under the contract; that is, the arbitrator must use the contract as the governing document in deciding disputes involving the contract's application. Where contract interpretation is the issue, the arbitrator uses "the law of the shop," examining past practices of the parties to give meaning to the contract's terms.

Judicial Deferral to an Arbitrator's Award

In three cases decided on the same day, the Supreme Court established a policy favoring judicial deferral to arbitration awards. These cases involved the United Steelworkers and collectively are called the *Steelworkers Trilogy*. The following case illustrates the breadth of the courts' deference to arbitration.

UNITED PAPERWORKERS INTERNATIONAL UNION V. MISCO, INC.
484 U.S. 29 (1987)

A collective bargaining agreement between the United Paperworkers Union (petitioner) and Misco, Inc. (respondent) required just cause to fire an employee. Misco fired Isiah Cooper, an employee who operated a machine that used sharp blades to cut rolling coils of paper, after police found Cooper in the back seat of his car in the Misco parking lot with marijuana smoke in the air and a lit marijuana cigarette in the front ashtray. Misco claimed that Cooper violated its Rule II.1, which provided for firing workers who possessed drugs on company property. Misco later learned that a police search of the car had found a plastic scales case and marijuana gleanings in the trunk.

Cooper grieved his discharge. An arbitrator refused to consider evidence from the police search of the trunk because Misco had not relied on it in firing Cooper and ruled that Misco failed to prove that Cooper possessed the marijuana cigarette. He ordered Cooper reinstated with full back pay.

Misco sued and the lower courts overturned the award on the ground that it conflicted with the public policy against operating dangerous machinery under the influence of drugs. The Supreme Court reversed.

Justice White

Collective-bargaining agreements commonly provide grievance procedures to settle disputes between union and employer with respect to the interpretation and application of the agreement and require binding arbitration for unsettled grievances. In such cases . . . the courts play only a limited role when asked to review the decision of an arbitrator. . . .

The courts have jurisdiction to enforce collective-bargaining contracts; but where the contract provides grievance and arbitration procedures, those procedures must first be exhausted and courts must order resort to the private settlement mechanisms without dealing with the merits of the dispute. Because the parties have contracted to have disputes settled by an arbitrator chosen by them rather than by a judge, it is the arbitrator's view of the facts and of the meaning of the contract that they have agreed to accept. To resolve disputes about the application of a collective-bargaining agreement, an arbitrator must find facts and a court may not reject those findings simply because it disagrees with them. The same is true of the arbitrator's interpretation of the contract. The arbitrator may not ignore the plain language of the contract; but the parties having authorized the arbitrator to give meaning to the language of the agreement, a court should not reject an award on the ground that the arbitrator misread the contract. . . . If the courts were free to intervene on these grounds, the speedy resolution of grievances by private mechanisms would be greatly undermined. Furthermore, it must be remembered that grievance and arbitration procedures are part and parcel of the ongoing process of collective bargaining. It is through these processes that the supplementary rules of the plant are established. As the Court has said, the arbitrator's award settling a dispute with respect to the interpretation or application of a labor agreement must draw its essence from the contract and cannot simply reflect the arbitrator's own notions of industrial justice. But as long as the arbitrator is even arguably construing or applying the contract and acting within the scope of his authority, that a court is convinced he committed serious error does not suffice to overturn his decision. . . .

The Company's position, simply put, is that the arbitrator committed grievous error in finding that the evidence was insufficient to prove that Cooper had possessed or used marijuana on company property. But . . . [n]o dishonesty is alleged; only improvident, even silly, fact-finding is claimed. This is hardly sufficient basis for disregarding what the agent appointed by the parties determined to be the historical facts.

■   ■   ■

[A] court may not enforce a collective-bargaining agreement that is contrary to public policy. . . . [A] court's refusal to enforce an arbitrator's interpretation of such contracts is limited to situations where the contract as interpreted would violate "some explicit public policy" that is "well defined and dominant, and is to be ascertained by reference to the laws and legal prece-

dents and not from general considerations of supposed public interests. . . ." At the very least . . . the violation of such a policy must be clearly shown if an award is not to be enforced.

As we see it, the formulation of public policy set out by the Court of Appeals did not comply with the [above standard]. . . . The Court of Appeals made no attempt to review existing laws and legal precedents in order to demonstrate that they establish a "well defined and dominant" policy against the operation of dangerous machinery while under the influence of drugs. Although certainly such a judgment is firmly rooted in common sense . . . a formulation of public policy based only on "general considerations of supposed public interests" is not the sort that permits a court to set aside an arbitration award that was entered in accordance with a valid collective-bargaining agreement.

Even if the Court of Appeals' formulation of public policy is to be accepted, no violation of that policy was clearly shown in this case. . . . [T]he assumed connection between the marijuana gleanings found in Cooper's car and Cooper's actual use of drugs in the workplace is tenuous at best and provides an insufficient basis for holding that his reinstatement would actually violate the public policy identified by the Court of Appeals "against the operation of dangerous machinery by persons under the influence of drugs or alcohol." A refusal to enforce an award must rest on more than speculation or assumption.

Case Questions

1. What was the just cause that Misco relied on to fire Cooper? Why did the arbitrator find that there was no just cause?

2. Give three reasons why the court of appeals refused to enforce the arbitrator's award. Why did the Supreme Court reject these reasons?

3. Which standard does a court apply when reviewing an arbitrator's award? Why is this standard used?

4. W. R. Grace and Co. has a collective bargaining agreement with the Rubber Workers Union. The agreement requires that layoffs be in reverse order of seniority. Female employees of Grace filed sex discrimination charges against Grace with the EEOC. Grace and the EEOC settled the charges by agreeing that layoffs would not reduce the percentage of Grace employees who were female. Grace laid off a large number of employees. To comply with the settlement agreement, Grace laid off some male employees while retaining some females who had less seniority. The male employees filed grievances.

Grace refused to arbitrate and sued in U.S. district court. The court held that the EEOC settlement agreement preempted the collective bargaining agreement. The union appealed. Grace then laid off additional employees, again laying off some males and retaining fewer senior females. After the males filed grievances, the court of appeals reversed the district court's decision. Grace reinstated the male employees. Their claims for back pay were presented to an arbitrator, who awarded them full back pay. Must Grace comply with the arbitrator's award? Explain.

5. The U.S. Postal Service fired a letter carrier after he was arrested, pled guilty, and received probation for unlawful delay of the mail. The letter carrier had been found with 3,500 pieces of mail in his home and car.

The letter carrier filed a grievance. An arbitrator found that his offense resulted from compulsive gambling. The arbitrator ordered the Postal Service to reinstate the letter carrier if, after a 60-day medical leave, the employee had successfully completed a gambling rehabilitation program. Must the Postal Service comply? Explain.

Strikes, Boycotts, and Picketing

Although the national labor policy promotes industrial peace through collective bargaining, occasionally bargaining efforts fail to produce agreement and the parties resort to their economic weapons. The economic weapon of labor is the strike. Employers' economic weapons include lockouts and hiring strike replacements.

The NLRA specifically guarantees employees the right to strike. Nevertheless, certain job actions are not protected. Violent conduct is not protected; neither are slowdowns, partial strikes, refusals to work overtime, or similar actions. Sometimes the line between protected and unprotected conduct is difficult to draw. For example, in one case technicians who were negotiating a new collective bargaining agreement with a television station distributed handbills accusing the station of airing outdated programs and giving viewers second-class treatment. The Supreme Court held that the handbilling was not protected activity because it was disloyal and unrelated to the dispute over a new contract.[2]

---

[2] NLRB v. Local 1229, Int'l Bhd. of Elec. Wkrs., 364 U.S. 464 (1953).

Illegal Job Actions

Some economic weapons that unions employ, in addition to being unprotected, are also unfair labor practices. These include secondary boycotts, work assignment picketing, and picketing for recognition.

Secondary Boycotts

Section 8(b)(4) prohibits secondary boycotts. A **secondary boycott** exerts union pressure to coerce a party with whom it has no dispute to cease dealing with a party with whom the union has a dispute. Secondary boycotts must be distinguished from lawful primary activity. For example, if the union has a dispute with XYZ Co. and goes on strike, the activity is primary and lawful, even though XYZ's customers find their supplies interrupted and take their business to XYZ's competitors. However, if the union pickets XYZ's customers to force them to cease doing business with XYZ, the activity is secondary and unlawful.

It is sometimes difficult to distinguish primary from secondary activity, particularly if two companies are located at the same site. Generally, the picketing is considered primary where four conditions are met:

- The picketing is limited to times when the primary employer is present.
- The primary employer is engaged in its normal business at the site.
- The picketing is restricted to places reasonably close to the primary employer.
- The picket signs clearly disclose that the dispute is with the primary employer.

A corollary to the common site situation is the "reserved gate rule." If an employer reserves a plant entrance for the exclusive use of outside contractors, a union on strike against the employer may not picket that entrance.

A **hot cargo agreement** is a form of secondary boycott and is therefore illegal. A hot cargo agreement provides that the employer not deal with nonunion employers or that employees need not handle nonunion goods.

Work Assignment Disputes

In a work assignment dispute, an employer is caught between conflicting claims of two unions. For example, assume that a contractor employs sheet metal workers represented by the Sheet Metal Workers Union and carpenters represented by the Carpenters Union. The company accepts a job to install a heating system that requires attaching metal duct work to wooden supports. If the employer assigns the work to its sheet metal workers, the carpenters will strike. If it assigns the work to its carpenters, the sheet metal workers will strike.

Section 8(b)(4) prohibits strikes and similar conduct to coerce the assignment of work to a particular group of employees. If such coercion is applied, the employer may file a charge with the NLRB. The NLRB must affirmatively resolve the work assignment dispute.

Recognition Picketing

A union that is not certified to represent a company's employees might picket to force the employer to recognize it or to force the employees to choose it as their representative.

Section 8(b)(7) bans such **recognition** or **organization picketing** in three situations: (1) another union has already been recognized by the employer as the employees' representative and the board cannot conduct an election because of an existing contract with the other union; (2) the employees voted in a valid board representation election within the preceding 12 months; or (3) the union pickets for more than 30 days without filing a petition for a representation election.

A union's informational picketing is protected. Informational picketing is picketing for the purpose of truthfully advising the public that an employer does not employ union members or have a contract with a labor organization. The protection given to informational picketing is lost where it induces individuals employed by others to refuse to pick up or deliver goods or perform other services.

Employer Responses to Strikes

If a strike or job action is illegal or unprotected, the employer may discharge the strikers. Protected strikes are of two types: economic strikes involving collective bargaining issues and unfair labor practice strikes caused or prolonged by an employer's unfair labor practices.

An employer may permanently replace economic strikers, and it need not fire the replacements when the strikers are ready to return to work. However, an employer cannot fire the strikers. Even those who have been replaced remain employees and must be recalled if positions open up for them. Unfair labor practice strikers may not be permanently replaced.

The legality of other employer actions depends on whether they are legitimate economic weapons or are inherently destructive of employee rights. For example, an employer may lock out, but it may not grant superseniority to replacements. Superseniority would guarantee replacements preferred treatment over strikers as long as they remain with the employer. The effects of superseniority remain long after the strike has ended and are necessarily destructive of employee rights.

Chapter Problems

1. Define the following terms:
    a. Concerted activity for mutual aid and protection
    b. Unfair labor practice
    c. Authorization cards

    d. Bargaining unit
    e. Laboratory conditions
    f. Mandatory subjects of bargaining
    g. Arbitration
    h. Secondary boycott
    i. Hot cargo agreement
    j. Recognition or organization picketing

2. Yellow Cab Co. leases taxi cabs to drivers. The lease agreement provides that the driver may lease the cab for a 12-hour day, a 12-hour night, or a 24-hour period. The driver pays for gasoline and must have a taxi driver's license from the state and city in which Yellow operates. The lease requires the driver to dress neatly and treat passengers courteously. The lease also requires the driver to follow specified procedures if involved in an accident.

   Drivers are not required to keep trip sheets or account to the company for the fares received. Over 90 percent of the fares result from people hailing cabs that cruise the streets; the rest result from telephone calls to the company's dispatchers. Drivers who wish to receive dispatch calls are required to report their location to the dispatcher at 30-minute intervals. A sign in every cab advises passengers to direct complaints to the company and gives the company's telephone number.

   You are the company president. Recently, a group of drivers has begun organizing a union. Your vice president has suggested refusing to lease cabs to union supporters and telling the drivers that they have no rights to join unions because they are not covered by the NLRA. Are these suggestions valid? Explain.

3. Consolidated Conglomerates, Inc. is a major conglomerate that wholly owns or has controlling interest in 45 different companies, one of which is Ace Widget Co. The Widget Workers Union began an organizing drive at Ace on January 2. On February 1, the union filed a representation petition with the NLRB. Consolidated administers a health insurance plan that covers all employees of Consolidated and its subsidiaries. On January 15, Consolidated decided to amend the plan, effective February 15, to provide dental benefits. The officials in charge of the plan were unaware of the organizing drive at Ace.

   A representation election is scheduled at Ace for March 15. Should Ace delay implementing the dental benefits until after March 15? What are the risks of implementing the plan at Ace on February 15? What are the risks of delaying implementation?

4. General Foods Corp. has established a job-enrichment program under which 30 employees are divided into four teams. The teams act by consensus and make job assignments to individual team members, assign job rotations, and schedule overtime among team members. They also interview job applicants.

General Foods has also retained a consultant to hold periodic meetings with team members and first-line supervisors in an effort to improve communications and build trust. At these meetings, complaints about the company and job conditions may be aired. Is General Foods in danger of violating Section 8(a)(2)? Explain.

5. Wilma Worker, an employee of the Lazy Acres Retirement Center, was openly soliciting her co-workers to join the Service Employees International Union. After a majority of the employees signed authorization cards, the union sent a telegram to Lazy Acres demanding recognition. Mary Manager, the Lazy Acres general manager, confronted Worker one day in the kitchen. Manager waved the telegram at her and yelled, "What's this about a union?" When Worker replied that the employees wanted a union, Manager said, "You know the owners will fight this and as part of management I will have to fight it, too."

    A week later the two owners confronted Worker in the kitchen. They asked why the employees wanted a union. Worker replied that it was because they were paid poorly. One of the owners asked if the union charged a fee to join. Worker replied yes, and the owner stated, "I will have to talk with Mary about this." Has Lazy Acres committed any unfair labor practices? Explain.

6. Ace Delivery Service employs 35 truck drivers, who are represented by Teamsters Local 123. Recently, three drivers were arrested and charged with selling cocaine out of their trucks. Ace now wants to begin a program of randomly testing truck drivers for drugs and of testing all job applicants for drugs. The test involves a chemical analysis of the driver's or applicant's urine. Must Ace bargain about this with the union? Explain.

7. The Service Employees Union has been on strike against Acme Janitorial Services for two weeks. Acme has hired 25 permanent replacements. The union demanded that Acme give it a list of the names and addresses of the new employees. Must Acme do so? Explain.

8. You are operations manager for Widget Manufacturing Inc. Your production workers are on strike and your plant is shut down. The labor relations department is trying to negotiate a new contract with the union and has predicted that the strike will last two to three weeks. You would like to use this time to have some major maintenance work done, including replastering and repainting walls and ceilings The construction company you use is unionized and its employees refuse to cross picket lines. What, if anything, can you do to insulate their work from the production workers' strike?

9. Several employees in the bargaining unit were receiving long-term disability benefits when the union went on strike. The employer wrote these employees asking if they supported the strike. When the employer received no responses, it wrote them stating that if they did not renounce the strike in writing, it would consider them on strike and cease paying them disability benefits. Did the employer violate the NLRA? Explain.

10. Due to a dispute over wages, High Tech Industries was struck by a union representing 75 of its employees. High Tech continued operating during the strike and further automated its operations. The strike was long and bitter. By the time it ended, High Tech had eliminated 35 of the 75 jobs. High Tech recalled 40 of the 75 employees. Of the remaining 35, 15 did not seek to return to their jobs, 15 were not recalled because they had assaulted supervisors and others who had crossed the union's picket lines, and 5 were not recalled because they were the union officers who led the strike. Did High Tech violate the NLRA? Why or why not?

VI BUSINESS AND THE MARKETPLACE

An Overview of the Antitrust Laws

Statute	Provision
Sherman Act	
Section 1	Prohibits agreements which restrain trade.
Section 2	Prohibits single-firm monopolization, attempts and conspiracies to monopolize.
Clayton Act	
Section 2	As amended by the Robinson-Patman Act, forbids price discrimination where the effect may be to injure or prevent competition.
Section 3	Prohibits exclusive dealing agreements and tie-in devices with regard to commodities where the effect may be to substantially lessen competition or tend to create a monopoly.
Section 7	Prohibits mergers where the effect may be to substantially lessen competition or tend to create a monopoly.
FTC Act	Prohibits unfair methods of competition and unfair or deceptive trade practices. Violations of the Sherman and Clayton Acts are also violations of the FTC Act.

The American economy relies primarily on competition to regulate the provision of goods and services in the marketplace. Antitrust laws protect competition from the private accumulation of economic power. These laws regulate conduct among competitors.

The Sherman Act, the Clayton Act, and the Federal Trade Commission Act protect the public from monopolistic control of the economy and facilitate, as well as regulate, competition. Chapters 19 and 20 explore these statutes in detail and their application to business. Chapter 19 considers restraints of trade; Chapter 20, monopolization and mergers; and Chapter 21 continues the examination by looking at antitrust regulation of pricing, franchising, and trade association activity.

The Sherman Act prohibits unreasonable restraints of trade and monopolistic behavior. Violations of the Sherman Act are both criminal and civil offenses. The Clayton Act regulates mergers that may substantially less competition, and it regulates price discrimination under specified circumstances. The FTC Act prohibits unfair methods of competition. Violations of the Clayton and FTC acts are civil offenses.

The Justice Department enforces civil provisions of both the Sherman and Clayton acts by seeking injunctive orders designed to remedy violations. Such orders may simply prohibit anticompetitive business practices or may require the defendant to take affirmative action, such as divesting itself of assets, divisions, or subsidiaries. The Justice Department also enforces the Sherman Act's criminal provisions.

Private individuals injured in their trade or business can sue alleged violators of the Sherman and Clayton acts and may recover treble damages, court costs, and attorneys' fees and, in some cases, obtain injunctive relief. Consumers are protected by the antitrust laws in two ways. First, under appropriate circumstances, they may sue the violators. Second, state attorneys general may bring actions on behalf of all injured individuals residing in their states.

The Federal Trade Commission enforces Section 5 of the Federal Trade Commission Act, which prohibits unfair methods of competition and unfair or deceptive trade practices. Unfair methods of competition include violations of the antitrust laws. The FTC's jurisdiction over unfair methods of competition, however, reaches conduct beyond that specifically outlawed in the Sherman and Clayton acts. The FTC proceeds by administrative adjudication, utilizing the methods discussed in Chapter 6.

19   RESTRAINTS OF TRADE

Learning Objectives

After learning this chapter the student should be able to:

- Recognize relationships with competitors that may result in antitrust liability.
- Analyze the risks of antitrust liability resulting from particular agreements with, and policies toward, suppliers, distributors, and franchisees.
- Assess the risk of liability arising from a firm or group of firms refusing to do business with another firm.

As explained in Chapter 7, under common law a court may not enforce a contract that is contrary to public policy. Contracts that unreasonably restrain trade are contrary to public policy.

Courts have taken two approaches to restraints of trade. Under the first approach, a court does not enforce a restraint that is the primary agreement. However, the court enforces a reasonable restraint that is a minor part of a broader agreement. These restraints are called *ancillary restraints*. Under the second approach, all reasonable restraints are enforced, whether they are primary or ancillary. In analyzing the reasonableness of restraints, the courts inquire into their purposes and effects. To be reasonable, a restraint must be justified by a legitimate business purpose and must not have an anticompetitive effect.

The common law is not an effective method of preventing restraints of trade. This is because a restraint is brought before a court only when one party seeks to enforce it against another. Many of the most anticompetitive restraints, such as agreements fixing prices or allocating markets, are never challenged. The parties voluntarily adhere to them. To remedy this, Congress passed the Sherman Act and the Clayton Act, authorizing the government and private parties to challenge these restraints.

This chapter considers the legality under the antitrust laws of agreements to restrain trade. It divides restraints into three primary categories: horizontal restraints, which are agreements among competitors; vertical restraints, which are agreements between customers and suppliers; and group boycotts, which are agreements not to deal with another party. All agreements are covered by Section 1 of the Sherman Act. Certain vertical agreements also involve Section 3 of the Clayton Act, which is discussed in the section dealing with vertical restraints.

Section 1 of the Sherman Act

> **Sherman Act, Section 1**
> Every contract, combination in the form of trust or otherwise, or conspiracy, in restraint of trade or commerce among the several states, or with foreign nations, is declared to be illegal. . . .

Section 1 of the Sherman Act prohibits every contract, combination, and conspiracy restraining trade in interstate or foreign commerce. The requirement that the restraint of trade involve interstate commerce is typical of federal regulatory legislation (and is discussed in detail in Chapter 5). The other two elements of a Sherman Act violation are (1) a contract, combination, or conspiracy; and (2) an unreasonable restraint of trade.

Contract, Combination, or Conspiracy

A contract is an agreement between two or more parties to do things that they were previously not obligated to do. A conspiracy conjures up visions of clandestine meetings and elaborate plans. A combination seems less sinister than a conspiracy and less formal than a contract.

In antitrust legislation, however, **contract, combination, or conspiracy** is a technical term meaning joint or concerted action. Section 1 of the Sherman Act prohibits two or more entities from pooling their economic power to restrain trade. Unilateral action does not violate Section 1, even though the identical action taken jointly would be illegal. The requirement of joint action is discussed in relation to intraenterprise activity and conscious parallelism.

Intraenterprise Doctrine

An intraenterprise arrangement is where two or more parts of the same enterprise agree to restrain trade. For example, a corporation may have many different divisions, each responsible for a different line of products. The divisions might compete with each other; however, the divisions are all part of the same corporation. There is only one legal entity, so there can be no conspiracy or agreement. Similarly, a corporation cannot conspire with its own officers or other employees when they are acting within the scope of their employment.

Conscious Parallelism

Conscious parallelism occurs when many competitors copy the actions of a market leader. When a few large producers dominate a highly concentrated market, the market is said to be *oligopolistic*. A change in the output of any one dominant firm affects market conditions substantially, causing competitors to follow suit. Consciously parallel behavior usually affects price. Competitors copy the leader's announced increases or decreases.

Consciously parallel behavior does not violate Section 1 as long as each competitor has made its own independent decision. However, certain circumstances may suggest that what appears to be a series of independent decisions to copy a price leader actually is the result of an agreement among competitors. The evidence may include meetings or other communications among competitors, parallel action that would benefit one competitor only if all others took the same action, and an overly complex series of consciously parallel steps. When this type of evidence is present, a jury may find that the competitors violated Section 1.

Restraints of Trade—The Rule of Reason

Section 1 of the Sherman Act prohibits "every contract, combination . . . or conspiracy that restrains trade. . . ." The statute cannot be interpreted literally because virtually every contract restrains trade to a certain extent. For example, assume that a buyer intends to order 100 widgets and that several sellers are competing for that order. As soon as the buyer contracts with one seller, the others can no longer compete for the order. The contract has literally restrained trade. Thus, a literal interpretation of Section 1 would result in declaring every contract to be illegal. This result was clearly not intended by Congress.

When Congress enacted the Sherman Act, it was aware of the common law approach to restraints of trade. Therefore, courts have developed a rule of reason for interpreting Section 1.

The Rule of Reason

Every agreement concerning trade, every regulation of trade restrains. To bind, to restrain, is of their very essence. The true test of legality is whether the restraint imposed is such as merely regulates and perhaps thereby promotes competition or whether it is such as may suppress or even destroy competition. *U.S. v. Chicago Board of Trade,* 246 U.S. 231 (1918).

The **rule of reason** requires that a restraint be scrutinized for its purpose, effect, intent, and the power it confers on the parties. To be reasonable, a restraint must be used for a competitive business purpose and not have an effect beyond that purpose. A restraint is unreasonable if the parties intended to suppress competition unlawfully, even though they could not or did not achieve that goal. A restraint is also unreasonable if it confers on the parties the power to substitute their judgment for the judgment of the marketplace.

Per Se Violations

Per se unreasonable restraints are those whose effects on competition are so harmful that they cannot be justified. When such a restraint is involved, to find a violation of Section 1 a court need only determine that the restraint exists. In this way, the court bypasses a rigorous inquiry into the restraint's reasonableness.

The per se rule serves a number of important functions. First, by declaring certain restraints per se illegal, the rule sets a standard of unreasonableness against which other restraints may be measured. This spares courts the necessity of performing complex economic analyses, for which they are ill-suited. Second, a standard of unreasonableness promotes the stability and predictability necessary for business planning.

It is tempting to label all restraints as requiring analysis under either the rule of reason or the per se rule. However, such a breakdown would be misleading, because the per se rule is a specific application of the rule of reason. Restraints that at first may not appear to be per se unreasonable may, after preliminary analysis, prove identical with per se violations.

Horizontal Restraints

Horizontal restraints involve agreements between two or more competitors to avoid competing with each other. When they occur among sellers of different brands, they are said to suppress *interbrand* competition. When they occur among sellers of the same brand, they are said to suppress *intrabrand* competition. The most common horizontal restraints are price fixes and divisions of territories, customers, and markets.

Price Fixing

The horizontal restraint first declared to be per se illegal was the **price fix**. In a free market economy, price is set by the interaction of supply and demand. When two or more competitors agree to fix the prices for their goods or services, they substitute their judgment for that of the marketplace. The Sherman Act is concerned with the power to manipulate prices as well as with the effect of artificially determined prices. Thus, the reasonableness of the fixed price is irrelevant. A reasonably fixed price today may become an unreasonable price tomorrow. All price-fixing agreements are per se illegal.

Price-fixing arrangements are not limited to agreements that specify prices; conspiracies to stabilize prices, set a floor under prices, or set a maximum level for prices are also per se illegal. Few restraints blatantly set forth an agreement to fix prices. Thus, it is necessary to determine whether a seemingly innocuous restraint results in a price fix. If the parties to the restraint intend to set prices, the restraint is per se illegal despite its appearance or its actual effect.

For example, a new car dealers' association circulated a list of suggested retail prices that were higher than the manufacturer's sticker prices. Their purpose was to set a starting point for use in bargaining with customers. Although most sales were made below the suggested prices, the use of the list was held to be an illegal price fix.[1]

Not all business arrangements that affect prices are condemned as per se price fixes; many legitimate business arrangements also have incidental effects on price. For example, a group of competing sellers may organize a buying cooperative to take advantage of bulk discounts. Such an arrangement may affect price, but its effects on price are incidental to its legitimate business purpose. Similarly, the use of joint selling agents by competitors may incidentally reduce price competition while achieving economies of scale for the participants. Other actions, such as an agreement not to advertise prices, may be indirect price fixes and therefore per se illegal.

Divisions of Territories, Customers, and Markets

When two or more competitors get together and agree to divide up territories or customers, they necessarily avoid competing with one another. Such arrangements are per se violations of Section 1, even if the parties are free to set their own prices

---

[1] Plymouth Dealers' Association v. United States, 279 F.2d 128 (9th Cir. 1960).

within their territories. Each competitor has eliminated the competitive forces within its territory that check its economic power.

Horizontal territorial or customer divisions are equally illegal, whether they occur among sellers of competing brands or among sellers of the same brand. An agreement between two Ford dealers to divide customers is as illegal as a comparable agreement between a Ford dealer and a Chevrolet dealer. The protection of intrabrand competition from horizontal restraints has a priority equal to the protection of interbrand competition.

A horizontal territorial division that restrains intrabrand competition cannot be justified even if it promotes interbrand competition. For example, in *United States v. Topco Associates, Inc.,* 25 independent supermarket chains formed Topco to enable them to compete with larger national chains.[2] They developed and marketed Topco products, thereby giving themselves a private label line of merchandise they could not otherwise offer. Each member received an exclusive territory for the sale of Topco products. The Supreme Court held that the exclusive territories were per se illegal because their elimination of intrabrand competition could not be justified by their promoting competition between Topco members and national chains.

Vertical Restraints

Vertical restraints are agreements between two or more parties at different levels of the distribution process. Typically, they are agreements between manufacturer and distributor or retailer, or between franchisor and franchisee. Vertical restraints frequently sacrifice some intrabrand competition to further interbrand competition. The most common vertical restraints are (1) territorial, customer, and market restraints; (2) resale price maintenance; (3) tying devices; and (4) exclusive dealing arrangements. The first two involve only the Sherman Act; the last two are also covered by Section 3 of the Clayton Act.

At one time, the courts analyzed vertical restraints no differently from horizontal restraints. However, in recent years the courts have looked more favorably on vertical restraints and have allowed restraints on intrabrand competition where they promote interbrand competition. This reevaluation of vertical restraints began with territorial and other market divisions. It has also affected the courts' approach to resale price maintenance and tying devices.

Territorial, Customer, and Market Restraints

Manufacturers and franchisors frequently impose territorial restraints on their distributors, retailers, or franchisees. These restraints may take the form of exclusive territories or customer divisions. Less restrictive restraints may also be used,

---

[2] 405 U.S. 596 (1972).

such as assigning areas of primary responsibility or designating the location of a dealer or franchisee. Vertical territorial or customer restraints differ from horizontal restraints in that they are designed for the benefit of the manufacturer or the franchisor rather than for the benefit of the competing retailers, distributors, or franchisees.

Vertical territorial or customer divisions have received varied treatment from the Supreme Court. In *United States v. Arnold Schwinn & Co.*, the Court concluded that vertical territorial divisions were per se illegal if the manufacturer parted with ownership and control of the product.[3] Where the manufacturer retained title to the product, however, exclusive territories were not per se unreasonable.

Many manufacturers found it impossible to change their distribution systems in a manner that would ensure their retention of legal title to their products. These manufacturers resorted to assigning areas of primary responsibility and employing dealer location clauses. One such manufacturer was GTE Sylvania, Inc.

CONTINENTAL TV, INC. V. GTE SYLVANIA, INC.
433 U.S. 36 (1977)

Continental TV was a licensed dealer of GTE Sylvania products. Its license contained a dealer location clause prohibiting Continental from selling Sylvania products at locations other than the one specified. Continental violated the location clause by establishing a new store at another location and transferring Sylvania products from the approved location to the new location. Sylvania canceled Continental's dealership and Continental sued, contending that the dealer location clause violated Section 1 of the Sherman Act. The lower courts held for Sylvania. The Supreme Court affirmed.

Justice Powell

We turn first to Continental's contention that Sylvania's restriction on retail locations is a per se violation of section one of the Sherman Act as interpreted in *Schwinn*. The restrictions at issue in *Schwinn* were part of the three-tier distribution system. . . .

In the present case, it is undisputed that title to the television sets passed from Sylvania to Continental. . . . [W]e are unable to find a principled basis for distinguishing *Schwinn* from the case now before us.

Both Schwinn and Sylvania sought to reduce but not to eliminate competition among their respective retailers through the adoption of a franchise system. . . . In intent and competitive impact, the retail-customer restriction in *Schwinn is* indistinguishable from the location restriction in the present case. In both cases the restrictions limited the freedom of the retailer to dispose of the purchased products as he desired. The fact that one restriction was addressed to territory and the other to customers is irrelevant to functional antitrust analysis and, indeed, to the language and broad thrust of the opinion in *Schwinn*.

---

[3] 388 U.S. 350 (1967).

Sylvania argues that if *Schwinn* cannot be distinguished, it should be reconsidered. Although *Schwinn* is supported by the principle of stare decisis, we are convinced that the need for clarification of the law in this area justifies reconsideration. . . . Since its announcement, *Schwinn* has been the subject of continuing controversy and confusion. . . . The great weight of scholarly opinion has been critical of the decision, and a number of the federal courts confronted with analogous vertical restrictions have sought to limit its reach. In our view, the experience of the past 10 years should be brought to bear on this subject of considerable commercial importance.

The market impact of vertical restrictions is complex because of their potential for a simultaneous reduction of intrabrand competition and stimulation of interbrand competition. . . .

Vertical restrictions reduce intrabrand competition by limiting the number of sellers of a particular product competing for the business of a given group of buyers. Location restrictions have this effect because of practical constraints on the effective marketing area of retail outlets. Although intrabrand competition may be reduced, the ability of retailers to exploit the resulting market may be limited both by the ability of consumers to travel to other franchised locations and, perhaps more importantly, to purchase the competing products of other manufacturers. None of these key variables, however, is affected by the form of the transaction by which a manufacturer conveys his products to the retailers.

Vertical restrictions promote interbrand competition by allowing the manufacturer to achieve certain efficiencies in the distribution of his products. These "redeeming virtues" are implicit in every decision sustaining vertical restrictions under the rule of reason. Economists have identified a number of ways in which manufacturers can use such restrictions to compete more effectively against other manufacturers: For example, new manufacturers and manufacturers entering new markets can use the restrictions in order to induce competent and aggressive retailers to make the kind of investment of capital and labor that is often required in the distribution of products unknown to the consumer. Established manufacturers can use them to induce retailers to engage in promotional activities or to provide service and repair facilities necessary to the efficient marketing of their products. . . . The availability and quality of such services affect a manufacturer's goodwill and the competitiveness of his product. Because of market imperfections such as the so-called "free rider" effect, services might not be provided by retailers in a purely competitive situation, despite the fact that each retailer's benefit would be greater if all provided the services than if none did.

Economists also have argued that manufacturers have an economic interest in maintaining as much intrabrand competition as is consistent with the efficient distribution of their products. . . .

Accordingly, we conclude that the *per se* rule stated in *Schwinn* must be overruled. . . . When anticompetitive effects are shown to result from particular vertical restrictions they can be adequately policed under the rule of reason, the standard traditionally applied for the majority of anticompetitive practices challenged under section one of the Act.

Case Questions

1. Why did the Court conclude that Sylvania's dealer location clause was indistinguishable from Schwinn's customer restrictions?

2. Which factors led the Court to conclude that *Schwinn* should be overruled?

3. Which justifications exist for the conclusion that vertical territorial restraints are reasonable?

4. Which factors might lead a court to conclude that a vertical market allocation is unreasonable?

Vertical exclusive territories are not per se illegal, while horizontal exclusive territories are per se illegal. However, many manufacturers compete with their distributors and retailers and many franchisors compete with their franchisees. Frequently these manufacturers and franchisors also create exclusive territories. Territorial restraints in these situations have both vertical and horizontal components. The manufacturer or franchisor has to establish that the restraints are intended to promote interbrand competition, thereby enabling a court to conclude that they serve a vertical rather than a horizontal purpose. If a court concludes that they serve a horizontal purpose, the court holds them to be per se illegal.

Resale Price Maintenance

Resale price maintenance occurs when a manufacturer tries to control the retail price of its product. A manufacturer may wish to set a maximum retail price on its product as part of an aggressive campaign to take customers away from competitors. In other cases, it may want to maintain a minimum price to create an aura of high quality for its goods. If the manufacturer and retailer agree to minimum or maximum resale prices, the contract is a vertical price fix. From 1911 to 2007, such agreements were per se illegal.

Ethical Dilemmas/Issues

Melissa Blackburn is the marketing director for Kiddo Clothing, Inc., which manufactures children's swimwear. Consolidated Stores is a national retail department store chain with stores located throughout the country, and is one of Kiddo's biggest customers. Anne Weilbacher is the buyer in charge of purchasing swimwear for Consolidated's stores.

Children's Castle is a chain of discount stores specializing in toys and children's clothing. Its stores are located throughout the northeastern United States. Children's Castle sells Kiddo swimwear at a discounted price.

Anne telephoned Melissa and pointed out that Children's Castle has taken swimwear sales away from Consolidated's stores in cities where Consolidated and Children's Castle compete with each other. Anne told Melissa that Consolidated will not purchase Kiddo's swimwear if Kiddo continues to sell to Children's Castle.

What are the ethical issues? What would you do?

In *Leegin Creative Leather Products Inc. v. PSKS Inc.*[4] the Supreme Court abandoned the flat ban, illegal per se approach to vertical price maintenance agreements. Vertical price restraints are now judged by the rule of reason. The

---

[4] 551 U.S. ___ (2007).

Court said that "Vertical agreements establishing minimum resale prices can have either pro-competitive or anticompetitive effects, depending upon circumstances in which they are formed." When considering vertical price maintenance agreements for possible antitrust violations courts apply the case-by-case approach of the rule of reason and assess their impact on competition.

Not all resale price maintenance activity violates the Sherman Act. Section 1 requires a contract, combination, or conspiracy for a violation. Where there is only unilateral action by the initial seller, there is no violation. Thus, a manufacturer may lawfully maintain retail prices by suggesting retail prices and unilaterally terminating or refusing to deal with retailers that sell below the suggested prices.

Tying Devices

Tying devices, also known as **tie-ins**, occur when a party offers to provide one good or service only to those who agree to accept another good or service. The desired good is called the *tying product,* and the one the buyer is forced to take is called the *tied product.* Section 3 of the Clayton Act applies when a party conditions the sale or lease of goods or commodities on the buyer's agreement not to deal in or use the goods of the seller's competitors. These conditions are illegal where they may tend to substantially lessen competition or to create a monopoly.

All tie-ins are restraints of trade under Section 1 of the Sherman Act. When the tying and tied products are tangible commodities, the tie-in is also covered by Section 3 of the Clayton Act. There are three requirements for a tie-in.

First, a substantial amount of commerce must be affected. If the amount of commerce affected is insignificant, the impact of the tie-in on competition is trivial.

Second, two separate products or services must be involved. A situation in which two or more products must be sold together does not necessarily signal an illegal tie-in. If the two products are totally unrelated, the two-product requirement is satisfied, but some combinations of products are not tie-ins. For example, no tie-in exists even though it is impossible to purchase a new car without a spare tire. In determining if a particular arrangement is a valid package of goods or an illegal tie-in, the courts consider whether (1) others in the field offer the products separately, (2) the number of pieces in each package varies considerably, (3) the purchaser is charged separately for each item, and (4) some of the items are available separately to other consumers.

Third, the defendant must have sufficient economic power in the tying product to enforce the tie-in. For example, if a supermarket refuses to sell eggs unless the customer also purchases bacon, no tie-in exists if the customer can buy eggs separately at a store down the street. If, however, the supermarket is the only local source of eggs, it probably possesses sufficient economic power to enforce the tie.

When the preceding three requirements are met, the tie-in is a per se violation of the antitrust laws. It restrains competition in the product that the customer is forced to purchase. The customer purchases the tied product only because of the coercion applied. Price, quality, service, and other characteristics in which sellers usually compete become largely irrelevant. The following case illustrates the Supreme Court's approach to tie-ins.

EASTMAN KODAK CO. V. IMAGE TECHNICAL SERVICES , INC.
112 S. Ct. 2072 (1992)

Kodak (petitioner) makes and sells photocopiers. It also provides service and replacement parts for its customers' copiers. Independent service organizations (ISOs; respondents) began servicing Kodak equipment and selling replacement parts to Kodak equipment. ISOs provided service at a price substantially lower than Kodak.

Kodak began a policy of selling replacement parts only to buyers of Kodak equipment who use Kodak service. Kodak also would not sell parts to ISOs.

ISOs were unable to obtain parts. Many were forced out of business, and others lost substantial revenue. Customers were forced to switch to Kodak service even though many preferred ISO services.

The ISOs sued Kodak, alleging that Kodak had unlawfully tied the sale of service for Kodak machines to the sale of parts. The district court granted summary judgment for Kodak. The Ninth Circuit Court of Appeals reversed the district court judgment. The Supreme Court affirmed the Ninth Circuit's decision.

Justice Blackmun

A tying arrangement is an agreement by a party to sell one product but only on the condition that the buyer also purchases a different (or tied) product, or at least agrees that he will not purchase that product from any other supplier. Such an arrangement violates Section I of the Sherman Act if the seller has "appreciable economic power" in the tying product market and if the arrangement affects a substantial volume of commerce in the tied market.

Kodak . . . challenge[d] . . . whether Kodak exercised "appreciable economic power" in the tying market. . . .

Market power is the power to force a purchaser to do something that he would not do in a competitive market. . . .

Respondents . . . allege that Kodak's control over the parts market has excluded service competition, boosted service prices, and forced unwilling consumption of Kodak service. Respondents offer evidence that consumers have switched to Kodak service even though they preferred ISO service, that Kodak service was of higher price and lower quality than the preferred ISO service, and that ISOs were driven out of business by Kodak's policies. Under our prior precedents, this evidence would be sufficient to entitle respondents to a trial on their claim of market power.

Kodak counters that . . . it cannot actually exercise the necessary market power for a Sherman Act violation. This is so, according to Kodak, because competition exists in the equipment market. Kodak argues that it could not have the ability to raise prices of service and parts above the level that would be charged in a competitive market because any increase in profits from a higher price in the aftermarkets at least would be offset by a corresponding loss in profits from lower equipment sales as consumers began purchasing equipment with more attractive service costs.

Kodak does not present any actual data on the equipment, service, or parts markets. Instead, it urges the adoption of a substantive legal rule that equipment competition precludes any finding of monopoly power in derivative aftermarkets. . . .

Legal presumptions that rest on formalistic distinctions rather than actual market realities are generally disfavored in antitrust law. This Court has preferred to resolve antitrust claims on a case-by-case basis, focusing on the particular facts disclosed by the record. In determining the existence of market power, and specifically the responsiveness of the sales of one product to price changes of the other, this Court has examined closely the economic reality of the market at issue.

Kodak contends that there is no need to examine the facts when the issue is market power in the aftermarkets. A legal presumption against a finding of market power is warranted in this situation, according to Kodak, because the existence of market power in the service and parts markets absent power in the equipment market simply makes no economic sense. . . .

Kodak . . . bears a substantial burden in showing that it is entitled to summary judgment. It must show that despite evidence of increased prices and excluded competition, an inference of market power is unreasonable. . . .

Does Kodak's theory describe actual market behavior so accurately that respondents' assertion of Kodak market power in the aftermarkets, if not impossible, is at least unreasonable?

To review Kodak's theory, it contends that higher service prices will lead to a disastrous drop in equipment sales. . . . Yet, according to the record . . . [s]ervice prices have risen for Kodak customers, but there is no evidence or assertion that Kodak equipment sales have dropped. . . .

Kodak and the United States attempt to reconcile Kodak's theory with the contrary actual results by describing a marketing strategy of spreading over time the total cost to the buyer of Kodak equipment. In other words, Kodak could charge subcompetitive prices for equipment and make up the difference with supracompetitive prices for service, resulting in an overall competitive price. This pricing strategy would provide an explanation for the theory's descriptive failings—if Kodak in fact had adopted it. But Kodak never has asserted that it prices its equipment or parts subcompetitively and recoups its profits through service. Instead, it claims that it prices its equipment comparably to its competitors, and intends that both its equipment sales and service divisions be profitable. . . . In sum, Kodak's theory does not explain the actual market behavior revealed in the record.

Respondents offer a forceful reason why Kodak's theory, although perhaps intuitively appealing, may not accurately explain the behavior of the primary and derivative markets for complex durable goods: the existence of significant information and switching costs. These costs could create a less responsive connection between service and parts prices and equipment sales.

For the service-market price to affect equipment demand, consumers must inform themselves of the total cost of the "package"—equipment, service and parts—at the time of purchase; that is, consumers must engage in accurate life-cycle pricing. Life-cycle pricing of complex, durable equipment is difficult and costly. . . .

During the life of a product, companies may change the service and parts prices, and develop products with more advanced features, a decreased need for repair, or new warranties. . . .

A second factor undermining Kodak's claim that supracompetitive prices in the service market lead to ruinous losses in equipment sales is the cost to current owners of switching to a different product. If the cost of switching is high, consumers who already have purchased the equipment, and are thus "locked-in," will tolerate some level of service-price increases before changing equipment brands. . . .

We conclude, then, that Kodak has failed to demonstrate that respondents' inference of market power in the service and parts markets is unreasonable, and that, consequently, Kodak is entitled to summary judgment. It is clearly reasonable to infer that Kodak has market power to raise prices and drive out competition in the aftermarkets, since respondents offer direct evidence that Kodak did so.

Case Questions

1. What is a tying agreement? When will a tying agreement violate the antitrust laws?
2. In order to obtain a summary judgment (and perhaps win at trial) what must Kodak (or any other business defendant) show in order to avoid liability for an illegal tie-in when there is evidence of increased prices and excluded competition resulting from its tie-in policy?
3. What is the potential impact of Kodak on the service and parts aftermarket in high-tech industries (which represent an enormous portion of the U.S. economy)?
4. What should a manufacturer that sells a product for which there is an aftermarket in parts and/or service do in response to Kodak? Explain.
5. What does the Court's opinion say about the role of naked economic theory and actual market conduct in antitrust law? Initial reaction to Kodak varied. A former assistant attorney general in charge of the Justice Department's Antitrust Division under the Reagan administration labeled the decision a return "to the dark ages of antitrust," and characterized the Court's opinion as a "dramatic departure from the economic enlightenment apparent in most of the Court's recent antitrust opinions." Another expert commented that the decision "promotes the interest of consumers in a way that is entirely consistent with the Court's recent opinions." With whom do you agree? Does Kodak signal less and less emphasis on economic analysis for the future? Consider the other cases included in this chapter. Does the Court's opinion represent a doctrinal shift in antitrust law? Explain.

Exclusive Dealing Agreements

Exclusive dealing agreements are contracts that require the buyer to purchase all of its requirements of a given commodity from the seller. Such arrangements may be made at the insistence of the seller or by mutual agreement. In the latter situation, the buyer is ensured of a constant supply, protected against price increases, and avoids the costs of storage; meanwhile, the seller reduces its selling expenses, is protected against market fluctuations, and is afforded a predictable market for its product. Exclusive dealing arrangements violate Section 3, where "competition has been foreclosed in a substantial share of the line of commerce affected." Exclusive dealing arrangements are more likely to be found legal where they are not imposed by a dominant party on a weaker party and where they are not industrywide practices.

Justice Department Guidelines

On January 23, 1985, for the first time in its history, the Justice Department issued vertical restraint guidelines. The following are the highlights of the guidelines:

1. Per se violations require express or circumstantial evidence of an explicit agreement to fix resale prices.

2. Restraints that are always lawful include selective distribution through a limited number of dealers, dealer location clauses, assigning areas of primary responsibility, and profit passover arrangements whereby a dealer selling in another dealer's area of primary responsibility must compensate that other dealer for promotional and servicing costs.

3. Territorial and exclusive dealing restraints are analyzed under a two-step approach.

   Step 1 requires calculating the vertical restraint index (VRI) by summing the squares of the market shares of each firm that is a party to an arrangement containing the restraint. For example, if two manufacturers use exclusive dealer territories and one has a 5 percent market share while the other has a 25 percent market share, the VRI = 25 + 625 = 650. Step 1 also requires calculating the coverage ratio, which is the percentage of each market involved in the restraint. In this example, the coverage ratio at the manufacturer's level is 30 percent. Under Step 1, the Justice Department does not challenge a restraint if the market share of the party imposing the restraint is 10 percent or less, or if each level of the market has a VRI of 1,200 or less or a coverage ratio below 60 percent.

   If the restraint does not pass Step 1, the department analyzes it further. Step 2 focuses on market structure, ease of entry, the VRIs and coverage ratios, whether market conditions are conducive to collusion, the exclusionary effects of the restraint, the intent of the parties, and the size of the firms.

4. The department does not challenge tie-ins where the firm's market share in the tying product is less than 30 percent.

Group Boycotts

An individual may refuse to deal with anyone without violating Section 1 of the Sherman Act. Many **group boycotts**, or concerted refusals to deal, however, are per se violations of the act.

The application of the per se rule to group boycotts arose from cases in which a group of firms at one level of the market coerced a group of firms at another level not to deal with competitors of the first group. For example, a group of retail lumber dealers circulated a blacklist to induce all retailers not to deal with wholesalers who also sold lumber at retail discount prices.[5] This practice was held illegal. Similarly, it was illegal for a group of automobile dealers to induce General Motors not to deal with competing discount outlets.[6]

Many group activities viewed literally are concerted refusals to deal. For example, a trade association might refuse to admit an applicant for membership. A buying or advertising cooperative might expel a member. For many years the law

[5] Eastern States Retail Lumber Dealers Assoc. v. United States, 193 U.S. 38 (1904).
[6] United States v. General Motors Corp., 384 U.S. 17 (1966).

was unclear concerning how these actions should be evaluated when challenged under the Sherman Act. In the following case, the Supreme Court sought to clarify the law.

NORTHWEST WHOLESALE STATIONERS, INC. v. PACIFIC STATIONERY & PRINTING CO.
472 U.S. 284 (1985)

Northwest (petitioner) was an office-supply wholesale-buying cooperative of which Pacific (respondent) was a member. Members were able to purchase products at effectively lower prices than nonmembers. Petitioner expelled respondent from membership, claiming that the expulsion was for failing to notify petitioner of a change in its ownership. Respondent maintained that the expulsion was for operating a competing wholesale operation.

The district court granted summary judgment for Northwest. The Ninth Circuit reversed, holding that the expulsion was a concerted refusal to deal, and, therefore, per se illegal. The Supreme Court reversed the Ninth Circuit.

Justice Brennan

This case . . . turns . . . on whether the decision to expel Pacific is properly viewed as a group boycott or concerted refusal to deal mandating per se invalidation. "Group boycotts" are often listed among the classes of economic activity that merit per se invalidation under §1. Exactly what types of activity fall within the forbidden category is, however, far from certain. . . . Some care is therefore necessary in defining the category of concerted refusals to deal that mandate per se condemnation.

Cases to which this Court has applied the per se approach have generally involved joint efforts by a firm or firms to disadvantage competitors by "either directly denying or persuading or coercing suppliers or customers to deny relationships the competitors need in the competitive struggle." In these cases, the boycott often cuts off access to a supply, facility, or market necessary to enable the boycotted firm to compete, and frequently the boycotting firms possessed a dominant position in the relevant market. In addition, the practices were generally not justified by plausible arguments that they were intended to enhance overall efficiency and make markets more competitive. Under such circumstances the likelihood of anticompetitive effects is clear and the possibility of countervailing procompetitive effects is remote.

Although a concerted refusal to deal need not necessarily possess all of these traits to merit per se treatment, not every cooperative activity involving a restraint or exclusion will share with the per se forbidden boycotts the likelihood of predominantly anticompetitive consequences. . . .

Wholesale purchasing cooperatives such as Northwest are not a form of concerted activity characteristically likely to result in predominantly anticompetitive effects. Rather, such cooperative arrangements would seem to be "designed to increase economic efficiency and render markets more, rather than less, competitive." The arrangement permits the participating retailers to achieve economies of scale in both the purchase and warehousing of wholesale supplies, and also ensures ready access to a stock of goods that might otherwise be unavailable on short notice. The cost savings and order-filling guarantees enable smaller retailers to reduce prices and maintain their retail stock so as to compete more effectively with larger retailers.

Pacific, of course, does not object to the existence of the cooperative arrangement, but rather raises an antitrust challenge to Northwest's decision to bar Pacific from continued membership. It is therefore the action of expulsion that must be evaluated to determine whether per se treatment is appropriate. The act of expulsion from a wholesale cooperative does not necessarily imply anticompetitive animus and thereby raise a probability of anticompetitive effect. Wholesale purchasing cooperatives must establish and enforce reasonable rules in order to function effectively. Disclosure rules, such as the one on which Northwest relies, may well provide the cooperative with a needed means for monitoring the credit worthiness of its members. Nor would the expulsion characteristically be likely to result in predominantly anticompetitive effects, at least in the type of situation this case presents. Unless the cooperative possesses market power or exclusive access to an element essential to effective competition, the conclusion that expulsion is virtually always likely to have an anticompetitive effect is not warranted. Absent such a showing with respect to a cooperative buying arrangement, courts should apply a rule-of-reason analysis. At no time has Pacific made a threshold showing that these structural characteristics are present in this case.

Case Questions

1. Which types of group boycotts are per se illegal? Why are they per se illegal?

2. What is a wholesale cooperative? Why is it not per se illegal?

3. Why is the expulsion from a wholesale cooperative usually not per se illegal?

4. Did the Supreme Court rule that Pacific's expulsion was legal? Why or why not?

International Antitrust

Competition law plays an important role in the international economy. U.S. antitrust enforcement extends beyond the borders of the United States. Where foreign cartels aimed at fixing prices or allocating markets in the United States are launched from abroad, the Justice Department and the Federal Trade Commission are empowered to prosecute their foreign as well as American participants.

Also, in an effort to increase competitiveness, other nations have adopted many of the antitrust concepts developed in American law. U.S. antitrust law has served as a model for competition law in the development of new capitalist economies in Eastern and Central Europe. The Justice Department and the FTC have sent lawyer/economist teams to provide technical assistance to the antitrust agencies in several countries that are developing market economies, such as Poland, Czechoslovakia, and the republics of the former Soviet Union. As a result, several countries now recognize price fixing as a serious economic threat.

There has additionally been an interest in the harmonization of competition law among nations. For example, a treaty between the European Community

(EC) (which enforces its own competition law) and the United States provides a mechanism for reinforcing each other's antitrust efforts. Under the treaty, the European Community and the United States have agreed to cooperate with each other and to coordinate antitrust enforcement in order to avoid or minimize any differences that may arise. This is important, because the basic objective of competition law in the European Community is the integration of the economies of the Community's member states, an objective that is not necessarily consistent with its secondary objective of promoting effective competition. The objective of U.S. antitrust law in recent years has been to enhance consumer welfare. These different objectives may determine the outcome of cases involving companies on both sides of the Atlantic. The treaty between the European Community and the United States provides a way to minimize potential differences arising out of different policy objectives between these international trading partners.

Chapter Problems

1. Define the following terms:
   a. Contract, combination, or conspiracy
   b. Conscious parallelism
   c. Rule of reason
   d. Per se unreasonable restraints
   e. Horizontal restraint
   f. Price fix
   g. Vertical restraint
   h. Resale price maintenance
   i. Tie-in
   j. Group boycott

2. Widget Works, Inc. is a holding company that wholly owns two subsidiaries: Alpha Widgets, Inc. and Beta Widgets, Inc. Alpha and Beta manufacture widgets and compete against each other. Alpha and Beta have agreed that neither will charge less than $22.50 per case of widgets. Does the agreement violate Section 1 of the Sherman Act? Why or why not?

3. Eight companies dominate the U.S. market in distributing motion picture films to movie theaters. They operate by licensing theaters to show the movies for a specified time period. Most movie manufacturers use more than one distributor for each movie. Each distributor received a letter from the largest movie theater chain asking it to refuse to do business with theaters that show double features. Two weeks after the letter was sent, two of the eight companies announced that they would refuse to license theaters that showed double features with first-run movies. One week later, the other six made similar announcements. Can a conspiracy among the eight be inferred from the preceding facts? Explain.

4. Wholesale beer distributors in California frequently have given retailers short-term, interest-free credit. Recently, a group of wholesalers have agreed to sell beer only if the purchasing retailer pays for the order at the time of or prior to delivery. The wholesalers believe that the agreement will stimulate competition by making price more visible to the retailers and by making it easier for new firms to enter the wholesale market. Evaluate the wholesalers' risk of Sherman Act liability.

5. Your corporation operates a national chain of discount department stores. You wish to induce independent food retailers to operate under the same roof and under the same name as your stores. You propose to license these retailers to use your company's name and to lease them space in your stores. You would limit the number and types of nonfood items they can sell and require them to charge competitive prices on all goods they sell. If they sell any items that you also sell, you require that they charge the same price that you charge. Will the proposal, if implemented, violate Section 1 of the Sherman Act? Explain.

6. Semolina wheat is used in the manufacture of macaroni. Most macaroni manufacturers use almost 100 percent semolina. Due to severe weather, the semolina harvest this year was poor. If all macaroni manufacturers continue to use 100 percent semolina, demand will far outstrip supply. Can the manufacturers agree to limit the semolina content of their macaroni without violating Section 1 of the Sherman Act? Explain.

7. You are vice president for marketing for a major furniture manufacturer. One of your marketing managers has advised you that many of your retail dealers in the Northeast, Midwest, and West have complained that two dealers in the South are offering discount prices nationwide through mail- and telephone-order catalogues. The manager suggested that the company impose a new policy prohibiting dealers from selling by mail or telephone to customers residing outside their states. The manager called the new policy "a pledge to our dealers to protect them from price cutters," and said that the complaining dealers agreed with the proposed new policy and had promised to help you enforce it. Evaluate the legality of implementing the manager's proposal.

8. East Jefferson Hospital is located in Jefferson Parish, Louisiana. Thirty percent of the patients residing in Jefferson Parish enter East Jefferson. The hospital agreed with Roux & Associates that Roux would provide all anesthesiology services needed by Jefferson patients. The hospital refused to allow any other anesthesiologists to provide these services to its patients. Hyde, another anesthesiologist, sued the hospital, claiming that the hospital's arrangement with Roux violates the antitrust laws. Is the hospital's agreement with Roux illegal? Explain.

9. You are the marketing manager for a distributor of first-run motion pictures. Your responsibility includes the Memphis, Tennessee area. The major theater chains in that area have advised you that they are willing to divide the

first-run motion pictures among themselves so that only one chain would bid on the rights to show any given movie in the Memphis area. They have asked your company to agree to deal only with their designated chain. If your company agrees to reject bids from independent theaters, they agree to match any independent bid that exceeds theirs. They also agree that if your company prefers a chain other than the one they selected to receive the picture, they would make the change. Evaluate your company's potential Sherman Act liability if it agrees to this arrangement.

10. A large group of banks recently met to discuss creating a new bank credit card. The banks would form a membership cooperative. All members would be entitled to issue the card, charge cardholders whatever interest rate and service fee they wish, and charge merchants whatever fee they wish for redeeming credit slips. The cooperative would serve as a clearinghouse to transfer funds between the banks that issued the card on which a purchase is charged and the bank that redeems the credit slip from the merchant. The cooperative would also run credit checks on credit card applicants, distribute to merchants lists of invalid cards, and provide similar services for member banks. Member banks would be prohibited from issuing a competing credit card, such as VISA or MasterCard. Will this prohibition be legal? Explain.

20 MONOPOLIES AND MERGERS

Learning Objectives

After learning this chapter the student
should be able to:

- Apply the three-step analysis used
  to determine whether a firm has
  violated Section 2 of the Sherman
  Act.

- Compare and contrast the following
  violations of Section 2 of the
  Sherman Act: (1) monopolization,
  (2) attempts to monopolize, and (3)
  combining or conspiring to
  monopolize.

- Apply the two-step process used to
  determine whether a merger
  violates Section 7 of the Clayton
  Act to (1) horizontal mergers, (2)
  vertical mergers, and (3)
  conglomerate mergers.

- Describe the defenses available
  under the Clayton Act to justify
  mergers.

- Describe the following enforcement
  procedures applied to mergers: (1)
  the Federal Trade Commission's
  premerger notification procedure;
  (2) the Justice Department's merger
  guidelines; and (3) court remedies.

The previous chapter discussed illegal trade restraints under the antitrust laws, focusing on anticompetitive trade practices. This chapter concerns problems of market structure that may lead to anticompetitive market conditions. Such conditions occur when one firm threatens to dominate a market either by becoming a monopolist or by merging with another firm. Thus, this chapter focuses both on monopolization, which is outlawed by Section 2 of the Sherman Act, and on illegal mergers, covered by Section 7 of the Clayton Act.

Monopolies: Section 2 of the Sherman Act

Section 2 of the Sherman Act prohibits (1) monopolizing, (2) attempts to monopolize, and (3) combining and conspiring with others to monopolize. Bigness alone is not prohibited, even if the firm is the largest in the industry. It is the anticompetitive exercise of economic power that the Sherman Act prohibits.

Courts have applied the rule of reason to Section 2, recognizing that success achieved through legitimate means should not be penalized. Thus, introducing superior products, giving better service, or setting more attractive prices are normally lawfully consistent with the goal of encouraging competition. When businesses use these acts or others with predatory intent to gain a monopoly of a particular product or geographic market, however, a Section 2 violation may occur. Under these circumstances, a company can be charged with violating Section 2 even though it may not be the largest company in its industry.

Sherman Act, Section 2

Every person who shall monopolize, or attempt to monopolize, or combine or conspire with any other person or persons, to monopolize any part of the trade or commerce among the several States, or with foreign nations, shall be deemed guilty of a felony. . . .

Monopolization

Section 2 of the Sherman Act does not outlaw monopolies; it is the act of **monopolization** that is forbidden. Monopolization is defined as the exercise of monopoly power within a relevant product and geographic market with the intent to monopolize. Determining whether a company has violated Section 2 involves a three-step analysis:

- Determining the relevant market (product and geographic).
- Determining if the firm has monopoly power within the relevant market.
- Determining whether the firm exercised monopoly power with intent to monopolize.

Determining the Relevant Market

To determine if a firm is a monopolist, one must first define the **relevant market** in which the firm operates. That market provides a framework for assessing a firm's economic power. This is a critically important factor in a monopolization case, because if a business can obtain a broad definition of the relevant market, it may be able to show that it has less economic power. Thus, in Section 2, one must first think of market by product and by place.

To determine if two or more products operate in the same relevant market, courts focus on the interchangeability or substitutability of one product for another. For example, suppose that the concern is whether the Seven-Up Company (7-Up) is a monopolist. Is the relevant product market lemon-lime soft drinks, all soda soft drinks (including cola drinks), all soft drinks (including such drinks as Kool-Aid), or all cold beverages (including alcoholic beverages)? Determining 7-Up's product market involves analyzing to what extent consumers substitute each of these beverages for 7-Up. The factors that courts consider include product differentiation (how functionally different the products are from one another), the barriers of entry into a market (in our example, a court may consider to what extent Kool-Aid can be marketed in bottles and cans), patterns of distribution, and consumer preference. Perhaps the two most important factors are functional interchangeability (how the products physically differ from one another) and consumer preference.

The relevant geographic market essentially is the place where sellers compete. For example, the soft drink manufacturers may sell their products nationwide, so the geographic market may be considered a national market. However, other products and services may be sold only in certain regions of the country, or may be sold only in cities of a certain size. In considering the relevant geographic market, courts take a practical approach and consider such factors as seller and buyer behavior, corporate organizational structures, distribution networks, and transportation costs.

Determining Monopoly Power

To be a monopolist under Section 2, a firm also must have **monopoly power** in its relevant market. **Monopoly power** is defined as the ability to raise prices and exclude competitors independent of the market forces of supply and demand.

The starting point for determining market power is to decide the alleged monopolist's **market share**, expressed as a percentage of production, units sold, or revenue. This is frequently the end point as well. A firm possessing a market share between 85 percent and 100 percent is deemed conclusively to have monopoly power, while a firm whose share is less than 50 percent would be found to lack such power. When a firm controls between 50 percent and 85 percent of the market, factors beyond percentage share of the market must be considered. These additional factors include the structure of the market, barriers to entry into the market, and the strength of the alleged monopolist's competitors. Conduct inconsistent with a competitive marketplace, such as the imposition of one-sided contract terms on customers or suppliers, is further evidence of monopoly power.

Prices charged or profits made, however, are generally not relevant to the determination.

Intent to Monopolize

The mere existence of monopoly power does not violate Section 2 of the Sherman Act. Bigness alone is not bad. The alleged monopolist must have acted with the intent to monopolize. This is sometimes referred to as the **purposeful act requirement**. That is, under Section 2, it is not illegal to be a monopoly; what is illegal is the act of monopolizing. Thus, a Section 2 violation requires monopoly power plus a purposeful act to either obtain or maintain that position. The purposeful act usually consists of some condemned or anticompetitive business behavior reflecting the firm's intent to monopolize.

Even when there is no specific intent behind a firm's actions, courts examine the reasonably foreseeable consequences of those actions. If monopoly power is a reasonably foreseeable consequence, courts find that the firm intended to monopolize. This standard of assessing market behavior is known as the **general intent** test.

Thus, a specific intent to violate Section 2 is not required for a firm to be guilty of monopolization; all that is required is for the firm to engage in conduct which foreseeably leads to the acquisition or maintenance of monopoly power. Many actions have, as their reasonably foreseeable consequences, the acquisition of monopoly power. These actions are not limited to predatory, immoral, or unfair practices. They encompass actions that, in the absence of monopoly power, would generally be regarded as good business practices. For example, long-term equipment leases have the foreseeable effect of maintaining a monopolist's dominant market share.

When a firm achieves monopoly power without intending to, it is a passive beneficiary of a monopoly because that monopoly has been thrust on it. Such monopolies are referred to as **passive monopolies**, or thrust-upon monopolies. These legal monopolies exist when the government confers a monopoly on a firm, as in the case of public utilities and patents. In some cases, a market is so small that only one firm can efficiently and profitably serve it. An example of this is a single movie theater in a town whose population can support only one theater. Other examples include changes in taste that drive out all but one producer, or a producer who develops a new product or technology and is the only firm in the market until other producers enter it. Finally, the alleged monopolist may have achieved its position as a result of a superior product or superior business acumen. In these instances, where as a result of **superior skill, foresight, and industry** one firm is the sole survivor of a group of active competitors, that firm is not viewed as a monopolist. Even so, thrust-upon monopolies, or those obtained through superior skill, foresight, and industry, take on a public service nature much like regulated industries. Thus, they may not undertake many normal business practices without falling suspect of monopolization. If the foreseeable result of a passive monopolist's business practice is to exclude competition, the practice violates Section 2 as a purposeful act of monopolization.

Monopoly power not otherwise unlawful may violate Section 2 if it was improperly obtained or is improperly used or maintained. For example, a firm may enter and compete for a market that can support only one company, but it violates Section 2 if it uses predatory or other unfair methods to drive out its competitors.

In some instances, a firm with a lawfully acquired monopoly may be required not only to refrain from using its power to gain a competitive advantage in another market but also to give its competitors access to its monopoly. Illustrative is *United States v. Terminal Railroad Association.*[1] Because of its geography, St. Louis could accommodate only one railroad terminal. Several railroads combined to form the Terminal Railroad Association, which owned and operated the city's sole terminal. The association required the unanimous consent of its members to allow nonmember railroads access to the facility. The court held that it violated Section 2 by refusing appropriate and equal use of the terminal to nonmember companies. The following case raises similar issues of misuse of monopoly power.

ASPEN SKIING COMPANY C. ASPEN HIGHLANDS SKIING CORPORATION
472 U.S. 585 (1985)

Aspen Skiing (Ski Co.) (petitioner) owned and operated three of the four skiing facilities in the Aspen, Colorado, area. Aspen Highlands (Highlands) (respondent) owned and operated the fourth. Ski Co. had over 80 percent of the market. For 15 years, the companies offered a six-day ticket that would admit the holder to all four areas and divided the proceeds based on usage. In 1977, Ski Co., however, refused to renew the arrangement unless Highlands agreed to take a fixed percentage of the proceeds. After negotiations the parties set Highlands's share at 15 percent.

The following year, Ski Co. demanded that Aspen Highlands reduce its share to 12.5 percent, an offer that Ski Co. knew Highlands could not accept. Ski Co. then terminated the arrangement and began selling a six-day ticket limited to its three mountains. Ski Co. also refused to sell Highlands tickets to Ski Co.'s properties, even when Highlands offered to pay full retail price. Highlands then developed a package consisting of a three-day lift ticket at Highlands's mountain and three vouchers each equal to the retail price of a one-day ticket at Ski Co.'s mountains. Although the vouchers were guaranteed by funds on deposit at an Aspen bank, Ski Co. refused to accept them.

Highland's share of the market declined steadily after that. It sued Ski Co. in federal district court, claiming that Ski Co. had monopolized the market for downhill skiing services at Aspen in violation of Section 2 of the Sherman Act. The jury found for Highlands, and the district judge awarded Highlands treble damages

---

[1] 284 U.S. 383 (1912).

(three times the monetary harm) of $7.5 million and attorney fees. Ski Co. appealed to the circuit court of appeals, which affirmed the trial court judgment, and to the Supreme Court of the United States, which also affirmed.

Justice Stevens

In her instructions to the jury, the District Judge explained that the offense of monopolization under Section 2 of the Sherman Act has two elements: (1) the possession of monopoly power in a relevant market, and (2) the willful acquisition, maintenance, or use of that power by anticompetitive or exclusionary means or for anticompetitive or exclusionary purposes. . . .

On the [second] element, the jury was instructed that it had to consider whether "Aspen Skiing Corporation willfully acquired, maintained, or used that power by anti-competitive or exclusionary means or for anti-competitive and exclusionary purposes." The instructions elaborated:

> In considering whether the means or purposes were anti-competitive or exclusionary, you must draw a distinction here between practices which tend to exclude or restrict competition on the one hand and the success of a business which reflects only a superior product, a well-run business, or luck, on the other. The line between legitimately gained monopoly, its proper use and maintenance, and improper conduct has been described in various ways. It has been said that obtaining or maintaining monopoly power cannot present monopolization if the power was gained and maintained by conduct that was honestly industrial. Or it is said that monopoly power which is thrust upon a firm due to its superior business ability and efficiency does not constitute monopolization.
>
> For example, a firm that has lawfully acquired a monopoly position is not barred from taking advantage of scale economies by constructing a large and efficient factory. These benefits are a consequence of size and not an exercise of monopoly power. Nor is a corporation which possesses monopoly power under a duty to cooperate with its

business rivals. Also a company which possesses monopoly power and which refuses to enter into a joint operating agreement with a competitor or otherwise refuses to deal with a competitor in some manner does not violate Section 2 if valid business reasons exist for that refusal.

> In other words, if there were legitimate business reasons for the refusal, then the defendant, even if he is found to possess monopoly power in a relevant market has not violated the law. We are concerned with conduct which unnecessarily excludes or handicaps competitors. This is conduct which does not benefit consumers by making a better product or service available—or in other ways—and instead has the effect of impairing competition.
>
> To sum up, you must determine whether Aspen Skiing Corporation gained, maintained, or used monopoly power in a relevant market by arrangements and policies which rather than being a consequence of a superior product, superior business sense, or historic element, were designed primarily to further any domination of the relevant market or submarket.

The jury answered a specific interrogatory finding the second element of the offense as defined in these instructions.

In this Court, Ski Co. contends that even a firm with monopoly power has no duty to engage in joint marketing with a competitor, that a violation of Section 2 cannot be established without evidence of substantial exclusionary conduct, and that none of its activities can be characterized as exclusionary. . . . [I]t is surely correct in submitting that even a firm with monopoly power has no general duty to engage in a joint marketing program with a competitor. Ski Co. is quite wrong, however, in suggesting that the judgment in this case rests on any such proposition of law. For the trial court unambiguously instructed the jury that a firm possessing monopoly power has no duty to cooperate with its business rivals.

The absence of an unqualified duty to cooperate does not mean that every time a firm declines to participate in a particular cooperative venture, that decision may not have evidentiary significance, or that it may not give rise to liability in certain circumstances. The absence of a duty to transact business with another firm is, in some respects, merely the counterpart of the independent businessman's cherished right to select his customers and his associates. The high value that we have placed on the right to refuse to deal with other firms does not mean that the right is unqualified. In *Lorain Journal,* we squarely held that the right was not unqualified. . . .

In *Lorain Journal,* the violation of Section 2 was an "attempt to monopolize," rather than monopolization, but the question of intent is relevant to both offenses. In the former case it is necessary to prove a "specific intent" to accomplish the forbidden objective—as Judge Hand explained, "an intent which goes beyond the mere intent to do the act." In the latter case evidence of intent is merely relevant to the question whether the challenged conduct is fairly characterized as "exclusionary" or "anticompetitive "—to use words in the trial court's instructions—or "predatory," to use a word that scholars seem to favor. Whichever label is used, there is agreement on the proposition that "no monopolist monopolizes unconscious of what he is doing." As Judge Bork stated more recently: "Improper exclusion (exclusion not the result of superior efficiency) is always deliberately intended."[2] . . .

In the actual case that we must decide, the monopolist did not merely reject a novel offer to participate in a cooperative venture that had been proposed by a competitor. Rather the monopolist elected to make an important change in a pattern of distribution that had originated in a competitive market and had persisted for several years. The all-Aspen, 6-day ticket with revenues allocated on the basis of usage was first developed when three independent companies operated three different ski mountains in the Aspen area. It continued to provide a desirable option for skiers when the market was enlarged to include four mountains, and when the character of the market was changed by Ski Co.'s acquisition of monopoly power. Moreover, since the record discloses that interchangeable tickets are used in other multi-mountain areas which apparently are competitive, it seems appropriate to infer that such tickets satisfy consumer demand in free competitive markets.

Ski Co.'s decision to terminate the all-Aspen ticket was thus a decision by a monopolist to make an important change in the character of the market.[3] Such a decision is not necessarily anticompetitive, and Ski Co. contends that neither its decision, nor the conduct in which it engaged to implement that decision, can fairly be characterized as exclusionary in this case. . . .

[W]e must assume that the jury followed the court's instructions. The jury must, therefore, have drawn a distinction "between practices which tend to exclude or restrict competition on the one hand, and the success of a business which reflects only a superior product, a well-run business, or luck, on the other hand." Since the jury was unambiguously instructed that Ski Co.'s refusal to deal with Highlands "does not violate section 2 if valid business reasons exist for that refusal," we must assume that the jury concluded that there were no valid business reasons for the

---

[2] R. Bork, The Antitrust Paradox 160 (1978) (hereinafter Bork).

[3] In any business, patterns of distribution develop over time; these may reasonably be thought to be more efficient than alternative patterns of distribution that do not develop. The patterns that do develop and persist we may call the optimal patterns. By disturbing optimal distributions one rival can impose costs on another, that is, force the other to accept higher costs. Bork at 156.

refusal. The question then is whether that conclusion finds support in the record.

The question whether Ski Co.'s conduct may properly be characterized as exclusionary cannot be answered by simply considering its effect on Highlands. In addition, it is relevant to consider its impact on consumers and whether it has impaired competition in an unnecessarily restrictive way.[4] If a firm has been "attempting to exclude rivals on some basis other than efficiency," it is fair to characterize its behavior as predatory. It is, accordingly, appropriate to examine the effect of the challenged pattern of conduct on consumers, on Ski Co.'s smaller rival, and on Ski Co. itself.

Over the years, [skiers] developed a strong demand for the 6-day, all-Aspen ticket in its various refinements. Most experienced skiers quite logically prefer to purchase their tickets at once for the whole period that they will spend at the resort; they can then spend more time on the slopes and enjoying apres-ski amenities and less time standing in ticket lines. . . .

The adverse impact of Ski Co.'s pattern of conduct on Highlands is not disputed in this Court. . . . Highlands' share of the relevant market steadily declined after the 4-area ticket was terminated. . . .

Perhaps most significant, however, is the evidence relating to Ski Co. itself, for Ski Co. did not persuade the jury that its conduct was justified by any normal business purpose. . . .

That conclusion is strongly supported by Ski Co.'s failure to offer any efficiency justification whatever for its pattern of conduct. In defending the decision to terminate the jointly offered ticket, Ski Co. claimed that usage could not be properly monitored. The evidence, however, established that Ski Co. itself monitored the use of the 3-area passes based on a count taken by lift operators, and distributed the revenues among its mountains on that basis. Ski Co. contended that coupons were administratively cumbersome. . . . Coupons, however, were no more burdensome than the credit cards accepted at Ski Co. ticket windows. Moreover, in other markets Ski Co. itself participated in interchangeable lift tickets using coupons.

Thus the evidence supports an inference that Ski Co. was not motivated by efficiency concerns and that it was willing to sacrifice short-run benefits and consumer good will in exchange for a perceived long-run impact on its smaller rival.

Because we are satisfied that the evidence in the record . . . is adequate to support the verdict under the instructions given by the trial court, the judgment of the Court of Appeals is affirmed.

Case Questions

1. What are the two elements of a Section 2 Sherman Act offense, as described in the *Aspen* opinion?

2. Which element was at issue in *Aspen?*

3. How is the line drawn between a firm's conduct that legitimately obtains and maintains monopoly power and a firm's conduct that constitutes illegal monopolization under Section 2 of the Sherman Act?

4. Does a firm with monopoly power have a duty to cooperate with its smaller rivals in a marketing arrangement to avoid violating Section 2 of the Sherman Act? Explain.

5. Why should the law treat a firm such as Ski Co. with monopoly power differently from firms without monopoly power? Explain.

---

[4] Thus, "exclusionary" comprehends at the most behavior that not only (1) tends to impair the opportunities of rivals, but also (2) either does not further competition on the merits or does so in an unnecessarily restrictive way. [3 P. Areeda & D. Turner, *Antitrust Law* 78 (1978).]

Attempts to Monopolize

Attempts to monopolize differ from monopolization. In an attempt to monopolize, the firm has not yet achieved monopoly power. In *American Tobacco Co. v. United States,* the Supreme Court said, "the phrase 'attempt to monopolize' means the employment of methods, means and practices which would, if successful, accomplish monopolization, and which, though falling short, nevertheless approach so close as to create a dangerous probability of it."[5] In the following case, the Supreme Court examines what is required to establish liability for an attempt to monopolize under the Sherman Act.

SPECTRUM SPORTS V. MCQUILLAN
113 S. Ct. 884 (1993)

Sorbothane, Inc. is the manufacturer of sorbothane—a polymer used in making shock absorber pads for horse shoes, athletic equipment, and in medical applications. Kenneth B. Leighton, Sr., is the president of Sorbothane, Inc. Spectrum Sports, Inc. (petitioner) is a distributor of sorbothane. The president of Spectrum, Kenneth B. Leighton, Jr., is the son of the president of Sorbothane, Inc.

Kenneth B. Leighton, Jr., threatened Shirley McQuillan (respondent), another regional distributor, that she would be "looking for work" if she did not sell her distributorship to Spectrum. When McQuillan refused, her distributorship was terminated by Sorbothane, Inc. McQuillan sued Spectrum, claiming that Spectrum's conduct constituted an attempt to monopolize in violation of Section 2 of the Sherman Act.

The jury found in favor of McQuillan and awarded here $1,743,000 in compensatory damages, which was trebled under a provision of the antitrust laws that permits treble damages for violations of the Sherman Act. The District Court also awarded nearly $1 million in attorneys' fees.

On appeal, Spectrum argued that sufficient evidence did not exist for the jury to find liability for attempting to monopolize because there was no evidence of the defendants' share of any relevant market. The Ninth Circuit Court of Appeals affirmed. In its view, the evidence was sufficient for the jury to conclude that the defendants engaged in unfair or predatory conduct, making it unnecessary for McQuillan to either define the relevant market or prove the defendants' market share. The Supreme Court reversed the lower court decisions.

Justice White

While Section 1 of the Sherman Act forbids contracts or conspiracies in restraint of trade or commerce, Section 2 addresses the actions of single firms that monopolize, as well as conspiracies and combinations to monopolize. Section 2 does not define the elements of the offense of attempted monopolization. Nor is there much guidance to be

---

[5] 328 U.S. 781 (1946).

had in the scant legislative history of that provision, which was added late in the legislative process. . . .

Consistent with our cases, it is generally required that to demonstrate attempted monopolization a plaintiff must prove (1) that the defendant has engaged in predatory or anticompetitive conduct with (2) a specific intent to monopolize and (3) a dangerous probability of achieving monopoly power. In order to determine whether there is a dangerous probability of monopolization, courts have found it necessary to consider the relevant market and the defendant's ability to lessen or destroy competition in that market. . . .

The purpose of the Act is not to protect businesses from the working of the market; it is to protect the public from the failure of the market. The law directs itself not against conduct which is competitive, even severely so, but against conduct which unfairly tends to destroy competition itself. It does so not out of solicitude for private concerns but out of concern for the public interest. Thus, this Court and other courts have been careful to avoid constructions of Section 2 which might chill competition, rather than foster it. It is sometimes difficult to distinguish robust competition from conduct with long-term anticompetitive effects; moreover, single-firm activity is unlike concerted activity covered by Section 1, which inherently is fraught with anticompetitive risk. For these reasons, Section 2 makes the conduct of a single firm unlawful only when it actually monopolizes or dangerously threatens to do so. The concern that Section 2 might be applied so as to further anticompetitive ends is plainly not met by inquiring only whether the defendant has engaged in "unfair" or "predatory" tactics. Such conduct may be sufficient to prove the necessary intent to monopolize, which is something more than an intent to compete vigorously, but demonstrating the dangerous probability of monopolization in an attempt case also requires inquiry into the relevant product and geographic market and the defendant's economic power in that market.

We hold that petitioners may not be liable for attempted monopolization under Section 2 of the Sherman Act absent proof of a dangerous probability that they would monopolize a particular market and specific intent to monopolize. In this case, the trial instructions allowed the jury to infer specific intent and dangerous probability of success from the defendant's predatory conduct, without any proof of the relevant market or of a realistic probability that the defendants could achieve monopoly power in that market. In this respect, the instructions misconstrued Section 2, as did the Court of Appeals in affirming the judgment of the District Court. [T]he judgment of the Court of Appeals is reversed, and the case is remanded for further proceedings consistent with this opinion.

Case Questions

1. What is required to prove that a business is liable for an attempt to monopolize in violation of Section 2 of the Sherman Act?

2. For whose benefit does the Court interpret the Sherman Act?

3. Why should the Court care what the market share is in a case of attempted monopolization?

4. Why should the same conduct be prohibited by a market player with an 80 percent share, yet permitted by a market player with a 2 percent market share?

Combining or Conspiring to Monopolize

Combining or conspiring to monopolize, as the terms imply, requires the action of two or more persons, unlike monopolization or attempts to monopolize, which can be committed by a single entity or person. Conspiracy to monopolize is a separate offense under Section 2 of the Sherman Act. It requires proof that two

Ethical Dilemmas/Issues

In February 1982, American Airlines and Braniff Airlines each had a major passenger complex at the Dallas-Fort Worth International Airport (DFW). The two airlines accounted for 76 percent of the monthly flights at DFW.

For some time before February 1982, American and Braniff were competing fiercely for passengers flying to, from, and through DFW by offering lower fares and better service. During a telephone conversation between Robert Crandall, American's president, and Howard Putnam, Braniff's president, the following exchange occurred:

Crandall: I think it's dumb . . . all right, to sit here and pound the . . . out of each other, and neither one of us making a . . . dime.
Putnam: Well. . . .
Crandall: I mean, you know . . . what the . . . is the point of it?
Putnam: Nobody asked American to serve Harlingen. Nobody asked American to serve Kansas City, and there were low fares in there, you know, before. So. . . .
Crandall: You better believe it, Howard. But, you, you, you know, the complex is here—ain't gonna change a . . . thing, all right. We can, we can both live here and there ain't no room for Delta. But there's, ah, no reason that I can see, all right, to put both companies out of business.
Putnam: But if you're going to overlay every route of American's on top of . . . every route that Braniff has—I can't just sit here and allow you to bury us without giving our best effort.
Crandall: Oh sure, but Eastern and Delta do the same thing in Atlanta and have for years.
Putnam: Do you have a suggestion for me?
Crandall: Yes. I have a suggestion for you. Raise your . . . fares 20 percent. I'll raise mine the next morning.
Putnam: Robert, we. . . .
Crandall: You'll make more money and I will, too.
Putnam: We can't talk about pricing.
Crandall: Oh, but . . . Howard. We can talk about any . . . thing we want to talk about.

Howard Putnam taped the telephone conversation.
What are the ethical issues? What would you do?

---

or more entities conspired with the specific intent of monopolizing. Proving such conspiracy is no different from proving conspiracy under Section I of the Sherman Act, while proving such intent is no different from proving intent in attempted monopolization cases.

Mergers and Acquisitions

A merger or acquisition combines two companies into one. Mergers and acquisitions can facilitate the flow of investment capital and channel business assets into areas of greater demand. They can replace ineffective managers with new leaders capable of revitalizing a failing company. However, mergers can also eliminate competitors, close markets, and raise barriers to new entries into existing markets.

Section 7 of the Clayton Act prohibits any merger where the effect "may be to substantially lessen competition, or tend to create a monopoly." Any business considering a merger must evaluate its legality under Section 7. That consideration involves a two-step process: determining the relevant market and assessing the competitive effects.

Determining the Relevant Market

Firms compete in marketplaces, so the effects of a merger must be evaluated in its marketplace. The first step in evaluating a merger's legality is to define the relevant market, in terms of both product and geographic markets.

Section 7 prohibits mergers that might tend to create a monopoly. Therefore, the relevant market determination focuses on markets capable of being monopolized. Courts consider the same factors used to determine relevant markets under Section 2 of the Sherman Act.

However, Section 7 also prohibits mergers that may substantially lessen competition. It prohibits mergers that may foster anticompetitive practices, such as other mergers or unreasonable restraints of trade. These practices can occur despite the presence of available substitutes; that is, they can occur in markets that are incapable of being monopolized. Therefore, a relevant market may have several submarkets. Section 7 is also concerned with protecting potential competition, including interindustry competition. A relevant market may thus be composed of two or more markets or submarkets.

A submarket can be viewed as an area subject to anticompetitive practices that fall short of monopolization. For example, a product may have many different uses, and demand for it may come from different types of buyers. Ninety percent of the buyers may have many available substitutes, which would be included within the relevant market. However, 10 percent may find it very difficult to substitute because they are dependent on the product's peculiar characteristics. They form a distinct group of customers. There may be distinct vendors who distribute the product to them. The price of the product may be somewhat sensitive to economic conditions affecting these distinct customers. Thus, the product itself would be a relevant submarket based on the remaining 10 percent of product demand.

Assessing the Competitive Effect

Once the relevant markets are defined, the Section 7 inquiry focuses on whether the merger may tend to lessen competition or may tend to create a monopoly. The appropriate concern is the merger's potential anticompetitive effects. Congress intended Section 7 to be a preventive measure. Therefore, even though a merger is not yet lessening competition it may violate Section 7 if it may lessen competition.

Each merger must be analyzed to predict its future impact on the relevant markets. Table 20–1 lists the various factors that courts look at in assessing the competitive effects of mergers in Section 7 cases.

Applying the Two-Step Process

Analysis of a merger or acquisition requires two steps: defining the relevant market and assessing the competitive impact. In applying the two-step process, courts classify mergers as horizontal, vertical, or conglomerate. Horizontal mergers involve firms selling the same good or service at the same level of distribution. Vertical mergers involve firms at different levels of distribution—usually a supplier and a customer. Conglomerate mergers involve firms whose products or services are not directly related.

Horizontal Mergers

Horizontal mergers have the most consistent and immediate anticompetitive potential because they replace two competitors with a single, stronger firm. The effects of a horizontal merger are illustrated in Figure 20–1.

When the industry in which a horizontal merger occurs is concentrated and the merger results in a company with an "undue market share," a rebuttable presumption arises that the merger is illegal. The levels of concentration and market share necessary to trigger this presumption are not very great. They may be particularly small where the industry has experienced a trend toward further concentration.

TABLE 20–1   **Factors Courts Consider in Assessing the Competitive Effects of Mergers**

- Whether the merger may result in the elimination of competition or deter potential competitors from entering the market.
- Whether the merger forecloses competitors from a significant portion of the market.
- Whether the merger may result in the entrenchment of a dominant competitor.
- Whether the merger may encourage reciprocal dealing between the merged firms.
- Market trends, such as a trend toward concentration.
- Postmerger evidence that the merger has actually adversely affected competition.

FIGURE 20–1   **Horizontal merger**

Premerger	Postmerger
A Versus B Versus C Versus D Versus E Versus	AB Versus C Versus D Versus E Versus

Analysis of a horizontal merger begins with statistical evidence of market concentration and market share. It may also end at that point if there is no evidence to rebut the presumption of illegality.

A presumption of illegality cannot be rebutted by showing that the merger would have procompetitive effects in another market. For example, when the second and third-largest commercial banks in Philadelphia merged, the Court refused to allow the banks to rebut the presumption of anticompetitive effects in metropolitan Philadelphia by showing that they could compete more effectively for national accounts against banks from other major cities.[6]

The rebuttal must focus on the characteristics and structure of the market concerned. It must emphasize characteristics contradicting the conclusion that a merger of two significant firms in a concentrated market is likely to trigger additional mergers, foreclose significant markets to competitors, or otherwise injure competition. In the following case, the Supreme Court found that a coal company had successfully rebutted the presumption.

UNITED STATES V. GENERAL DYNAMICS CORP.
415 U.S. 486 (1974)

The government (appellant) sued General Dynamics (appellee), the successor to Material Service Corporation, a deep-mining coal producer, complaining that Material Service's acquisition of United Coal Companies, a strip-mining coal producer, violated Section 7 of the Clayton Act.

The government's case consisted of production statistics indicating that in specified geographic markets the number of coal producers had been declining, that the markets for coal were concentrated, and that the acquisition substantially increased Material Service's market share. In finding that the merger would not substantially lessen competition, the trial court relied on evidence showing that United Electric's long-term reserves were almost depleted. The trial court rendered judgment for General Dynamics, and the government appealed. The Supreme Court affirmed.

Justice Stewart

In prior decisions involving horizontal mergers between competitors, the Court has found prima facie violators of section 7 of the Clayton Act

from aggregate statistics of the sort relied on by the United States in this case. . . .

The effect of adopting this approach to a determination of a "substantial" lessening of competition is to allow the Government to rest its case on

---

[6] United States v. Philadelphia National Bank, 374 U.S. 321 (1963).

a showing of even small increases of market share or market concentration in those industries or markets where concentration is already great or has been recently increasing, since "if concentration is already great, the importance of preventing even slight increases in concentration and preserving the possibility of eventual deconcentration is correspondingly great."

While the statistical showing proffered by the government in this case . . . would under this approach have sufficed to support a finding of "undue concentration" in the absence of other considerations, the question before us is whether the District Court was justified in finding that other pertinent factors affecting the coal industry and the business of the appellees mandated a conclusion that no substantial lessening of competition occurred or was threatened by the acquisition of United Electric. We are satisfied that the court's ultimate finding was not in error.

Much of the District Court's opinion was devoted to a description of the changes that have affected the coal industry since World War II. . . . First, it found that coal had become increasingly less able to compete with other sources of energy in many segments of the energy market. . . .

Second, the court found that to a growing extent since 1954, the electric utility industry has become the mainstay of coal consumption. . . .

Third, and most significantly, the court found that to an increasing degree, nearly all coal sold to utilities is transferred under long-term requirements contracts, under which coal producers promise to meet utilities' coal consumption requirements for a fixed period of time, and at predetermined prices. . . .

Because of these fundamental changes in the structure of the market for coal, the District Court was justified in viewing the statistics relied on by the Government as insufficient to sustain its case. Evidence of past production does not, as a matter of logic, necessarily give a proper picture of a company's future ability to compete. . . .

In the coal market . . . statistical evidence of coal production was of considerably less significance. The bulk of the coal produced is delivered under long-term requirements contracts, and such sales thus do not represent the exercise of competitive power but rather the obligation to fulfill previously negotiated contracts at a previously fixed price. The focus of competition in a given time frame is not on the disposition of coal already produced but on the procurement of new long-term supply contracts. . . . A more significant indicator of a company's power effectively to compete with other companies lies in the state of a company's uncommitted reserves of recoverable coal. . . .

The testimony and exhibits in the District Court revealed that United Electric's coal reserve prospects were "unpromising. . . ." Many of the reserves held by United had already been depleted at the time of trial, forcing the closing of some of United's Midwest mines. Even more significantly, the District Court found that of the 52,033,304 tons of currently minable reserves in Illinois, Indiana, and Kentucky controlled by United, only four million tons had not already been committed under long-term contracts. United was found to be facing the future with relatively depleted resources at its disposal, and with the vast majority of those resources already committed under contracts allowing no further adjustment in price. In addition, the District Court found that "United Electric has neither the possibility of acquiring more [reserves] nor the ability to develop deep coal reserves," and thus was not in a position to increase its reserves to replace those already depleted or committed. . . .

Irrespective of the company's size when viewed as a producer, its weakness as a competitor was properly analyzed by the District Court and fully substantiated that court's conclusion that its acquisition by Material Service would not "substantially . . . lessen competition. . . ."

Case Questions

1. What was the basis for the government's case that the merger might substantially lessen competition?

2. Was the government's evidence sufficient to raise a presumption that the merger was illegal? Explain.

3. What was the basis for rebutting the presumption?

Vertical Mergers

A vertical merger is a merger of firms that deal in the same product at different distribution levels. A widget manufacturer's acquisition of a widget wholesaler or retail widget chain would be a vertical merger. Vertical mergers may reflect a desire to realize economies in distribution, ensure the availability of supplies, or promote retail distribution of a manufacturer's product. Figure 20–2 illustrates a vertical merger.

Vertical mergers are more difficult to evaluate than horizontal mergers because the same number of competitors remain in both the supplier and customer markets. A vertical merger, however, may have anticompetitive effects on the markets of the supplier or the customer. The degree of market foreclosure is the starting point in analyzing any vertical merger. The larger the market the merger forecloses to the competitor of one of the merging firms, the greater is the likelihood that the merger would be held illegal. The intent of the parties to the merger is another important consideration. The level of concentration in the merging firm's markets and trends toward increasing concentration in either market can also prompt a finding that the merger is illegal. The concern of courts is particularly acute where there is a trend toward vertical integration. Since the 1960s there has been little enforcement against vertical mergers.

Conglomerate Mergers

Conglomerate mergers pose the smallest immediate threat to competition. They do not combine competitors into one, nor do they necessarily foreclose markets previously open to competitors. However, they may have other anticompetitive effects, particularly when they involve firms in similar or related industries.

FIGURE 20–2   Vertical merger

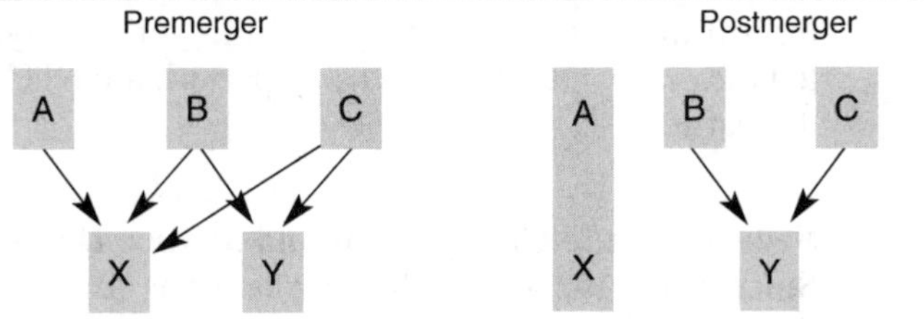

Defenses in Merger Cases

Most Section 7 cases are defended by attacking the plaintiff's definition of the relevant market and its evidence of anticompetitive effects. Two affirmative defenses are also recognized under Section 7: the failing company defense and the solely-for-investment defense. These defenses serve to legalize an otherwise illegal merger. The defendant bears the burden of proving them.

The Failing Company Defense
A merger that might otherwise violate Section 7 is considered lawful if one of the companies is failing. For this defense to apply, the failing company must be about to die, with no reasonable hope of survival short of merger. The acquiring company must either be the only company interested in purchasing the failing company or, if other companies are interested, it must be the company that poses the least threat to competition. Finally, it must be shown that methods to save the failing company short of merger have been tried and have failed or that such methods would be futile.

The Solely-for-Investment Defense
Section 7 does not apply to corporations purchasing stock in other corporations "solely for investment and not using [the stock] by voting or otherwise to bring about, or in attempting to bring about, the substantial lessening of competition." This is known as the *solely-for-investment defense*.

Enforcement

Section 7 violations, like all other Clayton Act violations, are civil offenses. Unlike Sherman Act violations, they are not crimes. Civil enforcement actions may be brought by private parties, the Justice Department, and the FTC.

FTC Premerger Notification
The Clayton Act includes a 30-day **premerger notification** program administered by the FTC. The purpose of the premerger notification is to allow the FTC and the Justice Department to enjoin mergers that they believe will have anticompetitive effects. If the acquiring company has sales of $100 million or more and the company to be acquired has sales or assets or $10 million or more, they must inform the FTC of the proposed merger 30 days before the merger is scheduled to take place. During the 30-day period, the FTC may request additional data from the parties.

Federal Trade Commission and Justice Department Merger Guidelines
Since 1968, the Justice Department has periodically issued guidelines to inform the business community of the analysis applied by the department to mergers. In

1992, the department and the Federal Trade Commission (referred together here as *the agency*) jointly issued revised merger guidelines. The guidelines do not have the effect of law. Nevertheless, they are useful for business planning in predicting the likely governmental response to a merger.

The guidelines define the relevant product and geographic markets as those in which a hypothetical monopolist impose a "small but significant nontransitory" increase in price. The agency will begin with each product and the location for each merging firm and ask what would happen if a monopolist imposed a small but significant nontransitory price increase. If the monopolist would not find it profitable because of a loss of sales to producers of substitute products at other locations, the agency will add those producers and locations to the definition of the product and geographic market.

Within the relevant markets, the guidelines rely on a formula known as the **Herfindahl-Hirschman Index** (HHI) to measure market concentration. The HHI is calculated by adding the squares of the individual market squares of all firms in the market. For example, in a pure monopoly, one firm has 100 percent of the market. The HHI equals 1002, or 10,000. If two firms each control 50 percent, the HHI is $50^2 + 50^2$, or 5,000. The smaller the HHI, the less concentrated the market. The guidelines classify markets as follows: unconcentrated = HHI below 1,000; moderately concentrated = HHI between 1,000 and 1,800; highly concentrated = HHI above 1,800.

In assessing market share, the guidelines recognize the impact of foreign competition. Foreign firms are assigned market shares in the same way as domestic firms; they are not excluded from the market solely because their sales are subject to import quotas.

The guidelines discuss horizontal mergers, vertical mergers, and mergers reducing potential competition. Generally, the agency is not likely to challenge horizontal mergers in unconcentrated markets; in moderately concentrated markets, the agency is not likely to challenge horizontal mergers that increase the HHI by fewer than 100 points; in highly concentrated markets, the agency is not likely to challenge horizontal mergers that increase the HHI by fewer than 50 points; and very likely to challenge those that increase the HHI by more than 100 points.

Market share and concentration data provide only the starting point for analyzing the competitive aspects of a merger. The presumption of illegality may be overcome by a showing that other factors in the guidelines analysis make anticompetitive effects unlikely. Other market factors include those that pertain to competitive effects, as well as market entry, efficiencies, and firm failure. For example, the agency will consider the ability of rival sellers to replace lost competition by repositioning their product lines. Also, a merger is not likely to enhance market power if entry into the market is so easy that market participants could not profitably maintain a price increase above premerger levels. Thus, the agency will consider the timeliness, likelihood, and sufficiency of the means of entry a potential entrant might practically employ. Because the primary benefit of mergers to the economy is their efficiency-enhancing potential, the guidelines allow firms to achieve available efficiencies (e.g., better integration of production facilities) without interference from the agency. The guidelines also permit mergers where one of the firms faces imminent failure.

Generally, the agency does not challenge vertical mergers unless they are likely to facilitate collusion or raise barriers to entry in the relevant market. The agency is not likely to challenge vertical mergers for facilitating collusion if the HHI is less than 1,800, nor is it likely to challenge mergers for raising barriers to entry unless the merger creates conditions where new entrants to one market must also enter a second market, where the need to enter the second market makes entry into the first market more difficult and less likely, and where the market structure is highly concentrated (HHI of 1,800 or greater).

In deciding whether to challenge mergers that reduce potential competition, the agency considers the ease of entry into the acquired firm's market, whether other firms similarly situated to the acquiring firms remain as potential entrants, the market share of the acquired firm, and market concentration. The agency is not likely to challenge these mergers in markets where the HHI is below 1,800.

Remedies

The remedies available in merger cases include preliminary injunctions, divestiture, and money damages. To obtain a preliminary injunction against a merger, the plaintiff must show that it is likely to win the lawsuit and that allowing the merger to proceed would irreparably harm competition.

Where a merger is not enjoined, or has already taken place before the lawsuit, then divestiture is possible. Divestiture occurs where a court orders a corporation to rid itself of the stock or property of another company.

As is true with other antitrust violations, successful parties in private civil lawsuits may recover three times the damages they have sustained, along with their litigation costs, including reasonable attorney fees.

International Mergers and Monopolies

Mergers and acquisitions commonly involve foreign buyers and sellers. Mergers between U.S. firms commonly transfer ownership of subsidiaries or operations, not only in the United States, but around the world. A merger may be reviewed not only by the U.S. Justice Department and the Federal Trade Commission, but by the antitrust agencies in other countries, such as Canada and the European Commission of the European Community. To avoid or minimize conflicts, treaties exist that call for cooperation and consultation. A treaty between the United States and the European Community attempts to avoid or minimize conflict in antitrust enforcement by calling for such consultation and cooperation.

Chapter Problems

1. Define the following terms:
   - *a.* Monopolization
   - *b.* Relevant market
   - *c.* Monopoly power
   - *d.* Market share
   - *e.* Purposeful act requirement
   - *f.* General intent
   - *g.* Passive monopoly
   - *h.* Superior skill, foresight, and industry
   - *i.* Premerger notification
   - *j.* Herfindahl-Hirschman Index

2. The Eastman Kodak Company is the world's largest manufacturer of film. Since 1952, its annual film sales have always exceeded 82 percent of the national volume and 88 percent of the national revenues. Kodak also produces instant-loading cameras designed for the mass market. Between 1954 and 1973, it never enjoyed less than 61 percent of the annual unit sales or less than 64 percent of the annual dollar volume, and in the peak year of 1964, Kodak cameras accounted for 90 percent of market revenues. Much of this success has been due to the firm's history of innovation.

   In 1963, Kodak first marketed the 126 Instamatic instant-loading camera, and in 1972, it came out with the much smaller 110 Pocket Instamatic. These small, light cameras employ film packaged in cartridges that can simply be dropped in the back, thus obviating the need to load and position a roll of film manually. The introduction of these cameras triggered successive revolutions in the industry. Amateur still-camera sales in the United States averaged 3.9 million units annually between 1954 and 1963, with little annual variation. In the first full year after Kodak's introduction of the 126, industry sales leaped 22 percent, and they took an even larger jump when the 110 came to market. Other camera manufacturers copied both of these cameras, but for several months after each was introduced, those who wished to buy one had to purchase a Kodak.

   When Kodak introduced the 110 Instamatic, it also introduced Kodacolor II film, which it marketed as a "remarkable new film" producing better pictures. Kodak made conscious decisions to introduce the new camera and film together, not to make the film available in the 126 format for 18 months, and not to provide its competitors with advance notice of the innovations. Kodak has also followed a consistent policy of refusing to make film available for formats other than those in which it makes cameras. Has Kodak violated Section 2? Explain.

3. IBM, facing stiff competition from newcomers to the market for peripheral data-processing devices, announced a series of price reductions designed to

eliminate that competition. IBM also announced that it would lease peripheral devices for a fixed term of years instead of allowing customers to cancel leases on 30 days' notice. The fixed-term leases were for periods of up
to two years, shorter in duration than those offered by IBM's competitors.
If these changes allow IBM to capture a monopolist's share of the market,
has IBM violated Section 2 of the Sherman Act? Explain.

4. Theater owners in Las Vegas submit bids to film distributors to get first-run
   movies. Successful bidders obtain an exhibition license specifying that a
   percentage of weekly house receipts are payable by the theater owner to the
   distributor.

   Raymond Syufy, a movie theater operator, entered the Las Vegas market in 1981 with a splash by opening a six-screen theater. Newly constructed and luxuriously furnished, it put existing facilities to shame.
   Syufy's entry into the Las Vegas market caused a stir, precipitating a bid-
   ding war. After a hard-fought battle among several contenders, Syufy
   gained the upper hand. By October 1984, Syufy had bought out all of his
   competitors except one, Roberts, a small exhibitor of mostly second-run
   films. Thus, Syufy captured 100 percent of the first-run film market in Las
   Vegas. That same month, however, a major movie distributor stopped doing
   business with Syufy, sending all of its first-run films to Roberts. Roberts
   took this as an invitation to step into the major leagues and, against all
   odds, began giving Syufy serious competition in the first-run market. By
   December 1986, Roberts was operating 28 screens, trading places with
   Syufy, who had only 23. In 1987, Roberts sold its theaters to the largest
   theater chain in the country, United Artists, and Syufy continued losing
   ground.

   The United States sued Syufy, alleging a violation of Section 2 of the
   Sherman Act. The Justice Department argues that "you may not get monopoly power by buying out your competitors." Syufy argues that he did not
   violate Section 2 because there were no significant barriers to entry. Who is
   right? Explain.

5. Plaza Theaters, Inc. owns all the movie theaters in a city with a population
   of 50,000. A rival corporation from the other end of the state has
   announced plans to build a new theater that will compete with Plaza. Plaza
   has warned the potential competitor: "If you open a theater here, Plaza will
   compete vigorously. It will go after all the first-run films and will offer
   them at the lowest possible prices. Plaza will make it impossible for you to
   survive in this town." If the rival cancels its plans to open the theater, has
   Plaza violated Section 2? Explain.

6. King Foods, Inc. is a large supermarket chain that grew steadily over the
   past decade. King's president, Anne Crowley, explains its success: "The
   supermarket industry is known to have low profit margins. To be successful
   in this business, a company must turn over large volumes of goods. King
   Foods has grown to its current proportions by doing just that." Upper man-

agement pushed for reinvestment of profits and obtained outside funds for further expansion. Crowley adds, "Because of our size, we can now enter a market and offer the consumer lower prices than previously existed." It is no secret that some of King's pricing activities contribute to its success. When King opens a new store, the grand opening sale lasts for six months, during which time the prices are consistently lower than those of area competitors. King maintains prices at a level that eventually forces small grocery stores to close. Once King has a dominant share of the new market, its prices gradually move up to the normal range. Has King violated Section 2 of the Sherman Act? Explain.

7. RSR Corporation acquired Quemetco, Inc. RSR produced secondary lead at smelting plants in Dallas, Texas, and Newark, New Jersey. Quemetco produced secondary lead at plants in Seattle, Washington; Indianapolis, Indiana; and City of Industry, California. Quemetco was building a fourth plant in Walkill, New York. After the merger, RSR closed its Newark plant.

    Secondary lead is recycled from scrap automobile batteries. It contains impurities and is generally used as hard or metallic lead. Primary lead is processed from lead ore. It is free of hardening impurities and is therefore used as soft lead. It can be hardened by adding metal, but the process is not economical. The principal users of primary and secondary lead are battery manufacturers. They use primary lead for battery oxides and secondary lead for posts and grids. Although secondary lead customarily sells for 10 percent less than primary, several commodities and metals exchanges do not distinguish between the two in quoting prices for trading in lead.

    Secondary lead producers try to ship their products to customers located within a few hundred miles of their plants to minimize trucking costs. However, secondary lead producers are willing to ship over greater distances when shipment is justified by fluctuations in market conditions, prices, and trucking costs. Define the relevant market(s) for analyzing the legality of the merger.

8. Amax, Inc. and Copper Range Company merged. Prior to the merger, Copper Range was the nation's seventh-largest producer of copper, with 4.6 percent of the market. Amax mined copper pursuant to a joint venture with another company and accounted for 1.4 percent of the market. All of Amax's reserves were obtained pursuant to joint ventures with other companies. Prior to the merger Amax announced its intention to expand its reserves and increase production. The copper industry was marked by high barriers to entry and high concentration, with the four largest companies holding 66 percent and the eight largest holding 90 percent. Did the merger violate Section 7? Explain.

9. Kennecott Copper Corporation, the largest copper producer in the country, accounting for 33 percent of the market, acquired Peabody Coal Company, the nation's largest coal producer, which had 10 percent of the market. Due to dwindling copper reserves Kennecott liquidated some of its assets, thus

obtaining a large amount of cash. It used this cash to buy Peabody. Kennecott made the purchase to diversify its operations in anticipation of the exhaustion of its copper reserves. Several years before the merger, Kennecott had acquired a small coal company to supply its own needs for coal. The coal market was not highly concentrated, but it did have very high barriers to entry. Did the merger violate Section 7? Explain.

10. ABC Gizmo Co. is the leading seller of gizmos in the country, with 36 percent of the market. The next leading company has 12 percent. The next four firms have 10 percent each. Three other firms have 3 percent each, and two others have 1.5 percent each. Can ABC acquire any other firm in the market without fear that the Justice Department could challenge the merger? Explain.

21 SPECIAL TOPICS IN ANTITRUST

Learning Objectives

After learning this chapter, the student should be able to:

- Recognize the pricing activities that may result in liability under the Robinson-Patman Act.
- Apply the Sherman Act to franchise relationships, and recognize when franchise relationships may result in antitrust liability.
- Explain the requirements of the Federal Trade Commission Franchise Rule.
- Analyze trade association activity under the Sherman Act, and recognize when such activity may result in antitrust liability.

This chapter deals with pricing, franchising, and trade association activity. All these activities are motivated by considerations of efficiency. The pricing of goods depends on how efficiently a firm produces, markets, and delivers its goods. Franchising is an efficient way of expanding a firm's sphere. Firms join trade associations to enhance the efficiency of their operations. All these activities are subject to antitrust regulation (see Table 21–1).

TABLE 21–1   Antitrust: Special Topics

Activity	Act	Prohibition
Pricing	Clayton 2	Price discrimination
Franchising	Sherman 1	Unreasonable restraint of trade
Franchising	FTC 5	Nondisclosure
Trade association	Sherman 1	Unreasonable restraint of trade

Price Discrimination

The Robinson-Patman Act prohibits sellers from practicing **price discrimination** and buyers from inducing sellers to engage in discrimination. It also prohibits price discrimination disguised as brokerage fees and requires that promotional allowances and services be available to all buyers on proportionally equal terms. The act's provisions are summarized in Table 21–2. Although the Robinson-Patman Act was aimed at abusive practices of large buyers and sellers, its prohibitions apply to all firms regardless of size.

Seller Discrimination

Section 2(a) of the Robinson-Patman Act contains the statute's basic prohibition against discrimination by a seller. For a violation of Section 2(a), there must be discrimination in price in the sale of commodities of like grade and quality in interstate commerce that results in competitive injury.

Discrimination in Price

Price discrimination is simply a difference in price. Price is computed on the basis of the purchaser's actual cost. The Robinson-Patman Act does not require that a

TABLE 21–2   The Robinson-Patman Act

Section	Prohibition	Defenses
2(a)	Seller discrimination in price, in the sale of commodities of like grade and quality, and in interstate commerce that causes competitive injury.	Meeting competition Cost justification Changing conditions
2(c)	Fictitious brokerage payments.	None
2(d)	Payments on allowances by seller to buyers for promotional services except where available to all buyers on proportionally equal terms.	Meeting competition
2(e)	Seller furnishing promotional services except where available to all buyers on proportionally equal terms.	Meeting competition
2(f)	Buyer-induced or knowing receipt of benefits of a Section 2(a) violation.	Same as for Section 2(a)

seller provide lower prices to wholesalers than to retailers or consumers; a seller who charges the same price to all buyers, regardless of their position in the chain of distribution, is not discriminating.

The Robinson-Patman Act equally prohibits indirect, as well as direct, price discrimination. Examples of indirect price discrimination include variations in the terms of delivery, sales returns, cash discounts, and warehousing.

Two Sales
A sale occurs only where there is an enforceable contract, and price discrimination can occur only when there are at least two completed sales. For example, a sale to customer X for $6 and an offer to sell to customer Y for $5 is not illegal, because only one sale has occurred. For the same reason, it does not violate the Robinson-Patman Act to sell to one party while refusing to sell to another.

Close in Time
Price discrimination occurs only when the two sales are reasonably close in time—a period determined by the circumstances surrounding the sale. In sales involving high-cost, low-volume products, such as jet engines, two sales a year apart may be considered close in time. On the other hand, sales of smaller items traded in high volume with great fluctuations in supply and demand may not be considered close in time, even though made within a few hours of each other.

Same Seller
The two sales must, of course, originate from the same seller before the Robinson-Patman Act applies. It is usually easy to tell whether this requirement has been met. The question becomes more difficult when a parent corporation and its subsidiary sell the same product at different prices to competing customers. The determining factor is often the degree of control exercised over the subsidiary by the parent corporation. As long as the parent and the subsidiary are independent entities in their pricing and distribution policies, they are not considered to be the same seller.

Commodities
The Robinson-Patman Act applies only to sales of commodities. Commodities are movable or tangible property. Such intangibles as services, leases, loans, mutual fund shares, and advertising are not commodities.

Like Grade and Quality
Illegal price discrimination occurs only when the two products sold are of like grade and quality. Thus, truck tires can be sold at a price different than bicycle tires. Goods, however, do not have to be of exactly the same grade and quality

for the act to apply. For example, juice containers that differ in size by only one-eighth inch are of like grade and quality because they are functionally similar in performance.

Like grade and quality refers to the physical properties of the commodity in question. Identical products sold under different labels are considered to be of like grade and quality. Although most marketing experts would say that customer preference for one brand over another differentiates physically identical products, the Supreme Court disagreed in *FTC v. Borden Co.*[1]

In the *Borden* case, Borden sold evaporated milk under the Borden brand and also under private labels. The private-brand milk was identical to the Borden-brand milk, but was marketed to Borden's customers at a lower price than the Borden-brand milk. The Supreme Court decided that the two different brands of physically identical milk were of like grade and quality, even though there was a distinct customer preference for the Borden brand over the other. The Court reasoned that the question of like grade and quality goes to whether the seller's pricing is covered by the statute. After a finding of like grade and quality, the inquiry does not end—competitive injury still must be proved. The real question becomes whether the preference, as created by the seller's advertising, results in competitive injury.

Competitive Injury
As mentioned earlier, a discrimination in price, by itself, does not violate the Robinson-Patman Act. The discrimination must tend to injure competition. Actual injury need not be shown; a probability of injury is sufficient to establish a violation. The requirement of competitive injury goes to the heart of Robinson-Patman analysis.

Following the Supreme Court's decision in *Borden* that the two brands of milk were of like grade and quality, the case was sent back to the circuit court of appeals to decide whether there was competitive injury. That court decided that the price differential did not result in competitive injury. Although there was testimony by customers that they lost sales to Borden, overall, Borden's competition experienced an increase in absolute sales. As to the lost sales that were testified to, there was no cause-and-effect relationship between the differences in price and those lost sales. Buyers were not injured, because all buyers were charged the same price for Borden-brand milk and all buyers were charged the same price for private-label milk. The competing sellers were not injured by the differences in price between the Borden-brand milk and Borden's private-label milk; they lost business to Borden because of the differentials in price between their own private labels and Borden's private labels.

In the following case, the Supreme Court addressed the competitive injury requirement of the Robinson-Patman Act.

---

[1] 383 U.S. 637 (1966).

TEXACO, INC. V. HASBROUCK
496 U.S. 543 (1990)

Between 1972 and 1981, Texaco, Inc. (petitioner) sold gasoline to Hasbrouck and other independent Texaco retailers (respondents) at its retail tank wagon prices (RTW) and delivered gasoline to those retailers. At the same time, Texaco offered substantial discounts to two distributors, Gull Oil Company and Dompier Oil Company, who picked up the gasoline from Texaco and delivered it to their own retailers. Gull resold the gasoline to retailers under its own name, and Dompier resold the gasoline to Texaco retailers. Texaco encouraged Dompier to enter the retail market directly by offering an additional discount for hauling. The sales of Gull and Dompier rose dramatically, while the sales of respondents declined dramatically. In 1976, respondents filed suit against Texaco, claiming that Texaco engaged in illegal price discrimination that violated Section 2(a) of the Robinson-Patman Act. The jury found for respondents. The court of appeals affirmed. The Supreme Court affirmed the lower courts' decisions.

Justice Stevens

We granted certiorari to consider Texaco's contention that legitimate functional discounts do not violate the Act because a seller is not responsible for its customers' independent resale pricing decisions. While we agree with the basic thrust of Texaco's argument, we conclude that in this case it is foreclosed by the facts of record.

In order to establish a violation of the Act, respondents had the burden of proving four facts: (1) that Texaco's sales to Gull and Dompier were made in interstate commerce; (2) that the gasoline sold to them was of the same grade and quality as that sold to respondents; (3) that Texaco discriminated in price as between Gull and Dompier on the one hand and respondents on the other; and (4) that the discrimination had a prohibited effect on competition. . . . Texaco . . . argue[s] . . . that, at least to the extent that Gull and Dompier acted as wholesalers, the price differentials did not injure competition. . . .

In *FTC v. Morton Salt* Co., we held that an injury to competition may be inferred from evidence that some purchasers had to pay their supplier "substantially more for their goods than their competitors had to pay." Texaco, supported by the United States and the Federal Trade Commission as amici curiae . . . argues that this presumption should not apply to differences between prices charged to wholesalers and those charged to retailers. Moreover, they argue that it would be inconsistent with fundamental antitrust policies to construe the Act as requiring a seller to control his customers' resale prices. The seller should not be held liable for the independent pricing decisions of his customers. . . .

[A] price differential "that merely accords due recognition and reimbursement for actual marketing functions" . . . is not illegal. In this case, however, both the District Court and the Court of Appeals concluded that even without viewing the evidence in the light most favorable to the respondents, there was no substantial evidence indicating that the discounts to Gull and Dompier constituted a reasonable reimbursement for the value to Texaco of their actual marketing functions. Indeed, Dompier was separately compensated for its hauling function, and neither Gull nor Dompier maintained any significant storage facilities.

Commentators have disagreed about the extent to which functional discounts are generally or presumptively allowable under the Robinson-Patman Act. They nevertheless tend to agree that in exceptional cases what is nominally a functional discount may be an unjustifiable price discrimination entirely within coverage of the Act. . . .

Both Gull and Dompier received the full discount on all their purchases even though most of their volume was resold directly to consumers. The extra margin on those sales obviously enabled them to price aggressively in both their retail and their wholesale marketing. To the extent that Dompier and Gull competed with respondents in the retail market, the presumption of adverse effect on competition recognized in the *Morton Salt* case becomes all the more appropriate. Their competitive advantage in that market also constitutes evidence tending to rebut any presumption of legality that would otherwise apply to their wholesale sales.

The evidence indicates, moreover, that Texaco affirmatively encouraged Dompier to expand its retail business and that Texaco was fully informed about the persistent and marketwide consequences of its own pricing policies. Indeed, its own executives recognized that the dramatic impact on the market was almost entirely attributable to the magnitude of the distributor discount and the hauling allowance. Yet at the same time that Texaco was encouraging Dompier to integrate downward, and supplying Dompier with a generous discount useful to such integration, Texaco was inhibiting upward integration by the respondents: two of the respondents sought permission from Texaco to haul their own fuel using their own tankwagons, but Texaco refused. The special facts of this case thus make it peculiarly difficult for Texaco to claim that it is being held liable for the independent pricing decisions of Gull or Dompier. . . .

"[T]he competitive injury component of a Robinson-Patman Act violation is not limited to the injury to competition between the favored and the disfavored purchaser; it also encompasses the injury to competition between their customers. . . ." Such indirect competitive effects surely may not be presumed automatically in every functional discount setting, and, indeed one would expect that most functional discounts will be legitimate discounts which do not cause harm to competition. At the least, a functional discount that constitutes a reasonable reimbursement for the purchasers' actual marketing functions will not violate the Act. When a functional discount is legitimate, the inference of injury to competition recognized in the *Morton Salt* case will simply not arise. Yet it is also true that not every functional discount is entitled to a judgment of legitimacy, and that it will sometimes be possible to produce evidence showing that a particular functional discount caused a price discrimination of the sort the Act prohibits. When such anticompetitive effects are proved—as we believe they were in this case—they are covered by the Act.

Case Questions

1. What is necessary to establish a violation of Section 2(a) of the Robinson-Patman Act?
2. What was Texaco's argument regarding the issue of injury to competition?
3. What is a functional discount?
4. Are functional discounts generally lawful under the Robinson-Patman Act? Why or why not?
5. Why did Texaco's functional discounts violate the Robinson-Patman Act?

Injury to competition prohibited by the Robinson-Patman Act can occur at various levels of the distribution process. The following discussion describes how competitive injury can occur at these various levels.

Primary-Line Injury. **Primary-line injury** (or injury at the seller's level) occurs when a seller suffers injury as a result of price discrimination by a competitor. This type of injury was alleged in the *Borden* case by Borden's competitors who had lost business to its private label. Primary-line injury normally occurs when a seller cuts prices to purchasers in one geographic area in an attempt to drive out a local competitor. The situation is demonstrated by Figure 21–1. S1 and S2 are competitors in Ohio. If S1 slashes its prices to Ohio buyers in an attempt to drive S2 out of business, without a corresponding decrease in price to its customers in Kentucky, Michigan, and Indiana, S2 may suffer a primary-line injury. Before a violation of the act can occur, S1's economic power must be sufficient to pose a probability of injury to S2.

Secondary-Line Injury. **Secondary-line injury** (or injury at the buyer's level) occurs when a seller discriminates in price between two competing buyers. This injury is illustrated in Figure 21–2. B1 and B2 are competing for the same customers. If S sells products at a lower price to B1 than to B2, then B2 is at a competitive disadvantage and may suffer competitive injury. However, in Figure 21–3 no such competitive injury occurs.

With no competition at the buyer level, there can be no buyer-level injury based on price discrimination. In such a case, S may discriminate in price between B1 and B2 without violating the act. Should B1 develop customers in Ohio, however, then S's more favorable treatment of B1 may cause competitive injury to B2 and thus violate the act.

Commerce

Most federal regulatory statutes apply to all parties engaging in or affecting interstate commerce. As discussed in Chapter 5, almost all business activity affects interstate commerce. The Robinson-Patman Act is not as broad as most other federal statutes. For Section 2(a) to apply, three conditions must be met. First, a violator must be engaged in interstate commerce. Second, discriminatory practices must occur in the course of interstate commerce. Third, either of the purchases must be made in interstate commerce.

Generally, a company that sells its goods intrastate has failed to meet the first test, that it be engaged in interstate commerce. However, if that firm resells goods

---

FIGURE 21–1   **An Example of Geographic-Based Price Cutting**

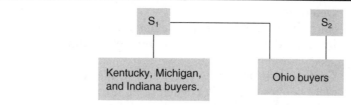

FIGURE 21–2   An Example of Price Discrimination between Competing Buyers

---

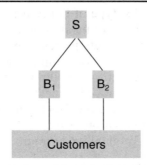

FIGURE 21–3   An Example of Price Discrepancy without Competitive Injury

---

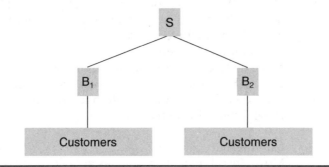

---

it received from outside the state, it may be treated as a firm engaged in interstate commerce. A sale made in interstate commerce is necessarily made in the course of interstate commerce and thereby satisfies the second test if the sale involves price discrimination. For the third test to be met, one of the purchases must be made in interstate commerce. It does not matter whether the sale to the favored or unfavored customer is interstate, as long as at least one of the two transactions generates discrimination across state lines. This requirement is met even if the objecting disfavored customer is a purely intrastate business, as long as the other sale that is the subject of the complaint is interstate.

Defenses
Three basic defenses to an alleged price discrimination are cost justification, meeting competition, and changing market conditions.

Cost Justification.   Section 2(a) of the Robinson-Patman Act provides a complete defense to a seller when price discrimination is justified by a difference in cost. This is a **cost justification defense**. This defense is available if the seller can link price differences to "differences in the cost of manufacture, sale, or delivery resulting from the differing methods [used] or quantities [sold]." A seller is not required to give a cost break to a buyer based on a cost saving, but it may do so as long as the cost saving is supported by a reliable cost study. If the seller gives a cost break to a particular buyer, the seller may not discriminate against other buyers; it must give similarly situated buyers the same break. The cost saving must be equally available to them.

To sustain a cost justification defense, the seller must prove that a price difference is based on a cost difference. Cost differences in manufacturing or distribution can justify differences in price. Assume, for example, that IBM sells 100 computers a year to a major university and 100 of the same model computers a year to a small computer distributor in a small city. IBM delivers all 100 computers to the university in one shipment; the delivery to the small distributor is made in many small shipments throughout the year. Here, the difference in transportation costs would justify a lower price for the university customer. Another type of justifiable price difference arises from a volume discount, when based on savings in sales personnel, travel, warehousing, or transportation.

Cost justification would in most instances be impossible to establish if not for the permissibility of placing customers in homogeneous groups to average the costs of selling to each group. The group classifications must be reasonable, and each group must have similar characteristics so that the average costs for the whole group are fairly representative of the costs of dealing with each of its members. Hence, IBM's computer purchasers who have the same number of deliveries to approximately the same location may be grouped together for the purposes of comparing their costs with other groups.

Meeting Competition.   The **meeting competition defense** is rooted in Section 2(b) of the Robinson-Patman Act. If the seller can show that the lower price "was made in good faith to meet an equally low price of a competitor," the seller will not be liable for price discrimination under the Act. The seller has the burden of proving the defense.

The statute is very clear that a seller may discriminate only to meet competition—beating competition is not allowed. This concept is more difficult to apply than it sounds. A price differentiation may not be justified where the seller of a premium product reduces its prices in a geographic area to the level charged by a competitor selling a nonpremium product. For example, Anheuser-Busch reduced the price of Budweiser beer in the St. Louis area from $2.93 per case to $2.35 per case in response to the price charged by three regional brewers that were selling their beer at $2.35 per case. In effect, Budweiser attempted to sell a premium product at a price that would have enabled it to compete against nonpremium products. Anheuser-Busch's meeting competition defense was rejected because the reduction was not necessary to hold its customers. The effect of the reduction was to beat competition rather than to meet it.[2]

Sellers must act in good faith when meeting competition. Their actions must be based on a reasonably prudent belief that responding by reducing prices is a

---

[2] FTC v. Anheuser-Busch, Inc., 363 U.S. 536 (1960).

competitive necessity. A seller that acts in good faith, though under an erroneous belief, is protected by the meeting competition defense. However, a seller has a duty to act with reasonable care in verifying competitive offers made to its prospective customers. When the competition is no longer a threat, the seller must cease discriminating in price. The operation of the meeting competition defense is illustrated by the following case.

FALLS CITY INDUSTRIES, INC. v. VANCO BEVERAGES, INC.
460 U.S. 428 (1983)

Vanco Beverages (respondent) was a wholesale distributor of beer produced by Falls City Industries (petitioner). Vanco was the sole Falls City wholesaler in Vanderburgh County, Indiana. Vanderburgh County included the city of Evansville and some Evansville suburbs. Other Evansville suburbs were located in Henderson County, Kentucky. Dawson Springs, Inc. was the sole Falls City wholesaler in Henderson County.

Falls City's competitors raised wholesale prices in Indiana but not in Kentucky. Falls City followed suit. As a result, Dawson Springs was charged a lower price than Vanco. Dawson Springs passed the savings on to its retailers, who were able to charge lower prices than retailers in Indiana. Many consumers in the Evansville metropolitan area switched their purchases of Falls City beer from Indiana to Kentucky retailers.

Alleging illegal price discrimination, Vanco sued Falls City. Falls City claimed that its lower prices in Kentucky were necessary to meet competition there. The district court rejected this defense and awarded damages to Vanco. The Seventh Circuit Court of Appeals affirmed. The Supreme Court reversed.

Justice Blackmun

On its face, Section 2(b) requires more than a showing of facts that would have led a reasonable person to believe that a lower price was available to the favored purchaser from a competitor. The showing required is that the "lower price . . . was made in good faith to meet" the competitor's low price. Thus, the defense requires that the seller offer the lower price in good faith for the purpose of meeting the competitor's price, that is, the lower price must actually have been a good faith response to that competing low price.

■   ■   ■

Vanco . . . [argues] that the existence of industrywide price discrimination within the single geographic retail market itself indicates "tacit or explicit collusion, or . . . market power" inconsistent with a good faith response. By its terms, however, the meeting-competition defense requires a seller to justify only its lower price. Thus, although the Sherman Act would provide a remedy if Falls City's higher Indiana price were set collusively, collusion is relevant to Vanco's Robinson-Patman Act claim only if it affects Falls City's lower Kentucky price. If Falls City set its lower price in good faith to meet an equally low price of a competitor, it did not violate the Robinson-Patman Act.

■   ■   ■

The Court of Appeals explicitly relied on two other factors in rejecting Falls City's meeting-competition defense: the price discrimination was created by raising rather than lowering prices, and Falls City raised its prices in order to increase its profits. Neither of these factors is controlling. Nothing in Section 2(b) requires a seller to lower its price in order to meet competition. On the contrary, Section 2(b) requires the defendant to show only that its "lower price . . . was made in good faith to meet an equally low price of a competitor.

A seller is required to justify a price difference by showing that it reasonably believed that an equally low price was available to the purchaser and that it offered the lower price for that reason; the seller is not required to show that the difference resulted from subtraction rather than addition.

A different rule would not only be contrary to the language of the statute, but also might stifle the only kind of legitimate price competition reasonably available in particular industries. In a period of generally rising prices, vigorous price competition for a particular customer or customers may take the form of smaller price increases rather than price cuts. Thus, a price discrimination created by selective price increases can result from a good faith effort to meet a competitor's low price.

Nor is the good faith with which the lower price is offered impugned if the prices raised, like those kept lower, respond to competitors' prices and are set with the goal of increasing the seller's profits. . . .

Section 2(a) does not require a seller, meeting in good faith a competitor's lower price to certain customers, to forgo the profits that otherwise would be available in sales to its remaining customers. The very purpose of the defense is to permit a seller to treat different competitive situations differently. The prudent businessman responding fairly to what he believes in good faith is a situation of competitive necessity might well raise his prices to some customers to increase his profits, while meeting competitors' prices by keeping his prices to other customers low.

■   ■   ■

The Court of Appeals also . . . [ruled] that the meeting-competition defense "places emphasis on individual [competitive] situations, rather than upon a general system of competition," and "does not justify the maintenance of discriminatory pricing among classes of customers that results merely from the adoption of a competitor's discriminatory pricing structure."

■   ■   ■

There is no evidence that Congress intended to limit the availability of Section 2(b) to customer-specific responses. . . . Congress intended to allow reasonable pricing responses on an area-specific basis where competitive circumstances warrant them. The purpose of the amendment was to "restric[t] the proviso to price differentials occurring in actual competition." We conclude that Congress did not intend to bar territorial price differences that are in fact responses to competitive conditions.

Section 2(b) specifically allows a "lower price . . . to any purchaser or purchasers" made in good faith to meet a competitor's equally low price. . . .

■   ■   ■

A seller may have good reason to believe that a competitor or competitors are charging lower prices throughout a particular region. In such circumstances, customer-by-customer negotiations would be unlikely to result in prices different from those set according to information relating to competitors' territorial prices. A customer-by-customer requirement might also make meaningful price competition unrealistically expensive for smaller firms such as Falls City, which was attempting to compete with larger national breweries in 13 separate States.

Of course, a seller must limit its lower price to that group of customers reasonably believed to have the lower price available to it from competitors. A response that is not reasonably tailored to the competitive situation as known to the buyer, or one that is based on inadequate verification, would not meet the standard of good faith. Similarly, the response may continue only as long as the competitive circumstances justifying it, as reasonably known by the seller, persist. One choosing to price on a territorial basis, rather than on a customer-by-customer basis, must show that this decision was a genuine, reasonable response to prevailing competitive circumstances. Unless the circumstances call into question the seller's good faith, this burden will be discharged by showing that a reasonable and prudent businessman would believe that the lower price he charged was generally available from his competitors throughout the territory and throughout the period in which he made the lower price available.

[The judgment of the district court and the court of appeals is reversed.]

Case Questions

1. Did Vanco and Dawson Springs compete with each other? Was there competitive injury caused by the different prices? Explain.

2. Which argument did Vanco make against Falls City's meeting competition defense? Why did the Supreme Court reject the argument?

3. Why did the court of appeals reject the meeting competition defense? Why did the Supreme Court reject the court of appeals' analysis?

4. Explain the difference between meeting competition on a customer-by-customer basis and meeting competition on a market-by-market basis.

5. What information would an executive want to have before raising or lowering prices in response to market competition?

Changing Market Conditions.   Sellers may reduce prices in response to changes in market conditions or in the marketability of their products. These changes are usually beyond the seller's control. Changing conditions include the threatened deterioration of perishable goods, the obsolescence of seasonal goods, distress sales under court process, and discontinuance of business in specified goods. The classic example of change in product marketability is provided by the automobile industry. Once automobile models for the new year become available, the old year's inventory becomes less marketable. In response, automobile manufacturers may reduce the price of the old year's models without fear of Robinson-Patman liability, because of the **changing market conditions defense**.

Buyer Discrimination

Section 2(f) of the Robinson-Patman Act makes it unlawful to knowingly induce or receive price discrimination in violation of Section 2(a). This section was designed to reach the high-volume purchasers in a position to extract large discriminatory price concessions from the seller. The application of Section 2(f) is illustrated in *Great Atlantic & Pacific Tea Co., Inc. v. FTC.*[3]

A&P, Borden's largest customer in the Chicago area, wished to change from selling brand-label milk to selling private-label milk. It communicated this desire to Borden, which offered A&P a discount on private-label milk. The offer would have saved A&P $410,000 per year. A&P then solicited offers from other dairies and received a more favorable bid from Bowman Dairy. It communicated this fact to Borden but refused to reveal the details of the Bowman bid. Borden, fearing the loss of A&P's business, responded with a new bid that would increase A&P's annual saving to $820,000. Borden stated that its new offer was designed to meet Bowman's bid. A&P accepted Borden's bid, knowing that it was better than Bowman's.

The FTC instituted a complaint against A&P, which included a charge that A&P violated Section 2(f) of the Robinson-Patman Act by knowingly inducing or receiving price discriminations from Borden. The FTC found that A&P knew or should have known that it was the beneficiary of unlawful price discrimination. A&P appealed the decision to the court of appeals, which affirmed the FTC decision. A&P sought review in the Supreme Court. The Supreme Court found in favor of A&P. The court reasoned that A&P could not be liable under Section 2(f) because Borden, the seller, had a valid meeting competition defense. Hence, a buyer cannot be guilty of Section 2(f) discrimination unless the seller is similarly guilty of Section 2(f) discrimination.

Ethical Dilemmas/Issues

Jennifer Blackburn is the manager of Jennifer's Flowers, Inc., a wholesale flower distributor in Chicago. One of the larger retail florists in Chicago has offered to place a large order for flowers with Blackburn. However, the retailer has demanded that she provide a discount that Jennifer's Flowers does not provide to other retailers.

Blackburn's attorney informs her that the retailer's demands cannot be accommodated without violating the Robinson-Patman Act's prohibition against price discrimination. Blackburn really wants to accommodate the retailer's demand, because it would increase business.

What are the ethical issues? What would you do?

Brokerage Payments

Section 2(c) prohibits making or receiving *brokerage payments* except when the payments are made for services actually performed. This section was intended to

---

[3] 440 U.S. 69 (1979).

eliminate dummy brokerage fees that large buyer chains extracted from sellers. The results of this practice were price concessions and, in reality, unfair price discriminations for favored buyers. A seller may not give a brokerage fee to the buyer's broker because the buyer's broker does not render services to the seller. To do so would violate Section 2(c).

Section 2(c) is self-containing and without reference to any other sections. As such, no cost justification, meeting competition, or changing market defenses appear to be available. A violation of Section 2(c) may result from a single transaction. There is no need for two sales, or any showing of competitive injury. All that is required for a violation is a brokerage fee flowing from buyer to seller, or vice versa, without supportive services rendered. However, recent cases have been chipping away at the traditional approach, so that more and more of Section 2(a) elements and the cost justification and meeting competition defenses are seeping into the case law.

Promotional Allowances and Services

Price concessions are not the only way a seller may favor one customer over another. The Robinson-Patman Act also encompasses discrimination related to promotional allowances, signs, displays, demonstrations, packaging, warehousing, return privileges, and a host of other merchandising services. These potential abuses are covered in Sections 2(d) and 2(e). Section 2(d) requires that any payments or allowances by a seller to a buyer for promotional services be available on proportionally equal terms to competing customers. Section 2(e) requires that any services furnished by a seller to a buyer be made available on proportionally equal terms to all competing customers.

Proportionally equal terms may be computed as a percentage of the dollar volume of goods sold or of the quantity of goods purchased. If a seller makes available to each customer an advertising allowance equal to 2 percent of annual purchases, the proportionally equal terms requirement would be satisfied. However, if the 2 percent allowance would not apply until a specified quantity of products were purchased, the allowance might violate the requirement if only a few large buyers could benefit from it.

The meeting competition defense is available under Section 2(d) or Section 2(e), but the cost justification and lack of competitive injury defenses are not available. Nonetheless, they have been considered by courts in determining whether a promotional plan is discriminatory.

Franchising

To the average person, franchising means fast-food chains along major streets. **Franchising**, however, includes a much broader segment of the marketplace. Franchises cover real estate brokerages, accounting and bookkeeping services, computer software, temporary help and other employment services, car rentals, building supplies, and many other areas. Virtually anything that has a marketing plan and can be packaged into something salable can be franchised.

Franchising has expanded tremendously in recent years, enabling franchisors to establish national distribution networks with minimal capital outlays. It also allows small local concerns to affiliate with nationally known operations. Franchisors are not, however, free from antitrust law concern.

Sherman Act: Application to Franchising

Sherman Section 1 and Clayton Section 3 (discussed in Chapter 19) regulate franchising activities. Franchisors are often faced with the same antitrust problems that confront other businesses. Consider, for example, the next case, which involves an alleged Section 1 automobile replacement parts tie-in violation.

METRIX WAREHOUSE, INC. V. MERCEDES-BENZ OF NORTH AMERICA, INC.
828 F.2d 1033 (4th Cir. 1987), *cert. denied,* 486 U.S. 1017 (1988)

Metrix Warehouse (plaintiff) was an independent wholesale distributor of "fast-moving" replacement automobile parts. Fast-moving parts were quick turnover items such as hoses, belts, and spark plugs. Plaintiff sued Mercedes Benz of North America (MBNA) and Diamler-Benz Aktiengesellschaft (DBAG), its German parent company (defendants), alleging that defendants' requirement that all Mercedes dealers buy their replacement parts from them violated the Sherman Act. A jury returned a verdict of $2.3 million, which the trial court refused to set aside. The Fourth Circuit Court of Appeals affirmed in relevant part and reversed on other grounds.

Circuit Judge Sprouse

In Metrix's case-in-chief, it principally tried to . . . show that MBNA officials linked new car access and other favorable treatment to the dealers' purchase of MBNA's "genuine" parts, creating a classic tying arrangement that was per se unreasonable. . . .

MBNA argues that its . . . tying arrangement was essential to preserve the goodwill of its customers, as well as to protect itself from its dealers' fraudulent behavior. . . .

■   ■   ■

An asserted business justification cannot salvage a tying arrangement that is otherwise per se unlawful without proof that means less restrictive than the tie-in were not feasible to achieve the desired protection. . . .

MBNA's . . . argument—that the tie-in was necessary to ensure the quality of the replacement parts sold by its dealerships—fails. . . . It was undisputed that DBAG issued product design specifications to the West German companies that manufactured over half of the fast-moving replacement parts that MBNA sold to the dealers. This evidence dispelled the notion that it was not feasible to designate preferred manufacturers and provide them with design specifications. . . .

MBNA next contends that its customers expected to receive "genuine parts" from MBNA-franchised dealerships and that this expectation constituted a valid justification for the tying arrangement. The evidence, however, suggests that MBNA could have satisfied its customers' expectations through less-restrictive means. Sufficient evidence was presented, for example, to support a finding that MBNA could have required its dealers to inform their customers of the origin of the parts sold and marshaled its efforts toward informing the consumer of the need to request MBNA's parts. In this manner, a customer who expected MBNA parts could have purchased them. It is not necessary, of course, to speculate on the jury's reasoning for rejecting MBNA's goodwill justifications. However, the evidence suggests that MBNA's judgment of its dealers and consumers ran contrary to the Sherman Act's policy that competition rule the markets of trade. As the Supreme Court observed, "any intrinsic superiority of the 'tied' product would convince freely choosing buyers to select it over others, anyway. Perceived consumer expectation, without more, will rarely justify an unlawful tie-in because it is "the public, acting through the market's impersonal judgment . . . [that] allocate[s] the Nation's resources and thus direct[s] the course its economic development will take."

In its final business justification argument, MBNA . . . maintains that, absent the restraint, its dealers would submit non-MBNA parts to MBNA for warranty reimbursement and asserts that its "right to protect itself against this fraudulent prac-

tice should be self-evident." While MBNA, of course, may protect itself against unfounded warranty claims, it cannot impose a tying arrangement when less-restrictive alternatives are reasonably available. MBNA failed to show that its "genuine" parts could not be distinguished from those of its competitors and that it could not avoid reimbursing dealers for its competitors' defective parts. Even assuming the parts were indistinguishable, MBNA presented no evidence that procedures such as stamping, inscribing, or numbering were infeasible alternatives to protect it against warranty "free-riding." Finally, MBNA did not establish that the tie-in was necessary to police dealer misconduct. . . .

Case Questions

1. Describe the tie-in presented in this case. What are the tying and tied products?
2. What was the basis for MBNA's defense?
3. Why did MBNA's business justification defense fail?
4. Would the court have come to a different conclusion if MBNA showed that it performed additional quality control tests on its replacement parts that made its parts more reliable than those sold by other dealers? Why or why not?

FTC Act: Application to Franchising

The relationship between the franchisor and its franchisees is usually governed by contract. The contract may violate Section 5 of the Federal Trade Commission Act. Section 5 prohibits unfair methods of competition and unfair or deceptive trade practices. Section 5 includes, but is broader than, the Sherman and Clayton acts. To implement Section 5, the FTC issues trade regulation rules setting basic standards of lawful business conduct. In response to widespread abuses by franchisors, the FTC has promulgated a rule governing the offering of franchises. The rule requires that all franchisors subject to it provide a prospective franchisee with a document containing specific disclosures.

The Rule's Coverage

The FTC rule is designed to cover all franchise systems, including retail business distribution rights for trademarked products and vending machine route programs. It defines franchises as two types of contractual relationships.

Type I franchises encompass what marketing experts have traditionally called a *franchise*—a marketing system centered on uniform standards and a trademark or tradename. Type I has three requirements:

1. The franchisee must operate under the franchisor's commercial symbol and distribute goods or services that are either identified by the franchisor's symbol or required to meet the franchisor's quality standards. A Coca-Cola bottler is covered because, although the bottler may operate under its own name, it distributes soft drinks identified by the franchisor's trademarks, such as Coca-Cola, Tab, and Sprite. A franchisee operating a Century 21 real estate brokerage franchise is also covered because, although it does not distribute any trademarked items, it must meet the franchisor's quality standards and operates under the Century 21 trademark. A McDonald's franchisee would meet both alternatives of this requirement. It offers food for sale under such commercial symbols as Big Mac and Egg McMuffin. It must meet the franchisor's standards governing the quality of food served and operates under the McDonald's name using commercial symbols such as golden arches.

2. The franchisor exercises significant control over the franchisee's methods of operation or gives the franchisee significant assistance in its operation. Areas of significant control or assistance include the franchisee's business organization, promotional activities, management, or marketing plan.

3. The franchisee is obligated to pay a fee of at least $500 to the franchisor within six months after starting business.

Type II franchises involve such business opportunities as middle-level distributorship and vending-machine supply contracts, even when they are not centered on specific trademarks or subject to uniform standards. Type II also has three requirements:

1. The franchisee offers, sells, or distributes goods, commodities, or services supplied either by the franchisor or by another party with whom the franchisee is required to deal.

2. The franchisor secures for the franchisee retail outlets, accounts, or sites for vending machines, rack displays, or similar sales displays.

3. The franchisee is obligated to pay a fee of at least $500 to the franchisor within six months after starting business.

Both types of franchises are covered only if the franchisee is required to pay the franchisor $500 or more within six months after starting business. This is because the rule is aimed at the prerule practices of some franchisors who received large franchise fees after making unrealistic or even fraudulent promises.

A franchisor is not subject to the rule if the total of all required franchise payments in the first six months is less than $500. The $500 limit includes not only payments made for the right to have a franchise but also payments for tools, equipment, promotional material, and other noninventory goods and services provided by the franchisor. However, it does not include franchisee payments for inventory, optional franchisee payments, and franchisee payments required after the first six months.

Payments for Inventory.   The typical retail franchisee is required to establish an initial inventory. For example, franchisors require new automobile dealerships to purchase an initial inventory of vehicles, parts, and accessories. Inventory purchases are not considered required payments if they are made in quantities a reasonable entrepreneur would require and at fair wholesale prices. Where inventory requirements are unreasonable in price or quantity, however, the FTC may view them as required payments.

Optional Payments.   Franchisees frequently purchase noninventory goods or services from the franchisor. To avoid inclusion of these purchases within the $500 limit, franchisors can allow their franchisees to obtain these goods and services from alternative sources. If the franchisee chooses to obtain them from the franchisor anyway, the franchisee's payments to the franchisor are considered optional. The franchisee's option to purchase from alternative sources must be realistic in light of the industry and community.

The FTC has indicated that it is particularly suspicious of real estate purchases and leases where the franchisor has considerable incentive to require the franchisee to use franchisor-owned property that would otherwise be vacant. For example, the FTC considers service station leases to be required payments, even though the franchisee has the option of leasing a station from other sources, purchasing an existing station, or constructing a new station. Traffic pattern, traffic access, and zoning restrictions give existing leases a comparative advantage over other alternatives, while the initial capital required and uncertainties in financing make the purchase or construction of a new station a dubious possibility for new franchisees.[4]

Payment Required after the First Six Months.   The FTC's franchise rule assumes that in six months the franchisee will become sufficiently familiar with the franchisor to be able to make informed judgments about the relationship. Thus, payments to be made after the first six months are not counted in determining the rule's applicability. A franchisor can avoid the rule's operation by accepting a promissory note payable later than six months from the start of business. For the note to be effective, the franchisor must not be able to discount it and thus destroy the franchisee's ability to assert legal defenses in the collection process.

---

[4] FTC Franchise Advisory Opinions Nos. 17 and 18 to Sinclair Marketing, Inc. and Marathon Oil Co. (October 1, 1979, and October 5, 1979).

Required Disclosure

All franchisors covered by the FTC rule must furnish a disclosure document to prospective franchisees. The rule does not provide for prior review of the document by the FTC. The cover of the required document appears in Figure 21–4.

The document must then set forth the franchisor's name and address and the names of its officers and directors. It must give the following information about its officers and directors:

- Their business experience.
- Their felony convictions, if any, for fraud, embezzlement, fraudulent conversion, misappropriation of property, or restraint of trade.
- All of their involvements in civil or administrative agency litigation concerning fraud, dishonesty, or the franchise relationship.
- Any bankruptcy proceedings in which they have been involved.

The document must also:

- Describe the franchise, including its trademarks, format, the market for its goods or services, and its expected competition.
- Disclose the requirements of franchisees, including required payments, obligations to purchase goods from the franchisor, and personal participation in operating the franchise.
- Disclose the restrictions on franchise territories, customers, or site selection.
- Describe the financing and training made available by the franchisor.

Finally, the document must include information specifying the grounds for terminating the franchise or denying its renewal, statistics of the number of franchisees terminated in the past year, and balance sheets and income statements for

---

FIGURE 21–4   Information for Prospective Franchisees Required by the Federal Trade Commission

To protect you, we've required your franchiser to give you this information. *We haven't checked it and don't know if it's correct.* It should help you make up your mind. Study it carefully. While it includes some information about your contract, don't rely on it alone to understand your contract. Read all of your contract carefully. Buying a franchise is a complicated investment. Take your time to decide. If possible, show your contract and this information to an advisor, like a lawyer or an accountant. If you find anything you think may be wrong or anything important that's been left out, you should let us know about it. It may be against the law.

There may also be laws on franchising in your state. Ask your state agencies about them.

Federal Trade Commission Washington, D.C. 20580

the last three years. The financial statements need not be certified, but they must be prepared in accordance with generally accepted accounting procedures.

Earning Predictions

If the franchisor suggests that the franchisee may achieve a specific level of potential sales, income, or profit, there must be a reasonable basis for the representations. The material supporting the predictions must be made available to prospective franchisees and the FTC. The predictions must be made in a separate document containing all bases and assumptions, the number and percentage of franchise outlets known to have at least equaled the predicted record, and the dates on which that record was attained. The document must also contain the following statement:

CAUTION

These figures are only estimates of what we think you may earn. There is no assurance you'll do as well. If you rely upon our figures, you must accept the risk of not doing so well.

Instead of predicting what prospective franchisees may earn, some franchisors advise them of the sales, income, or profits of existing outlets. In that way, franchisors lead the prospects to infer that they can do as well. These statements must also be given in a separate document that contains the following:

CAUTION

Some outlets have (sold) (earned) this amount. There is no assurance you'll do as well. If you rely upon our figures, you must accept the risk of not doing so well.

All such earnings statements must have cover sheets containing statement similar to that in Figure 21–4.

Trade Show Exemption

The FTC has carved out an exemption for disclosure by trade show promoters who make arrangements with franchisors to offer franchise or business opportunities at their shows. Trade show promoters are exempt from the disclosure requirements applying to franchise brokers if they distribute either of two precautionary notices to each attendee at the show.

Penalties

Franchisors who violate the FTC rule are subject to civil fines of up to $10,000. The FTC may also bring actions for damages on behalf of franchisees in federal district court.

Trade Association Behavior

Trade associations are organizations of competitors with common interests and business pursuits. Section 1 of the Sherman Act has had a severe impact on many trade association activities, several of which are explored in the following sections.

Membership Qualifications

Trade associations often provide services that assist their members' businesses and thereby enhance their abilities to compete. Consequently, their membership criteria are subject to Sherman Act scrutiny under the rule of reason. Unreasonable restraints of trade result from membership requirements not related to the functioning of the service and from membership fees set so high that they raise barriers to entry.

An example of trade association service is the multiple listing of houses maintained by most real estate associations. Each member broker lists houses for sale with the multiple listing service and has access to the houses listed by all other members. Thus, a member broker has the competitive advantage of access to the listings of many other brokers. Simply listing a seller's house enables a broker to make the house available for consideration by many buyers' brokers. Denial of admission to a real estate association results in denial of access to the multiple listing service. This makes it more difficult for a nonmember broker to compete for the business of buyers and sellers. Not all denials of membership are unlawful; however, the criteria on which an exclusion rests must be analyzed under the rule of reason.

Requirements that members approve applications of prospective members, that exclude part-time brokers from membership, or that freeze membership are unrelated to the functioning of the multiple listing service. Such requirements place nonmember competitors at a disadvantage and, accordingly, have been found to unreasonably restrain trade. On the other hand, objective membership requirements that ensure the high integrity and reliability of all users of the service have been found reasonable in light of each member's responsibility for the actions of other members.

Statistical Reporting and Price Exchanges

Among the most important functions of American trade associations are the collection and dissemination of data providing a statistical profile of their industries. In an otherwise perfect market, greater access to information enhances competition. Data-gathering activity, however, may also signal association members about pricing policies they have previously agreed on. A trade association may lawfully gather and disseminate information on costs, volume of production, stocks on hand, and past transactions. Association members may meet and discuss such information, provided that no effort is made to reach any agreement on prices, units of production, or other restraints on competition. Data-gathering schemes are viewed as price fixes, however, when they involve daily reporting or reveal the identities of participating companies, the information furnished by each, or use audits to ensure accurate reporting.

Product Standardization

Product standardization campaigns can have a procompetitive effect by eliminating consumer confusion and focusing consumer attention on price. Where products are standardized, however, prices frequently tend toward uniformity. The problem posed is whether that uniformity is a natural market response to standardization or whether standardization is a method of fixing prices.

In addition to facilitating price fixing, standardization may inhibit innovation. Generally, the degree of standardization plays a leading role in determining whether a particular program unlawfully inhibits innovation. Standards that are recommended and confined to legitimate aims, such as improved safety, usually survive antitrust attacks. However, where a program attempts to standardize color, design, size, or similar features, or where such a program imposes sanctions for deviations, the program may stifle innovation and violate the Sherman Act.

Codes of Ethics

Trade associations frequently promulgate ethical codes to accomplish industry self-regulation. Some code provisions, such as those fixing minimum fees, blatantly violate Section 1. Others, such as those advising against fraudulent or deceptive advertising, are clearly reasonable. Code provisions between these extremes must be assessed under the rule of reason to determine whether they violate the Sherman Act. Code provisions must be justified as either procompetitive or as serving legitimate business purposes with no substantial restraints on competition.

Some codes of ethics are simply advisory in nature. Each association member must follow its own conscience in deciding whether to comply. Many codes, however, contain sanctions for violations. The sanctions may range from reprimands through suspension to expulsion from the trade association. If a sanction is, in effect, a group boycott, it is a per se violation. Thus, an antitrust violation may result from the enforcement of a code provision that is otherwise lawful.

Activities Aimed at Customers or Suppliers

Some associational activities dealing with customers and suppliers are per se illegal group boycotts under the Sherman Act. Sometimes boycott activity is blatant. For example, in an effort to combat style piracy, the members of an association of women's clothing designers agreed to boycott retailers that sold copies of their originals.[5] Similarly, the American Medical Association was found to have violated the Sherman Act by pressuring hospitals to boycott doctors who worked for a nonprofit health maintenance organization.[6]

Association activities that do not involve direct contact with customers or suppliers but are aimed at them do not violate the Sherman Act if they serve legitimate purposes and do not involve price fixing, boycotts, or other unreasonable restraints. The most common activity of this kind is credit reporting. Many companies are too small to carry out their own credit checks economically. These companies may band together through their trade association to achieve an economy of scale that enables them to establish a credit reporting service. Credit reporting generally does not violate Section 1 unless it is accompanied by agreements to fix credit terms or to deny credit to particular customers.

Joint selling and buying activities may result in price fixing, which is a per se violation of Section 1 of the Sherman Act. They may, however, simply represent reasonable efforts to secure a greater market share. As long as market forces continue to set prices, the restraints are reasonable.

Chapter Problems

1. Define the following concepts and terms:
   a. Price discrimination
   b. Like grade and quality
   c. Primary-line injury
   d. Secondary-line injury
   e. Cost justification defense
   f. Meeting competition defense
   g. Changing market conditions defense
   h. Business justification defense
   i. Franchising
   j. Trade association

2. The *Bismarck Tribune* is a daily newspaper based in Bismarck, North Dakota. The *Morning Pioneer* is a daily newspaper based in Mandan, North Dakota, which is about seven miles from Bismarck. The two newspapers have a long history of coexistence, each serving its own market area without attempting to infringe the market of the other.

   Recent developments have caused this amicable relationship to break down, and the *Tribune* is now waging an active campaign to capture the Mandan market. In its attempt to win the *Pioneer*'s customers, the *Tribune* has reduced the price of its newspaper delivered in Mandan below the Bis-

---

[5] Fashion Originators Guild v. FTC, 312 U.S. 457 (1941).
[6] American Medical Association v. United States, 317 U.S. 519 (1943).

marck price. The *Tribune* delivered in Mandan contains older news than the *Tribune* delivered in Bismarck. Also, the *Tribune* advertisements are valuable only to those persons who shop in Bismarck. The *Pioneer* has brought an action to prevent the *Tribune* from engaging in what the *Pioneer* considers illegal activity in violation of Section 2(a) of the Robinson-Patman Act. What is the *Pioneer's* argument? What is the *Tribune's* counterargument? Has the Tribune violated Section 2(a)? Explain.

3. The Folger Company, manufacturer of Folger's Coffee, is considering undertaking a major promotional campaign whereby it will give directly to consumers free samples, refunds, and coupons good for 50 cents off on purchases of a two-pound can. Although Folger's coffee is sold nationwide, the company plans to limit its promotional campaign to the metropolitan Chicago area. Will this limitation violate Section 2(a) of the Robinson-Patman Act? Explain.

4. Continental Baking Co. manufactures white bread, which it markets under the label *Wonder Bread.* Continental sells Wonder Bread to supermarket chains and independent groceries. Many independents have formed a buying cooperative. Continental has agreed to sell the cooperative a private-label bread at 20 percent below the price it charges for Wonder Bread. Members of the cooperative will market it as Tender Crust Bread. The private-label bread is identical to Wonder Bread except for its brand name. The cooperative has also agreed that its members will give Wonder Bread preferred shelf space over competing brands. Has Continental violated the Robinson-Patman Act? Why or why not?

5. Morton Salt Company manufactures and sells different brands of table salt to wholesalers and larger retail grocery chains. Its finest brand, Blue Label, is sold on a standard quantity discount system. Blue Label purchasers pay a delivered price based on the quantities bought:

Purchases	Price per Case
Less than carload	$1.60
Carload	1.50
5,000 cases in any consecutive 12 months	1.40
50,000 cases in any consecutive 12 months	1.35

Only five companies operating large chains of retail stores have been able to buy Blue Label at $1.35 per case. Because of the discount these companies command, they are able to sell Blue Label at retail cheaper than the wholesaler purchasers can sell it to independently operated retail stores. Many of those independently operated stores compete directly with the retail outlets of the five large chains. The FTC seeks to enjoin Morton from sales of salt under this discount system. Identify and discuss the key issues.

6. Kroger Company operates a chain of more than 1,400 retail grocery stores in 19 states. Its sales exceed $2 billion a year. The competitors of Kroger's Charleston Division include national and regional chains and independent supermarkets. Beatrice Foods, a large U.S. dairy company, has $569 million in annual sales. Beatrice supplies Kroger's Charleston Division. Kroger decided to sell private-label brands to become more competitive. It invited companies to submit bids for bottling Kroger-label milk for its Charleston Division. Broughton submitted the first bid. Beatrice officials then met with Kroger representatives in the hope of making a successful bid for bottling Kroger's private-brand milk. When a Beatrice official said that his company would offer a 15 percent discount, the Kroger representative replied, "Well, forget it—I've already got one at 20 percent off the list price." Actually, Kroger had not received any bid lower than the Beatrice offer. Beatrice then offered to meet the 20 percent discount, and Kroger accepted the offer. Is Beatrice in violation of the Robinson-Patman Act? Why or why not? Is Kroger in violation of the act? Why or why not?

7. You are the vice president for North American sales for NEC, a major manufacturer of telephone equipment. As vice president, you have negotiated volume discounts of 8 to 12 percent with existing customers. Recently, NEC upgraded its 6140 line of telephones to include more programmable features. NEC has approximately $1 million of the older, less programmable telephone equipment in its inventory. Bob Wright, a regional sales manager, called you, saying that he has found a buyer for the older equipment if you are prepared to sell it below cost. What should you tell Bob?

8. A franchisor of hardware stores wishes to use a table that shows potential franchisees what the investor's gross profits would be if a particular number of items are sold in a given period of time from certain retail locations. What liability might result from the use of the table? What must it do to avoid liability?

9. Comprehensive Accounting Corporation (CAC) franchises accountants to provide services in CAC's name. CAC's services to its franchisees include data processing. CAC generates accounting reports from its large computer. Its franchisees pay for this service. CAC, by contract, permits its franchisees to use other data processing services only if those services "produce reports that look exactly like those Comprehensive produces." Many of CAC's franchisees have small computers, but those computers, although they come close, do not duplicate CAC's data processing with respect to forms. Nonetheless, several franchisees used their own computer systems. May CAC terminate them without violating the antitrust laws? Explain.

10. A trade association of china manufacturers conducted a cost-accounting survey of its members. The study was conducted to enable members to bring their prices more nearly in line with costs. It was intended to replace an outdated study that had been conducted by a member of the association. The study's results were discussed at association meetings and unanimously adopted by members as their basis for determining prices. There are more than 1,700 sizes, shapes, and colors of china. China prices have never tended toward uniformity. Has the association violated the Sherman Act?

A THE CONSTITUTION OF THE UNITED STATES OF AMERICA

Preamble

We the People of the United States, in Order to form a more perfect Union, establish Justice, insure domestic Tranquility, provide for the common defence, promote the general Welfare, and secure the Blessings of Liberty to ourselves and our Posterity, do ordain and establish this Constitution for the United States of America.

Article I

Bicameral legislature

Section 1 All legislative Powers herein granted shall be vested in a Congress of the United States which shall consist of a Senate and House of Representatives.

House of Representatives

Section 2 The House of Representatives shall be composed of Members chosen every second Year by the People of the several States, and the Electors in each State shall have the Qualifications requisite for Electors of the most numerous Branch of the State Legislature.

No Person shall be a Representative who shall not have attained to the age of twenty five Years, and been seven Years a Citizen of the United States, and who shall not, when elected, be an Inhabitant of that State in which he shall be chosen.

Representatives and direct Taxes shall be apportioned among the several States which may be included within this Union, according to their respective Numbers, which shall be determined by adding to the whole Number of free Persons, including those bound to Service for a Term of Years, and excluding Indians not taxed, three fifths of all other Persons.[1] The actual Enumeration shall be made within three Years after the first Meeting of the Congress of the United States, and within every subsequent Term of ten Years, in such Manner as they shall by Law direct.

---

[1] Changed by the Fourteenth Amendment.

The Number of Representatives shall not exceed one for every thirty Thousand, but each State shall have at Least one Representative; and until such enumeration shall be made, the State of New Hampshire shall be entitled to chuse three, Massachusetts eight, Rhode-Island and Providence Plantations one, Connecticut five, New-York six, New Jersey four, Pennsylvania eight, Delaware one, Maryland six, Virginia ten, North Carolina five, South Carolina five, and Georgia three.

When vacancies happen in the Representation from any State, the Executive Authority thereof shall issue Writs of Election to fill such Vacancies.

The House of Representatives shall chuse their Speaker and other Officers; and shall have the sole Power of Impeachment.

Senate

Section 3   The Senate of the United States shall be composed of two Senators from each State, chosen by the Legislature thereof,[2] for six Years; and each Senator shall have one Vote.

Immediately after they shall be assembled in Consequence of the first Election, they shall be divided as equally as may be into three Classes. The Seats of the Senators of the first Class shall be vacated at the Expiration of the second Year, of the second Class at the Expiration of the fourth Year, and of the third Class at the Expiration of the sixth Year, so that one third may be chosen every second Year; and if Vacancies happen by Resignation, or otherwise, during the Recess of the Legislature of any State, the Executive thereof may make temporary Appointments until the next Meeting of the Legislature, which shall then fill such Vacancies.[3]

No Person shall be a Senator who shall not have attained to the Age of thirty Years, and been nine Years a Citizen of the United States, and who shall not, when elected, be an Inhabitant of that State for which he shall be chosen.

The Vice President of the United States shall be President of the Senate, but shall have no Vote, unless they be equally divided.

The Senate shall chuse their other Officers, and also a President pro tempore, in the Absence of the Vice President, or when he shall exercise the Office of President of the United States.

The Senate shall have the sole Power to try all Impeachments. When sitting for that Purpose, they shall be on Oath or Affirmation. When the President of the United States is tried, the Chief Justice shall preside: And no Person shall be convicted without the Concurrence of two thirds of the Members present.

Judgment in Cases of Impeachment shall not extend further than to removal from Office, and disqualification to hold and enjoy any Office of honor, Trust or Profit under the United States: but the Party convicted shall nevertheless be liable and subject to Indictment, Trial, Judgment and Punishment, according to Law.

Congressional elections

Section 4   The Times, Places and Manner of holding Elections for Senators and Representatives, shall be prescribed in each State by the Legislature thereof; but

---

[2] Changed by the Seventeenth Amendment.
[3] Changed by the Seventeenth Amendment.

the Congress may at any time by Law make or alter such Regulations, except as to the Places of chusing Senators.

The Congress shall assemble at least once in every Year, and such Meeting shall be on the first Monday in December, unless they shall by Law appoint a different Day.[4]

Powers and duties of Congress

Section 5   Each House shall be the Judge of the Elections, Returns and Qualifications of its own Members, and a Majority of each shall constitute a Quorum to do Business; but a smaller Number may adjourn from day to day, and may be authorized to compel the Attendance of absent Members, in such Manner, and under such Penalties as each House may provide.

Each House may determine the Rules of its Proceedings, punish its Members for disorderly Behavior, and, with the Concurrence of two thirds, expel a Member.

Each House shall keep a Journal of its Proceedings, and from time to time publish the same, excepting such Parts as may in their Judgment require Secrecy; and the Yeas and Nays of the Members of either House on any question shall, at the Desire of one fifth of those Present, be entered on the Journal.

Neither House, during the Session of Congress, shall, without the Consent of the other, adjourn for more than three days, not to any other Place than that in which the two Houses shall be sitting.

Compensation, immunities, restrictions—members of Congress

Section 6   The Senators and Representatives shall receive a Compensation for their Services, to be ascertained by Law, and paid out of the Treasury of the United States. They shall in all Cases, except Treason, Felony and Breach of the Peace, be privileged from Arrest during their Attendance at the Session of their respective Houses, and in going to and returning from the same; and for any Speech or Debate in either House, they shall not be questioned in any other Place.

No Senator or Representative shall, during the Time for which he was elected, be appointed to any civil Office under the Authority of the United States, which shall have been created, or the Emoluments whereof shall have been increased during such time; and no Person holding any Office under the United States, shall be a Member of either House during his continuance in Office.

Legislative procedures

Section 7   All Bills for raising Revenue shall originate in the House of Representatives; but the Senate may propose or concur with Amendments as on other Bills.

Every Bill which shall have passed the House of Representatives and the Senate, shall, before it become a Law, be presented to the President of the United States; if he approves he shall sign it, but if not he shall return it, with his Objections to that House in which it shall have originated, who shall enter the Objections at large on their Journal, and proceed to reconsider it. If after such Reconsideration two thirds of that House shall agree to pass the Bill, it shall be

---

[4] Changed by the Twentieth Amendment.

sent, together with the Objections, to the other House, by which it shall likewise be reconsidered, and if approved by two thirds of that House, it shall become a Law. But in all such Cases the Votes of both Houses shall be determined by Yeas and Nays, and the Names of the Persons voting for and against the Bill shall be entered on the Journal of each House respectively. If any Bill shall not be returned by the President within ten Days (Sundays excepted) after it shall have been presented to him, the Same shall be a Law, in like Manner as if he had signed it, unless the Congress by their Adjournment prevent its Return, in which Case it shall not be a Law:

Every order, Resolution, or Vote to which the Concurrence of the Senate and House of Representatives may be necessary (except on a question of Adjournment) shall be presented to the President of the United States; and before the Same shall take Effect, shall be approved by him, or being disapproved by him, shall be repassed by two thirds of the Senate and House of Representatives, according to the Rules and Limitations prescribed in the Case of a Bill.

Powers of Congress   **Section 8**   The Congress shall have Power To lay and collect Taxes, Duties, Imposts and Excises, to pay the Debts and provide for the common Defence and general Welfare of the United States; but all Duties, Imposts and Excises shall be uniform throughout the United States;

To borrow Money on the credit of the United States;

To regulate Commerce with foreign Nations, and among the several States, and with the Indian Tribes;

To establish an uniform Rule of Naturalization, and uniform Laws on the subject of Bankruptcies throughout the United States;

To coin Money, regulate the Value thereof, and of foreign Coin, and fix the Standard of Weights and Measures;

To provide for the Punishment of counterfeiting the Securities and current Coin of the United States;

To establish Post Offices and post Roads;

To promote the Progress of Science and useful Arts, by securing for limited Times to Authors and Inventors the exclusive Right to their respective Writings and Discoveries;

To constitute Tribunals inferior to the supreme Court;

To define and punish Piracies and Felonies committed on the high Seas, and Offences against the Law of Nations;

To declare War, grant Letters of Marque and Reprisal, and make Rules concerning Captures on Land and Water;

To raise and support Armies, but no Appropriation of Money to that Use shall be for a longer Term than two Years;

To provide and maintain a Navy;

To make Rules for the Government and Regulation of the land and naval Forces;

To provide for calling forth the Militia to execute the Laws of the Union, suppress Insurrections and repel Invasions;

To provide for organizing, arming, and disciplining the Militia, and for governing such Part of them as may be employed in the Service of the United States, reserving to the States respectively, the Appointment of the Officers, and the Authority of training the militia according to the discipline prescribed by Congress;

To exercise exclusive Legislation in all Cases whatsoever, over such District (not exceeding ten Miles square) as may, by Cession of Particular States, and the Acceptance of Congress, become the Seat of the Government of the United States, and to exercise like Authority over all Places purchased by the Consent of the Legislature of the State in which the Same shall be, for the Erection of Forts, Magazines, Arsenals, dock-Yards, and other needful Buildings;—And

To make all Laws which shall be necessary and proper for carrying into Execution the foregoing Powers, and all other Powers vested by this Constitution in the Government of the United States, or in any Department or Officer thereof.

Limits on congressional powers

Section 9   The Migration or Importation of such Persons as any of the States now existing shall think proper to admit, shall not be prohibited by the Congress prior to the Year one thousand eight hundred and eight, but a Tax or duty may be imposed on such Importation, not exceeding ten dollars for each Person.

The Privilege of the Writ of Habeas Corpus shall not be suspended, unless when in Cases of Rebellion or Invasion the public Safety may require it.

No Bill of Attainder or ex post facto Law shall be passed.

No Capitation, or other direct, Tax shall be laid, unless in Proportion to the Census of Enumeration herein before directed to be taken.[5]

No Tax or Duty shall be laid on Articles exported from any State.

No Preference shall be given by any Regulation of Commerce or Revenue to the Ports of one State over those of another; nor shall Vessels bound to, or from, one State, be obliged to enter, clear or pay Duties in another.

No Money shall be drawn from the Treasury, but on Consequence of Appropriations made by Law; and a regular Statement and Account of the Receipts and Expenditures of all public Money shall be published from time to time.

No Title of Nobility shall be granted by the United States: And no Person holding any Office of Profit or Trust under them, shall, without the Consent of the Congress, accept of any present, Emolument, Office, or Title, of any kind whatever, from any King, Prince, or foreign State.

Limits on powers of states

Section 10   No State shall enter into any Treaty, Alliance, or Confederation; grant Letters of Marque and Reprisal; coin Money; emit Bills of Credit; make any Thing but gold and silver Coin a Tender in Payment of Debts; pass any Bill of Attainder, ex post facto Law, or Law impairing the Obligation of Contracts, or grant any Title of Nobility.

No State shall, without the Consent of the Congress, lay any Imposts or Duties on Imports or Exports, except what may be absolutely necessary for executing its

---

[5] Changed by the Sixteenth Amendment.

inspection Laws: and the net Produce of all Duties and Imposts, laid by any State on Imports or Exports, shall be for the Use of the Treasury of the United States; and all such Laws shall be subject to the Revision and Control of the Congress.

No State shall, without the consent of Congress, lay any Duty of Tonnage, keep Troops, or Ships of War in time of Peace, enter into any Agreement or Compact with another State, or with a foreign Power, or engage in War, unless actually invaded, or in such imminent Danger as will not admit of delay.

Article II

Presidency

Section 1   The executive Power shall be vested in a President of the United States of America. He shall hold his Office during the Term of four Years, and, together with the Vice President, chosen for the same Term, be elected, as follows:

Each State shall appoint, in such Manner as the Legislature thereof may direct, a Number of Electors, equal to the whole Number of Senators and Representatives to which the State may be entitled in Congress: but no Senator or Representative, or Person holding an Office of Trust or Profit under the United States, shall be appointed an Elector.

The Electors shall meet in their respective States, and vote by Ballot for two Persons, of whom one at least shall not be an Inhabitant of the same State with themselves. And they shall make a List of all the Persons voted for, and of the Number of Votes for each; which List they shall sign and certify, and transmit sealed to the Seat of the Government of the United States, directed to the President of the Senate. The President of the Senate shall, in the Presence of the Senate and House of Representatives, open all the Certificates, and the Votes shall then be counted. The Person having the greatest Number of Votes shall be the President, if such Number be a Majority of the whole Number of Electors' appointed; and if there be more than one who have such Majority, and have an equal Number of Votes, then the House of Representatives shall immediately chuse by Ballot one of them for President; and if no Person have a Majority, then from the five highest on the List the said House shall in like Manner chuse the President. But in chusing the President, the Votes shall be taken by States, the Representation from each State having one Vote; a quorum for this Purpose shall consist of a Member or Members from two thirds of the States, and a Majority of all the States shall be necessary to a Choice. In every Case, after the Choice of the President, the Person having the greatest Number of Votes of the Electors shall be the Vice President. But if there should remain two or more who have equal Votes, the Senate shall chuse from them by Ballot the Vice President.[6]

The Congress may determine the Time of chusing the Electors, and the Day on which they shall be given their Votes; which Day shall be the same throughout the United States.

---

[6] Changed by the Twelfth Amendment.

No Person except a natural born Citizen, or a Citizen of the United States, at the time of the Adoption of this Constitution, shall be eligible to the Office of President; neither shall any person be eligible to that Office who shall not have attained to the Age of thirty five Years, and been fourteen Years a Resident within the United States.

In Case of the Removal of the President from Office, or of his Death, Resignation, or Inability to discharge the Powers and Duties of the said Office, the Same shall devolve on the Vice President, and the Congress may by Law provide for the Case of Removal, Death, Resignation or Inability, both of the President and Vice President, declaring what Officer shall then act as President, and such Officer shall act accordingly, until the Disability be removed, or a President shall be elected.[7]

The President shall, at stated Times, receive for his Services, a Compensation, which shall neither be increased nor diminished during the period for which he shall have been elected, and he shall not receive within that Period any other Emolument from the United States, or any of them.

Before he enter on the Execution of his Office, he shall take the following Oath or Affirmation:—"I do solemnly swear (or affirm) that I will faithfully execute the Office of President of the United States, and will to the best of my Ability, preserve, protect and defend the Constitution of the United States."

Presidential powers   **Section 2**   The President shall be Commander in Chief of the Army and Navy of the United States, and of the Militia of the several States, when called into the actual Service of the United States; he may require the Opinion, in writing, of the principal Officer in each of the executive Departments, upon any Subject relating to the Duties of their respective Offices, and he shall have Power to grant Reprieves and Pardons for Offences against the United States, except in Cases of Impeachment.

He shall have Power, by and with the Advice and Consent of the Senate, to make Treaties, provided two thirds of the Senators present concur; and he shall nominate, and by and with the Advice and Consent of the Senate, shall appoint Ambassadors, other public Ministers and Consuls, Judges of the supreme Court, and all other Officers of the United States, whose Appointments are not herein otherwise provided for, and which shall be established by Law: but the Congress may by Law vest the Appointment of such inferior Officers, as they think proper, in the President alone, in the Courts of Law, or in the Heads of Departments.

The President shall have Power to fill up all Vacancies that may happen during the Recess of the Senate, by granting Commissions which shall expire at the End of their next Session.

Section 3   He shall from time to time give to the Congress Information of the State of the Union, and recommend to their Consideration such Measures as he shall judge necessary and expedient; he may, on extraordinary Occasions, convene both Houses, or either of them, and in Case of Disagreement between them,

---

[7] Changed by the Twenty-fifth Amendment.

with Respect to the Time of Adjournment, he may adjourn them to such Time as he shall think proper; he shall receive Ambassadors and other public Ministers; he shall take Care that the Laws be faithfully executed, and shall Commission all the Officers of the United States.

Impeachment

Section 4   The President, Vice President and all civil Officers of the United States, shall be removed from Office on Impeachment for, and Conviction of, Treason, Bribery, or other high Crimes and Misdemeanors.

Article III

Judiciary

Section 1   The judicial Power of the United States, shall be vested in one supreme Court, and in such inferior Courts as the Congress may from time to time ordain and establish. The Judges, both of the supreme and inferior Courts, shall hold their Offices during good Behaviour, and shall, at stated Times, receive for their Services, a Compensation, which shall not be diminished during their Continuance in Office.

Jurisdiction

Section 2   The judicial Power shall extend to all Cases, in Law and Equity, arising under this Constitution, the Laws of the United States, and Treaties made, or which shall be made, under their Authority;—to all Cases affecting Ambassadors, other public Ministers and Consuls; to all Cases of admiralty and maritime Jurisdiction;—to Controversies to which the United States shall be a party; to Controversies between two or more States; between a State and Citizens of another State;[8]—between Citizens of different States;—between Citizens of the same State claiming Lands under Grants of different States, and between a State, or the Citizens thereof, and foreign States, Citizens or Subjects.

In all Cases affecting Ambassadors, other public Ministers and Consuls, and those in which a State shall be Part, the supreme Court shall have original Jurisdiction. In all the other Cases before mentioned, the supreme Court shall have appellate Jurisdiction, both as to Law and Fact, with such Exceptions, and under such Regulations as the Congress shall make.

The Trial of all Crimes, except in Cases of Impeachment, shall be by Jury; and such Trial shall be held in the State where the said Crimes shall have been committed; but when not committed within any State, the Trial shall be at such Place or Places as the Congress may by Law have directed.

Treason

Section 3   Treason against the United States, shall consist only in levying War against them, or in adhering to the Enemies, giving them Aid and Comfort. No Person shall be convicted of Treason unless on the Testimony of two Witnesses to the same overt Act, or on Confession in open Court.

---

[8] Changed by the Eleventh Amendment.

The Congress shall have Power to declare the Punishment of Treason, but no Attainder of Treason shall work Corruption of Blood, or Forfeiture except during the Life of the Person attainted.

Article IV

Full faith and credit

Section I   Full Faith and Credit shall be given in each State to the public Acts, Records, and judicial Proceedings of every other State. And the Congress may by general Laws prescribe the Manner in which such Acts, Records and Proceedings shall be proved, and the Effect thereof.

Privileges and immunities, extradition

Section 2   The Citizens of each State shall be entitled to all Privileges and Immunities of Citizens in the several States.

A person charged in any State with Treason, Felony, or other Crime, who shall flee from Justice, and be found in another State, shall on Demand of the executive Authority of the State from which he fled, be delivered up, to be removed to the State having Jurisdiction of the Crime.

No Person held to Service or Labour in one State, under the Laws thereof, escaping into another, shall, in Consequence of any Law or Regulation therein, be discharged from such Service or Labour, but shall be delivered up on Claim of the Party to whom such Service or Labour may be due.[9]

New states

Section 3   New States may be admitted by the Congress into this Union; but no new State shall be formed or erected within the Jurisdiction of any other State; nor any State be formed by the Junction of two or more States, or Parts of States, without the Consent of the Legislatures of the States concerned as well as of the Congress.

The Congress shall have Power to dispose of and make all needful Rules and Regulations respecting the Territory or other Property belonging to the United States; and nothing in this Constitution shall be so construed as to Prejudice any Claims of the United States, or of any particular State.

Protection of states

Section 4   The United States shall guarantee to every State in this Union a Republican Form of Government, and shall protect each of them against Invasion; and on Application of the Legislature, or of the Executive (when the Legislature cannot be convened) against domestic Violence.

Amendment procedures

Article V

The Congress, whenever two thirds of both Houses shall deem it necessary, shall propose Amendments to this Constitution, or, on the Application of the Legislatures

---

[9] Changed by the Thirteenth Amendment.

of two thirds of the several States, shall call a Convention for proposing Amendments, which, in either Case, shall be valid to all Intents and Purposes, as Part of this Constitution, when ratified by the Legislatures of three fourths of the several States, or by Conventions in three fourths thereof, as the one or the other Mode of Ratification may be proposed by the Congress; Provided that no Amendment which may be made prior to the Year One thousand eight hundred and eight shall in any Manner affect the first and fourth Clauses in the Ninth Section of the first Article; and that no State, without its Consent, shall be deprived of its equal Suffrage in the Senate.

Supremacy of federal laws

Article VI

All Debts contracted and Engagements entered into, before the Adoption of this Constitution, shall be as valid against the United States under this Constitution, as under the Confederation.

This Constitution, and the Laws of the United States which shall be made in Pursuance thereof; and all Treaties made, or which shall be made, under the Authority of the United States, shall be the supreme Law of the Land; and the Judges in every State shall be bound thereby, any Thing in the Constitution or Laws of any State to the Contrary notwithstanding.

The Senators and Representatives before mentioned, and the Members of the several State Legislatures, and all executive and judicial Officers, both of the United States and of the several States, shall be bound by Oath or Affirmation, to support this Constitution; but no religious Test shall ever be required as a Qualification to any Office or public Trust under the United States.

Ratification

Article VII

The Ratification of the Conventions of nine States shall be sufficient for the Establishment of this Constitution between the States so ratifying the Same.

Done in Convention by the Unanimous Consent of the States present the Seventeenth Day of September in the Year of our Lord one thousand seven hundred and Eighty seven and of the Independence of the United States of America the Twelfth. In witness whereof We have hereunto subscribed our Names.

■   ■   ■

The first ten amendments, the "Bill of Rights," were ratified in 1791.

Freedom of religion, speech, press, assembly

Amendment 1

Congress shall make no law respecting an establishment of religion, or prohibiting the free exercise thereof; or abridging the freedom of speech, or of the press; or the right of the people peaceably to assemble, and to petition the Government for a redress of grievances.

Right to bear arms

Amendment 2

A well regulated Militia, being necessary to the security of a free State, the right of the people to keep and bear Arms, shall not be infringed.

Quartering soldiers

Amendment 3

No Soldier shall, in time of peace be quartered in any house, without the consent of the Owner, nor in time of war, but in a manner to be prescribed by law.

Searches and seizures

Amendment 4

The right of the people to be secure in their persons, houses, papers, and effects, against unreasonable searches and seizures, shall not be violated, and no Warrants shall issue, but upon probable cause, supported by Oath or affirmation, and particularly describing the place to be searched, and the persons or things to be seized.

Rights of accused, due process

Amendment 5

No person shall be held to answer for a capital, or otherwise infamous crime, unless on a presentment or indictment of a Grand Jury, except in cases arising in the land or naval forces, or in the Militia, when in actual service in time of War or public danger; nor shall any person be subject for the same offence to be twice put in jeopardy of life or limb; nor shall be compelled in any criminal case to be a witness against himself, nor be deprived of life, liberty, or property, without due process of law; nor shall private property be taken for public use, without just compensation.

Criminal prosecution

Amendment 6

In all criminal prosecutions, the accused shall enjoy the right to a speedy and public trial, by an impartial jury of the State and district wherein the crime shall have been committed, which district shall have been previously ascertained by law, and to be informed of the nature and cause of the accusation; to be confronted with the witnesses against him; to have compulsory process for obtaining witnesses in his favor, and to have Assistance of Counsel for his defence.

Common-law suits

Amendment 7

In Suits at common law, where the value in controversy shall exceed twenty dollars, the right of trial by jury shall be preserved, and no fact tried by a jury, shall be otherwise reexamined in any Court of the United States, than according to the rules of the common law.

**Bail, cruel and un-
usual punishment**

Amendment 8

Excessive bail shall not be required, nor excessive fines imposed, nor cruel and unusual punishments inflicted.

**Unenumerated
rights**

Amendment 9

The enumeration in the Constitution, of certain rights, shall not be construed to deny or disparage others retained by the people.

**Powers reserved
to states**

Amendment 10

The powers not delegated to the United States by the Constitution, nor prohibited by it to the States, are reserved to the States respectively, or to the people.

Suits against states

Amendment 11 [Ratified 1795]

The Judicial power of the United States shall not be construed to extend to any suit in law or equity, commenced or prosecuted against one of the United States by Citizens of another State, or by Citizens or Subjects of any Foreign State.

Presidential elections

Amendment 12 [Ratified 1804]

The Electors shall meet in their respective states and vote by ballot for President and Vice President, one of whom, at least, shall not be an inhabitant of the same state with themselves; they shall name in their ballots the person voted for as President, and in distinct ballots the person voted for as Vice President, and they shall make distinct lists of all persons voted for as President, and of all persons voted for as Vice President, and of the number of votes for each, which lists they shall sign and certify, and transmit sealed to the seat of the government of the United States, directed to the President of the Senate; The President of the Senate shall, in the presence of the Senate and House of Representatives, open all the certificates and the votes shall then be counted;—The person having the greatest number of votes for President, shall be the President, if such number be a majority of the whole number of Electors appointed; and if no person have such majority, then from the persons having the highest numbers not exceeding three on the list of those voted for as President, the House of Representatives shall choose immediately, by ballot, the President. But in choosing the President, the votes shall be taken by states, the representation from each state having one vote; a quorum for this purpose shall consist of a member or members from two-thirds of the states, and a majority of all the states shall be necessary to a choice. And if the House of Representatives shall not choose a President whenever the right of choice shall devolve upon them, before the fourth day of March next following, then the Vice

President shall act as President, as in the case of the death or other constitutional disability of the President.[10] The person having the greatest number of votes as Vice President, shall be the Vice President, if such number be a majority of the whole number of Electors appointed, and if no person have a majority, then from the two highest numbers on the list, the Senate shall choose the Vice President; a quorum for the purpose shall consist of two-thirds of the whole number of Senators, and a majority of the whole number shall be necessary to a choice. But no person constitutionally ineligible to the office of President shall be eligible to that of Vice President of the United States.

Prohibition of Slavery

Amendment 13 [Ratified 1865]

Section 1   Neither slavery nor involuntary servitude, except as a punishment for crime whereof the party shall have been duly convicted, shall exist within the United States, or any place subject to their jurisdiction.

Section 2   Congress shall have power to enforce this article by appropriate legislation.

Citizenship, due process applied to the states, equal protection of the laws

Amendment 14 [Ratified 1868]

Section 1   All persons born or naturalized in the United States and subject to the jurisdiction thereof, are citizens of the United States and of the State wherein they reside. No State shall make or enforce any law which shall abridge the privileges or immunities of citizens of the United States; nor shall any State deprive any person of life, liberty, or property, without due process of law; nor deny to any person within its jurisdiction the equal protection of the laws.

Section 2   Representatives shall be apportioned among the several States according to their respective numbers, counting the whole number of persons in each State, excluding Indians not taxed. But when the right to vote at any election for the choice of electors for President and Vice President of the United States, Representatives in Congress, the Executive and Judicial officers of a State, or the members of the Legislature thereof, is denied to any of the male inhabitants of such State, being twenty-one[11] years of age, and citizens of the United States, or in any way abridged, except for participation in rebellion, or other crime, the basis of representation therein shall be reduced in the proportion which the number of such male citizens shall bear to the whole number of male citizens twenty-one years of age in such State.

Section 3   No person shall be a Senator or Representative in Congress, or elector of President and Vice President, or hold any office, civil or military, under

---

[10] Changed by the Twentieth Amendment.
[11] Changed by the Twenty-sixth Amendment.

the United States, or under any State, who, having previously taken an oath, as a member of Congress, or as an officer of the United States, or as a member of any State legislature, or as an executive or judicial officer of any State, to support the Constitution of the United States, shall have engaged in insurrection or rebellion against the same, or given aid or comfort to the enemies thereof. But Congress may by a vote of two-thirds of each House, remove such disability.

Section 4   The validity of the public debt of the United States, authorized by law, including debts incurred for payment of pensions and bounties for services in suppressing insurrection or rebellion, shall not be questioned. But neither the United States nor any State shall assume or pay any debt or obligation incurred in aid of insurrection or rebellion against the United States, or any claim for the loss or emancipation of any slave; but all such debts, obligations and claims shall be held illegal and void.

Section 5   The Congress shall have power to enforce, by appropriate legislation, the provisions of this article.

Right to vote

Amendment 15 [Ratified 1870]

Section 1   The right of citizens of the United States to vote shall not be denied or abridged by the United States or by any State on account of race, color, or previous condition of servitude.

Section 2   The Congress shall have power to enforce this article by appropriate legislation.

Income taxes

Amendment 16 [Ratified 1913]

The Congress shall have power to lay and collect taxes on incomes, from whatever source derived, without apportionment among the several States, and without regard to any census or enumeration.

Direct election of senators

Amendment 17 [Ratified 1913]

The Senate of the United States shall be composed of two Senators from each State, elected by the people thereof, for six years; and each Senator shall have one vote. The electors in each State shall have the qualifications requisite for electors of the most numerous branch of the State legislatures.

When vacancies happen in the representation of any State in the Senate, the executive authority of such State shall issue writs of election to fill such vacancies: *Provided,* That the legislature of any State may empower the executive thereof to make temporary appointments until the people fill the vacancies by election as the legislature may direct.

This amendment shall not be so construed as to affect the election or term of any Senator chosen before it becomes valid as part of the Constitution.

Prohibition

Amendment 18 [Ratified 1919]

Section 1   After one year from the ratification of this article, the manufacture, sale, or transportation of intoxicating liquors within, the importation thereof into, or the exportation thereof from the United States and all territory subject to the jurisdiction thereof for beverage purposes is hereby prohibited.

Section 2   The Congress and the several States shall have concurrent power to enforce this article by appropriate legislation.

Section 3   This article shall be inoperative unless it shall have been ratified as an amendment to the Constitution by the legislatures of the several States, as provided in the Constitution, within seven years from the date of the submission hereof to the States by the Congress.[12]

Right to vote for women

Amendment 19 [Ratified 1920]

The right of citizens of the United States to vote shall not be denied or abridged by the United States or by any State on account of sex.
Congress shall have power to enforce this article by appropriate legislation.

Terms of office

Amendment 20 [Ratified 1933]

Section 1   The terms of the President and Vice President shall end at noon on the 20th day of January, and the terms of Senators and Representatives at noon on the 3d day of January, of the years in which such terms would have ended if this article had not been ratified; and the terms of their successors shall then begin.

Section 2   The Congress shall assemble at least once in every year, and such meeting shall begin at noon on the 3d day of January, unless they shall by law appoint a different day.

Emergency presidential succession

Section 3   If, at the time fixed for the beginning of the term of the President, the President elect shall have died, the Vice President elect shall become President. If a President shall not have been chosen before the time fixed for the beginning of his term, or if the President elect shall have failed to qualify, then the Vice President elect shall act as President until a President shall have qualified; and the Congress may by law provide for the case wherein neither a President elect nor a Vice President elect shall have qualified, declaring who shall then act as President,

---

[12] Repealed by the Twenty-first Amendment.

or the manner in which one who is to act shall be selected, and such person shall act accordingly until a President or Vice President shall have qualified.

Section 4   The Congress may by law provide for the case of the death of any of the persons from whom the House of Representatives may choose a President whenever the right of choice shall have devolved upon them, and for the case of the death of any of the persons from whom the Senate may choose a Vice President whenever the right of choice shall have devolved upon them.

Section 5   Sections 1 and 2 shall take effect on the 15th day of October following the ratification of this article.

Section 6   This article shall be inoperative unless it shall have been ratified as an amendment to the Constitution by the legislatures of three-fourths of the several States within seven years from the date of its submission.

Repeal of Prohibition

Amendment 21 [Ratified 1933]

Section 1   The eighteenth article of amendment to the Constitution of the United States is hereby repealed.

Section 2   The transportation or importation into any State, Territory, or possession of the United States for delivery or use therein of intoxicating liquors, in violation of the laws thereof, is hereby prohibited.

Section 3   This article shall be inoperative unless it shall have been ratified as an amendment to the Constitution by conventions in the several States, as provided in the Constitution, within seven years from the date of the submission hereof to the States by the Congress.

Number of terms for president

Amendment 22 [Ratified 1951]

Section 1   No person shall be elected to the office of the President more than twice, and no person who has held the office of President, or acted as President, for more than two years of a term to which some other person was elected President shall be elected to the office of the President more than once. But this Article shall not apply to any person holding the office of President when this Article was proposed by the Congress, and shall not prevent any person who may be holding the office of President, or acting as President, during the term within which this Article becomes operative from holding the office of President or acting as President during the remainder of such term.

Section 2   This Article shall be inoperative unless it shall have been ratified as an amendment to the Constitution by the legislatures of three-fourths of the several States within seven years from the date of its submission to the States by the Congress.

Presidential elections, District of Columbia

Amendment 23 [Ratified 1961]

Section 1 The District constituting the seat of Government of the United States shall appoint in such manner as the Congress may direct:

A number of electors of President and Vice President equal to the whole number of Senators and Representatives in Congress to which the District would be entitled if it were a State, but in no event more than the least populous State; they shall be in addition to those appointed by the States, but they shall be considered, for the purposes of the election of President and Vice President, to be electors appointed by a State; and they shall meet in the District and perform such duties as provided by the twelfth article of amendment.

Section 2 The Congress shall have power to enforce this article by appropriate legislation.

Prohibition of poll taxes

Amendment 24 [Ratified 1964]

Section 1 The right of citizens of the United States to vote in any primary or other election for President or Vice President, for electors for President or Vice President, or for Senator or Representative in Congress, shall not be denied or abridged by the United States or any State by reason of failure to pay any poll tax or other tax.

Section 2 The Congress shall have power to enforce this article by appropriate legislation.

Presidential disability and succession

Amendment 25 [Ratified 1967]

Section 1 In case of the removal of the President from office or of his death or resignation, the Vice President shall become President.

Section 2 Whenever there is a vacancy in the office of the Vice President, the President shall nominate a Vice President who shall take office upon confirmation by a majority vote of both Houses of Congress.

Section 3 Whenever the President transmits to the President pro tempore of the Senate and the Speaker of the House of Representatives his written declaration that he is unable to discharge the powers and duties of his office, and until he transmits to them a written declaration to the contrary, such powers and duties shall be discharged by the Vice President as Acting President.

Section 4   Whenever the Vice President and a majority of either the principal officers of the executive departments or of such other body as Congress may by law provide, transmit to the President pro tempore of the Senate and the Speaker of the House of Representatives their written declaration that the President is unable to discharge the powers and duties of his office, the Vice President shall immediately assume the powers and duties of the office as Acting President.

Thereafter, when the President transmits to the President pro tempore of the Senate and the Speaker of the House of Representatives his written declaration that no inability exists, he shall resume the powers and duties of his office unless the Vice President and a majority of either the principal officers of the executive department or of such other body as Congress may by law provide, transmit within four days to the President pro tempore of the Senate and the Speaker of the House of Representatives their written declaration that the President is unable to discharge the powers and duties of his office. Thereupon Congress shall decide the issue, assembling within forty-eight hours for that purpose if not in session. If the Congress, within twenty-one days after receipt of the latter written declaration, or, if Congress is not in session, within twenty-one days after Congress is required to assemble, determines by two-thirds vote of both Houses that the President is unable to discharge the powers and duties of his office, the Vice President shall continue to discharge the same as Acting President; otherwise, the President shall resume the powers and duties of his office.

Eighteen-year-old voting age

Amendment 26 [Ratified 1971]

Section 1   The right of citizens of the United States, who are eighteen years of age or older, to vote shall not be denied or abridged by the United States or by any State on account of age.

Section 2   The Congress shall have power to enforce this article by appropriate legislation.

Congressional compensation

Amendment 27 [1992]

No law, varying the compensation for the services of the Senators and Representatives, shall take effect, until an election of Representatives shall have intervened.

B SECURITIES ACT OF 1933*

Definitions

Section 2 When used in this title, unless the context requires—

(1) The term "security" means any note, stock, treasury stock, bond, debenture, evidence of indebtedness, certificate of interest or participation in any profit-sharing agreement, collateral-trust certificate, preorganization certificate or subscription, transferable share, investment contract, voting-trust certificate, certificate of deposit for a security, fractional undivided interest in oil, gas, or other mineral rights, any put, call, straddle, option, or privilege on any security, certificate of deposit, or group or index of securities (including any interest therein or based on the value thereof), or any put, call, straddle, option, or privilege entered into on a national securities exchange relating to foreign currency, or, in general, any interest or instrument commonly known as a "security," or any certificate of interest or participation in, temporary or interim certificate for, receipt for, guarantee of, or warrant or right to subscribe to or purchase, any of the foregoing.

Exempted securities

Section 3 (a) Except as hereinafter expressly provided the provisions of this securities title shall not apply to any of the following classes of securities:

■   ■   ■

(2) Any security issued or guaranteed by the United States or any territory thereof, or by the District of Columbia, or by any State of the United States, or by any political subdivision of a State or Territory, or by any public instrumentality of one or more States or Territories, or by any person controlled or supervised by and acting as an instrumentality of the Government of the United States pursuant to authority granted by the Congress of the United States; or any certificate of deposit for any of the foregoing; or any security issued or guaranteed by any bank; or any security issued by or representing an interest in or a direct obligation of a Federal Reserve bank. . . .

---

* This material is excerpted from the Securities Act of 1933, as amended.

(3) Any note, draft, bill of exchange, or banker's acceptance which arises out of a current transaction or the proceeds of which have been or are to be used for current transactions, and which has a maturity at the time of issuance of not exceeding nine months, exclusive of days of grace, or any renewal thereof the maturity of which is likewise limited;

(4) Any security issued by a person organized and operated exclusively for religious, educational, benevolent, fraternal, charitable, or reformatory purposes and not for pecuniary profit, and no part of the net earnings of which inures to the benefit of any person, private stockholder, or individual;

■   ■   ■

(11) Any security which is a part of an issue offered and sold only to persons resident within a single State or Territory, where the issuer of such security is a person resident and doing business within, or, if a corporation, incorporated by and doing business within, such State or Territory.

(b) The Commission may from time to time by its rules and regulations and subject to such terms and conditions as may be described therein, add any class of securities to the securities exempted as provided in this section, if it finds that the enforcement of this title with respect to such securities is not necessary in the public interest and for the protection of investors by reason of the small amount involved or the limited character of the public offering; but no issue of securities shall be exempted under this subsection where the aggregate amount at which such issue is offered to the public exceeds $5,000,000.

Exempted transactions

Section 4   The provisions of section 5 shall not apply to—

(1) transactions by any person other than an isssuer, underwriter, or dealer.

(2) transactions by an issuer not involving any public offering.

(3) transactions by a dealer (including an underwriter no longer acting as an underwriter in respect of the security involved in such transactions), except—

(A) transactions taking place prior to the expiration of forty days after the first date upon which the security was bona fide offered to the public by the issuer or by or through an underwriter,

(B) transactions in a security as to which a registration statement has been filed taking place prior to the expiration of forty days after the effective date of such registration statement or prior to the expiration of forty days after the first date upon which the security was bona fide offered to the public by the issuer or by or through an underwriter after such effective date, whichever is later (excluding in the computation of such forty days any time during which a stop order issued under section 8 is in effect as to the security), or such shorter period as the Commission may specify by rules and regulations or order, and

(C) transactions as to securities constituting the whole or a part of an unsold allotment to or subscription by such dealer as a participant in the distribution of such securities by the issuer or by or through an underwriter.

With respect to transactions referred to in clause (B), if securities of the issuer have not previously been sold pursuant to an earlier effective registration statement the applicable period, instead of forty days, shall be ninety days, or such shorter period as the Commission may specify by rules and regulations or order.

(4) brokers' transactions, executed upon customers' orders on any exchange or in the over-the-counter market but not the solicitation of such orders.

■   ■   ■

(6) transactions involving offers or sales by an issuer solely to one or more accredited investors, if the aggregate offering price of an issue of securities offered in reliance on this paragraph does not exceed the amount allowed under section 3(b) of this title, if there is no advertising or public solicitation in connection with the transaction by the issuer or anyone acting on the issuer's behalf, and if the issuer files such notice with the Commission as the Commission shall prescribe.

Prohibitions relating to interstate commerce and the mails

Section 5   (a) Unless a registration statement is in effect as to a security, it shall be unlawful for any person, directly or indirectly—

(1) to make use of any means or instruments of transportation or communication in interstate commerce or of the mails to sell such security through the use or medium of any prospectus or otherwise; or

(2) to carry or cause to be carried through the mails or in interstate commerce, by any means or instruments of transportation, any such security for the purpose of sale or for delivery after sale.

(b) It shall be unlawful for any person, directly or indirectly—

(1) to make use of any means or instruments of transportation or communication in interstate commerce or of the mails to carry or transmit any prospectus relating to any security with respect to which a registration statement has been filed under this title, unless such prospectus meets the requirements of section 10, or

(2) to carry or to cause to be carried through the mails or in interstate commerce any such security for the purpose of sale or for delivery after sale, unless accompanied or preceded by a prospectus that meets the requirements of subsection (a) of section 10.

(c) It shall be unlawful for any person, directly or indirectly, to make use of any means or instruments of transportation or communication in interstate commerce or of the mails to offer to sell or offer to buy through the use or medium of any prospectus or otherwise any security, unless a registration statement has been filed as to such security, or while the registration statement is the subject of a refusal order or stop order or (prior to the effective date of the registration statement) any public proceeding of examination under section 8.

C SECURITIES EXCHANGE ACT OF 1934*

Definitions and application of title

Section 3   (a) When used in this title, unless the context otherwise requires—

■   ■   ■

(4) The term "broker" means any person engaged in the business of effecting transactions in securities for the account of others, but does not include a bank.

(5) The term "dealer" means any person engaged in the business of buying and selling securities for his own account, through a broker or otherwise, but does not include a bank, or any person insofar as he buys or sells securities for his own account, either individually or in some fiduciary capacity, but not as part of a regular business.

■   ■   ■

(7) The term "director" means any director of a corporation or any person performing similar functions with respect to any organization, whether incorporated or unincorporated.

(8) The term "issuer" means any person who issues or proposes to issue any security; except that with respect to certificates of deposit for securities, voting trust certificates, or collateral-trust certificates, or with respect to certificates of interest or shares in an unincorporated investment trust not having a board of directors or the fixed, restricted management, or unit type, the term "issuer" means the person or persons performing the acts and assuming the duties of depositor or manager pursuant to the provisions of the trust or other agreement or instrument under which such securities are issued; and except that with respect to equipment-trust certificates or like securities, the term "issuer" means the person by whom the equipment or property is, or is to be, used.

(9) The term "person" means a natural person, company, government, or political subdivision, agency, or instrumentality of a government.

---

* This material is excerpted from the Securities Exchange Act of 1934, as amended.

Regulation of the use of manipulative and deceptive devices

Section 10   It shall be unlawful for any person, directly or indirectly, by the use of means or instrumentality of interstate commerce or of the mails, or of any and deceptive facility of any national securities exchange—

(a) To effect a short sale, or to use or employ any stop-loss order in connection with the purchase or sale, of any security registered on a national securities exchange, in contravention of such rules and regulations as the Commission may prescribe as necessary or appropriate in the public interest or for the protection of investors.

(b) To use or employ, in connection with the purchase or sale of any security registered on a national securities exchange or any security not so registered, any manipulative or deceptive device or contrivance in contravention of such rules and regulations as the Commission may prescribe as necessary or appropriate in the public interest or for the protection of investors.

D THE SHERMAN ACT*

Restraints of trade prohibited

Section 1　Trusts, etc., in Restraint of Trade Illegal; Penalty.　Every contract, combination in the form of trust or otherwise, or conspiracy, in restraint of trade or commerce among the several States, or with foreign nations, is declared to be illegal. Every person who shall make any contract or engage in any combination or conspiracy declared by sections 1 to 7 of this title to be illegal shall be deemed guilty of a felony, and, on conviction thereof, shall be punished by fine not exceeding one million dollars if a corporation, or if any other person, one hundred thousand dollars, or by imprisonment not exceeding three years, or both said punishments, in the discretion of the court.

Monopolizing prohibited

Section 2　Monopolizing Trade a Felony; Penalty.　Every person who shall monopolize, or attempt to monopolize, or combine or conspire with any other person or persons, to monopolize any part of the trade or commerce among the several States, or with foreign nations, shall be deemed guilty of a felony, and, on conviction thereof, shall be punished by fine not exceeding one million dollars if a corporation, or, if any other person, one hundred thousand dollars, or by imprisonment not exceeding three years, or by both said punishments, in the discretion of the court.

---

* This material is excerpted from the Sherman Act, as amended.

E   THE CLAYTON ACT*

Refusals to deal

Section 3   Sale, etc., on Agreement not to Use Goods of Competitor. It shall be unlawful for any person engaged in commerce, in the course of such commerce, to lease or make a sale or contract for sale of goods, wares, merchandise, machinery, supplies, or other commodities, whether patented or unpatented, for use, consumption, or resale within the United States or any Territory thereof or the District of Columbia or any insular possession or other place under the jurisdiction of the United States, or fix a price charged thereof, or discount from, or rebate upon, such price, on the condition, agreement, or understanding that the lessee or purchaser thereof shall not use or deal in the goods, wares, merchandise, machinery, supplies, or other commodities of a competitor or competitors of the lessor or seller, where the effect of such lease, sale, or contract for sale or such condition, agreement or understanding may be to substantially lessen competition or tend to create a monopoly in any line of commerce.

Private suits

Section 4   Suits by Persons Injured; Amount of Recovery. Any person who shall be injured in his business or property by reason of anything forbidden in the antitrust laws may sue therefor in any district court of the United States in the district in which the defendant resides or is found or has an agent, without respect to the amount in controversy, and shall recover threefold the damages by him sustained, and the cost of suit, including a reasonable attorney's fee. . . .

Mergers

Section 7   Acquisition by One Corporation of Stock of Another. No corporation engaged in commerce shall acquire, directly or indirectly, the whole or any part of the stock or other share capital and no corporation subject to the jurisdiction of the Federal Trade Commission shall acquire the whole or any part of the assets of another corporation engaged also in commerce, where in any line of commerce in any section of the country, the effect of such acquisition may be substantially to lessen competition, or to tend to create a monopoly.

---

* This material is excerpted from the Clayton Act, as amended.

No corporation shall acquire, directly or indirectly, the whole or any part of the stock or other share capital and no corporation subject to the jurisdiction of the Federal Trade Commission shall acquire the whole or any part of the assets of one or more corporations engaged in commerce, where in any line of commerce in any section of the country, the effect of such acquisition, of such stocks or assets, or of the use of such stock by the voting or granting of proxies or otherwise, may be substantially to lessen competition, or to tend to create a monopoly.

This section shall not apply to corporations purchasing such stock solely for investment and not using the same by voting or otherwise to bring about, or in attempting to bring about, the substantial lessening of competition. Nor shall anything contained in this section prevent a corporation engaged in commerce from causing the formation of subsidiary corporations for the actual carrying on of their immediate lawful business, or the natural and legitimate branches or extensions thereof, or from owning and holding all or part of the stock of such subsidiary corporations, when the effect of such formation is not to substantially lessen competition.

Interlocking directorates

Section 8   Interlocking Directorates and Officers . . .   No person at the same time shall be a director in any two or more corporations, any one of which has capital, surplus, and undivided profits aggregating more than $1,000,000, engaged in whole or in part in commerce, other than banks, banking associations, trust companies, and common carriers subject to the Act to regulate commerce approved February fourth, eighteen hundred and eighty-seven, if such corporations are or shall have been theretofore, by virtue of their business and location or operation, competitors, so that the elimination of competition by agreement between them would constitute a violation of any of the provisions of any of the antitrust laws. The eligibility of a director under the foregoing provision shall be determined by the aggregate amount of the capital, surplus, and undivided profits, exclusive of dividends declared but not paid to stockholders, at the end of the fiscal year of said corporation next preceding the election of directors, and when a director has been elected in accordance with the provisions of this Act it shall be lawful for him to continue as such for one year thereafter.

F   THE FEDERAL TRADE COMMISSION ACT*

Unfair methods of competition prohibited

Section 5   Unfair Methods of Competition Unlawful; Prevention by Commission—Declaration.   Declaration of unlawfullness; power to prohibit unfair practices.

(a)(1) Unfair methods of competition in or affecting commerce, and unfair or deceptive acts or practices in or affecting commerce, are declared unlawful. . . .

Penalty for violation of order, injunctions and other appropriate equitable relief.

(b) Any person, partnership, or corporation who violates an order of the Commission to cease and desist after it has become final, and while such order is in effect, shall forfeit and pay to the United States a civil penalty of not more than $5,000 for each violation, which shall accrue to the United States and may be recovered in a civil action brought by the Attorney General of the United States. Each separate violation of such an order shall be a separate offense, except that in the case of a violation through continuing failure or neglect to obey a final order of the Commission each day of continuance of such failure or neglect shall be deemed a separate offense.

---

* This material is excerpted from the Federal Trade Commission Act, as amended.

G   THE ROBINSON-PATMAN ACT*

Price discrimination; cost justification; changing conditions

Section 2   Discrimination in Price, Services, or Facilities.   (a) Price: selection of customers.

It shall be unlawful for any person engaged in commerce, in the course of such commerce, either directly or indirectly, to discriminate in price between different purchasers of commodities of like grade and quality, where either or any of the purchasers involved in such discrimination are in commerce, where such commodities are sold for use, consumption, or resale within the United States or any Territory thereof or the District of Columbia or any insular possession or other place under the jurisdiction of the United States, and where the effect of such discrimination may be substantially to lessen competition or tend to create a monopoly in any line of commerce, or to injure, destroy, or prevent competition with any person who either grants or knowingly receives the benefit of such discrimination, or, with customers of either of them: *Provided,* That nothing herein contained shall prevent differentials which make only due allowance for differences in the cost of manufacture, sale, or delivery resulting from the differing methods or quantities in which such commodities are to such purchasers sold or delivered: *Provided, however,* That the Federal Trade Commission may, after due investigation and hearing to all interested parties, fix and establish quantity limits, and revise the same as it finds necessary as to particular commodities or classes of commodities, where it finds that available purchasers in greater quantities are so few as to render differentials on account thereof unjustly discriminatory or promotive of monopoly in any line of commerce; and the foregoing shall then not be construed to permit differentials based on differences in quantities greater than those so fixed and established: *And provided further,* That nothing herein contained shall prevent persons engaged in selling goods, wares, or merchandise in commerce from selecting their own customers in bona fide transactions and not in restraint of trade: And *provided further,* That nothing herein contained shall prevent price changes from time to time where in response to changing conditions affecting the market

---

* This material is excerpted from the Robinson-Patman Act, as amended.

for or the market-ability of the goods concerned, such as but not limited to actual or imminent deterioration of perishable goods, obsolescence of seasonal goods, distress sales under court process, or sales in good faith in discontinuance of business in the goods concerned.

Meeting competition

(b) Burden of rebutting prima-facie case of discrimination.

Upon proof being made, at any hearing on a complaint under this section, that there has been discrimination in price or services or facilities furnished, the burden of rebutting the prima-facie case thus made by showing justification shall be upon the person charged with a violation of this section, and unless justification shall be affirmatively shown, the Commission is authorized to issue an order terminating the discrimination: *Provided, however,* That nothing herein contained shall prevent a seller rebutting the prima-facie case thus made by showing that his lower price or the furnishing of services or facilities to any purchaser or purchasers was made in good faith to meet an equally low price of a competitor, or the services or facilities furnished by a competitor.

Brokerage payments

(c) Payment or acceptance of commission, brokerage or other compensation.

It shall be unlawful for any person engaged in commerce, in the course of such commerce, to pay or grant, or to receive or accept, anything of value as a commission, brokerage, or other compensation, or any allowance of discount in lieu thereof, except for services rendered in connection with the sale or purchase of goods, wares, or merchandise, either to the other party to such transaction or to an agent, representative, or other intermediary therein where such intermediary is acting in fact for or in behalf, or is subject to the direct or indirect control, of any party to such transaction other than the person by whom such compensation is so granted or paid.

Promotional allowances

(d) Payment for services or facilities for processing or sale.

It shall be unlawful for any person engaged in commerce to pay or contract for the payment of anything of value to or for the benefit of a customer of such person in the course of such commerce as compensation or in consideration for any services or facilities furnished by or through such customer in connection with the processing, handling, sale, or offering for sale of any products or commodities manufactured, sold, or offered for sale by such person, unless such payment of consideration is available on proportionally equal terms to all other customers competing in the distribution of such products or commodities.

Promotional services

(e) Furnishing services or facilities for processing, handling, etc.

It shall be unlawful for any person to discriminate in favor of one purchaser against another purchaser or purchasers of a commodity bought for resale, with or without processing, by contracting to furnish or furnishings, or by contributing to the furnishing of, any services or facilities connected with the processing, handling, sale, or offering for sale of such commodity so purchased upon terms not accorded to all purchasers on proportionally equal terms.

Buyer discrimination

(f) Knowingly inducing or receiving discriminatory price.

It shall be unlawful for any person engaged in commerce, in the course of such commerce, knowingly to induce or receive a discrimination in price which is prohibited by this section.

Predatory practices

Section 3   Discrimination in Rebates, Discounts, or Advertising Service Charges; Underselling in Particular Localities; Penalties.   It shall be unlawful for any person engaged in commerce, in the course of such commerce, to be a party to, or assist in, any transaction of sale, or contract to sell, which discriminates to his knowledge against competitors of the purchaser, in that, any discount, rebate, allowance, or advertising service charge is granted to the purchaser over and above any discount, rebate, allowance, or advertising service charge available at the time of such transaction to said competitors in respect of a sale of goods of like grade, quality, and quantity; to sell, or contract to sell, goods in any part of the United States at prices lower than those exacted by said person elsewhere in the United States for the purpose of destroying competition, or eliminating a competitor in such part of the United States; or, to sell, or contract to sell, goods at unreasonably low prices for the purpose of destroying competition or eliminating a competitor.

Any person violating any of the provisions of this section shall, upon conviction, thereof, be fined not more than $5,000 or imprisoned not more than one year, or both.

H   NATIONAL LABOR RELATIONS ACT*

Definitions

Section 2   When used in this Act—

(2) The term "employer" includes any person acting as an agent of an employer, directly or indirectly, but shall not include the United States or any wholly owned Government corporation, or any Federal Reserve Bank, or any State or political subdivision thereof, or any person subject to the Railway Labor Act, as amended from time to time, or any labor organization (other than when acting as an employer), or anyone acting in the capacity of officer or agent of such labor organization.

(3) The term "employee" shall include any employee, and shall not be limited to the employees of a particular employer, unless the Act explicitly states otherwise, and shall include any individual whose work has ceased as a consequence of, or in connection with, any current labor dispute or because of any unfair labor practice, and who has not obtained any other regular and substantially equivalent employment, but shall not include any individual employed as an agricultural laborer, or in the domestic service of any family or person at his home, or any individual employed by his parent or spouse, or any individual having the status of an independent contractor, or any individual employed as a supervisor, or any individual employed by an employer subject to the Railway Labor Act, as amended from time to time, or by any other person who is not an employer as herein defined.

(11) The term "supervisor" means any individual having authority, in the interest of the employer, to hire, transfer, suspend, lay off, recall, promote, discharge, assign, reward, or discipline other employees, or responsibly to direct them, or to adjust their grievances, or effectively to recommend such action, if in connection with the foregoing the exercise of such authority is not of a merely routine or clerical nature, but requires the use of independent judgment.

---

* This material is excerpted from the National Labor Relations Act, as amended.

(12) The term "professional employee" mean—

(a) any employee engaged in work (i) predominantly intellectual and varied in character as opposed to routine mental, manual, mechanical, or physical work; (ii) involving the consistent exercise of discretion and judgment in its performance; (iii) of such a character that the output produced or the result accomplished cannot be standardized in relation to a given period of time; (iv) requiring knowledge of an advanced type in a field of science or learning customarily acquired by a prolonged course of specialized intellectual instruction and study in an institution of higher learning or a hospital, as distinguished from a general academic education or from an apprenticeship or from training in the performance of routine mental, manual, or physical processes; or

(b) any employee, who (i) has completed the courses of specialized intellectual instruction and study described in clause (iv) of paragraph (a), and (ii) is performing related work under the supervision of a professional person to qualify himself to become a professional employee as defined in paragraph (a).

Rights of employees

Section 7   Employees shall have the right to self-organization, to form, join, or assist labor organizations, to bargain collectively through representatives of their own choosing, and to engage in other concerted activities for the purpose of collective bargaining or other mutual aid or protection, and shall also have the right to refrain from any or all of such activities except to the extent that such right may be affected by an agreement requiring membership in a labor organization as a condition of employment as authorized in section 8(a)(3).

Unfair labor practices

Section 8   (a) It shall be an unfair labor practice for an employer—

(1) to interfere with, restrain, or coerce employees in the exercise of the rights guaranteed in section 7;

(2) to dominate or interfere with the formation or administration of any labor organization or contribute financial or other support to it: *Provided,* That subject to rules and regulations made and published by the Board pursuant to section 6, an employer shall not be prohibited from permitting employees to confer with him during working hours without loss of time or pay;

(3) by discrimination in regard to hire or tenure of employment or any term or condition of employment to encourage or discourage membership in any labor organization: *Provided,* That nothing in this Act, or in any other statute of the United States, shall preclude an employer from making an agreement with a labor organization (not established, maintained, or assisted by any action defined in section 8(a) of this Act as an unfair labor practice) to require as a condition of employment membership therein on or after the thirtieth day following the beginning of such employment or the effective date of such agreement, whichever is the later, (i) if such labor organization is the representative of the employees as provided in section 9(a), in the appropriate collective bargaining unit covered by such agreement when made, and (ii) unless following an election held as provided in section 9(e) within one year preceding the effective date of such agreement, the Board shall have certified that at least a majority of the employees eligible to vote in such

election have voted to rescind the authority of such labor organization to make such an agreement: *Provided further,* That no employer shall justify any discrimination against an employee for nonmembership in a labor organization (A) if he has reasonable grounds for believing that such membership was not available to the employee on the same terms and conditions generally applicable to other members, or (B) if he had reasonable grounds for believing that membership was denied or terminated for reasons other than the failure of the employee to tender the periodic dues and the initiation fees uniformly required as a condition of acquiring or retaining membership;

(4) to discharge or otherwise discriminate against an employee because he has filed charges or given testimony under this Act;

(5) to refuse to bargain collectively with the representatives of his employees, subject to the provisions of section 9(a).

(b) It shall be an unfair labor practice for a labor organization or its agents—

(1) to restrain or coerce (A) employees in the exercise of the rights guaranteed in section 7: *Provided,* That this paragraph shall not impair the right of a labor organization to prescribe its own rules with respect to the acquisition or retention of membership therein; or (B) an employer in the selection of his representatives for the purposes of collective bargaining or the adjustment of grievances;

(2) to cause or attempt to cause an employer to discriminate against an employee in violation of subsection (a)(3) or to discriminate against an employee with respect to whom membership in such organization has been denied or terminated on some ground other than his failure to tender the periodic dues and the initiation fees uniformly required as a condition of acquiring or retaining membership;

(3) to refuse to bargain collectively with an employer, provided it is the representative of his employees subject to the provisions of section 9(a);

(4)(i) to engage in, or to induce or encourage any individual employed by any person engaged in commerce or in an industry affecting commerce to engage in, a strike or a refusal in the course of his employment to use, manufacture, process, transport, or otherwise handle or work on any goods, articles, materials, or commodities or to perform any services; or (ii) to threaten, coerce, or restrain any person engaged in commerce or in an industry affecting commerce, where in either case an object thereof is—

(A) forcing or requiring any employer or self-employed person to join any labor or employer organization or to enter into any agreement which is prohibited by section 8(e);

(B) forcing or requiring any person to cease using, selling, handling, transporting, or otherwise dealing in the products of any other producer, processor, or manufacturer, or to cease doing business with any other person, or forcing or requiring any other employer to recognize or bargain with a labor organization as the representative of his employees unless such labor organization has been certified as the representative of such employees under the provisions of section 9: *Provided,* That nothing contained in this clause

(B) shall be construed to make unlawful, where not otherwise unlawful, any primary strike or primary picketing;

(C) forcing or requiring any employer to recognize or bargain with a particular labor organization as the representative of his employees if another labor organization has been certified as the representative of such employees under the provisions of section 9;

(D) forcing or requiring any employer to assign particular work to employees in a particular labor organization or in a particular trade, craft, or class rather than to employees in another labor organization or in another trade, craft, or class, unless such employer is failing to conform to an order or certification of the Board determining the bargaining representative for employees performing such work:

Provided, That nothing contained in this subsection (b) shall be construed to make unlawful a refusal by any person to enter upon the premises of any employer (other than his own employer), if the employees of such employer are engaged in a strike ratified or approved by a representative of such employees whom such employer is required to recognize under this Act: *Provided further,* That for the purposes of this paragraph (4) only, nothing contained in such paragraph shall be construed to prohibit publicity, other than picketing, for the purpose of truthfully advising the public, including consumers and members of a labor organization, that a product or products are produced by an employer with whom the labor organization has a primary dispute and are distributed by another employer, as long as such publicity does not have an effect of inducing any individual employed by any person other than the primary employer in the course of his employment to refuse to pick up, deliver, or transport any goods, or not to perform any services, at the establishment of the employer engaged in such distribution:

(5) to require of employees covered by an agreement authorized under subsection (a)(3) the payment, as a condition precedent to becoming a member of such organization, of a fee in an amount which the Board finds excessive or discriminatory under all the circumstances. In making such a finding, the Board shall consider, among other relevant factors, the practices and customs of labor organizations in the particular industry, and the wages currently paid to the employees affected;

(6) to cause or attempt to cause an employer to pay or deliver or agree to pay or deliver any money or other thing of value, in the nature of an exaction, for services which are not performed or not to be performed; and

(7) To picket or cause to be picketed, or threatened to picket or cause to be picketed, any employer where an object thereof is forcing or requiring an employer to recognize or bargain with a labor organization as the representative of his employees, or forcing or requiring the employees of an employer to accept or select such labor organization as their collective bargaining representative, unless such labor organization is currently certified as the representative of such employees:

(A) where the employer has lawfully recognized in accordance with this Act any other labor organization and a question concerning representation may not appropriately be raised under section 9(c) of this Act;

(B) where within the preceding twelve months a valid election under section 9(c) of this Act has been conducted, or

(C) where such picketing has been conducted without a petition under section 9(c) being filed within a reasonable period of time not to exceed thirty days from the commencement of such picketing; *Provided,* That when such a petition has been filed the Board shall forthwith, without regard to the provisions of section 9(c)(1) or the absence of a showing of a substantial interest on the part of the labor organization, direct an election in such unit as the Board finds to be appropriate and shall certify the results thereof: *Provided further,* That nothing in this subparagraph (C) shall be construed to prohibit any picketing or other publicity for the purpose of truthfully advising the public (including consumers) that an employer does not employ members of, or have a contract with, a labor organization, unless an effect of such picketing is to induce any individual employed by any other person in the course of his employment, not to pick up, deliver or transport any goods or not to perform any services.

Nothing in this paragraph (7) shall be construed to permit any act which would otherwise be an unfair labor practice under this section 8(b).

(c) The expressing of any views, argument, or opinion, or the dissemination thereof, whether in written, printed, graphic, or visual form, shall not constitute or be evidence of an unfair labor practice under any of the provisions of this Act, if such expression contains no threat of reprisal or force or promise of benefit.

(d) For the purposes of this section, to bargain collectively is the performance of the mutual obligation of the employer and the representative of the employees to meet at reasonable times and confer in good faith with respect to wages, hours, and other terms and conditions of employment, or the negotiation of an agreement, or any question arising thereunder, and the execution of a written contract incorporating any agreement reached if requested by either party, but such obligation does not compel either party to agree to a proposal or require the making of a concession: *Provided,* That where there is in effect a collective-bargaining contract covering employees in an industry affecting commerce, the duty to bargain collectively shall also mean that no party to such contract shall terminate or modify such contract, unless the party desiring such termination or modification—

(1) serves a written notice upon the other party to the contract of the proposed termination or modification sixty days prior to the expiration date thereof, or in the event such contract contains no expiration date, sixty days prior to the time it is proposed to make such termination or modification;

(2) offers to meet and confer with the other party for the purpose of negotiating a new contract or a contract containing the proposed modifications;

(3) notifies the Federal Mediation and Conciliation Service within thirty days after such notice of the existence of a dispute, and simultaneously therewith notifies

any State or Territorial agency established to mediate and conciliate disputes within the State or Territory where the dispute occurred, provided no agreement has been reached by that time; and

(4) continues in full force and effect, without resorting to strike or lockout, all the terms and conditions of the existing contract for a period of sixty days after such notice is given or until the expiration date of such contract, whichever occurs later:

The duties imposed upon employers, employees, and labor organizations by paragraphs (2), (3), and (4) shall become inapplicable upon an intervening certification of the Board, under which the labor organization or individual, which is a party to the contract, has been superseded as or ceased to be the representative of the employees subject to the provisions of section 9(a), and the duties so imposed shall not be construed as requiring either party to discuss or agree to any modification of the terms and conditions contained in a contract for a fixed period, if such modification is to become effective before such terms and conditions can be reopened under the provisions of the contract. Any employee who engages in a strike within any notice periods specified in this subsection, or who engages in any strike within the appropriate period specified in subsection (g) of this section, shall lose his status as an employee of the employer engaged in the particular labor dispute, for the purposes of sections 8, 9, and 10 of this Act, but such loss of status for such employee shall terminate if and when he is reemployed by such employer. Whenever the collective bargaining involves employees of a health care institution, the provisions of this section 8(d) shall be modified as follows:

(A) The notice of section 8(d)(1) shall be ninety days; the notice of section 8(d)(3) shall be sixty days; and the contract period of section 8(d)(4) shall be ninety days.

(B) Where the bargaining is for an initial agreement following certification or recognition, at least thirty days' notice of the existence of a dispute shall be given by the labor organization to the agencies set forth in section 8(d)(3).

(C) After notice is given to the Federal Mediation and Conciliation Service under either clause (A) or (B) of this sentence, the Service shall promptly communicate with the parties and use its best efforts, by mediation and conciliation, to bring them to agreement. The parties shall participate fully and promptly in such meetings as may be undertaken by the Service for the purpose of aiding in a settlement of the dispute.

(e) It shall be an unfair labor practice for any labor organization and any employer to enter into any contract or agreement, express or implied, whereby such employer ceases or refrains or agrees to cease or refrain from handling, using, selling, transporting, or otherwise dealing in any of the products of any other employer, or to cease doing business with any other person, and any contract or agreement entered into heretofore or hereafter containing such an agreement shall be to such extent unenforceable and void: *Provided,* That nothing in this subsection (e) shall apply to an agreement between a labor organization and an employer in the construction industry relating to the contracting or subcontracting of work to be done at the site of the construction, alteration, painting, or repair of a building, structure, or other work: *Provided further,* That for the purposes of this subsection (e) and section 8(b)(4)(B) the terms "any employer," "any person engaged in commerce or any industry affecting other producer, processor, or manufacturer," "any other employer," or "any other person" shall not include persons in the relation of a jobber, manufacturer, contractor, or subcontractor working on the goods or premises of the jobber or manufacturer or performing parts of an integrated process of production in the apparel and clothing industry: *Provided further,* That nothing in this Act shall prohibit the enforcement of any agreement which is within the foregoing exception.

(f) It shall not be an unfair labor practice under subsections (a) and (b) of this section for an employer engaged primarily in the building and construction industry to make an agreement covering employees engaged (or who, upon their employment, will be engaged) in the building and construction industry with a labor organization of which building and construction employees are members (not established, maintained, or assisted by any action defined in section 8(a) of this Act as an unfair labor practice) because (1) the majority status of such labor organizations has not been established under the provisions of section 9 of this Act prior to the making of such agreement, or (2) such agreement requires as a condition of employment, membership in such labor organization after the seventh day following the beginning of such employment or the effective date of the agreement, whichever is later, or (3) such agreement requires the employer to notify such labor organization of opportunities for employment with such employer, or gives such labor organization an opportunity to refer qualified applicants for such employment, or (4) such agreement specifies minimum training or experience qualifications for employment or provides for priority in opportunities for employment based upon length of service with such employer, in the industry or in the particular geographical area: *Provided,* That nothing in this subsection shall set aside the final proviso to section 8(a)(3) of this Act: *Provided further,* That any agreement which would be invalid, but for clause (1) of this subsection, shall not be a bar to a petition filed pursuant to section 9(c) or 9(e).

(g) A labor organization before engaging in any strike, picketing, or other concerted refusal to work at any health care institution shall, not less than ten days prior to such action, notify the institution in writing and the Federal Mediation and Conciliation Service of that intention, except that in the case of bargaining for an initial agreement following certification or recognition the notice required by this subsection shall not be given until the expiration of the period specified in clause (b) of the last sentence of section 8(d) of this Act. The notice shall state the date and time that such action will commence. The notice, once given, may be extended by the written agreement of both parties.

I   TITLE VII OF THE CIVIL RIGHTS ACT OF 1964[*]

Definitions

Section 701   Definitions [For the purposes of this subchapter]—

(b) The term "employer" means a person engaged in an industry affecting commerce who has fifteen or more employees for each working day in each of twenty or more calendar weeks in the current or preceding calendar year, and any agent of such a person, but such term does not include (1) the United States, a corporation wholly owned by the Government of the United States, an Indian tribe, or any department or agency of the District of Columbia subject by statute to procedures of the competitive service (as defined in section 2102 of Title 5), or (2) a bona fide private membership club (other than a labor organization) which is exempt from taxation under section 501(c) of Title 26, except that during the first year after March 24, 1972, persons having fewer than twenty-five employees (and their agents) shall not be considered employers.

(j) The term "religion" includes all aspects of religious observance and practice, as well as belief, unless an employer demonstrates that he is unable to reasonably accommodate to an employee's or prospective employee's religious observance or practice without undue hardship on the conduct of the employer's business.

(k) The terms "because of sex" or "on the basis of sex" include, but are not limited to, because of or on the basis of pregnancy, childbirth, or related medical conditions; and women affected by pregnancy, childbirth, or related medical conditions shall be treated the same for all employment-related purposes, including receipt of benefits under fringe benefit programs, as other persons not so affected but similar in their ability or inability to work, and nothing in section 2000e-2(h) of this title shall be interpreted to permit otherwise. This subsection shall not require an employer to pay for health insurance benefits for abortion, except where the life of the mother would be endangered if the fetus were carried to term, or except where medical complications have arisen from an abortion: *Provided,* That

---

* This material is excerpted from Title VII of the Civil Rights Act of 1964, as amended.

nothing herein shall preclude an employer from providing abortion benefits or otherwise affect bargaining agreements in regard to abortion.

Section 703

Employer Practices

(a) It shall be an unlawful employment practice for an employer—

(1) to fail or refuse to hire or to discharge any individual, or otherwise to discriminate against any individual with respect to his compensation, terms, conditions, or privileges of employment, because of such individual's race, color, religion, sex, or national origin; or

(2) to limit, segregate, or classify his employees or applicants for employment in any way which would deprive or tend to deprive any individual of employment opportunities or otherwise adversely affect his status as an employee, because of such individual's race, color, religion, sex, or national origin.

Employment Agency Practices

(b) It shall be an unlawful employment practice for an employment agency to fail or refuse to refer for employment, or otherwise to discriminate against, any individual because of his race, color, religion, sex, or national origin, or to classify or refer for employment any individual on the basis of his race, color, religion sex, or national origin.

Labor Organization Practices

(c) It shall be an unlawful employment practice for a labor organization—

(1) to exclude or to expel from its membership, or otherwise to discriminate against, any individual because of his race, color, religion, sex, or national origin:

(2) to limit, segregate, or classify its membership or applicants for membership, or to classify or fail or refuse to refer for employment any individual, in any way which would deprive or tend to deprive any individual of employment opportunities, or would limit such employment opportunities or otherwise adversely affect his status as an employee or as an applicant for employment, because of such individual's race, color, religion, sex, or national origin; or

(3) to cause or attempt to cause an employer to discriminate against an individual in violation of this section.

Training Programs

(d) It shall be an unlawful employment practice for any employer, labor organization, or joint labor-management committee controlling apprenticeship or other training or retraining, including on-the-job training programs to discriminate against any individual because of his race, color, religion, sex, or national origin in admission to, or employment in, any program established to provide apprenticeship or other training.

Businesses or Enterprises with Personnel Qualified on Basis of Religion, Sex, or National Origin; Educational Institutions with Personnel of Particular Religion

(e) Notwithstanding any other provision of this subchapter, (1) it shall not be an unlawful employment practice for an employer to hire and employ employees, for an employment agency to classify, or refer for employment any individual, for a labor organization to classify its membership or to classify or refer for employment any individual, or for an employer, labor organization, or joint labor-management committee controlling apprenticeship or other training or retraining programs to admit or employ any individual in any such program, on the basis of his religion, sex, or national origin in those certain instances where religion, sex, or national origin is a bona fide occupational qualification reasonably necessary to the normal operation of that particular business or enterprise, and (2) it shall not be an unlawful employment practice for a school, college, university, or other educational institution or institution of learning to hire and employ employees of a particular religion if such school, college, university, or other educational institution or institution of learning is, in whole or in substantial part, owned, supported, controlled, or managed by a particular religion or by a particular religious corporation, association, or society, or if the curriculum of such school, college, university, or other educational institution or institution of learning is directed toward the propagation of a particular religion.

Members of Communist Party or Communist-action or Communist-front Organizations

(f) As used in this subchapter, the phrase "unlawful employment practice" shall not be deemed to include any action or measure taken by an employer, labor organization, joint labor-management committee, or employment agency with respect to an individual who is a member of the Communist Party of the United States or of any other organization required to register as a Communist-action or Communist-front organization by final order of the Subversive Activities Control Board pursuant to the Subversive Activities Control Act of 1950.

National Security

(g) Notwithstanding any other provision of this subchapter, it shall not be an unlawful employment practice for an employer to fail or refuse to hire and employ any individual for any position, for an employer to discharge any individual from any position, or for an employment agency to fail or refuse to refer any individual for employment in any position, or for a labor organization to fail or refuse to refer any individual for employment in any position, if—

(1) the occupancy of such position, or access to the premises in or upon which any part of the duties of such position is performed or is to be performed, is subject to any requirement imposed in the interest of the national security of the United

States under any security program in effect pursuant to or administered under any statute of the United States or any Executive order of the President; and

(2) such individual has not fulfilled or has ceased to fulfill that requirement.

Seniority or Merit System; Quantity or Quality of Production; Ability Tests; Compensation Based on Sex and Authorized by Minimum Wage Provisions

(h) Notwithstanding any other provision of this subchapter, it shall not be an unlawful employment practice for an employer to apply different standards of compensation, or different terms, conditions, or privileges of employment pursuant to a bona fide seniority or merit system, or a system which measures earnings by quantity or quality of production or to employees who work in different locations, provided that such differences are not the result of an intention to discriminate because of race, color, religion, sex, or national origin, nor shall it be an unlawful employment practice for an employer to give and to act upon the results of any professionally developed ability test provided that such test, its administration or action upon the results is not designed, intended or used to discriminate because of race, color, religion, sex or national origin. It shall not be an unlawful employment practice under this subchapter for any employer to differentiate upon the basis of sex in determining the amount of the wages or compensation paid or to be paid to employees of such employer if such differentiation is authorized by the provisions of section 206(d) of Title 29.

Businesses or Enterprises Extending Preferential Treatment to Indians

(i) Nothing contained in this subchapter shall apply to any business or enterprise on or near an Indian reservation with respect to any publicly announced employment practice of such business or enterprise under which a preferential treatment is given to any individual because he is an Indian living on or near a reservation.

Preferential Treatment not to be Granted on Account of Existing Number or Percentage Imbalance

(j) Nothing contained in this subchapter shall be interpreted to require any employer, employment agency, labor organization, or joint labor-management committee subject to this subchapter to grant preferential treatment to any individual or to any group because of the race, color, religion, sex, or national origin of such individual or group on account of an imbalance which may exist with respect to the total number or percentage of persons of any race, color, religion, sex, or national origin employed by any employer, referred or classified for employment by any employment agency or labor organization, admitted to membership or classified by any labor organization, or admitted to, or employed in, any apprenticeship or other training program, in comparison with the total number or percentage of persons of such race, color, religion, sex, or national origin in any community, State, section, or other area, or in the available work force in any community, State, section, or other area.

(k) Disparate impact as basis of practice

(1)(A) An unlawful employment practice based on disparate impact is established under this subchapter only if—

(i) a complaining party demonstrates that a respondent uses a particular employment practice that causes a disparate impact on the basis of race, color, religion, sex, or national origin and the respondent fails to demonstrate that the challenged practice is job related for the position in question and consistent with business necessity; or

(ii) The complaining party makes the demonstration described in subparagraph (C) with respect to an alternative employment practice and the respondent refuses to adopt such alternative employment practice.

(B)(i) With respect to demonstrating that a particular employment practice causes a disparate impact as described in subparagraph (A)(i), the complaining party shall demonstrate that each particular challenged employment practice causes a disparate impact, except that if the complaining party can demonstrate to the court that the elements of a respondent's decisionmaking process are not capable of separation for analysis, the decisionmaking process may be analyzed as one employment practice.

(ii) If the respondent demonstrates that a specific employment practice does not cause the disparate impact, the respondent shall not be required to demonstrate that such practice is required by business necessity.

(C) The demonstration referred to by subparagraph (A)(ii) shall be in accordance with the law as it existed on June 4, 1989, with respect to the concept of "alternative employment practice."

(2) A demonstration that an employment practice is required by business necessity may not be used as a defense against a claim of intentional discrimination under this subchapter.

(3) Notwithstanding any other provision of this subchapter, a rule barring the employment of an individual who currently and knowingly uses or possesses a controlled substance, as defined in schedules I and II of section 102(6) of the Controlled Substances Act (21 U.S.C. 802(6)), other than the use or possession of a drug taken under the supervision of a licensed health care professional, or any other use or possession authorized by the Controlled Substances Act or any other provision of Federal law, shall be considered an unlawful employment practice under this subchapter only if such rule is adopted or applied with an intent to discriminate because of race, color, religion, sex, or national origin.

(l) Alteration of test results

It shall be an unlawful employment practice for a respondent, in connection with the selection or referral of applicants or candidates for employment or promotion, to adjust the scores of, use different cutoff scores for, or otherwise alter the results of, employment related tests on the basis of race, color, religion, sex, or national origin.

(m) Motivations for practice

Except as otherwise provided in this subchapter, an unlawful employment practice is established when the complaining party demonstrates that race, color, religion, sex, or national origin was a motivating factor for any employment practice, even though other factors also motivated the practice.

(n) Challenges to practices implementing litigated or consent judgments or orders

(1)(A) Notwithstanding any other provision of law, and except as provided in paragraph (2), an employment practice that implements and is within the scope of a litigated or consent judgment or order that resolves a claim of employment discrimination under the Constitution or Federal civil rights laws may not be challenged under the circumstances described in subparagraph (B).

(B) A practice described in subparagraph (A) may not be challenged in a claim under the Constitution or Federal civil rights laws—.

(i) by a person who, prior to the entry of the judgment or order described in subparagraph (A), had—

(I) actual notice of the proposed judgment or order sufficient to apprise such person that such judgment or order might adversely affect the interests and legal rights of such person and that an opportunity was available to present objections to such judgment or order by a future date certain; and

(II) a reasonable opportunity to present objections to such judgment or order; or

(ii) by a person whose interests were adequately represented by another person who had previously challenged the judgment or order on the same legal grounds and with a similar factual situation, unless there has been an intervening change in law or fact.

(2) Nothing in this subsection shall be construed to—

(A) alter the standards for intervention under rule 24 of the Federal Rules of Civil Procedure or apply to the rights of parties who had successfully intervened pursuant to such rule in the proceeding in which the parties intervened;

(B) apply to the rights of parties to the action in which a litigated or consent judgment or order was entered, or of members of a class represented or sought to be represented in such action, or of members of a group on whose behalf relief was sought in such action by the Federal Government;

(C) prevent challenges to a litigated or consent judgment or order on the ground that such judgment or order was obtained through collusion or fraud, or is transparently invalid or was entered by a court lacking subject matter jurisdiction; or

(D) authorize or permit the denial to any person of the due process of law required by the Constitution.

(3) Any action not precluded under this subsection that challenges an employment consent judgment or order described in paragraph (1) shall be brought in the court, and if possible before the judge, that entered such judgment or order. Nothing in this subsection shall preclude a transfer of such action pursuant to section 1404 of Title 28.

Section 704

Discrimination for Making Charges, Testifying, Assisting, or Participating in Enforcement Proceedings

(a) It shall be an unlawful employment practice for an employer to discriminate against any of his employees or applicants for employment, for an employment agency, or joint labor-management committee controlling apprenticeship or other training or retraining, including on-the-job training programs, to discriminate against any individual, or for a labor organization to discriminate against any member thereof or applicant for membership, because he has opposed any practice made an unlawful employment practice by this subchapter, or because he has made a charge, testified, assisted, or participated in any manner in an investigation, proceeding, or hearing under this subchapter.

Printing or Publication of Notices or Advertisements Indicating Prohibited Preference, Limitation, Specification, or Discrimination; Occupational Qualification Exception

(b) It shall be an unlawful employment practice for an employer, labor organization, employment agency, or joint labor-management committee controlling apprenticeship or other training or retraining, including on-the-job training programs, to print or publish or cause to be printed or published any notice or advertisement relating to employment by such an employer or membership in or any classification or referral for employment by such a labor organization, or relating to any classification or referral for employment by such an employment agency, or relating to admission to, or employment in, any program established to provide apprenticeship or other training by such a joint labor-management committee, indicating any preference, limitation, specification, or discrimination, based on race, color, religion, sex, or national origin, except that such a notice or advertisement may indicate a preference, limitation, specification, or discrimination based on religion, sex, or national origin when religion, sex, or national origin is a bona fide occupational qualification for employment.

J TITLE I OF THE AMERICANS WITH DISABILITIES ACT

Definitions

Section 101 Definitions As used in this title:

(1) Commission—The term "Commission" means the Equal Employment Opportunity Commission established by section 705 of the Civil Rights Act of 1964 (42 U.S.C. 2000e-4).

(2) Covered entity—The term "covered entity" means an employer, employment agency, labor organization, or joint labor-management committee.

(3) Direct threat—The term "direct threat" means a significant risk to the health or safety of others that cannot be eliminated by reasonable accommodation.

(4) Employee—The term "employee" means an individual employed by an employer.

(5) Employer—

(A) In general—The term "employer" means a person engaged in an industry affecting commerce who has 15 or more employees for each working day in each of 20 or more calendar weeks in the current or preceding calendar year, and any agent of such person, except that, for two years following the effective date of this title, an employer means a person engaged in an industry affecting commerce who has 25 or more employees for each working day in each of 20 or more calendar weeks in the current or preceding year, and any agent of such person.

(B) Exceptions—The term "employer" does not include—

(i) the United States, a corporation wholly owned by the government of the United States, or an Indian tribe; or

(ii) a bona fide private membership club (other than a labor organization) that is exempt from taxation under section 501(c) of the Internal Revenue Code of 1986.

(6) Illegal use of drugs

(A) In general—The term "illegal use of drugs" means the use of drugs, the possession or distribution of which is unlawful under the Controlled Substances Act (21 U.S.C. 812). Such term does not include the use of a drug taken under supervision by a licensed health care professional, or other uses authorized by the Controlled Substances Act or other provisions of Federal law.

(B) Drugs—The term "drug" means a controlled substance, as defined in schedules I through V of section 202 of the Controlled Substances Act.

(7) Person, etc—The terms "person", "labor organization", "employment agency", "commerce", and "industry affecting commerce", shall have the same meaning given such terms in section 701 of the Civil Rights Act of 1964 (42 (U.S.C. 2000e).

(8) Qualified individual with a disability—The term "qualified individual with a disability" means an individual with a disability who with or without reasonable accommodation, can perform the essential functions of the employment position that such individual holds or desires. For the purposes of this title, consideration shall be given to the employer's judgment as to what functions of a job are essential, and if an employer has prepared a written description before advertising or interviewing applicants for the job, this description shall be considered evidence of the essential functions of the job.

(9) Reasonable accommodation—The term "reasonable accommodation" may include—

(A) making existing facilities used by employees readily accessible to and usable by individuals with disabilities; and

(B) job restructuring, part-time or modified work schedules, reassignment to a vacant position, acquisition or modification of equipment or devices, appropriate adjustment or modifications of examinations, training materials or policies, the provision of qualified readers or interpreters, and other similar accommodations for individuals with disabilities.

(10) Undue hardship—

(A) In general—The term "undue hardship" means an action requiring significant difficulty or expense, when considered in light of the factors set forth in subparagraph (B).

(B) Factors to be considered—In determining whether an accommodation would impose an undue hardship on a covered entity, factors to be considered include—

(i) the nature and costs of the accommodation needed under this Act;

(ii) the overall financial resources of the facility or facilities involved in the provision of the reasonable accommodation; the number of persons employed at such facility; the effect on expenses and resources, or the impact otherwise of such accommodation upon the operation of the facility;

(iii) the overall financial resources of the covered entity; the overall size of the business of a covered entity with respect to the number of its employees; the number, type, and location of its facilities; and

(iv) the type of operation or operations of the covered entity, including the composition, structure, and functions of the workforce of such entity; the geographic separateness, administrative, or fiscal relationship of the facility or facilities in question to the covered entity.

Discrimination

Section 102 Discrimination   (a) General Rule—No covered entity shall discriminate against a qualified individual with a disability because of the disability of such individual in regard to job application procedures, the hiring, advancement, or discharge of employees, employee compensation, job training, and other terms, conditions, and privileges of employment.

(b) Construction—As used in subsection (a), the term "discriminate" includes—

(1) limiting, segregating, or classifying a job applicant or employee in a way that adversely affects the opportunities or status of such applicant or employee because of the disability of such applicant or employee;

(2) participating in a contractual or other arrangement or relationship that has the effect of subjecting a covered entity's qualified applicant or employee with a disability to the discrimination prohibited by this title (such relationship includes a relationship with an employment or referral agency, labor union, an organization providing fringe benefits to an employee of the covered entity, or an organization providing training and apprenticeship programs);

(3) utilizing standards, criteria, or methods of administration

(A) that have the effect of discrimination on the basis of disability; or

(B) that perpetuate the discrimination of others who are subject to common administrative control;

(4) excluding or otherwise denying equal jobs or benefits to a qualified individual because of the known disability of an individual with whom the qualified individual is known to have a relationship or association;

(5)(A) not making reasonable accommodations to the known physical or mental limitations of an otherwise qualified individual with a disability who is an applicant or employee, unless such covered entity can demonstrate that the accommodation would impose an undue hardship on the operation of the business of such covered entity; or

(B) denying employment opportunities to a job applicant or employee who is an otherwise qualified individual with a disability, if such denial is based on the need of such covered entity to make reasonable accommodation to the physical or mental impairments of the employee or applicant;

(6) using qualification standards, employment tests or other selection criteria that screen out or tend to screen out an individual with a disability or a class of individuals with disabilities unless the standard, test or other selection criteria, as used by the covered entity, is shown to be job-related for the position in question and is consistent with business necessity; and

(7) failing to select and administer tests concerning employment in the most effective manner to ensure that, when such test is administered to a job applicant or employee who has a disability that impairs sensory, manual, or speaking skills, such test results accurately reflect the skills, aptitude, or whatever other factor of such applicant or employee that such test purports to measure, rather than reflecting the impaired sensory, manual, or speaking skills of such employee or applicant (except where such skills are the factors that the test purports to measure).

(c) Medical Examinations and Inquiries—

(1) In general—The prohibition against discrimination as referred to in subsection (a) shall include medical examinations and inquiries.

(2) Preemployment—

(A) Prohibited examination or inquiry—Except as provided in paragraph (3), a covered entity shall not conduct a medical examination or make inquiries of a job applicant as to whether such applicant is an individual with a disability or as to the nature or severity of such disability.

(B) Acceptable Inquiry—A covered entity may make preemployment inquiries into the ability of an applicant to perform job-related functions.

(3) Employment entrance examination-A covered entity may require a medical examination after an offer of employment has been made to a job applicant and prior to the commencement of the employment duties of such applicant, and may condition an offer of employment on the results of such examination, if—

(A) all entering employees are subjected to such an examination regardless of disability;

(B) information obtained regarding the medical condition or history of the applicant is collected and maintained on separate forms and in separate medical files and is treated as a confidential medical record, except that—

(i) supervisors and managers may be informed regarding necessary restrictions on the work or duties of the employee and necessary accommodations:

(ii) first aid and safety personnel may be informed, when appropriate, if the disability might require emergency treatment; and

(iii) government officials investigating compliance with this Act shall be provided relevant information on request; and

(C) the results of such examination are used only in accordance with this title.

(4) Examination and Inquiry—

(A) Prohibited examinations and inquiries—A covered entity shall not require a medical examination and shall not make inquiries of an employee as to whether such employee is an individual with a disability or as to the nature or severity of the disability, unless such examination or inquiry is shown to be job-related and consistent with business necessity.

(B) Acceptable examinations and inquiries—. A covered entity may conduct voluntary medical examinations, including voluntary medical histories, which are part of an employee health program available to employees at that work site. A covered entity may make inquiries into the ability of an employee to perform job-related functions.

(C) Requirement—Information obtained under subparagraph (B) regarding the medical condition or history of any employee are subject to the requirements of subparagraphs (B) and (C) of paragraph (3).

Defenses

Section 103   Defenses   (a) In general—It may be a defense to a charge of discrimination under this Act that an alleged application of qualification standards, tests, or selection criteria that screen out or tend to screen out or otherwise deny a job or benefit to an individual with a disability has been shown to be job-related and consistent with business necessity, and such performance cannot be accomplished by reasonable accommodation, as required under this title.

(b) Qualification Standards—The term "qualification standards" may include a requirement that an individual shall not pose a direct threat to the health or safety of other individuals in the workplace.

(c) Religious Entities—

(1) In general—This title shall not prohibit a religious corporation, association, educational institution, or society from giving preference in employment to individuals of a particular religion to perform work connected with the carrying on by such corporation, association, educational institution, or society of its activities.

(2) Religious tenets requirement-Under this title, a religious organization may require that all applicants and employees conform the religious tenets of such organization.

(d) List of Infectious and Communicable Diseases—

(1) In general—The Secretary of Health and Human Services, not later than 6 months after the date of enactment of this Act, shall—

(A) review all infectious and communicable diseases which may be transmitted through handling the food supply;

(B) publish a list of infectious and communicable diseases which are transmitted through handling the food supply;

(C) publish the methods by which such diseases are transmitted; and

(D) widely disseminate such information regarding the list of diseases and their modes of transmissability to the general public. Such list shall be updated annually.

(2) Applications—In any case in which an individual has an infectious or communicable disease that is transmitted to others through the handling of food, that is included on the list developed by the Secretary of Health and Human Services under paragraph (1), and which cannot be eliminated by reasonable accommodation, a covered entity may refuse to assign or continue to assign such individual to a job involving food handling.

(3) Construction—Nothing in this Act shall be construed to preempt, modify, or amend any State, county, or local law, ordinance, or regulation applicable to food handling which is designed to protect the public health from individuals who pose a significant risk to the health or safety of others, which cannot be eliminated by reasonable accommodation, pursuant to the list of infectious or communicable diseases and the modes of transmissability published by the Secretary of Health and Human Services.

Drugs and alcohol   **Section 104   Illegal Use of Drugs and Alcohol**   (a) Qualified Individual With a Disability—For purposes of this title, the term "qualified individual with a disability" shall not include any employee or applicant who is currently engaging in the illegal use of drugs, when the covered entity acts on the basis of such use.

(b) Rules of Construction—Nothing in subsection (a) shall be construed to exclude as a qualified individual with a disability an individual who—

(1) has successfully completed a supervised drug rehabilitation program and is no longer engaging in the illegal use of drugs, or has otherwise been rehabilitated successfully and is no longer engaging in such use;

(2) is participating in a supervised rehabilitation program and is no longer engaging in such use; or

(3) is erroneously regarded as engaging in such use, but is not engaging in such use;

except that it shall not be a violation of this Act for a covered entity to adopt or administer reasonable policies or procedures, including but not limited to drug testing, designed to ensure that an individual described in paragraph (1) or (2) is no longer engaging in the illegal use of drugs.

(c) Authority of Covered Entity—A covered entity—

(1) may prohibit the illegal use of drugs and the use of alcohol at the workplace by all employees;

(2) may require that employees shall not be under the influence of alcohol or be engaging in the illegal use of drugs at the workplace;

(3) may require that employees behave in conformance with the requirements established under the Drug-Free Workplace Act of 1988 (41 U.S.C. 701 et seq.);

(4) may hold an employee who engages in the illegal use of drugs or who is an alcoholic to the same qualification standards for employment or job performance and behavior that such entity holds other employees, even if any unsatisfactory performance or behavior is related to the drug use or alcoholism of such employee; and

(5) may, with respect to Federal regulations regarding alcohol and the illegal use of drugs, require that—

(A) employees comply with the standards established in such regulations of the Department of Defense, if the employees of the covered entity are employed in an industry subject to such regulations, including complying with regulations (if any) that apply to employment in sensitive positions, in such an industry, in the case of employees of the covered entity who are employed in such positions (as defined in the regulations of the Department of Defense);

(B) employees comply with the standards established in such regulations of the Nuclear Regulatory Commission, if the employees of the covered entity are employed in an industry subject to such regulations, including complying with regulations (if any) that apply to employment in sensitive positions in such an industry, in the case of employees of the covered entity who are employed in such positions (as defined in the regulations of the Nuclear Regulatory Commission); and

(C) employees comply with the standards established in such regulations of the Department of Transportation, if the employees of the covered entity are employed in a transportation industry subject to such regulations, including complying with such regulations (if any) that apply to employment in sensitive positions in such an industry, in the case of employees of the covered entity who are employed in such positions (as defined in the regulations of the Department of Transportation).

(d) Drug Testing

(1) In general—For purposes of this title, a test to determine the illegal use of drugs shall not be considered a medical examination.

(2) Construction—Nothing in this title shall be construed to encourage, prohibit, or authorize the conducting of drug testing for the illegal use of drugs by job applicants or employees or making employment decisions based on such test results.

(e) Transportation Employees—Nothing in this title shall be construed to encourage, prohibit, restrict, or authorize the otherwise lawful exercise by entities subject to the jurisdiction of the Department of Transportation of authority to—

(1) test employees of such entities in, and applicants for, positions involving safety-sensitive duties for the illegal use of drugs and for on-duty impairment by alcohol; and

(2) remove such persons who test positive for illegal use of drugs and on-duty impairments by alcohol pursuant to paragraph (1) from safety-sensitive duties in implementing subsection (c).

Notices

Section 105   Posting Notices   Every employer, employment agency, labor organization, or joint labor-management committee covered under this title shall post notices in an accessible format to applicants, employees, and members describing the applicable provisions of this Act, in the manner prescribed by section 711 of the Civil Rights Act of 1964 (42 U.S.C. 2000e-10).

K   RESPONSES TO ETHICS OPINION POLL

The following excerpts report the responses given by those questioned in the Gallup Organization poll, described in the Ethical Dilemmas/Issues box on page 22. The excerpts are from Ricklefs, "Ethics in America," *The Wall Street Journal,* November 27, 1983. Reprinted by permission of The Wall Street Journal, Dow Jones & Company, Inc. All rights reserved.

To obtain this data, Gallup . . . polled a representative national general-public sample of 1,558 adults and a sample of 398 middle-level big-company executives. It interviewed the general citizens in person and mailed confidential questionnaires to the executives. The polling organization figures there is a sampling error of up to 3 percent in the general-public poll and up to 5 percent in the smaller executive poll.

Here is how the people Gallup surveyed say they would handle the dilemmas:

Family versus Ethics

More often than not, both executives and general citizens say family responsibilities should take precedence. Roughly half—49 percent of the public and 52 percent of the executives—thinks Jim should disregard his discovery to protect his family. About 34 percent of both the executives and the public think he should report the owners.

The money involved "isn't worth the loss of a job," says a manufacturing executive in his 50s. "Hundreds of thousands could make a difference." A company controller urges disregarding the cheating and adds: "The IRS has auditors to catch this kind of thing."

A financial executive says that to disregard the cheating "is not my real answer, but the chances of a 58-year-old whistleblower finding employment in this society might be difficult." Some executives suggest options that weren't offered in the question: resign or look for another job.

The Roundabout Raise

Though the public took a permissive approach to some of the other dilemmas, it decisively rejected the roundabout raise—and the executives rejected it even more overwhelmingly. Some 65 percent of the general citizens and 91 percent of the executives say Joe should turn down the circuitous raise. Only 25 percent of the public and 7 percent of the executives think he should "take this as authorization to pad his expense account."

The Faked Degree

More executives recommend dismissing Bill (50 percent) than overlooking the claim (43 percent). The general public decisively recommends (66 percent to 22 percent) overlooking the false claim rather than dismissing Bill. Within the general public, however, 33 percent of those with professional occupations recommend dismissal. Gallup points out that academic credentials might be particularly important to people in these occupations.

In an otherwise identical question asked of a subsample, Bill didn't merely fail to graduate—he never attended college at all. But the distinction didn't seem to matter. Both subsamples gave similar answers to the question.

Sneaking Phone Calls

In an otherwise identical question asked of part of the sample, Gallup has the employee making only $10 a month worth of personal long-distance calls instead of $100.

The difference matters, especially to executives. When the employee is sneaking $100 a month of calls, 64 percent of the public and 76 percent of the executives think that Helen should report him. Some 28 percent of the public and 19 percent of executives favor disregarding the calls.

But when the amount involved is $10 a month, 47 percent of the public and 48 percent of the executives favor disregarding the calls.

Put another way, when $100 a month is involved, the executives are tougher than the public. But when the figure is only $10 a month, the executives are more inclined to disregard the calls.

Abusive discharge   A tort, recognized in some states, committed when an employer discharges an employee in violation of a clear expression of public policy.

Acceleration clause   A provision in a credit agreement that allows the creditor to demand full payment of the debt if the debtor does not make timely payments or otherwise fails to comply with the terms of the agreement.

Acceptance   The offeree's assent to the terms of an offer to enter into a contract.

Act of state doctrine   Principle preventing judicial examination of certain acts of a foreign government.

Action   A suit brought in a court.

Actionable   A term used to show that acts provide a basis or legal reason for a lawsuit.

Adequate protection   Usually an amount of money paid by the trustee in bankruptcy to a secured creditor to compensate for depreciation or other loss to property in which the secured creditor has a security interest.

Adjudication   The determination of a controversy and pronouncement of a judgment or decree in a case.

Administrative agency   An agency of the government charged with administering particular legislation.

Administrative law judge   An officer who presides at the initial hearing on matters litigated before an administrative agency. He or she is independent of the agency staff.

Administrative Procedure Act   A statute establishing the procedural rules governing how federal agencies operate.

Affectation doctrine   A doctrine, developed by the Supreme Court in interpreting the Commerce Clause of the Constitution of the United States, whereby Congress has the power to regulate any activity that has an appreciable effect on interstate commerce.

Affidavit   A written declaration or statement of facts, sworn before a person who has the authority to administer such an oath.

Affirm   To agree with. An appellate court affirms a lower court decision when it declares the decision valid.

Affirmative action   The aggressive search to hire qualified minorities or those underrepresented in the workplace. An obligation undertaken by federal contractors to make special efforts to hire women and minorities. It is also a remedy which a court may decree under Title VII of the Civil Rights Act of 1964 and which the National Labor Relations Board is authorized to make under the National Labor Relations Act to effectuate the policies of those statutes.

Affirmative defense   An assertion that, if true, relieves a defendant of liability or limits a plaintiff's recovery.

Agent   One who acts for a principal.

Allegation   In a pleading, a declaration or statement by a party to a suit.

Allege   To make a statement of fact, an assertion, or a charge.

Amicus curiae   Latin, "Friend of the court." An individual or corporation that, because of strong interest in a case, petitions the court for permission to file a brief.

657

Answer   A pleading of the defendant which responds to a complaint by either admitting or denying the allegations contained in the complaint.

Antitakeover statutes   Statutes that benefit incumbent management of a corporation in the event of a corporate takeover attempt.

Apparent authority   A doctrine whereby an agent binds a principal to a third party because the principal invests the agent with the appearance of authority, even though actual authority is absent.

Appeal   The process by which a party asks a higher court to review alleged errors made by a lower court or an agency.

Appellant   The party that takes an appeal from one court to another.

Appellate court   A court having jurisdiction of appeal and review.

Appellee   The party in a case who responds to an appeal.

Appraisal rights   Rights of minority shareholders to have their interests appraised and sold to the corporation at the appraised value.

Arbitrary and capricious standard of review   The standard of judicial review of agency action whereby a court sets aside agency action if the agency failed to consider relevant evidence or made a clear error in judgment.

Arbitration   A process wherein a dispute is submitted to a mutually acceptable person or board, each party to the dispute having agreed beforehand to comply with the decision.

Arguendo   For the sake of the purposes of argument. A statement or observation made as a matter of argument or hypothetical illustration.

Arraignment   A proceeding wherein the accused is formally informed of the charge(s) and is asked to plead guilty, not guilty, or nolo contendere.

Articles of Confederation   The name of the document embodying the compact made among the 13 original states of the Union, before the adoption of the present Constitution.

Assault   The intentional tort of causing another person to be apprehensive of a battery.

Assumption of the risk   An affirmative defense raised by the defendant that defeats the plaintiff's recovery because the plaintiff knowingly and volun-tarily exposed himself or herself to the danger that caused the injury.

Attachment   The act or process of taking, apprehending, or seizing persons or property by virtue of a judicial process for the purpose of securing satisfaction of a judgment.

Attempt   In criminal law, an effort to accomplish a crime, amounting to more than mere preparation or planning for it, which, if not prevented, would have resulted in the full consummation of the attempted act, but which, in fact, does not bring to pass the party's ultimate design. In civil matters, an attempt ordinarily means an intent combined with an act falling short of the thing intended.

At-will employee   An employee who may be discharged by the employer for any reason without liability.

Authorization cards   Cards signed by employees in favor of a particular union as their collective bargaining representative.

Aver   To set out, assert, or allege in a formal complaint before a court of law.

Bailment   A delivery of goods by one person (bailor) to another (bailee) in trust for the accomplishment of a specific purpose involving the goods (e.g., repair) on an express or implied contract to carry out such trust and subsequently return the goods to the bailor.

Bailor   One who entrusts goods to another under a bailment.

Bait and switch   A method of selling in which a seller advertises at a low price a product that the seller does not intend to sell (the bait) and then disparages that product to the prospective buyer and directs the buyer to a higher-priced product (the switch) which the seller intended to sell all along.

Banc   French, "The full court." A court sits *en banc* when all the judges making up the court hear the case in contradistinction to having the case decided by one judge or a portion of the judges of the court.

Bargaining order   An order of the National Labor Relations Board directing an employer to bargain with a union. A bargaining order is made to remedy employer conduct during a board conducted election to decide whether the employees want a union to be their representative. The employer's conduct must be so serious an interference with employees' free choice as to render a new election incapable of being conducted.

Bargaining unit The group of employees sharing a community of interest and making up a unit for purposes of union representation and collective bargaining. Barred Obstruction; subject to a hindrance that prevents legal redress or recovery.

Battery The intentional tort of performing an unwanted touching.

Beneficiary One for whose benefit a trust is created.

Best efforts underwriting A type of underwriting whereby an underwriter agrees to use its best efforts to sell securities of an issuer to brokers in return for a commission on the sales that it makes. Under this type of distribution the underwriter is not obligated to sell any designated quantity of securities.

Bill The draft of an act of the legislature before it becomes law.

Bill of information A formal accusation of the commission of a crime made by a prosecutor in place of a grand jury indictment.

Bill of lading A document issued by a person engaged in the business of shipping goods. It serves as a receipt of goods received, a memorandum of the sales contract between seller and shipper, and a document of title evidencing ownership of the goods described in the bill of lading.

Blue sky laws State statutes regulating the sale of securities.

Bona fide Latin, "In good faith." Honestly, sincerely.

Bona fide occupational qualification A statutory exception to employment practices that might otherwise violate equal employment laws; it allows an employer to discriminate in its hiring where religion, national origin, sex, or age is reasonably necessary to the normal operation of a business.

Bona fide seniority system A seniority system which applies equally to all employees regardless of membership in a protected class, was not established or maintained for the purpose of discriminating, and operates rationally in accord with the practice in the industry.

Bond (security) A certificate issued by a governmental body or a corporation to represent a debt owed to the bondholder as well as a promise to pay interest.

Boycott A conspiracy or confederation to prevent anyone from carrying on business, or to injure anyone's business, by preventing potential customers from doing business with him or her.

Breach of contract Failure, without legal excuse, to perform any promise which forms the whole or part of a contract.

Bribe Anything given in value with the corrupt intent to induce or influence a public official in the performance of his or her duties.

Broker An agent who bargains, carries on negotiations, and makes contracts on behalf of his or her employer for compensation; also, a dealer in securities issued by others.

Brokerage The compensation of a broker, including wages and commission.

Bubble concept The treatment of all pollution-emitting devices collectively within an area, thus permitting increased pollution from sources as long as there is an equivalent decrease in pollution from other sources under the bubble.

Burden of proof The necessity or duty of affirmatively proving the fact or facts in dispute on an issue raised between the parties to a suit in court.

Business judgment rule A rule that affords board members of a corporation wide latitude in decisionmaking.

Canons of ethics Standards for the professional conduct expected of a lawyer, comprising the Code of Professional Responsibility. Initially adopted by the American Bar Association, it has been enacted into law in most states.

Capitalist model of justice A model based on the theory of economic justice that any distribution of things of value which results from unfettered economic competition is just.

Case law The law as developed or laid down in decided cases, as opposed to statutes.

Case of first impression A case which has no precedent on which the court may rely.

Cause of action The facts which evidence a civil wrong, thereby giving rise to a right to judicial relief.

Cease and desist order An order by an agency or a court directing someone to stop doing something.

Certiorari A means of obtaining appellate review by petition; a writ issued by an appellate court to an inferior court commanding the record to be certified to the appellate court for judicial review.

Charging party A person who files a complaint with a government agency alleging that there has been a violation of law. In labor law, the person who files an unfair labor practice charge with the National Labor Relations Board is called a charging party. Also, a person who files a charge with the Equal Employment Opportunity Commission, alleging that someone has violated one of the federal employment laws prohibiting employment discrimination, is called the charging party.

Checks and balances A system of government whose branches provide checks and balances against each other.

Choice-of-forum provision A provision in a contract specifying a jurisdiction's court to which the parties agree to submit any disputes that may arise under the contract.

Choice-of-law provision A clause in a contract specifying the body of law the parties to the contract agree will govern their contract.

Churning Abuse of a customer's confidence by a broker who initiates excessive transactions for the customer for personal gain.

Circumstantial evidence Evidence of an indirect nature; evidence from which the existence of a fact is inferred.

Civil law That body of law concerned with civil or private rights. Contrast *Criminal law.*

Claim A cause of action.

Class action An action brought by one or more persons as representatives of a large group of similarly situated persons.

Close corporation A corporation with a small number of shareholders who are family members or otherwise related.

Closed-end credit Refers to specific amount of credit for a definite time with loans repaid in installments.

Codetermination A process of management in which employers and employees share in the decision making.

Collateral Property pledged as security for the satisfaction of a debt.

Collective entity doctrine A doctrine of constitutional law holding that the Fifth Amendment's privilege against self-incrimination is a personal right and does not apply to corporations or other collective entities.

Collusion An agreement between two or more persons to commit a wrongful act.

Commerce The exchange of goods, products, or property of any kind.

Commercial speech A term used in constitutional law to refer to economic speech, such as advertising.

Commodity A movable article of commerce, especially merchandise.

Common carrier One that transports persons or property for compensation, providing such services to the general public.

Common law The principles and rules which derive solely from custom or from the judgments and decisions of courts. It is judge-made law.

Comparative negligence The doctrine under which a plaintiff's negligence as a factor in his or her own injury is assigned a percentage value, and his or her recovery from the defendant is reduced proportionately. Contrast with *Contributory negligence.*

Compensable Capable of being compensated.

Compensable damages Damages which compensate the victim for a loss; damages that put the victim in the position he or she was in before the injury occurred.

Compensable injury Within workers' compensation statutes, compensation to an employee for injury arising out of and in the course of employment.

Compensatory damages Damages compensating an injured party for the injury sustained, and nothing more; such compensation as will simply make good or replace the loss caused by a wrong or injury.

Competitive injury An injury to competition or to a competitor.

Complaint The first pleading by the plaintiff in a civil case. Its purpose is to give the defendant the information on which the plaintiff relies to support its demand. In a complaint, the plaintiff sets out a cause of action, consisting of a formal allegation or charge presented to the appropriate court.

Composition plan A plan whereby a debtor pays a pro rata share to each creditor in satisfaction of debt.

Concerted action Action that has been planned, arranged, adjusted, agreed on, or settled between parties acting together pursuant to some design or scheme.

Conciliation The proceeding in which litigants are brought together by a third party.

Concur To agree.

Concurring opinion A printed opinion in which a judge agrees with the decision of the majority of the court for a different reason. With reference to appellate court opinions, a concurring opinion is one written by a judge who may agree with the majority opinion's conclusion, but for different reasons, and therefore writes a separate opinion.

Confederation A league or compact for mutual support, particularly of nations or states. Such was the colonial government during the American Revolution.

Confirmed letter of credit A letter of credit sent to a bank near the seller's place of business, indicating another bank representing the buyer will pay on presentation of required documents.

Conglomerate merger A merger among firms that operate in separate or distinct markets.

Conscious parallelism When a competitor copies the actions of a market leader absent contract, combination, or conspiracy.

Consent decree A decree entered by consent of the parties. It is not a judicial sentence, but is an agreement of the parties made under the sanction of the court.

Consent order An agreement by the defendant to cease activities which the government asserts are illegal. Also known as consent decree.

Consequential damages Damage or injury that is not a direct, immediate, or predictable result of a party's act, but is nevertheless shown to be a consequence of it.

Consideration Something given in exchange for a promise which makes the promise legally enforceable. Consideration consists of doing or promising to do that which the giver was not previously obligated to do or refraining from doing or promising to refrain from doing that which the giver had a legal right to do.

Consignee One to whom goods are consigned for sale or safekeeping.

Consignment Property delivered by a consignor to an agent for sale where title is held by the consignor until the property is sold.

Consignor One who delivers goods to another on consignment.

Conspiracy A combination or confederation between two or more persons formed for the purpose of committing, by their joint efforts, some unlawful or criminal act.

Construction defect In a product liability action, a defect which results from the negligent manufacture of a particular item rather than from a defect in its design.

Constructive conditions Conditions that the law implies into a contract based on the order of performance under the contract.

Consumer credit Credit that is extended primarily for personal, family, or household purposes.

Consumer Product Safety Commission A federal administrative agency which supervises and regulates consumer products.

Consumer product safety standard Performance or labeling standard, voluntarily assumed by product manufacturers, or imposed by the CPSC on product manufacturers.

Contempt A willful disregard or disobedience of a public authority.

Contempt of court An act which disturbs or obstructs a court or is intended to detract from its authority or dignity.

Continuing trespass A type of trespass that occurs over an extended period of time.

Contract An agreement that a court enforces.

Contributory negligence Conduct by the plaintiff which is a contributing factor in his or her injury, thus barring any recovery against the defendant. Contrast *Comparative negligence.*

Conversion An unauthorized assumption and exercise of ownership over goods belonging to another, to the alteration of their condition or the exclusion of the owner's rights.

Conviction The result of a criminal trial which ends in a judgment that the prisoner is guilty as charged.

Copyright A limited monopoly granted by the federal government to protect literary type works.

Corporate opportunity An opportunity that arises because of a corporation's business or situation; a doctrine which prevents corporate officials from personally appropriating an opportunity which belongs to the corporation.

Corporation   A business organization which is a legal entity formed in compliance with statutory law whose owners enjoy limited liability.

Corrective advertising   A remedy of the Federal Trade Commission by which one found guilty of violating the Federal Trade Commission Act with regard to unlawful advertising is ordered to correct the lasting impression of the advertising on the public by engaging in advertising that repudiates the earlier advertising.

Cost justification defense   The justification of price discrimination under the Robinson-Patman Act based on the difference in cost.

Counterclaim   A claim presented by a defendant which, if successful, defeats or reduces the plaintiff's recovery.

Countervailing duties   A tax imposed by an importing country on goods to counter-act a subsidy given by the exporting country to the manufacture of the goods.

Court judgment   The official decision of a court determining the respective rights and claims of the parties in a lawsuit.

Credit bureau   An establishment that makes a business of collecting information relating to the credit, character, responsibility, and reputation of individuals and businesses for the purpose of furnishing the information to subscribers.

Creditor   A person to whom a debt is owed.

Criminal law   That body of law, commonly codified into penal codes, which declares what conduct is criminal and provides punishment for such conduct to protect society from harm. Contrast Civil law.

Criminal penalty   Punishment attached to the conviction of a crime.

Cross claim   A claim made in the course of an action by a defendant against a codefendant or by a plaintiff against a coplaintiff.

Cross elasticity of demand   An economic measure of the relationship between price changes and demand changes for a particular good.

Cross-examination   The examination of a witness at a trial or hearing, or on taking a deposition, by the party opposed to the one that produced said witness, on his or her evidence given in chief, to test its truth, to further develop it, or for other purposes.

Data   acts from which to draw a conclusion. De facto In fact; in deed; actually.

De jure corporation   A lawfully recognized corporation.

De minimis   Something small or trifling.

De novo   Latin, "To begin anew." Usually refers to the necessity of a new hearing on the same facts and law previously litigated.

Debt security   Bonds, notes, debentures, and any other corporate securities which represent a debt owed to the holder.

Debtor   One who owes money.

Deceit   A fraudulent misrepresentation used by one person to deceive or trick another, who is ignorant of the facts, to the damage of the latter.

Decertify   In labor law, to decertify a union is to take away its status as the exclusive bargaining agent of the employees of an employer. Decertification occurs usually after an election is conducted by the National Labor Relations Board to determine whether the employees wish to continue to have a particular union act as their exclusive bargaining agent.

Declaratory judgment   A judgment which simply declares the rights of the parties or expresses the opinion of the court on a question of law without ordering anything to be done.

Defamation   The disparagement of one's reputation; the offense of injuring a person's character, fame, or reputation by oral or written publication.

Default   Failure; omission to perform a legal or contractual duty; the failure of a party to appear in court after being properly served with process.

Defendant   The party against which an action is brought in a civil case; the accused in a criminal case.

Defense   An assertion offered by a defendant which, if successful, relieves him or her of liability, reduces the plaintiff's recovery, or defeats a criminal charge.

Defined benefit plan   A retirement plan that provides specific retirement benefits based on age and length of employment.

Defined contribution plan   A pension plan whose benefits are based on the amount in the retirement account.

Demand   The amount of a particular good that consumers buy in a given period of time.

Deposition Pretrial testimony of a witness taken orally and under oath before an officer of the court (but not in open court), subject to cross-examination and reduced to writing.

Design defect In the law of product liability, a defect in a product resulting from its design, so that every one produced is similarly defective. Contrast with *Construction defect.*

Dicta Plural of *dictum.* Opinions of a judge that do not embody the resolution or determination of the court.

Dictum The word is generally used as an abbreviated form of obiter dictum (a remark by the way). An observation or remark made by a judge in pronouncing an opinion in a case, concerning some rule, principle, or application of law, or the solution of a question suggested by the case, but not necessarily involved in the case or essential to its determination.

Disclosure The act of disclosing. In several areas of government regulation of business, it refers to the act of revealing required information to consumers, investors, and employees.

Discovery Devices that may be used by one party to obtain information about the case from the other party in preparation for trial.

Disparagement An untrue or misleading statement about a competitor's business or goods made to influence, or tending to influence, the public not to buy from the competitor.

Disparate impact The imposition of a rule of employment which disproportionately affects a protected class.

Disparate treatment The treatment of one employee or prospective employee less favorably than another because of race, sex, religion, national origin, age, or handicap.

Disposable earnings The portion of a person's income that he or she is free to spend or invest as he or she sees fit after payment of taxes and other obligations.

Dissenting opinion An opinion wherein a judge disagrees with the result reached by the majority of the court. Contrast Concurring opinion.

Distress sale A "going out of business" sale in which the seller receives less for the goods than would be received under normal conditions.

Distributive justice Theories of justice dictating the morally proper way to distribute things of value in society.

Diversity jurisdiction The jurisdiction of the federal courts to hear cases in which the parties are citizens of different states or one of the parties is an alien and the amount in controversy exceeds $50,000.

Diversity of citizenship A phrase used with reference to the jurisdiction of the federal courts, which, under Article III, Section 2, of the Constitution of the United States, extends to cases between citizens of different states. See diversity jurisdiction.

Dividend The share allotted to each of several persons entitled to participate in a division of profits or property. Dividends are what a shareholder earns from the stock owned in a corporation.

Draft A written order by the first party, called the drawer, instructing a second party, called the drawee (such as a bank), to pay a third party, called the payee. Due diligence defense A defense to a securities violation which requires a defendant to prove that he or she exercised ordinary prudence, but nonetheless was unaware of a material misrepresentation contained in the registration statement.

Effluent limitation The amount of pollutants legally dischargeable from a particular source.

Electronic Funds Transfer Act A federal statute that requires financial institutions to disclose the terms of electronic funds transfer services, establishes a procedure for error resolution, and specifies penalties for violations.

Eminent domain The power of a sovereign to take private property for public use, necessitating just compensation.

Emission limitation A specific rule that operators of pollutant sources must follow to reduce emissions.

Emissions offset policy A policy under the Clean Air Act whereby increased emissions are permitted by the applicant at a source in a nonattainment area as long as sufficient reductions in emission occur in the same area.

Employment-at-will doctrine The legal doctrine that holds that whenever an employment relationship is of an indefinite duration, either party—the employer or the employee—may terminate the relationship at will, for good cause or bad, in good faith or with malice.

Enabling legislation A term applied to any statute that enables agencies, corporations, or persons to do something they could not do before. Such statutes confer a lawful power in an agency to act on a given matter.

Enactment The process by which a bill becomes a statute.

Enterprise coverage A type of coverage of the federal Fair Labor Standards Act whereby that act covers all the employees of a firm that engages in commerce.

Entrepreneur Someone who organizes, manages, or assumes the risk of a business.

Environmental impact statement A statement that details the environmental impact of proposed administrative action. The statement must be prepared by an agency whenever it plans or engages in major federal actions significantly affecting the quality of human environment.

Equal Credit Opportunity Act A federal statute that prohibits discrimination in credit extension on the basis of sex, race, religion, national origin, age, and other protected statuses.

Equitable relief Injunction, specific performance, restraining orders, and the like, as opposed to money damages.

Equity security A share in a corporation, usually referred to as stock.

Escrow A writing, deed, stock, or property delivered to a third person, to be held by that person until the fulfillment of a condition and then delivered to its owner.

Ethicist One versed in the study of how moral decisions are justified.

Ethics The study of how moral decisions are justified.

Ex parte On the application of one party only. A judicial proceeding is ex pane when it is taken or granted at the request of, or for the benefit of, one party only, and without notice to, or contestation by, any person adversely interested.

Exclusive dealing agreements Contracts on which the buyer is obligated to purchase all of its requirements of a given commodity from the seller.

Executive agencies Federal agencies that are under the direct control of the president. Appointments to executive agencies do not need Senate approval.

Executive order An order by the chief executive of a government affecting the administration of the executive branch of government.

Exhaustion A doctrine requiring that a party utilize remedies provided within an agency before seeking review by a court.

Exonerate To exculpate; to remove a responsibility or duty.

Experience rating provision A rating of an employer, based on historical unemployment data, which determines the employer's state unemployment compensation tax contribution.

Export trading company A company that acts as an intermediary in the marketing of goods overseas.

Express conditions Conditions inserted in a contract by the parties that must be fulfilled before a party has a duty to perform or that when fulfilled relieve a party of a duty to perform.

Express warranty A warranty which the seller creates by making a representation or a promise relating to goods or by showing the buyer a sample or model of them, regardless of whether such words as guaranty or warranty are used.

Expropriation An act by which a foreign government takes over ownership of an American company or American property located in the foreign government.

Expunge To destroy; to strike out wholly. "Expungement of the record" refers to the process whereby a record of a criminal conviction is sealed or destroyed after a designated period of time.

Extension plan A plan whereby a debtor extends the time for payments to creditors past the due date.

Fair Credit Reporting Act A federal statute that regulates consumer reporting agencies.

Fair use A doctrine under copyright law which permits reasonable use of copyrighted works for limited purposes, such as criticism, news, reporting, teaching and research.

False imprisonment The intentional tort of interfering with another person's freedom of movement.

Federal question jurisdiction The jurisdiction of the federal courts to hear cases arising under the U.S. Constitution, acts of Congress, or treaties.

Federal Register A federal publication providing notice of federal rulemaking by federal agencies.

Federalism The relationship between the states and the federal government whereby responsibility and autonomy is divided between them.

Fellow servant doctrine A common-law doctrine, now abrogated by all workers' compensation acts, that an employee injured by the negligent act of a fellow employee cannot recover damages from his or her employer.

Fiduciary A person having a duty, created by his or her undertaking, to act primarily for another's benefit.

Fiduciary duty The duty which arises whenever one person is in a special relationship of trust to another, such as the duty an attorney owes to a client.

Firm commitment underwriting A type of underwriting of securities whereby the underwriter is obligated to purchase a designated number of shares of securities from an issuer at a specified price.

Fixture Personal property that has been affixed to reality in such a manner as to become part of the realty. Foreign corporation A corporation doing business in any state other than the one in which it is incorporated.

Foreign Corrupt Practices Act A federal statute which prohibits bribing a foreign official, and establishes accounting procedures designed to discover, such briberies.

Form 10-K A form that must be filed with the SEC within 90 days after the end of the fiscal period and which contains current audited financial statements and information regarding the operations of the business and the status of its securities.

Forum non conveniens, doctrine of The power of a court to decline jurisdiction when the convenience of the parties and the ends of justice would be better served by bringing the action in another court.

Franchise A special privilege conferred on someone.

Franchisee A holder of a franchise.

Franchisor A party granting a franchise.

Fungible goods Goods of any type which are by nature considered to be the equivalent of any other good of that type.

Garnishee The person on whom a garnishment is served; one who has in his or her possession the property of someone who owes a debt to another person.

Garnishment A proceeding in which money, property, or credits of a debtor in possession of a third person, the garnishee, are applied to the payment of debts. The process is available only where it is authorized by statute.

GATT The abbreviation for General Agreement on Tariffs and Trade. Treaty covering the treatment of exports and imports for adopting nations.

General intent An intention, purpose, or design, either without a specific plan or without a particular object.

Golden parachutes Lucrative compensation benefits granted to corporate executives in the event they are terminated after a takeover.

Good Under the Uniform Commercial Code, any tangible item capable of being moved other than money, securities, and real estate.

Good faith An intangible quality encompassing honesty, sincerity, and the lack of intent to defraud or take advantage of another.

Goodwill The propensity of customers to return to a business. The patronage of a particular business. As such, it is an intangible asset of a business.

Gratuity A gift.

Gross negligence A conscious or intentional act or omission likely to result in harm to a person or property; a higher level of culpability than simple negligence.

Group boycott A per se violation of the Sherman Antitrust Act which amounts to a refusal to economically deal by two or more.

Handicap A physical or mental impairment that substantially limits one or more of life's major activities.

Hazard communication standard An OSHA standard requiring chemical manufacturers and importers to evaluate the hazards of all chemicals they produce or import, to develop material safety data sheets for each chemical, to label containers holding chemicals with information concerning the chemicals and their hazards, and to so advise their employees about the hazards.

Horizontal merger Acquisition of one company by another company producing the same product or similar product and selling it in the same geographic market.

Horizontal restraint An agreement between two or more competitors to avoid competing with each other.

Hot cargo agreement A form of a secondary boycott involving an illegal agreement that the employer will not deal with nonunion employers or that the employees need not handle nonunion goods.

Imminent hazard An immediate danger resulting from a product defect.

Impeach To challenge the credibility of a witness.

Impleader A procedure whereby a defendant brings a new party into an action on the basis that the new party may be liable to that party.

Implied contract A contract not explicitly created by the parties, but inferred, as a matter of reason and justice, from the circumstances.

Implied warranty A warranty which arises by operation of law although the seller does not express it; for example, that a product is fit for the purpose for which it is intended.

In camera In chambers; in private. A cause is said to be heard in camera either when the hearing is held before a judge or agency official in his or her private office or when all spectators are excluded from the courtroom or agency hearing room.

Incidental damages Damages resulting from a buyer's breach of contract, such as the costs of stopping delivery and reselling the goods; damages resulting from a seller's breach, including the expenses incurred in returning rightfully rejected goods and procuring a replacement.

Incorporation doctrine A doctrine developed by the Supreme Court whereby it has interpreted the Due Process Clause of the 14th Amendment of the Constitution of the United States as incorporating, or absorbing, selected provisions of the Bill of Rights (the first 10 amendments) and thus applying them to the states. Prior to the incorporation doctrine, the Bill of Rights applied only to the federal government.

Independent contractor One who contracts to do work for a principal and maintains the means, method, and manner of accomplishing the result.

Independent regulatory agency A federal agency to which appointments require Senate approval.

Indict *See Indictment.*

Indictment A formal accusation made by a grand jury which charges that a person has committed a crime.

Information *See Bill of information.*

Injunction An order of the court directing someone to do or not to do something.

In personam jurisdiction The power which a court has over the defendant's personas opposed to the power of a court over property.

Insider With respect to federal regulation of securities, an insider is anyone who has knowledge of facts not available to the general public. With regard to Section 16 of the Exchange Act of 1934, an insider is specifically defined as an officer, director, or any security holder owning at least 10 percent of the stock of a corporation.

Inside trading Gains derived by trading on inside information.

Intent A conscious and purposeful state of mind with which a person acts.

Intentional infliction of emotional distress An intentional tort action providing redress to the victims of outrageous conduct that causes severe psychological injury.

Intentional torts A category of civil wrongs giving redress to the victims of willful wrongdoing.

Interpretive rules Rules of a federal agency rendering interpretations of the agency's enabling legislation. Such rules are not binding on the courts. Such rules do not need to be issued according to the procedures of the federal Administrative Procedure Act.

Interpretivism A theory of constitutional law maintaining that the Constitution should be interpreted by resort to its literal language or the intent of the framers, as found in historical accounts of the drafting of the Constitution.

Interrogatories A discovery device consisting of a series of written questions directed by one party to another party.

Interstate commerce Commercial trading, traffic, or the transportation of persons or property from a point in one state to points in other states.

Intervention The act of a nonparty becoming a party to a lawsuit on his/her own initiative.

Intrastate commerce Commerce that is carried out wholly within the limits of a single state.

Invasion of privacy An intentional tort providing redress to the victims whose privacy has been unreasonably intruded on.

Investigative consumer report Information gathered through personal interviews with neighbors, friends, associates, or others.

Involuntary corporate dissolution The dissolution of a corporation by the state for noncompliance of administrative requirements.

Irrevocable letter of credit A letter of credit that cannot be cancelled without the agreement of both buyer and seller.

Judgment non obstante verdicto (judgment n.o.v.) *See Judgment notwithstanding the verdict.*

Judgment notwithstanding the verdict A judge's judgment that is contrary to the verdict of the jury.

Judicial review The process by which the Supreme Court of the United States reviews legislation and refuses to enforce those laws that it declares to be unconstitutional.

Jurisdiction The power of a court or a judicial officer to decide a case; the geographic area of a court's authority.

Jurisdictional standards Standards issued by the National Labor Relations Board for particular industries for purposes of determining whether the board will assert jurisdiction.

Jurisprudence The philosophy of law; the science which studies the principles of law and legal relations.

Labeling defect In the law of product liability, a defect in a product resulting from inadequate labeling.

Labeling standard A standard issued by the Consumer Product Safety Commission requiring that a warning label be attached to a product.

Laboratory conditions Conditions regulated by the National Labor Relations Board to ensure a fair determination of the uninhibited wishes of the employees, during an election campaign.

Labor organization An organization of employees organized for the purpose of dealing with their employer.

Laissez-faire economics A policy whereby government takes a hands-off posture toward economic planning.

Lanham Act A federal act that prohibits the use of any false description or representation in connection with any goods or services introduced into commerce.

Legal relief Money damages. Contrast *Equitable relief.*

Legislation The act of enacting laws; the making of laws by express decree; sometimes means a statute or statutes.

Legislative history The background and events leading up to the enactment of a statute; for example, committee reports and floor debates. Courts use the legislative history of a statute in determining the legislature's intent in enacting it.

Legislative rules Regulations issued by federal agencies pursuant to the federal Administrative Procedure Act. Such rules are binding on courts.

Legislator One who makes laws; a member of a legislative body.

Legislature The department, assembly, or body of government that makes laws for a state or nation.

Letter of credit A letter authorizing one person to pay money or extend credit to another on the credit of the writer.

Libel To defame or injure a person's reputation by a published writing.

License A permit granted by a government authority, person, or business to pursue some occupation or to carry on some business.

Lien A security interest in another's property, usually exercisable on the nonpayment of a debt.

Like grade and quality An element in a price discrimination offense under the Robinson-Patman Act requiring two products that are the subject of price discrimination to be of like grade and quality

Limited partnership A special form of partnership whereby the business is managed by general partners and financed by limited partners who do not participate in the management and who enjoy limited liability.

Liquidation The act or process by which a party settles his or her debt by converting all assets into cash and making distribution to creditors. The term is also used in connection with a Chapter 7 straight bankruptcy proceeding.

Lobbying Attempts, including personal solicitation, to induce legislators to vote in a certain way or to introduce legislation.

Long-arm statute A state statute subjecting a nonresident or a foreign corporation to the state's jurisdiction if the person or corporation has committed a tortious wrong or conducted business within the state, or has otherwise had minimal contacts within the state.

Magistrate A term for a public officer. Commonly, however, the term is applied to judicial officers with limited authority, such as justices of the peace.

Magnuson-Moss Warranty Act A federal statute that requires certain disclosures in connection with written warranties, imposes restrictions on disclaimers of implied warranties, and establishes a procedure through which consumers may more effectively enforce their warranty rights.

Mandatory subjects of bargaining Under the National Labor Relations Act, bargaining on wages, hours, and other terms and conditions of employment, including retirement benefits, vacations, rest periods, and work assignments.

Marxist model of justice A model based on the theory of economic justice: "from each according to his ability, to each according to his needs."

Mediation The act of a third person who attempts to persuade disputing parties to adjust their positions so as to resolve their dispute.

Meeting competition defense A defense to price discrimination under the Robinson-Patman Act when the seller's lower price was made in good faith to meet the equally low price of a competitor.

Merchantable Of good quality; of the quality fit for the purpose for which the good is intended.

Merger The fusion or absorption of one thing or right into another. For example, a merger occurs when one corporation becomes a part of another corporation.

Merit model of justice A model based on a concept of justice holding that if any distribution of things of value is based on merit, the distribution is just.

Misrepresentation An untrue statement that justifies the rescission of a contract.

Modification A change.

Monopoly The ownership or control of so large a part of the market supply of a given commodity as to stifle competition and ensure control over prices and competition.

Moot A question which is no longer a controversy because the issue involved is no longer in dispute.

Morals Judgments regarding what is right or wrong, good or evil.

Mortgage A pledge or security of particular property for the payment of a debt.

Most-favored-nation clause A clause found in most treaties providing that the citizens or subjects of contracting nations may enjoy the privileges accorded by either nation to those of the most favored nation.

Motion A request to a court or judge for a rule or order favorable to the requesting party, generally made within the course of an existing lawsuit.

Motion for directed verdict A request that the judge order the entry of a verdict for one party on the grounds that the opposing party has failed to present sufficient evidence for any other verdict.

Nationalization The act whereby a host country takes the property of an alien for a public purpose.

Natural law Conception of law as a system of rules and principles for the guidance of human conduct which, independently of enacted law or of the systems peculiar to any one people, might be discovered by the rational intelligence of man, and would be found to grow out of and conform to man's nature.

Necessary and Proper Clause Clause in U.S. Constitution which authorizes Congress to make all laws necessary and proper to carry out the enumerated powers of Congress and all other powers vested in the federal government.

Negligence The omission to do something that a reasonable and prudent person, guided by those considerations which ordinarily regulate human affairs, would do, or the doing of something that a reasonable and prudent person would not do.

Negligence per se Imputation of negligence when the defendant's violation of a statute results in injury to a person who is within the class of persons the statute is designed to protect and which injury is the type the statute is designed to protect against.

Nolo contendere Latin, "I will not contest it." A plea in a criminal action often having the same effect as a guilty plea, except that it may not be used against the defendant in a subsequent civil action. Also known as a no-contest plea.

Nonattainment area An area that has not met the national standards for air quality established under the federal Clean Air Act.

Noninterpretivism A theory of constitutional interpretation maintaining that the Supreme Court may make the determination of constitutionality by referring to values other than those constitutionalized by the framers.

Non-obviousness One of the characteristics of an invention that makes it patentable; if the state of the art at the time of the development was such that the "invention" was obvious, it will not be patentable.

Nonpoint source Nondiscernible and unconfined conveyance, such as overflows from irrigated agriculture.

Nuisance A class of torts that arise from the unreasonable, unwarrantable, or unlawful use by a person of his or her property, or from unlawful personal conduct, which obstructs or injures the rights of another.

Obiter dictum See Dictum.

Offer A proposal or act on the part of one person whereby he or she gives to another the legal power to create a contract.

Offeror Someone who makes an offer.

Oligopolistic A market in which a few large producers dominate.

Open-end credit Revolving charges and credit cards which permit the consumer to pay a part of what is owed.

Opinion of the court The statement by a judge or court of the decision reached in regard to a cause tried or argued before them, expounding the law as applied to the case, and detailing the reasons on which the judgment is based.

Order A command or direction authoritatively given.

Order for relief An order of a court or an administrative agency providing a remedy to someone.

OSHRC Occupational Safety and Health Review Commission; a federal administrative agency established under the Occupational Safety and Health Act; it hears appeals from OSH Act violations.

Over-the-counter market The market for securities traded off the floor of a stock exchange and usually sold through brokerage houses.

Palming off To impose by fraud; to pass off a product as another product by unfair means.

Parent corporation A company which owns over 50 percent of the voting stock of another company, known as its subsidiary.

Parliament The supreme legislative assembly of Great Britain.

Parole evidence Evidence of terms of a written contract other than the written document. When the written document is intended as the parties' final expression of their contract, parole evidence of prior agreements or representations cannot be used to vary the terms of the document.

Partnership An association of two or more persons to carry on as co-owners of a business for profit.

Partnership by estoppel A partnership arising when third parties are erroneously led to rely on the existence of a partnership.

Patent A limited monopoly granted by the federal government to make, use, and sell an invention.

Pattern or practice of discrimination A general policy of treating members of a protected class less favorably than other employees, proved by circumstantial evidence.

Per curiam Latin, "By the court." Used to indicate an opinion by the entire court rather than a single judge. Sometimes refers to a brief statement of the court's decision unaccompanied by any written opinion.

Per se Latin, "By itself." Inherently.

Performance standard A standard issued by the Consumer Product Safety Commission specifying minimum performance criteria for a product.

Personal property That property which has no fixed site and is moveable.

Petitioner A party that files a petition with a court, applying in writing for a court order; a party that takes an appeal from a judgment; a party that initiates an equity action.

Plain meaning rule A rule of statutory construction which requires that the meaning of words in a statute be assigned their plain import unless to do so would result in an absurdity.

Plaintiff   A person who brings an action or complaint against a defendant; the party who initiates a suit.

Plea   An answer to a complaint or to a material allegation of fact therein. In criminal procedure, the answer of the accused in response to the criminal charge.

Pleadings   The formal allegations by the parties of their respective claims and defenses; the complaint, answer, and reply.

Plenary   Full; entire; complete; absolute; perfect.

Point source   Any discernible and confirmed conveyance of water, such as a pipe, ditch, well, or canal.

Police power   The inherent power of a state over persons and property which enables the state to regulate the health, safety, and welfare of society.

Positive Law   Law actually or specifically enacted or adopted by proper authority for the government of a society.

Possession   The control or custody of property, for one's use and enjoyment, to the exclusion of all others.

Post hoc   Hereafter; after this time.

Power of Attorney   A written instrument investing an agent with authority to act for a principal.

Precedent   A previously decided court case which serves as authority for a subsequent similar case.

Predatory intent   An attempt to drive competitors out of business by sacrificing present revenues in the hope of recouping losses through future high prices.

Preemption doctrine   The doctrine adopted by the U.S. Supreme Court holding that certain matters are of such a national, as opposed to local, character that federal laws take precedence over state laws. As such, a state may not pass a law inconsistent with the federal law.

Preferential transfer   A transfer made during the 90-day period before an insolvent debtor's bankruptcy petition is filed, in which the debtor transfers to the creditor a greater percentage of the debt than would have been received under the distribution provision of the act.

Prejudicial error   An error made during a trial which materially affects the rights of a party and thus may be grounds for a reversal of judgment or a new trial.

Premises rule   A rule of worker's compensation law that holds that an employee who is injured while on the employer's premises may recover even though the employee was going to or coming from the work site.

Price discrimination   Selling to one customer at a price and refusing to sell to another at the same price by someone engaged in interstate commerce.

Price fix   The act of establishing a price; a per se violation of the Sherman Antitrust Act, as an unreasonable restraint of trade.

Prima facie   Latin, "At first sight." A fact presumed to be true unless disproved by evidence to the contrary.

Prima facie case   A case which has proceeded on sufficient proof to that stage at which it supports a judicial finding if evidence to the contrary is disregarded. A litigating party is said to have a prima facie case when the evidence in its favor is sufficiently strong for its opponent to be called on to answer it. A prima facie case, then, is one which is established by sufficient evidence and which can be overthrown only be rebutting evidence adduced on the other side.

Primary-fine injury   Injury that occurs when a seller suffers damages as a result of price discrimination by a competitor.

Principal   In agency law, the party for whom an agent acts.

Private law   As used in contrast to public law, the term means that part of the law which is administered between citizen and citizen or which is concerned with the definition and enforcement of rights in cases where both the person in whom the right inheres and the person on whom the obligation is incident are private individuals.

Private placement   An exemption under the Securities Act for transactions by an issuer not involving any public offering.

Privilege   A right or advantage particular to an individual or a class.

Privity   A mutual or successive relationship,, for example, the relationship between the parties to a contract.

Pro rata   Proportionately.

Probable cause   Reasonable grounds for belief in the existence of facts. In criminal procedure, reasonable grounds for the belief that a person should be arrested or a warrant issued.

Procedural justice   A form of justice that deals with the process used in deciding outcomes.

Procedural law   The part of law which concerns the method or process of enforcing rights.

Procedural rules   Rules adopted by an administrative agency to govern its internal procedures, such as the handling of charges, the holding of hearings, and the timing of investigations and hearings.

Promissory estoppel   A legal theory that allows a promise to be enforced without consideration. The theory applies where the promisee reasonably relies on a promise to his or her detriment and when that reliance is foreseeable to the promisor.

Prosecution   A criminal action. The term is also frequently used with respect to civil litigation and includes every step from commencement to final determination.

Prospectus   A pamphlet that capsulizes the information contained in the registration statement.

Proximate cause   Event(s) or action which, in natural and unbroken sequence, produce an injury that would not have occurred absent the event(s) or action.

Proxy   Written authorization given by a shareholder to vote his or her shares at a shareholders' meeting.

Proxy statement   A statement containing prescribed information that must be supplied to shareholders before proxies are solicited.

Public law   The branch of law concerned with administrative and constitutional law.

Publicly held corporation   A corporation whose stock is in the hands of many.

Punitive damages   Damages awarded to a plaintiff greater than the amount necessary to compensate his or her loss. They are generally granted where the wrong involves intent, violence, fraud, malice, or other aggravated circumstances.

Quid pro quo   The giving of one valuable thing for another.

Real property   Land and anything that is permanently attached to land.

Realist conception   A conception of law that holds that law is not embodied in abstract principles but in the process of deciding disputes.

Recognition picketing   The picketing of an employer by a noncertified union to force the employer to recognize it or the employees to choose it as their representative.

Reconstruction period   Period following the Civil War during which the states of the former Confederacy were reintegrated into the Union.

Red herring prospectus   In securities law, an advance copy of the statement (prospectus) to be filed with the Securities and Exchange Commission preceding an issue of securities. The copy is marked in red ink, "not a solicitation, for information only."

Redlining   The practice of denying mortgage loans to finance property located in specific neighborhoods.

Redress   The receiving of satisfaction for an injury sustained.

Relevant market   The geographic market composed of products that have reasonable interchangeability for purposes for which they are produced, considering their price, use, and quality. The term, in relation to a case involving an alleged violation of the Sherman Act or the Clayton Act, consists of both a product market and a geographic market.

Reliance damages   A measure of money damages for breach of contract that places the victim of the breach in the economic position he or she would have been in had the contract not been made.

Remand   To send back. The sending of a case back to the same court out of which it came, for the purpose of having some action taken on it.

Reorganization   A type of bankruptcy that permits a financially disturbed business to continue while arrangements for the adjustment of debts are made with creditors.

Res ipsa loquitur   Latin, "The thing speaks for itself." Rule of evidence whereby negligence of the defendant is inferred from the circumstances as the result of a reasonable belief that the injury could not have happened without such negligence.

Res judicata   Latin, "A matter adjudged." A thing judicially acted on or decided; a rule that a final judgment or decree on the merits by a court of competent jurisdiction is conclusive of the rights of the parties or their privies in all later suits on points and matters determined in the former suit.

Respondeat superior   Latin, "Let the master answer." Doctrine which provides that an employer or master is responsible for the acts of an employee or servant committed within the scope of the employment.

Respondent   The party that contends against an appeal.

Response costs The costs of federal or state environmental cleanups for which the violator may be ordered to pay.

Restatement A book published by the American Law Institute consisting of that body's restatement of the law in one of several areas, such as torts, contracts, and agency.

Restitution The avoidance of unjust enrichment, accomplished by requiring the recipient of a benefit to pay the reasonable value of the benefit to the party that conferred the benefit.

Restraining order An injunction; a court order prohibiting a party from doing something.

Restraint of trade Contracts or combinations which tend, or are designed, to eliminate or stifle competition, effect a monopoly, artificially maintain prices, or otherwise obstruct commerce as it would be carried on if left to the control of natural or economic forces.

Reverse To overthrow, vacate, set aside, make void, annul, repeal, or revoke, as to reverse a judgment.

Reviewability A term addressing whether a court has the power to review an administrative agency's action.

Revocation The recall of some power, authority, or thing granted.

RICO Racketeer Influenced and Corrupt Organizations Act; a federal statute that makes it a crime to acquire or operate an enterprise by a pattern of racketeering.

Rights model Ethical justification holding that decisions least disruptive of human rights are to be preferred.

Right to know provision A provision within the superfund law requiring owners and occupiers of facilities which produce, use, and store hazardous chemicals to file with local and state officials a material safety data sheet for each hazardous chemical.

Right to sue letter A letter issued by the Equal Employment Opportunity Commission to a complainant after finding probable cause of discrimination and when attempts to conciliate the dispute have failed.

Rulemaking A function of most federal agencies that allows interested parties to comment on proposed rules of an agency before their promulgation.

Rule of reason A restraint against trade that has a procompetitive business purpose and a competitive restraint not beyond that business purpose.

Rule 10b-5 An SEC rule that prohibits fraud in connection with any sale or purchase of securities.

Sale of business doctrine A doctrine rejected by the United States Supreme Court; it holds that the sale of 100 percent of the stock of a business is not a sale of a security for purposes of federal securities law.

Scalping The practice of a securities broker whereby the broker recommends the purchase of a stock for the purpose of inflating its value so that the broker, who had purchased the same stock previously, capitalizes on its sale.

Scienter Knowledge; intent to deceive or defraud.

Secondary boycott In labor law, the term refers to a refusal by union employees to work for, purchase from, or handle products of a secondary employer with whom the union has no dispute, with the object of forcing such employer to stop doing business with the primary employer with whom the union has a dispute.

Secondary meaning A trademark that has developed a new meaning in which it serves to identify specific goods. For example, Nantuckett has a primary meaning of a geographical location; however, it has a secondary meaning—a specific manufacturer's shirts.

Secondary-line injury Injury that occurs when a seller discriminates in price between two competing buyers.

Security A stock, bond, note, investment contract, or other interest involving an investment in a common enterprise with the expectation of a profit to be derived from the efforts of someone other than the investor; an obligation given by a debtor to assure payment of a debt by providing the creditor with a resource that the creditor can use if the debtor defaults on the debt.

Security interest A type of interest held by a creditor in a debtor's property such that the property could be sold on the debtor's default to satisfy the debt.

Seniority By seniority, the oldest worker in point of service, ability, and fitness for the job is the first to be given a choice of jobs, is the first to be promoted within a range of jobs subject to seniority, and is the last to be laid off. This proceeding is followed down the line to the youngest worker in point of service.

Separation of powers A phrase referring to the division of the federal government into three departments or branches: the legislative, which is empowered to make laws; the executive, which is required to carry out the laws; and the judiciary, which is charged with interpreting the laws and adjudicating disputes under the laws. One branch is not permitted to intrude on the domain of another.

Shareholder A person who owns stock in a corporation.

Shipping terms Terms in a contract which govern the shipment of goods. Shipping terms determine such matters as when risk of loss passes and when performance is complete.

Short-swing profits Profits made by an insider through the sale or other disposition of the corporate stock within six months after purchase.

Single trespass A trespass of a single instance.

Situs Situation or location.

Slander The tort of oral defamation.

Social audit A report of a company's social behavior.

Social balance sheet A report in which a company shares information on its social behavior.

Sole proprietorship A business owned by one person.

Sovereign An independent body or state; a chief ruler with supreme power, such as a king.

Sovereign immunity Doctrine preventing a litigant from asserting an otherwise meritorious claim against a sovereign (government).

Specific intent Exercise of intelligent will to commit a crime.

Specific performance A remedy for breach of contract that requires the breaching party to actually perform what he or she had promised to perform in the contract.

Squeeze out The elimination of minority shareholders by the majority shareholders.

Standard deviation A statistical method of measuring the probability that a given result occurred by chance.

Standing A stake in a controversy sufficient to entitle a person to sue and obtain judicial resolution of the controversy.

Stare decisis Latin, "Let the decision stand." Doctrine under which courts stand by precedent and do not disturb a settled point. Under this doctrine, once a court has laid down a principle of law as applied to a certain state of facts, the court adheres to that principle and

applies to it all future cases in which the facts are substantially the same.

State action In constitutional law, the term is used to designate governmental action that is necessary for purposes of bringing a constitutional challenge to such action.

State right-to-work statute A state statute authorized by the Taft-Hartley Act whereby an employee may lawfully refuse to join a union certified as the bargaining representative of the employer's employees.

Status quo ante Latin, "The state of things before."

Statute An act of a legislature declaring, commanding, or prohibiting something; a particular law enacted by the legislative department of government. Sometimes the word is used to designate codified law as opposed to case law.

Statute of frauds A statute requiring that certain contracts be supported by written memoranda.

Statute of limitations A statute prescribing the length of time after an event in which a suit must be brought or a criminal charge filed.

Statutory law Law consisting of statutes as opposed to common law, which is judge-made law.

Stay To stop, arrest, or forbear. To stay an order or decree means to hold it in abeyance or to refrain from enforcing it.

Stop order The name of a Securities and Exchange Commission order directing that the effectiveness of a registration statement be suspended. The order also suspends a security issuer's license to use the mails and warns the investing public that the SEC has found the registration statement to be unreliable.

Strict liability Liability without fault. A case is one of strict liability when neither care nor negligence, neither good nor bad faith, neither knowledge nor ignorance exonerate the defendant.

Subject matter jurisdiction A court's authority to hear a particular type of case.

Subpoena A writ ordering a person to appear and give testimony or to bring documents in his or her control.

Subsidiary corporation A corporation of whose shares at least a majority are owned by another corporation, which thus has control over it.

Substantial evidence standard of review The standard of judicial review of agency action whereby a court examines the administrative record to determine if substantial evidence exists to support the agency determination.

Substantiation A requirement imposed on advertisers by the Federal Trade Commission that they be able to substantiate the truth of their advertising claims.

Substantive law That part of law which creates, defines, and regulates rights, as opposed to procedural law, which prescribes the methods for enforcing the rights.

Summary judgment A pretrial decision reached by a trial court, after considering the pleadings, affidavits, depositions, and other documents, on the ground that no genuine issue of fact has been raised.

Summary plan description Under the Employee Retirement Income Security Act, a statement of any material modifications to a pension plan, annual reports including certified financial statements, and terminal and supplementary reports, if the plan is to be terminated.

Summons An instrument served on a defendant in a civil proceeding to give the defendant notice that he or she has been sued.

Sunset legislation A statute which provides that an agency's authority shall expire on a given date unless the legislative body acts to extend it.

Supremacy Clause A clause in the U.S. Constitution providing that all laws made by the federal government pursuant to the Constitution are the supreme law of the land and are superior to and conflicting state law.

Takeover bid A bid to assume control or management of a corporation; a tender offer.

Target company The company intended to be taken over in a takover bid.

Tender offer An offer to purchase shares of stock, usually made in an attempt to obtain a controlling interest in a corporation.

Terminable at will The normal employment relationship, absent a contract, whereby an employer may discharge an employee for any nondiscriminatory reason.

Tie-in When a party offers to provide one good or service only to those who agree to accept another good or service.

Tombstone ad An advertisement of a stock offering containing language to the effect that the announcement is neither an offer to sell nor a solicitation of an offer to buy any of the securities listed. The actual offer is made only by the prospectus.

Tort A civil wrong or injury, other than a breach of contract, committed against the person or property of another.

Tortfeasor A person who has committed a tort.

Trade association Organizations of competitors with common interests and business pursuits.

Trademark A word, name, symbol or device used by a manufacturer or merchant to identify goods and distinguish them from those manufactured by others.

Treatise A book that expounds on a broad area of a subject.

Treaty An agreement between nations.

Treble damages Three times actual damages. The remedy provided to a successful plaintiff in certain actions, including antitrust suits.

Trespass A tort action affording redress for injury committed to the plaintiff by the unauthorized entry on another's land or the interference with another's personal property.

Trust A legal arrangement whereby property or other assets are secured for beneficiaries by placing legal title and usually management responsibility in a trustee.

Trustee The person appointed to execute a trust.

Truth in Lending Act A federal statute that regulates consumer credit by requiring lenders to disclose certain credit terms in a standard way and regulates the cancellation of credit agreements, consumer leasing, and credit card extension and use.

Unconscionable So unfair or one-sided as to oppress or unfairly surprise a party.

Unfair labor practices Those practices contained in sections 8(a) and (b) of the NLRA that prohibit specified employer and employee practices, for example, refusing to bargain in good faith.

Uniform Commercial Code A comprehensive code, drafted by the National Conference of Commissioners on Uniform State Laws, which has been enacted in all of the states.

Union certification The process by which the National Labor Relations Board certifies a union as the exclusive bargaining representative of a unit of employees in the employer's work force.

Utility model Ethical justification holding that acts or rules that provide the greatest benefit to the greatest number of people are right or good.

Validation A statistical corroboration of a selection procedure that has an adverse impact on a protected group.

Variance Permission to depart from the literal requirements of an administrative regulation

Venue The particular county or geographic location in which a court with jurisdiction may hear a case.

Vertical merger A merger between two firms that have a buyer-seller relationship.

Vertical restraint An agreement between two or more parties at different levels of the distribution process to restrain trade by, for example, inhibiting intrabrand competition.

Vested Fixed, settled, absolute. Having the character of absolute ownership. With regard to pension plan benefits, vested benefits are not contingent on the employee continuing to work for the employer.

Veto Latin, "I forbid." The refusal of assent by the executive officer whose assent is necessary to perfect a law which a legislative body has passed.

Vicarious liability See *Respondeat superior.*

Vis-à-vis Face to face. One of two things or persons opposite or corresponding to each other. In relation to each other.

Void Null; ineffectual; having no legal force.

Warrant A writ from a competent authority in pursuance of law which directs the doing of an act, is addressed to an officer or person competent to do the act, and affords that officer or person protection from damage if he or she does it. In particular, writs are issued by a magistrate or justice, and addressed to a sheriff, constable, or other officer, requiring the latter to arrest someone or to search someone's person or property and seize items of evidence.

Warranty A promise that a statement is true. In contracts, a written or verbal undertaking or stipulation that a certain statement in relation to the subject matter of the contract is or shall be as it is stated or promised to be.

White collar exemptions Those executive, administrative, and professional personnel, who are salaried and meet other specified requirements and who are exempt from coverage of the Fair Labor Standards Act.

Work-product doctrine The doctrine by which certain material prepared by an attorney in anticipation of litigation is protected from discovery.

Work councils Plant-level committees consisting of supervisory personnel and workers, which decide plant-level matters.

Writ A court order directing a person to do something.

Wrongful discharge See *Abusive discharge.*